The Elite Leadership Course

The Elite Leadership Course

Life at Sandhurst

Garry McCarthy

Pen & Sword
MILITARY

First published in Great Britain in 2021 by
Pen & Sword Military
An imprint of
Pen & Sword Books Ltd
Yorkshire – Philadelphia

Copyright © Garry McCarthy 2021

ISBN 978 1 52679 049 1

The right of Garry McCarthy to be identified as Author of this work has been asserted by him in accordance with the Copyright, Designs and Patents Act 1988.

A CIP catalogue record for this book is
available from the British Library.

All rights reserved. No part of this book may be reproduced or transmitted in any form or by any means, electronic or mechanical including photocopying, recording or by any information storage and retrieval system, without permission from the Publisher in writing.

Typeset by Mac Style
Printed and bound in the UK Printed and bound in the UK by CPI Group (UK) Ltd, Croydon, CR0 4YY1.

Pen & Sword Books Limited incorporates the imprints of Atlas, Archaeology, Aviation, Discovery, Family History, Fiction, History, Maritime, Military, Military Classics, Politics, Select, Transport, True Crime, Air World, Frontline Publishing, Leo Cooper, Remember When, Seaforth Publishing, The Praetorian Press, Wharncliffe Local History, Wharncliffe Transport, Wharncliffe True Crime
and White Owl.

For a complete list of Pen & Sword titles please contact

PEN & SWORD BOOKS LIMITED
47 Church Street, Barnsley, South Yorkshire, S70 2AS, England
E-mail: enquiries@pen-and-sword.co.uk
Website: www.pen-and-sword.co.uk

Or

PEN AND SWORD BOOKS
1950 Lawrence Rd, Havertown, PA 19083, USA
E-mail: Uspen-and-sword@casematepublishers.com
Website: www.penandswordbooks.com

Contents

Preface		vi
Introduction		vii
Foreword		ix
Chapter 1	Reception Day	1
Chapter 2	Male Bonding	34
Chapter 3	Character Reassignment	87
Chapter 4	Week Two	104
Chapter 5	Every Day a School Day	114
Chapter 6	Ice Breaker	132
Chapter 7	Compass Rose	167
Chapter 8	Dear John	212
Chapter 9	Plain Jane	249
Chapter 10	Calm Before the Storm	297
Chapter 11	Exercise Red Light	314
Chapter 12	Brecon Brenda	354
Chapter 13	Brecon Bimble	374
Chapter 14	Where are they Now?	402
Acknowledgements		410
Index		411

Preface

Much has changed since this book was written. In no way does it reflect life at the Royal Military Academy today. Unknown to us all, the officer of the late 1990s would face war waged at a rate of attrition that was, at times, higher than that of the Great War. Regardless of the flaws in the techniques used to train officers at this time, this book is a historical record of how one group were trained for the impending wars in Iraq and Afghanistan in the following decade.

This is the extraordinary true story of twenty-one young men battling their way through the greatest challenge any young leader could possibly undertake. It is a unique insight into the industry of making leaders and commanders of the British Army, the likes of which has never been told before. Physically brutal, emotionally draining, the intensity of scrutiny is not replicated in any other form of leadership training. For the precious few who make it through, they reflect on this period of their lives as the most defining. They form a special group of men carrying the torch of every leader that fought in both World Wars.

Thirty years have elapsed since the chain of command denied publication of this account, and much has changed; this account has very little in common with what happens at Sandhurst today. Training servicemen and women for modern-day conflict is now highly regulated and scientific. But during the desperate times of war, when time is at a premium, we turn to our experiences to deliver what is needed. Leadership training must change with the times and synergize with global and regional atmospherics. Sandhurst has exemplified this concept and constantly reassessed course content and training methods to meet these changing dynamics. Consequently, there is little correlation between the content of this book and how training is delivered at Sandhurst today.

This story captures the most unique period during one of these changes. Built around the principles of Lord Rowallan's Highland Fieldcraft Training Centre, established in 1943 to develop character, Sandhurst introduced its own version of the course in 1977. The course remained unchanged until it was disbanded in 1999, although it has made several reappearances in different disguises ever since.

The people in this story are real, although to protect their identities names have been changed and characters merged. The account is as accurate as possible, given the lapse of thirty years since these events occurred. Some events and dates are deliberately skewed to prevent causing offence to those involved or still serving. In addition, some locations and theatres of operations have been substituted for similar environments that keep the events believable.

Introduction

It is hard to imagine a time when a book on leadership could be more relevant. The pandemic created by the spread of COVID 19 will change many things in the world, and not simply what we do and how we do it. It will equally influence our view of the world and our place in it. As assessments of the national and international consequences of the virus begin, a critical eye will be focused on the quality of decision-making and the effectiveness of leadership within governments and institutions. It will be important to analyse how governments and institutions reacted to the spread of the virus and to determine how effective had been the preparation for such an event.

'Decision-making' and 'leadership' are two crucial components of military 'Command'. Outside the military and other emergency services, leadership is seldom considered an integral part of education or training. More often than not, such matters are covered in any depth only when individuals are about to undertake what might be deemed to be 'leadership roles'. Even then, the focus is likely to be on what leaders have to 'do' rather than what they have to 'be', whereas behavioural characteristics are regarded by the military as an essential element of the 'moral component' of military capability. They are the basis of selection and a persistent training theme throughout a soldier's service.

It is easy to forget that leadership skills are a necessity at every level of an organization and that small group leadership is essential if higher level leadership is to be effective. It is no accident that military training focuses on developing command ability at the earliest stages of training: from Officer Cadet and Junior Non-Commissioned Officer upwards. And yet what are the practical, legal and moral expectations placed upon those who are being led? During initial training, soldiers are being given the practical skills they require to do their job. They are also being taught how to follow. 'Followship' (if it can be termed that) can be defined as the acceptance of the authority of another person and willingness to carry out their instructions. Such authority may be derived from the State or an institution, or it may be informal. Good 'followship' is born of good leadership; but 'leadership' and 'followship' are two sides of the same coin. During an era in which the concept of the individual is in the ascendency, it is too easy for the idea of 'followship' to be associated with disempowerment and lack of autonomy, even servility, discrimination and exploitation, and tag them with a label marked 'bad'. Yet without the practice of 'followship', effective leadership is, at best, very difficult and, at worst, quickly undermined.

If leaders are required to 'act' in response to direction or to circumstance, then so too must those who follow. Good leadership and effective 'followship' demands that individuals accept responsibility for their actions, and act in accordance with circumstances as they are and not how they might wish them to be.

The Sandhurst motto of 'Serve to Lead' expresses the essence of military leadership training in two distinct ways. Firstly, you cannot lead until you have learned to serve. Secondly, and perhaps counter-intuitively, leaders are the servants of those they lead. In this book we follow the journey of a group of young men seeking to understand service and duty, learning to serve and lead, striving to understand how to create unity of purpose, without which success is elusive. It is tough and uncompromising, but for these future leaders, the price of getting it wrong will be failure, resulting perhaps in death and destruction, and even social breakdown, destroyed economies and political instability. In recent times, it may be that we have neglected the values of 'leadership' and 'followship'. Perhaps now more than ever, we need to forge a route that reconnects society as a whole with the values which continue to underpin the military way.

General Sir Jack Deverell KCB OBE
Commandant, Royal Military Academy Sandhurst, 1995–97

Foreword

No dissertation or doctorate is capable of scripting the definitive formula for successful leadership, because it doesn't exist. Theologians debate nature or nurture, while professors lecture about types and characteristics. But from a personal experience, it is a cocktail of institutional brilliance, not a science. British military leadership, at all levels, has been forged in the fires of monumental failures and glorious victories. We have sought to learn more from our failure than we do from our success. The British Non-Commissioned Officer is a mosaic derived from 300 years of triumph and defeat; no one else is better placed to distinguish the difference between good and bad leadership. It is nothing short of genius to employ these men and women to instruct officers in the art of leadership at Sandhurst. It's a cliché, but 'you reap what you sow'. Like no one else in the world, the British Army invests heavily in the leadership training of the Non-Commissioned Officer. They are taught from day one to think for themselves, to improvise, adapt and overcome. The best of them can identify all that is necessary and dismiss anything that's not. Most crucially, they are taught to understand the higher commander's intent; to lead from the front so they may inspire everyone around them. The return on this investment is the best officer corps in the world.

This is a brilliant account of how leadership is made. Leadership is intimate. Professional relationships built on trust, integrity, commitment and belief are unbeatable. The bond between an officer and their soldiers is the most intimate professional collaboration on the planet. Get it right, and soldiers will follow you into the fires of hell and certain death without questioning your logic. Get it wrong, and infamy awaits.

Andy McNab CBE DCM MM DArts
The Genesis of Military Leadership

Chapter One

Reception Day

'**M**arvellous! Marvellous! Absolutely bloody marvellous, don't you just love reception day. Great to have you on board Gaz, welcome to Row-Co!'

Pat's voice bounced off the magnolia walls of the cellar accommodation deep below the grandeur of Sandhurst's Old College building. Purposefully, walking at pace heading to his office, he continued to reminisce about previous courses: 'You know, if the students had the smallest inclination of what they were letting themselves in for, they wouldn't turn up.'

I was perplexed by his comment, which was contrary to my understanding. My belief was that anyone winning a place at Sandhurst knew exactly what to expect. If anyone should be worried, it was me. Prior to attending the selection course for potential instructors at Sandhurst, my research into the 'Officer Development' courses proved fruitless. The only literature available was a short pamphlet written in the late seventies explaining that Rowallan Company was a descendant of the Highland Fieldcraft Training Centre, or a bespoke course designed for developing leadership in young men wishing to become Army officers. There was nothing sinister that would substantiate Pat's comments. Confused by his statement, I pressed him for an explanation: 'Hang about Sir! The Regular Commissions Board [RCB] briefs everyone about Rowallan. Surely all of the students are prepared before they arrive?'

'True Gaz,' Pat replied. 'Very true. But those who know better won't fall for the claptrap spouted by the selectors at RCB. They will be easy to identify!'

'How?' I enquired.

'They will be the ones that don't turn up!' Pat laughed psychotically as he rubbed his hands vigorously and hunched his back like an archetypal villain.

Pat was typical Parachute Regiment. Although physically small, his powerful frame was dwarfed only by the enormity of his character. A soldier of twenty madcap years, his quick wit and black humour were frequently exercised at the expense of others. Having excelled as a Colour Sergeant Instructor in the previous two years, the Commandant of Sandhurst had singled him out for promotion to Warrant Officer Class Two and installed him as the Company Sergeant Major of the most notorious training organization in the British Army. Rowallan Company – also known as 'Row-Co' – was the primary source of all horror stories associated with Sandhurst. The Commandant could not have chosen a better man to keep these stories alive.

First impressions of Pat were hugely misleading. With wild blue eyes, an errant bouffant, out-of-control eyebrows and a crazy expression permanently fixed to his face, all complemented by his carefree use of politically incorrect words, it was easy to jump to the wrong conclusion and cast him as a typical Para. But Pat was an expert in human behaviour. Although there were no recognized academic credentials or post-nominal, he crafted his unique style through life experience. Always likely to say or do something that would leave you puzzled, astonished or bent over double on the floor in fits of laughter, he played to the audience for effect. But misjudge the moment at your peril. Astute and as driven as any other professional 'strutting his stuff' around the Academy, Pat had an awesome reputation within the Special Forces world.

The very first time we met, he was dressed in ill-fitting scruffy combat trousers and cheap desert boots with his last four digits of his Army number neatly stencilled on the heel. Like all off-duty Paras, he wore an ageing maroon T-shirt emblazoned with one of those rebellious slogans like 'shoot them all and let God sort it out!'. 'Ah, you must be Gaz! Marvellous!' Shaking my hand and nearly breaking my fingers in the process, he was pleased I had volunteered for the job.

> 'The OC is out on a run, but welcome aboard buddy. I would love to stop and chat but I've just received my divorce papers in the post. I'm running off to ask my girlfriend if she would like to get married today. If she behaves herself, she can take me up on the offer. Just in case she is crazy enough to say "yes", I have booked the registry office in the Shot [Aldershot]! Hang around and meet the team, I won't be long. Moneypenny will square you away!'

With a smile as large as a house, and dressed just a little smarter than when he left, he reappeared four hours later. 'Well let's hope this marriage lasts a bit longer than my first two!' he yelled, whilst roaring with laughter.

Pat held court exceptionally well. He explained to the training team who had assembled to congratulate him that it was imperative he got this marriage off to a good start. So, soon after they left the registrar's office, they rushed home to consummate their marriage.

Pat delivered an impromptu Benny Hill skit: 'I asked Sara to try on my trousers. She squeezed into my army lightweights and waltzed around the flat pretending to be a soldier, barking orders and saluting like a crazed cadet. "That's the last time you wear the trousers in this house," I told her!'

Sara, a woman with a sharp, sarcastic wit and cut from the same crazy cloth as her new husband, was not one to shy from confrontation. She slipped off a pair of skimpy Ann Summers knickers, twirled them around her fingers and flung them at Pat.

'Can you get into these?' she asked. Two minutes of uncontrollable excitement and anticipation elapsed as Pat battled to ease the lacey lingerie over his huge thighs. 'You're having a laugh. I can't get in them.'

'No, you're right,' she shot back. 'And you never will with that chauvinistic attitude! Best you buck your ideas up cupcake, or this marriage will be shorter than you!' It was a sign of what to expect in the weeks ahead.

* * *

The smell of shoe polish and burnt beeswax mixed with the acidic aroma of industrial floor polish filled the air as the training team finalized their preparations for reception day. The central hub for Company planning and administration was at the far end of what would be the students' accommodation. The first of three small offices belonged to the Company Sergeant Major, and was shared with the company clerk and the Company second-in-command. Pat had two volumes on his voice: loud and very loud! When he spoke, his voice penetrated every empty inch of the cellar accommodation. He could be heard relentlessly poking fun at the company clerk who sat at the adjacent desk in the small office.

'Moneypenny! You tart, have you got all the attestations squared away for the reception?'

Corporal Davis mumbled quietly to himself before answering. He saw himself as much more than just a company clerk, more a soldier first and HR specialist second. If this perception was challenged, it offended him hugely. In his defence, he was forced to do every arduous task everyone else did, which was impressive for a company clerk. But despite this, life with Pat was never going to be easy for anyone who was not part of the airborne elite.

'Yes Sir. I am all over it!' he grunted, in a vain attempt to rebel against the oppressive relationship he had with Pat.

Pat would be quick to pick up on his despondent attitude, and played on it mercilessly. 'What's wrong Moneypenny, that time of the month is it?'

Davis wouldn't respond, for fear of receiving more of Pat's wayward attention. Collecting his paperwork, he left for the Indian Army Memorial Room to ready himself for the arrival of the first students. Meaningfully, he scuttled down the corridor, his heel tips angrily striking the polished floor. Filling the empty accommodation with the familiar metallic sound of hobnailed boots, Corporal Davis charged off in his own little rage. Moving as quickly as possible whilst carrying a box of stationery, Pat's overtones chastised him for several minutes even after he was long gone.

The Directing Staff, commonly known as the 'DS', consisted of one major, three captains, one Company Sergeant Major and three Colour Sergeants. Collectively, we busied ourselves preparing ceremonial uniforms in the staff wing of the accommodation. The staff wing ran parallel to the students' rooms, one of many wings in a maze of corridors, forming a classic herringbone shape of lodgings. With low ceilings covered by heavy-duty service pipes and wiring, it resembled the inner workings of a Chinese laundry rather than the historic elite Military Academy it professed to be. The cellar accommodation was meant to be temporary, but its miserable, damp, dungeon-like appearance gave it an oppressive atmosphere that played to the advantage of the course atmospherics. Ironically, it would be the site of much physical and mental torture, mainly self-inflicted but nonetheless just as miserable.

With the arrival of the students imminent, there was much personal preparation in its final stages. In the DS corridor, the atmosphere was full of light-hearted banter mixed with the jangling of swords, clinking of medals and crunching of hobnailed boots. I called out to Pat, who was now three doors away in his changing room: 'What time do you think they'll start arriving Sir?'

'Well, the smart ones will turn up with five minutes to spare, but those that believe the garbage printed in the glossy brochure we sent them are probably here already. Mummy and Daddy included.'

Major Gordon Gray, the Officer Commanding Rowallan Company – known to all as the OC – was quick to identify Pat's condescending tones: 'Sergeant Major! Surely you're not suggesting that we have deliberately misled anyone are you?'

Identifying the OC's thinly veiled sarcasm, the corridor erupted into laughter. As OC, Major Gray was charged with setting the standards we would all be invited to achieve. Not just those of fitness and commitment, but also of morality and integrity. Without mercy, the OC was bombarded with comments berating his lame attempt to defend the glossy brochure sent to all students ahead of their arrival.

'Misled did you say? Bollocks! Out and out lied is what we've done. Best work of fiction since that old dude wrote the Bible,' giggled Pat.

'I thought that was the whole idea of it!' shouted Captain Dunn, the appointed Commander of No. 2 Platoon and the officer to whom I would be subordinate. Glancing at Captain Dunn, who was chuckling to himself in his room opposite mine, it was clear he had a mischievous streak. Peering from behind his door, he winked and offered a wry smile whilst simultaneously polishing his medals. Fishing for more banter, he patrolled the corridor to see if anyone would take the bait. Young, tall and athletic, Captain Dunn was bubbling with excitement.

His broad shoulders and huge arms blocked the light as he ambled across the corridor and stood in my doorway.

> 'I'm serious, Colour!' A huge grin was fixed on his face. 'Ten years ago, they sent me that very same brochure two weeks before the course started. I remember thinking, "how exciting". I couldn't wait to start at Rowallan, it looked great fun. It was full of pictures of adventure training, climbing, canoeing, hill walking and people having fun. Mind you, at 19 you are very gullible. The brochure is pure propaganda! It is no surprise that they keep it under lock and key. Worst of all, there is a happy-looking Saudi prince on the back cover looking like a million dollars. I recall thinking if that dude could do it, I could. Little did I know that overseas students are not allowed to do the course, and the prince never once set foot near Rowallan.'

Pat urged the team to leave their rooms and assemble at the entrance of the accommodation. Talking to no one specifically, he walked around rattling off instructions to ensure we understood our duties. One by one, the DS gathered just inside the swinging doors for one final check. More in the pursuit of vanity, loosely disguised as professional pride, we jostled around the long mirror at the entrance for one final check. With ties straightened, buttons squared and belts pulled tight, Pat gave an approving nod to depart. Swords and pace sticks to hand, the complete training team weaved their way through the labyrinth of corridors leading to the Grand Entrance. It was just before 1000hrs on Monday, 3rd January.

The portico of Old College stands alone as a global symbol of elitism. Six huge fluted pillars grace the forward edge of the wide white stone stairs. Imposing and impressive in equal measure, this iconic entrance is accessible to only the most privileged people on the planet. Designed by John Sanders in 1808 and guarded by six brass cannons that saw action at Waterloo, just the sight of the building stirs an emotional sense of pride deep in the soul. The ten steps leading to the heavy oak doors droop in the centre, worn-down by the hoofs of the Academy Adjutant's grey charger. Famously, the horse ascends the stairs at the conclusion of every Sovereign's Parade, a tradition that was started by Captain Frederick Browning. Legend has it that in 1924, whilst he was the Academy Adjutant, Captain Browning was so angry at the poor performance of officer cadets during the parade that he charged up the stairs after the cadets on his horse to issue a fierce rebuke. He would later go on to make the rank of lieutenant general and command 1 Airborne Corps during the Second World War. If ever there was a sight capable of intimidating someone and inspiring at the same moment, watching the Academy Adjutant follow cadets up the stairs was it. In nearly every painting of Sandhurst, or any journal of military leadership, the Grand Entrance features. You get the privilege of walking these steps twice in a lifetime: once on the day you arrive, and once on the day you finish.

It was just short of 1100hrs before the first of the forty-six listed students arrived. Clutching four bags and an ironing board, a slightly overweight individual stumbled up the steps to the reception area. Pat stood watching at the top of the steps, impatiently tapping his pace stick on the floor and scouring for parents. Robotically, his head flicked left to right repeatedly before stopping and fixing a cold stare on the first arrival. Seizing the moment, Pat heckled him between fits of laughter: 'Have you come dressed as a hippy surfing clown? You do know this is the Royal Military Academy Sandhurst and not Thorpe Park?'

The expression on the young man's face spoke volumes. Shocked and offended, confusion gave way to resignation. Showing sympathy, I held the large oak door open as the young lad juggled his baggage and pushed by me.

'Ha! Marvellous; bloody marvellous! That will be a string vest offence, the first of the year, Gaz!' laughed Pat.

'What? What do you mean string vest offence?' I asked. Pat pointed his pace stick at me before inviting the rest of the DS to explain.

He was not short of takers. Captain Dunn struggled to contain his laughter, and Paddy began to nod wisely with approval before everyone voiced an explanation. The string vest was a badge of dishonour. It was awarded to an instructor or member of staff for violation of Row-Co code of practice. Only worn during physical fitness periods, it indicated to the world that one of the strict codes of conduct enforced upon the Rowallan Company instructor had been breached. The concept was designed to humiliate and coerce the instructor to adhere to the stringent code of tough love. Such embarrassment encouraged the kind of teaching environment that gave Rowallan its reputation.

'Live by the sword, die by the sword!' someone chirped from the far end of the cold, grey-stoned corridor. The vest made you look a complete prat, but worse still, the owner continued to wear it until someone else committed a 'string vest offence'.

Although a staff code of conduct didn't exist on paper, and therefore it was unreasonable for me to have been aware of it, my plea with Pat for clemency on day one went unheard. How did anyone know what would constitute a violation and what didn't? I tried to summon support from Paddy, who was the appointed Colour Sergeant of No. 1 Platoon, and his Platoon Commander Captain Watts. But both had been with Rowallan for two terms and were quietly pleased not to be the first to wear the string vest at the start of the course. Surely the OC would help?

'Sir, this is unfair. How can it be allowed? We can't discredit staff with a made-up code of conduct. It took me a year to train for this job, added to the selection course which has a 75 per cent failure rate; what flawed logic has you humiliating the DS like this? This is not the time to discover that there is some sort of Masonic-like set of rules for me to adhere to! What are the rules and where are they written down?'

My frustration was evident.

'Well, Colour, it's like this. At Rowallan we do things very different to the rest of the Academy.'

Before the OC could continue, Captain Dunn interrupted him mid-flow:

'We don't have the luxury of time here. Nor do we have space in our lives for the fancy frills the normal cadets get. The students need to see your dark side, and we have to ensure it's always on display. You need to cram twenty years of hardship into three months. They need to sample the worst we have to offer. It's a tough gig and the only way to achieve this is to keep the pressure on everyone. That includes you and me, the Sergeant Major, the OC, the store-man and the clerk; everyone. The Row-Co Colour Sergeant must be feared. A cold-hearted, uncompromising, mace-wielding psychopathic type of character. No airs or graces, just ruthless. It's quite simple really, you don't need it written down. The string vest is the tool we use to prevent your human side accidentally slipping out. No one likes wearing it; you will learn it's an effective tool of motivation. It will eventually make sense.'

'Mace-wielding nutter! That being the case, how should they see you, sir?' I asked.

'Oh you know, approachable, caring and interested,' he replied. 'The sort of person you would like your sister to marry. A knowledgeable surrogate father figure, if you like. Or as I see it, just an all-round good egg.'

Major Gray shook his head in disbelief at what Captain Dunn had just blurted out, before shooting him down in flames: 'James, what a load of rubbish! You're no more an all-round good egg than I am an Olympic athlete. Colour, I shouldn't listen to him. You will figure it out as the course goes on.'

Reception had become busy. Upon arrival, a student was given a name tag, displaying only his surname, before being ushered into a long grey slate stone corridor while his paperwork was completed. More often than not, a student would arrive with his parents. A well-rehearsed drill would see one of the three captains greet the mother and father and escort them into the impressive Indian Army Memorial Room. Parents were served – with polite conversation and reassurance – tea, coffee and sticky cakes. Simultaneously, the Colour Sergeant would marshal the student into the corridor of no return. The high ceilings and historical military art adorning the walls induced an atmosphere more akin to a museum than a busy military academy. Occasionally, the silence would be shattered with the shrill of orders being barked out by the DS: 'Stand still! Stop fidgeting! Shut up! Face your front! Do nothing until I tell you to.'

My opposite number, Paddy, constantly patrolled the corridor, waiting to accumulate enough students to move onto the next phase of reception.

Paddy was a Colour Sergeant in the Foot Guards. Six foot two and hard as nails, he had the meticulous attention to detail that you only ever find in a Guardsman. Like most army nicknames, there was a simple correlation between Paddy and his heritage. In Paddy's case, fifteen years in the Irish Guards skewed his Belfast accent into an abrupt mixture of modern-day Saxon with Celtic overtones. With heartless cold eyes, Paddy scrutinized every student as he patrolled the corridor. Systematically inspecting them from head to toe, an assessment was made of everyone as they stood in the corridor. His eyes seemed to be turbocharged, continuously scanning students for their imperfections. Relentlessly, he would highlight their failings, holding nothing back. He could be brutal with his words: 'Stomach in lad! Shoulders back youngin! Stop looking around and face your front. Have some dignity and pride. Stomach in; keep it in fatty.'

Blurting out meaningless instructions just to break the silence seemed to help his concentration. 'Look at me, look away, look at me! Stop twitching man. Steady! What's wrong with you?' Bizarrely, it seemed to fit the scenario and before too long I was doing the same.

With sufficient students processed by the administrators, they were primed to move to the accommodation via the Company Quartermaster Sergeants' stores.

'Pick up all your kit and follow me.' Devoid of emotion, trying hard to fit into Captain Dunn's perceived persona of a Rowallan Colour Sergeant, my tone was curt. Deliberately setting off at a blistering pace, it was impossible for the students to keep up. Through the network of corridors, the clunking of ironing boards and luggage could be heard negotiating steps and doors. Exiting the rear of the building, we walked into the confines of Chapel Square. It was awash with suitcases, ironing boards and large holdalls as the students struggled to maintain the unreasonable pace.

'For crying out loud, if I go any slower, I'll bloody well stop. Now keep up.' Before they had time to reassemble, we were off again.

Fifty metres later we arrived at the Company stores, another cold, damp sub-surface corner of Old College. The stores were an Aladdin's cave of domestic and specialist equipment required for the course. The Company store was run by a small team euphemistically known as the 'Q Party', 'Q' being a common military reference to anything belonging to the Quartermasters department. A store's trained Colour Sergeant or equivalent would normally lead each 'Q Party', and for his sins, Pete was our Company Quartermaster Sergeant. Within two minutes, his slick organization would see him issue all the students with a crimson red tracksuit and matching rugby shirt, as well as a climbing harness plus toggle rope, one rucksack containing waterproof clothing, one helmet and one packed lunch. Before they could depart, Pete also issued a few sharp words of wisdom on loss or damage to items that belonged to the Crown. In the blink of an eye, Pete then shooed them out of his store.

The issued tracksuits were the property of the Quartermaster. Like most military kit, they would be handed down from person to person until beyond economical repair. The tracksuit came in one of two sizes – too little or too big. There was little chance of owning one that fitted correctly. Every tracksuit carried the names of the previous owners, written and crossed out with indelible ink, somewhere close to the nape of the jacket. Visibly, battle scars covered the tracksuit. Like campaign medals, each tracksuit had its own story to tell. Bleached by sun and sweat, ground-in dirt, blood or rope burns, each stain was evidence of an epic event likely to be repeated by the new owner. Once issued with their basic needs, the students were rushed into their accommodation. Keeping explanations to a minimum, the students received their next instructions: 'Get changed into your red tracksuit immediately. Eat your lunch, and at 1230hrs you will be taken to the gym for your initial fitness assessment. So go easy on the packed lunch.'

Twenty minutes later, the next group were wheeled in and given the same brief. There were almost twenty students crammed into the narrow corridor that would be their home for the next three months. It was flight or fight time. The loss of personal space, which was now shared with total strangers whilst trying to don an ill-fitting red tracksuit and simultaneously eating a packed lunch, heightened everyone's anxiety. The floor was littered with baggage, expensive suits, empty coke cans, ironing boards and other items, making it virtually impassable. It was already a far cry from the grand arrival most had enjoyed just an hour previously.

Five students failed to show up, which wasn't uncommon. Fully assembled and dressed in red tracksuits, forty-two students paraded in a side street just off Chapel Square at the rear of Old College. It was an area purposely selected to remain hidden from the inquisitive eyes of the routine Sandhurst Cadets who were enjoying the Commissioning Course. At Row-Co, extraordinary efforts were taken to create an atmosphere of mystery in order to distance the student from the real functions of the Academy. To further enforce this secrecy, Officer Cadets on the normal Commissioning Courses were forbidden to interact with a Rowallan student. This was mainly to retain the initiative in a war of attrition and maintain the secrecy of what went on in the Company. Whenever an Officer Cadet saw a student from Rowallan Company, he would be in one of three conditions: going on physical fitness, returning from physical fitness or sitting in the medical centre suffering from too much physical fitness! These visions would send shivers down the spines of the cadets on the regular Commissioning Course, for everyone knew that if you were 'Back-Termed' from term one of the Commissioning Course, a place on Row-Co was waiting for you.

The prospect of being 'Back-Termed' to Rowallan Company was the ultimate nightmare. Any person destined for Sandhurst will have heard the horror stories about life in Row-Co. Most of these stories are spine-tinglingly terrifying, but the worst part of it is, they're mostly true! Seventy-five per cent of the training was completely unorthodox, and was frowned upon by many who felt the methods were archaic.

For a Row-Co student, life changed forever the moment he walked up the steps of the Grand Entrance. He embarked on a voyage of self-discovery, and the vehicle he travelled in was called 'the good ship misery'. He would be tested to breaking point, and then taken one step further. Every facet of his behaviour would be analysed to within one inch of his life. Mannerisms, character flaws and personal foibles would be pawed over and kicked around publicly for all to discuss. With no place to hide, it was emotionally uncomfortable, physically demoralizing and mentally intolerable. Finding himself facing impossible situations, more suited to a Laurel & Hardy sketch or a Peter Cushing horror classic, few would survive. From the very start, all students were alienated for a very specific effect. If a student was to be successful on Row-Co, he would need to quickly develop self-sufficiency, build his own strength of character and acquire a will of iron, and forge successful relationships combined with the desire to win. Leadership comes from many life skills; learning what these skills are and knowing how to merge them into a formula for success was the ultimate end state for those on the course. The approach was infamously referred to as 'the quickening'. You either fought for your life or lost your head, and a place in the Army in the process.

The course was sold to the outside world as 'Leadership Development'. By constantly contriving ways to build a person's character, and in some cases dismantle it in order to rebuild it, there was nothing else like it in the world. The aim of Rowallan Company was to convert an individual selected at risk by RCB into a successful candidate on the routine Commissioning Course. One complete calendar year in length, the Commissioning Course thoroughly prepared a cadet for the role of a young officer in the modern, high-tempo British Army. But it couldn't waste spaces on the course. It sought to attain a 99 per cent success rate by only selecting those they were certain could endure the rigours of the programme. In comparison to the Rowallan course, which lasted only fourteen weeks, the Commissioning Course ran at a leisurely pace. When selected as a potential army officer at RCB, students were graded as a pass or fail. If RCB had a student that they had doubts about, but identified a spark of potential, they offered the individual a Row-Co pass. This meant that after successful completion of fourteen weeks of leadership training, they could advance to the start of the Commissioning Course.

There were many reasons why someone could be sent to Row-Co, and despite RCB's best efforts, diligence, analytical approach and success, they were human and didn't always get it right. For the selectors, it was easy to identify those who were too arrogant, cocky, under-confident or immature. But working on the principle that you can fool some of the people some of the time, it was possible to fool the board and make it through the selection process. Conversely, there were those who ended up not demonstrating their true character and ability, merely because of group atmospherics and dynamics; some of these ended up at Row-Co. The Regular Commissions Board made its decision, never telling the student why they had been sent to Row-Co, and from the moment they arrived, the DS treated everyone with the same level of contempt, irrespective of why they were on the course.

* * *

Down the side road just off Chapel Square, Pat was standing on the courtyard dwarf wall to elevate himself to a point that afforded him eye contact with all those assembled. Loosely gathered in a military fashion, Pat spoke to the course.

> 'Right you ugly bunch of wannabes, we're off to the gym. That's G. Y. M for some of you tubbies out there who are wondering what I am talking about. From this moment on, whenever you move around the Academy you will march in a smart soldier-like manner. There is no time to teach you how to march properly, so you'll have to pick it up as we go along. Turn and face your left.'

The moment the students turned, there was an instant eruption of shouting. It appeared to come from everywhere as screams rebounded off the high walls of Old College, trapped by the hollow square of the courtyard. The intensity of the moment could be seen on the shocked faces of the students. Every member of staff, storemen and clerks included, began screaming marching instructions. Students were set upon randomly to receive a few seconds of personal attention. This was the Row-Co 'hothouse' method of learning foot drill on the move. By the time they reached the gym, the students had been taught as much marching drill as they would need to know in order to survive the course. Eventually, the course came to a halt outside the gymnasium, puffing and panting more through angst than exertion. As odd as this may sound, if delivered with a high tempo, and the conditions are right, marching is physically hard.

The time was 1240hrs, and the last student had arrived less than thirty minutes previously. Standing silent in three ranks outside the gymnasium, there was a gentle wisp of perspiration rising from the foreheads of most. Unwittingly, several parents walked by, enjoying a stroll around the grounds, oblivious to the fact that it was their children they were passing dressed in ragged red tracksuits, waiting patiently to start their assessment. Wallowing in the glory of their child's achievement, they ambled around the Academy, blissfully unaware that their most cherished possession had been processed, administrated and changed for their first test, all in the same time it took to walk from the coffee shop to the car park. In less than forty minutes, we had taken their pride and joy, cut the apron strings and thrust them into the harshest of all military regimes. Exploiting the shock of capture, the staff maximized every opportunity to induce a feeling of vulnerability or fear. Trepidation, anxiety and confusion are a consequence of short-notice dislocation and the sudden loss of comfort and control. The process of character assessment had begun.

'Stand up straight and stop looking around!' Paddy repeatedly snapped at everyone, irrespective of whether they warranted it. One student caught Paddy's eye, and before the student was able to break eye contact, Paddy had burst his way through the rank and file to stand toe-to-toe with him.

'What about yee, wee man?' The student attempted to answer, stuttering a few incoherent words. Paddy pushed his nose into the face of the student.

'Name?' he screamed.

The student tried frantically to avoid eye contact. 'Sir. Hudson!'

Paddy edged even closer and whispered in Hudson's ear: 'Royalty are you, Hudson? Eyeball me again, Hudson, I will rip your arms off and bash you over the head with the soggy ends. Do you understand me, wee man? The Queen wouldn't even look at me the way you just did, see!'

'Sir. Yes Sir!' Hudson blurted. Paddy walked towards me with a big smile on his face and, with his back to the students, gave a knowing wink.

'Did you see that cheeky toe-rag, Gaz? He's got an attitude problem, believe you me. That arse thinks he's going to be Chief of the General Staff someday! He will not think that this time next week.'

Major Gray appeared from behind the double doors of the gymnasium annex. His infectious enthusiasm for physical fitness was borderline obsessive. Stood on the small steps in front of the intake, he raised a huge smile and greeted everyone with excitable overtones. Bubbling with enthusiasm, he explained that they were about to undergo an initial assessment on their fitness. This was for several reasons, the most important of which was to arm the staff with sufficient information to divide the course members into two platoons of equal fitness ability. Each platoon would have an equal share of fit and unfit students. This balance was crucial to the fundamental mechanics of how the course would work and essential to everything it sought to achieve, which was based on competition, success and failure through physical effort. The major said the premise of the course was firmly rooted in the lessons Lord Rowallan learnt during two World Wars. Throughout the course, both platoons would compete against each other for the privilege of not being punished: a stark contrast to the conventional thinking of rewarding someone for winning.

As the OC finished his explanation, the physical training instructor (PTI) dedicated to the course emerged from the gym. 'Daz' was a PTI with a difference. Although a young man, Staff Sergeant Dazzell had silver hair and a permanently weathered expression that suggested he had been partying all night. A veteran of six courses, Daz never gave the students an inch. Ruthlessly dispassionate, a word or a movement out of place was punished with hard physical activities. Daz basked in his position of authority, epitomizing that crazy mace-wielding oddball image synonymous with Captain Dunn's vision.

'Welcome to the house of God,' said Daz. 'This is the most important building in the Academy, and you need to behave with total respect whilst in it. You will come to learn who I am, but for now, all you need to know is I don't take prisoners!'

Daz stood sideways on, wearing a starched white singlet vest with crossed clubs to denote his official qualification. He chose to wear his thin vest to show off his finely tuned upper body, despite the bitter cold and the yielding ground frost.

He continued: 'Before we do this small and pathetic little assessment, we will warm the body up with a few laps around the inside of the sports hall, so none of you faggots pull a muscle.'

Daz couldn't open his mouth without belittling the students. Even by his normal standards, he overplayed his dislike for the new arrivals. With a burst of insults, he quickly ushered everyone into the gym. Like a ringmaster orchestrating a procession of circus animals, he set them off running clockwise around the hall. Standing in the centre on his own, screaming instructions to keep the pressure on, Daz reinforced the shock of capture. Handpicked for this task, his broad Liverpudlian accent shrilled loudly inside the large hall to pronounced effect. Although Daz's words were losing definition amongst the bare walls and high ceiling, you immediately felt his authority through the urgency of his delivery.

Standing in the corner of the gym with my Platoon Commander, Captain Dunn, we watched the students complete lap after lap. Using what my wife would call 'people watching', we focused our attention on the physical appearance of several students. As foolhardy as it is to judge someone by their appearance, there was no harm in exercising your thoughts privately.

'Colour, we don't want him in the platoon. I can tell at just one glance he's not up for it!' Captain Dunn pointed out a wiry, anaemic-looking character who was gurning awkwardly and glowing bright red as he struggled to keep up.

'Let's not be too judgmental just yet, Sir!' I replied, trying to maintain a positive outlook.

'Bollocks, Colour! Take another look. The man has got "failure" stamped across his forehead in bold capital letters, as well as a neon light hanging around his neck saying "look at the failure sign in bold capitals stamped on my forehead. It says failure!" As sure as Elvis is dead, he won't last the course!'

Hearing the suppressed laughter, Pat joined the conversation. Without even knowing why we were laughing, Pat broke out into a manic giggle: 'You've clocked the pipe cleaner, Gaz, am I right? I am, aren't I? This is my favourite game.'

'Yes. Captain Dunn reckons the kid won't last the course,' I replied.

Pat took another look at him. 'You're wrong, Sir. He won't last the week.'

They had been running around the sports hall for less than fifteen minutes, and already some students were finding it hard. Daz opened a fire exit door and marshalled everyone out into the cold January air. He explained that the assessment was a 3-mile run, split into two phases. Phase one was a mile-and-a-half run-walk, completed as a squad in under fifteen minutes; phase two was a mile-and-a-half individual best effort. Although officially an assessment, there was a pass mark to achieve: runners needed to complete the individual run in under ten minutes and thirty seconds.

Perspiration, dripping gently from the heads of the students, collided with the cold air to form a shallow cloud above the group. The students followed behind Daz as he made his way to the start line of the assessment. We set off at a leisurely pace, but having travelled no more than 400 metres, Pat was already giving someone some special attention. It was no surprise that the skinny kid who was struggling in the gym was in a state of distress. Pat dragged him out of the squad. Bright red and looking very vulnerable, Pat bombarded him with questions and accusations:

> 'What's your name? What's your problem, were you going to Lego Land but took the wrong junction on the M25? What do you think you are doing here? Deluded you are son, absolutely deluded. If you have been sent by Jeremy Beadle to take the piss, it won't work! Have you been sent to test me? Do you know what the hell is going on here?'

Failing to understand the rhetorical nature of the questions, the skinny kid offered as many answers as he thought useful: 'No, Sir. Hays, Sir, Hays. Yes, Sir.'

Hays appeared to be hyperventilating. With erratic shallow breathing, restless limbs and panic etched on his face, the lad was not going any further. His head began to flop back and forth, then side to side, as he stared up to the sky and collapsed to the floor. By now the colour had drained from his face and his symptoms became hypothermia-like. Hays grabbed hold of Pat's arm in a token effort to raise himself. With just the whites of his eyes showing, he was on the verge of fainting.

'Gaz! Gaz!' Pat shouted at me, despite being less than a foot away. 'Come and get this joker off me. Take him to the medical centre before he passes out, or I may just knock him out. Bluffing little shit! There's nothing wrong with him!'

Incomprehensively, as if someone had just flicked a switch, Hays sprang back to life. He gently let go of Pat and began to regain his composure. Stumbling to his feet, he reached out and grabbed my arm, clinging to me like a limpet mine.

'Sorry, Sir, I'm sorry. I don't know what came over me,' Hays moaned as Pat ran off to catch up with the rest of the squad, who were by now disappearing into the distance.

Breaking the grip Hays had on my arm, the thought of getting him to carry on with the test entered my mind. But at the suggestion, his bottom lip wobbled and tears rolled down his face. Seconds later, the full waterworks appeared. Accompanied by mumbling and gesticulation, it was getting close to a full-scale emotional breakdown.

Bollocks! This was the last thing I needed. Just yards from Old College Headquarters, under the watchful eyes of the College Commander and Regimental Sergeant Major, the tables had turned, and it was me who felt vulnerable. There is no training to help DS deal with this scenario. Whilst I had some experience handling people suffering from hysteria, never had it been induced by a fitness session.

'Pull yourself together, soft-lad, you're making a show of the both of us. It's embarrassing.' My voice was calm and quiet, hoping a less aggressive approach would work, but Hays just cried louder. The whining was accompanied by increased grappling at my arm and buckling at the knees. So intense was his efforts to hold on tight to me, it was reminiscent of a phenomenon known as 'crag-fast', a disposition associated with fear, anxiety or emotional trauma.

Emotional breakdowns are not to be toyed with. Even if this was a little theatrical, it was clear that Hays had gone over the edge. The military are better now than ever before at recognizing and dealing with emotional stress. Servicemen can suffer emotional breakdowns before, during or after any kind of intense activity. From the classic *Blackadder* sketch of wearing underpants on the head and pencils up the nose to dishing out extreme violence, a breakdown emerges in many disguises.

My thought process was as blurred as a Turner Art prize as the rapidly developing scenario was digested. Analysing the options open to me, there were two courses of action available. Firstly, I could revert to type, shout at him, reduce him to a complete wreck and recover the dignity lost in front of the term-three students who had stopped to watch the situation unfold. The other option was to gently encourage him in a concerned father-like manner to stop crying, sit him down on the kerbstone until he regained composure, explain all was not lost and look to rebuild his confidence. By the time all outcomes had been processed, a small crowd of senior-term Officer Cadets transiting between lessons had gathered to ogle at the commotion. It was 'Catch 22'. Hays was threatening to unpick the Rowallan reputation in front of cadets on the Commissioning Course. Yet his fragile confidence would crumble under any more pressure.

Like watching a gladiator in the Coliseum, the onlooking cadets were expecting Hays to be put to the sword. The lad left me with no choice. Snatching hold of his forearm, he was dragged to his feet. With a violent jolt forward, Hays began to run. Fighting every step of the way, the crying stopped as his concentration switched to breathing and staying on his feet. 'Stop! Stop! Please stop!' Hays yelled repeatedly. Two minutes later, we crashed through the thick swing doors of the Medical Centre and Hays flopped onto the floor. A medical orderly glanced at me, raised a sarcastic smile and announced to all within earshot: 'I think Row-Co has started!'

'When you have fixed him, give me a ring at Row-Co,' I said. 'Someone will come back and collect him.' The medic looked at me disapprovingly, his eyes fixed on my exit. As the doors clattered behind me, Hays could be heard pleading with the medic: 'Don't let him come back for me. I can't go back there.'

Having missed the assessment, it was prudent of me to head for the finish line. Pat and Major Gray were leading the race, with the nearest students 10 metres behind. The remainder of the DS were encouraging the students at the rear of the run. As they passed the finish point, their times were recorded and called out by Daz. The fastest runner behind the OC completed the mile-and-a-half in eight minutes and thirty seconds, while the last few struggled across the line with times of twelve minutes or more. Over 50 per cent of the students failed to make it under ten-and-a-half minutes. Names and times duly recorded, Daz departed to his office to consolidate and analyse the results.

No sooner had they caught their breath, than Paddy doubled them back to the accommodation. For some, the exertion had been too much. Under the watchful eye of Corporal Davis, two students vomited uncontrollably. With little sympathy, once they had finished, they were ushered back into the ranks outside the accommodation, where their running times were read out. All those who completed the run within the allocated time were immediately released and rewarded with an early shower. Those who had not made the ten minutes and thirty seconds pass time, Pat punished with a 'fartleck' session. The rear of Old College – a square, grassed area with four equal sides – lends itself well to this style of interval training. Pat explained they would run down one side, walk the next, run the next and so on. One lap would be approximately 200 metres. Pat stood in the middle of the square, within easy reach of anyone failing to apply maximum effort. Ten laps, 2km and an angry Sergeant Major was a sight to strike fear into the heart of every onlooker.

This was the Rowallan way. The reward for success was not being punished. It was designed to make you fear failure and strive for success; simply put, if you failed at anything, you were punished. If you came second, you were punished. This would continue until you became obsessed with succeeding or you decided to quit. Everything a student was invited to do, was turned into a contest to identify the strong, ostracize the weak and create a winning mentality. Even eating was a contest. If you arrived last in the dinner queue, you were expected to be first out of dinner. Irrespective of what activity you had just completed, no matter the time of day, the weather or the circumstances, everything was a race. No exceptions, no excuses! Failing was not tolerated; moreover, it was always punished.

By mid-afternoon, the results of the fitness assessment had been analysed and the students divided into two platoons. Whilst divvying up the students was not rocket science, it was a closely guarded secret as to why people were sent to which platoon. Ultimately, Pat and the OC would make the decision based on experience and intuition. There was no scientific explanation for this skill.

* * *

Leading scholars have failed to explain how servicemen have the ability to assess a person's character and intuitively know how to get the best out of him. This may seem unremarkable until the skill is seen in action. Accurately assessing an individual's strengths and weaknesses in the space of a heartbeat, and adjusting the style of leadership to suit the moment, is unique and inexplicable. Many soldiers develop a heightened emotional intelligence that becomes so finely tuned that no thesis can specifically capture where it comes from or how it develops. Maybe it's a combination of dealing with multifaceted problems or the regular contact with human diversity, hardships or complex scenarios.

At best, academics describe five styles of leadership: participative, transactional, transformational, autocratic and laissez-faire. In a very clinical way, scholars would like us all to fit into one of these categories. It is fair to note that most military leaders conform to more than one of these flavours of leadership. But my observation has been that the best military leaders employ a selection of styles, one that is fit for the moment (selectional, if you like). There are times to be autocratic, periods to be transformational and even laissez-faire. In the right circumstances, a talented military leader will display every recognized style of leadership, and most of the associated characteristics in the dynamic space of a 'wicked problem'. But the true unidentifiable ingredient, the agile edge, knowing which styles to blend in order to achieve the desired effect or outcome, comes from heightened emotional intelligence. Fluid and ever-evolving, it morphs and changes several times, right up to the point of realizing success. Selectional leadership is consistently agile, with multiple interchangeable parallels, all tailored to meet the scenario but delivered with mental agility, or a level of emotional intelligence that is born from a broad understanding and depth of experience.

Military leaders and academics may not recognize selectional leadership, because it is not understood. Educators have boxed it between transformational or transactional styles. The closest any leadership journals have come to explaining it has been the emergence of 'situational leadership'. At a glance, it may appear that situational and selectional are the same, but this is far from the truth. Situational leadership is rigid in its end-state and is closer to leadership habits than it is styles. In contrast, selectional leadership has no definite end-state, just a continuous loop of learning, adaptation, blending formulas and implementation. It is truly a polar opposite to situational. Its main strength lays in its agility. It is comfortable in chaos, happy to detour, never hamstrung by think-tank formulas or scientific forecasting. In short, it remains human, with emotional intelligence acting as the gyroscope.

In humble circles, it is frequently mooted that the fundamental flaw in the planning for the second war in Iraq, known as Operation Telic, was the inability to adapt in a timely fashion with a rapidly changing situation. By definition, situational leadership is fixed by the situation. That is to say, the here and now, or in military language, the current battle. To mitigate this constraint, it is common to employ others to think beyond the current situation, ironically dislodging them from the current situation. The end result is the inability to provide a coherent solution to a quickly changing problem. In Iraq, UK and US forces failed to transition from war-fighting to peacekeeping in a coherent fashion. Sitting in my truck heading north through Basra in June 2003, I recall vividly watching the mass exodus of Coalition forces. Never-ending convoys were triumphantly heading home, unwittingly setting the ideal conditions for insurgents, semi-quasi political groups and criminals to fill the power vacuum. In recent history, this is the best example of the limitations of situational leadership.

Possibly the biggest difference between these two styles is the speed at which situational leadership can become toxic without noticing. When the situation demands, all leaders shift through the gears of command, searching for the right drive ratio. Occasionally, one must employ the ruthless efficiency of autocracy, because the situation demands it. But this is fraught with danger. The perils of autocracy lay unnoticed, like a dormant cancer. Success from autocracy is infectious. It needs no empathy, no morality, no human complexity. It is easy to understand why leaders and their deputies find it easy to employ. But beyond autocracy waits toxicity, and from this, there is no recovery.

* * *

Standing outside the accommodation at the muster point, the drizzle swirled in the high wind. No. 2 Platoon was now assembled and placed under the command of Captain Dunn, with me as his assistant. Captain Dunn welcomed them to his command whilst I stood silently surveying the list of names handed to me by Pat. Instantly, the name 'Hays' jumped off the page. Surely he wouldn't make it out of the Medical Centre! The thought of having to nurse him through the course drove me to despair. Without even knowing the lad, it was certain his inclusion would cause more trouble than a second-hand motor bought from Botch-it & Scarper! Hays conformed to the '80/20' rule, where 80 per cent of instructional time is monopolized by 20 per cent of the people.

Recruiting soldiers has always been problematic, and always will be. I knew that in the current recruiting climate, it would not be easy to get Hays removed from training. The cost of recruiting one volunteer in the 1980s or 1990s was quoted as £15,000, but in truth, the MoD would have invested much more in nurturing potential officers at universities prior to arriving at Sandhurst. No matter how poor a student, or how physically weak he may be, it was seen as the instructor's responsibility to find a way to bring him up to the required standard. We knew Hays would need many hours of 'one to one' instruction, and even then, he may have been a lost cause. Not that the task was unachievable, but there was a penalty for this monopoly. Dedicating a disproportionate time to one student denies others their fair share of attention. But in a world that strives to be politically correct, the British Army will always strive to harmonize with social trends, for if it fails to do so, the demographic pool from which it fishes will run dry. It was obvious that Hays did not have the ingredients to make a soldier, let alone an officer. Even if he was 6ft 2in and had eagle eyes with realistic hair and gripping hands, he was never going to look like a man of action! Mentally, he was weak, and physically underdeveloped, so there was little chance of success

After Captain Dunn finished delivering a mini inspirational leadership speech to the platoon, I called the nominal roll with a long hard look at each individual as his name was read out. They attempted to stand to attention and acknowledge the roll call, replying with 'Yes, Colour Sergeant!', just as Paddy had taught them. Eventually, Hays' name was read out. Mercifully there was no answer; the lad was still at the Medical Centre. My mind imagined him whining to the Medical Officer (MO) and getting a ten-day sick note. But just then, as if it was being orchestrated by a cruel prankster, he walked around the corner, bold as brass. Looking totally refreshed, almost pleased with his contribution thus far, Hays' arrival caught me off-guard.

'Ay up, Colour Sergeant,' Hays chirped at me in a thick Yorkshire accent. His squeaking voice cut me to the bone. 'The Medical Officer said I wah ok! He gave me the thumbs-up to rejoin training.'

Showing a bit of compassion, I asked what the MO had thought the problem was. Hays rolled his eyes back, canted his head to the left and tutted before offering an answer: 'He said I were probably putting in too much effort – close to exhaustion.'

'What! What? Say that again, he said fucking what?' I needed to check my anger. Colour Sergeant instructors are regularly sacked for using vulgar or abusive language, but Hays had taken me to boiling point.

Struggling to hide my contempt, I openly joked and cursed at nothing in particular, stopping only when my head hurt from listening to my own ranting. Gritting my teeth and trying to control my temper, I mustered just enough polite words to direct Hays to stand with the rest of the platoon. After a short wait, the photographer turned up to record on film for eternity those who started course number 4/93. Dressed in their red tracksuits, they tentatively posed with just the faintest of smiles. The next time they were to have a platoon photograph, the picture would record the faces of those who passed one of the hardest tests the military had to offer. In the meantime, the current picture would be used to identify individuals as we learnt who they were and serve as a crude 'chuff chart', crossing out the faces of those who failed.

By four o'clock that afternoon, the students were ready to receive the official opening address from the Company Commander. Major Gray had been a Row-Co student in the early Eighties. Now in his late 30s, he loved the outdoors and was incredibly fit, not to mention being the fastest member of the Directing Staff over a flat mile. Running was like a religion to him, with every spare minute committed to his own personal fitness training. He possessed the finest qualities of a modern-day officer. An effortless ability to mix intelligence and common-sense made him very approachable. To place this observation into context, it is worth noting that not all Army officers are approachable or intelligent. Like all walks of life, the corps of officers occasionally attracts its fair share of undesirables, despite the industry's greatest efforts to ensure their proven pedigree. Additionally, one should never confuse intelligence with education. Some of the most brilliant minds have changed the world on little more than a state education: Bill Gates and Steve Jobs spring to mind. Therefore, it will not be a surprise to learn that the British Army has its fair share of cussed characters that eventually end up in positions of importance. As hard as it may be to believe, there are officers in command of many hundreds of soldiers who should never be allowed to be in charge of more people than they could share a ride on a unicycle with, let alone a battalion of squaddies. Whilst all military commanders are selected through due process before they earn the privilege to lead servicemen, the selection is not made by measuring their ability to lead. Consequently, a good number of leaders fail to connect intellectually or emotionally with real soldiers for fear of compromising their authority.

Major Gray, however, was a 'Master of Leadership' and knew how to galvanise a team. Despite the serious nature of his job, he enjoyed the occasional team joke. The training team would regularly plot childlike antics, with hilarious results. In the weeks before the course formed up, the Directing Staff conducted a detailed reconnaissance of all routes we would use during the course. On one occasion we took a trip around Snowdonia to rehearse the running routes for the final exercise. Halfway up the 'Pig-Trail', we stopped to discuss the procedures to be followed should we suffer casualties. Having removed our rucksacks and boiled our brews, pored over the maps and likely scenarios, Pat distracted Major Gray while Captain Dunn stuffed his rucksack with several chunks of Welsh slate. It wasn't until we had completed the walk that Major Gray twigged that his rucksack had become much heavier. Watching him dig out rock after rock from the deepest recesses of his rucksack, bemused by their sudden appearance, only made us laugh harder. Mercilessly, Pat ridiculed him for leaving his kit unattended in the presence of his juvenile understudies. Desperately defending his pride, the OC then tried to convince Captain Dunn that he had placed the slate in the rucksack himself and the rocks were all part of his personal training regime!

The students assembled in Mons Hall, a small all-seated theatre used for briefings and lectures. In front of them sat the complete training team. Standing behind the lectern, acting as master of ceremonies, Major Gray introduced his staff one by one:

'By now you will have already seen a fair bit of Company Sergeant Major Swift. Until recently, he was a Colour Sergeant in New College before being selected for promotion to Warrant Officer Class Two, and winning the appointment of Company Sergeant Major, Rowallan Company. He is a hugely experienced soldier, who has served with all three battalions of the Parachute Regiment. Previously, the Sergeant Major instructed at the famed Para Depot, and at the Parachute Training Company also known as P Company. His operational service is exceptional and includes Northern Ireland, the Falkland Islands, Bosnia and Cyprus to name just a few theatres. For those who are unfamiliar with the role of the CSM, please be advised that he is my right-hand man. If he issues an instruction, assume it has come from my office. He is by far the busiest man in this organization, so please don't waste his time with niff-naff and trivia; it will only make him angrier than he already is.

'Platoon Commander of No. 1 Platoon is Captain Tom Watts. Captain Watts is on loan to Sandhurst from the Special Air Service, where he has just finished serving as a Troop Commander. During the recent Gulf War, he played a pivotal role in locating and destroying Saddam Hussein's Scud

Missile sites and mobile launchers. During the early phases of the Bosnia conflict, Captain Watts collated vital intelligence, leading to numerous successful military operations against one of the world's most tyrannical leaders and undoubtedly saving countless lives and preventing further ethnic cleansing.

'He is assisted by Colour Sergeant Jones of the Irish Guards. This is his third course, making him the longest-serving member of Rowallan Company. Colour Sergeant Jones has been at Sandhurst for nearly two years, previously serving as one of the key personnel with the prestigious F Company, organizing ceremonial duties at Buckingham Palace and preparing others for public pageants. A soldier of distinction, he has stood before Her Majesty the Queen no fewer than ten times Trooping the Colour.

'Captain James Dunn commands No. 2 Platoon. A member of the Airborne Forces, he has been extremely busy prior to his arrival at Sandhurst. His operational portfolio includes tours of Cyprus with the UN, Bosnia and the recent Gulf War. More recently, Captain Dunn has just completed his second tour of Northern Ireland. In his spare time, he is an international athlete, representing the country on numerous occasions.

'Assisting him is Colour Sergeant McCarthy. A member of the Light Division, he has just returned from Central Africa. As part of the British Military Mission, he was tasked with establishing a new Defence Force for the protection of Mozambique. Training two warring factions, 'RENAMO' and 'FRELIMO', makes him one of only a handful of soldiers to successfully partake in executing the Rome Peace Accord. A veteran of multiple tours of Northern Ireland, Colour Sergeant McCarthy is an accomplished Counter-Revolutionary Warfare Instructor.'

It was an impressive gathering of military personnel who understood life at the 'coal face' of a busy army. As we listened attentively to Major Gray's opening address, we all sat motionless and devoid of expression, whilst surveying the students in the lecture hall. Without exception, they all appeared flustered and anxious. Most of them were still red and sweating from their earlier exertions. On the huge silver screen, they watched a short homemade video compiled by the Company Second-in-Command. This showed a few highlights of previous courses, including students mountain climbing and abseiling in the driving rain.

In one clip, a number of students were hill-walking in a snow blizzard. As a student tried to negotiate a wire mesh fence by straddling it, he slipped and fell face-first into the snow-covered elephant grass. His trailing leg got hung up on the top single strand of barbed wire and his trousers ripped wide open. With the howling wind obliterating the modulation, the student lay motionless calling for assistance. When it failed to arrive, he flipped himself over and came to rest laying on his rucksack, ripping the leg of his trousers clean off. Like a stranded tortoise, he lay still for a short while, legs and arms splayed in different directions, a naked leg exposed to the elements with steam slowly rising from the bulk of his torso and head. Agonisingly slowly, he started to move; first his legs kicked out in search of a foothold, then his hands searched for an anchor point. With a sudden jerk, the forlorn figure rolled back over on to his belly and tucked his knees up to his chest so the heavy rucksack was centrally balanced on his back. The camera zoomed in on his face until the screen was filled with nothing other than his expressions of pain, hunger, tiredness and dejection. The audience shook their heads in disbelief, whilst some began mumbling to themselves. They were mesmerized by the video, almost living the pain of the student in the clip. In any other context, the video clip would have been hilarious, even a contender for *You've Been Framed*. But armed with the knowledge that this was the very thing they were about to be invited to partake in, there was nothing but empathy and respect emanating from those sat watching. Silence descended on the lecture hall as the video finished and the OC switched on the lights before continuing:

> 'Don't freak out! If you have the ability, we will find it and develop it. But I give you fair warning, a lot of you will not pass this course. The average failure rate is 60 per cent. Leading soldiers into war, just like Captain Watts and Dunn have been doing, is not for the deluded fantasizing about the grandeur of the Officers' Mess. There is no drinking G&Ts on the balcony watching the war go by as a manservant fetches and carries for you. It's about developing the ability to beat a vicious adversary in the most unimaginable circumstances, simultaneously remaining composed enough to inspire thirty battle-weary soldiers. It's a test of character, resolve and fortitude, and for those who are able to see the course to its conclusion, you will be better equipped to cope with life's trials and tribulations no matter your employment.'

That final statement struck me as being peculiar: 'no matter your employment.' What other employment could there be after you get to the end of the course?

The OC added: 'I am aware that at this moment in time, you will not be able to see the light at the end of the tunnel. In a feeble effort to reassure you all, please let me introduce Officer Cadet Reed, recipient of the Highland Trophy and top Rowallan student from course 6/92.'

If the OC thought that Reed was going to ease anxiety, he was hugely mistaken. The Final Term cadet described the course in his own uncensored words – 'exhausting', 'terrifying' and 'relentless pressure' were mentioned in his opening lines. It was an astonishing confession of pain, misery and endurance.

Reed finished by quoting a number of statistics: 'We averaged 50km running every week. We averaged four hours of sleep each night. At least one person left every day in the first two weeks of the course. Most significantly, less than 40 per cent of those who started passed.' Reed left the audience stunned. He offered just one more piece of advice: 'Learn quickly and win at all cost, or life becomes insufferable.'

Major Gray grabbed his briefing notes, gave an awkward wink to his staff and walked past Pat, who was about to take centre stage. Pat flicked open his notebook, slammed it on top of the lectern and started to talk about discipline and camp trivia in his own unique style. Eventually, he finished by explaining what happens for the rest of the day:

'Next on the agenda at fun school is kit search. Your Colour Sergeant will take you to your accommodation and sanitize your entire luggage. He will remove the following items, as they will now be considered as contraband. Chocolate! Credit cards! Money! Sweets! Pictures! Medicine! Smoking material! Additional military material! Books, radios or anything else we think you would like to keep. That equals anything that may bring you pleasure or make you laugh or reminisce.'

Known as discombobulation, this is a common technique used by the military. It is specifically designed to cause disorientation. Special Forces use this practice to maintain the 'shock of capture' and retain the initiative with people they are interrogating. Deprivation is a crucial tool used by the DS to speed up the process of team bonding. By creating a level playing field and putting everyone through the same discomfort, the students develop inherent mutual respect for each other and develop a unified focus and common goal. The average person will cringe with the perceived level of cruelty inflicted on these young men, but knowing what depths of despair war brings on young officers, it was best they learnt to manage this kind of treatment in the comforts of a training environment, rather than realize they can't cope whilst on operations fighting an evil enemy in a far-flung corner of the world.

As we marched back to the accommodation, the dark winter afternoon had robbed us of daylight. Forward five steps, turnabout, march back four steps, turnabout, march forward five steps, turnabout, march back four, and suddenly 100 metres became 1,000 metres. By the time we made it back to the accommodation, the sweat had begun to flow freely down the foreheads of several students.

'What's wrong with you lot?' I barked, showing my displeasure at their efforts. 'We've only walked 100 metres, and most of you are close to dropping down dead. PlayStations and Game Boys; the only thing fit about you lot is your thumbs.'

As part of the indoctrination process, no matter how demanding an event or task may be, the DS would seek to trivialize it, belittle the size of the achievement and effort. There was a method in the madness of this approach. Firstly, military history has demonstrated that no plan has ever survived contact with the enemy. It is essential that all officers develop resilience capable of withstanding the cruellest twist of fate or the hardest physical challenge, yet retain an analytical focus to pick their way through the most complicated of problems while simultaneously enduring incredible levels of stress. Moreover, leadership is at times all about perception, and even when all around you there is panic, a leader must be the epitome of composure. Surreptitiously, the DS coached students to grow a mask of command to prepare them for the loneliest place on the planet, being in command when it all goes disastrously wrong.

The students were crammed into the platoon corridor and the kit search got underway. With Pat hanging around to check my performance, I put on the 'angry Colour Sergeant' act. Pat was still to be won over. My predecessor had let him down massively, and he was still hurting from a trust betrayed. To prevent a reoccurrence, his antennae were now tuning into my credentials.

'OK you bunch of dreamers, empty your suitcases and bags onto the floor where you stand. I need to see everything!' I shouted.

Instantly, the floor was covered with all sorts of items, from clothes to hair dryers, even the occasional teddy bear, before I continued: 'As I search your kit, state your name and give me a quick brief on your background. Who you are, where you've been, what school you went to and anything else of interest!'

The background brief was essential to achieving a balance of attitude and ability throughout the platoon. By what was said, and how it was delivered, I could gain a huge insight into someone's character. Conceptually, by pairing the Etonian with the rough and ready Yorkshireman, we merge together opposite ends of the social spectrum. A form of social engineering, the idea was to heighten the experience. The rooms originally built for one person were better described as a large broom cupboard, affording no space for privacy. Coping with this heightened level of proximity is an ergonomic nightmare in its own right. However, being crammed in a small room with a total stranger, learning to deal with each other's most annoying habits is an important part of personal development. It bleeds away any selfish attitudes and educates individuals to consider others, as well as providing a partner to work with and share in your misery. Of course, there are those who can't tolerate this kind of cohabitation. Inevitably, they would drift towards violence, the old-fashioned way of reconciling differences. Although never encouraged, and if discovered it would be punishable by instant dismissal, it was recognized as a learning process in its own right.

Having listened to a number of briefs, I arranged my first pairing. Standing nearest to me was Weston, an affluent young man who eloquently repeated tales of exotic countries and safaris in Kenya, Zimbabwe and South Africa. The young man had attended Winchester College and proudly wore his house tie just to ensure everyone knew it. If he told me once that it was thanks to his father's cheque book, he told me a thousand times. As if to enforce his standing in the hierarchical order of wealth, he requested a safe place for the Rolex Submariner watch he waved in front of me. Endlessly dropping names of the rich and famous like they were going out of fashion, his new friends seemed impressed. Instantly, it was easy to see why the selectors at RCB sent him to Rowallan. Visions of the staff at RCB laughing as they referred him to Row-Co whizzed around my brain. His arrogance made him the ideal person to bunk with Mathews. Born and bred in Hereford, he spoke with a broad farmer's accent, with everything appearing to start and end with an 'errrr'! Short, with a powerful frame, Mathews appeared keen to advertise his rugby talents. Judging by his cauliflower ears and bent nose, he was overdue a rest from the game!

Opposite their room, Haigh and Packman were paired. Dressed like an Oxford history teacher, complete with pen marks around the pockets and grubby elbow patches, Haigh was intellectually very sharp. With two firsts – one in theology, the other in history – he was an odd candidate for the Army. Slightly older than the average student at the age of 27, he spoke in long and convoluted sentences, never risking a simple word if ten would fit. For all his obvious intelligence, there was a nervousness about his behaviour. Comically, his edgy twitch suited his personality. Despite this disposition, there was clear potential hidden under the pile of theological claptrap he spouted. Packman appeared well prepared: coherent answers efficiently fended all my intrusive questions, unwittingly making me suspicious. A big grin on his face gave him a smug look, not amounting to arrogance, but he was clearly keen to get started. Something we both had in common. His preparation comprised some form of previous military experience, and this would be the ideal crutch for Haigh. My eyes were drawn to a selection of tablets in a 'girly' make-up bag. All the usual suspects, from Imodium to Tiger Balm. Purchased without prescription, the collection was hiding something else. He was proud of his medical kit, but despite agreeing that it was prudent to have all these items, it irked me that he had arrived with such an array of medicines. A feeling of distrust was bubbling just below the surface of his character.

Stone and Watson were thrown into the next room. Both were very similar in character, despite Stone coming from Merseyside and Watson from Kent. An occasional hint of uncorroborated arrogance surfaced in Watson's voice as we discussed his background. In his suitcase was no end of contraband, which he surrendered quickly. Even items he was told not to bring featured amongst his belongings. Subconsciously, I had him pegged as a chancer, someone likely to take a shortcut, the kind who parks in the disabled bay at Tesco's because it's convenient. If this was true, the course would break him early.

Stone had obvious issues. With buck teeth, a face full of acne and freckles framed by a mop of ginger hair, he had an unfortunate gormless expression. There was an uneasy manner about him; he would not have been out of place selling knock-off DVDs in the local pub. He giggled at the misfortune of his peers, failing to understand that this was a shared predicament. Overly keen to placate my questions, my 'spider senses' tingled every time he spoke. It was unfortunate that his demeanour was irksome; consequently, he would draw attention just by being present. This wasn't the best pairing, but time was pressing and there was still much to achieve. At the first opportunity, these two needed to be separated to prevent mutual destruction.

Squeezed into the room opposite were Rideout and Murphy. Rideout was of Mediterranean heritage. With a healthy glow to his skin, thick-set black hair and dark eyes, he stumbled his way through his brief. Flustered by my every question, he constantly flapped his arms and screwed his face up whilst delivering his answers. His eyes bounced frantically around his head and his hands continued to fidget long after the talking ceased, exemplifying his selection to Row-Co. Suffering from 'stupid expression syndrome', a permanently startled look on his face denied him the ability to be taken seriously. His new roommate, Murphy, was the complete opposite. He appeared to be a calm and collected young man, but I knew that he was neither. I could sniff an act a mile away, and quickly placed him into the apathetic box of my notional character sorting lexicon. Choosing his words carefully, there was a lack of sincerity with his attentiveness. This was a young man who was well-drilled by someone to get protocols and replies in all the right places. Despite his engaging character, the lack of substance compromised his disposition. Nevertheless, it was a good start; perhaps too good, as any normal person would have been at least a little anxious.

Puddick was the son of a serving barrister. Quick to inform me of his First-Class Honours in law at Oxford, the clothes in his suitcase suggested he hadn't given up hope of following in his father's footsteps. Wearing an expensive suit cut in Savile Row, he definitely looked the part. The pinstripe suit with crimson silk lining, with matching tie and handkerchief, must have cost a fortune. But for all this refinery, his words lacked conviction. He appeared keen enough; maybe it was nothing more than the shock of capture. Puddick shared with Boyle, who was a typical Scouser. Cheeky, with a quick wit, he was streetwise and keen to show it. I removed lots of his personal belongings, just to test the boundaries and identify a weak point. The more that was removed, the broader his smile. It was my mischievous character that paired these together. Succumbing to my inner demon, they were bound to have conflicting views on the application of the judicial system! He oozed eagerness, and for geographical reasons I took an instant shine to him, but his gullible disposition suggested he was an affirmed conformer. You could have told him black was white and Boyle would have swallowed it. When I spoke to him, his expression peeled his face backwards like he was caught in a wind tunnel. When I stopped, the smile disappeared and his face turned to jelly. It was like playing with a new toy, watching his eyebrows raise and fall with the pitch of my voice.

Next was Williams, a North Yorkshire lad, who appeared to be a little wet and lacking in confidence. Williams was aged 19, with greasy hair and mild acne. He reminded me of a TV character called 'Tory boy'. Full of spittle and misplaced clichés, his mouth was an odd shape, full of cockeyed teeth that appeared to be constantly on display. His gangly gait was going to be an issue with some of the physical demands. An eclectic academic background left him with a confused accent. It was more Lancashire than Yorkshire, but every so often he would clip his T's and compromise his lineage. His new roommate, Francis, carried more than his fair share of 'puppy fat'. His physical appearance was secondary to his nervous and clumsy demeanour. Despite being eloquent with his responses, there was an underlying nervousness. Pleasingly, he possessed a sense of humour and a keen wit. There was a warmth about his personality that was infectious and easy to relate to. If we could tighten up his body tone and overall confidence, he would do well.

At the halfway point of searching and pairing, people were slowly claiming their own space on the emptying corridor. Hays was by now at the far end by the fire escape, occupying a large space of his own. There was no attempt to keep connected with the rest of the students; he just stood there gawping at what was going on. This was a concerning indication, which was quickly picked up by the others. Before moving into his room, Boyle had twice tried to encourage him to join the rest of the platoon and include him in the fold. But Hays appeared content with his isolated position, almost revelling at being divorced from the group.

Next to be paired were an ex-serving soldier and a military virgin. King was confident and well-prepared, mainly due to the five years of service with the Royal Engineers. It was an unwritten rule for RCB to send ex-rankers to Rowallan, so it made sense to pair him with Witherspoon. King's presence in the platoon was a real bonus. Having someone who could interpret military peculiarities and impart his knowledge in my absence would be worth its weight in gold. On the other hand, military virgins struggle the most in the early stages, both emotionally and physically. They fail to understand some of the seemingly pointless tasks and one-dimensional conversations. Incapable of comprehending the requirement to cooperate in communal activities, as well as sharing responsibilities for everything, was their biggest downfall. This is not to say they didn't accept this sort of lifestyle, but acceptance occasionally presents problems. This sudden change to their life order can manifest a desire to question everything and somehow expect justification. The military institution is quick to stereotype this behaviour if someone fails to conform. By the ignorant, they are labelled as mavericks or rebels. This is not entirely accurate, and the use of these phrases conversely says more about the user than the victim. Mavericks and rebels can be force-multipliers, if well led. There is a degree of tolerance required before it can be determined if they are truly trouble-starters or geniuses in waiting.

Across the corridor, Danner and Trollope shared the smallest of all the rooms. Their bunk backed onto the utility room, subsequently losing space to the industrial plumbing that fed the water to the showers, sinks and toilets. Danner, clearly an Etonian, was the size of a small mountain, although most of his weight was puppy fat. The flab was creeping up on him. It showed around the cheeks and below the chin. In every way, he was typical of other Etonians I had instructed previously. Intellectually quick, his tortured English was hard for me to decipher. Every answer came with hand gestures and emphasized by facial contortions. He needed to give each answer some form of an analogy in a slightly patronizing fashion, albeit innocently. It was hard not to pass comment on the clothes in his case. The glare from the bright yellow corduroy trousers, grotesque multi-coloured shirts and emerald green low-cut slip-on shoes nearly burnt the retinas out of my eyes. It was most likely that he was just too idle to dress sensibly. With the contents of his suitcase sprawled across the floor, the yellows, blues and reds intertwined to resemble an award-winning piece of abstract art.

Similar in build and gait to Danner, Trollope also carried a bit too much weight around his waist. The beginnings of a tyre flopping over his trousers was unsightly. He was distinctly unhappy with the experience thus far. Although coming from the north of England, his grumpy aura didn't surprise me. His discomfort was understandable, but once again, it was hard to figure out why he thought he would enjoy Army life. This despondency would not survive the course and if it persisted, he wouldn't last much more than a week. It appeared Trollope was suffering more than the shock of capture; he was drowning in the disappointment of reality.

Equally unhappy was Goldson. Deflated and resigned from the start, there was a distinct lack of interest and a hint of subversion in his body language. The second such attitude in quick order, there was a compelling need to ask him why he had decided to join the forces. Lethargically, he explained it was always his aspiration to be in the Army and follow in his father's footsteps. Not wanting to shoot him down on his first solo flight, I humoured him, but secretly felt his days were already numbered. He was paired with Moore for no reason other than they both wore that 'disappointed child at Christmas' expression on their face. With dour expressions and lethargic gait, they were dubbed 'grumpy and grumpier'! At least they both smiled in agreeance with me when they were told.

For a moment it occurred to me that maybe all was not lost. The year before arriving at Sandhurst, Moore had been rejected by the Royal Marines. Retelling the story of how the Marines suspected he had homosexual tendencies made everyone giggle. At a time when the military feared that gay men and lesbians would undermine its fighting spirit and cohesion, he was a victim of 'military irrational fear'. Notwithstanding the stupidity of those who refused him entry, one glance at Moore and the way he dressed and you could understand why the Marines had jumped to this conclusion. He was a little camp, with too much attention paid to personal grooming, but nothing more than that. There was a steadfast, determined character waiting to get out, and his tale about the Marines confirmed my initial impression.

Long before it was made legal for homosexuals to join the British Army in 2000, I never subscribed to marginalizing people for their differences. Specifically, should an individual feel the desire to volunteer to put his life on the line for democracy or other honourable reasons, he has a divine right to choose his own path in life. What is the national debt owed to Alan Turing? What would the outcome have been if he had been prosecuted for his homosexuality before breaking the Enigma code? A conservative guess is that his work saved 14 million lives and shortened the war by two years. Moore had slightly effeminate features mixed with a Blackadder rubberized face. Sometimes initial impressions are misleading, and this was certainly the case with Moore. His words carried a hint of authority that others had lacked, whilst his efforts to maintain eye contact displayed a clear sign of confidence; he was calmly assured. Although there wouldn't be much fun in that room, it was a good pairing.

Three students were left, and it was clear that they had self-selected who they wanted to bunk with. Barns and Lane stood side by side. Cheekily, they gathered their kit and moved into the last-but-one room without any words from me. Barns was a tall, thin and gangly lad who wore a fixed grin. A well-travelled character despite his mummy's boy appearance, apart from some early nerves – which were not a bad thing – he had potential written all over him. Slightly pale, with deep-set eyes and jet-black hair, I could see him growing into an old brigadier in charge of the village fete fifty years from now! Zealously, he answered my questions on his recent exploits whilst treading carefully not to make it appear he had been on the biggest holiday of his life. There was a lack of muscular build to support his tall frame: the first few weeks were probably going to be his toughest. Getting over the physical pounding he was about to receive would be his greatest challenge. His roommate Lane was a young, inexperienced lad with no evident character to identify with. Devoid of spark, the prominent northern accent, mixed with colloquial language, did little to mask a pitiful image. It was not hard to see that the lad was already out of his depth. Uneasy in my presence, uncomfortable in this environment, his body language screamed 'failure'. He had no contraband in his bags, not even one additional item of toiletries. With the persona and mannerisms of a young offender, getting him through the course was going to be tough.

Unintentionally, but understandably, Hays occupied the last room on his own. For some reason, this didn't strike me as a huge problem for the time being. People would be moved around on a weekly basis, and it would be useful for him to get acclimatized slowly. Almost pleased that he had made it to the end of his first day at Sandhurst, he dutifully surrendered a bagful of medicine for inspection. A beaming smile accompanied his attempt to explain the reason for each of the containers: 'These are iron tablets to increase my low energy. This is a multi-vitamin supplement to protect me from scabies and scurvy. This one is …'……

I snapped at Hays and interrupted him mid-flow: 'You're taking the piss out of me, Hays! Why do you have all these medicines?'

Failing to understand the rhetorical nature of my question, Hays repeated his answer. This time he was allowed to finish. It was important that he knew his needs had been heard. After the conclusion of his mind-numbing waffle, it was time to spell out the Sergeant Major's directions.

'Which one of these medicines do you have a prescription for?'

'The family doctor advised me to take them. Every one is for a specific reason.'

'That's not what I asked! This is not a game of "guess what I take"! I just need to know, which of these twenty tubs of tablets and creams have been given to you by a doctor using a prescription?'

'None, Sir!'

'OK, at last, an answer. You can have them all back once you finish the course.'

Hays withdrew his chin and bit his lip, fighting the desire to say another word. He wasn't exactly a hypochondriac, but it was hard to understand how someone of his age could have such a large collection of medicines. To put him in a room on his own, professionally, was a poor judgment call. He had already marginalized himself from his peers; leaving him in a room on his own, his fate had been sealed. With hindsight, Hays should have been put into a room with a stronger character. More than anything, he needed to be with someone who could inspire him. Maybe, subconsciously he was already written off: his behaviour had confirmed my bias too early. It matters not that he was always going to fail, only that he had been failed by me on day one, something that took me a few months to realize.

With all the students busy settling into their rooms, the accommodation lights blazed into the night sky. Muted conversations seeped through the sash windows, occasionally interrupted by the slamming of a collapsed ironing board or falling loo seat. A quick look up and down the corridor confirmed that most people understood the implied tasking, and the order was given to stop for the evening meal. A short walk to the canteen, and the students were given twenty minutes to eat their supper before they were escorted back to their new homes. Before the day had finished, Captain Dunn addressed the platoon in our study hall. It was less of a hall and more of a large classroom, and would be the central hub for most of the platoon's activities. Housing everything from exercise planning to academic studies, the hall would eventually become their second home. Where possible, Captain Dunn and I would impart much of our knowledge in the comfort of the classroom environment.

He reintroduced himself by giving a more detailed synopsis of his career, finishing off by explaining the concept of the 'Chain of Command' and why it was relevant to everyone from this point forward. Although this process is not unique to the military, only the military guard it so parochially. Further explained was the protocol and etiquette for the many encounters with the staff at the Academy. After fifteen minutes or so, Captain Dunn's day was complete.

I made my way back to the DS corridor, where Captain Dunn was just changing into his civilian clothing, getting ready to do some personal fitness training. He had an important race which was only a week away, and his dedication was unrivalled.

'Boss, I'm not holding much hope for one or two of those characters,' I said.

'Agreed, Colour. Hays won't last the duration.'

'Not just Hays. I was picking up a handful of bad vibes from a few other characters.' At this early stage, neither of us could put names to faces, so we just went by descriptions: 'The tubby lad is going to struggle.'

'Who? Do you mean Mr Blobby?' laughed Captain Dunn.

Just then, the DS corridor burst into a chorus of 'Blobby, Blobby, Blobby' calls, made famous by Noel Edmonds' TV programme. Captain Watts, who was also getting changed into his fizz kit, shouted out that he also had a Mr Blobby. For a short time, we all argued who had the fattest student. Finally, Captain Dunn conceded and christened our overweight student (Trollope) 'Half Blobby', while Captain Watts called his student 'Full Blobby'. The use of nicknames, despite being unorthodox and frowned upon, was very useful during the early stages of the course. It described and identified people with relative ease, negating the need for biographies and pictures. Although risky and unacceptable by today's standards, for Rowallan it worked.

Captain Dunn locked his door, hid the key above the door frame and headed to the gym. It would be midnight before he got to bed. At nearly 2200hrs, my preparation for the next day was complete, less my diary. Keeping an accurate account of how people were performing was pivotal to developing a bespoke approach for their future development. As I headed out of the accommodation, the students were still bumping into each other in their tiny rooms as they politely searched for personal space. Best they get used to it quickly, for despite the feeling of high intensity, training is the easiest part of soldiering; the real thing is harder and the consequences of getting it wrong are much more sinister.

It was less than a quarter of a mile to my bunk in the Warrant Officers and Sergeants' Mess. I walked slowly across the forbidden grass at the rear of the College, safe in the knowledge that the Academy Sergeant Major would be tucked up in his bed, so there was no one around to shout at me. Life is paradoxical at the best of times, but Sandhurst was even more so. For the twenty-one students of No. 2 Platoon, I had just become their tin god. They would fear, love, hate and enjoy my company in the weeks ahead. Having played this role before, the power and influence an instructor has over his charges could be mutually intoxicating. What they wouldn't know was that every move I made, every decision or order issued, someone in the Academy was assessing me and watching me, keen to scalp me if I got it wrong. All instructors at Sandhurst are known as 'Survivors'. This is for two reasons. Firstly, they must survive the intensity of the selection cadre, which lasts more than two months and crams in every arduous event the regular Commissioning Course endures. Ordinarily, there are nearly 200 candidates starting the selection process, with as few as twenty-eight places available. Secondly, to become a real survivor, they must complete the two-year posting without being sacked. On average, the Academy would sack two instructors each year. No one was ever under any illusions; the Academy Sergeant Major was fearsome. Any indiscretion, no matter how trivial, would attract his attention. In a parallel universe, this made him my tin god.

Chapter Two

Male Bonding

Rain pelting against the window of my bunk woke me long before the alarm clock burst into life. It was five o'clock, and winter's welcome gift to the course was Hurricane Abigail, the first of several storms being forecast. Before setting off to the Dungeon, I took a quick shower, more to kick-start my senses than for hygiene purposes. The swirling rain danced on the flooded tarmac roads as I took the short walk to the student accommodation. My jacket offered little protection as water slowly trickled down my neck. As I edged closer to the accommodation, the buzz of activity sliced through the noise of the rain gushing from drainpipes and overflowing gutters. From behind rain-splashed windows, brilliant white fluorescent lights pierced the morning gloom as shadows scurried frantically past the frosted glass of the shower block. Swing doors banging, toilets flushing and extractor fans whirling loudly, the cacophony of communal living emphasized the busy start to the day. Conspicuous by the absence of light, one room remained idle, but in the confusion of the previous day's activities, there was no guarantee that the room was occupied.

Students rushed about the accommodation half-dressed and a little disorientated, clearly still overwhelmed by their new surroundings. Checking on the darkened room, the expectation was an unoccupied bed. I turned the handle and pushed open the door. In a millisecond, fury and rage consumed me. A tidal wave of anger ransacked my calm exterior as the fluorescent lights flickered into full illumination. Hays was peacefully sleeping, wearing an annoyingly big grin on his face. Indignantly, he was ripped from his bed by his sideboards and dragged into the corridor. Like an errant falcon tethered to its trainer's glove, he flapped erratically at my hand as he was frog-marched to the washroom. Still clad in his paisley-patterned pyjamas, I thrust him into the shower. Bewildered and dazed, he initially protested with a feeble struggle. It was too late; I was committed, and his objections were lost in a blur of irrepressible disappointment.

With Hays pinned against the white tiles of the shower cubical, cold water pouring over the pair of us, the red mist cleared. I had overstepped the mark, truly in danger of being dishonourably dismissed from the Academy. Easing my grip, I tried to recover the violation by rationalizing with him. It was a pathetic attempt to mitigate my behaviour. To this day, I am not too sure who benefited the most from the soaking. My actions were overenthusiastic by a country mile, and the event produced a soaking for the pair of us. Being drenched whilst playing judge, jury and executioner had more than a feeling of déjà vu. Having regained my composure and berated myself for letting the incident develop unbridled, the cause and effects were reviewed in my mind. Trying to justify my actions by convincing myself 'this is what would have happened in the good old days' whilst simultaneously acknowledging that 'this is no way to train anyone, let alone a future leader' was nothing short of pitiful! The sight of the hapless boy cowering under the cold water in his paisley pyjamas had a sobering effect. My resolve for instructing needed recalibrating. The reaction was disproportionate to the problem; if it wasn't addressed immediately, it would be me who wouldn't last the course.

As an instructor on a course as intense as Row-Co, you give your heart and soul to your students, as you demand their heart and soul in return. It is a unique and privileged position, with dynamics that are hard for the general public to understand. For a short yet defining period of their life, you become their surrogate father, and they your adopted child. To this end, the sense of disappointment when you are let down is hard to accept – frequently the response is twisted by the emotion. I note this not to justify my numerous indiscretions, but to acknowledge that the cause and effect are not aligned like a mathematical formula. Consequently, the human factor contributes hugely to the intensity of this kind of relationship. From flash to bang, Hays had me at 'silly point' in the blink of an eye.

By 0600hrs, the course had paraded outside the accommodation before being swiftly marched to breakfast. All meals were taken at a frantic pace on Row-Co, and breakfast was no exception. Within ten minutes of arriving at the canteen, the students were given a one-minute warning order by Paddy, who, like me, would escort his students to every meal for the first four weeks. Paddy's voice reverberated around the huge canteen, which was empty apart from our students: 'One minute to be outside. Be there or be square.'

Even if you were the only person in the canteen, this amount of time was totally unfeasible. Forty-two students trying to get served all at once was never going to be ergonomically possible. Predictably, only a few students made it outside on time having eaten breakfast. It took a further five minutes for the remainder of the course to eventually assemble outside of the canteen. Paddy stood in front of forty-two bemused faces, his arms crossed and frowning with disapproval:

> 'You civi wankers, you think that rules are made to be broken. Well at UOTC maybe, but no in my army. When I say something, I mean it, so when I said "outside in one minute", I meant outside in one minute, not four! Not five minutes. So get this inta your wee heads! Failing to comply warrants a punishment.'

Paddy's strong Belfast accent was menacing even when he wasn't angry; add a hint of disappointment to his tone, and it was terrifying. For the next five minutes, Paddy inflicted a punishment, Rowallan-style: press-ups, sit-ups, burpees and squat thrusts. Followed by more press-ups, more sit-ups and more burpees or squat thrusts. By the time he had finished, several students were looking decidedly pale, while others struggled to keep down their breakfast. But just for good measure, we ran all the way back to the accommodation, the long way around.

As daylight filled Chapel Square, the rest of the Academy woke. There remained a few hours of administration to complete before the course could truly get underway. I couldn't wait; the first day of a new course, and it was time for a baptism of fire. Pat walked the corridors, bellowing instructions at the top of his voice: 'Get outside. Five minutes, outside. Red rugby shirts, lightweight trousers and boots.'

Captain Dunn chatted away randomly to anyone who would listen as he was swamped by students pushing past him heading for the exit. Outside, Major Gray manoeuvred through the assembling crowd and into a position to address the course. He explained that they were all about to go for their first collective jog. This was not entirely correct, depending on whose perspective you took. The golden thread of an officer's education is integrity. Should he lie, all trust would be irrefutably lost. It is unthinkable and unacceptable for an officer to lie. However, a masterful play on words would be essential if the DS were to keep the upper hand during the course. The exact truth would have been 'we are going on a 6km run, stopping to do various physical exercises on the route.' But to let the student know this would be to give him knowledge, and be better placed to make assumptions and predictions that would disarm our influence. It was critical that no one had the ability to assess how much effort was required during fitness sessions. At this early stage we wanted full-blooded commitment, for only then could we assess the best way to develop an individual's suitability for leadership.

Careful management and manipulation of information kept students at a high state of readiness. The aim was to develop an individual's self-reliance, build resilience, nurture initiative and unite them through misery. Concerted discombobulation was the core premise of the approved programme. Professionally, it is official military doctrine, used to disorientate, confuse and dislodge an opponent in order to retain the initiative; at Rowallan, it was an effective tool which was exploited to within an inch of its legitimacy.

Daz, the PT instructor, appeared from inside the accommodation. Walking around the three formed ranks, he randomly insulted anyone who caught his eye. Predictably, he began to crack crude jokes at the expense of Corporal Davis, who was stretching off, ready for the run. Davis was dressed in Lycra trousers with a skin-tight T-shirt. Despite most of the staff giggling at the tirade of abuse, Davis remained composed, so Daz turned his attention back to the students: 'Gaz! What did the Medical Officer say about sticky the stick insect yesterday?'

We didn't need to look at the students – we all knew he was talking about Hays. Ironically, he did resemble a stick insect, with his sunken collar bones, scrawny arms and retractable chin. Even the small rugby shirt hung loosely around his frame! Captain Dunn couldn't help but hear the question, and immediately seized on the opportunity to turn the tables on Daz: 'Good question, Staff! Apparently, it was your fault. The warm-up prior to yesterday's run was too exhausting for him. You hadn't considered that it was his first day in training. At least that's what he said to the M.O.'

If this statement was true, Daz would be in serious trouble. Furthermore, the M.O. would be seeking a formal investigation into the training Daz delivered. Physical training is a science-mad business, and for all Daz's rough edges, he was meticulous in his planning. Sandhurst was under serious pressure to reduce its injury rate, which was running at approximately 46 per cent for those in their first fourteen weeks. There was no such thing as just running people ragged for the sake of it. Lessons were rehearsed, planned and executed to a precise formula. Despite it appearing and feeling like it was random, this was just an illusion: the DS make it appear chaotic and unplanned in order to prevent students from developing instructor knowledge.

Daz paused for a while before he caught on to Captain Dunn's ploy: 'Well this time I'll do a better job, Sir. On this jaunt, we'll lose him out on the training area for good. With all the other stick-like creatures out there, he will be right at home.'

Pat butted in: 'What makes you think he'll make the training area? As I recall, he was blubbering after 200 yards yesterday.'

Someone offered to run a sweepstake, and before it could be halted several notional bets were being placed. Daz offered £5 if he made it beyond the ammunition compound, which was half a mile onto the training area. Captain Dunn and Pat both agreed £5 should Hays make it to the halfway point. Jokingly, I offered a tenner if he made it within sight of the back gate, or a little less than half a mile.

Leading from the front of the Company, Major Gray set the pace. For safety reasons, we would always be followed closely by the 'Jack Wagon', a substitute ambulance. We frequently referred to this vehicle as the Jack Wagon because it was tasked with collecting those who gave up whilst running. The term 'Jack', although not exclusive to military language, normally refers to someone who takes an individualistic approach during team events or life in general. To 'Jack something in' or to 'Jack on someone' just means to give up. Giving up on any activity in the Army is universally known as 'Jacking'. We had covered less than

200 metres before the Jack Wagon received its first customer. Running at a leisurely warm-up pace towards the rear gate, the blurred figure of a student tumbled out of the ranks and into a small clearing at the roadside. Crumpled in a heap, bellowing expletives and clutching several parts of his body, was Hays. My initial concern for his wellbeing vanished after I deduced that there was more than a hint of serendipity in where he landed. The narrow lane of entangled trees, nettles and thorn bushes had just one small clearing, and somehow Hays had fallen into it.

It was more than luck. The cushioned landing space was less than 3ft wide. The odds of him hitting that gap were a million to one. Either this was a minor miracle or a cold and calculated attempt to avoid participating in the physical fitness session. Corporal Davis made several attempts to get Hays back on his feet. As expected, and with great theatrical expertize, Hays protested as he once more crumpled to the floor as if hit by a sniper. Decisively, Captain Dunn instructed the driver of the Jack Wagon to put him in the vehicle. A young soldier from the local transport squadron stepped out of the comfort of his long wheelbase Land Rover and helped Hays into the back of his vehicle.

Daz dropped off the front of the group just in time to see Hays climb aboard the Jack Wagon. Captain Dunn, Corporal Davis and I sprinted and caught up with the main group.

'Gaz! Don't think you're getting a penny out of me. You must have staged that! Was he in on the bet?' I demanded.

For a short while, Hays' ignominious display got to me. You can't help but take these things personally. He exhibited the worst possible characteristics for anyone vying for a position of responsibility, let alone that of a serving officer wishing to protect the nation from its enemies. It was confirmation that Hays would not be successful on the course; no matter what happened next, we had seen enough, and more importantly, so had everyone else. I dwelt on the realization for a moment and gave myself a reality check. I looked for the positives to come out of Hays' demise before settling for some black humour: 'Pat, that's a tenner you owe me, and Daz and the boss, in fact, the lot of you owe me. I said he wouldn't make it within sight of the gate, so get your cash out!'

So pathetic was my attempt to extort money from everyone, even Corporal Davis laughed at me! Wow, great! Hays caves in, Moneypenny laughs at me and to make it worse, the shitty string vest was starting to rub under my arms!

With less than half a mile covered, several students began to struggle. It was little surprise to see the two blobbies at the rear. Captain Dunn was running alongside half-blobby, quizzing him on how he had become so overweight: 'Trollope, the Directing Staff have given you a nickname. Guess what it is?'

Trollope was too busy concentrating on breathing and trying to keep up with the rapidly disappearing squad. He tried to answer, but struggled to complete a coherent sentence as he fought for breath. Eventually, he resorted to shaking his head and grunting to answer.

'Time's up!' Captain Dunn laughed out loud. 'Let me help you; it is Half Blobby! Now I know that sounds bad, but don't be too disappointed at this. If you look behind, you will see the student we've christened Full Blobby, or Blobby Blobby for short.'

It was just what Trollope didn't need. The unwanted attention proved too much for him and he broke into a walk.

'Don't dare walk!' shouted Captain Dunn. 'You won't like what the Colour Sergeant has for those who give in.'

He responded for a nanosecond before giving in again.

'Well Trollope, don't say I didn't warn you! Colour Sergeant, come and give Blobby some of your special encouragement.'

'Too many kebabs after the beer and not enough self-motivation,' I explained. 'That's why you have been sent here, Blobby.' Placing my hand in the small of Trollope's back, it took a gargantuan effort to push him into a jog.

'How much further are we going, Colour Sergeant?' Trollope muttered. He was close to his limit of effort, despite the fact we had covered less than 2km.

'Shut up Blobby! You've done nothing yet! If you haven't noticed, I've been pushing you for the last mile. Look behind you, the only thing in sight is the Jack Wagon. I'm going to stop pushing. If you don't continue to run on your own, you're on the Jack Wagon.'

Trollope's face was covered in the residue of his efforts. His contorted expression was testimony to the fact that he had surpassed his limit. The instant I stopped pushing, Trollope sank to his knees.

'Get up! Keep going, Blobby, don't give up so soon,' I shouted. Trollope staggered to his feet, then tried to run, but it was useless. One final shove to kick him into life was a bridge too far. His tubby frame collapsed spreadeagled on the ground. It was a hard fall, peeling back the skin on the palms of his hands as they hit the ground. It was his last act before being placed on the Jack Wagon. Along with five other students, Trollope cut a pitiful figure. As I turned away from the vehicle, Hays could be seen grinning at everyone from the passenger seat. He had moved into the front of the Jack Wagon and switched the heater on to full blast. Clean, dry and with not even a hint of sympathy for his peers shivering in the back, Hays was the epitome of a selfish, deluded dreamer.

Even with a recalibrated approach, it required phenomenal levels of restraint not to resort to violence. With my temper under control, I dragged Hays out of the vehicle by the scruff of his neck and shoved him into the back of the Jack Wagon. Once again, Hays had taken me to the edge of the abyss in trying to control my urge to thump him. Keeping this emotion under control was proving more difficult than it appeared, especially in anticipation of him antagonizing me further. Staring into his eyes, from a distance of just 2 inches, there was nothing. No disappointment, dejection or confusion; he just looked back with an infuriating smirk, oblivious of his crime. Disgusted beyond understanding, I released my grip and instructed him to sit at the back of the vehicle and not speak to the other students.

* * *

Thumping students is an old-school concept, and something one grows out of with age and experience, but that doesn't mean the desire cannot sometimes get the better of you. Soldiers need an aggressive streak; it's the ingredient that gives you the edge in combat. Understanding how to train it into someone is as complex as training someone how to control it. Whilst training recruits at the Rifle Depot (Winchester) in the 1980s, I was entrusted with ten young potential soldiers. A few weeks into the course, we became aware of pilfering within the squad. The thief was picking padlocks and stealing money from personal lockers. So, with the help of the Platoon Sergeant, I set out to catch the thief. Before paying the recruits, we marked their bank notes using an ultraviolet pen. Two days later, one of my recruits reported some of his money had been stolen. I paraded my squad in their section room, then, in their presence, searched their belongings. Scanning their money using the ultraviolet detector, first to be checked was my most trusted trainee. Confident it would reveal nothing, his money was placed under the detector. To my horror, the check showed positive. Betrayed by the look in my eyes, the young Cockney lad knew he had been caught. Saying nothing, and feeling the remainder of the search was pointless, the next recruit was checked. Disappointment and disbelief filled my head as the search also proved positive. A third pound note was later discovered in the possession of another very good student.

Three of my best recruits had been thieving. It was a serious offence. If the Platoon Commander was to learn of this, he would have no choice but to kick them out, no questions asked. But despite the seriousness of the offence, which warranted a punishment, declaring my findings would be catastrophic. To condemn three recruits to a dishonourable discharge before realizing the opportunity to teach them right from wrong just wasn't economically sound. Such a moral dilemma gave me sleepless nights. On the one hand, this was a deplorable act. On the other, they were good recruits, a commodity that infantry battalions were desperately short of. For a few days, the hunt for a solution occupied my every thought. Then a philosophy from my days growing up on the council estates of Kirby came back to me – 'Better a thief than a liar'. The more the words ran through my mind, the more it became obvious that this was the way out. Undeniably it was a subconscious way of justifying how to find the resolution, but there was truth in the hypothesis. The thought behind this philosophy was simple; you could always know when someone is thieving, but you don't always know when someone is lying.

Eventually, it dawned on me that it would be acceptable to repeat a punishment administered to me under similar circumstances during my time as a new recruit. Universally known as a 'Regimental Bath', it was used for various crimes contrary to the good conduct of soldiering, and this particular crime fitted the bill. A Regimental Bath is being forcefully dumped into a bath by a group of your peers after a 'Kangaroo Court'. The accused was given a choice of local summary punishment or punishment by due process! No one ever chose due process for fear of discharge or a hefty fine.

Not wishing to implicate my fellow instructors, I thought through the mechanics of delivering this punishment on my own. Using a small windowless bathroom, I would switch the light off and surreptitiously manoeuvre the individual to the edge of an overflowing bath, then close the door to achieve total darkness. While the victim struggled to adjust his eyes to the surroundings, he would receive the option of judicial process or summary justice. Confident he would choose the latter, I would deliver a short sharp punch to the solar plexus. Breathless and disorientated, the follow through of the punch would carry him into the bath. That would be the end of it, penance paid. Right or wrong, I naively thought there was substantial credibility in this kind of summary justice, and something a little noble about delivering it.

Having rehearsed the drill late that Sunday evening, the three recruits were summoned to my office. They were informed that there was irrefutable evidence that identified them as thieves. For five minutes, there was blame and counter-blame, embarrassment, denial and remorse. Eventually, there were tears and confessions. In my capacity as their tin god, all possible options were explained in detail. Firstly, we could inform the Platoon Commander and the end result would probably be a dishonourable discharge. Alternatively, we could tell the civilian police, and this could be doubly worse. Or they could be tried by Kangaroo Court and take my punishment. Without hesitation, they opted for the trial. Relieved and intoxicated by my own self-importance, all three recruits were marched to the bathroom for punishment. The first recruit was ushered in. The young Londoner nervously walked through the door and was shepherded into position. Calf muscles flush against the open end of the overflowing bath, he had no idea what was going on. Standing directly in front of him, with just enough manoeuvre space to deliver a rabbit punch to the chest, the young lad began to quiver. With a disappointed tone, his crime was read out and he pleaded 'guilty'. As he started to plead for forgiveness, the drawcord of the light switch was pulled. One swift punch square on to the solar plexus and the lad was sent tumbling into the bath. With the wind knocked out of him, bewildered and drenched, it was old-school discipline at its best.

There was no pain from the punch. In fact, it is fair to say that it was more a shove than a punch. It was the overwhelming sense of embarrassment and loss of self-esteem that caused the hurt. How was this 'wide boy cockney' going to explain to his peers how he came to be soaked from head to toe? Suffering from the shock of what just happened, the young lad hauled himself out of the bath, water spilling everywhere. The door was opened, and a shard of light guided him out of the bathroom so he could make good his escape. The remaining pair looked at each other with fear written across their face. Priceless; the stunt had worked brilliantly, causing the hairs on the back of my neck to stand on end.

'Next!' I screamed, high on adrenaline.

A short, stocky lad from Newcastle scuttled into the bathroom. Skilfully, he was steered to the bath's end. It was the same drill, his calf muscles up tight to the end of the bath so it could act as the crucial cantilever that would topple him neatly into the bath. As silence fell, he was offered the same deal as his mate. Again, without hesitation, he opted for the quick solution. A flick of the switch, a slam of the door, then bam! One punch, and two seconds later, splash! It was going like clockwork! Keeping the lads in training, keeping them in the Army, defending the realm and – to cap it all – they had been dealt a respected punishment! Feeling like Roy of the Rovers after scoring the winning goal in the FA Cup Final, complacency crept in as the last man was guided into the ambush position.

A young spotty-faced Cornishman stood anxiously at the end of the bath. Constantly fidgeting with his military glasses, his eyes were fixed on the water that continued to lap from side to side in the bath. It is clear to me now that he had figured out what was about to take place, but my arrogance had blinded me. After a short discussion, we struck a deal on a suitable punishment for his crime. The light was doused, the door slammed shut. Fist clenched, arm cocked back, I lunged forward, searching for his chest. Anticipating a thud followed sharply by a splash, my whole bodyweight had shifted forward. In the dark, the young lad ducked just as the punch was delivered. Committed to the thrust, the momentum of my missed punch pulled me forward, stumbling head over heels and sending me tumbling into the bath face-first. With a mixture of disbelief and embarrassment, I turned to see my intended target flee through the door and into the relative sanctuary of his eight-man room. Mortified by failure, it was best not to chase after him. Suffering the indignity of explaining the reason for my drowned rat appearance was not the outcome this plan had envisaged.

In hindsight, my decision to dish out this old-school punishment was misguided and derived more from my lack of personal development than any perceived 'defender of the realm' stance. I often speculate how the three lads reflected on my leadership. The lad from London went on to have a very successful career in the Special Forces and played a pivotal role in thwarting a massive terrorist attack in the centre of London. Would he say, 'McCarthy, what a bully'? Or would he say, 'if it wasn't for McCarthy, I wouldn't be here now'?

Like 99 per cent of all recruits who went through training before it was well regulated, I was ill-treated, constantly abused and bullied by my instructor, and up to that point, this was my only point of reference. Although I would continue to get things wrong whilst training recruits, the soaking was the best thing to happen to me during my two years at Winchester. It forced me to look for better ways of developing young people and move out of the Dark Ages. Corporal punishment in lieu of fair justice was a thing of the past, despite many people advocating its effectiveness. It was time to contemplate a more receptive form of management that would see me circumnavigate such predicaments in the future. It was no small task, given the fact that my job was to teach people how to 'close with and kill the Queen's enemies' and you can't do this by pillow fighting. One key theme of basic training is to heighten the aggressive instinct. Subsequently, you need aggressive practices. These are fraught with danger, as the path to controlled aggression is conducive to misuse and misinterpretation. Do too little and you underachieve; do too much and you produce a monster. Moreover, get away with it and you underpin an institution with a flawed philosophy. Learning where the balance lies is complex and doesn't happen overnight.

* * *

At the 3km mark, Daz halted the squad in order to regroup, allowing the less-fit students to catch up. But there would be no rest for those at the front, with press-ups and star jumps for the fitter students as they waited. Everyone was verbally encouraged to do better, constantly pushed to do more than the person next to him. After he had achieved that, the process was repeated. In contrast to other courses, the instructors did not have the mandate to churn out a common standard. Rowallan was about facilitating individual achievement at the expense of collective attainment. There was no discussion of minimum standard, no minimum pass score; it was all about doing more than the next man, finding your own limit just so you had a benchmark to improve upon.

The Jack Wagon was near to capacity as Paddy put more of his students on board. Four kilometres into the run, No. 2 Platoon had plenty of strugglers to choose from. Danner was 'running' at a speed slower than walking pace, if that was possible. I paused beside him for a short while, mainly to have a second look at his unorthodox running style: 'Danner, you're shaped like a cheeseburger. You've spent far too much money in McDonald's over the past couple of years. Isn't that right, softlad?'

'Yes, Colour Sergeant, but my father worked very hard for that money.' It was a cheeky answer, followed by an even cheekier grin. It took some effort not to laugh at what he declared.

'I wouldn't laugh, big lad, you do realize that you are beginning to look like Ronny McDonald. You already have the size 14 shoes and big stupid nose.'

Danner raised a smile and tried to keep running. This lad was likeable, with character in abundance, but we faced an uphill struggle if he was going to make it through the course. Moreover, a greater effort would be required to turn him into a young leader of men and knock him out of the 'class clown' persona he hid behind. Personality will get you so far, but at some stage, the Army will demand more than charisma.

Danner was at the rear of the squad. Although not struggling for breath, he was just unable to go any faster. For now, this would be enough to stay on the course.

Weston limped along just in front of Danner. 'What's your problem, softlad?' I barked. Weston screwed his face up and explained he had a long-standing problem with his knees.

'And they let you join the Army? That is surprising! If you've got a problem with your knees, how do you think you are going to get through the course?'

Weston had a self-assured look on his face as he answered my question: 'I feel I have enough determination to get through the course, Colour Sergeant.'

Weston continued to hobble, wincing with each step, but there was something missing. Maybe it was the lack of sincerity in his answer. Initially, it was hard to put a finger on it, even though years of meeting weird and wonderful people had gifted me the ability to make swift character assessments. Seldom would this be wrong, but it was taking longer to understand Weston. One hundred metres later, he had done enough. If there really was a problem with his knees, there was no sense in making it worse. For now, he could get on the Jack Wagon.

Major Gray continued to set the pace at the front, leading the course up and down the largest hills on the training area. With less than half a kilometre to go before we arrived at Wishmoore Bottom swamp, Pat was becoming excited. Heavy winter rains caused the swamp to swell into a 50-metre-wide lake. Sitting amongst the fallen leaves and bare trees, the black mirrored surface reflected picturesque silver-grey skies with a pretence of innocence. Only the overpowering stench of wet peat compromised its true identity. Pat regrouped the intake at the head of the swamp. Silver birch trees lurched over the water. Branches gently swaying, their reflection looked like gargoyles guarding an evil lair. With their toes touching the forward edge of the water, the front rank could see their own reflection shimmer on the glossy black surface. Behind them, their fellow students slowly amassed.

'Right, you bunch of ugly tarts, start jogging on the spot while we wait for the fatties to catch up.' Pat called for the Directing Staff to move to the front;

the harsh language he used was alien to me, but it served a purpose. Gathered at the front of the students, we supervised some additional fitness for those who were establishing themselves as the stronger members. With the course reassembled, apart from those on the Jack Wagon, Pat called out at the top of his voice: 'Company will advance! Forward!' Directly on hearing Pat's command, the Staff charged into the swamp. Captain Dunn and Watts ran hard into the water until they were at chest height, with the OC just behind. Pat sprinted through the murk until he lost speed, then dived headlong into the dark mass. With a huge splash, he disappeared below the surface before emerging, belly up, 20 metres later. Theatrically, he promptly broke out into the backstroke, yelling: 'Marvellous. Bloody marvellous. Get in here, you bunch of fannies.'

Baltic-cold water caused the flow of blood in my thighs to stall, instantly turning my legs into dead weights. With a glance behind, it was pleasing to see Mathews launch himself into the swamp. Instantaneously, it swallowed him whole, with dirty brown debris bubbling in his wake. He stayed under longer than expected, and for a short time we watched and worried. It was a brave commitment, displaying complete trust in the Staff by being the first student to jump in. With a burst of relief, he reappeared 10 metres further up the swamp. Breaking the surface gasping for air and in a mild panic, it was as comical as it was impressive. The freezing conditions made it difficult for him to fill his lungs, and the sound of rapid breathing and splashing water echoed idly in the empty woodland. With a fistful of expletives, the diminutive figure battled his way to the far end. The remainder of the course followed, desperately kicking their way through the murk as it quickly began to change into a thick sludge. Paddy and I returned to the start of the swamp in anticipation of a few swamp-shy individuals refusing to take the plunge.

Watson entered the swamp cautiously. Avoiding the centre, he waded along the side, where the water was knee-high. Wearing an expression that compromised his discomfort, he was the first to receive my encouragement: 'Hoy, softlad! Move into the centre, where the bodies are buried and the going is tough.'

Watson responded with a look of irritation, sighed, and continued to hog the side of the swamp.

'Williams! Williams!' Eventually, Watson looked at me. 'Do you mean me? I am Watson!'

'Yes, Watson. I mean you. There may be a language barrier here; I speak English, and you may struggle with this on the planet Zorg, or wherever you come from. However, everyone else has gone down the centre of the swamp, so you do the same.'

Watson stopped and glanced skyward before he answered: 'What's the point in going down the middle? I'm sure it's not necessary.'

If I couldn't remember his name before, I was not going to forget it now. Briefly, I recalled the manner in which Watson had spoken to me on reception day: aloof and arrogant. Unequivocally, this is the ugliest character trait in an officer, and probably the hardest to coach out of a student, mainly because arrogance infers superiority. But the development of a young officer in his early years relies on taking advice from subordinates such as Non-Commissioned Officers. Fail to consider this experienced advice, and you just might get a heap of people killed. History is littered with examples of commanders failing to take advice, with disastrous consequences. Infamously, The Battle of Hattin (1187) may be the most poignant. Despite the advice from Templar Knights and nobles, King Guy of Lusignan marched his army into a certain trap just outside of modern-day Jerusalem. His arrogance cost the Crusaders dearly. King Guy did not lose this battle because of poor tactics; he lost it through arrogance. His narcissistic leadership marginalized his advisors and he marched his force into annihilation.

Paddy stared at me with a look that reassured me that what I was about to do was right. Wading across to Watson, I grabbed him by the white collar of his red rugby top and dragged him out of the swamp, back to the start, where I told him: 'Running through the swamp is not pointless, Watson! Do as your peers do and you will forge a meaningful relationship. Do it better and you will earn their respect. However, repeating something because you didn't do it right the first time, now that's pointless.'

Holding on to the cotton collar of his rugby top, I leapt into the swamp, pulling Watson with me. The sudden jolt shocked him, and his feet failed to advance. With a thud, he belly-flopped into the murky water and submerged for the briefest of moments. In a state of total panic, he reappeared, spitting mud and gasping for air, arms flailing and searching for something to hold on to.

'Colour Sergeant! My eyes are stinging. I can't see! I can't see!'

'Of course you can't see, softlad, your eyes are full of swamp shit. Did you think you were immune to it?'

Watson started to ease his way through the swamp, rubbing his eyes, and mumbling unintelligibly. Feigning exhaustion, he was the last man to exit. Mustering sufficient energy to high-five those waiting for him, a smile beamed from his face and he spontaneously screamed salutations. Maybe there was hope for him after all!

Less those on the Jack Wagon, the course had battled their way through the swamp and were now doing more physical exercises on the far end of the swell. Pat stood in front of them, steam rising from his thighs and shoulders. With a crazy smile on his face, he screamed out to everyone: 'Are you having fun? Well are you having fun or not?'

'Yes, Sir!'

'Louder,' demanded Pat, and the course dutifully obliged.

'Better! Who wants to do that again?' A few students raised their hands. 'OK, all those with their hands raised, stand still. Those with their hands lowered, follow me.'

Pat rounded them up and sprinted back to the start of the swamp, with the rest of the DS trailing. Without looking back, he plunged into the overflowing mass with another dive, but the agitated water had changed viscosity, Pat slapped the surface as it slowly parted and he sank! Several students realized what was required and without hesitation followed their Sergeant Major. Those who hesitated attracted the wrath of the Staff who had returned for a second go.

As we exited the water, Mathews was stood nearest to the edge. He said: 'Can we go again please, Colour Sergeant?' He wasn't trying to impress, he was just wishing to join in the fun. Sadly, we were out of time. Pat barked more orders and the DS rallied around to ensure people complied.

Surrounded by a cloud of steam, we gently jogged back through the rear gate of the camp. Frozen muscles and saturated clothes hindered free movement of the legs, while the heavy clothes sapped the final remnants of energy. Deliberately, Major Gray took a detour as we headed into the centre of the Academy. Those who had stayed with the squad deserved the privilege of running across New College square for the entire world to see. Horrified officer cadets undertaking the Commissioning Course looked on. Mesmerized by the sight of Rowallan students covered head to toe in black slime and enveloped by an insufferable stench, they stopped to watch in admiration. Swamp residue dripping from the students left a black snail trail, much to the horror of the groundstaff. Their battered and dishevelled condition was confirmation that they had experienced the most unpleasant yet gratifying start to the morning's activities.

Having arrived at the accommodation, the students were brought to a halt. The OC, Pat and the Q party disappeared for a shower. Paddy issued simple instructions to the students: 'Fifteen minutes and let's have you all outside, showered and changed, ready for lunch. Get away! Run away! Get away now.' Paddy shouted louder and louder, intentionally instilling urgency and pressure. The students raced for the door. With only three shower cubicles per platoon, no one dare waste a second. Not that they needed additional encouragement, but the final man to pass through the door was dragged back to be punished for being last.

The Directing Staff had the luxury of one shower between two, so it was no great effort to be ready before the students. With ten minutes gone, few of the students stood outside, ready to go to lunch. Those who failed to make it on time were punished with push-ups and burpees. Lunch lasted twenty minutes; this time the students were ready for the frantic charge. Adapting to the pace of life, they all managed to eat a sizeable meal, hoping that it would digest later.

Forty-five minutes after returning from the swamp run, they were showered, fed, administrated and ready for lessons.

There wouldn't be a more important subject imparted to the students than that of first aid. It was crucial that the student was fully trained in casualty handling, as we could guarantee the need to use it during the course. At some stage, they would all find themselves in life-threatening situations, and it was inevitable that someone would get injured. The first aid lesson started with a standard military training video made during the Vietnam War. Graphic and unpleasant, blood flowed from start to finish as soldiers with horrendous injuries were carried in and out of a Mobile Army Surgical Hospital. Stone sniggered at those who struggled to watch the vivid pictures of arterial blood squirting uncontrollably from gunshot wounds and grenade injuries. He was now drawing my attention constantly. There is nothing more disingenuous than a student mocking the discomfort of his peers. Stone was shaping my thoughts on his social bearings, and they weren't good.

After two hours of fake blood, triangular bandages and gory stories, Paddy and I delivered a joint lesson on the art of rucksack packing. Standard Operational Procedures (SOPs) had everyone packing their kit in a specific way. Top of the agenda was waterproofing, better known as the skill of wrapping one's clothes in watertight bags. They were also shown how to make an emergency first aid kit, as well as the art of keeping everything clean and free from germs. Equally important was water management and survival equipment, and where it should be stowed. Their rucksack would be their mobile home, and it had to be organized with precision, ready to go anywhere, at any time. Being ready for any eventuality at short notice was known as 'bug-out ready'. To conclude the session, they were shown how essential command and control equipment such as maps, compass, protractor and whistle needed to be managed with greater care and be carried on the body.

Sitting with the Sergeant Major at his desk completing an injury report for Weston, Paddy knocked on the door frame to get our attention: 'Gaz, I've just sent one of your blokes to your office. He's wanting away.'

'About time,' I replied.

'I knew it wouldn't be long before Hays would throw his hand in.' Pat looked up, interested in Paddy's words.

'No! No! It's no him. Oh no, it's the wee fat guy.' Paddy imitated a 'fat guy' by puffing up his chest, inflating his cheeks and wobbling from side to side with his arms outstretched like a Sumo wrestler.

'No, you need to be more specific Paddy, they're all fat. You have just described half the course,' Pat said sarcastically.

Puzzled by Paddy's description, I headed to my office. It wasn't a total surprise to see Trollope was standing outside. 'What's the problem, Blobby?'

Trollope sprung to attention. 'Well Colour Sergeant, I am having second thoughts about wanting to be in the Army, so I'd like to leave.'

This knee-jerk statement irritated me. Offended and disappointed, my mood took a swing for the worse. I took it as a personal insult as my mind raced with conflicting thoughts. Why did he want to leave the Army? Didn't he realize what a massive privilege it was to be a leader of men? I looked Trollope square in the eye and contemplated my words.

'I understand this is uncomfortable for you. You may not think you will make a good officer, and you're probably right, but after only two days you can't possibly know.'

Trollope lowered his head with embarrassment; he knew I was right. There was a desire to be a British Army officer, but no interest in working hard for the privilege. He tried to explain his decision to leave and offered several excuses, but I stopped him mid-sentence:

'Blobby, shut up! My ears are bleeding. You are not at a Chinese takeaway. This is not the supermarket of job convenience. You can't chop and change your mind after you have made a commitment. Leave or stay? Do you want to free the oppressed and protect the nation or do you want to flip stocks and shares and rob old ladies of their savings? Be noble or be a knob? There is no second chance here, we treat you like men, you say leave and you're gone!'

'Leave, Colour Sergeant, I wish to leave,' Trollope muttered under his breath. I shook my head and stared hard at the body language of his dejected figure before saying:

'Blobby, the sad fact is, you have not given this a chance. Nor have you given me the opportunity to help you realize your true ability. In years to come, you will regret this moment. We don't give places at Sandhurst away for free. You have robbed someone else of an opportunity. But the greatest indignity is, you have cheated yourself of the only true chance to discover who you are.'

As quick as he was enlisted, he was gone: packed off to a holding company before discharge, like cutting out cancer before it spreads. Once someone had given notice to Voluntarily Withdraw (VW), time was of the essence. There must be no chance to spread despondency amongst the remaining students. Most recruit courses have a time bar that prevents an individual from leaving before the end of week four, and we knew a few students would be wavering on the same decision. Our swift actions were a countermeasure to avoid a mass panic setting in. Number 2 Platoon was down to twenty students, and it was disappointing that Trollope was the first to go.

The last period of instruction that evening saw me explain the requirement for personal hygiene. It may sound like teaching people to suck eggs, but the younger generation seldom understand the finer details of keeping clean whilst living in communal areas. Everything from demonstrating how to shower correctly to flossing was taught. Standing in the washrooms with twenty students, wind-burnt and blurry eyed, I finished my teaching and offered my last words of the day:

> 'I shall summarize by saying that it is imperative that not only can you look after your personal hygiene, but as a leader of men you must also look after those whom you command. When you are tired, hungry and sodden wet, your output and focus will suffer. You must learn the skills of enforcing hygiene in difficult scenarios. We will always enforce the highest standards of hygiene and punish you if they fall short of our expectations. Later in your service, you will be familiar with this phrase, "My weapon. My men. Me." For now, enjoy the luxury of only needing to look after yourself.'

Pulling back the shower curtain of the end cubicle, I reached inside and pulled out a large wooden box. Like a magician, I put my hand inside and produced eight bright white pet rabbits, complete with floppy ears and crimson red eyes.

'I shall leave these rabbits here; spread them out amongst the platoon,' I said. 'It is now your responsibility to care for, feed and clean them, from now until the end of the course.'

I left the students cuddling and stroking their new friends. Another day done and one student lighter, it had been a cracking day and we could feel the platoon bonding. The warm glow of success distracted me from the feeling of cold still lingering deep inside my thighs. Walking back to my bunk, the child in me was still giggling at the thought of Pat doing the backstroke in the swamp. It was not only the students who were buzzing with excitement. For me, tomorrow couldn't come quick enough.

The following morning, at 0530hrs, Hays greeted me. He had been standing outside the accommodation in the drizzle, and judging by how wet his clothes were, he'd been there some time. Soaked to the bone, he snapped to attention and water bounced from his shoulders as he said: 'Good morning Colour Sergeant, is it possible that I could have a small word please?'

'Don't tell me, you want to go sick.' I couldn't help but be sarcastic.

'Erm, no, Colour Sergeant, I want to leave.'

I paused and checked my arcs to see if anyone was within earshot. The next words from my mouth would get me sacked if heard by the wrong person: 'Excellent news Hays, you are making a good decision.'

Hays didn't answer; he just smiled, and I smiled with him.

'Go wait outside the Sergeant Major's office and explain to him when he arrives,' I said.

The smile slipped away from Hays' face, to be replaced by an expression of concern and anxiety. 'Could I not just get on and go, Colour Sergeant? I'm already packed. My mother is on her way. We are trying to leave after breakfast.'

I replied:

'Hays, I want to ask what planet you are on, but I fear you would say Earth! That would mean you and I are the same species. You can't imagine how much that would depress me! There is no one keener to see you leave than me. But we have a moral obligation to ensure you leave in good order. It will take some time to see you out of Sandhurst.'

Hays began to well up. His bottom lip wobbled as his face flushed bright red. 'But Trollope left five minutes after asking to leave. My mum is on her way.'

'No, softlad, he didn't. It may have looked that way, but Trollope is currently cleaning sinks and mirrors in the washrooms of Dettingen Company accommodation. We don't just send you home. Fuck me, Hays, what is going through your mind? This is not Butlin's and I am no Redcoat! You can't choose to check out when the fun stops!'

The opportunity was there for me to offload on Hays. There was an overwhelming urge to issue a wake-up call. Just at the point where my words were becoming more offensive, Corporal Davis arrived to rescue me from myself. Day three of the course and we were down to nineteen. If they continued to fall at this frequency, there would be no one to train by the end of week three!

The first serial of the day was room inspection. Despite previously explaining the requirement and what to expect, this was their first attempt and expectations were low. My first room was Weston's. Almost insultingly, he slouched to attention, while his roommate, Mathews, shot his heels together at double-speed. Whilst looking through their attempt to organize their room, I asked how they were enjoying the course. Weston responded to each question with lethargy and disinterest. It was becoming increasingly obvious that Weston had a stinking attitude.

'Weston, where is this shitty attitude coming from?' I asked. 'Countless times you have received instruction on how to interact with a member of staff, so why are you behaving like a scolded child by not conforming?'

'Sorry, I am in pain,' he replied. 'It's hard to think straight. It's my knee, Colour Sergeant. The pain is excruciating after the run yesterday.'

'I fail to see how a pain in your knee affects the tongue in your head.' A smirk covered Weston's face: a glimpse into his soul unmasked a hidden agenda.

'Colour, do you mind if I see the Quack after this?'

With swathes of blonde hair wildly out of control and an unbelievable arrogance, he had flicked my angry switch.

'Colour! Colour, fucking Colour!' The pitch of my voice crept ever higher:

'Who on this planet do you think you are? I am not sure if you are thick, stupid or just trying to test the boundaries. Last warning; you follow the instructions like everyone else. Stick to the script, Weston. Address me as Colour Sergeant. If you cut corners like that again, you will get a personal values and standards lesson. I'm not your personal mess hand. You won't need to ask to see a doctor, he will visit you at A&E. Promise.'

Weston rolled his eyes and began to quote his right to see a doctor.

'Bloody hell. You are unbelievable, Weston. I am standing right here. Don't roll your eyes back and expect me to do shag all about it. You are sailing too close to the wind. Go stand outside the Sergeant Major's office. Explain to him why you have a shitty attitude before you ask to visit the medical centre. Be sure to tell him you felt the need to remind me of your rights! There is nothing he loves more than a cocky student gobbing off about his entitlements!'

Weston sneered. Nonchalantly walking towards the Sergeant Major's office, the lad misjudged his predicament. From the far end of the corridor, he could hear Hays suffering a tirade of insults. Pictures bounced on their hooks and windows rattled as Pat got into full swing with an old-fashioned 1950s-style dressing down. Weston paused in the centre of the corridor and turned back to check where I was.

'Shall I try a bit later, Colour Sergeant, I think the Sergeant Major's busy?' he pleaded. But it was too late for Weston. The jump had been made from the pan into the fire. I smirked at Weston, just as he had smirked at me seconds before. There was nothing to say as he turned about and headed in the direction of the Sergeant Major's office. Pat had already clocked Weston. From experience, he knew where this relationship was headed. Weston hadn't been in the office five seconds before Pat hit the highest decibels possible for a human. Veins burst from Pat's forehead as his tone became ever more aggressive. Not holding back with his assessment of Weston, it was uncomfortable listening. Whatever it was Weston said, Pat took offence. Corporal Davis quickly left the office to take refuge in my hall of study. Not sure whether to laugh or be afraid, Corporal Davis' eyes bulged whilst describing how Pat's veins were close to bursting as Weston waltzed into the Sergeant Major and started the conversation with, 'The

Colour boy said …' He didn't even get the opportunity to explain his presence before Pat exploded!

Mathews, now on his own, stood rigid to attention in the centre of the room. He was shaking and straining with the effort exerted trying to remain still.

'How's the rabbit, Mathews?' I asked.

'Good, Sir! I mean he's good, Colour Sergeant. I've called him Rabbit.'

'Very original, but it smells like piss in here. Make sure he's had a bath on the next room inspection!'

Producing a 12-inch ruler from my A4 notebook, the size of his bed block was measured: 'Three inches too high. Eight inches too short! As saggy as my granny's tits. Reshow!' Both bed blocks were thrown out of the room and into the corridor as I continued:

> 'Make sure you repeat this to Weston when he returns. Your bed block is a reflection of personal discipline and attention to detail. All corners are 90 degrees, sheets folded at a depth of exactly one inch deep and 24 inches square. Blankets are 2 inches deep, 24 inches square and flat as a pancake. I won't accept this shoddy workmanship. The clothes in your locker need to be ironed like they were on display at Harrods and not on the rail of a thrift shop.'

For good measure, the contents of all the draws were emptied onto the floor before leaving Mathews to contemplate his failings.

Packman and Haigh were already standing to attention as I entered their room.

'How are you two getting on with the rabbit?' Packman nodded and smiled at nothing specific, but Haigh wore a puzzled expression. 'What's wrong, big fella?' I asked. Haigh took a short, sharp breath.

'Well, Colour Sergeant, I am grateful you asked. The relevance of the requirement is understood. It is clear that the need for personal hygiene is integrated with that of the supervisory skills in identifying the failings of others, but …'

I stopped Haigh in full flow: 'It's not a science lesson, Haigh. There are no points for your word count. Are you asking me why you have the rabbit?'

'Erm, yes,' gulped Haigh.

'Because I say so, numb-nuts. It will help you develop your administration of others. And one more thing, speak in plain English. We can't wait all day for you to get your point out.'

Looking at their bed block, both students had fallen short of what we would expect. For dramatic effect, all bedding and the remaining contents of their room were thrown into the corridor next to Mathews'.

It didn't take long to get through the rest of the rooms. The main aim of this first inspection was to develop an understanding of attention to detail. We set the bar at an unachievable height, and from that moment on they were invited to achieve it. For anyone who has been through basic military training, bed blocks are notoriously a focus of detestation. You needed to allow twenty minutes to achieve a bed block that would pass muster. Folding crumpled bed linen to exactly 24 inches squared to produce a crazy piece of linen origami was tiresome. But most importantly, it took a significant amount of time, which would become the most valuable commodity to a Rowallan student. With every minute of sleep precious, losing such a valuable commodity to the misery of making a bed block was infuriating. Mercilessly, every bed block was dismantled during the room inspection. That was with the exception of Danner, who spent the second night of the course on his own.

It was reasonable to expect him to be a little subdued after Trollope moved out, but to my surprise, he was upbeat and positive. Inspecting his wardrobe, it was faultless.

'Well, Danner, I am impressed. This bed block is like the rest of them, but your locker has surprised me. You must have got up early?'

Danner wore a pleased grin on his face and proceeded to tell me he roused with everyone else, but was just a quick worker! Ripping his bed block to the floor, it dawned on me that if his locker was so tidy, why was his bed block so bad? A second look at all his drawers fuelled my suspicions further.

'Why have you only got one pair of boxer shorts? And only two pairs of socks; in fact, where is your towel as well as your washing and shaving kit? Come to that, where are the rest of your civilian clothes and all of your belongings?'

Curiosity had got the better of me. What was going on? I pulled open the departed Trollope's locker door, expecting to see it empty. As the door eased open, an explosion of clothes and bedding fell out. I didn't know if I should congratulate Danner for his initiative or punish him for his cheek. Either way, this was going to get ugly. Opening the window of his room, the contents were thrown into the street. Everything apart from his mattress was slung as far as they would travel. Intentionally, the items were strewn across the wet road for all to see. If he retrieved them quickly enough, just the items on the rain-drenched floor would be wet and dirty. Tonight, he would spend more time than his peers doing additional washing, drying and ironing. Before leaving his room, it was prudent to offer some quick advice.

'You're not clever enough to know where to take risk, Danner, or when to take it. My advice to you, lad, is play it by the book until you understand what is what, in the military. On your current display, don't get your hopes up for the next ten years.'

The first teaching period of the day was part two of the first aid lessons: how to make an improvised emergency stretcher. Using ropes, sticks, guns, ponchos, slings and first field dressings, they learnt the art of building crude stretchers.

But this lesson was masking other activities: there was an ulterior motive behind this session. Upon conclusion of the lesson, the course would be introduced to the first of many inter-platoon competitions. Having been shown how to build an improvised stretcher, the students were taken to Monkey Hill wood, a small tump at the rear of Old College. Hidden between the cemetery and stables, this obscure woodland provided the branches suitable for a makeshift stretcher. Monkey Hill wood is only 50 metres in diameter, but under the canopy was hidden a very steep tump. After some leisurely coaching and advice on construction techniques, they assembled at the base of the hill.

The remaining Staff appeared from the shadows of the adjacent stables, and immediately the gig was up. The students knew something was coming, but just for confirmation, Stone alerted his buddies. Sneakily, he had been watching my every move, studying my body language and trying to read my intentions. DS-watching is the phrase we use to describe this behaviour, but Stone was too inexperienced to understand that studying the Staff was a double-edge sword. As Major Gray announced the first official competition, it surprised nobody that it would involve their improvised stretchers. Monkey Hill had to be conquered ten times, the equivalent to running uphill for a kilometre carrying a stretcher loaded with a casualty. Not that the students needed it, but Pat felt compelled to remind everyone that the reward for victory was not to be punished.

Before the start, Murphy was placed in command. His first task was to select two members of the platoon to act as casualties and have them ride it out on the stretcher. Before anyone had time to speak, Stone volunteered, and Murphy happily accepted his services. Captain Dunn took the opportunity to issue a pre-race pep talk:

> 'OK fellas, this is where the course really starts! You can be a disciple, or you can be the leader, it's up to you. There is no middle ground here, no shadows in which to hide: leader or follower. Your choice. It is here that you discover that the privilege of leading has a price, and it is to be better than everyone else. Give 100 per cent effort. Don't leave anything in reserve and don't be last!'

Each platoon had made two stretchers. For the first stretcher, Murphy used Witherspoon, Lane, King and Haigh. Failing to give them clear guidance, the four of them argued about the best carriage technique. 'Two and two,' Lane ordered. 'No, that won't be enough, we have to go with all four at once,' blurted an irritated King. The second stretcher, with Weston as the casualty, was carried by Danner, Mathews, Packman and Watson. Like stretcher one, they failed to nail down the order of attack as Murphy neglected to issue his vision. This was not going to end well. Murphy had not got a grip of this task, and his direction to his team lacked conviction.

Standing on the main transit road through the camp at the base of Monkey Hill, Major Gray explained the race rules for the final time before handing over the event to the PTI. Daz issued a few insults before starting the competition off by sounding an air horn. The cracking of fallen branches and leaves being trampled on was deafening as the teams crashed through the wooded tump. Stumbling and dropping the stretcher as they hit the first major incline, confusion reigned. By the time they had hit the crest of the hill for the first time, the race began to take shape. In due course, they would come to learn that the stretcher race is the Monaco Grand Prix of all military races. In any stretcher race, once you have the lead, it's yours to lose. Your only hope is to have a better rotation drill for stretcher bearers. Two minutes after the start, the pattern was established, and Murphy's charges were third and fourth.

'Murphy, don't let the other platoon's stretchers get away from you, or you'll never catch them again,' shouted Captain Dunn.

Murphy responded instantly. He shouted at Puddick to change with Lane, hoping for an injection of energy. It was a good idea but poorly executed, and consequently it backfired. Without coordination, Lane became confused and dropped his end of the stretcher. Frustration, exacerbated by the leading edge becoming stuck in the ground, and panic gripped the team. Then just like a comedy sketch, the second stretcher tumbled over the first, crumpling into a heap on the floor. Getting both stretchers moving again seemed to take an age. The second stretcher had fallen apart, and mayhem had broken out amongst the students. By the time both stretchers had got themselves together, No. 1 Platoon had long gone. They had established a massive lead that proved too big to overhaul. With huge excitement, the winners were boisterously celebrating Major Gray's announcement of winning their first three points as we were left to contemplate where it all went wrong.

Captain Dunn summoned the platoon to the base of the hill. 'Fellas, you didn't listen to me,' he said. 'I did say, you don't want to come last because the losers get punished. It's jungle rules here fellas! You need to take this on board quickly. If you don't, you won't see the end of this course. Colour, do you want to explain where it all went wrong?'

'Yes please, Sir, but can I have twenty minutes with them first?' Captain Dunn smiled and nodded.

'OK team,' I said. 'Pick up what remains of your stretchers and head back to the start line.'

Standing in silence, the platoon half expected me to sympathize with their failure. They were wrong.

'So, that took you twenty minutes and fifteen seconds. No. 1 Platoon achieved it in nineteen flat. We will now do it again, and you need to cross in eighteen minutes something, or we'll do it a third time. Murphy, you're sacked! Boyle, you're in command. Don't mess up. Before you start, organize, think through the plan and manage the execution.'

Boyle set about rearranging the students on each of the stretchers. In contrast to Murphy, he chose to station the changeovers in a relay fashion, enforcing rotations at the top and the bottom of the hill. This leapfrog effect would work well, provided the direction was clear. They all knew how far they had to run, and when changeovers would happen. Boyle danced around both groups like Tigger from *Winnie the Pooh*. His enthusiasm was infectious, which served to heighten the excitement of his peers. Seconds after crossing the start line, Danner began to struggle, still not fully recovered from yesterday's exertions. The stretcher was being passed around smoothly, but the tempo suffered from the earlier effort. They needed an injection of pace, or they would fail again.

'Boyle, you need to get these people moving, or they ain't going to make the grade,' I barked. He heard my comment and immediately set about accusing people of malingering. In a fit of anger, he grabbed hold of the lead stretcher, let out a Comanche warrior like scream and kicked fresh energy into the stretchers.

'Good! Much better,' Captain Dunn said loudly. Chasing the rear stretcher over the top of the woods, the praise spurred them all on, crashing over the finish line in eighteen minutes ten seconds. Several students fell to the ground, wheezing and gasping for air.

'Get up! Get the hell up!' I shouted. 'This is no egg and spoon race at a school open day. If you'd put that much effort in the first time around, you would have won by fifty seconds and not needed to do this again.' They were wise words, although at this late stage of the event, they fell on deaf ears. Captain Dunn and I allowed the platoon to gather their thoughts for a while as we discussed who had performed well. It had not escaped our attention that Stone had opted to stay on the stretcher for the punishment. Also, Weston did little more than follow behind, limping. Perhaps the most encouraging sign of the race was Witherspoon. Contrary to yesterday's performance, he dug in deep and never once took a break. Although we would not show it, we were both quietly impressed.

Gathered at the base of the hill, students in three ranks, Captain Dunn read through a list of failings:

'Insufficient energy. No hunger or desire. Far too nice about the way you ran the race. In terms of command, let me summarize by saying this. Murphy, you can't afford to just hope things will work out. It's clear you tried to organize, but in the limited time you had, you needed to be more direct.

Start at the autocratic end of the leadership lexicon, then climb down to situational. Organize, plan and execute. Then it's all about inspiring people in the moment. You didn't do enough. The lesson here is preparation, and when that begins to fail, effect change. You nearly achieved this, but for some shoddy coordination. Boyle, you benefited from seeing what went wrong on the first attempt. So what? You organized and communicated well. It's just a shame we needed two goes to get it right.'

A huge smile filled Boyle's face, but no quicker did it arrive than it disappeared as Dunn continued: 'Of course, any leader worth his salt would never have allowed Stone to ride on the stretcher twice. You could have used his energy on the second attempt. Had you plucked your head out of your arse, you would have lessened the pain you inflicted on your team! Colour, anything to add?'

'When time is tight, you need to analyse the task quickly,' I interjected. 'Consider the SWOT analysis technique. It is quick and easy. Tally up the Strengths at your disposal. Assess the Weaknesses. You will then be able to list the Opportunities that lead to mitigating Threats.'

For some, this was a new concept. Nodding with approval, the mood lifted slightly and the students retired to retrieve slings, ropes and other items dropped during the race. It was pleasing to see they were hurting with disappointment as well as fatigue. Failure is part of the critical path to becoming a good leader, something the students would come to learn.

Having had a short break, the students went back up Monkey Hill for a bushcraft and survival lesson. Captain Watts, a jungle warfare expert and qualified escape and evasion instructor, was the best person to deliver this lesson. During the Gulf War, he found himself in a real fight for survival. Surrounded by Saddam Hussein's elite Republican Guard, it took all the cunningness of a fox to evade capture on several occasions. His first demonstration was basic techniques for building improvised shelters using brushwood and leaves. Ingeniously, he then demonstrated the ability to navigate by using an analogue watch, the sun and the stars. Trick after trick, Captain Watts kept the students amazed at the art of survival. There was a real edge to his delivery, and the students were mesmerized by a succession of improvised weapons used for hunting.

After an hour passed, the subject of food and water became the main subject. A stack of examples was systematically laid out on a 6ft wooden table. One by one, the means of capturing wildlife was explained in graphic detail.

'On occasions, your food may be alive. You need to kill it. Kill it before it gets away. Kill it before it kills you. Snakes, for example, are full of nutrition, but idle in its presence and you will become the food.'

Captain Watts produced a tatty brown sandbag containing something inside trying desperately to escape. The course eased backwards in anticipation of a snake leaping out. Thankfully, rustling around inside the large hessian sack was nothing more than a chicken. Captain Watts placed it calmly on the table. Then, like a magician, he hypnotized the chicken by holding its head down and repeatedly drawing a line under its nose. The students gasped in amazement; you could sense they didn't know what was coming next.

Calmness personified, he tucked the chicken under his arm, stroked its head and slowly extended the chicken's neck. At the point of resistance, he gave a huge corkscrew push, and the chicken's neck came clean off its body. Tucked up tight under his arm, the chicken continued to kick and twitch whilst defecating down the back of Captain Watts' leg. Gaps appeared amongst the crowd as several students vomited the moment the severed head of the chicken was tossed onto the table, crashing down with a thud, its eyes still staring at the crowd. With the dead chicken at rest, it was prepared for cooking. Captain Watts explained the process of preparing any animal, no matter how big or small, was the same: skin it or pluck it, get rid of its guts and nuts, then cook it. The students were totally absorbed by his every action. Starstruck and transfixed by the Special Forces officer, they loved being taught survival techniques. More animals were placed on the table, but students could not take their eyes off the dead chicken's head. Finally, the lesson finished with a demonstration of approved methods for dispatching other small creatures, which included fish and a rabbit.

With time being so tight, there was no opportunity to head back to the canteen for lunch. This would become the norm for the students, as the course squeezed twenty weeks of training into twelve. Lunch would be delivered by the Q party in the form of a packed meal. It would arrive in a flimsy white cardboard box, 6 inches square and 3 inches deep. Typically, it would contain processed cheese sandwiches, crisps, a hard green bitter apple and a Blue Riband chocolate bar. In the interest of morale, a large container of tea and one of coffee would be shared by both platoons. There were just five minutes to eat lunch before it was time for the compulsory military swim test.

Sandhurst Academy swimming pool sat on the edge of the visitors' car park, and close to Monkey Hill. The weary, 1960s-style building looked as inviting as a dog's dinner. The test sounded simple. Dressed in military shirt and trousers, the first part of the test was four lengths of the pool without touching the sides or the floor. With no break, it was straight into treading water for five minutes. Finally, without assistance or rest, the student had to make a survival flotation pack by transforming his trousers into a buoyancy aid. Removing the trousers and tying knots at the base of each leg, the trick was to quickly whip them over the head and capture the air in the garment whilst treading water. For the heavier student, this would prove difficult.

Once the formalities of the test were finished, Daz put the students through a swimming session designed to bring the students face-to-face with total energy collapse. Standing at the side of the pool, Daz ordered everyone to swim from one end to the other, get out, complete ten press-ups, ten sit-ups, ten star jumps, then sprint to the start and do it again. There was no rest at any stage and no opportunity to skive. The Staff strategically positioned themselves at the corners of the pool to ensure the student never got the chance to slack. It didn't take long before the symptoms of fatigue appeared. Barns clearly didn't enjoy being in the water and was stuck at the deep end. His arms had become so tired and heavy, there was no energy left to pull himself out of the pool. Barely keeping his head above the water, he had to be dragged out by Captain Watts. There was no mercy or sympathy as Barns was unceremoniously dragged out by the scruff of his neck. Exhausted, many were barely able to get changed ahead of the next lesson.

As the final lesson of the day arrived, the students were dog-tired. The scheduled evening lecture on the realities of war was an enormous struggle for most. An outstanding presentation by a fellow Colour Sergeant from 2 Para, who was shot aged only 18 during the Falklands War, was wasted on their tired minds. As fascinating as it was, most of my time was spent waking students up as they succumbed to the conditions of a warm lecture theatre and exhausted body. After it finished, the platoon was assembled in the corridor. They needed to better understand what they were going through, so I imparted my thoughts on the day's efforts.

> 'For those who are just experiencing the real army for the first time, today has been physically very tough, but it doesn't get easier. In fact, it's going to get harder. Yesterday your body was telling you it can't go on. But today, it did go on. If it is telling you now that it can't go on, know that tomorrow it will go on, and that's a promise. You will be amazed at the body's resilience; in time you will learn how far it can be pushed. I tell you this because the battle you face is not physical. It is a mental fight. Convince yourself mentally that you can cope, and your body will fall into line.'

Tired faces gawked back at me, but there was an imperative need to reflect on the start of the day:

> 'Finally, let's review the stretcher race. If you lose any inter-platoon race, you are punished. You got off lightly today. In the future, punishments will be harsher. So, from this point forward, we need to keep an eye on your mental health. At the end of each day, you are to make an entry into a personal journal. You must complete at least one side of A4, in the issued Banner book. You should reflect on the day's activities and how you have managed, or not. Include what lessons you have learnt and grade your performance. The contents will be read by the Platoon Commander and me every Sunday.'

As I was about to leave, Murphy raised his hand. 'Colour Sergeant, when is the next race?'

It was obvious what was going through his mind. Murphy was thinking about why he had been sacked after the stretcher race, and he was fishing for some feedback.

'Look, you all know the score by now,' I said. 'No one is told anything until it's about to happen. If there is a race tomorrow, I'll tell you just before it happens.'

'So how do we know what we need to have ready for tomorrow, Colour Sergeant?' replied Murphy.

'Learn from today. Study what you did well and what you didn't. Think about the words Captain Dunn issued. Then be ready for anything. It's that easy; you can't go wrong. Revise the use of SWOT. Once you learn how to use it, you will find it an invaluable tool for analysis.'

Making a swift exit, the boys were left to contemplate the day ahead.

Intentionally, the following morning got off to a slow start, specifically programmed to allow the body time to recover from the recent exertions. But even by Commissioning Course standards, it dragged on. Faraday Hall is the centre of intellectual excellence at the Academy, but this being their first encounter with the course, one academic lecture was followed by another, then another. There are doctors, authors, historians and professors galore kicking around the building, aptly dubbed 'Far-Away Hall'. This was due to its distance from the accommodation, although some Senior Term Cadets suggested that maybe it was because the Staff were so far removed from reality, the nickname referenced their disconnection; there was no denying their intellectual prowess. I always felt like I was returning the stolen church collection when I delivered the students to Faraday Hall. For me, an angry Colour Sergeant scowling at being deprived of his students, leadership couldn't be found in a book. But for the students it was viewed as respite, knowing the rest of the day would bring more physical exertion.

When the students returned to the accommodation, they were given a packed lunch and five minutes to themselves before being instructed to change into their indoor PT kit and jog to the gymnasium. A subdued atmosphere was quickly banished as Daz welcomed them loudly into the main hall. He had set up the gym floor for circuit training, and it looked like more misery for the students. Blue exercise mats lay around the edges of the gym. At the head of the matt was a laminated sign with exercise instructions and quantities required: twenty sit-ups, twenty press-ups, twenty heaves, 20-metre sprints and twenty dips set out down the left-hand side of the gym. On a crash mat down the other side were dead weight pushes, tyre drags, squats and – worst of all – knees to the chest. After twenty minutes thrashing, with no rest, the students were looking ragged after the first circuit. Daz blew his whistle and the circuits came to an end. It had been short and sharp but effective, as the dishevelled state of the students would testify. Daz rounded up the intake and walked to the larger hall to the rear of the main gym. He had set up an indoor assault course, designed more to build camaraderie than improve fitness. It consisted of thirty obstacles, each contrived to slow down the user, force communication and incite raw emotions and tensions.

'OK, you ugly lot.' It was one of Daz's favourite sayings. 'This is a relay assault course. It is also the second inter-platoon race. The rules are simple. Only one member of the platoon is allowed on the course at any one time. Each member must finish the course before the next starts. If a team member fails to complete the course, the team is disqualified.'

Captain Dunn corralled the students into the corner for a pep-talk: 'Fellas, we are already three points behind in this competition. If you don't win this one, you will be putting yourselves under needless pressure over the next few days. This is a must win. Think on the advice we gave you last time. Colour, have you got anything to add?'

The platoon looked at me sheepishly. It was difficult to hide the disappointment of yesterday's loss. Vexingly staring at the group, they needed to lock onto my every word. The body language of those who refused to fix their gaze back at me compromised their weak mental strength. While Murphy's eyes were wide open, screaming 'choose me to lead this race', Mathews and Boyle fidgeted with nervous energy, and Goldson, Lane and Weston clearly wanted to be elsewhere. I stated:

'Think back to yesterday! Your second effort was quicker than No. 1 Platoon's first. Why was that? It's a state of mind. Both platoons are equally balanced; you need to develop tough mental agility. If you wish to win this race, focus on just this race and hold nothing back. Encourage each other; if needed, kick each other up the backside to achieve it! Here's your chance to get it right, be positive, think about the best way to tackle the obstacles and disseminate this information as best practice when you return. Organize, plan and execute. Most of all, be calm and don't panic. OK! Rideout! This is your big moment. You are the commander. Remember, it is the commander that makes the difference in a team event. You must be clear with communications, decisive with decisions and lead by example!'

Rideout proceeded to do the exact opposite. Almost right away he burst into a blind panic, and total pandemonium ensued: chaotically trying to organize everyone into a start place, with absolutely no application of anything previously taught. For someone who had never organized so much as a bus trip previously, it was a steep learning curve. His focus was on achieving a straight line at the start point. Like a dogmatic school prefect, he manhandled people, one behind the other, laser straight. Uninspiring, and struggling to convince anyone of his leadership, the seeds of failure were sown. He generated more panic amongst the platoon than Daz ever did. Weak leadership is ripe for mutiny, and before long he had been pushed into the background as the stronger students began to offer their advice. Rideout had lost control and was now ineffective as a leader. If this race was to be won, it would be through the efforts of individuals acting independently.

The rule for the Directing Staff at Row-Co was no interfering with the competition once it got underway. Encouragement was acceptable, but no advice and no reorganization specifically designed to help the platoon win. They must make this journey on their own, as often lessons learnt the hard way are the ones we remember best. Teaching officers to avoid the pitfalls of 'blame culture' by examining their own failure set Rowallan apart from every other military course. We stood quietly watching from a distance, conferring and cross-referring our observations.

'Boss, Rideout is losing the plot here, he's being overrun by everyone, including Stone.' Captain Dunn nodded in agreement with me as he stared at those who demanded to be the centre of attention. The information gleaned by appointing individuals into command positions was extremely valuable to the DS. Principally, it afforded an intimate insight into the individual's personality and the flaws in his leadership potential. It highlighted strengths and betrayed weakness; pivotally, it helped the DS to formulate an action plan for the development of the individual. But it was not just about being a leader; sometimes we learned far more by watching those who should be in support. Unwittingly, when off-guard, they could also display their true colours. For example, if a student displayed obstructive, argumentative or subversive characteristics, it's likely that he would behave like this during his career. This character trait must be confronted. Officers need to be team players, build healthy relationships and work collaboratively. If in the early days of training, rogue characteristics are left unchecked, eventually they morph into one side of the toxic triangle.

There was no science used during these assessments. It was not an exact art or even well-understood by academics authorized to script this kind of training. The judgment on who was doing things right or wrong was left to the experience of the Platoon Commander and the Colour Sergeant. It was not difficult to see why the intensive selection process took nearly two years, for those who aspired to be a Colour Sergeant Instructor at the Academy.

Unlike the stretcher race, where we needed to be in the middle of the event to conduct our evaluations, this race gifted us plenty of opportunity to observe from afar. From a distance, we could absorb every aspect of the group dynamics and study behaviours with impunity.

Captain Dunn highlighted character flaws that caught his eye in several students: 'Colour, have a look at him hiding in the background, what's his name?'

'Yeah, Watson that is, Sir. He's got a funny attitude. There is something suspicious about him that is hard to pinpoint.'

'How do you mean, Colour?'

'It is too early to nail down, but he's too confident. Maybe he is just full of arrogance! It is not something specific, just a feeling. You would think he would be keen to please, but instead, he's full of apathy. Most curiously, he celebrates his own mediocrity, almost trying to convince himself that his challenge was greater than anyone else's! The swamp run being a good example!'

'Well, Colour, I may be able to shed some light on that. His father is a serving senior officer, and there will be disappointment he has not gone directly onto the Commissioning Course. There will be a belief that he just needs to attend Rowallan and a pass is assured, no matter what.'

It was a brave statement by Captain Dunn. In those few words, he had convinced me that he was honest, forthright and tightly bound by pure integrity. Uniquely, his loyalty was not constrained to an upward trajectory. If he could acknowledge the flaws of this nature to an NCO, the acid test for honesty had been passed. Other officers would have dismissed my viewpoint, fearful that the truth would undermine authority, something known as 'opaque' integrity. But Captain Dunn was not anchored by a class category, a truly rare quality amongst army officers. I had come from the toughest of backgrounds in Liverpool, and nothing came for free. The notion of Watson getting a free ride had me grinding my teeth.

'However, Colour, there is a long way to go. The lad will still need to make it to the end of this course. As it stands, his chance of survival is 50 per cent, and that's before the end of week one. My advice, Colour: let nature take its course.' Captain Dunn chuckled and offered a knowing smile.

The race started and No. 2 Platoon got off to a fantastic start. King, the ex-Sapper, had taken it on himself to run the first leg. His experience helped to create a lead of half the gym's length. The second person to negotiate the obstacles was Mathews. His powerpack gait was ideal for this event as he flew around the course with great ease, extending the lead further. Packman, Barns and Boyle all had good runs, and despite the gangly frame of Barns getting trussed up like a Christmas turkey by the cargo net, they retained the lead. It was looking positive, despite the middle order of Weston, Danner, Stone and Haigh losing ground. Exuberantly, Rideout was busy trying to organize the final runners. Arms flailing wildly with excitement, head uncontrollably bobbing, he ran around like the proverbial headless chicken. Turning to the final two runners, Puddick was told to go next and Watson briefed to do the last leg. But Watson protested furiously: 'Bollocks, no! Why should I go last? Put someone else last!'

We watched on as the confrontation escalated. We were keen to see how Rideout would handle it, and how far Watson would contest it. Watson claimed he was not going to carry the can if he came last, and violently remonstrated with those who had already been. Eventually, Rideout succumbed to the louder personality, and Watson went next. He performed brilliantly, although No. 1 Platoon had organized their finishers tactfully, and by the time the final student set off, the lead was slender. Puddick's small, stocky frame attacked the first obstacles with great energy. Scuttling under the cargo net, head down, nose in front, the cheers of his teammates filled the gym. Slowly, the distance between him and his opponent grew. At the 10ft rope climb, it was hard to see any other outcome than a victory. Anxiously, the platoon continued to shout and dance with every obstacle successfully negotiated. With just the final hurdle to clear, disaster struck. Puddick flung himself off the top of the pommel horse, landing awkwardly. Clipping the edge of the mat, his ankle buckled beneath him as he screamed out in pain. So severe was the landing, we knew immediately that he was not going to get up. Laying on the floor in agony, tears streaming down his face, his opposite number jogged by to take the chequered flag and another three points. No. 1 Platoon was now six points ahead.

It was a demoralizing blow for our students. They had done well, but they had come in last, and with this came punishment. No. 1 Platoon departed the gym, jubilant and raucously cheering whilst high fives were dished out en masse. As punishment for their failure, No. 2 Platoon received three extra laps of the course, delivered by Daz, who was bereft of compassion or empathy. He had sent Puddick off to the Medical Centre in an ambulance before pushing the defeated students to their limits around the course. For good measure, he then made them collapse the obstacle course and return equipment to its rightful place, robbing them of vital rest and administration time.

As would be the pattern for the weeks ahead, I wandered around the accommodation to check the students' wellbeing. The atmosphere was very subdued. Unfortunately, things didn't get any better. News had reached us that Puddick's ankle was badly damaged and hospitalization was inevitable. The Medical Officer made it clear that he wouldn't take any further part on the course. Even though the course had just started, Puddick had established himself as a popular figure, so his premature departure had a massive effect on platoon morale. It was unfortunate; anyone can land awkwardly, but there was a suspicion that it may not have happened had he not run the final leg. As devastated as the platoon was, there was no hiding the emergence of the dislike they were developing for Watson.

Wanting to check on Rideout's mental state, I walked through the accommodation and called into his room. Intuitively, it was easy to assess the cumulative pain of the platoon's loss. It didn't help that Mathews took the loss personally, and this made it feel apocalyptic.

'OK, Rideout, where did it go wrong?' Mathews talked over him, offering his version of events, but this just earned him a quick rebuke. Rideout then had space to compose his thoughts and tried again.

'Maybe we were just unlucky, Colour Sergeant,' he said, but I'd have none of that:

> 'No, not true. You make your own luck in everything you do. Today you failed to be decisive when it mattered most. Well, that's being kind. The start was unorganized and chaotic. The middle part lacked structure and understanding. But it was the end that saw you throw away the initiative. You had made the right decision and then allowed yourself to be persuaded otherwise. Your biggest problem is you are not seeing the end-state! All the exercises and fitness sessions are a sideshow to developing your ability to lead, to command and control. The difference between you and a soldier has to be your ability to bring assured clarity to the chaos of war. What we needed from you was a structure, a plan, control, foresight and, when it was required, a steely-eyed warrior, unflinching and decisive with his commands. What we got was George from *Rainbow*. That said, it's early days. So, don't mope, don't blame your luck, don't blame others. In peace, there is no failure, just lessons learnt.'

Picking up his journal, I looked through the past few entries while Rideout digested my blunt assessment. He had not completed today's reflection, which presented me with an opportunity:

> 'Rideout, you are going to write me a SWOT analysis. Imagine you must run the race again tomorrow. List the Strengths, Weakness, Opportunities and Threats of all those taking part in the race. Then write the running order of the platoon. Compare it against the running order that went in the race today. Then do some self-analysis. Grade your communication, instruction, evaluation and re-evaluation. Finally, write a note on how you controlled your group and dealt with conflicting opinions and ideas.'

With the briefest of smiles, Rideout was left to complete my request. Intentionally, my body language was less aggressive; it was essential he knew he was on the right track. Critical to this journey he was on, was his ability to separate the gamesmanship and the learning points of the course. That brief smile upon my exit offered him just a hint of encouragement, which he gratefully received.

My last act of the day was to get Danner and Boyle to move rooms. With Puddick's injury being terminal and Trollope's VW, both students needed new roommates. Searching for Boyle, he was not in his room, but his voice could be heard further down the corridor. Morale was emanating from Danner's room as the two students ironed their uniform. The opportunity for a bit of eavesdropping presented itself. Quietly standing by the door, I could hear they were discussing their peers. Insightful and funny, it was such a pity to break it up, although they had already become suspicious of my presence. Danner peered out of the door and saw me standing there. He dashed back into the room, raised a smile and clumsily came to attention.

'Sounds like you two are having fun?' I ventured.

Boyle was quick to defend their exchange as banter, and that they were truly devastated to learn of Puddick's departure. Irreverently, Danner interjected with a request to move in with Boyle. Although this was the very reason for my visit, Danner could not be allowed to feel victorious by getting something he requested. Consequently, his request was denied: 'You would like that wouldn't you, Danner? So, no! Boyle, you grab your kit and move in with Danner.'

Later that evening, it dawned on me that Danner was smart enough to realize that would have been my response: anticipating my authoritative disposition, he had offered to move in with Boyle, knowing I would find it too cheeky and decline it. This saved Danner a heap of work. I cursed myself, knowing he had played me like a fiddle! Even so, his cunning impressed me. Tomorrow would be another day, and retribution would be on my mind.

After a swift breakfast, the course was marched out to the backdoor training area, which was by now becoming a very familiar place for the students. The purpose of this event was to learn the most important skill for any commander – map reading. Barossa training area at the rear of the Academy provides the students with an uninterrupted low-level training environment. With undulating woodland, fern-covered hills, open expanses and peat bogs full of water, it was perfect for the early days of the course. The criss-crossing tracks, pylons and firebreaks offered excellent topographical examples to teach basic navigation. It was large enough to host most of the Academy on it at any one time, and consequently it was always busy.

The mood in the platoon was lifting, and this simple introduction was deliberately designed to be a leisurely event. The students entertained Captain Dunn with their attempts to decipher map coordinates, symbols and demarcation lines. By midday, we had walked the length and breadth of Barossa, visiting every spur, re-entrant and contour of interest. Williams offered the most entertaining of answers when he described a church with a tower as 'a church with a flat spire'. Curiously, it kind of made sense, and there is nothing wrong with unconventional; at the very least, no one ever confused the three different church symbols again.

However, the real reason for walking all around the training area was far more sinister than map reading tuition. The hidden agenda was to end up at the start point of the Wish Stream run. One of the most revered events at Row-Co, it was a work of pure genius. The event was deliberately placed at the end of the first week, when morale was dipping and students were feeling dislocated. The principal aim was simple: unite the Company and replace the dislocation with an unbreakable male bond. The by-product of this was mutual respect, self-confidence and emotional strength. All these attributes formed the foundations for surviving the first four weeks; specifically, emotional strength. This attribute above all would become essential during the many dark, desperate moments of the course. The next hour was assigned to facilitate male bonding on an unprecedented scale.

Gathered together about 4km south of the camp, on the crest of a windswept hill, Major Gray held the students' attention, discussing the benefits of good navigation. If nothing else, he said, an officer is expected to be excellent at map reading. The students were aware that something was afoot. The influx of a plethora of new faces roused their suspicions. But the absence of any formal brief, or the by now formal pep-talk, contrived to deceive and generate a false sense of security. Adding to the facade, the CQMS had set up the most elaborate tea party imaginable. Pete invited the students to help themselves to the tea, coffee and cakes laid out on several 6ft tables covered with a fancy white cloth.

With smiles, chatter, giggling and a seemingly disinterested Directing Staff, the students were fooled into relaxing. They were enjoying the moment, as well as the cream cakes. With the students deceived – hook, line and sinker – Pat detonated a thunder-flash. The pyrotechnic produced a deafeningly loud bang, simultaneously lighting up the dim woodland with a blinding flash. Four more ear-piercing cracks brought an abrupt end to the festivities. The students were stunned. An acrid smell of burnt gunpowder filled the damp air, while the noise continued to reverberate around Barossa. By the time they had the inclination to look up and see where it came from, they discovered that they had been surrounded by nearly twenty members of Academy Staff, all of whom were screaming and ushering the course in the direction of Pat's voice. The look on Haigh's face was priceless. He looked at Pat, looked at the cake, then looked at Pat again. Like the inner workings of an old grandfather clock, I could see the cogs in his head turning slowly to a conclusion.

'No, no way. Not now! Not during high tea! No way,' he repeated several times, genuinely irritated by the interruption.

With the sound of the thunder-flash replaced by that of the DS, purposely yelling to induce pandemonium, Pat disappeared into the Wish Stream, screaming at the top of his voice, 'Follow me! Everyone follow me. Let's go!' Amongst the chaos, my suspicions turned to Pat's new language. Where had all the obscenities gone? A wall of famous blue Rowallan T-shirts – each adorned with a stag's head sitting over the wearer's heart – chased the students in the direction of Pat's call. Forming an impenetrable Row-Co wall, we squeezed a tight circle around the students to heighten the panic and intensify the interruption. The noise produced by the Staff as they repeatedly screamed at the students was thunderous. With coffee in hand and cake in mouth, Haigh was the first to vanish into the woods. Screaming as he jumped into the stream, he was immediately tripped face-first by the deadfall and sludge. The remaining students were hot on his heels. Leaving a trail of paper cups and half-eaten fancy cakes, they splashed their way through the deepening mud and water.

At its narrowest, the stream was less than 3ft in width and 3ft deep, more akin to an irrigation ditch than a stream. Yet once you were in it, there was no escape. Silt sucked your feet deep into the base, and the sides were flanked by trees and thick scrub. Exit was impossible. At irregular intervals, the stream was choked by overgrown tree roots and fallen branches. These obstructions created natural chokepoints. Frustratingly for some students, it prevented anyone from gaining any speed or free space in which to run. Inevitably, the friction at each chokepoint was increased by the DS, as they heightened the sense of urgency by shouting at anything standing still.

At the chokepoints, the students were encouraged to exit the stream and battle through the thick hedgerows instead of waiting for queues to clear. But this was a deliberate ploy to confuse the students. No sooner had they left the stream than another member of the Staff barked instructions to get back in the water. For a little over 2km, the students constantly pushed and fought each other, trying to squeeze past the man in front, only to be caught at the next obstacle and overtaken. At one stage a full-scale fist fight broke out between a few students who had lost control of their emotions as the pressure became unbearable. With a kilometre still remaining, everyone was tiring fast and covered head to toe in stinking peat water. To the rear of the Company, the Academy Adjutant and others were berating someone. Blissfully unaware that we were due to be visited by Academy staff, it never dawned on me to think twice to check who it was. They were having problems with a student who had decided enough was enough, but by this stage, both Paddy and I were locked into the stream and couldn't move back to help. They would need to deal with it themselves. My mind ran riot asking who the student could be and who was picking up the pieces.

The stream began to widen and deepen as we neared the fence line of the Academy. The stronger students were able to run two astride for the final 500 metres before they reached the security fence. But the stream didn't lead to a gate or convenient bridge; instead it ran through a narrow culvert. It was the penultimate obstacle to be negotiated before the event finished. The swollen stream flowed quickly through the culvert, with precious little room at the top for air to pass. First to go through the culvert was Pat. Taking one deep breath, he squeezed into the concrete tube and kicked his way through to the other side. With a huge splash, he fell 1.5 metres into a large overflow pond. Shortly after, one by one, the students were guided into the culvert, with no time to contemplate what was at the other end. The presence of so many bodies at the head of the culvert caused the water to swell. With every passing second, the water became deeper and faster. Now at chest height, and running level with the top of the culvert, there was little mud to contend with, but the smell was insufferable. Mathews was the first student to reach the entrance from No. 2 Platoon.

Wrestling with the elements, he struggled to guide himself into the culvert. A combination of the water rushing to funnel through the constriction and a fallen tree inhibited his movement. Scrambling his way into the mouth of the concrete tube, he pushed his face high up against the roof of the tunnel and inched his way to the other side. Reaching the point of exit, he flung himself into the clearer water of the overflow pond. His exit was accompanied by the thunderous roar of escaping water trapped behind him. Hitting the catchment at pace in a flurry of white foam, the lad disappeared as a cloud of silt rose from the base of the ditch. Two seconds later, triumphantly, his head and shoulders broke the surface and a frantic scramble to the steep sides of the pond followed. To his horror, he discovered that getting out wasn't as easy as it first appeared. The sides of the pond had deteriorated in the bad weather. Failing to gain traction with his wet boots and clothes laden with peat water, extracting from the pond needed a team effort. Mathews would have to wait for help to arrive before negotiating the final obstacle.

As the course members filtered through the culvert, I walked back to see who was where in the queue to get through the chokepoint. Still waiting to pass through was Danner. The big lad was not coping well. Whilst the course syllabus would address his fitness, it would be his mischievous tendencies that would need coaching. Barns and Goldson were near the rear, making little effort to get through the tunnel. For Barns, it was a case of adapting to the physical challenges of his new life, but Goldson had deeper issues. Worryingly, Haigh was aimlessly walking around the water, allowing himself to be pushed and shoved aside. He was first to follow Pat from the start, but now it was telling to see him this far back. Curiously, he wasn't unhappy; indeed, a huge smile suggested a perverse enjoyment of the situation. The usual suspects who previously struggled at the rear of each run were poised to exit the culvert last.

The Staff had by now gathered around the entry and exit points to increase the urgency. With just a few students remaining, one of Paddy's platoon became stuck halfway through the culvert and broke out into a panic. Terrifying screams escaped from both ends of the tunnel. Distressingly, the sound of someone choking on water was the only noise preventing further screams. Both Captain Dunn and Major Gray were trying to calm him down, but their words had no impact. Pat, deciding enough was enough, jumped back into the water, climbing up through the exit point of the culvert. The sudden arrival of Pat's body caused the wash-back to completely flood the culvert. The student lost his air pocket and the screams fell silent. The situation became desperate, as neither Pat nor the student could breathe. Captain Watts launched himself into the water, but thankfully, just before he got into the tunnel, a gush of white foaming water spat out two bodies. First to emerge from the water was a student. Spitting black water as he jumped high into the air, our relief at his safe extraction was evident. With just a hint of concern, the OC scoured the water around the student looking for Pat. But he had swum the length of the pond underwater before emerging at the far end, belly up and face just breaking the surface, shouting his favourite words: 'Marvellous! Marvellous! Absolutely bloody marvellous! You're getting paid for this. Come on you lot, smile!'

Students littered the edge of the water catchment, scrambling up the steep bank. Pat stayed in the water, wading around the sides, quietly chastising slower members of the course. With the Company clear of the water, they assembled at the car park in the shadow of Victory College. Jogging on the spot, steam continuously surged off their shoulders as body heat escaped the grip of the wet clothes. Intentionally grouped in a tight formation to heighten the experience, they had just completed the Wishstream run. The sound of water sloshing inside everyone's boots with each step harmonized with the melodic tones of soggy clothes slapping against flesh. The sight, sound and smells emanating from the assembled mass were nothing short of inspiring.

When you say it out loud, the thought of running through an ice-cold stream for nearly 4km, swimming through flooded culverts and water catchments, sounds frightening. Yet the truth of the matter was that the whole thing was little more than a trick to boost confidence. The event was so carefully stage-managed that it could even fool the visiting staff. The mud and close proximity of the group prevented maximum exertion. The propinquity was a substitute for effort, the purpose being to intensify the feeling of moving quickly. It was impossible to gain speed, and the pulse rate rarely hit 130. To distract the students from identifying that they couldn't run quickly, the number of Directing Staff in attendance was hyper-inflated. Rent-a-crowd formed the Row-Co wall, and pressure was maintained by berating and encouraging. Uncomfortable, awkward, smelly and mostly intimidating, yes; but physically demanding it wasn't, not that the students realized this.

The short jog home to the accommodation was executed with immense pride. Each student had gained a newfound self-belief, and the feeling was palpable. They had finished the run at the same time as each other. It was the first time no one dropped out, and the perceived thrashing had been survived by all! Just when they didn't think it could get better, there was one final surprise. Out from the group of visiting Directing Staff, numbering nearly twenty in total, stepped a man in his early fifties. A puzzled expression spanned the mud-splashed faces of the students.

'Well, gentlemen, well done,' he said in a distinguished, commanding tone. There was real sincerity in his voice, which came with a knowing smile as he continued:

> 'If I had said to you a week ago, that you would be thrashed to within an inch of your lives running up a frozen stream on a Saturday afternoon, and that you would enjoy it, you would have thought me mad. But, gentlemen, that is what you have just done. And done it brilliantly; very well done. I'm sure you will remember today for many years to come. I make the effort to come along on this event because it epitomizes everything Rowallan represents – team spirit, selflessness and whole-hearted commitment. If you haven't deduced who I am yet, I'll help you out. For my sins, I'm the Academy Commandant, Major General Deverell. I hope to see you on several occasions over the coming weeks and look forward to sharing similar successes as we have enjoyed today.'

Stunned by the appearance of a major general soaked from head to toe and covered in mud, it was a jaw-dropping moment. Visibly glowing with pride, simultaneously coming to terms with their achievement, the moment was masterfully orchestrated. The Commandant knew that his presence was critical at this stage. He was one of Britain's finest officers, a man who had experienced the greatest challenges of command. With a blend of humility and razor-sharp intellect, his reputation amongst the students was on a level other generals could only drool over. This was more than demonstrating leadership through example; this was a lesson on Values-Based Leadership (VBL). The Commandant valued selflessness, commitment and endeavour, and in the space of thirty minutes, he demonstrated that fact. Not to be confused with values and standards, VBL is about consistently practising what you preach, then stopping preaching when you can't practise. It's about identifying where your leadership adds value to someone under your charge, or amidst your professional sphere of influence. Deft, intuitive and inspirational, the general had just connected with these young students and inspired them to keep going. He had done what he was asking people to do; this was the Rowallan way, and VBL personified.

Dutifully, wherever the Commandant went, so did the Academy Sergeant Major. Making a beeline for me, scowling with intent, my spider senses tingled as he addressed me: 'Colour Sergeant. Stand still! What are you wearing on your feet? Are you in the Gurkhas? You're small enough to be a Gurkha. Jungle boots are for Gurkhas, regiments of the line wear boots combat-high! You are treading a fine line, Colour Sergeant!'

Braced to attention, chastised and immured by embarrassment, the Academy Sergeant Major had just kicked the enthusiasm clean out of me. Up until that moment, it had been a great day. Left to make sense of the pointless tirade, my focus was temporarily lost.

'Wow. He really doesn't like you, does he, Colour?' chirped Captain Dunn.

'Not sure that is the case,' I replied. 'Maybe he dislikes everyone?' This was at least my hope.

It had been a long week for the students, and their faces exhibited fatigue with every swing of their arms as they marched back to their rooms. With Captain Dunn already in the shower, the platoon was assembled in the study hall so they could receive a warning order from me:

'OK team, here is the agenda for the rest of the day. You are to get your kit washed, dried and ironed. Get your journal up to date, and at some stage, on Sunday, either Captain Dunn or I will collect them. Finally, the Company Sergeant Major will be inspecting your rooms tomorrow. You will get five minutes' warning, but be ready from 0830hrs onwards. Ensure you are ready for him and don't get caught out.'

There was a flurry of questions, which I dodged without answering. No unnecessary clarity, a skill I perfected when dealing with Merseyside Police as a kid. Notwithstanding the need to guard against unintentionally giving away information, the importance of entertaining their questions was more about calming down their nerves and demonstrating that, despite what they may have thought, I was very human, and they needed to see that side of me. Over the weeks ahead, the Q&A sessions would be a tactic that helped me get to know the true character of each man. But for now, the plethora of questions needed fending off with a nondescript response, so the interpersonal exchanges could be saved for another day.

Leaving the students to their own devices, it was time to start the solemn task of analysing each character with Captain Dunn and crafting a bespoke approach for individual problems. But before I could make good my escape, Weston limped out of the door after me.

'Excuse me, Colour Sergeant, can I nip to see the MO again? My knees are dreadfully painful.'

'Yes, Weston, I'm sure you're on first-name terms with her now. Go and see the Company Sergeant Major first; he needs to fill in a sick note. Take it with you, and make sure you wear your red tracksuit, so they know you are from Rowallan Company!'

Suspicions remained high. Unconvincing, with a lack of conviction in his request, it was best to send him to the MO to be safe. To get this wrong would be unforgivable for any instructor. If he was genuinely in pain, medical help was prudent.

Captain Dunn was idling around the staff accommodation, looking for someone, to harass when I returned.

'Hey, Colour, are you ready to start the end-of-week review? Where shall we start? How about alphabetical order, or as they come?'

I grabbed my notebook and settled into an old wooden school chair next to his desk. 'As they come please, boss!'

Captain Dunn took a long look at the list, sighed deeply and then began: 'Murphy! He's a likeable chap. Got a bit of go in him! No great problems at this early stage. What do you think, Colour?'

'Undecided, boss, he has impressed in fits and starts,' I replied. 'There is obvious potential on display. You recall he was sacked during the stretcher race, but that was more to motivate the others as opposed to punish his performance. Actually, all things considered, as a first attempt, it was good. He would have learnt much about himself and the tools of command during the stretcher race. It would make sense for one of us to remind and revise the tools of command with everyone next week. They are learning them as if they were physical objects; they need to understand the concept first.'

'Agreed, Colour. There is a fantastic opportunity to re-run the stretcher race on the first exercise. Let's populate the Command Appointment Matrix and shape it so he lands that appointment. A second crack at it will hopefully rectify the mistakes he made on Monkey Hill.'

Flicking through his paperwork, Captain Dunn was selecting an uncontested path to ease us both into the marathon session. 'Good! Let's talk about Barns next. We've seen him struggling this week!'

'Not wrong, Sir,' I agreed. 'To be honest, my alarm bells are ringing with this lad. It is a simple issue, so the answer is readily available; we don't need a bespoke scheme of manoeuvre for him. But if his fitness doesn't improve rapidly, he won't keep pace with the course. If that happens, we could lose him too early.'

'That's true enough, Colour. It's tricky, that's for sure. What are your initial thoughts?'

'We aren't quite at the "kid gloves" stage with him yet, but we need to be conscious that we don't knock the stuffing out of him before he becomes strong enough to cope with the rigours of the course,' I suggested. 'During the next few fitness sessions, I'll pay a bit more attention to him. Being so tall and thin has its issues. His strength and conditioning haven't kept pace with his physical development. There is the likeability factor about him – you could see soldiers thriving under his command.'

'I am not that convinced, Colour! He really is struggling with the simplest of physical tasks. Gaining the stamina required in such a short time is hard.'

'Sir, you could be right. Should we park our concerns until we see how he copes with week two? There is mental strength and that rare quality of emotional intelligence. I am not disagreeing with your assessment, and your observations make sense, but I think he has something.'

'OK, let's see what next week brings. Let's move on to Boyle. A bit of a grey man, Colour? But he is keen enough.'

'Yes, Sir. Although greyish, not quite grey. Once out of his shell, he will settle in nicely. A little quiet, but committed; no immediate problems. Of course, there is something affable about him, and that's half the battle. If anything, maybe he is still suffering the shock of capture. Wouldn't be surprisd if we begin to see the real Boyle soon now Danner is his roommate.'

'You only like him because he supports Everton! What would you say about him if Liverpool was his chosen team?'

'No. Not true, boss. However, if he told me that he wanted to join the Royal Logistic Corps, I could take a dislike to him.'

'Cheeky! You would be surprised by the RLC, Colour, we are a talented bunch, even if it is only being the best at eating Yorkie bars and flipping burgers. Oh, and I don't see you wearing airborne wings!'

It was a fair point. I never had any desire to jump out of a perfectly serviceable aeroplane. Despite the simple description of the Logistic Corps, the opportunities for soldiers and officers to diversify and join the murky world of Special Forces are ample. Captain Dunn had done P Company with the Paras early in his service, and enjoyed teasing others who hadn't.

'Boss, I take my hat off to you for earning your wings, but when you land on the DZ, what are you doing next? Getting the egg banjos on or refuelling the trucks!'

'Mmm, is that a bite? Are you a little jealous of the Corps? We'd better move on to Francis before you apply to transfer! He has started well, Colour; reminds me of myself when I went through the course.'

'How so? Do you mean you were tubby and resembled a rabbit caught in the headlights, or you were so gullible you believed the propaganda booklet you were sent?'

By now, Captain Dunn and I were just looking for any excuse to exchange banter.

'True, although it's less like a rabbit caught in the headlights and more like a headless chicken,' admitted Dunn. 'I gave Francis a small task on day two, and he was close to crumbling under the pressure. That's not a good sign. Then, during his interview, he just grinned nervously and rambled on about rugby. There is a good character waiting for the right moment to prove it. I am confident he has what it takes. We should focus on controlling his flapping, Colour.'

'Understood, boss! Whilst he does flap, this is just compensating for his lack of knowledge and understanding; he is not a natural flapper. More small tasks and a bit of responsibility mixed with close supervision will help. I'll make him the duty student a few times on the bounce – this will get him use to added pressures, help him practise using authority.'

Captain Dunn burst into laughter, nearly choking on his coffee. 'You're taking the piss aren't you, Colour? Are you mad? The Sergeant Major will eat him alive. Picture each morning when he issues his duty student brief. No, that's a lousy plan!'

Captain Dunn was right. Pat would instantly identify that Francis flapped under pressure and toy with him. The thought of Pat exploiting Francis' weakness conjured up images of Francis melting away in a pool of perspiration as Pat smashed him with press-ups, squats and star jumps.

'OK boss, you're right, that's not such a good idea. I'll think up a few confidence-building tasks over the weekend. Let me work up the plan.'

Smiling like the cat who got the cream, Captain Dunn continued: 'You don't like it when I am right, do you, Colour? It hurts when the little Platoon Commander gets one over on the Colour Sergeant! Shall I continue with King next, Colour?'

I rubbed my face and sighed; more because I should have thought through the duty student solution for Francis than the fact Captain Dunn identified the flaw before me.

'Err, King. He's doing just what he needs to and no more, isn't he?' Captain Dunn looked at me quizzically. Further explanation was required.

'My observation is that King knows exactly what we're looking for and he's doing nothing more than what he needs to do, in order to stay out of trouble.' Captain Dunn nodded and agreed.

'The problem we face with King is, the experience and knowledge he has as a soldier gives him a degree of parity with us. Our tricks will not fool him all the time. He will have suffered most of them before, so he knows our constraints. Testing him and forcing his weaknesses into full view will be a challenge. Maybe we need to develop something bespoke for him.'

'True, Colour, we just need to play this another way. Let's chat with the academics to see how he copes with an intellectual challenge as opposed to the physical. We know he copes with the physical friction, but how does he think when he is tired? Let me fix a scheme of manoeuvre for him.'

'Moore! A nice easy one for you, Colour, would you like to start?'

'No obvious problems this week. He appears to have his head screwed on, although he's a little effeminate!'

'The word you are looking for is "boring", Colour. There is no spark, no pulse. The lad needs to live a little, let his hair down, if he had any. At his age, Colour, I'd travelled the world, commanded a troop in Northern Ireland, stood on the baseline during riots on the streets of Belfast and gone to war in Iraq, done a tour with the United Nations. There were medals, women and good times everywhere.'

Captain Dunn struggled to get his stories out as he indulged himself reminiscing his time as a young Platoon Commander.

'Boss, don't bore me with your war stories. It's late, and if you get me started on tours of Northern Ireland, you may just discover it was probably me throwing rocks at you on the baseline in Belfast.'

Captain Dunn's eyes opened widely as a look of disbelief covered his face. As bored squaddies, our favourite pastime was to jump the fence of North Howard Street Mill operations base, just off the Falls Road, and stone our mates as they passed the segment gates. Occasionally, and depending on where the riot was, we would join in just for the fun of it. As a young soldier, Belfast was my second home. I had come to know it well. Youth, and the feeling of invincibility that it brought, suppressed the stupidity of these actions. One of those bumps along the way to maturity is the best way to explain it.

'No way. You started your very own riots?' I gave him the look that compromised my own mischievous beginnings. We both burst into fits of laughter. It was my turn to reminisce, explaining that lots of soldiers bunked out of the forts dotted around Belfast to do what young people do in a bustling big city. Stoning soldiers was definitely one of the lesser crimes. Meeting up with girls and sneaking into football matches were not uncommon. One day someone will write a book about the scams and fun during wars.

It was an excellent understanding that we had developed; the banter was part of an infectious formula that engendered loyalty, honesty and mutual respect. Sometimes a student would do something stupid or brilliant, and with no need to compare notes, one sideways glance was confirmation we were thinking the same. In the private confines of our room or out of earshot of anyone else, Captain Dunn was referred to as 'boss'. This is a term of endearment and respect, but it does have its critics. Frowned upon by some officers who refer to it as 'Boss Culture' to stigmatize its use, it can be contentious. Envious of what it stands for, some seek to suppress close relationships, worried it could undermine authority. They couldn't be further from the truth. In the right environment, relaxing boundaries enhances relationships. For those officers who still think that respect comes free with a badge of rank, they struggle with close relationships. 'Boss culture' is a misnomer; it's the propaganda of toxic leadership, the kind that seeks to keep everyone in their place.

'Fair point, Colour,' grinned Captain Dunn, before returning to the subject of Moore. 'But do you think he looks a bit like Rowan Atkinson?'

'No!'

'OK, Blackadder then?'

'Still no!'

'Do you not think he has that rubbery-face look, you know, that Mr Bean image?'

'No, no and erm, no. OK, that's enough, or we will never finish. Let's move swiftly on, Sir, who's next?'

'Such a killjoy, Colour. Let's talk about Rideout! Now here's a character. He reminds me of a Thunderbirds puppet, always bobbing and weaving with a grin the size of a Cheshire cat. I swear there is only one word in his vocabulary – "Yes".'

'Ha, spot on. He's got problems alright, but nothing a bit of Sandhurst micromanagement wouldn't sort out. He wants to do well and is keen to improve and impress. Clearly very fit, the lad has a stomach like a washboard, but he was underwhelming in command of the assault course race. That said, it was not all his fault. What's your assessment, Sir?'

Captain Dunn reverted to tapping his pencil on the desk, deep in thought. This was always the first sign that he had reservations. Sometimes he would search for a turn of phrase that would be inoffensive as he disagreed with my view.

'His journal is quite informative. There is no denying his intellect. Have you read it yet? If you get a chance, Colour, have a look at the SWOT analysis he drafted. He knows his stuff and can think straight, knows how to analyse a problem for sure, but we will need to help him control his flapping. Not sure we can overcome this. Maybe he's your best candidate for duty student next week. The Sergeant Major will undoubtedly thrash some sense into him, but knowing he is a fit lad he will be able to handle it. By the time the week is done, we will be better placed to see if we can save him. Thrash him to within an inch of his life and he will realize there is no need to flap, because he can cope. This will be a journey of self-discovery, but the answer may not be what he wants to hear. Can you chat with the Sergeant Major so he understands what we are trying to do with Rideout?'

Captain Dunn then asked: 'How about Witherspoon, or should I say Wetspoon?'

'Mmm, "wet" is an accurate description. Although there have been glimpses of potential, we are some distance off the ingredients of an Army officer.'

Captain Dunn paused and considered his reply. 'He needs a rocket up his arse, Colour. The next two weeks may just sort him out. So, I won't put him on the endangered list just yet, but he is heading in that direction. Let us both try and smoke him out of his cocoon this week coming.'

'Roger that, boss. I will try and rattle his cage until we can see his fighting spirit. He will need to get a move on though. The next week is a test for all; it will be mountainous for him. If he doesn't spark we should bring him in early for a warning, or we may just get stuck with him later during the course.'

'Fair enough, Colour. Let's turn our thoughts to Mathews. The cauliflower-eared scrum-half from Hereford. I like the cut of his jib. He always appears to be ready for action. What do you think?'

'He's keen enough, and fit – can't ask for much more at this stage. At times, I see a bull terrier when he gets going; we need to polish that out of him. There is much there for us to work with, but it's easy to see why he has been sent here. At times there is a lack of conviction, but he tries to effect a change when change is needed. This tells me he is constantly evaluating things. When he has been faced with two options – do nothing or do something – he has chosen wisely. We can teach someone when it's right to do something, but it's much harder to teach someone the emotional intelligence to do nothing.'

Corporal Davis appeared at the door. 'Sir. Colour. Sorry to interrupt your Progress Board, but the MO has just been on the phone. He needs to speak with the Platoon Commander of No. 2 Platoon.'

Captain Dunn disappeared in the direction of the Company office, leaving me to make more coffee and raid the biscuit jar. Calories were everything to a Row-Co instructor. The Staff kept a jar of high-calorie goodies in each room, normally Blue Riband biscuits that had been left behind by students. Fifteen minutes and four Blue Ribands later, Captain Dunn reappeared, surrounded by doom and gloom.

'Bad news I'm afraid, Colour. Weston is to be MD'd [medical discharged]. The upside is, that brings the total losses up to four this week! That's not a bad average, mind you. I had lost five by this stage on the last course. And as a bonus, one less report to write. Things are looking up.'

Despite the bravado, I could tell by the tone of his voice that the captain didn't mean a single word he had just said. The Rowallan myths were the main source of its legendary status. Stories which leaked about how students couldn't cope, or that instructors thrashed people into obscurity, often had little substance. But leaked stories had a useful purpose. There was an expectation that no one, even the students, wanted to see compromised. This was the notion that Rowallan was the toughest course the British Army could offer a young officer. We both sat still at the desk for a moment, deep in thought, as Captain Dunn tucked into his first Blue Riband biscuit, so I notched up number five.

'We'd better crack on with Haigh. Can you start, Colour?'

'That's not fair, boss! Why me? Surely you should start with a problem child?'

'Well, you love it, Colour. The challenge of dealing with over-educated military virgins is what keeps you ticking.' Captain Dunn burst into a fit of giggles, barely keeping the chocolate biscuit in his mouth.

Pausing to gather my thoughts on Haigh, finding the right words would be important. It would be very easy to give someone the wrong impression of this lad, as he constantly asked stupid questions and wore a bemused look on his face. It was his relentless quest for justification that made him appear different from the rest of his cohort. It would have driven me to distraction but for the fact he was being serious and sincere. He would quickly understand complexity before scoffing at the notion of a simple alternative. The consequence was causing him to become alienated from his peers and provoked constant criticism.

'Haigh is suffering from an identity crisis,' I said. 'At times, he lacks self-belief, and possibly commitment, yet in the same breath, demonstrates remarkable clarity of thought when dealing with wicked problems. My greatest fear is the lad's a sitting duck for ridicule! John Lennon sang "They hate you if you're clever and they despise a fool." Haigh comes across as both. However, he has displayed a glimmer of hope, and I'll keep on trying to educate and protect him from those who exploit his unorthodox understanding. He will need to take the advice on board quickly. My opinion is for you to challenge his thinking style, try and match his intellect. He needs help in shortening his thinking time, to become more intuitive and less mathematical.'

Pensively, Captain Dunn looked at me. Haigh's inquisitive manner, coupled with his oddly shaped body, made him an easy target for cheap jibes. The rest of the students had nicknamed him 'Clyde', the orangutan made famous by Clint Eastwood in the film *Every Which Way But Loose*. It took every ounce of restraint for the DS at Row-Co not to crack jokes at Haigh's expense; if we were to do so, all hope would be lost. We both agreed that whilst it would be fair game to apply pressure on others, we needed to ensure the DS did not escalate his isolation from the platoon.

Students similar to Haigh had challenged my instructional abilities in the past. They are unique, talented but prone to unmilitary behaviour. Such a cohort exists in the military under the disguise of the Professionally Qualified Officers (PQO). These are officers who have qualified in professional disciplines such as medicine, theology or as vets. Sometimes sponsored by the service and sometimes through vocation, they join the military. In the nicest possible way, they are a peculiar bunch of people: incredibly intelligent, very professional, fully committed and occasionally good at soldiering. But having lived in the logical world of academia, some may struggle with the world of basic military logic, and this can lead to high anxiety or trigger irrational responses.

Five months earlier, deep in the middle of Barossa, whilst teaching a PQO course basic battle procedures, these two worlds collided. The exercise involved little more than identifying the location of an enemy during an advance to contact. To make it easy, we gave the enemy a fluorescent red hat and sat him at the base of a lone large tree. Firing a machine gun that was over-oiled and producing clouds of white smoke, it couldn't get much easier to spot him. Figuring out how to attack the enemy by analysing the ground was a simple procedure which had been explained to the course several times in a leisurely fashion. Up to this point, the day had been going very well. It was a summer course, with late starts and early finishes. My appointed commander was a young dentist, the youngest ever qualified and allegedly the brightest medical mind Oxford produced. He was intense and full of energy. His eyes beamed lasers, no matter how turgid the subject. You could not have wished to meet a more attentive student. As he lay behind a fallen tree, all was going to plan. He had control of his section, comprising four nurses, three padres and a vet.

With everyone assembled in a small fold behind the tree, all that was required was a swift appreciation of the ground before he launched a quick attack. To put this in context, it was the kind of problem we would give to a 16-year-old CCF student. But the young dentist began to dally. To force a decision and keep some momentum, I encouraged him to make his move. 'Left or right, Sir, what do you think?'

'I don't know, Colour Sergeant!' he replied. 'If we go left, we all die. If we go right, most of us die. We can go straight, but that's suicidal.'

'Correct, Sir, that's the pressure of command, but stay here any longer and the enemy will bring down artillery fire on you and you will all die anyway. Or you run out of ammunition and they will come and attack you. Either way, someone is dying!'

Tears began to stream down his face. He shook his head violently before ripping off his helmet and throwing it to the floor. The speed of transition from calm to distraught indicated deeper problems.

'You can't expect me to work like this! You can't expect answers this quickly. It's intolerable; you're intolerable. No one can work like this.'

Caught off-guard by his reaction, words were hard to find. He took my silence as disapproval and ran off into the undergrowth, disappearing from view. His battle buddies were blissfully unaware of his meltdown, and kept calling to him for answers. Following him into the undergrowth, I found him kneeling down, head pressed up against a tree with his fingers in his ears, repeatedly saying 'shut up, shut up!'.

This was not a man who struggled under pressure. Nor was he mentally weak – in fact, he was the total opposite – but that didn't mean he could separate relevance and irrelevance when it appeared intertwined. There was no logic in running directly into the killing zone of an enemy machine gun, but the risk of complete annihilation is mitigated with sound tactical planning. This is why command can feel like the loneliest place on the planet.

Haigh shared similar characteristics to the young dentist. He cared less about what people thought, and more about the need to focus on doing the best he could. If he couldn't understand it, he asked questions repeatedly. Only when it was presented in micro-sections, where he could dissect it into digestible chunks, would he be content. From my experience, people like this cope well with the illogical nature of the military, but only for the briefest of occasions before imploding or leaving. If we wished to retain Haigh, we would need a combination of kid gloves and tough love.

Captain Dunn finished his notes on Haigh and looked up. The nervous tapping of the pencil and pensive looks had returned as he flicked through the pages of jottings.

'Seeing as you don't like going first to offer your thoughts with those who have personality challenges, I'll start first on this one, Colour. See if you can guess who I am talking about. This character, despite being well educated, is not for the Army. He lacks drive, commitment, desire and interest, but his major ailment is that he is incredibly boring and uninspirational.'

'Lane?'

'Yes, Colour, he's a problem child all right, isn't he?'

'Well, boss, you have sussed him out quickly. It is safe to say he will not make it to the end of the course. He is unfit, uninterested and unworkable. Intervention is required, and I would urge that we do it now. We must flag him up to the OC and see if we could get shot of him.'

'Yes, Colour, I hear you, but the OC won't have it. After only five days, he will say we haven't given him a chance. It's not that easy either; there is significant pressure from the College Commander to improve our retention.'

'Why's that, boss?'

'Well, this doesn't go any further, Colour; if it does, I'm in big trouble. The Army Training Division is not too pleased with the number of students we have lost in recent courses. Every year the Academy looks at efficiency measures, and cutting Rowallan as a course would save a chunk of money. It's hard to convince people that we are good value for money, specifically when we get through students at a rate of one a day!'

'Well that's understandable, boss, but there is nothing new about this. It is a perennial problem which all stems from the selection process. We shouldn't look to share the blame here! If we carry Lane to the end of the course, he's not likely to be successful thereafter. This is obvious to all.'

'Again, Colour, I hear you loud and clear. I shall chat to the OC and see what his thoughts are, but don't expect too much.'

'You know he won't get any resistance from the Commandant.'

Captain Dunn looked at me puzzled. 'How do you mean?'

'Well, this morning when we ran down the Wishstream, and the general was at the rear, he was pushing Lane all the way, but Lane kept on throwing himself to the floor crying that he couldn't go on. By the time we finished, the general was fairly annoyed, as well as being virtually exhausted. There is no way the general will want to experience that next time.'

The major general enjoyed being out of his office, and Rowallan was full of opportunity. Although we didn't know it at the time, he fought the civil servants counting the pennies relentlessly to prevent them from cutting Rowallan. The general visited every course at Sandhurst: the first term, intermediate and final terms. He was well placed to observe the impact Row-Co students had on the Commissioning Course. When he came out running with Row-Co, he identified those who would go on to do well and challenge for top honours in the year ahead. He would frequently talk of the valuable contribution Rowallan graduates made during the first fourteen weeks of the Commissioning Course. Steadying the nerves of new Officer Cadets and providing the glue to galvanize thirty strangers was invaluable. Having survived the worst that could be thrown at them, they quickly became the ballast of a platoon throughout all three terms.

Moving on, Captain Dunn said: 'You will have empathy with this one, Colour: Stone. A fellow northerner like you. This will be interesting!'

'Thanks for reminding me of that fact, boss. At the risk of being stereotypical of young men from the north, he is a slacker, constantly looking for the easy way out. Doesn't like hard work, but most of all, what he writes in his journal is frightening. We don't hide the fact we both read the journals, but whether he is deliberately trying to wind us up with his sarcastic and immature comments, or he's attempting to be witty, he is misjudging the moment. In one of his entries this week there is a comment about fitness with Staff Dazzell being too easy. If Staff Dazzell knew that, the whole Company would be run into the ground as punishment.'

Captain Dunn nodded in agreement. 'You're right about his maturity, Colour. But let's not lose sight that he is an intelligent boy. His interlocutors thus far have all been teenagers, subsequently he still thinks like the school child smoking a crafty fag behind the bike shed. His adult interaction and social awareness are so underdeveloped, it is a real issue. I am not sure we need to develop an approach just yet; we need to get hard evidence before we shape our decision with reason. The solution will lay amidst some crafty social engineering!'

'Kind of agree, but he needs to grow up sharpish if he's going to be of any use to his peers. Maybe a chat with Daz about that comment in the journal? Or maybe we invite Stone to explain his thoughts to Daz?'

Captain Dunn suggested: 'Firstly, we need to be very careful with how we use the information in their journals. If students became aware that we used their words to shape our decisions, they will stop writing their true feelings. My other thought is we don't share too much information with anyone outside our little empire. Interference by someone who is only seeing our students occasionally will have an adverse effect. If Staff Daz knew what was in the journal, you are right, he would take his revenge on everyone. So, can I suggest we do nothing just yet? We keep our powder dry. If he progresses through the course, we will see greater evidence and better understand how to tackle his immaturity.'

Both our cups had been dry for a while – it was time to fill them with strong coffee and search for a fresh supply of Blue Ribands. After a brief interlude, we both sat back down in our school chairs and the captain took up where we left off.

'Now here's an interesting if not difficult character, Watson. Let me read what I have written down here over the past few days, Colour.'

'Surly', 'arrogant', 'aloof' and 'socially awkward' were all mentioned, Captain Dunn struggling to raise a smile as the mood darkened.

'Watson has some serious character flaws,' I admitted.

'Hold on, Colour, I haven't finished. Selfish, idle and a little grubby. Now it's your turn.'

'Sir, there is little good to say about him. He is demonstrating all the signs of a narcissist, borderline deluded. I'm afraid we will need to put a lot of work into reshaping his outlook on life. Do you know what they call him?'

Captain Dunn raised his head, stopped twirling his pencil and stared at me. 'No. What?'

'Vic!'

'Why Vic? Is that his first name, Victor?'

'No, they call him Vic because he gets up everyone's nose, just like one of those vapour tubes you buy from the chemist!'

'The answer, Colour, is to bring him down to size at a rapid rate of knots, and do it publicly. With any luck, it will open his eyes to the fact that he is quickly becoming the most unpopular person on the course. If that doesn't work, I'll tell him straight during his first progress interview next week. In the meantime, could I ask you to get a grip of his turnout and bearing? He may also need a few pointers on managing his spots. That's not acne he's suffering from, it's a lack of personal hygiene.'

Pat was readying himself for a cycle ride home. As he stopped at the door to bid us farewell, he listened to the end of the conversation.

'Watson,' he said. 'That's one of the few names I've learnt. Let's see how he handles tomorrow's fun and games.' Captain Dunn was surprised to hear Pat's voice.

'That will be the Sergeant Major developing lock-on with Watson then, boss,' I said.

Pat departed towards his office, filling the corridor with a crazy laugh as Captain Dunn sunk his face into his hands. 'God only knows what will greet us after the Sergeant Major spends a full day alone with all the students. OK, let's crack on! Danner – he's a cheeky bugger isn't he, Colour? Do you want to kick it off?'

'Cheeky is one way to describe him. Although that's not always a bad thing. I am more concerned about his commitment and fitness. I'm a little puzzled why he wants to be here. It is obvious he's not in it for the money, and he isn't in it for a lasting career. I'm a bit puzzled by him at the moment. He has struggled with every event we've done, but hasn't displayed any hint of discontent. In fact, he smiled at me today as if we were the best of mates.'

'I can see that disappoints you, Colour,' giggled Captain Dunn.

'We may be lucky with Danner. Provided he keeps at it, just staying on the course will whip him into line without too much effort from us. If there is a concern, it would be to keep his cheek in check.'

'Three remaining,' said Captain Dunn. 'Goldson, Packman and Williams: who first?'

'Packman, boss; he's has proved to be a very capable young lad. On the events to date, he has given it his best and finished high up in the pecking order each time. I'm pleased with his contribution at the end of week one.'

'Yeah, but you know, it's a little strange, Colour.'

'Why? What is?'

'Well, Packman is also from Welbeck College. That's the school for potential officers, a bit like a young apprenticeship scheme. They tend to be very bright but extremely immature. We have another Welbecksian in the platoon – guess who it is.'

'So, I am looking for someone who is very immature and lacks life experience you mean, boss. Stone?'

'Spot on, Colour. He is typical of what Welbeck College produce: intelligent kids, but they don't always integrate quickly or as well as we would like.'

'How come they are so different?'

'It is hard to say, but more often than not, they look more like Stone than Packman. So I'm pleasantly surprised with Packman.'

Captain Dunn had a file on every student. Most of the information was collected prior to the student arriving, including a summary of school life and other achievements. I never asked to see what was inside these files, for fear that it would prejudice my judgment. It is hard to recover from a first impression, and if that was the written word, it can be harder still. The pen is truly mightier than the sword and should never be underestimated, but it is as much about the author as it is the subject.

Captain Dunn forced a smile before he summed up: 'I think Packman will be fine in the first few weeks, but after he has endured some real hardships, we will be better placed to assess his potential. OK, Colour, nearly there. Goldson. This lad doesn't have what it takes. He is lethargic or docile; not even a spark from him when it's required. In fact, I am surprised he has lasted this long. I felt sure he would have sacked it by now. Thoughts?'

'Not much more to add, other than he is unfit, and that is going to cause us a huge problem if he sticks with it. We need to target him next week. I will adjust the Command Appointment Matrix to ensure Goldson features nice and early, but I am a little embarrassed at the lack of my observations.'

Captain Dunn scribbled more notes. 'Finally, Williams, Colour! I'd love to start, but it would be hard for me to pick him out of a line-up. Can't recollect what he looks like!'

Captain Dunn pulled out the large platoon photograph and searched the names scribbled on the chalkboard held in their hands. 'Jesus Christ, even with his name written on a board, it's hard to pick him out.'

'That's a bonus, boss, because I don't know what he looks like either.'

With greater scrutiny, we both scoured the photograph. The students stood in three ranks, wearing red tracksuits and holding up name boards just as they would do in an American jail.

'Yes! Got him; there he is on the back row.' Captain Dunn raised his fist in a victory salute, and the full smile had returned to his face.

'No, I haven't seen anything of him, boss.'

'Well, this is going to be easy! Let's have a look at his test results.' The captain flicked through the small mountain of paperwork we had accumulated. 'Run, 10:25; dips, seven; press-ups, twenty-two; sit-ups, twenty-nine. Not great, but not the worst. There is nothing here to start panicking over. He seems very middle of the road, although I haven't interviewed him yet. It doesn't help that his name is Williams! Definitely another candidate for an early appearance on the command tasks next week please, Colour.'

'Puddick, Weston, Trollope and Hays all gone! So, let us see what we've deduced,' Captain Dunn said, once again flicking back and forth through his notes. 'The people we need to look at over the next few days are: Williams – obviously – Goldson, Watson, Witherspoon, Stone, Haigh, Francis, Rideout and Lane. Anyone else do you think, Colour?'

'Yes, Barns and Danner, boss.'

'Barns! Yes, nearly forgot about him.'

Captain Dunn finished scribbling his notes before slamming them closed in his book. 'So, from twenty-one down to seventeen; not a bad week at the office. Well, that's me, Colour, I'm going to start writing these reports up and then I must get some training in. See you Monday.'

Wasting no time, Captain Dunn left.

Chapter Three

Character Reassignment

'Rideout! Rideout!' My shout echoed up and down the empty corridor as other students repeated my command like a First World War trench announcement. Standing impatiently waiting for Rideout to appear, he could be heard crashing around in his room trying to hasten his arrival. The partition doors between the accommodation and the main corridor crashed open, spitting the student out in the process. He was red-faced and flustered: 'Yes, Sir! No, I mean! Yes, Colour Sergeant. I mean Sir.'

'You don't know what you mean, do you, softlad?'

'No, Sir; I mean yes, Sir,' he blurted out.

I shook my head in the realization that this may be harder than initially appeared.

'Ten press-ups, softlad. Each press-up needs to be accompanied by the words: "I must learn the military ranks." My rank is not "Sir", it's "Colour Sergeant"! After you have done your press-ups, assemble the platoon in the study hall so we can go through the requirements for Sunday.'

Rideout was now receiving the character reconstruction we had agreed in a bid to cure his flapping character – more responsibility, more micro-tasks in which he would have to exercise authority and achieve his aim. The plan was to desensitize the feeling of intimidation and make him comfortable in chaos. With the platoon assembled in the study hall and each student sitting at his designated desk, the conditions were starting to shape up. Military authority was becoming second nature, and mutual respect was seeping through at all levels. I took the time to have a good stare at everyone, allowing them the same opportunity, not that anyone took it. Purposefully silent, there was a dramatic pause before I explained the events of Sunday:

> 'OK, tomorrow's a big day for you lot. Over the past few days, we have inspected your rooms and you seem to be getting a grip of the attention to detail that's required. That said, there is much more work to be done. Tomorrow, the Company Sergeant Major will conduct his first room inspection. He will inspect your rooms first thing in the morning, so tonight you must concentrate on organizing your lockers, ironing your kit and mastering the bed block. Oh, and by the way, Rideout, it's your responsibility to ensure it is all ready for the CSM in the morning. Don't

get it wrong. If it was me, there would be a pre-inspection before the Sergeant Major arrives, and don't let anyone get away with slacking!'

Once again, the tactic was to deliberately walk out of the study hall and back to my office quickly, giving the students no opportunity to ask questions. There is only one thing worse than not knowing what is about to happen, and that is 'the waiting'. It was to be a busy night for the students, cleaning and polishing with just a hint of trepidation. They were not to know that the CSM would spend less than thirty seconds in each room. This would be ample time to achieve the desired effect of this particular event. The outcome was predetermined, the effect identified long before they had even turned up at the front gate.

It was close to 2100hrs by the time my notes were finished and the appointment matrix was rewritten ready for the next week. Having prepared my kit, it was time to go home. There was still a buzz of activity radiating from the accommodation, triggering an impromptu walk around their rooms; wandering from room to room, saying nothing, just listening to student conversations until compromised. It may have been a bit unfair to do this, but the unguarded information was invaluable. Having listened to Stone complaining about everything and nothing, I stepped into his room to give him some gentle words of encouragement. Halfway through my fatherly chat, the double doors swung open wildly and Weston's voice filled the corridor. Loud and full of arrogance, he let loose a triumphant cry.

'Yea ha!' he yelled. 'I am out of here. I've got the ticket I came for: unfit for military service.'

Puzzled and uncertain of what had just been said, I peered from behind the door and along the corridor. Weston was walking away from me, minus his limp. Above his head, he waved a letter. Unable to fathom out what was going on, I decided to say nothing and watch things develop, intrigued to hear what else he was going to say. Danner was at the far end of the accommodation, and Weston walked in that direction, vigorously waving the paper.

'Dan! Dan! Told you. Look! Look at this bad boy.' The expression on Danner's face compromised my presence. Weston turned around and saw me standing in the doorway of Stone's room. There was no need for words, no need for me to shout; my expression said everything Weston needed to know. Caught red-handed, he had deliberately set out to con his way out of the Army via a medical discharge. The reason for his actions was irrelevant at that precise moment in time. For a few seconds, there descended an eerie silence as the whole platoon realized what had just occurred. Weston limped towards me, offering his slip of paper, accompanied by some incoherent mumblings. He stopped a few inches short of me and gawked awkwardly. Showing no emotions and saying nothing, I left the accommodation, leaving Weston standing alienated and in the dark.

Unable to concentrate, my walk to the Sergeants' Mess took me forever. This was a moral dilemma to which there was no easy solution. Telling Captain Dunn about Weston would not change the outcome. Just letting him go was morally wrong, but if he went without a fuss, it would save everyone a heap of heartache. He was cheating the system, and such audacity needed to be exposed. But what would the consequences be? To accuse a potential officer of lying was a big thing, as Sandhurst is fuelled on integrity. If it was proven that he was conning the system by pretending to have a bad knee, he would be hauled in front of the Commanding Officer. The result would either be the indignation of a dishonourable discharge or, worse, being forced to see out his contract. If the latter happened, a year down the road he would be a commissioned officer, in charge of thirty soldiers in Bosnia, Kosovo or Belfast, but he would still be a lying fraudster. That was a truly dangerous prospect. Even if the accusation could be proved – which would be problematic and nigh-on impossible – was the squeeze worth the juice?

Moral dilemmas are part and parcel of life, be it military or civilian. But the values and standards demanded of serving the Queen make for some difficult moments. The cultural and demographic diversities are sufficient to guarantee a huge mix of social and domestic challenges. Officers and soldiers are drawn from across the Commonwealth, and this brings flavour to our identity. Yet it is these differences that frequently cause conflict and threaten the good order of unit cohesion, affecting the fighting spirit. The issue with Weston was not that different, even if it was almost surreal. On the walk back to my room, I racked my brain for a reference point, a similar issue during my career that would help me get my bearings with this problem. The memories came flooding back of a dilemma that could have been produced by a scriptwriter for the soap opera *EastEnders*.

* * *

Whilst serving a two-year operational tour of Northern Ireland as a platoon sergeant, my relationship with the soldiers had become close. Frequently we worked fourteen hours a day under relentless pressures, and genuinely feared for our lives on a daily basis. These kinds of experiences force you to learn far more about each other than perhaps you would do back in England. One of the Riflemen had been very quiet over an extended period of time. Kenny was a typical 19-year-old Londoner. He was cocky, witty and loud, but a hard worker. Always keen to do his job well, he never shied away from hard work; a real likeable lad. After the end of another long patrol in the Mourne Mountains, we sat down on my patrol pack and cracked open my flask as we waited to be picked up by a helicopter. Whilst sharing my brew, I seized the moment to ask him what was wrong. Kenny denied having any dramas, insisting everything was 'rosy'. I knew it wasn't the truth, but to force the issue would be to make it worse, so the subject was dropped.

The following morning, Kenny was loitering outside my office. 'Morning, Sarge,' he said. 'Your iron not working?'

It was a typical cheeky comment from Kenny, which was not funny or well timed. Insinuating that my shirt hadn't been ironed served to do little more than vex me. But the tone and delivery lacked authenticity, so he escaped the tongue-lashing he deserved. Kenny walked into the office behind me, making small-talk about football. He was gearing up to tell me he had a problem, so I listened to how Arsenal were the best team in the world – no easy task for an Evertonian. Eventually, it came out.

'Sarge, you're a man of the world. I'm in a bit of trouble like! Could do with some pointers.'

'OK, Kenny, what is it?'

Kenny pulled up a chair and made himself comfortable in my office. 'I've caught a dose. You know, the clap,' giggled Kenny.

It was hard to see the funny side of the statement. He was engaged to be married to a really nice local girl, Ann-Marie. She was a devout Catholic, and it was evident Kenny had been messing around.

Thirty seconds elapsed before my thoughts were offered. 'Well, softlad, how long have you known?'

'About a few weeks, Sarge!'

'The blessing here is, we have both been stuck on the border doing patrols for a few weeks, so you haven't passed this on to Ann-Marie.'

Kenny's silence said it all. He looked at me for a fraction of a second, then looked down at the floor.

'Well, Kenny, you're going to have to come clean with this one. Get down to see the MO now. As soon as you can, you need to get Ann-Marie to see a doctor.'

'That's a nonstarter, Sarge! There is no way in the world I can tell her. She would be devastated. We have only ever had sex once, and that wasn't until I'd given her the engagement ring. If I tell her, she'll call off the wedding and her brothers will kill me.'

Kenny had dismissed my advice without pausing to consider it.

'Well, Kenny, there is nothing we can do. You have just got to be honest and take what is coming. Explain that you have been a complete idiot, and then beg for her forgiveness and maybe your honesty can salvage something.'

'No, Sarge, there is a way you can help me. I've been thinking this through for the last week. If the MO gives me the penicillin and stuff to get rid of the dose, you can phone him later to say that it got lost during a patrol or sum-fing like that.'

'Don't be bloody stupid, softlad, what good will that do?'

'Well, because you're a sergeant and that, the MO will believe you and give me a second lot of tablets. Then I'll give them to Ann-Marie without her noticing. Dead clever really.'

'If this wasn't so serious, softlad, I would laugh. How do you intend to convince her to take the medicine? Remove the label of the bottle and replace it with one that says "beauty therapy treatment – Take one tablet three times a day after meals"?'

Kenny looked at me, confused and annoyed. 'No! My plan was to mix the medicine with drinks of tea and that, you know, disguise the taste. Or cover the tablets with chocolate! A mate of mine said it would work; he has done it to his girlfriend.'

'Kenny, don't be daft. For a starter, you don't even know if she has caught the bloody thing.'

'She has got it all right, Sarge.'

'How do you know?'

'She has told her sister about the symptoms, and her sister has got the dose and is on medication for it.'

'What does her sister have to do with all this, and how do you know she's caught a dose?'

As soon as the last words left my lips, it all began to make perfect sense. 'Kenny, no. Please tell me I am wrong. Please tell me you have not been shagging Ann-Marie's sister.'

His eyes began to well, as the magnitude of the problem dawned. Ann-Marie's sister was married to a corporal in our platoon. The corporal was in Wales on a promotion course and wasn't due back for several weeks. Now I was facing a serious moral dilemma. From a simple problem of a sexually transmitted disease, it was now on the brink of an internal disaster. This kind of behaviour is catastrophic to unit cohesion. Friends of Corporal Phillips would lynch Kenny for what he had done. Before you knew it there would be carnage in the small team and we would be ineffective fighting terrorism. Needing to think this through, Kenny was sent away for a few hours. There was no easy solution. It was rapidly developing into a case of damage limitation. One thing we could guarantee was there would be tears before the night was out. I knew everyone involved very well. In the past couple of months, there had been a reason to deal with the occasional domestic argument involving them all. There was only one way to stop the problem escalating, and that was to tell everyone involved to visit the MO.

I called Kenny into my office and explained his options:

'Kenny. You have to do one of two things.

'One: you can try and scam Ann-Marie. Lie about a fling with some tart downtown. Then go with her to the MO and get the required treatment.

With any luck, she won't put two and two together and you should come away with just a kicking from Ann-Marie's brothers, then live in fear of the truth getting out for the rest of your life.

'Two: you could come clean, live in hell for about six months, but at least you will have been honest and not have to live in fear of the truth catching you up. And that is the key issue in this problem. Your lack of honesty, lack of integrity and selfish behaviour are set to cause further pain for all involved.'

Kenny sat in my office for a few minutes while he considered what had been said. He could see this was coming to a head.

'Kenny! Listen, take the day off and get it sorted. Come back in the morning and let me know the result.'

'Cheers, Sarge.' He left, visibly upset.

The following morning, Kenny duly appeared at my office with a big grin on his face. 'Got it sorted, Sarge.'

'Good, Kenny, how did she take it?'

'Take it? God no, I didn't tell her, Sarge. I told Ann-Marie's sister that I wouldn't see her any more unless she convinced Ann-Marie to take the medicine with her. Kind of sisters united! She's going to tell her it's breast enlargement medicine or something.' Kenny wore a large grin, signifying his perceived success.

The red mist descended and I dragged Kenny into my office by the scruff of his neck, slamming the door shut behind him. His expression changed immediately.

'What's the drama, Sarge?'

'Kenny, you've been shagging your Section Commander's wife. Is that not a problem?'

The blank look in his eyes told me that he didn't consider it so. She was renowned for extra-marital affairs, so why shouldn't he share in the fun?

Kenny received my ultimatum: 'If you see Corporal Phillips' wife once more, I'll have your arse booted out of the Army. That's a promise. Now get yourself down to Ann-Marie and clean up this mess before you ruin someone else's life.'

It was not a request. I threw him out of the office as quickly as he entered. Kenny could not be trusted, and it was time for me to tell my boss and the Company Sergeant Major. Together, we contrived to post Corporal Phillips back to England and send Kenny to Germany. It may ruin his engagement with Ann-Marie, but it might save Corporal Phillips' marriage.

But before we could implement the plan, the truth leaked out. Ann-Marie had sussed her sister's plan and figured it out. The company clerk ran over to the Sergeant Major's office to find me, and told me that Ann-Marie was looking for Kenny to give him some bad news. Eventually, they all converged on the

NAAFI, where a full-scale fist fight ensued. Kenny lost most of his hair, as well as receiving a black eye and a cut lip. Corporal Phillips returned from his course early, having heard the news from a friend. Shortly after his return, he split from his wife and started drinking heavily, causing me a catalogue of other problems. He failed to earn promotion and left the Army shortly after with his life in ruins.

Several months after it all calmed down, we set up a makeshift boxing ring during a gym session. Under the pretence of coaching fighters for an upcoming boxing match, Kenny was invited to spar with me. There was no coaching done that day. My disappointment in Kenny was vented in a legally delivered battering. Failing to stop at the bell, the fight continued until Kenny could take no more. He was left in his corner nursing two black eyes and a bloody nose. Removing my gloves, I slung them at him where he fell. Kenny knew he had given me and all his fellow Riflemen a heap of trouble. He had let himself down, and all those who had kept him alive over the past twenty-four months. He had wrecked two families, ruined Corporal Phillips' career and broke up the unique bond of an effective fighting unit. After our little encounter, he had grown up at a rapid pace, albeit six months too late. He had lost his friends and lost the respect of his commanders, as well as every girl he knew in the small military community. Struggling to come to terms with the enormity of his misdemeanour, Kenny left the Army nine months after the incident. It was a sad and sorry tale.

*   *   *

With Weston, the dilemma was on a smaller scale: the worst-case scenario would be a decision to retain him. Although confident he would not make it to the end of the course, it couldn't be discounted. Being commanded by a man with a dubious character is something not to be enjoyed. The thought of what he was prepared to do in order to save his own backside began to scare me. Responsibility is a heavy burden in the military; one wrong decision can cost someone his life. There was little sleep that night as I tossed and turned trying to arrive at the right decision.

Sunday morning, at 0700hrs, I jumped onto my bike and headed over to the dungeon to ensure things were going smoothly. Pat was planning a surprise walk around the accommodation at 0800hrs before his inspection. Rideout was dressed and flapping around the students' rooms. It was not what we had in mind for Rideout, but it was a start. I took him into the study hall for a closed-door chat and explained how important it was to appear calm in front of those he led, even if deep down inside he was in a blind panic. It is a simple tactic that can inspire confidence in those around you. It's not bluff and it's not bullshit; it's composure under pressure. Recognize the symptoms of panic, so you know when it is taking hold of you, then begin to manage it.

'Listen, analyse, decide and brief,' I advised him. 'Keep saying this to yourself when you engage with Academy staff and it will help you calm down.'

Quietly, Rideout acknowledged the advice.

Some students had been overzealous and stayed up until four in the morning, cleaning and polishing anything and everything. The students had worked hard in a vain effort to impress the Sergeant Major. Ironically, Pat was not keen on inspections in camp; to him, they proved nothing. 'Any fool can keep his kit clean in camp,' Pat would say. But the programme said he was to do a room inspection, so he did it, in his own unique style. He never requested any of the other DS to come in on a Sunday, and volunteered to occupy the students on his own. However, with this being my first course, I wanted to understand how this all glued together.

'Stand by, Row-Co scum-bags!' Pat's menacing tones rattled the windows, sending everyone into a blind last-minute panic. He stood in the centre of the accommodation so he could see both of the platoon duty students, who were standing to attention at the entrance of their respective platoon corridors.

'Which one of you two is brave enough to tell me that you're ready to be inspected?' said Pat. Neither of the students dared to blink in case it was seen as an acknowledgement.

'Come on! Have some bloody courage, or can't you handle the responsibility?' Pat was becoming irate.

'Weak tossers, both of you. Go back to your rooms and wait for me to call for you.'

One of the cleverest military skills is the art of using procrastination. War is a terrible thing, but waiting for the battle to start is possibly the worst feeling in the world. Fear and anxiety grips you and plays tricks on the mind. Gaps in your thought process are filled with the most unpleasant thoughts, and like a cancer, it can consume you until you are either cured or you succumb. Making people wait was a tactic used very effectively in Rowallan. For the DS, it was important to have a mechanism to measure tolerance. This tactic helped identify someone's breaking point. Once you knew where the threshold of tolerance was, it became possible to coach people past it and build a strength of character from the identified control point.

'Rideout!' Pat yelled from the comfort of his office.

Rideout came running. 'Here, Sir.'

'Here, Sir,' Pat repeated in a girl's voice. Rideout was physically shaking with the effort he was expending stood to attention. Completely intimidated by Pat's presence, beads of sweat dripped from his forehead.

'Stop shaking like a lunatic or I'll throw you in a bath of hot soapy water with my dirty laundry and you can make like a Zanussi. You lunatic.'

'Yes, Sir,' replied Rideout, marginally more composed.

'That's better,' Pat said patronizingly. 'Now, let's go into one of these rooms that you have diligently prepared for me to inspect.'

Pat loved to play mind games with the students. He would make statements that were so obviously untrue that they were ridiculous. He continued to exaggerate his statements until eventually it was understood that his words had no relevance to his actions.

'Whose room first, Rideout? Take me to the best room. If it is good enough, I won't inspect the rest of the platoon. Who first?'

Rideout considered the question. He was trying to apply the 'listen, analyse, decide and brief' technique we discussed earlier. But this wasn't a real-life scenario; this event was about dislocating the student. Pat gave him no time to respond and jumped into the first room he came across.

'Name, scum bag,' Pat demanded.

'Moore, Sir.'

'Don't pout your lips at me, Moore,' snapped Pat, offended by his smile. 'How do you expect to be taken seriously with that rubber face you've got?'

Without even looking at the room, Pat reached for Moore's bed, ripped the mattress clean off and threw it to the floor, wrecking the bed block in the process. Moore didn't change his expression, but his roommate Goldson was completely shell-shocked. Terrified, he stared motionless at what was happening to the room he had spent all night cleaning. Goldson had not gone to sleep during the night. He stayed awake perfecting his locker layout and bed block; everything was polished to within an inch of its life. The inside of the drawers, the welts of the windows, the inside of the bin, the underneath of the bin, even the welt of the bin. Everything was perfect. But Pat had no interest in anything. He looked at nothing. Without pausing, he just threw everything onto the floor and kicked it into the corridor. In less than thirty seconds, the room was trashed beyond recognition. No surface was left unmolested, no drawer still filled or locker still containing clothing. Goldson was by now close to tears. Visibly holding back his anger and straining at the neck to hold his body still, Pat's actions had shaken him to the core.

As Pat was leaving, he turned to Goldson and said: 'Don't get upset by this, cupcake, there is far worse to come.'

Goldson could no longer hold back the tears. His eyes were flooded, and his bottom lip withdrew far into his mouth in a desperate attempt to conceal his hurt. Before I got a chance to tell Goldson to get a grip of himself, Pat was trashing the next room and I felt it best to join him.

Danner was an expert at bluffing room inspections, having endured a few in his time with his University Officer Training Corps. He sprayed deodorant around the room before Pat entered, hoping to make it smell nice and throw the Sergeant Major off the scent. He spoke calmly to Pat and welcomed him into the room, but if he was trying to disarm Pat, it had the reverse effect.

'Marvellous! Absolutely bloody marvellous!' shouted Pat. 'What's that smell? Have one of you two stolen a whore's handbag? You both look like drag queens. Are you sure you don't want to join the Navy?'

Danner's composure broke as Pat opened the window and threw the entire contents of his wardrobe into the cold January air. His mouth was moving in time with his hands, but only jumbled half-words made it beyond his lips. That was until his mattress was squeezed through the window and exploded like a party popper as it shot out into the courtyard.

'Well, really! Is that absolutely necessary" Danner asked.

'What did you say your name was, fat lad?'

'Danner, Sir.'

'Fancy yourself as some kind of English Che Guevara? Let me show you how we deal with rebels at Sandhurst.'

Pat also grabbed Boyle's bedding, including his mattress, and forced it all through the small window. In a frenzy, everything but the two students had been hurled into the courtyard and onto the street – even the bin. Standing in an empty room, with absolutely nothing in it that wasn't screwed to the wall, Pat issued one more insult: 'If you weren't so fucking fat, you would have gone through the window too!'

Pat moved on to the next room, and we could hear Boyle rip into Danner. He was genuinely traumatized by the additional thrashing Danner's comment had generated. Less than fifteen minutes had elapsed, and Pat had clinically dismantled the whole platoon's efforts. The corridor was a mosaic of clothing and bed linen. Bags, boots, shoes and the remnants of bed blocks were strewn everywhere. As quickly as he had arrived, Pat left the accommodation, leaving behind him a group of baffled, confused and angry individuals. The silence slowly gave way to the scuffling of people sifting through the entangled bed sheets and clothes as students tried to separate the mess and identify their personal belongings.

'Oh my god,' Mathews whispered. 'What the fuck just happened? It looks like the Tasmanian Devil has stayed the night with his friends and decided to decorate the room with my bedding.'

'Yeah, the little bugger must have stayed in my room too,' added Danner. He briefly reached through his window to reclaim items of his clothing off the floor, then decided to drop them back where they lay.

'Shh! Listen to that lot get it next door,' Barns said as he started an infectious laugh. Soon the whole platoon began to laugh, with the exception of Haigh. His face oozed bewilderment, as he turned to Mathews.

'What was funny about staying up all night, only to have your room viciously dismantled in less than thirty seconds by someone called the Tasmanian Devil?'

Mathews shrugged his shoulders and smirked. 'You have got to agree, that was crazy. Look, my mattress is stuck halfway out of the window. My Nike trainers are hanging on the tree outside!'

A dour expression from Haigh compromised his emotions. He was openly disappointed by the experience as he declared that 'it wasn't funny – it was pointless'.

The students were still suffering from what they had nicknamed a 'Tazing' when they were summoned outside. As was the tradition on a Sunday at Sandhurst, all students attended church. Dressed in their Sunday best, we swiftly marched over to the Academy Chapel and sat down in the sanctuary of the rear pews. Covertly squeezed into the back arch of this magnificent building, we kept the Row-Co students separated from the remainder of the congregation. With the service finished, the students were quickly extracted and placed back in the accommodation without anyone knowing we were there. The accommodation remained unchanged. It was total carnage. The Tasmanian Devil analogy made sense. Pat knew where the pressure points were and how to generate hard work. Talcum powder spilt in the carpet, finger smudges on mirrors and windows, pencil cases kicked around the room – he deployed every trick in the book. The mess would take a day to clean up.

Rideout was busily trying to gather the contents of a wash bag Pat had emptied out. It was the ideal time for me to read his journal and make small talk about getting the rooms back to their normal state. Captain Dunn had spoken about the SWOT Rideout had written, and it was impressive. In the margins of a turbulent day, the fact he had been tasked to do a SWOT had been forgotten. It was hugely gratifying to read that he had thought the problem through correctly. He'd analysed who should do what, noted why they were best suited to the task and even had a schematic explaining when he should re-evaluate his plan. Not that he was aware of this, but he had sketched the basis of human terrain analysis, demonstrating high levels of intelligence.

'What do you think, Colour Sergeant?' Rideout enquired. 'Would that have been the formula to have won the assault course race?'

'Well, you don't need a comment from me. The Platoon Commander has written here that you have done this well.'

Rideout proceeded to tell me that he fully understood the SWOT and would use it to formulate his decisions in the future.

'Rideout, the SWOT is just a tool, so be wary of using a screwdriver instead of a spanner. It is in support of your understanding, it is not the template for understanding. Use this tool on its own or think it to be the panacea to the problem, and it will backfire.'

There was a need to give him an example of how it can cause more problems than it resolves, which gave me the opportunity to repeat a story of a SWOT that inadvertently compounded a simple problem.

Some years earlier, whilst serving with the British Military Mission in Mozambique, I was entrusted to train 100 soldiers from each side of the two warring factions of the Mozambique civil war. My students were drafted from the Mozambique Liberation Front (FRELIMO) and the Mozambique Resistance Movement (RENAMO), with fifty from each. These two organizations had been killing each other by the tens of thousands ever since the regime of Estado Novo was overthrown in 1974. The British Military Mission commander insisted that the first part of the training comprised education, fitness and social reform. The fitness and education were easy tasks, but the social reform was the responsibility of the commander and his deputy to organize. Their great plan was to lay on free transport, take the soldiers into the local township and let them loose in the bars so they could do some social bonding.

The initial assessment of this idea appeared successful. Morale went sky high, tensions were defused and previous indiscretions all but forgotten. Then, four weeks after the start of the social reform, the attendance in training dropped as the soldiers spent more and more time at the medical centre. Frustrated by the low numbers, one afternoon I visited the doctor to discuss what kind of injuries were keeping the soldiers from training.

'Injuries? No, there are no injuries. They all have sexually transmitted disease,' the doctor explained to me.

Surprised by this news, at the next Command Conference, the training team briefed the commander on the days lost through sickness and explained that the high number was attributable to the social reform programme. The colonel in charge was old-school: he summoned the training team and dictated a SWOT. It was the first time I had witnessed it, but the commander seemed to know what to do. The colonel stated that the positive influence resulting from the visits into town was something we didn't wish to lose; lost training days through STDs was the problem. So, how were we to stop soldiers contracting STDs? 'Genius, that's the answer,' the commander declared after looking at the SWOT. 'Let's issue condoms at the front gate and the soldiers will be able to have safe sex with the free women in the township.'

That made sense to me, as the analysis indicated that STDs were the root cause. What was not easy to understand was how the commander had made the mental leap from the problem to the solution. Despite the very eloquent words on the chalkboard, not one of the findings suggested that more sex was the answer! But he was the commander; we never challenged his analysis, we trusted his judgment and fully expected it to work. His many years of command and training fooled me into thinking that the colonel must be right!

Dutifully, we all ensured that soldiers were taking condoms into town and that there was a healthy supply held at the guardroom. We even placed supplies on the bus that took them into town, just in case someone was caught short. We were topping up the supplies daily, and it appeared that these guys were having huge amounts of sex downtown. Bizarrely, a few weeks later the STD problem had morphed into an epidemic. It took a huge effort to discover what had gone wrong, but eventually, a more detailed analysis discovered that we had inadvertently brought this STD epidemic upon ourselves.

During the late 1980s and early 1990s, Africa was being ravaged by two diseases – Acquired Immunodeficiency Syndrome and Human Immunodeficiency Virus, better known as AIDS and HIV. Unbeknown to us, condoms were as rare as unicorns and locals traded them like hard cash. For these battle-weary soldiers, who had previously spent ten years risking their lives in the most violent of civil wars, unprotected sex presented no risk at all; in fact, it was a reasonable trade-off. The soldiers were taking the condoms downtown and selling them to the locals. This gave them more money to buy beer and spend more time in the brothels. We had increased the unprotected sex in the township three-fold. In this instance, the SWOT was poorly applied. The colonel failed to go beyond the second and third order effects because he had already come up with his decision. It's not quite Newton's third law of physics, but you must analyse in totality; like a mathematical problem, you seek to arrive at the lowest common denominator.

For many years, it was a conundrum that remained a mystery. Five young intelligent captains hungry for promotion, three accomplished majors and six sergeants had sat in on the SWOT analysis, so why did it go so wrong? It took twenty years of teaching leadership to discover the answer, which was that the colonel dictated his order and – as weak as the solution was – no one wished to challenge his command. Fear of embarrassment or a loss of reputation prevented contribution. The commander saw himself as an individual, and his team feared retribution and negative evaluation if they spoke out. We came to recognize this as cockpit culture, a team afraid to tell the experienced man he is about to kill everyone! The theory is not unique to pilots: it fits perfectly with any small team led by a poor commander.

My anecdote over, Rideout paused and asked me several questions in a clear and calm manner. He was taken by my little dit. As flattering as it was, I needed to keep my guard up or Rideout would have me telling him more than he needed to know. With the skill of a politician, I avoided directly answering his questions. Some stuff he had to learn himself, and it would do him the world of good to fail at some of it. The real reason behind me speaking to him was to gauge his composure after the morning's activities. He was en route to success; if he could get through the rest of the morning without Pat crucifying him, the signs would look promising.

With lunch still resting heavy in the stomach, the course was standing to attention at the edge of Chapel Square awaiting Pat's next instructions. Pat had dressed down and was wearing an old grey tracksuit top and bottoms. Nonchalantly, he ambled along the sidewalk in the direction of the Company.

'Hands up here if you know what a changing parade is?' A few students raised their hands. 'Good, in that case, I don't need to explain it to you. I want you back here in five minutes changed into combat trousers and combat jacket. Four minutes fifty-nine, four minutes fifty-eight, four minutes fifty-seven. What are you waiting for? Four minutes fifty-six.'...

The students broke ranks and darted for the main door. Nearly forty bodies fighting for space at the main entrance was an ugly sight, and in desperation, people started to climb through windows. No. 2 Platoon were closest to the front door, so it was little surprise to see Danner, Mathews, Boyle and Rideout emerging from the accommodation first. It took a further twelve minutes before the last of the students appeared.

Pat sat on the stairs leading up to the floor above our accommodation, tapping his watch. 'Twelve minutes! If I knew you were going to be that long, I'd have gone home and made my tea, got changed and still beat most of you back here. Five laps of Chapel Square – go!'

It was remarkable that the course had accepted their fate so quickly. There were no discerning comments or protests, just blind obedience. I was further impressed that few people seemed to become separated as they ran around the square. Pat turned to me and pointed this out: 'You see how they are grouping together. They are becoming a herd – safety in numbers – but we can't let this take hold. Group thinking is not what we are looking for. The weak will sneak through and the strong will dumb down their development. Next time around, I will get the little buggers.'

With the Company back at the start point, Pat gave them five minutes to reappear in full marching equipment. This dress was used for field exercises and needed the student to carry his rucksack. Again, it was No. 2 Platoon that emerged first, but less than ten people made it out in under five minutes.

Pat put on his angry voice. He mocked the state of the rucksacks that failed to sit correctly on the shoulders of most students, before issuing another punishment: 'We are going to play fives. No, not that poncey game played by public schools too tight to give out squash rackets, but the first five people to run around Chapel Square don't have to do it a second time. Go, go – get going.'

Fully laden with rucksacks, the students charged around the square. This time gaps opened up everywhere. Barns, Danner and Witherspoon stood out to the rear. Impressively, Rideout flew ahead of everyone and was the first to hit the finish line. Pat removed the first five students and dispatched the remainder around the square again. Now, Mathews, King and Moore were leading the group. By the time the Company had been whittled down to the last group, Barns, Goldson and Haigh made up the majority, with just two from No. 1 Platoon. Pat proceeded to conduct these parades for a full hour. Each time the students emerged from the accommodation wearing an entire outfit that had only just been rescued from the trashing it received during the early-morning inspection. Pat had no sympathy for the students. He instructed them to parade in their lounge suits, and when they failed to achieve the five-minute cut-off, he sent them all running around the square in the expensive outfits.

This time, however, as they were running around the rear of Old College, Pat took me into the accommodation. He looked in a few rooms and started to laugh maniacally. 'Marvellous, look at that. It will take them weeks to straighten this crap out. I think we are nearly there!'

As the Company began to reassemble, we could see that they were dead on their feet. There was a fear that Haigh, Barns and a few of the other stragglers would throw their hands in. Daringly, my thoughts were offered to Pat: 'Do you think we need to give them more time, Pat?'

'Gaz, worry about what you do, not what I do. I have been doing this shit for a long time; don't give me your advice.'

Pat's voice went up a couple of octaves as he issued his next instructions. I had clearly annoyed him. 'PT kit. White PT vest, blue shorts, socks and trainers. Go!'

Pat stormed off in the direction of the accommodation and let loose on everyone and anyone. He was taking his anger out on the students, even though the cause of it was me. 'We are going to be at this all bloody day, unless you make it out in less than five minutes. Get a shagging move on!'

The urgency in his voice seemed to have the desired effect. They had returned agonizingly close to the allotted five minutes, the quickest time so far. But that was not good enough, and Pat delivered a Churchillian speech:

> 'No one will remember the name of the man who came second. No one will support the ideas of the man who almost won. This is your moment. This is when you define yourself as a leader of men. Not any old group of men, but the most feared men on the planet. The British soldier accepts nothing but the best from his leaders, and you are failing to deliver that. You must work harder. You need to find twenty-three seconds in order to get out here on time and bring an end to these endless changing parades. I have all day. Hands up if you know what Mess Tin Order is?'

A few students raised their hands. 'Good; you know the drill. Stand by. Five minutes back outside in Mess Tin Order. If you are one second over, everyone runs around the square and we will do another changing parade. Go!'

By now there were windows and fire escapes open all around the block. The students had perfected the ability to squeeze into the accommodation in less than ten seconds. Remarkably, it was less than thirty seconds later before the first ten or so students made it back on parade. They wore nothing more than their underpants and a mess tin stuffed down the front to protect their manhood. Barechested, white-legged and with 'dayglo' boxer shorts, the last man out was Haigh.

Pat held up his stopwatch. He shook his head in order to disguise what he was about to say: 'I said you needed to get on parade in less than five minutes or you would be stuck here all day. You have done it in four minutes fifteen seconds.'

Several students screamed out in exhilaration, and Pat released a knowing smile. The Company looked ridiculous stood to attention in nothing other than boxer shorts and a mess tin shoved down the front, but to a man, they smiled proudly – heads high, shoulders back, eyes beaming with achievement.

Pat afforded them a little praise: 'See, I knew you fannies could do it. You have earned the rest of the day off. Get your rooms squared away and prepare yourself for tomorrow. If you are not out of my sight in ten seconds, I will change my mind. Nine, eight, seven...'

In less than five seconds, the last man had vanished as Pat walked off in the direction of the car park without so much as a goodbye.

Feeling a little sorry for myself, it was time to prepare for tomorrow's events. Dejectedly, I walked back to my office. I had spoken too soon. The inability to listen and observe right up to the end before opening my mouth had plagued me ever since I stepped off the train at Winchester. What Pat had done was genius. Once the desired effect had been achieved, he brought the requirement down to a near achievable standard and then rallied the troops with his speech. Then, by giving the students a dress code that demanded that all they needed to do was get undressed, they achieved what appeared to be the impossible. Pat's plan had unified the platoons through the misery of shared hardships, and again made it appear as if they had worked hard to overcome the impossible. In the process, this perceived victory had the effect of galvanizing team spirit and enhancing growing morale. Back in the accommodation, Rideout was walking around urging everyone in a very diligent, duty-like fashion to reassemble their rooms. He had stopped flapping, and that pleased me and served to boost my morale. The change in his character was obvious. I left the students to their own devices, weaving my way through the mess back to the DS corridor.

Captain Dunn was in his office, collecting a paddle and splash deck for his canoe. He was about to take part in a competition, and sneaked in through the rear of the accommodation so as not to disturb Pat's activities. I hadn't expected to see him, but I seized the chance to talk about Weston.

'Boss, I know you're in a rush, but we could do with a quick chat about Weston.'

Captain Dunn raised a half-smile; he knew this would happen:

'He's playing his ticket, Colour! It's as simple as that, and the doctor also knows it. You will probably find his father has threatened to cut the size of his enormous allowance if he doesn't follow in the family footsteps and join the Cavalry. This convenient injury means he can now go back to sponging off his parents or get a job in daddy's business as an executive who knows nothing about the job. To be honest, Colour, the Army is better off without people like Weston, don't you think?'

Captain Dunn didn't even stop as he delivered his assessment.

'I am sorry, I am mega-late already. It's no consolation, but he would have probably failed anyway. He's an arrogant plonker. Don't get emotionally attached! See you in the morning, Colour,' he yelled from outside the accommodation, making his exit.

Weston was fooling his family, but he wasn't fooling Captain Dunn or me. It was, however, hard for me to accept. All my military career had been underpinned with the belief that those who served to lead were honest, honourable, noble members of the elite. The realization that the officer corps had its fair share of undesirables was a stark reality that shook my faith in the system. Whilst I had encountered poor leaders and poor officers previously, I never for one moment thought there would be deceitful characters getting through RCB. Yet Captain Dunn took it in his stride; he had seen all this before. But for me, the lowly Colour Sergeant, this was a new world, and one that was proving difficult to understand.

Chapter Four

Week Two

It was Monday morning, the start of week two, and the introduction to the most feared punishment at Sandhurst was just hours away. The 'Mean Machine' was infamously renowned for destroying the souls of all those fed through it. It was a deserved reputation, earned by bringing its victims to exhaustion or forcing them to crumble into submission. To the untrained eye, it looked like an eclectic mix of harmless tat abandoned in a courtyard. Visually scruffy, it appeared to be nothing more than some scaffolding bars, yellow boxes and the occasional traffic cone. But to the student on Row-Co, it represented intense pain, endless sweat, blood, real tears and misery.

The Mean Machine occupied a space no larger than half a tennis court, three sides of which were accommodation walls. Three floors high and made of common brown London bricks, with evenly spaced white wooden sash windows and a cast-iron spiral fire escape, there was a hint of the 'Dickens' about it. The hollow square courtyard captured the worst of the winter elements and never felt the warmth of the sun. The windows on the floors above the Mean Machine remained firmly closed, and the curtains were drawn. It was widely known that, should an officer cadet on the Commissioning Course dare sneak a view of events, the penalty would be instant participation. In the centre of the courtyard, there was a small rock garden with a few overgrown shrubs.

Around the edge of the courtyard, at intervals of 5 yards, lay pieces of makeshift gym equipment. There was a scaffolding bar for doing pull-ups, accompanied by a hand-painted sign denoting the exercise required, as well as the number of repetitions to attain. There was also a contraption to keep the feet steady during sit-ups, and mats for press-ups, squat thrusts and star jumps. Rock-filled H83 ammunition boxes were painted bright yellow and had the narrowest of carriage handles. Each box weighed about 15lb and was employed during numerous exercises, the worst of which was to hold the box outstretched whilst squatting in the stress position. With both hands grasping the narrow handle of the box, the student would raise it to shoulder level while keeping his arms fully extended in front of him. It was followed closely by carrying two boxes up the spiral fire escape, at the same time as another student. A thick gym rope hung down from the second level of the fire escape and was used for rope climbing. The total number of exercises would vary depending on how many people were available at the time, although it was never lower than twenty, in order to expend at least a minute's worth of effort on each piece of equipment.

Every exercise was specifically designed to be gruelling, with no rest between rotations. For increased intensity, students were micromanaged by the DS, with additional staff drafted in to elevate stress levels. The high walls of the courtyard trapped and amplified the cacophony of sounds emanating from the Mean Machine. Unrelenting demands, obstinately bellowed by the Directing Staff, resulted in ear-piercing screams of pain as students tried to adhere to instructions. For the passer-by, it made for uncomfortable listening. The most menacing sound came from the metallic thud of the yellow ammunition box crashing to the ground as students lost their grip on one of the many exercises involving the burden. Add to the noise the occasional sound of vomiting or a member of the Staff becoming frustrated at the lack of application of a student, the infamous reputation of this contraption was easy to understand. If you didn't know any better, you would be forgiven for thinking this was more a torture chamber than a tool for developing stamina.

Major Gray explained the purpose of the Mean Machine to the course, informing everyone that it was normally only used for punishment. However, to ensure everyone knew how to use the equipment correctly, it would masquerade as the day's first formal fitness session. With an awkward smile, he handed the proceedings to Daz, who quickly demonstrated each exercise. Two minutes later, the machine was in full use and students began to engage in personal battles with each piece of equipment encountered. Barns was enduring an isometric squat, with his legs at a perfect right angle, back straight pressed up against a wall, arms fully extended holding onto a yellow burden; he frequently lost his battle with the laws of physics. For the taller student, keeping the dead weight held outstretched transferred excruciating pain directly to his quadriceps. Haigh typically pulled faces with each attempt at an exercise, failing to achieve a satisfactory standard and attracting the attention of Pete the CQMS. In the shadows, Lane demonstrated that his problem was worse than we had feared. He was failing to complete more than five or six exercises per minute, sometimes unable to achieve even one at the right standard. He was unable to complete one pull-up or one rope climb, which infuriated Corporal Davis, who was supervising that particular exercise.

After fifteen minutes, Daz paused the proceedings, blowing a long whistle blast so as to be heard over the screams of pain and clanking of metal. The course stopped rotating and the courtyard filled with a chorus of panting, coughing and the occasional breakfast being regurgitated. Standing in the middle of the courtyard, balancing on several boulders in the rock garden, Daz summoned Stone to join him. Slightly confused, Stone made his way to Daz's side. With everyone watching, Daz addressed the course:

'Stone here thinks he is fit enough and doesn't need to do fitness with you lot, therefore he can miss out the next half of this exercise. Instead, he can stand here and watch you guys go through the pain and torture of another twenty minutes. Because he is so good, he can keep the time and blow the whistle to initiate the changeovers.'

Captain Dunn stared at me across the courtyard. With his arms outstretched, he mouthed, 'What the fuck?'

I shook my head back at him, and in a similar fashion shrugged my shoulders. I didn't know how Daz had got this information, but it was too late to do anything about it. Daz had entered into retribution mode. A big smile appeared on Stone's face, affirming his naivety. He truly believed what Daz said. Thinking he had moved to legendary status, Stone twirled the cord of the whistle around his hand and continued to grin. But instead, he had just become further ostracized. Daz restarted the session on the Mean Machine and Stone stood front and centre, purchased high on the rocks in the garden. It was Daz's intention to make Stone the villain and allow the jungle rules to come into play once the DS had finished. But the overtones emanating from the students' mumblings as they rotated between exercises confirmed our fears. It was exacerbated by the glowing grin on Stone's face, which offered more evidence that this approach would fail. It would take much more than this to knock the immaturity out of him. He was not ready for responsibility and accountability. With no shame, Stone enjoyed a break from the session, just as he did on the stretcher race in week one.

Captain Dunn crossed the courtyard. 'Colour Sergeant, did you tell Staff Sergeant Dazzell about the journal entry?'

The unabridged use of rank and name told me that Captain Dunn had the hump with what we were witnessing.

My response was rudely emphatic: 'No, bollocks did I!'

I was equally surprised by Daz's actions, and a little miffed the boss thought I had not followed the agreed plan for developing Stone. We both watched on as it became more uncomfortable by the minute as the students suffered the ferocity of Daz's session and Stone blew the whistle to signify a change of exercise. Our assessment of Stone's attitude was woefully inaccurate, and the problem was greater than we understood. It was now clear to both of us that the task with Stone was probably beyond our means.

King was doing 50-metre sprints up and down the road, with Moore on burpees, Packman on chin-ups and Williams climbing the 15ft rope. Mathews was in the crucifix position with a yellow ammunition container in each hand. There were step-ups for Francis and shuttles up and down the stairs carrying two yellow burdens for Goldson. A shrill on the whistle and they all moved 5 metres to the right, took up a new exercise and started again. Staff stood in the gap between each exercise so they could berate two students simultaneously. There was no rest: relentless barracking and the pains of using unorthodox equipment made this exercise intimidating and miserable from start to finish. If someone struggled to lift, push or pull quickly enough, he was thrown onto the road to do sprints until his arms recovered sufficiently.

Having endured the Mean Machine once, the conditions were set for the DS to use it as a form of 'on the spot' punishment whenever there was a need. The aim of the first encounter with the improvised contraption was two-fold. Firstly, any future sessions would not need Daz to be present. More crucially, it physically pushed the student as far as possible so he had a benchmark of physical attainment engraved deep into his memory. For good measure, the immediate reminder would be delivered through the accumulations of cuts, bruises and blisters administrated by the crude improvised equipment. Few people made it to the end of a Mean Machine session unless the DS wanted them to. Those who proved to be fitter than their peers were singled out and pushed harder to prevent them from surviving the ordeal. In order to maintain the Mean Machine as an effective punishment, it needed to have a reputation that would strike fear into the very psyche of those who walked by.

The Mean Machine yielded varied results. Most fruitful was the ability to assess individual attitudes, which were fully exposed after less than two minutes of micromanaged physical exertion. Students would break down or just resign themselves to damning verbal abuse because they could not achieve the standard demanded. Tearful attempts at keeping pace with Daz's whistle were interspersed with the DS encouraging protagonists to work harder. Others would rise to the challenge, trying to accomplish the demands dictated by the fierce pace of the event. Regularly, a student would screech loudly, swearing and cursing at nothing in particular or just trying to distract himself from the unremitting pain.

A final blow on the whistle by Stone, and Daz called an end to the session. Standing in three ranks on the side street off Chapel Square, the familiar cloud of steam rose from the sweat-soaked red rugby shirts as bodies began to cool down in the freezing cold temperature.

Major Gray stood in front of the students, rubbing his chilled hands and wearing a huge grin. 'Well, who didn't enjoy that?'

It was a predictable humorous comment that the students failed to understand. They responded with a chorus of coughs as they took deep breaths of cold air, which would react adversely with their heated lungs. They were dead on their feet, but Pat had no compassion. At the top of his voice, he yelled for silence, then berated students for their poor discipline and wimpish behaviour.

'I hope that is the only time we need to go through the Mean Machine over the next few weeks,' said Major Gray. 'However, now you know what this is all about. Bear this in mind, if you fail to achieve the required standard during any event, the punishment will be a Mean Machine session upon return to the Academy.'

Paddy and I collected our respective platoons and briefed them on the day's remaining events. We had hugely different styles in managing our students, the main reason for this being the difference in our regimental backgrounds. Paddy would normally have his students standing rigidly to attention in three ranks while he paced up and down, threateningly cutting through the ranks to keep a firm grip on those failing to listen to his formal brief. My style looked to achieve the same outcome in a relaxed manner. For me, this was a successful formula that had galvanized trust, belief and mutual respect. Neither style was wrong; each had its strengths and weaknesses, but the contrast was easy for all to see.

We instructed the students to collect their ponchos, maps and compasses, and assemble on the sports pitch in front of New College. As the students disappeared into the accommodation at warp factor seven, I tugged Daz on the arm and walked in the opposite direction.

'Mate, what was that all about with Stone. Have you been reading their journals?'

'No, Gaz, you know I am not that interested in what they write.'

'How did you know what Stone had written?' I asked.

'I was in the loo on the crapper and he was trapping off to the rest of the boys about how he could manipulate the Staff through his journal. The dick droned on about getting me to slack off during the sessions. I couldn't let it go unpunished. That lad is in for a tough ride from now until we finish. With any luck, his mates are giving him a pummelling in the washrooms right now.'

Captain Dunn had changed and walked to the sports fields, ready to deliver his first lesson of the week. He received the students with a huge smile and cracked a few jokes, telling everyone that the Mean Machine was their own personal gymnasium. Still giggling at his own joke, he began to teach the rudimentary skill of plotting bearings. This skill is one of the most valuable to any military commander. Coordinating firepower for fighter jets, attack helicopters, artillery and mortars depends on an individual's ability to accurately calculate a bearing. At night, bearings are critical to navigation. Leading a battalion of soldiers to the start line of a battle depends on the navigation of a young Platoon Commander. This skill needs to be matched with an ability to accurately judge distance whilst marching on a specific bearing.

Having practised marching on bearings and calculating the true north and magnetic north equations which were factored into individual compass errors, the final exercise was explained. This confirmation of the instruction gave the DS great amusement, so much so that some people came to watch the bizarre sight of the Night Exercise Without Darkness (NEWD). Once deemed competent with the skill, the student would confirm his understanding by taking part in a small assessment. He would set a bearing from one end of the sports ground to the other and walk the exact distance between checkpoints. Unaided, he needed to stop in a small square marked out on the floor which was exactly 300 metres away. At first, the students all looked confident with everything Captain Dunn explained. It didn't sound so difficult, to walk 300 metres on a bearing and stop in a small area that was marked out in luminous orange mine tape.

The students noted down the bearings and applied their individual adjustments.

'All ready to go, fellas?' smiled Captain Dunn.

A few polite nods and encouraging words fell from the huddled mass.

'OK. Pull out your ponchos!'

Baffled and a little curious, the students reached for their ponchos and shook them out in front of us. The dark green plastic sheet released a stale smell of rain, mud and forestry blocks. It was an old piece of equipment that was once used as a soldier's waterproof jacket, but now it was used for making a tent, otherwise known as a basher. On this day, however, it was about to be used as the critical component for the NEWD.

Captain Dunn continued:

'Grab the hood of your poncho – it's somewhere in the middle – and tie a knot in it. Place a bungee cord on the floor by your feet, then drape the poncho over your head. Make sure you have enough space under the poncho to read your compass. Once you have yourself orientated, the Colour Sergeant and I will tie the bottom of your poncho tight with your bungee cord. Confirm to us that you have no light creeping into your poncho, and you are free to march on a bearing using only your compass and pacing skills.'

Apart from making the individual look like an escaped alien from a *Star Trek* film, it would also simulate the reading of a compass by night. Needless to say, if you had calculated the magnetic variation wrongly or failed to apply the individual compass error, you would head in the wrong direction. Fail to count your paces and you would not end up in the square marked out by Captain Dunn. Later in the course, students would need to use these skills on a daily basis, by day and night, whilst hungry and tired. Mastering these skills was essential to surviving the distance. On Dartmoor or Salisbury Plain, getting them wrong is disastrous, but in the confines of the sports grounds of Sandhurst, the penalty for missing the target would be decided by the geography of the surrounding lakes and streams. Occasionally, it was likely that a wayward student would encounter sports equipment dotted around the estate: cricket nets, football goals, rugby posts and polo pitch markers all presented a hazard.

Barns was one of the first to declare himself ready to practice his new-found skill.

'OK, Barns, let me check your compass bearing!' Barns offered me his compass without speaking.

'Cat got your tongue, Barns?' I asked.

'No, Colour Sergeant. I am not feeling too good after this morning's PT.'

I seized the opportunity to tell Barns about his poor standard of fitness: 'Barns, it's only right to tell you that your fitness is very poor. You will have to work harder than the rest of the students just to keep your head above water. It's a sad fact that if you don't improve at a rapid rate you won't make it to the end of the course.'

Barns looked me square in the eyes and nodded in agreement. 'I will, Colour Sergeant, promise.'

He appeared to be disappointed by my lack of faith in him, but secretly the outlook was not good. It was not the conversation Barns needed at that present moment in time. He was struggling with his map-reading instruction and the past few days had left him jaded. But the look he gave me was not one that suggested he was here to fail. There was sincerity in everything he had said thus far, and something likeable about him that soldiers would warm to. He convinced me of his desire to lead soldiers, and that was enough to secure every ounce of my support.

He pulled the thick green plastic poncho over his head and the bottom was secured using a bungee cord. Barns was in a very vulnerable position. At that very moment in time, he was low on morale, tired and heavy-legged, facing a long struggle to improve his fitness, rounded off nicely with the prospect of being one of the favourites to fail the course. He needed a confidence boost to keep his desire to pass the course alive. With his bearing checked and his poncho shutting out all the light, he was ready.

'OK, Barns, can you see any light creeping into the poncho?'

'No, Colour Sergeant.'

'Good. How far have you got to go?'

'About 300 metres, Colour Sergeant.'

'No, Barns, there is no "about". What did you calculate it to be on the map?'

'Three hundred metres. Or 180 consecutive double strides, Colour Sergeant.'

'Better. Much better. Now trust the compass and take your time. Set off when you're ready, big lad.'

It wasn't long before Barns was heading in the wrong direction.

'Stop! Barns, look at your compass. Is the needle sat on the bearing reading you set?'

Barns rustled frantically inside his poncho. He was breathing heavily; the anxiety could be heard seeping out of his poncho.

'I am going to remove the bungee cord, Barns. We are then going back to the start point. Take a moment to compose yourself. Consolidate your thoughts once more and start again. Let me know when you are ready.'

'Yes, Colour Sergeant.'

'Do you realize how silly you look dressed like this? Have a look at them over there; what do they look like?'

Barns giggled and smiled. His breathing relaxed and his hands stopped trembling. It was a good sign. Although he was mumbling to himself, it was at least coherent. This was the first big test for Barns, and one he needed to pass. As irrational as it sounds, he was in danger of suffering death by a thousand cuts, and just one more failure could break his resolve. If he made the mental leap from wanting to make it to wanting to quit, the fight would be over before it started.

'If you need to adjust the compass, do it now. Concentrate on keeping the needle fixed on the bearing, and don't rush, softlad.'

I grabbed hold of his shoulder and steered him in the right direction for the first five paces. Every so often he would veer off track and a surreptitious nudge from me would get him back on course. His loud counting alerted me to what he was thinking. Eventually, he stood still and screamed 'target!', signalling he had arrived at his destination. Barns stood still as he waited for someone to tap him on the back so he could remove the poncho from his body. I stood beside him and made out I didn't know who it was.

'Who's that?'

'Barns, Colour Sergeant. I think I'm at the finish point now.'

'Do you now, Barns?' I replied, trying to build the suspense. Unfastening his poncho to survey the point at which he stopped, his eyes adjusted slowly to the light and he focused on his surroundings. A quick glance at his map, and Barns began to realize he was at the exact position he had plotted, smack bang in the centre of the orange mine tape.

'It works, it actually works. I can't believe it. Brilliant.'

Barns had just won a small victory in his war to survive Row-Co. Despite the fact it was orchestrated, he had sampled success. His elation was palpable. Barns was beside himself with this achievement, which served as a timely reminder that this young man was here to fulfil his dreams and it was my job not to trample on them.

'Don't celebrate too soon, big lad. You have three more checkpoints to visit.'

Barns came back to earth with a bump.

Watson was close by. His poncho was faded and old, making it easy for us to identify him. The first checkpoint was by now full of poncho-clad students, all waiting for permission to defrock. I cut through the statues and tapped on Watson's back.

'How is it going, Watson?'

'No problem, Colour Sergeant, it's basic navigation to be honest. I studied geography at uni, so this is just a bit of revision.'

Watson's answer was as arrogant as you could get. It was full of his typical egotism. Now he could see everyone else. Mid-conversation, he began to giggle, pointing at a fellow student who had become snarled up amongst the cricket nets. The student was visibly frustrated at his inability to escape from the catchment. Misjudging the moment, Watson tried to share the humour of the predicament. This truly irritated me.

'OK, Watson, this one will test you. Plot this grid reference on your map – 6449 1989. Now set a bearing from here to that grid.'

He dropped onto his knees and pulled out his protractor. Busily, he began calculating the route. Once he was ready, his poncho tied tightly around his body, he was sent on his way. The bearing would take him parallel with one of the many streams at Sandhurst and finish up short of the lake. Watson set off on his bearing with confidence, and even had the cheek to bid me goodbye. I had to bite my tongue as I imagined my sinister plot coming to fruition.

Watson's direction was extremely accurate, avoiding the possibility of walking into the stream.

'Watson! Stop!' I shouted.

Watson came to a halt.

'What is it, Colour Sergeant?'

'Nothing to worry about, Watson, there are a few people in front of you, they are just struggling a bit. Wait here for a while. I'll give you a shout when you are clear to go on.'

After leaving Watson on his own for nearly twenty minutes with the poncho over him, I returned. It was all part of the plan hatched to humble his arrogance.

'OK, Watson, it's about 125 metres to your checkpoint. On you go.'

Watson stood still, and his poncho rustled as he got the compass closer to his eyes.

'One hundred and twenty-five metres, Colour Sergeant?' asked Watson, but I didn't answer him. There was a hope he would have forgotten how far he had travelled and how far he had to go. But if he wasn't already unsure, I'd given him an incorrect distance to sow the seed of doubt. Watson called for me a few more times before setting off. It was less than 90 metres to the lake. If Watson was as good as he professed, he would stop just short. If he wasn't, he would end up in the lake. Jogging back towards Captain Dunn, keen to share my plot, it was hard to contain my excitement. En route, we stopped several students and told them to take off their ponchos and watch the solitary figure heading towards the lake. Captain Dunn and I stood some 60 metres away, eagerly watching Watson stride confidently towards the water. Like two delinquent school kids who had played a cheap trick on a teacher, we giggled at the prospect of Watson overshooting the target. To rapturous applause, Watson obliged and disappeared into the lake with a scream and a splash.

When Watson surfaced, he was confronted by an audience of highly amused students, who bombarded him with sarcastic comments, reminding him that he was supposed to be an ace map reader. My scheme had achieved the desired result, to show Watson he was as vulnerable as the next man. Previously, this tactic had worked superbly with other potential officers; it was my hope that Watson was smart enough to realize this. If nothing else, his mishap had served to raise the morale of all those around him. Remarkably, he emerged from his poncho blaming the compass. It was just as we had suspected. I had to confront this immediately and get him to see that the error was all his.

'What happened, Watson?'

'I am uncertain, Colour Sergeant. Maybe the compass fluid froze or something. I can't understand where it went wrong. The bearing was exactly right.'

'Do you think you overshot the target, you know, miscounted your steps?'

'No, Colour Sergeant, I was bang on.'

'If you were bang on the distance, you would have stopped short of the lake. You walked beyond the target, and that is a counting error. You may have even forgotten how far you had travelled before you stopped. But above all, listen to your peers and what they are saying. You have set yourself up for a fall with your cockiness. There is a fine line between confident and cocky. Get it wrong, and your leadership quickly morphs into delusion and the slippery road to toxicity.'

As we marched back to the accommodation, there was a profound feeling of unity forming throughout the platoon. The winter snow had returned with vengeance, swirling viciously before blanketing the Academy in a frozen white quilt. The awe-inspiring sight of New College framed beautifully by the winter setting stirred the pride of the marching troops. Chests out, heads high, necks rammed into the collar and shoulders pulled back – the magic had begun to work. As we reached the edge of the accommodation, the platoon knew what was coming next. They needed to be the first to get showered, changed and back out on parade. Intuitively, they picked up the pace in anticipation of the next command being 'Get away. Run away. Go!'

To our surprise, it was less than ten seconds before the road was empty and showers were running.

Chapter Five

Every Day a School Day

Thawing snow filled the gutters and clung to life around the edges of Chapel Square as the weekend's covering slowly succumbed to the arrival of sleet. In the silence of a sleeping Academy, the Directing Staff gathered in the shadows of the church. It was close to midnight as Major Gray appeared from one of the many doorways peppered around the rear of Old College.

'Hello, chaps!' Major Gray, typically upbeat, announced his arrival. Paddy sprung to attention.

'Hello, Sir, it's all quiet over there, Sir.' Upright, arms pinned to his side and as rigid as a statue, Paddy looked out of the corner of his eyes at the accommodation. It was still cold enough for the moisture in his breath to freeze and turn to vapour as he greeted the OC. The ambience of the orange street lights was amplified by the surviving white patches of snow, giving Chapel Square a sinister feel. An eerie silence descended on the DS as they became hypnotized by the shadows scurrying around the inside of the students' accommodation. Room lights were still blazing, and noise from drying machines endlessly whirling radiated from utility rooms, echoing around Chapel Square. Occasionally, machines and chatter would fall silent and you could hear the drizzle trying to break through the cold before a blast of pure rain would hit the ground. The battle of a changing climate saw the cold rain re-form into sleet.

'Poor fellas,' giggled Captain Dunn. 'If they had any idea of what was about to happen, half of them would throw in the towel right now.'

'Talking of what is about to happen, let me just reiterate what the aim of this small exercise is,' said the OC, huddling everyone closer to summarize the plan:

> 'Hopefully, your instructions and checks will have ensured the students have the correct equipment packed in their rucksacks. From experience, the big problem we had on the last course was the lack of maps being correctly waterproofed. If there is anything you should check twice, I recommend you have sufficient map cases. If they leave camp without waterproof maps, it's game over! With any luck, our OpSec [operational security] has been tight enough and none of the students has a clue about what is planned.'

Major Gray looked towards his Colour Sergeants, and all three nodded in agreement.

'Good. So, the aim of the next few hours are to expose any flaws in personal preparation, administration and equipment packing. Also, also, also – may I add – we must introduce them to what we expect from a bugout. So maximum effort please.'

Militarily, the phrase 'bugout' is used to express a quick extraction from any given location. Bugouts are intense affairs. They occur when you least expect it or at the least appropriate moment. In training, they are used to simulate the sudden arrival of the enemy, which in turn practises your state of readiness. There is never any warning before a bugout, but one thing is for sure: when it's called, it is accompanied by alarm and confusion, leading to pandemonium. Depending on what you are doing at that very moment in time, it can be the funniest or most stressful of experiences.

'My lot will get the good news,' laughed Captain Watts. 'I can't wait to see the look on their faces.'

Major Gray was quick to follow this comment:

'Tom, this is the first major shock to the system for most of these students. While I subscribe to some theatrics to sharpen their senses, please guard against taking the charade too far. So, to that end, this is the way it should happen. Just after midnight, the Platoon Colour Sergeants will bounce into the accommodation and kick everyone out of bed. After they have achieved the desired effect, Platoon Commanders should strategically place themselves outside the main entrance and guide your respective students to their designated form-up points ready for a kit inspection. All Staff, please get involved. Execute the kit check, with emphasis on waterproofing everything. They need to be as watertight as a stevedore's wallet. Especially maps! Use the issued kit list to check they all have the correct equipment as per the packing instruction. If everything goes well, it shouldn't take more than two hours. Happy? Any questions?'

Paddy nodded and asked for clarity on the punishment policy. Major Gray scratched his head and giggled quietly. 'What did we do on the previous course?'

'Names, Sir. That is the traditional Highland Fieldcraft punishment from days of yore,' Captain Dunn was quick to reply.

'Aye. So it was. Names it was, Sir. Aye, Sir, it's always been names,' added Paddy.

It was hard not to laugh out loud before asking, 'What hideous crime does that innocent statement mask?'

Paddy gave a knowing laugh before volunteering the answer: 'Well you see, Gaz, it's several stress exercises rolled into one. At the same time as its execution, the student must shout out his crime.'

'Good; it sounds like fun.'

Paddy continued: 'You get the student to adopt the press-up position. He does one press-up, one squat thrust, one knees to chest and finally one star jump. No stopping in between, just one swift movement.'

Paddy proceeded to give everyone a demonstration. His muscular physique made the exercise look easy, and before too long, all the Staff were down on the wet ground perfecting the exercise, dreaming up ways to make it more difficult.

'Don't you think they should wear their rucksacks at the same time?' suggested Captain Watts. A mixture of laughs and sarcastic comments flooded in from the Staff. Captain Watts argued his case for a few minutes. Failing to win support, he labelled all the DS a bunch of softies before repeating several stories of the punishments he suffered during his SAS selection course.

'That's the problem with this man's Army; we're too soft on recruits. We need to bring back public flogging.'

This comment stunned everyone into silence. Captain Watts' face compromised the tongue-in-cheek comment, affirmed by a quick wink and knowing grin. Hysterically, Paddy failed to identify the lack of sincerity and immediately jumped in to support his Platoon Commander's comments, agreeing we needed to introduce corporal punishment.

'Ay, dead on, Sir, you're right, that's what we should do; flog them if they get it wrong. No with a belt and that, but something that doesn't mark.'

The sincerity of his comment sent everyone into stitches of laughter, mainly because we genuinely believed that if he had his way, he would bring back flogging or an equivalent punishment.

'That's time, everyone!' said Major Gray. 'Midnight. If the Colour Sergeants would like to go and do their bit, we can get this show on the road.'

Paddy and I made our way through the main entrance. The accommodation was still fairly busy, with students trying to prepare their kit for the next few days' activities. We stopped by the door and listened to the students chatting away, keen to discover if they knew what was about to happen. Several of them were talking about the instructors, so we paused to take in their stories. Neither of us could identify the students' voices, but their chatter amused us.

'Is Captain Watts your Platoon Commander?'

'Yes.'

'He looks a right evil bastard. Is he?'

'He actually doesn't say much, he just looks at you with a death stare. I have a friend at uni who knows him. Apparently, he had killed ten Iraqi Republican Guard in a shootout during the Gulf War.'

'Do you believe him?'

'God knows what the SAS are capable of doing, but the OC said on his introduction that Captain Watts was instrumental in bringing down Saddam Hussein's Scud missile units.'

We were struggling to contain our laughter. Desperately trying to avoid compromising our position, we both turned away to take a deep breath and laugh quietly.

* * *

Stories like this were good fun to listen to. A good friend of mine was serving with the Special Air Service during the Gulf War and was forever repeating his favourite mythical story. Having attentively listened to him regale the tale several times, it was easy to see how such rumours became captivating.

Mick and Al were experienced blades serving with Mobility Squadron 22 SAS. They had been tasked with the reconnaissance of an Iraqi airfield and to assess its weaknesses. Eventually, they decided to target the fuel storage dump well behind enemy lines. For several days they observed the fuel dump from a distance of 2km, using the most sophisticated surveillance equipment available. As normal during stand-off surveillance, they began to exhaust the amount of information obtainable. Of greater concern, it looked as if they were on the move. Higher command instructed the patrol to destroy the fuel. The pair agreed to get into the compound via a blind spot and sabotage as much of the critical infrastructure as possible.

Mick continues the story:

'Twenty-four hours of meticulous military planning had preceded our first move. Previous missions had identified several blind spots in the airfield security. A total of eight men would be involved in the operation, but only me and Al would enter the fuel dump and place explosive charges on a time delay. The plan was simple. We would split into three groups: cover group A and cover group B, with me and Al as the assault group. Under the protection of the cover groups, Al would crawl up to the fence, breach it, and neutralize any surveillance devices between the large fuel dump and the fence line. Meanwhile, I would provide close protection from behind a disused outbuilding near the perimeter fence surrounding the 50-gallon containers. Once Al was inside the compound, I would join him, and together we would place several delay charges, setting them on a five-minute delay. Our secondary target was the living quarters where the pilots slept. If time permitted, we would also leave a few calling cards in one or two other places in order to create as much confusion as possible. This would hopefully mask our escape.

'Early hours on a winter's morning in the middle of the desert, the temperature falls to sub-zero. This certainly was the case as we set out on our sabotage mission. We crammed as much weaponry and ammunition into our kit as possible, then climbed aboard our pinky, which contained an assortment of cannons and grenade launchers. Approximately 5km away from the airfield, we dismounted from our vehicles and set off into the night, heading for a large wadi: eight highly trained Special Air Service blades, equipped with enough weaponry to start a small war. It was exhilarating. Confidence was high as the patrol moved undetected into the final positions.

'From behind a sand dune we were able to locate the outbuilding and confirm exactly what we had planned. With the cover groups in their positions, the signal to go was given. Me and Al began to crawl on our bellies, heading for the outbuilding, when Al suddenly stopped dead in his tracks.

'"What's up, Al?" I whispered.

'"There's a sentry sat by the fuel."

'I crawled level with Al and looked through my weapon sight. I took a long, hard look at the sentry, but couldn't believe what I saw.

'"He's sleeping! Monging it big time. Have a look."

'"He bloody is as well. I can't believe that. What do you want to do?"

'"I've spent a lot of time on this job. I ain't turning back now, I'd not live it down. The boys would have a field day, taking the piss. Let's just watch him for a short while; see if he is replaced or wakes up and goes."

'After nearly an hour, the situation was exactly the same. Al pointed out that time was getting tight, and if we delayed our decision any longer we would get caught in the light. I had to re-evaluate the plan. I thought through every possible scenario in quick time, and decided we would have to eliminate the sentry then continue with the mission.

'"OK. Al, we're going to have to do him. Let's get a move on."

'We started to crawl in the direction of the sentry. My body was frozen stiff after being still for nearly two hours – just moving felt good. The sentry was sitting with his back against a low rocky outcrop located to the rear of an outbuilding. With the weather as cold as it was, the Arab sentry was well protected from the elements, wearing several layers of clothing, as well as a thick Parka-type coat. His head, neck and ears all covered with a blanket, he had left just enough space for his eyes to peer out of. I stopped about 5 metres short of the sleeping guard and brought my weapon into the aim.

'"OK Al," I whispered as I listened to the sentry snore his head off.

'"OK Al what?"

'"Do him!"

'"I've not done anyone like this before. Why don't you do him?"

'For the next two minutes, we argued over who was going to kill the sleeping sentry, before I finally relented and decided to take the responsibility. I gave Al a good slagging down. I had suckered myself and decided to do the dirty work.

'"Mick, it needs to be quiet. Don't shoot him."

'"What? Just slit his throat?"

'"No, you can't, it's covered up with his scarf and the hood of his Parka. If you shoot him, you will wake the whole camp up."

'After another lengthy debate, I finally decided to knock him out by hitting him over the back of the head with the butt of my rifle. The sentry had kindly removed his helmet before nodding off to sleep, and this was perfect for a quiet kill. I crawled up to within striking distance of the Iraqi soldier, thinking what a prat he was – fancy falling asleep while on sentry. I psyched myself up and convinced myself that one big "baseball bat" swing should do the trick. With any luck, he might even survive to tell the tale to his grandchildren. With every ounce of energy, I swung my rifle and caught the sentry square on the back of his head. The hood of his Weston muffled the thud, and the sentry slumped to the floor. I was about to praise myself on a job well done when the sentry let out an almighty scream.

'"Aaahhhh!.Wa-Allahee! Wa-Allahee!"

'The sentry rolled around on the floor, clutching his head. "Aaahhhh! Wa-Allahee! Allahee!"

'"What the fuck are you doing?" Al whispered loudly. I hit the sentry again and again, but each time I hit him, he screamed louder. The airfield burst into life, with sirens and searchlights appearing all over the place. Al started to fire at the guards as they began to follow the noise, and at the same time the cover groups opened fire on the partially dressed guards leaving their sleeping quarters. I gave the signal to extract at a rapid rate. For the next few hours, we skirmished across the desert, chased by what felt like a battalion of the Iraqi Republican Guard, which by now was at full alert. After we had broken contact with the enemy, we made our emergency rendezvous close to the vehicles, where a quick head check identified that everyone had returned safely. No one spoke, and for a brief moment, everyone just focused their sights on the horizon. Spontaneously, we all burst out into fits of laughter. I tried to explain to everyone what had happened, but I couldn't get a word in for the slagging down I was receiving. I couldn't help thinking, "I hope no one ever gets to hear about this cock-up", although I was sure I wouldn't hear the last of it. Sometimes even the greatest fighting force in the world can get it wrong, as the best-laid plans fail to survive contact with the enemy.'

During numerous nights out, Mick repeated this story. Each time he added more to it. Eventually, it grew so big he must have won the war single-handed. Whether the story was true or not, it served a purpose: it kept the myth alive and the fear of the Special Forces real.

* * *

Chuckling to myself and daydreaming, normality was restored as Paddy flung open the main door and burst into the accommodation.

'Bugout! Bugout! Grab your kit and get outside now!' His Irish accent filled the role of terrorizer to great effect. I regained my concentration and, following Paddy's lead, I was screaming too: 'Bugout! Bugout! Get your kit together and get outside right now!'

Haigh, the first person to appear from his room, was clearly dazed by what was happening.

'Excuse me, Colour Sergeant, what time is it?'

'Midnight, just gone, now get your kit together and get outside. Hurry up!'

Haigh frowned and frantically rubbed his forehead, trying to comprehend the situation. For the first time, the reason why his peers called him Clyde was evident. The large forehead, receding hairline and frown had an uncanny resemblance to the *Every Which Way But Loose* character. It was not the words that he struggled with, more their lack of logic and justification. Momentarily, he disappeared into a stupor.

'Haigh!' I shouted. 'Get a move on. Look lively.' Like a light had just been switched on, he instantly began to get himself organized.

Less than a minute after Paddy and I entered the accommodation, it was bedlam. Doors swung open and slammed closed at a furious pace, while half-dressed bodies scampered from one room to the next, ferrying kit around like Nepalese Sherpas. Danner and Moore collided with each other in passing, spilling kit across the floor. Simultaneously, they bent down to retrieve their dropped equipment, banging their heads in the process. An angry exchange followed and intervention was required.

'Hey! Laurel and Hardy, pack it in. When you have finished with the comedy show, get your kit together and get outside.'

Danner came to his senses instantly. Apologizing profusely, his big frame continued to block the main exit and more apologies were offered.

Rideout passed me four times within the space of a minute: wearing only his socks and boxer shorts the first time, half-dressed the second, fully clothed the third and finally fully dressed and dragging his equipment behind him, heading for the exit. Bouncing from one room to another with the intention of flustering ill-prepared students with repeated cries to 'bugout', my initial assessment was pleasing until Witherspoon caught my eye. With him still in his pyjamas trying to pack his rucksack whilst attempting to wash and shave at the same time, my frustrations mounted.

'Bloody hell, Witherspoon! What are you up to?' Witherspoon stood in silence, a vacant look filling his eyes.

'Answer me then, softlad.'

'Well the truth is, Colour Sergeant, I don't know.'

Witherspoon's answer caught me by surprise. It was the last thing I expected him to say. There was no faulting his honesty, but even I knew what he was doing. He was failing to prioritize – a perennial problem for military commanders. Competing priorities poorly managed will cause maximum frustration all around. For the individual, he becomes flustered, while for his subordinates, they become frustrated. Poor leadership will issue multiple priorities, masking them under many disguises, from 'Main Effort' to 'Out-puts' and 'Inspections'. Subordinates become discouraged and efforts are needlessly trebled in order to cover all bases; it is 'bad busy', working hard on everything, because everything is the commander's priority. Witherspoon was suffering from this, but in a microcosm. His Main Effort was to get out of the building, but he had replaced it with superficial compliance tasks, such as shaving, which was done at the expense of getting dressed. This incident had greater meaning for me. In any business, it is intuition that one needs if one is to be a good commander or leader. Common sense will always prevail, but adherence to regulation in such a dogmatic fashion is potentially disastrous.

'If you don't know what you're doing, stop doing it and do as you're being told. Get your kit together and move outside with the rest of the course!'

'With everything, Colour Sergeant?'

'Yes, Witherspoon, with everything!'

'Including my rabbit?'

'What?'

'My rabbit, Colour Sergeant. Do I take him or leave it behind?'

'Leave it.'

'How about food? Shall I leave him some food or will we not be gone for long?'

I had no answer to Witherspoon's endless questions. Unable to think quickly enough, I resorted to the archaic art of shouting verbal abuse at an inaudible level to intimidate the lad into silence. It worked. Witherspoon grabbed a small amount of equipment and headed for the exit, dressed in only his boxer shorts.

As the students vacated the building, I made a quick survey of their rooms, keen to see if they had been left tidy. The first room was worse now than it was after Pat's Tazing. Each room had been left open, with personal belongings flung in all four corners. Upon reaching Mathews' room, I was greeted by the rabbit he had been entrusted with. It was wearing a makeshift collar with a name tag that simply read 'Rabbit'! Mathews had made a home for his new friend in the shape of a cardboard box, furnishing it with two parts of a soap dish masquerading as food and water trays.

Leaving the accommodation and making my way to Chapel Square, Captain Dunn had the students prepared for inspection. The dark winter sky was broken by the random flickering of a street light, the orange flashes creating a psychedelic feel to the illuminations around Chapel Square. If you took away the disorderly students, the scene was picturesque, reminiscent of a sombre Christmas card. The platoon stood in a hollow square under the supervision of Captain Dunn. Most were busy trying to adjust their state of dress, preparing for a 'Type A' field inspection.

'Type A' field inspections were used as the preferred method for delivering student education and character development, as well as enhancing the opportunity to sharpen personal administration. For a 'Type A' field inspection, every item carried in the rucksack needed to be laid out at the feet of the student in a set format. Firstly, the student would fold his poncho into an exact square – no deviation. On top of it, spare clothing would be folded, again into a perfect square, then placed in a specific sequence. The socks, underwear, waterproof jacket and trousers were laid out an inch from the top edge. Then along the bottom were the red rugby top, training shoes and toggle rope for the events that would require such forms of dress. Meticulous attention to detail was paramount in organizing the layout. Washing and shaving kit, mess tins and eating utensils sat in the centre. Punishment loomed if anything was found to be out of place or dirty. Maps, rations, sleeping bag and cooking kit were also to be displayed. In total, the student packed nearly 50lb of equipment in the rucksack, and every item had an exact place to be stored.

Time was ticking by as we walked around the three sides of the square, watching the students frantically arranging then rearranging their equipment.

'Gaz. Have you checked the rooms?' Pat shouted.

'Yes, Sir, I had a quick look around. They're in scruff order.'

'Paddy, how was your side?'

'Good, Sir, spot on. Blue-red-blue-tickity-boo, Sir.'

Pat stormed off in the direction of the accommodation, reappearing a short time later, and was clearly unimpressed with what he had seen.

'Colour Sergeant!' he shouted. Using my rank instead of my name was a clear indication that all was not well. In regiments like Pat's and mine, rank is rarely used amongst peer groups; but when it is, it's normally because a reprimand is imminent.

'I'm not impressed with the state of those rooms,' Pat said. 'You need to stick some of those scum bags into the Rembrandt. That is way short of the standard we expect.'

Pat stormed off to speak to the OC. Left with my tail between my legs, it wasn't the start to the exercise that I would have liked. A quick glance over at Paddy's students revealed that they appeared better organized and generally more prepared in comparison to mine. I began to curse my bad luck, wondering how the situation had arisen. Examining my own performance first, maybe more could have been done.

Captain Dunn walked across to see what was said.

'What was that about, Colour?'

'The Sergeant Major has a sad on with the state of the accommodation. It's in a hell of a mess, and I'm sure he's not too pleased with the performance of this lot during the bugout.'

'Well, Colour, don't get too upset about that just yet. You need to prepare yourself for the state of their attempt at a kit layout.'

Captain Dunn walked down the line, shaking his head in despair. He stopped in front of Lane and pointed down at a bare poncho. Lane's expression was full of self-pity, an insight into his mental fragility.

'Lane, where are your spare clothes, food, washing kit, command kit … in fact, why can't I see anything of use?' Lane failed to reply.

'OK, too hard a question. How about your emergency rations, maps, survival kit or water?'

'In my room, Colour Sergeant.' With teeth clenched in frustration, it was difficult to assess what was going on in Lane's mind.

'Lane! Look down at your poncho. Apart from your sleeping bag and red rugby top, you have got nothing at all. How do you expect to survive in the mountains of Wales or Scotland with nothing more than a sleeping bag?'

Lane began stuttering his answer, but before he had the chance to complete a sentence, Captain Dunn snapped.

'You are a complete liability, Lane! A bloody hindrance. Colour Sergeant, fifty names for this idle individual.'

I demonstrated the exercise to Lane and then supervised him until he could execute the punishment correctly. Once he had grasped the exercise, he stood in front of all the students to demonstrate the punishment. Activities were paused so the platoon understood the requirement.

'Lane! Failure to pack the correct equipment, one! Lane! Failure to pack the correct equipment, two!' And so it went on.

Lane paced the chorus to the speed of his exercises. At the top of his voice, he shouted the exercise number just as he leapt into the air to complete the star jump. We left him in front of the platoon to complete his fifty names and carried on with the inspection. The next student in the line was Stone. He stood to attention, proud of his kit layout. A smile suggested he was confident.

'Stone, why have you not waterproofed your kit as you were taught?'

'Well, it's not raining hard enough for all my kit to get wet, Sir.'

'Wow, that is an interesting concept, Stone,' said Captain Dunn. 'But how about if I drag you through the nearest river? Which is what I am likely to do if ever you come up with a smart-arse answer like that again. Thirty names, Stone. "I must waterproof my kit." Take this as a stern warning. You need to wake up and smell the coffee before it's too late. You're not as special as you think you are.'

Stone began his punishment: 'Stone! I must waterproof my kit, one! Stone! I must waterproof my kit, two!'

The bugout visibly flustered Rideout. He had laid out his kit correctly, but nervously scanned the lines to see if he had done it right.

'Brought all your kit with you, Rideout?' asked Captain Dunn.

'Err, yes, Colour Sergeant; no, I mean yes, Sir.'

'Is that a "yes" or a "no", Rideout?'

'Sir!'

'Rideout, get a grip of yourself. Let's start from the beginning. Have you got all your equipment?'

Rideout took a deep breath. 'Yes, I have.'

'Well, Rideout, that has impressed me. It appears you have. It's reasonably well laid out; the first to do so. However, after nearly fifteen years' service, two wars and four operational tours, I've earned the right to be called "Sir" by a young pretender like you.'

'Sorry, Sir. I did mean to say "Sir", Sir. It just didn't come out. Sorry, Sir.'

'Well, best you start to concentrate harder because as it stands you are heading for a painful ride through the course. Thirty names. "I must concentrate harder." Oh, I am sorry Rideout; I did mean to tell you that we were going to turn up at midnight and drag you out of your bed on a cold February morning, but it just didn't come out!'

Major Gray was patrolling the ranks, giggling uncontrollably as Captain Dunn hit his sarcastic best. He had stopped to inspect Haigh's kit, struggling to identify what had gone wrong. While the poncho was full of equipment, none of it was the correct stuff.

'Haigh, where are your waterproofs?' Captain Dunn demanded.

'I am wearing them, Sir.'

'OK, where is your washing and shaving kit?'

'In my pocket, Sir.'

'I see! Are these new rules or are you just inventing new stuff to test me?'

'Well, Sir, it is raining so the waterproofs are prudent. The calamitous manner of our departure prevented the opportunity to wash and shave, hence my aspiration to attend to my dishevelled look on the move.'

'Haigh, Haigh, Haigh! Stop talking.'

Captain Dunn had to persist before silence fell and he continued: 'Fifty names, "I must do the same as everyone else".'

Reluctantly, Haigh emptied his pockets and resentfully began his punishment.

The inspection continued in a familiar pattern. Every student would fail our scrutiny and a varying number of 'names' would be issued. In general, the turnout was not as poor as it could have been, despite the odd shocker. We set out to catch the students by surprise, and we succeeded. If we had deployed after the inspection, some students would not last the night, while others would last twenty-four hours and no more. Witherspoon was the least well prepared. He stood in the snow, shivering uncontrollably. Captain Dunn stood in front of him, trying to digest the poor state of Witherspoon and his equipment.

'You're clearly not in the Rembrandt, are you, Witherspoon?'

Teeth chattering and wearing a befuddled look, Witherspoon stood in silence.

'Answer the Platoon Commander then, softlad.'

Witherspoon struggled to speak: a combination of cold and shock had him stupefied. 'I am not sure what you mean by that question, Sir,' he said.

'Bloody hell, Witherspoon. Who's Rembrandt?'

'He's a p-p-p-painter, Colour Sergeant.'

'Painter, picture – made the connection yet?' For the next few minutes, I tried to explain to the young man from Birmingham the connection, but the cold had gripped him. I began to regret my decision to chase him out of the accommodation in just his boxer shorts. Witherspoon had truly been caught unprepared for the bugout, and was physically suffering as a result. But despite his predicament, he was still punished with thirty names for poor personal administration.

With the exercise achieving its main aim, Pat called to all the students to leave their equipment where it was and gather around Major Gray for a debrief. Standing underneath the orange glow of a street lamp, the OC explained the aim of the exercise was to test and rehearse the bugout procedure.

'Who isn't enjoying himself?' asked the OC, whilst looking at an audience of frozen faces. 'Well, let me ask you something else. What do you think is going to happen next?'

A student raised his hand: 'We are going on a ten-day exercise, Sir.'

Major Gray smiled. It was confirmation his exercise had achieved its aim. He continued:

'Ok, some of you will be pleased to hear that we are not actually going anywhere tonight. In fact, you are shortly going back to bed, as tonight has only been a dress rehearsal to demonstrate to you what we all should expect the next time you get bugged-out. Be prepared, be packed and be ready for almost anything. The next time we bugout, you will get straight onto the trucks. If you forget something, we leave it behind and it stays left behind.'

The OC glanced at Pat and disappeared into the night. Pat took centre stage to address the students:

'Some of you throbbers may live like tramps at home, but take this as the final warning. If ever you leave your rooms in such poor order again, or you leave them open, you will need to recover the entire contents from one of the surrounding lakes. Take heed. Gaz, Paddy, put these children to bed. Gaz, come see me once you are done!'

The platoon assembled just outside the main doors of the accommodation and Captain Dunn spoke to them first:

'Fellas, a quick debrief. If we were to go on a weeklong trip, some of you would end up in hospital. Believe me when I say it, this happens frequently, and I am sure it will happen to at least one of you here. People have forgotten waterproofs, command equipment, emergency food and water, not to mention the basic clothing requirements. I will leave the rest to the Colour Sergeant, but if you have learnt anything from tonight, it should be this: stay packed and stay prepared to go anywhere at any time. There are no more second chances.'

Captain Dunn turned to look at me. 'Colour Sergeant, I am seriously unhappy; we will chat in the morning!'

Without wishing anyone goodnight, he walked off in the direction of his home, leaving me to tidy up. Captain Dunn's comments to me were manufactured and prearranged, designed to give the impression that he had been let down. It's a simple trick, a bit like emotional blackmail, designed to make the students feel guilty about their poor effort. Being disappointed in himself will induce a desire to do better. A side-effect of this was to give us a good excuse to put the students through the Mean Machine.

There was much to say to the students about administration, but Witherspoon was displaying all the signs of hypothermia and my priorities changed. He was on the threshold of serious injury, with his eyes rolling backwards, and I caught hold of him just before he fainted. His lips, ears, toes and fingers had turned a deep shade of blue. The only thing to do was to put him straight into a warm shower. Secretly, during the course of the inspection, my concerns had distracted me; he had been in the cold too long. Desperately keen not to upset Pat again, my decision to act sooner had been repressed. After nearly twenty minutes in the shower, slowly increasing the temperature to hot, Witherspoon began to show signs of recovery. He had certainly more to talk about than most of his companions. Once Witherspoon had gained full control of his body and a trip to A&E had been averted, it was time to get some sleep. It was nearly three in the morning, and the night had been more eventful than need be. Relieved there was no lasting damage to Witherspoon, and angry and disappointed in myself for not intervening earlier, it would be a restless night for me.

There is a fine line between pushing someone beyond their limits and pushing them over the edge. With Witherspoon, only by luck was disaster averted. We came within a hair's breadth of getting it wrong. Leaving things to chance when you can absolutely see they are not going well demands early intervention. Distracted by Pat's anger and the poor state of the inspection, I failed to properly consider the seriousness of Witherspoon's predicament. Worse still, when it did cross my mind, the courage to change priorities deserted me. Irrelevant distractions masked the moment when the situation had changed; although true dangers had been seen, the priorities had been lost amidst personal ambition. It was a pivotal occurrence that would shape all my thoughts thereafter and fine-tune my understanding of dealing with a changing situation. Some years later, faced with a situation that changed in the blink of an eye, my reactions had much improved, having learnt from the Witherspoon experience.

* * *

Shortly after the 1st UK Armoured Division took part in the invasion of Iraq, I found myself at the very front of every evil event the conflict had to offer. There were very few Arabic speakers in the British Army in 2003 and consequently, the few of us who were available were much in demand. Even after the fighting finished, and the transition was afoot, trouble pursued me across the country. As UK troops departed the country in mid-July, my job was to establish the interim Police force of Iraq. Under the command of the Provost Marshal of Basra and Mason Provinces, he tasked me to run basic law enforcement courses and establish police stations from Safwan on the border of Kuwait all the way to the northern tip of the British Area of Responsibility in Mason Province.

Long and difficult days were proving frustrating and complex. Routinely, I would call into the Provost Marshal's office and update him on my progress. On one particular day, the Basra project officer for the Royal Military Police asked me for some assistance. Captain Helen Taylor was in her late twenties, a committed officer with a fantastic reputation. She was a real force to be reckoned with inside the headquarters of the Military Police. Tenacious and intelligent, there was fire in her belly and a determination to be successful in pursuit of bringing peace to her patch in the centre of Basra. When she spoke, people listened. Tall, with a commanding demeanour, she was everything the British Army was proud of. Analytical, mentally robust and passionate about democracy and freedom, she was an inspirational role model to all under her charge.

Amidst the busiest of days, her request for help sounded simple. Despite being close to exhaustion, and needing to make the long journey north, I agreed to interpret her conversation with a local family that had moved into an abandoned Ba'ath Party headquarters. After a short drive through the centre of the city we arrived at a palatial building with a walled garden and five floors. In the doorway, children innocently played football with coke cans and anything else that would roll. On the first and second floors, there were more children and a large number of women cooking rice and making bread. It was becoming clear that this was not one family as we understood it, but the whole family, extended members, aunties and uncles as well.

We made our way to the rooftop, where the family elders were sitting cross-legged on the floor. More children were playing, with a few women washing and hanging bedding out on makeshift washing lines. The project officer introduced me to the family elder, Abdul Aziz, who spoke some broken English. His weather-beaten face matched his brown teeth and bloodshot eyes: Abdul had not enjoyed an easy life. Evenly spaced scars on his arms, blunt trauma marks on his forehead and cigarette burns on the back of his hands told me he had been the victim of the brutal deposed regime. Despite the coalition force destroying his city, he remained upbeat and positive about the future. After a few pleasant exchanges, it soon became apparent that there had been several visits before mine, and the initial part of the conversation was cordial. The British Army had sent a medical team a few days earlier to administer some health care to a baby, and the civilian-military cooperation group (CIMIC) had tried to find the family a new home.

'Mr McCarthy, could you please translate the following for me?' asked Captain Taylor. 'Please explain to the head of the family that the building he is occupying is to be requisitioned for the new police force of Iraq. We gave his family one week to move out and find a new home and it is now time they left.'

Caught by surprise, I took a deep breath before translating the words. Instantly, the mood changed. The captain continued: 'Please add that CIMIC have offered them a house on the outskirts of the city and they need to move into it. Should the family fail to move in the next twenty-four hours, we will have no option but to remove the family through force.'

It was an unpleasant task the captain had been given, and she was not enjoying its execution.

In typical Arab fashion, Abdul thanked God – for nothing in particular – and explained that the house CIMIC had offered him had been struck by tanks, and chemical residue (depleted uranium) would cause serious illness to his family if he moved there. He continued to explain that to move to this house would mean certain death. But the tall, ginger-haired Captain Taylor was impassive as she asked me to repeat the fact that Abdul had to leave in the next twenty-four hours. By this time the women had gathered around us, along with the younger men. The pair of us were trapped in a vulnerable position on the rooftop, detached from our force protection downstairs that was securing the entry and exit points.

Abdul suddenly said, 'Mashay Allah, Mashay Allah' (an Arabic phrase to ward off evil) and fell into a trance. With alarming frequency, he paced along the edge of the roof, excessively reciting Quranic verses. His tone became aggressive as he cursed Saddam Hussein for the misery he had brought on his family. 'Sakeenee! Sakeenee! [Where's my knife, where's my knife?] I kill Saddam, I kill he.' Mixing his broken English with his native tongue, the repetition of every phrase was the final indicator that Abdul was no longer thinking straight. 'Kill me now, kill me now. We go to new house we all die, so kill me now.'

With every passing second, the crowd became more and more agitated; within a minute, the women were wailing, the men shouting and the children crying.

Abdul snapped. In a fit of rage, he grabbed the nearest child. A girl, approximately aged 3, startled and confused, was dragged close to his body. With scraggy auburn hair and faded brown dress with gold braiding, she was devoid of emotion as her grandfather shuffled towards the edge of the flat roof. With a tight grip around her left wrist, he bent down to grab her left ankle. In one swift move, he hauled the child over the small safety wall and dangled her over the side. It was at least a 50ft drop to the concrete floor below. There was foam frothing from his mouth and an unswerving look on his face.

'I kill my children. One by one, I will kill all children. Better we die here with my family than die from your poison.'

Shaking the child below the height of the safety wall, for one terrifying moment, the fear she had been dropped consumed me.

I moved a foot closer to Abdul to confirm the girl was still in his grasp. Her emerald eyes sat deep in her Mesopotamian features as the sunlight faded. At peace with her fate, she calmly used her free hand to stop her dress fluttering in the wind. With the savage nature of life in Iraq threatening to turn one more innocent soul into a senseless victim, my emotional tolerance flew off the scale. The girl was neither angry nor upset; she just dangled, quietly resigned to her destiny. Maybe she didn't understand the danger she was in, but for me, the situation had changed. Abdul's behaviour seemed to be accepted by his family.

This was the moment the Witherspoon incident came flooding back to me. Morally, my reactions should have been quicker with him. Irrespective of the group's aim on that night, I should have got Witherspoon out of danger and faced the consequences later.

Now on the rooftop in downtown Basra, the needs of the British Army needed to be forgotten or there would be certain death for this beautiful child. With my eyes fixed on Abdul, I repeated 'Allah Raheem, Allah Raheem' (God is merciful, God is merciful). It was crucial to connect with Abdul; he needed to see me as a person, as a father, as a solution, not the problem. He was not bluffing. If the previous two months in Iraq had taught me anything, it was that man can be evil and merciful in the same breath, and that one man's act of mercy is another man's act of evil. No one has the divine right to judge unless you have walked in the shoes of every person on the planet.

But this was not just about the turbulence of another family move, nor the realistic prospect of dying from depleted uranium poisoning. At that very moment in time, we were witnessing Arab culture at its most extreme. This was no longer an issue of where to live, more an education to his family on how to live. Whilst fighting the Irish Republican Army, we were often told by the terrorists we encountered that it was 'better to die on your feet than to live on your knees'; with the Arab, there was a parallel they simply called honour. In the Gulf, the man is unrivalled, and women must not disgrace his standing. This was not about the house, this was about Abdul Aziz not losing his standing in the hierarchy of his home. He would happily kill every female in the family to maintain his standing. What's more, his community would agree with his actions, wife including. From bitter experience and many years of soldiering in the Middle East, there is no winning a debate with an angry male desperately defending his honour.

'Abdul, my brother,' I said. 'We don't want that. This is not what the Army came here for. What will it take to bring the child back to her mother?'

'Nothing. Allah Raheem. Allah wa Barakatu.' (God is merciful, and God offers his blessing).

'Abdul, my brother. Hear me please. This is your building. I will inform the captain that this is your home, that you can't move. She will understand; she is a mother and knows you love your family. We can make this right if you bring the child back to her mother.'

Abdul finally lifted the girl over the wall and stepped away from the edge. Nonchalantly, he dropped the child at his feet, but retained a tight grip of her wrist. The mother ran to the aid of the child, but suffered an angry rebuke from Abdul. 'It's for the good of the family,' he screamed at the mother, still refusing to release the child.

Adopting a subservient posture, I held out my hand. Fixing my eyes with Abdul's trance-like gaze, it was time to plead for forgiveness.

'My brother, I am serious, please take my hand. It is my word, my honour. Take my life, I offer it to you.'

It felt like an age before Abdul grabbed it. Grasping his hand, with all my adrenaline running wild, emotions got the better of me. I had deployed to Iraq only a few days after the birth of my own daughter. After several near misses, I felt my luck was going to run out sooner or later, and maybe this was the moment. My paternal instincts made a mess of my straight thinking. Like an old black and white TV flicking between channels, my mind skipped between thoughts of never seeing my daughter and watching Abdul's child plunge to her death. Seeing the girl sprawled out motionless on the floor, having escaped death, was no easy sight.

'We will not return, my brother, but please know this,' I told Abdul. 'There are many other Iraqis that want this building, and they are not as kind as us. Please don't stay here longer than you must. God is great, he is merciful; may you travel safely with God's blessing.'

Captain Taylor stood 5 yards behind me. Her face had turned ashen with what had just occurred. I could hear nothing but my heart pounding in my inner ear as we left Abdul. Whatever words left my mouth as we walked down the stairs would not have been coherent. At the door to the walled garden, two RMP soldiers played improvised football by kicking cans and stones around with some of Abdul's kids, totally oblivious to what had just taken place. We mounted up into the Toyota Land Cruisers and headed back to the HQ. There was nothing to say. Desperation would have seen Abdul drop that child off the roof, and that was not worth the cost of a new police station at that moment in time. Internally, I was an emotional wreck. With so much loss of life endured so far, how could someone willingly sling his children off the roof of a five-storey building? It took me a while to understand this, but desperation distorts logic, and passion is no practical solution to physical problems.

Although Witherspoon would never learn of these events, it was our encounter on the practice bugout that undoubtedly saved the life of the young Iraqi girl. Her beautiful green eyes, set in the most peaceful of expressions as she dangled from the rooftop, will linger with me forever. Of all the death experienced in several wars, it is this image that consistently emerges from the shadows of a quiet moment to haunt me. Mesmerized by her innocence, the lessons learnt during that intervention have calibrated my emotional intelligence. At times, this has been viewed as a weakness; on other days, a life-changing skill. Emotional intelligence cannot be taught – it has to be learnt the hard way. There is no electronic simulator or online substitute for the development of this skill. It is operational experience, and this comes at a cost to the reservoir of the emotions we own. Once that reservoir is empty or poisoned, there is little left other than selfishness, dispassion and an easy path to toxic leadership.

Chapter Six

Ice Breaker

It was 0545 hours the morning after the first bugout rehearsal and I'd managed a full two hours sleep before reveille was called. The grounds between the accommodation and the Warrant Officers and Sergeants' Mess had received another unwelcome covering of heavy snowfall in the few hours we had been asleep. With the intention of rousing the students, I entered my half of the accommodation, only to be greeted by several students who were already up and moving about.

'Who woke you lot up?' I asked.

'No one,' replied Francis, who was just heading towards the washroom. 'We've been preparing our kit in case we get bugged out again, Colour Sergeant.'

'Whose stupid idea was that?'

'Well, no one's really, we just think we might get bugged out today.'

How Francis had come to his conclusion worried me. Staying at this level of alertness would exhaust them before they left the camp.

'Francis, you can't stay up every night, from now until the end of the course, just in case you get bugged out again.'

Walking the length of the accommodation, I discovered that every student had remained awake, busying himself with kit packing. This was the last thing we needed: a bunch of students who had not slept for twenty-four hours. It was difficult enough trying to teach when they were fully rested; it would be nearly impossible when they were deprived of sleep. And if the students were not tired enough, it was just about to get a whole lot worse.

'Francis, tell the platoon to put on their red rugby tops and move out to the Mean Machine!' Baffled by my comment, he looked at me in disbelief, staring silently in expectation of another order.

'Well get to it, softlad!'

Francis set about his task of rallying his fellow students. Ten minutes later, they had formed up outside the Mean Machine. Most of the equipment was buried beneath a fresh layer of snow. Individuals began to clear small areas of working space, some having to search hard before locating equipment that had been completely covered.

'Two people on a piece of equipment!' I shouted. 'Thirty seconds hard work on each item, and it will be all over in fifteen minutes. Skive, and we'll do it again! Stand by!'

One long whistle blast and we were underway. The courtyard filled with the groans of physical exertion and warm exhaled air, which began to create a light fog captured inside the courtyard.

Barns grimaced as droplets of snow and ice fell off the pull-up bar and ran down his back. Mathews' small, powerful frame flapped frantically at the rope climb, finding it virtually impossible to gain a grip on the frozen rope. Murphy was looking tired, annoyed and confused as he battled his way up the spiral staircase carrying two yellow burdens, one in each hand. He was paired with Williams, who was struggling behind. Another long whistle blast and the exercise stopped.

'Change exercise!'

One long whistle blast and a new exercise began. Pat appeared from a side door, having heard the commotion. Enthusiastically, he immediately began to scold the nearest student.

'Watson. Oi, Watson, get your head up. Come on, princess, try harder. What's wrong, didn't you get enough sleep last night, Watson?'

I burst out laughing and Pat frowned at me. 'What?' he snapped.

'Nothing, but that's King. The dude in the stress position is Watson.'

Pat moved towards Watson and dished out a venomous tirade of abuse. 'Did you hear me, Watson? Straighten your arms and stop skiving, you homo!'

Pat developed a dislike for some people very quickly. But if you didn't crumble under his barracking, there was a good chance he would leave you alone and not bother learning your name.

After we had completed one full lap of the circuit, they had done enough and Pat was content.

'Marvellous, that's how to start your day. I love the Mean Machine,' he shouted as he disappeared back through the side door, and instantly began to shout at someone from Paddy's platoon. The students were ushered out of the courtyard and into the side street. Their faces conveyed dejection, fatigue and failure. It wasn't the right time to issue a standard military-style telling off, but something had to be said.

'What do you think that was for?'

Mathews sprung to attention, raising his hand at the same time. 'Because we were in poor order last night during the bugout, Colour Sergeant.'

'Spot on, Mathews. It's becoming tiresome telling you this. You must fully understand the system will punish you for failing to meet the required standards, regardless of where you are, how you are feeling or what time of day it is. Fail and pay the consequences. It is not an idle threat, it's a promise. You have five minutes to get showered and ready for breakfast. Go!'

The first lesson after breakfast was delivered by the Platoon Commander. He introduced the students to the Formal Orders process and taught them how the procedure worked. In order to achieve a mission given to you by a higher commander, you need to devise a plan and work out your own scheme of manoeuvre. The plan, along with the scheme of manoeuvre, needs to be explained to those who will execute the practicalities of the task. Normally imparted as a formal brief known in the military as 'Orders', they are events sequenced logically, whilst progressively achieving tasks by passing through set goals. It is vital a student not only understands how the orders are processed, but can apply the formula with common sense, intelligence and just a hint of creativity. In Rowallan, an orders process template was used specifically to allow a student the opportunity to practice four tools of command: Planning, Briefing, Command and Control, and Evaluation/Re-evaluation. Later in life, this would morph into the OODA loop, fashioned so successfully by American strategist John Boyd: Observe, Orientate, Decide and Act is a continuum evaluation model proven to win wars when used correctly, but first, one must master the basics.

Planning is an art that good academics find easy to articulate from the comfort of their classrooms. But for students in the infancy of learning, the subject of planning can appear to be a black art. For this reason, many obvious mistakes are made on the road to becoming a good planner. At Rowallan, mistakes were encouraged, even if they were punished. We learn best from our mistakes, especially when they can be associated with some kind of misery. In teaching the students the basic skills of planning, the instructors would seek to deliver simple tools and models that could be easily explained. Thereafter, they would seek to develop the skills through practice and self-learning. Although the formal 'Orders' process is an advanced tool of command, it was used at Row-Co to enhance leadership exercises. Students would need to develop the ability to conduct quick analysis, using simple tools like SWOT or METS (Manning Equipment Training Sustainment), then brief their findings using the framework of command tools we had given them.

The penultimate planning tool taught by Captain Dunn was the skill of evaluation and re-evaluation. The ability to evaluate a task is the product of education, punctuated with emerging trends as well as understanding cause and effects. Critically, the most important commodity is knowing your own strengths and weaknesses, which will help you avoid sleepwalking into a monumental blunder. It is for this reason that Rowallan focused much of their tuition on the art of re-evaluation. The ability to rescue an enormous error and turn it into a near miss comes from understanding how to use this tool.

Identifying the point at which re-evaluation is required is not difficult, but having the courage to re-evaluate and change direction is complex. The fear and dread of failure are unthinkable as a military commander. But in truth, few operations ever go as planned and there is always going to be a need to test and adjust as missions evolve. Occasionally there will be a need to go back to the start point. During the course, we mitigated a reluctance to re-evaluate by surreptitiously introducing tasks that could not be achieved. Exercises designed to fail will produce several opportunities to re-evaluate. This would allow the DS the opportunity to coach a student to have the courage to re-evaluate when failure was looming large. These lessons are priceless. There are too few studies examining the reasons why we don't admit our mistakes. Psychology likes to focus on proven tangibles. Explaining why we just say sorry instead of admitting we were wrong is a difficult task. One good reason is that get it wrong in the military and lives are lost.

Finally, the students received an overview of how to command and control people effectively. The skills involved with command and control are by far the hardest to master, primarily because it is as much about style and character as it is about substance. It is the ability to fuse a myriad of disciplines and skills into one harmonious direction, balanced with speed of thought, intuition and insightfulness. The ability to predict second and third order effects arising from your own decision (which is more than likely a second order effect of someone else's primary decision) and countering the effect before it comes to fruition is, to me, a little 'sci-fi'. Second and third order effects are mathematical equations, and, in many respects, can be calculated through specific formulas and analysis, but there is no substitute for experience. Education and knowledge tells you which formula would be best suited, but experience will tell you if it's right. The adage that education is knowing a tomato is a fruit, but experience is knowing not to use it in a fruit salad, remains extant.

As the lesson was summarized, there was a feeling of progression in the air. Everyone wanted to command; they joined the Army to be in charge and lead soldiers into battle. Captain Dunn's lesson offered numerous examples of command tools and how they were best utilized. As exciting as it was, it was only theory. It was important not to let the notion of greatness blur the practicalities of command. Command can be lonely and frustrating, and for the military it often results in a heavy heart. There will be very few commanders in today's British Army who have not written a condolence letter to the wife or mother of a soldier under their command; indeed, most will have written many.

Having finished the lesson, the students changed into T-shirts and combat jackets before being marched to the assault course. With its many obstacles, the assault course area was the ideal place to teach the fundamentals of command by participating in command tasks. For many, this would be their first time encountering 'Command Tools', and for most, the realization that theory and practice is a complex mosaic of issues that have few parallels. It is a serious subject, and Major Gray was quick to recognize that for a young man, command can bring unprecedented pressure. To reduce this feeling, the Directing Staff delivered a slapstick demonstration on how not to use command tools, by reenacting some of the funnier moments witnessed on previous courses. Taking charge of a simple command task, Major Gray played commander and narrator, with his Staff playing the role of students. The command task was to scale a 12ft wall.

The OC delivered a poor brief to Private Smith (played by Paddy). He pointed to a lead weight and climbing rope before telling Private Smith to tie the rope to the weight and throw it over the wall. Paddy followed the instructions verbatim. Tying the rope to the heavy weight, it was slung over the obstacle. Major Gray then told everyone else to climb over the wall using the rope. Comically, a fight then broke out when it was discovered that Paddy threw it over the wall along with the weight attached. With Paddy protesting his innocence, explaining that he did exactly as he was told, the rest of the DS challenged Major Gray for control. The whole episode descended into farce, with hilarious consequences.

Intentionally, the OC lost command and control as the DS overacted their parts in the charade. Pat played the school fool and kept trying to pull down everyone's trousers, while Pete went off reservation by pulling out a camping stove and beginning to make tea! The final result was calamitous, culminating in one of the team being pushed into the large fishing lake that dominated the assault course area. During this particular demonstration, it was the turn of Captain Watts to take the plunge. We had rehearsed the stunt the month before the students arrived, and the climax was meant to be spectacular. Enter stage left Captain Watts standing at the edge of the lake waiting for Captain Dunn to execute a 360 turn whilst holding a long plank of wood. With impeccable timing, the plank swung around and knocked Captain Watts somersaulting towards the lake. We paused in anticipation of a huge splash, but he just bounced on the ice and slid for 20 yards. With added comedic value, he then struggled to extract himself off the lake, slipping twice and falling on his face. The whole pretence produced a loud burst of laughter and a minute's applause. It was purposely designed that way, in order to show the students the lighter side of the Rowallan Staff whilst delivering a serious lesson. For the first time during the course, the Staff and students shared a good laugh as Captain Watts complained about back pain and a massive headache whilst bemoaning his inability to get off the lake. Paddy and I then finished the lesson by demonstrating the correct way to execute a command task, while Major Gray narrated the event, this time with a serious tone. Occasionally, he paused the action to highlight crucial areas, common mistakes and good tips for command and control.

Straight after lunch, life was back to normal. Red rugby tops and green denim trousers were donned for physical fitness, with strength and endurance training by virtue of a 7km run. No. 2 Platoon's order of merit was well and truly established in the league of fitness. Moore, Mathews, King and Rideout worked hard enough to avoid catching unwanted attention. At the other end of the spectrum, Haigh, Barns, Danner, Lane, Goldson and Watson began to attract all the DS attention. Occasionally, the 'grey' men would drift into one of the two hot zones. If you were at the rear, you were a 'waster' and took abuse for it. If you were at the front, you were a 'smart ass' and took abuse for that. Boyle, Williams and Witherspoon found small hiding places amongst the faces of other 'grey' men, while Stone was beginning to master the art of DS watching, putting in just enough effort to keep the Staff off his back.

The run included 'fartlek' interval sessions, with the rear runners continuously having to sprint to the front of the squad. With the squad being approximately 25 metres in length and covering 25 metres in distance whilst you ran from rear to front, it was a 50-metre sprint that came around every three minutes. Professionally, fartlek training is tough, but as everyone had come to expect, we gave it an added twist. Canals and water ditches somehow found their way into the session, just to ensure the threshold of misery had been attained. Characteristically, this run finished with a swim through one of the small water catchments at the rear of Academy headquarters. Although the water stretched less than 20 metres, it still required great physical effort to get through it. Hitting the cold water with warm muscles caused contractions and cramp the moment contact was made. Wind chill heightened the intensity of the cold, and 'charley horse' wreaked havoc with the legs once a successful extraction from the water had been made.

Soaking wet and dripping peat mud wherever they went, the students returned to the accommodation. Despite their sorry state, a five-minute time limit was placed on everyone to return, be showered and changed into red tracksuits, carrying their local area map, compass and Belt Order. Major Gray briefly explained that they were about to do a navigation competition. Instinctively, we could see this took the students by surprise. They assumed that there had been as much running as was possible in one day. The OC started off by reading out the inter-platoon score, which was currently six points to zero in favour of No. 1 Platoon. With his sinister grin, he reminded everyone of the consequences of coming second and handed the course over to Colour Sergeant Edwards.

Colour Sergeant Edwards, or Eddie as he was known, was in charge of organizing military skills competitions. His daytime job was to provide the Row-Co DS with key support and ease the burden by sharing the administration and logistic duties. Most importantly, it was his responsibility to organize all Navigation Training, tests and assessments for the duration of the course. With the students on parade, he issued the rules of the competition. The route was over 8km long, most of which would be cross-country, avoiding tracks and roads. The scoring system was simple: the more checkpoints you visited, the more points you scored. There were ten checkpoints to visit in total and a time limit of two hours and thirty minutes to achieve it. Students were dispatched at random, and at intervals of two minutes. One hour after the start, the complete course was out searching for checkpoints. For some of them it was to be a test of stamina, for others a lesson in poor advanced preparation. Darkness falls quickly during the late days of January and early February, and most of the students would have failed to consider this prior to setting off. As the first runners began to return to the control tent, darkness had descended. Six of Paddy's students had returned before the first of my platoon made it back to camp. Rideout had returned, having collected all the required checkpoints and with twenty minutes to spare. He had done brilliantly, the first student to make all the checkpoints and arrive back in time. Elation was creeping in as we learnt that Paddy's students had incurred penalty points for being over the allotted time. Rideout stood to attention in front of Colour Sergeant Edwards at the finish point.

'Let's have your control card then, Rideout.'

With a great sense of achievement, Rideout offered Eddie his card. He was still breathing hard and soaked in a mixture of damp and sweat as he waited for his final score. His card was closely inspected, ensuring he had collected all the checkpoints.

'Gaz, do you want to have a quick check of this?' Surprised by the invitation, I took the control card off Eddie and looked hard for missed checkpoints.

'Looks good to me, Eddie?'

'Well, he's got all the checkpoints, Gaz, and his time is outstanding, but he has punched his card in the wrong place for eight of his checkpoints. It was explained in my brief at the start.'

A second look at the card to see how wrong Rideout had got it confirmed Eddie's comments.

'So, Rideout, tell me this: when you got to checkpoint one, why did you clip your control card in the box marked checkpoint five?'

Rideout looked at me in total disbelief.

'Answer me then, softlad'

There was no answer to give. A quivering lip and a huge frown said all that was needed. My elation evaporated as it dawned on me that my platoon was about to get another thrashing, and I immediately took it out on Rideout.

'Did you think this was a game of Where's Wally? What was the reason for stamping your card like it was a bar-chit? Answer me, fuck-wit. How on earth did you get that simple task wrong?'

'Lack of application, Colour Sergeant.'

'Application my arse. What a lot of crap. You can start running around Chapel Square until you can apply a better answer. Get going!' My voice got louder and louder, advertising my anxiety as he started to jog away.

Rideout set off totally dejected, running around Chapel Square. Each lap would take him more than three minutes. He never once blinked or looked in the direction of the control tent as he completed lap after lap of his punishment, watching everyone else disappear for a shower. Thirty minutes later, the majority of the students had returned. Eddie would remove their cards and inspect them before issuing a score. I was getting nervous and agitated as he locked himself away to do his sums.

'How are my lads looking, Eddie?'

'Well, I would say it was about neck and neck. It will all depend on the last runners. But you know, it is likely to come down to Rideout failing to hit the correct punch holes on his control card!'

I took a jog out to the training area with the view to encouraging the stragglers. At the entrance, my attention was drawn to a small stash of discarded military equipment that clearly belonged to a Row-Co student. 'Belt Order' contained a water bottle plus a utility pouch with basic first aid kit and emergency rations. Its total weight was probably less than 6lb, but a student would find it cumbersome. Ditching it would relieve the wearer of the annoying water bottle that constantly chafed the waist. Each item on the belt would be marked with the name and the regimental number of its owner, but to my amazement, the name on the belt was not one of my students. Maybe it belonged to a student on a different course. Placing it back down where it was found, my attention turned back to searching for stragglers. But just before leaving the back gate and heading out to the first checkpoint, another abandoned Belt Order caught my eye. This time the name on it was 'Francis', in large black letters. This was hugely disappointing. Carefully, the belt was replaced where it was found, and I carried on chasing the last runners.

Having done as much as possible, it was time to return to the control tent and wait for Francis. Eventually, he appeared, puffing and panting and covered in sweat and brambles. Francis handed in his scorecard, but before he was issued his tally, I dragged him out of earshot of everyone else.

'Francis, tell me. What do you carry in your Belt Order?' The fatigued look on his face was replaced by that of a guilty expression.

'Water, food and a first aid kit, Colour Sergeant.'

'Good start, Francis. Now explain why we carry them?'

'In case of an emergency, Colour Sergeant?'

'Very good so far. So, something like an urgent need for a first aid kit! Urgent need for water! With that in mind, would it be stupid to abandon this equipment whilst running around a dangerous training area littered with trip hazards, unexploded pyrotechnics etc?'

Like all students when confronted by such a blunt question, Francis failed to answer. Conveniently, Rideout was just passing me, having done more laps of Chapel Square than he should have. Without a second thought, I stopped Rideout and instructed Francis to take his place running around the square until he was told to stop. Chapel Square was over-watched by the control tent, so we would keep an eye on him as we analysed the scores, but between Francis and Rideout, they had taken me to the point of depression.

'Rideout!' I screamed, and out of the student accommodation he appeared. Having calmed down, he needed to hear a considered response to what went wrong:

> 'Thirty minutes spent running around Chapel Square is thirty minutes of sleep you have just lost. You need to concentrate harder, Rideout. If you want to make the grade, listen more than you talk. Tonight, contemplate the qualities of a good leader. Slow yourself down. In your mind, you must tell yourself that you are susceptible to errors when you try and do things quickly. You must be more considered in everything you do.'

Rideout made for the shower, while the DS gathered at the control point.

'Hey Eddie, have you finalized the scores yet?' I enquired.

'No, Gaz, there is a bit of a problem working out the average run time. Can you give me a hand please, buddy?'

For the next twenty minutes, we worked the calculators hard until we came up with the final results. It was very close; our running time was faster than Paddy's platoon, but several of our scorecards had been incorrectly marked. Eddie read out the final scores as we sat in the office drinking coffee. It was odd that only my students marked the cards wrongly, but everyone attended the same brief. Eddie explained that he mentioned it and couldn't understand why it was just No. 2 Platoon who got it wrong. He handed me the script, and there it was in black and white. Hidden amongst the blurb of the marking system and mathematical equations for average run times was the statement, 'incorrect punching of control cards will be marked with zero'.

Upset that we had been beaten on a technicality, and aware that the gap on the scoreboard had now reached the embarrassing total of nine points, my train of thought lost its way. Driven to distraction, my uniform was pressed to within an inch of its life during kit preparation. Busying myself with tedious work such as file updates and exercise instructions helped to ease the pain of the loss. Still sulking in my room, Pat appeared at my door, dripping wet.

'Ah, Gaz. Absolutely marvellous, buddy. Good to see you have finally settled into the Rowallan spirit of punishment by running your students into the ground in the pissing rain. Love it – welcome aboard.'

Pat had been out running with the OC. They both enjoyed their fitness, and training with raw recruits didn't satisfy their appetite. Although the quantity of fitness the students endured outnumbered that of the Commissioning Course, it was still well below that of a highly motivated and accomplished officer or soldier.

To avoid the loss of personal fitness standards, they sometimes enjoyed two or three sessions a day. On the odd occasion, they would use Rowallan activities as an opportunity to do more fitness, and the navigation exercise had done just that.

'What do you mean, Sir?' I asked, thinking a reprimand was afoot.

'Ha, like you don't know! One of your students is running around the square outside, and he's collected a sizeable audience. He was there when we left over an hour ago. He must have really pissed you off!'

'Oh my God! Francis! Bloody hell, he's been out there for way over an hour and a half.'

Pat giggled ominously as I walked out to Chapel Square, trying to remain cool and calculated in a pathetic effort to mask the fact that I had forgotten about Francis running around the square.

Francis was on his chinstrap – totally exhausted. Too tired to run, it was more a shuffle or an exaggerated forward lean to force his feet to keep moving. The young man deserved an apology, but that would compromise my 'heartless instructor' persona. Several young officer cadets were gawking out of windows at Francis as he completed lap after lap. In an effort to fool Francis that it was all part of the punishment, I stood in the centre of the square, arms clasped behind my back in classic Prince Charles fashion and watched him awkwardly chugging around the square.

'Don't slow down, Francis, or you will stay here all night.'

Francis was too tired to answer me; too tired even to look at me. One lap later and his pains were brought to a halt.

'Francis, go and stand outside my office and think about what you want to say to me.' Hunchbacked and gingerly wriggling his feet outside my office, his soaking wet clothes clinging to him, he was the epitome of dejection.

'Can you explain why you discarded your Belt Order on the training area, softlad?'

'Yes, Colour Sergeant, it was down to my naivety and my desire to do well. I thought I could run faster by leaving it behind, but in retrospect, my thoughts were poorly judged.'

Although Francis was yet to learn how to balance risk versus reward, his assessment made sense and the fact he knew he got it wrong was very promising, but this was a lesson for another day.

'Yes, you have got that right, softlad, naive is apt. What makes it worse is the fact that you have punched the wrong holes on your scorecard, and as a result you have been disqualified, causing the platoon to lose the competition.'

Francis' face began to contort, and for a brief moment it looked like he would burst into tears. Unexpectedly, he broke out into raucous laughter. Under normal circumstances, this would have me doing backflips in anger, but after what Francis had been through, I calmly asked him to explain his actions.

'If I didn't laugh I would cry,' he giggled further.

It was Francis' first self-taught lesson of gallows humour, the fuel that keeps soldiers going during their dark hours. Several times in a soldier's career, he will be faced with overwhelming odds. The crucial ingredient in managing insurmountable odds lies deep within an individual's attitude. I laughed with Francis for a short while and reminded him of a phrase that soldiers often use: 'Laugh, and the world laughs with you. Cry, and you'll shrink your face because no one gives a shit!'

After a short break for evening meal, the course assembled in one of the Academy's many theatres to take part in a debate. For Sandhurst students, debates are used as the vehicle for a cerebral stretch, helping them to view tough, persistent and wicked problems through conflicting lenses. Additionally, they are a clever way of placing students in awkward academic situations, in order to see how their mind thinks. Are they group thinkers? Do they think in isolation or are they completely random? The first of many debates was led by the Company's academic tutor. Professor Emily Lee was typical of those who lived in 'Far-Away Hall': incredibly bright, but a little distant when it came to idle chat. Petite, slim and always dressed in black, she gave the impression of a lady who secretly enjoyed a conga at the local disco. She challenged Danner, and his Etonian heritage, to defend state schools and the low achievements recently reported in the news. Simultaneously, she invited Boyle, with his state school certificates, to argue that elitism is the only way to ensure we don't dumb down education or accidentally drift into Marxism. Both individuals launched scathing attacks on the opposite institution, sparking a violently contested debate. It was a work of masterful intellect by Professor Emily. Having previously said very little, the platoon was in full meltdown contesting each other's views.

At first glance, Sandhurst debates appeared meaningless. Full of hot air, there was a suspicion that they were only there to fill the programme. As an NCO, it took me some time to understand the value of constructing a coherent argument in order to articulate an effective viewpoint. Faraday Hall used multifaceted and contentious scenarios, packed with emotion, to replicate similar conundrums likely to challenge a young officer in a politically charged environment. Supporting controversial policies that one may not wholeheartedly believe in, whilst remaining sufficiently motivated to convince and lead subordinates, needs to be nurtured. In conflict, it is easy to lose faith in the chain of command and politicians alike, so prudence demands the Officer Corps practise the art of managing tensions and removing the emotions when most vulnerable.

The debating exercise finished at 2000hrs and had been an enormous success. Danner, incredulous having lost the argument, learnt the importance of dispassionate logic, conviction and concise delivery. Boyle, despite having won the majority of votes, failed to remain composed when confronted by provocative statements. He realized that swearing and arguing more loudly than his opponent did little more than dissuade the audience from believing in his leadership. The students were feeling euphoric, buzzing with energy retained from the boisterous exchanges. It had not gone unnoticed that they all enjoyed the company of an attractive professor, who had skilfully manipulated the debate to retain momentum and tempo. There was plenty of chatter amongst the ranks as they marched back from 'Far-away Hall'. The hum of enthusiasm quickly disappeared as we marched beyond the front door and down the side street to the home of the Mean Machine and I told them:.

> 'Well, it will come as no surprise to everyone that we lost the Navigation Competition. We are now three competitions without a win, that's nine points to zero, for those struggling with the maths. And you all know the penalty for failure. You have two minutes to get changed into your red rugby tops and be back out here ready for a session of punishment PT.'

One of the principles of war is the maintenance of morale. It was evident that this punishment was screaming this principle at me. The issue of morale is a tricky subject to master. Like most things, it is all about balance, perception and understanding. Whilst guiding a scuba diving expedition to the South of France, I recall a number of soldiers telling me morale was low. Furthermore, the disgruntled group informed me, it was all down to my decision to ban drinking alcohol before the evening meal. Sitting on a beautiful beach in Cannes, surrounded by half-naked bronzed goddesses and enjoying the warm water of the French Riviera, the issue was not one of morale; it was one of discipline. The answer was education on why discipline needs to be enforced; sometimes it is done to save people from themselves. This is where command can become lonely. An international incident would make the headlines if a drunken soldier died on the French Riviera. Loose women, cheap booze, global terrorism and organized crime hid around every corner. It was only me who understood the consequences of mixing so many volatile scenarios in an international setting. Many members of the expedition refused to talk to me for the rest of the trip. It would take a further three years for the lead protagonists to confess they got it wrong, but only after they suffered similar experiences as they ascended through the appointments of command.

With a session on the Mean Machine pending, I could see morale was about to come crashing down. This punishment needed to be tempered with emotional intelligence, with one eye on what lay ahead. There was little explanation required. The platoon knew the consequences of coming last. They quietly made their way to their respective start positions before enduring the punishment without complaint. Standing under the glow of the orange street lights, there was little sense in labouring the point one more time. As the session came to an end, the students quietly dispersed, and it was time for me to take my rest back in the Sergeants' Mess.

It felt like a microsecond before the alarm clock had me awake and back at work. With the DS gathered outside the Company Quartermaster's stores, just out of sight of the accommodation, it was 0500hrs on the second Friday of the course. Major Gray's brief was short and simple. Emphasizing the lessons learnt from the practice bugout, it was stressed that there would be no return to the accommodation to retrieve forgotten equipment. It was essential that, during the confusion caused by the bugout, we all stress the need for students to deploy fully equipped. With a tired grin and a subdued rub of his hands, the OC dispatched his staff to unleash merry hell on the sleeping students.

With nothing else said, Paddy and I burst into the accommodation and set about evicting students from their rooms. Rapidly moving from room to room, I swung open each door and screamed at the sleeping occupants: 'Bugout! Get outside now! Gather your kit. Make sure you have it all. Maps! Rations! Waterproofs!'

Three or four rooms later, the remainder of the students had heard the commotion and started to leave the building. Outside the main entrance, Captain Dunn received everyone and set them out ready for a 'Type A' field inspection. By 0530hrs, most of the students were busy doing names as a punishment for forgetting items of equipment, only this time the quantity issued was much greater than previously.

Long before the rest of the Academy heard reveille, Rowallan Company were walking out to the training area. Carrying their rucksacks, dressed in full marching kit, the Company eased out of the camp in single file. Like one large snake half a kilometre long, slowly cutting its way through an urban melee, we passed each of the historic buildings en route to the back gate. The walk to our destination was 5km in total, just long enough to test the stamina of most students. After less than 2km, the line became broken as gaps appeared between the fit and the unfit. It was the usual suspects at the rear: Barns, Haigh, Stone, Lane and Goldson. Disappointed and increasingly frustrated by the fact that nearly all the students at the rear belonged to me, my fuse began to burn quickly. Putting my hands on the back of their rucksacks, I pushed Barns and Haigh alternately to keep them from falling too far behind. They responded by increasing their effort for a short distance, so I switched to Stone and Goldson, both of whom rejected my positive encouragement. The Platoon Commander berated Packman and Williams, who idled behind Danner, who was already soaked in sweat.

'Williams, what are you doing back here?' he asked. Williams blurted a few jumbled words with no great conviction. The boss then grabbed hold of his arm and began to pull him at a faster pace, and for a short while Williams kept up.

Francis was just drifting towards the rear. A short, sharp shove from Eddie and he increased his pace to stay out of our reach. At the finish point, Pat was busy issuing press-ups to those who had stayed the distance at his pace, emphasizing his 'no resting' policy.

'How many behind you, Gaz?' Pat asked.

'About three or four.'

'Was anyone on the Jack Wagon?'

'No. At least not while I was chasing up the stragglers.'

The tail-enders began to appear, firstly Barns, who was obviously trying but wasn't achieving anything much above the minimum. Haigh followed closely behind, and in the distance was Goldson. Looking bored and showing no signs of trying, Goldson reached the finish. Pat summoned Goldson and asked him to explain why he was nearly ten minutes behind everyone else. Unhappy with the answer, Pat delivered a tongue lashing followed swiftly by an extra physical fitness training session in a one-to-one environment. Onlookers grimaced at Goldson's ordeal. Pat wasn't impressed by Goldson's contribution, and typically widened the search for a reaction.

'Everybody join in. Press-up position, down! Twenty press-ups to Goldson's timings! Shout them out, tough guy. And if they're not good enough, it will be another twenty.' Pat looked to incentivize Goldson through guilt and peer pressure. Effective and brutally efficient, Goldson tried much harder.

The Jack Wagon appeared as Goldson played master of ceremonies for the press-ups. We weren't expecting to see anyone on board, so it caught us all by surprise when Stone stepped off the back. Still wearing a stupid smug grin on his face, he walked towards his fellow students. Captain Dunn and I watched from a distance. Stone showed no obvious signs of an injury, which made everyone even more baffled as to his need to board the wagon. Danner immediately began to accuse him of malingering, to which Stone offered little defence. As tensions began to rise between the pair, I summoned Stone to come and explain his problem. Our presence caught him off-guard, and suddenly he developed a limp.

'Why did you get on the Jack Wagon, Stone?' I demanded.

'I've pulled my hamstring.'

'Wow, you are multi-talented. I didn't know you were a qualified doctor. Does this injury come and go at random, or is it consistent?'

'It's consistent!'

'Does it affect your manners.'

'No,' he replied, with a puzzled look.

'If that's the case, the next time you address me, use my rank. Secondly, how come you have only just started to limp?'

'I haven't, Colour Sergeant. I've been limping all the time.'

Not keen to get into an argument with the lad, he was dispatched to see a medic before Captain Dunn and I discussed Stone's integrity. We both felt he was lying, but proving it would be impossible. The medic was duty-bound to believe Stone's complaint. Two days of light duties issued by the medic was the solution, which prohibited him from taking any further part in the exercise. If it wasn't for the guppy-faced grin, we may have believed him, but he had previous and it was now affecting our judgment.

At the edge of a large wood on the training area, the students were introduced to the skills of living in the field and surviving on the contents of their rucksacks. Life-sustainment skills such as building shelters and cooking rations played second fiddle to the main events of the morning: pre-training for command tasks. In order to succeed with most command tasks during the course, the students needed to learn a plethora of rope skills, including how to make a safety harness using a small rope. Critically, they were also required to practise building an aerial ropeway using an 'A-Frame'. Finally, we introduced everyone to the fundamentals of mechanical advantage: pulley wheels, parbuckles and cantilevers would all be central to the success of the more complex task.

With the fundamentals of rope skills and 'A-frames' out of the way, we concentrated on building character and trust amongst the platoon, using an old-school Special Forces technique. In an unorthodox fashion, the Staff delivered an exercise designed to heighten senses, intuition and trust. Uniquely, stretching a student out of his comfort zone in unusual ways helped to sharpen his speed of thought. With the students gathered into a tight circle, we instructed them to remove the balaclava from their rucksacks. Haigh's curiosity was mounting. We instructed the platoon to place their balaclavas on their heads, with the opening to the rear, and to pull the hood of their jacket high up over their head. Captain Dunn and I then wrapped thick black masking tape around the area of the eyes to guarantee that the student couldn't see a shred of light. Conditions were set. Vision was denied, just as it would be if you were a Platoon Commander in war, waiting patiently for friendly forces to assault an enemy position. The mind has to work at double speed. Calculating risk and pre-empting mistakes before they lead to failure are a job requirement only a military commander has to meet.

For the next hour, we silently manhandled and frogmarched the students for 10 or 20 metres in different directions in order to disorientate and confuse their senses. Additionally, they would be placed into low-level stress positions, to frustrate, tire and elevate their agitation. The whole event was executed by hand signals to give the student no indication of what was happening. When conditions were met, and the students processed sufficiently, we placed everyone onto a 4-ton truck. The silence was only broken as the tailgate of the vehicle was slammed shut, and Captain Dunn offered me warm clothing for the long journey whilst I was sitting on the truck with the platoon. It was, of course, a bluff; I never got on the back of the truck. In yet another effort to confuse the students, the vehicle was then driven out of the Academy gates and on to the M3 motorway. The sounds of motorway traffic would give the perception of a long journey. After 10 miles it returned to the Academy assault course via the rear dirt track, close to the beagle kennels. For the whole duration, the students remained sitting on the floor of the vehicle, hands on heads, in total silence.

After the elaborate charade, we arrived at the assault course less than a kilometre from their accommodation. The students were carefully debussed from the vehicle, then fitted into a climbing harness and clipped onto a thick guide rope. Still in total silence, we needed to keep the students guessing as to their destiny. Slowly, they were manhandled into a long queue waiting to be guided through the Rowallan 'confidence course'. Exclusive to Row-Co, the course was like nothing else ever seen at Sandhurst. It was full of unusual obstacles and designed to challenge your mental strength, not your physicality. The rope was taut and travelled at waist height. It passed through, round or over most of the obstacles on the assault course before leading to the confidence obstacles constructed by Eddie and Pete. With the illusion set and the students fooled into thinking they had been shipped out to somewhere unfamiliar, instructions were whispered to one person at a time. He was told to follow the rope wherever it took him. Additionally, he was told he would encounter a few obstacles that should be negotiated without hesitation. To intensify pressure, the student was warned that if he stood still for more than five seconds, an electric shock from a cattle prodder would be used to encourage quicker movement.

The by-product of this short exercise was two-fold. Firstly, it would give the DS an understanding of how confident someone truly was. Secondly, it was a crafty opportunity to balance out the hierarchical order of merit within the platoon. Thus far, those who had been part of UOTC would have experienced some military training and understand the requirement we were searching for. But this kind of exercise was reserved for specialists, and it was unlikely anyone would have previous experience. This created a level playing field. What the DS was hoping to see was the uninhibited emotions of those who had so far kept their nerve. Row-Co was only useful if it exposed the true character of the participant. If the events on the course were timid and easy, people would bluff their way through, undermining the concept. Of all the exercises on the course, this was possibly the most informative for the DS.

Standing at the start of what was euphemistically called the 'confidence course', the picture was bizarre. Over thirty people, hooded and blindfolded, silently stood in a straight line waiting anxiously to learn what lay ahead. Fixed to the rope by his harness, no student would ever be in any danger. Fear would be self-generated, and it is the management of this irrational fear that is critical to a commander's learning. To ensure safety, a member of the Staff accompanied everyone who undertook the event. Predominantly, this was to keep up the pretence that the student remained in a dangerous predicament. The key to the success of this event was to maintain the illusion of a hazardous situation so the DS could analyse behaviour under stress. Disorientation on its own was sufficient to bring an individual's fears to the surface; add it to the rest of the charade, and most were at breaking point before they even stepped off.

First in line was King. It was possible that as a former soldier, he may have experienced something similar in the past. If it appeared that he was managing to cope with ease, it was my intention to increase the fear factor. After checking the security of his harness, he was issued a brief and instructed to walk the course. Nervously, King eased himself forward, guided by the rope. He reached the first obstruction after two minutes of ghost walking and set about feeling its shape and size. High anxiety seeped from under his hood as he worked hard to identify the obstacle. King could feel the outline of a large round opening, but couldn't interpret what it was. I placed my hand on his head and guided him into a drainage tunnel. After a short while, he figured it out and began to feel his way through the concrete tube. A gentle trickle of water hinted at what lay ahead. He reappeared at the far end and stopped in the mouth of the exit, unable to feel the floor, walls or roof ahead of him. His senses were working overtime to identify his surroundings. Below him was a water catchment full of freezing water. Having failed to make contact with any hard surface at the end of the cylindrical concrete obstacle where the rope went slack, King knew where he was. Holding on to his nose, he leapt feet-first into the water. Soaked to the skin and covered in mud, panting quickly in reaction to the freezing temperature, King had impressed me. Even if he had experienced this before, that leap of faith affirmed his trust and commitment.

Next, the rope guided him alongside a large kitchen table. It was manned by two Gurkha soldiers, who spoke forcefully in their native tongue. Close-up and personal, they set about King trying to intimidate him. One of the Gurkhas gripped his hands and prevented him from moving, while the other lifted the front of his balaclava and force-fed him herbs, peppers and spicy vegetables. In broken English, one said, 'You like cockroach! You like cockroach? Swallow cockroach, swallow. I say swallow, you swallow. Swallow!'

With a small chunk of potato and herbs cut in the shape of a cockroach shoved into King's mouth, the Gurkhas held onto his nose until he swallowed the offering. King opened his mouth to show it was free of food.

'Good. You drink. You drink now!' Homemade alcoholic drink similar to poteen was poured into his mouth. King refused to swallow it, and the Gurkhas became physically forceful until he obliged.

Released by the Gurkhas, King followed the beaten track whilst feverishly gripping the guide rope. By now the young student was ready for almost anything.

You could see the confidence growing as he adjusted to the surroundings. The rope guided him through a group of suspended tractor tyres and across a few small streams, eventually arriving at the first of his major tests of confidence. With my hand gripping the forearm of King, we walked onto a small irrigation dam wall. The dam controlled the water levels between the main lake and a large tributary. Slightly elevated, the top of the wall was approximately 2ft above the main lake and 4ft above the river it filled. The wall was 4ft wide and 6ft long. To retain a sense of peril, a plank 8 inches wide and 10ft long was placed on bricks and laid over the wall, with the final 6ft straddled by crash mats and soft ground. As King mounted the plank, he was told that it was a narrow high bridge. There was a long fall to his left, so if he felt that he might fall off the bridge, he should dive to the right, where the water was deep enough to break his fall. In a further effort to give credit to the charade, his belt was unclipped from the guide rope and he was told it was too dangerous to stay clipped in at such a height.

Easing forward 6 inches, his toes tentatively felt for the perimeter of his new boundaries. Poised precariously at the start of the plank, King waved his hands around, searching for something to grab hold of. The deception was working brilliantly; he was showing signs of nerves. You could tell by his body language that he was full of fear, but working hard to contain it. I walked alongside him on the dam wall. It took an age for the lad to reach the middle of the crossing. Standing level with him, I paused his progress and moved his arms into the crucifix position. A stone was placed in his right hand.

'Drop the stone and listen,' I whispered in his ear. Listening intently, the stone was released. But with my hands cupped just below his, it fell into my grasp. One second later it was allowed to continue its fall. The time lapse between drop and splash contrived to give the impression that he was high above the water. If there was any doubt before, King was now convinced he was high up on a narrow plank, with nothing but water below. A combination of the wind thrashing at the trees and the water rushing over the flood gate of the dam contrived to give the moment a menacing feel. Notably, this had affected King as he began to mumble before he continued to edge forward.

The end of the plank approached, and the final stage of this confidence challenge was put into action. As he was feeling for the end of the plank, one of the supporting staff brushed his left side with a large branch to knock King off balance. A combination of surprise, shock and fear saw the student pirouette sharply, trying to maintain his balance. At that very moment, the safety rope was dragged across the right of his body, causing him to topple to the left. Under the impression he needed to fall to the right, King frantically grabbed and flapped at the rope, trying to prevent himself from falling left. At the point of no return, King let out an ear-piercing scream in anticipation of what he thought would be a long fall. After just 6 inches, he hit the ground, landing smack bang in the centre of the crash mat. To stifled laughter and giggling, he rolled off the matt and onto soft thick moss. Instantly, he realized he had been duped and broke into a chorus of cursing and swearing, not holding back his feelings. While the student picked himself up and dusted himself off, the Staff struggled to maintain their silence, holding back the laughter. I fixed King back on to the guide rope, patted him on the back, gave faint praise and told him to continue following the rope.

The final test of confidence stretched over 100 metres. Terrifying and bordering on torture, this stunt was as cruel as it was ingenious. A member of the Directing Staff stood poised to stop the student 100 metres short of the finish line. Breaking the strict code of silence, the DS would pretend that the safety vehicle had run out of fuel. It would then be explained that, for safety reasons, it needed to be refuelled before he could proceed. Saying nothing more, a metal jerry can of petrol was opened in close proximity to the student. With his senses heightened, clean water would be splashed over his legs and an empty jerry can dropped to the floor. Frantically apologizing, the Staff claimed the can fell off the tailgate of the Land Rover. All the time, a small rag soaked in petrol was kept close to the nose of the student. Deprived of sight, legs dripping wet and nostrils flooded with the smell of petrol, the illusion was set. The final part of the deception was to start the Rover and rev it loudly, signalling the all-clear for the student to continue on his way.

A number of easy obstacles would then be encountered: stepping stones, under-over hurdles and a long wooden maze complete with dead ends. At the exit point of the maze, the unmistakable crackling noise of a large fire could be heard. The guide rope ran towards the centre of the crackling, as the smoke wafted over the student. On the far side, the Company Sergeant Major would take control. Shouting to the student to run fast and not stop, Pat would repeatedly scream at him 'prepare to jump'. Whilst the rope never ran near the fire, the student would be absolutely convinced that he was doused in petrol and being told to leap over a fire.

King cautiously approached the Sergeant Major. He could sense the heat getting greater and hear the spitting and cracking of damp wood burning. 'Spider senses' tingling, he eventually came to a halt. Shaking his head, he refused to continue.

'Are you fucking mad or what? I am covered in petrol! I am not jumping anywhere.'

Pat calmed the student. This considered, passive demeanour was a huge change from the angry disciplinarian the intake had come to fear. 'Trust me, fella! Keep your speed high, don't stop, and jump with all your strength when I shout "jump".'

It was a perfect piece of psychological manipulation. Would King trust the Sergeant Major, the course, the Army? Or would he flatly refuse?

With a quick word of encouragement and a gentle shove from me, King was sent running and screaming in the direction of the flames. Goose-stepping and kicking his legs high in the air to avoid prolonged contact with the fire, he was desperate to hear the command 'jump'. But the instruction was never going to be delivered, and King would have to decide to keep running or jump when he felt the urge. Combining all options, he invented a skip-jump-run motion that had Pat in stitches with laughter. Less than five seconds after King had done his first skip-cum-jump, Pat reverted to his angry self and bombarded King with insults. As if he was intentionally trying to add to the comedy moment, King replied in kind, swearing and repeating his obscenities with each skip and jump. His insults were tolerated by Pat, who was quietly impressed by King's attitude.

After King had covered 20 metres, Pete, the CQMS, rugby-tackled him to the ground to avoid a collision with the post holding the end of the guide rope. Quickly, Pete ripped off the balaclava and calm descended in an instant. King scanned the area to see where the fire was. Promptly, he discovered that there was some distance between him and the danger. The whole thing was a confidence trick which had started way back when he was doused in water. He felt his legs and smelt his hand, then began to laugh.

'Well done, King, you wuss,' growled Pat. It was a welcome insult for the experienced student. Pat rarely handed out praise, and if it came with an insult, that would be good enough. Wearing a huge smile on his face, King was left to bemoan, reminisce and rejoice while I returned to the start line and collected another student.

Making my way back along the route to the start, the exercise was in full flow. Accompanied by a member of the DS, students were spaced out at intervals of approximately 20 metres. Attached to the never-ending rope by their harnesses, few were enjoying the experience. Eddie was guiding Goldson, who was encountering great problems. Twice he ripped off his balaclava and refused to tackle the obstacles. Each time he tore off his mask, the obstruction was compromised and the illusion defused. This allowed him the opportunity to view the problem and negotiate it without induced fear or concern. During the plank walk, he broke down and refused to soldier on. After some tactful encouragement from Eddie, his determination to hold onto the rope for so long spoilt the illusion. He was attracting a lot of bad press, and this behaviour was making him an easy target for ridicule. The intensity of his complaining was greater than we had come to expect. Possibly a mental blockage or a subconscious decision to distrust the Staff, the concerns for Goldson mounted.

Witherspoon, on the other hand, surprised everyone. Captain Dunn was guiding him around. He had expected the lad to be full of fear and trepidation, but remarkably, he flew through the course showing no signs of nerves. Amazingly, as he was pushed from the plank, he tried to perform a swallow dive because the boss had convinced him he was 10ft in the air. Captain Dunn nearly wet himself laughing as the hooded figure landed head first on the crash mat. To Pat's annoyance, he gently jogged past the last obstacle as if there was no threat of catching fire. As Pat launched into a tirade of abuse, accusing Witherspoon of being able to see through his blindfold, the student disarmed Pat and explained the confidence trick was fundamentally flawed. He said when the Land Rover was started up, confirming it was safe to continue, it was clearly a diesel engine. It made no sense to be carrying petrol in a vehicle that used diesel. The attempt to fool everyone of a refuel had been compromised by the wrong fuel. If nothing else, we had identified a strength in Witherspoon: he could think straight under pressure. He could be analytical and capable of logical assessments, able to block out misplaced information. Even Pat was impressed, so much so that he gave Eddie a slagging down for not noticing it during the rehearsals. At the end of the exercise, the students were given a piece of A4 paper and told to describe their experiences. Moore wrote only two words on his sheet: 'Totally violated!'

Before the exercise, the boss reminded me of those we identified as needing a lift in confidence: Francis, Williams, Witherspoon, Rideout, Barns and Lane. Their journey through the course was micromanaged so we could work on building their self-assurance. Whilst other members of the Staff guided students around the circuit, only myself or the boss would guide these individuals. Conversely, the tougher students and more confident characters – Mathews, Boyle, Moore and Packman – were all given a rough ride, with every event extended and exaggerated for maximum impact. Much of this was amateur psychology and dramatics, derived from a wealth of understanding how people and soldiers think. We sought to employ a simple piece of reverse psychology, knowing that the students would swap stories at the earliest opportunity. They would be keen to measure their own performance against that of their peers. During these conversations, the strong characters would talk about how frightened they had been during a particular event, or how hard they found it. By a process of self-analysis, the weaker character would assume he had been dealt the same treatment and would believe he had coped with the ordeal better than the stronger personalities. From this, his confidence would grow and the gap between the respective groups would narrow. Of course, it was understood by the Staff that this was no panacea for the multifaceted problem of developing young commanders, but it did provide the foundations from which we could begin.

The evening appeared to arrive early, offering the chance to begin the night-time events sooner than scheduled. Colour Sergeant Edwards had set out a simple night-time orienteering course that covered 3km. The main idea was to give the student a taste of map reading by night. The temperature had plummeted as Eddie set the students off in a fashion they had now become familiar with – scorecards, set times and regular intervals. It was gone midnight as the final student completed the course. Predictably, this was not the end to their day. Military officers must think clearly, even when exhausted and hungry, and always be ready for an additional task. There is only one way to learn how to develop this skill, and that is to practise it. So once a student had completed the orienteering, he was given map coordinates to his sleeping location and told to navigate his way home. In amongst this order was the instruction to be ready for a 'Type A' field inspection by 0555hrs the following morning. After he had verified the location with the supporting Staff and drawn up a route card which would be checked, the student was left to his own devices to survive the night unaided. With the exception of Stone, that is, who was wrapped up warm and snoring in a sleeping bag next to the Jack Wagon, enjoying the benefits of a sick chit!

It seemed 0500hrs arrived seconds after my eyes had closed. With it came the worst of the February weather. Ice had formed on my sleeping bag, mainly produced by the moisture rising from my damp clothes. A wimpish peek from the comfort of my four seasons North Face cocoon and Barossa looked like a winter wonderland. Yesterday's sleet and snow had frozen solid and been topped with a dollop of fresh snow. Branches on the surrounding trees drooped with icicles, reflecting the dawn light spreading quickly across a clear sky. Eddie was already up, cooking breakfast on the tailgate of the Land Rover. In small training teams like ours, it was usually the role of the supporting Colour Sergeant to provide luxuries such as endless brews, bacon butties and occasionally breakfast.

'Morning, Gaz! Fancy some sausage and beans before we go down and do the field inspection?' Every word from Eddie's mouth was accompanied by a cloud of mist as his warm breath mixed with the sub-zero temperature, further dissuading my desire to crack open the seal of my sleeping bag on such a bitterly cold morning! Clutching a plastic mug of black coffee made by Eddie, I wriggled from the comfort of my sleeping system and sat on the back of the Land Rover. The gas stove, still gushing heat, seemed a nice place to start my day. It wasn't long before Paddy joined our huddle in the rear of the vehicle, all of us making small talk about how cold the night had been.

'I don't know about you two, but there was no sleep to be taken last night. I woke up every thirty minutes or so shivering. Disappointed in my arctic sleeping bag, that's for sure!'

Not yet fully awake, I just nodded in agreement to Paddy's remarks. A lack of sleep and limited blood circulating around my body suppressed my response. Eddie dished out the boil-in-the-bag breakfast, and all three of us squeezed into the rear of the vehicle and ate our rapidly cooling sausage and beans. It looked as if we had all been out on the town for a week. The lack of blood near the extremities gave us the appearance of the walking dead. Huddled in the rear of the Land Rover, faces rubberized and pillow-marked, it didn't feel like we were the backbone of this elite Academy.

In the distance, we could hear a faint humming noise. Intermittent and mechanical, it was familiar.

'Paddy, can you hear that noise?' Paddy stopped eating so that he could concentrate on the distant humming.

'I do, Gaz, I hear it like; it's no something I recognize though.'

For a moment, all three of us concentrated on the noise, a low humming that peeked and dipped at irregular intervals. It had to be something to do with the military because it was on the training area, but it truly baffled us all. Muffled, chainsaw-like, it was being manually handled. As quick as it started, it stopped, and the echo fell silent, allowing us to get on with the start of the day.

Paddy and I walked down to the concentration area, where the students had spent the night under their bashers. The distance wasn't great; depending on the route, it was less than a kilometre. From a distance of about 50 metres, we were pleasantly surprised to see that the students had complied with our directions. On a track junction, in the centre of a sparse wood, the students had laid out their kit in anticipation of our arrival. For a short while, I delayed my inspection to take my usual long look at the students. Each face told its own story of how they coped with the night, just like mine. Goldson was wearing nearly every item of spare clothing he owned. Stubble on his face and sleep in his eye, more would be expected from a vagrant. Lane was in a similar position. Looking ragged and tired, he stood over his kit, dishevelled, disinterested and shivering. At this very moment, he was not fit to lead a sleeping party, let alone a raiding party.

The 'Type A' field inspection took the normal format, although this time there was no orchestration of punishments. This time around it was black and white. Good administration meant no punishment, poor administration meant lots of punishment. For the first time, praise was overtly given to individuals who had successfully survived the night and administrated themselves to a good standard. Packman had displayed just such a standard, having taken in all the lessons we had delivered over the previous two weeks. During the inspection, his kit was found to be near perfect. Determined to catch him out, I told him to remove his boots, checking to see if he had powdered his feet. To my amazement, his feet were powdered like a baby's bum! It was good to have such a sharp student, and Packman avoided any punishment. Mathews had made several fundamental errors that would see him punished. There was no hiding the fact that Mathews had a scruffy appearance, which meant he would always attract the eye of an inspecting officer. He had left dirty and wet clothes at the top of his rucksack. Unprotected and inside his waterproof layer, the entire contents of his rucksack had been contaminated. The one thing that prevented Mathews from receiving a greater number of names was the happy expression on his face.

Despite the things we had subjected him to, he still appeared pleased to see us; it was a character trait that would win him great favour with everyone.

Goldson underwent punishment even before his inspection started.

'Why haven't you shaved, Goldson?'

'I couldn't get a fire started to boil the water, Colour Sergeant.'

'So how did you cook your breakfast?'

'I haven't had breakfast, Colour Sergeant.'

'So how do you think you are going to get through a day of strenuous activity?'

Goldson didn't answer. He just stood waiting for the instruction to begin his punishment, and I obliged.

'Fifty names, "I must shave every morning". Fifty names, "I should not forego food for sleep", and fifty names, "I'm behaving like a prize prat".'

It was the ideal time for Captain Dunn to turn up. He and the rest of the officers had been at the beginning of the training area, waiting for the Academy Commandant to arrive in preparation for the next event. The boss stood over Goldson, issuing him with a career brief. Captain Dunn spoke deliberately loudly, with the intention that everyone would hear what was being said and take heed. Specifically, he was keen that the Commandant heard Goldson receive another bollocking.

'Goldson, ask yourself a question. In your present state of poor personal administration, who do you think you could inspire?'

Goldson didn't answer; he just continued with his punishment. Not convinced he had taken on board what the boss had said, I stopped his punishment to deliver a more formal military buttonholing.

'Stand to attention, Goldson! You are trying my patience, lad. Do you really think that you stand a bloody chance of passing this course with your lethargic attitude?'

The rhetorical question had no impact, so I continued.

'If you are serious about becoming an Army officer, becoming a leader of men, a man amongst men, you need to change your attitude. Because presently, not even a fool would follow you out of curiosity, let alone into a combat situation. Now pick up your razor and remove that pathetic stubble from your face.'

Goldson had wound me up to my limit of tolerance. His nonchalant approach to the course was not only irritating, it was also offensive. He was heading for a fail, and despite being told this several times, he continued to do nothing about it. Goldson began to dry shave, and with every movement of the blade, his face contorted and grimaced with discomfort. A dry shave is extremely unpleasant, but this was the standard punishment for anyone who failed to shave.

The sight of the general was the signal to get the students to put on their red rugby tops and pack away all the contents of their rucksacks. Intentionally, the DS set about causing alarm and despondency, harrying and denying everyone time to stow items away correctly. There was a hidden motive for this act of intimidation. If the student had listened to our instruction, his kit would be stowed quickly and waterproofed. Reducing time would practise the discipline of kit packing and emphasize the reason why soldiers pack kit in a specific order, paying close attention to keeping it dry. The brighter student had made a connection and knew the reason for this chaotic charade, but there was no time for it to be discussed with peers. It was now survival of the fittest. As soon as the last man had put his rucksack on his back, Pat demanded they follow behind him as he immediately began to speed-walk up a large hill heading back towards camp.

Wearing nearly 50lb of equipment, both the DS and the students trailed in his wake. Getting the legs working after being standing still in the cold for nearly two hours was hard. The lack of warm blood in the leg muscles and the heavy kit caused everyone to struggle. Haigh was the last man in a long line of stragglers, gurning and faltering as he battled to the top of the hill.

'Haigh, what's your excuse for being at the back of the Company?' I asked.

'I can't get my legs going. I think I have frostbite; they just won't function correctly, Colour Sergeant!'

Haigh made it to the top of the hill, then broke out into a slow jog. Without warning, I grabbed hold of his waist belt and began to run down the other side, dragging him with me. Slowly, we began to pass the normal tailenders, catching up with the general and his entourage.

'Do you know what your problem is, Haigh?' Struggling for breath, he was unable to answer my question.

'I'll tell you what it is, softlad. You are a tart! You can't cope with hard physical work unless you're supervised. Unless there is someone there to encourage you! Now we both know what your problem is, Haigh, we can work on it. The next time you are found hiding at the rear of the Company, standby for special treatment.'

It hit a raw nerve with Haigh. His instant response was to screw up his face and sprint. It had the required effect. As a reward, he was left alone, and my attention switched to someone else. It was 3km back to the camp, and as we approached it, the strange noise that confused us earlier was now getting louder. Paddy came jogging up behind me.

'Gaz, that humming noise is back. Any idea what it is yet?'

Glancing at the boss, offering him the opportunity to comment, he just held his hands up and shook his head. The frontrunners of the Company were being held at the Academy back gate. Predictably, Pat was conducting blanket punishment while waiting for the arrival of the backmarkers. This was my cue to leave the Company and run ahead of everyone to prepare for the next event.

We had planned to play a trick on the students, and the prop that was to be used needed careful preparation. Eddie was at the gate, waiting for me to arrive. He had that look of concern on his face that automatically said there was a problem.

'What's wrong, Eddie?'

'Nothing much.'

'But something is – it's as plain as the nose on your face.'

'Yeah, it's the fish. I am sorry, Gaz, but it's dead. We put it in a bucket of water overnight and left it just below the water line in the bathing lake, ready for this morning's fun and games. But when I went to move it to the island, the lake had frozen up. Unfortunately, the water in the bucket also froze and the fish wasn't able to escape the freeze.' Eddie offered me the half-frozen, dead fish.

'Well, it will still work, it just won't be as effective,' I said.

The dead trout was stashed in my map pocket, but there was no concealing my disappointment that the fish had died. This trick had previously worked brilliantly; it would be less convincing with a dead fish.

'Well, you might not be able to use it anyway if Pete can't clear a path through the lake,' Eddie said, trying to cushion the blow.

'What do you mean?'

'For the last two hours, he has been trying to break up the ice with the bow of the rigid raider. It's driving him mad, as the water is freezing up as quick as he can clear it.' Suddenly the penny dropped. That's what the strange noise was, a Jonson 40cc boat engine on the back of the military raiding craft. I immediately thought that if the water was that cold, the OC wouldn't let the students cross it for fear that they might get muscle seizure and someone would drown.

Fish in pocket, I rejoined the rest of the DS as the OC was delivering his brief on the next stage. It was his standard co-ordinating brief detailing who was to do what and when. After he finished, he offered the chance for questions and I felt sure that someone would ask if it was safe to cross the lake with the temperature as low as it was. There was a long pause before Captain Watts finally broke the silence. Saved by the bell, I thought, he is going to give the OC the benefit of his Special Forces training and advise him not to do the lake crossing.

'Gordon, why can't me and James be the first to jump into the lake instead of the Colour Sergeants?' The OC quickly answered.

'Because, Tom, if the Colour Sergeants drowned, you have to write the death report. However, if a Platoon Commander drowns, well that's me writing the report. Seriously, Tom, that will ruin my weekend.'

Dunn and Watts burst out laughing at the answer, as did the Commandant, but for a brief moment, my sense of humour deserted me. That water was bloody freezing and the truth was, I didn't want to get in.

'OK, Colour Sergeants. Lead on, let's do it.' Major Gray waved us away in the direction of the students. Immediately, Paddy and I began screaming wildly at our platoons. This was as much to enthuse myself as it was to kick-start the platoon into a long run and jump into the lake.

'On me. On me. Let's go, follow me!'

Running off in the direction of the lake, several of the fitter students were tight on my heels. Pushing our way through the heavy undergrowth that surrounded the lake, we eventually arrived at a suitable launching point where the ice was broken. Without hesitation, I hurled myself into the lake. In a well-rehearsed drill, my rucksack was whizzed off my back and slung in the water first. The rucksack bobbed up and down, acting as my buoyancy aid, as my legs kicked frantically behind me. The shock of the cold water was like being hit over the head with a mallet. Stunned into silence, adrenaline contracting into my vital organs, the body immediately wanted to shut down. My arm and leg movements slowed as the freeze took hold, but that wasn't my biggest worry. Pete, who was operating the motorboat, had broken the ice into large chunks, and each chunk was at least 4 inches thick. Dangerously, they drifted in front of me, blocking my route to the pontoon situated in the centre of the lake. Pete realized the hazard and began to shove them out of the way with the nose of the boat. As helpful as this was, he inadvertently created large waves as he piloted the boat forward and backwards, pushing my flotation aid in the other direction.

Relieved to make the island, my attention turned to the students. Several remained on the far bank, too concerned to take the leap. It wasn't long before Captain Watts appeared to incentivize the students, despite their protests. Mathews, King, Rideout, Moore and a few of Paddy's students were the first to join us on the pontoon. As soon as they arrived, they began running on the spot to prevent freezing up. Eventually, every member of the course was crammed onto the small man-made wooden island in the centre of the lake. Orchestrated by Pat, the course was running and jumping on the spot and occasionally breaking into a ten-second sprint. With every student screaming at the top of his voice, they counted down from ten to one whilst sprinting at full pace on the same spot. There was no need to encourage the sprints; everyone was keen to warm up and shake the cold water off their bodies. The wooden island became wrapped in a fog of steam billowing in all directions from fifty bodies generating heat.

From the centre of the pontoon, Major Gray had to call repeatedly for silence so he could gain everyone's attention. It was our signal for a bit of play acting.

'OK you lot, listen up. Before you get to the home bank, you must first catch at least one fish each. If you catch a fish, you can have the rest of the day off. Catch two fish, two days off. Three gives you three days off. You get the picture? Any questions?'

Haigh raised his hand, as we knew someone would.

'Are there fish in there, Sir? It doesn't look like it's been stocked. Maybe ever!

The students laughed, and someone demanded to know what kind of fish lived in the lake. Doubt rumbled loudly from the crowd as they huddled together on the pontoon.

'Colour Sergeant McCarthy, where are you? Raise your hand please,' Major Gray, unable to see me due to the fact we were all crammed on the island, called out to me.

'Sir. I'm here near the edge, Sir.'

'Good, that's handy, Colour Sergeant. Can you jump in the lake and catch me a fish, please? We need to see what kind it is! I think they are carp!'

'Sorry, Sir! Did you say catch me a fish? Can't you just take my word for it, Sir? The lake is full of trout!'

'No, Colour Sergeant. My integrity is in question here. I am surrounded by thirty-eight doubting Thomases. Quickly, if you will. Heaven forbid the students don't believe me that there are fish in the lake.'

'OK, Sir, but are you sure? It's going to be a little tricky with the water being so cold!'

'Come on, Colour Sergeant. We need to get a move on!'

The improbability of trout living in a blackwater lake was not lost on the students. With much mumbling and doubt, I leapt into the lake. The students shuffled around to the edges to see what was happening. Holding my breath and clinging to the retention chains of the pontoon to stay at the bottom of the lake for as long as possible, the dead trout was plucked from my pocket. At my limit, mustering as much of a jump as possible, I reappeared with a huge splash and began flapping the 12-inch fish in an effort to convince the students that it was still alive. The tall figure of Captain Dunn was near the front, and I tossed the fish to him. Theatrically, he juggled the fish just long enough for them to identify it as a trout. To maintain our deception, he dropped the slippery fish back into the water as if it had made a getaway. The students let out a deafening cheer, spontaneously leapt into the water and began searching for fish. Laughing so much, I struggled to swim. Ten feet from the bank, the lake became shallow and I stood up, turning around to see the students splashing around frantically looking for fish. If we didn't do something quickly, they would probably stay there until they froze or drowned.

'Hey, you lot! That's it! Time's up! In you come before you all freeze to death.' Major Gray jumped in and chased everyone back to shore.

Having retrieved the students and their rucksacks, we huddled together in a small clearing overlooking the lake. It was critical to get everyone to change into their dry clothes. Collectively, the DS and the students began to remove their wet clothes and change into their dry kit in full view of everyone. It was imperative that the students saw the DS open their wet rucksacks and produce dry clothing, and then quickly change into it. It was as much for our credibility as it was proof of concept. The trick was to de-kit quickly and avoid losing body heat to the heavy wet clothes. Every member of the training team and every student stood stark naked rummaging through their rucksacks, desperately keen to don the dry clothing.

Danner's voice was the first to break the silence. He could be heard asking his fellow students for spare clothing. Naked and gingerly manoeuvring around barefooted, he was getting no response from those around him.

'Danner, what are you whingeing about?' I asked.

'It's absolutely preposterous, Colour Sergeant. My spare clothes, they're wetter than the ones I am wearing.'

It was no surprise his clothes were wet. In fact, it was virtually guaranteed that everyone else's clothes would be soaked. The whole lake-crossing exercise was designed to demonstrate the need to be diligent when packing your rucksack, and to have an efficient waterproof system.

Despite the peculiar surroundings and bizarre sight of forty grown men stark naked at the side of a wood, morale was high. From the side pouch of my rucksack, I produced a large bottle of port. Not something that would normally be carried, but pulling out a bottle of Sergeants' Mess port would be stylish and welcoming. Black mugs shivering in the hands of the students, each man smiled as they slurped at the red liquor.

'Well, Danner, you know what they say about that, don't you?'

'No, Colour Sergeant!'

I offered him another splash of port, which he gratefully accepted, before continuing, 'Seven Ps. Prior Planning and Preparation Prevents Piss-Poor Performance! Look at my clothes; bone dry. We all did exactly the same swim, we all ran the same distance. There is nothing different between your kit and mine.'

Danner nodded in agreement. The truth of the matter was, the DS knew this was coming; consequently, we had spent a good ten minutes ensuring everything was watertight. The students had a little under sixty seconds and were still in the learning stages. Still, the point was proven and the valuable lesson of keeping equipment dry had been learnt.

We had been out of the lake for nearly fifteen minutes and it was time to check the health of the platoon. Using the port as a distraction from the cold, Captain Dunn whipped up enthusiasm in preparation for the next serial. Lane was some way behind the rest of the platoon, still struggling to get dressed while the majority of people had finished and were now packing away wet clothes. I gave Lane another splash of port, then asked him what the holdup was.

'My fingers are so numb, Colour Sergeant. I can't feel a thing. I can't do up my boot laces, my buttons, I can't even grip the zip on my jacket.'

One look at Lane and you could see there was little effort or thought being applied.

'Lane, how do you think the others coped? We are all going through the same experience, and the only difference is attitude. At this moment, Lane, yours is weak, very weak.'

His expression was blank, soulless, with no spark, but this was not the time for a heated exchange. He needed the reason why and the solution.

'OK, Lane. We have taught you how to analyse problems. We have taught you how to evaluate and re-evaluate. So, let's do this together. 'Issue: fingers don't work because they are cold. Solution: get them warm so they work.'

'Yes, Colour Sergeant.'

'Good. How are we going to do this?'

'Rub them?'

'I am sure you have done that, and it didn't work. So, what? Re-evaluate the solution.'

'Light a fire.'

'Good thinking, but we don't have time. Next.'

'Share body heat with a friend?'

'Well done, this is about generating body heat, but everyone is too busy to share theirs. So, what?'

'Make my own body heat, Colour Sergeant!'

There was nothing more to say. He had found the answer. Lane started to sprint on the spot. His blood warmed up and brought back the feeling in his fingertips. Thirty seconds later, he buttoned up his shirt. Repeating the process with small sprints, soon his boot laces were fastened and we were ready to go. Lane got a rare smile out of me. He had shifted through the gears of analysis with a little help and achieved his aim. If he could continue to do this, just maybe there was hope.

Pete was struggling to extract the boat out of the lake and was in need of a helping hand. The CQMS is often the forgotten hero in any military organization. All the hard, ugly work is done by him and his team. There is no fun running around after students, Staff and other members of the supporting cast.

'Hi, Pete, let me give you a hand. Did we get away with our trick with the fish? Did it look convincing?'

'Yes, Gaz, even Corporal Davis was fooled. It looked good from where we sat. The students were definitely hoodwinked. Did you let it go?'

'It's in the bin, mate. It died. Frozen in the bucket overnight.'

'No wonder. I had to break the ice with a pickaxe this morning before we could launch the rigid raider. I'm shocked the OC let you do the crossing. You know the lake is out of bounds to the rest of the Academy? I thought someone might have said something to him.'

I shook my head at Pete and raised a big smile. 'Yeah, me too, but it is a little late now, and the Commandant joined in so they must have been confident it was a risk worth taking!'

It was a timely reminder for me. Despite my years of teaching all types of soldiers from all around the globe, someone else would always know best. Sometimes we all need to be taken out of our comfort zone, and that may take a little push or a little risk. Retrospectively, it was the right thing to do as it forged a unity like no other event on the course.

The mood was subdued by the cold as the course tabbed (marched with equipment) from the assault course area. The well-trodden route back to the accommodation took less than twenty minutes. In recognition of the hardship they had just suffered, they received one full hour to administrate themselves before lunch. But that was as much sympathy as they were allowed. In the canteen, it was business as usual: twenty minutes for all to be fed, watered and ready for the next lesson. In the study hall, Captain Dunn revised the platoon on the Orders Process before explaining the common methods of adjusting the procedure to meet an unusual or unspecified task, such as organizing public events similar to the Queen's birthday parade or state funerals. Having completed his lesson, the Platoon Commander discussed varying scenarios and made rough estimates on how they could be tackled. Each student would get the opportunity to do some analysis on a generic problem, and then brief everyone on his solution using the formal orders process.

One hour into the lesson, Moore was the third student to deliver his analysis using the orders template. He was mid-flow, delivering his plan to a make-believe situation, when Pat burst into our study hall.

'Right, stop what you're doing and move into the classroom next-door now!' His face was beaming with excitement and anticipation. After all the students had crammed into Paddy's classroom, Pat made an announcement.

'The Company Commander has been summoned by Thames Valley Police. There has been a break out from Broadmoor secure prison and several inmates have escaped. They are dangerous and on the loose in the local area.' The colour started to drain from the faces of the students as Pat continued with the announcement.

'You will all know that Broadmoor prison backs on to our military training area and that Broadmoor is home to some of the country's most notorious mentally disturbed criminals, including the Yorkshire Ripper.'

As the students broke out in spontaneous conversation, Major Gray walked into the classroom and introduced a policeman to the students.

The policeman gave a description of three escaped prisoners. To assist with situational awareness, details of their crimes were briefed to the audience, including their psychopathic tendencies. He summarized by theorizing that these men were likely to be hiding out on the training area. The first phase of the recovery operation had been established, with the police manning roadblocks in the surrounding villages and towns. With that statement, the OC announced that the Commandant had given the Thames Valley Chief Constable permission to use all available manpower currently at the Academy. Because it was a long weekend for everyone else, that only left Rowallan Company. With that, he gave the students five minutes to prepare themselves for a brief followed by an immediate deployment, likely to last 24 hours. The students disappeared to their rooms and busily gathered what they thought they might need during the search, or at least what was useable given a significant amount of kit was still sodden from the lake crossing.

With mild chaos, they all reassembled in classroom two. Major Gray delivered a comprehensive plan. He divided the students into four groups, two in each platoon. Following military doctrine, areas of responsibility, coordinating instructions, boundaries, report lines, timings, control measures and emergency procedures were issued. It was a detailed brief containing every eventuality, from what to do if you got lost or injured to what happened if you discovered an escaped prisoner. Once the orders had been confirmed and students understood the task, they were dispatched to look for the convicts. It took nearly an hour to walk out to the start point of the search, which was in the exact centre of Barossa. Captain Dunn then nominated two students as commanders of their respective search parties. Lane and Goldson were given ten minutes to gather their thoughts before they had to deliver a set of orders outlining their plan.

The boss would go with Goldson, which would leave me to escort Lane and his group. Collectively, the group helped Lane draft his orders brief and landscape a model of the terrain in miniature using branches, foot powder, grass and rocks. Fifteen minutes later, with the students gathered in a semicircle around the ground model of the area, the brief was issued. Lane began his orders lacking confidence and conviction. With the details that Lane had to deliver, and given the nature of the task at hand, it was hoped his orders would have been detailed, lasting approximately twenty minutes. Staggeringly, at the four-minute point, he told the students to stand up and begin the search.

There was no way the students could be sent out on a mission with so little information. With my head in my hands, a halt was brought to the proceedings and everyone was sat back down before I summarized what Lane had briefed.

'Well, do we all feel ready to deal with these dangerous people we are searching for? Have you been given clear guidance on who does what and what actions are required at what stage? How about the control measures? What measures are in place to prevent repeating activities in the same area, wasting valuable time and light?'

There was a deadly silence. Student loyalty prevented criticism or even calculated comment. The brief had not been good, and everyone knew it. I continued:

'Ok, if no one has the moral courage to speak out, let me. If you hadn't guessed it by now, let me stick you all in the Rembrandt. There are no escaped prisoners and there will be no search. The whole episode has been part of an elaborate hoax to exercise you in applying the orders process in a scenario other than command tasks. Judging by Lane's orders, it may not have worked very well.'

The students were becoming accustomed to misinformation and deception, so no one was surprised by my announcement. Murphy giggled and explained he knew it was a bluff from the start because the policeman was actually the Colour Sergeant from the girls' platoon. Only a few days ago he had received a bollocking from him whilst they were standing outside the accommodation waiting to march to breakfast.

We all had a little giggle at the acting of Colour Sergeant Mort, who had played the policeman, before I got back to the standard of orders delivered by Lane:

'Let's examine how much information has been missed. Command and control, or C2 as we'll call it, not one aspect of it was explained. Cut-off times, actions on, limits of exploitations, emergency RVs! The list is endless. In truth, it's frightening how much has been missed. If you briefed real soldiers like this, they would eat you alive. Soldiers are not shy when it comes to C2; if your plan stinks, they will be brutal with their response. They will rip you apart. You will lose credibility and the Platoon Sergeant will disown you.'

It took thirty minutes to highlight the crucial points Lane had failed to address. He had neglected to inform his audience of how the search would be conducted, who was responsible for what tasks and – critically – the control measures and cut-off timings. Limitations such as time, daylight, equipment and logistical support, all have an effect on the operation. What would be the action taken if an escaped prisoner needed to be detained? How were we going to inform Major Gray of our progress? The debrief to the group finished with me delivering an example of how it should have been done before we all joined Captain Dunn to listen to his debrief to Goldson. Predictably, he was highlighting the same points. With the exercise complete, we marched back to camp.

'How did Goldson do, boss?' I asked. A look of despair filled his face.

'Not good, Colour; it's hard to find anything positive to say. Regrettably, and of greater concern, during my debrief he thought he had done well. He just kept smiling and nodding at me. I'm concerned about his mental stability.'

'How do you mean?'

'I'm not sure. Maybe it's the vacant look he wears or the random questions he asks. You can tell he has not kept pace with the conversation by his vague answers. It's difficult to put my finger on what it is exactly. Never mind, it will come out in the wash. Anyway, another day another dollar, Colour. I'm heading off to do some training – UK championships coming up. Are you going back to the accommodation?'

'Yeah, boss.'

'Can you just mention our conversation with the OC. We need to let him know how this exercise went, specifically my comments on Goldson. We need to prep the ground with this issue. It must not come as a shock to the OC at the first Company Progress Board.'

It was now very dark and silent around the Academy. The college was on a long weekend and the only people moving around the camp came from Rowallan. As we returned to the accommodation, it was time to change the duty student. For obvious reasons, Stone was selected. He was briefed on what was expected over the next few hours. There was precious little to say other than there would be a twelve-hour period of grace. They should dry and re-pack their kit in this time, as it may be required very soon after the twelve hours elapsed. The irony of this was that Stone's kit was dry, having not taken full part in the exercise due to his mystery injury. Danner was close by and immediately chanced his arm with a speculative question. But before he asked, he couldn't refrain from having a snipe at Stone for looking so fresh and clean. Secretly, his sarcastic comments about Stone made me want to burst out laughing. Danner was a comedian at heart and his wit was razor sharp.

'Colour Sergeant, the next bugout wouldn't be tomorrow whilst we're eating supper by any chance?' he said.

This unashamed attempt by Danner to squeeze information from me would upset other members of the DS had they received it. But the duel of wits with Danner kept us both keen. He could sense there was a game being played by me; he was doing little more than trying to discover the rules. It was not a bad thing to see him develop this cheeky disposition, knowing full well, during difficult times, it would pay dividends. Unsure if his question was based on good information or rumour, it was tactfully avoided by using the Rowallan DS 'get out of jail free' clause, better known as on-the-spot punishment!

'Fifty press-ups, Danner. Moore, you can count them out, nice and loud so they can be heard from my office.' Danner adopted the press-up position, but continued to pursue an answer.

'There must be an element of truth in that question, Colour Sergeant, or you would have given me a bigger punishment for my cheek.'

'Yes, you're right, Danner: 100 press-ups, on you go.' Moore burst out laughing at Danner's predicament, but they both knew that Danner's persistence was with justification.

The canteen was shared with the Academy drivers and support staff, so rumours would always be rife after a visit to the cookhouse. Although the chefs were all briefed not to talk to the students, they were often sympathetic to their cause. Sometimes a chef would inadvertently let it slip that the course was not booked in for certain meals. On other occasions the students could see the chefs preparing the packed meals destined for Row-Co. Any act different from the normal generated rumours of a bugout within the next twenty-four hours. But Danner was trying to narrow down the window of opportunity and find the exact time of the bugout. Despite his 100 press-ups, Danner's cheek had paid off. My actions had compromised the imminent likelihood of a bugout, which only served to elevate the anxiety.

Chapter Seven

Compass Rose

The Academy was just beginning to bubble back to life as the Commissioning Course returned from their long weekend. Cars double-parked at the rear of Old College as officer cadets ran in and out of doorways, hoping not to get caught illegally parked. It was 1500hrs on the third Sunday, and the Staff had gathered at the rear of the Chapel. Paddy couldn't help himself – every time he saw someone illegally parked outside the accommodation, he jumped out of the shadows and issued a bollocking. At one stage, he followed three female cadets into their accommodation just so he could tell them off. Had it not been for the intervention of the OC, Paddy would have spent the whole night enforcing the Academy Sergeant Major's laws on parking and loving every minute of it.

Out of sight and earshot, the OC delivered an abridged bugout brief. This was bugout number three; there was no need for lengthy details, just a quick chat about the tempo he wished to kick-start this five-day trip with.

'Everything ready to go, Q?' he asked Pete.

'Just one problem. We have not been given spare wheels, so if anyone gets a puncture it's tough luck!'

Pete issued this statement as if it was second nature, but it generated more questions than it answered.

'Why are there no spares?' Pat chuntered.

'It's a training piece of kit; they don't do spares anymore. If you get a puncture, I will come and recover you. Having tried it before, it's game over if the tyre goes flat, so don't even try to do anything other than wait for me to arrive.'

Pete glanced around to catch everyone's eye. He wanted to be sure we all understood what he said.

'It's a little archaic, don't you think, Pete? Are we that hard up for Land Rover spares?'

Captain Watts giggled at my comment, as did Pat, then Paddy followed suit. Pete looked at me as if I had two heads, and the conversation died into an awkward silence.

Captain Dunn chatted to Major Gray about Goldson. he was keen for the OC to understand his concerns about the lad's mental wellbeing. The conversation was sombre and serious, with long pauses and plenty of half-finished sentences. It was clear they both thought there would be further problems. But to eject a student from the course on the grounds that the DS thought he was barking mad, wouldn't be acceptable. More importantly, if he was suffering issues, this course would not help him get better. We found ourselves in a position familiar to every other training team delivering phase one training: the challenge of business efficiencies and value for money versus the training teams' standards. Goldson was a problem child, but it would take a lot of time and effort to prove this to the Academy Headquarters before they would agree to his removal. Pat interrupted the conversation and prompted Major Gray to give the go-ahead for Paddy and me to start the bugout, which he dutifully did.

This time, we were expected. There was none of the screaming and shouting that preceded the previous bugout, when just the sight of the DS appearing together at an unusual hour was enough to start the students off. Francis was the first to see the Staff enter the corridor this time. He was prepared for what was coming, but still broke out into a blind panic when the reality of our presence was confirmed. In quick order, though, the accommodation was cleared and Exercise Compass Rose was underway.

Standing in a hollow square, an inspection of Command equipment was critical to the success of the exercise: maps, torch, compass, protractor and watch, all of which the students stowed on their bodies. Other essential equipment carried in their rucksacks, such as waterproofs, spare clothing and first aid kits, were also accounted for. True to our promise, anything forgotten was left behind. Several students had either forgotten or, in an effort to reduce weight, didn't pack their emergency rations, a decision they would come to regret. With the kit inspection complete, Pete loaded all the rucksacks onto the back of his Bedford 4-ton truck. By 1530hrs, the course was formed up in three ranks ready to deploy. With little fuss, Pat marched all the students to the training area, where they would be greeted with the biggest physical test so far. We were about to find out if our fitness training had paid off.

The test would begin with a competition: a challenge that needed as much command and control as it required physical exertion. Having reached the rear gate of the Academy at the front of the squad, Pat stood on a hard-standing waiting for the last of the students to arrive. Behind him, two massive cannons lingered menacingly. Wearing a huge smile, he welcomed the Company to the start of the exercise.

'Marvellous, absolutely marvellous! Gentlemen, let me introduce you to "Pain and Gain".'

Mounted proudly on their carriages, the artillery guns stared at the squad like a pair of angry English bull terriers. The old 25-pounder weighed 1.1 tons and had long been retired from service. Renowned for its accuracy, the ability to depress the barrel so low allowed the weapon to be used in the direct fire role. Nowadays, this remarkable cannon sits innocently on plinths outside cadet camps and museums. A few are used as gate guardians, passionately placed outside Regimental Headquarters, quietly acknowledging the contribution of such an iconic weapons system. Nowhere better is this exemplified than the cannon that greets you as you enter the Headquarters of 22 SAS. The 25-pounder fired by Sergeant Labalaba as he held off 250 enemy single-handed during the Battle of Mirbat in Oman in 1972 stands proudly to honour his bravery and that of his fellow 'Blades' who fought with him that day. For the students of Row-Co, however, both guns represented something more menacing. Over the years, they had been well kept, but there was nothing ergonomically easy about pushing them.

This competition was a 5km run with the guns over rough and undulating ground. Before they started, Daz demonstrated how to pull and push the 25-pounders. It was a necessary safety brief, issued deliberately to warn students not to disrespect or mishandle their heavy guns. There were no jokes, no sarcastic comments, just repeated words of caution: 'Danger, don't do this ... Dangerous, don't do that ... Under no circumstances stand in front of the cannon when it is moving downhill!' He was nervous; you could hear it in his voice. Having witnessed broken legs and arms in previous races, Daz recounted the story of a student being run over twice in the space of fifteen seconds, once by his own gun and then by the gun following behind. He said ropes were attached to both sides of the carriage. On the flat and going uphill, they were used to tow the cannon; going downhill, they became the braking system. Time after time, Daz warned of the dangers involved whilst towing a piece of artillery. Eventually, he finished with a warm-up and stretch before giving the students a two-minute warning.

Captain Dunn corralled his charges and launched into a rousing speech. He issued a warning to Barns, Stone, Watson, Lane, Goldson and Danner, accusing them of not giving 100 per cent effort during past events. In addition, he advised the students of the need for coordination balanced with disciplined command and control.

'This is all about gut-wrenching effort and intelligent management using the command tools,' he said.

Solemnly, he stared at each member of the platoon before nominating Haigh as the commander for the opening event. Having not won a race so far, the boss directed me to go easy on the students in my pep talk in an attempt to boost confidence and morale. He didn't need to say this to me; it was obvious that this was not the moment for the Alex Ferguson hairdryer treatment. I therefore told them:

> 'Nine points adrift! It's time to start the comeback. You proved several times that you are faster and fitter than the other platoon, but where you let yourselves down is on teamwork, personal application and intelligence.

You must work as a team and play to win. If you don't win, it ain't worth playing. Listen to the Platoon Commander's words of wisdom: it's as much about C2 as it is about effort. Think back to the stretcher race – get the changeover right and we will win with an easy margin. Haigh! It can't be stressed enough: it is critical that you come up with a solid plan to win this race because if you don't, I will sack you on the spot! Promise! Anybody got any questions? No? Good; let's do it!'

After a glance at the boss to ensure he approved of my tone, my focus switched to the race commander.

'Haigh, a quick word.' Haigh ran over to me and sprang to attention.

'Yes, Colour Sergeant.'

'Two pieces of advice for you. Firstly, volunteers are better than pressed men, so be careful who you tell to do what. Remember, this is all about C2. Secondly, get in front early and you will have the psychological edge. Leave nothing out there. Everything needs to be spent on this race.'

Haigh gathered his troops for a brief and we listened intently.

'I want to get off to a good start. Who would like to volunteer to pull the gun into the lead?'

Rideout, Francis, Mathews and Moore raised their hands. Haigh added Danner, King and himself to the list.

'No, Haigh!' I shouted. 'You can't command if you are pulling the fucking thing. What did we say to you thirty seconds ago? This is as much about command and control as it is about physical effort! Get a grip and task someone else, for Christ's sake!'

My anxiety could be heard in the reproach.

'Yes, of course,' said Haigh. 'Sorry, Colour Sergeant, of course I can't pull the gun. Barns, you start.'

He continued: 'The first changeover will be Boyle, Packman, Witherspoon, Lane, Watson and Murphy. That leaves Williams, Stone and Goldson to act as the brakes for the first major obstacle. Any questions? Moore, you are second in command. Stone, you are the timekeeper – call the time out after every minute.'

The students gathered themselves into a rugby-style scrum and began shouting and screaming encouragement at each other in an effort to increase the hype.

'That's a promising start, Colour,' said Captain Dunn. 'Don't know why they're doing it, but it looks good.'

Haigh's brief had brought a warm glow to my mood. He was a little unorthodox, but there was something in there that had caught our attention, even if it was just curiosity. For a short while, we laughed at Haigh's ungainly figure. Some of the odd shapes he and the rest of our students cut were a sight to behold. Danner, with his wide waist, had a look of early pregnancy about him; Witherspoon's hunched shoulders made him look like a tall, skinny version of Quasimodo, the hunchback of Notre Dame; and Stone cowered from the light breeze like Old Mother Hubbard.

Daz was standing in front of the guns at the start line. There was some kind of safety hold-up, and nervous tension crept in. Inexplicably, Haigh then started to contradict his earlier orders. We watched in disbelief as he dished out numbers and dictated exact locations for his team. He then picked an argument with Barns about how the rope should be held in the hand. Such dictatorship was not required. Stifling the thinking of his peers and behaving like a playschool dinner lady would undermine cohesion. My earlier confidence began to ebb away as he countered his initial brief. His previous plan became lost and confused amidst his new direction. It was immediately obvious that things were not going to run smoothly. With a look of dejection, Captain Dunn shook his head at me. We both knew Haigh was about to fail his first key appointment, even before he started.

Daz summoned Paddy's students to bring their 25-pounder to the start line and explained that, due to the dangers of pulling a gun at high speeds through narrow tracks and paths, the teams would now start at an interval of sixty seconds, which undermined my advice to get in front early, but was eminently sensible. With the crack of Daz's starter pistol, Paddy's students got their gun moving with an eighteen-man tow. Haigh ushered his team to the start line. Rideout, Francis, Mathews and Moore gathered around the front of the gun. Their eyes were fixed on the other students disappearing up the hill and around the first bend. Haigh then changed his mind yet again and told the remainder of the students to find a vacant position on the gun and push with all their might. Mathews started to scream encouragement to anyone that would listen. This started a chain reaction, and it wasn't long before everyone was screaming and shouting, eventually silenced by the second crack of Daz's starter pistol.

Responding to another chorus of motivational calls, the students set off pulling and pushing the gun. The impressive start was short-lived, as after covering less than 50 metres, the gun came to a grinding halt. The front of the carriage was unmanageable. The cast iron chassis and its large towing eye was too heavy for Rideout and Moore to prevent it nose-diving into the ground. Despite the gun barrel pointing rearwards, most of the weight was leaning forward on the chassis, causing it to constantly dip forward. To find the gun's equilibrium, the front part of the carriage needed to be raised higher. The problem for Rideout and Moore was that they could not balance the gun and pull at the same time; it had to be one or the other. Haigh's immediate thought was to put more people up to the front of the gun to assist with carrying the weight. Consequently, the front of the carriage became congested and no one could get sufficient purchase to pull and run.

'It's too crowded!' shouted Francis. 'There are too many people crowding the front portion.' He was getting angry at Haigh.

Once again the gun came to a grinding halt. From the melee, Packman offered advice on achieving the right balance. As innocent as his intentions were, his pompous overtones angered Mathews, who just wanted to get the gun moving. All the while, the gun remained still. Valuable time slipped away, and with it the platoon's morale. As tempers frayed, Haigh's command and control vanished.

Captain Dunn became increasingly annoyed at Haigh's dithering. This was the moment for re-evaluation, but he had to figure it out for himself. Tensions mounted, and not only with the students. With the gap already at an impossible nine points, surely it would be twelve in the next hour. Unusually, Captain Dunn lost his cool. On several occasions when the gun stopped moving, he erupted in a burst of angry, insult-littered criticism. It is a tricky hurdle to negotiate when a student begins to fail an appointment. Normally, the pressure is placed on the instructor to ensure success, so Captain Dunn's actions were an indication of how bad things were getting. Questions, as innocent as they were, had already been raised about the performance of No. 2 Platoon, and both Captain Dunn and I were feeling the heat. There was a simple solution to Haigh's problem, but he couldn't see it, despite Captain Dunn doing his utmost to point him in the right direction.

As the gun once again travelled for a short distance and then crashed, Haigh had learnt as much as he could under the circumstances. It was time to give someone else an opportunity. The boss gave me the nod to remove Haigh from command. If he could not bring about swift change, it would be Packman to take charge. Hauling him out of the line, we ran alongside the gun as he received my brief:

> 'You gave Haigh advice before, and it was good advice. Your idea made sense and should work. The reason Haigh didn't listen to you is that your inter-personal skills stink. If Haigh doesn't get a grip, you will be put in command. My advice is to watch your tone, select your words better and respect those you command. There is a time to inspire and a time to perspire; don't get them confused.'

Haigh got one more opportunity to succeed. In an act of desperation to get the gun moving again, he grabbed hold of the front rope and frantically began pulling it.

'Haigh, we don't want you to apply effort, we want you to apply thought and command!' I shouted. Haigh pulled an angry face to declare his dissatisfaction. It was the final straw and enough reason to sack him as promised.

'Haigh, don't pull that spanked child look, you can't inspire people that way. You're sacked. Stop talking from this point forward. There you go, now you can pull the gun all you want! Packman, you're in charge. Get a grip of this fiasco and get the gun moving now!'

Feverishly, Packman reorganized the students around the gun, then instructed Lane to climb onto the barrel and shuffle to the end, acting as a counterbalance. This found the gun's equilibrium, which made the front raise off the ground. It was just the answer the problem required. Now the gun would travel without it nosediving into the road. A huge effort then went into pushing and pulling the gun, and at the 3km point, they saw the other platoon for the first time since the start. Their gun had crashed, but they were still three minutes ahead. With a roar of encouragement and hope, the ropes creaked under No. 1 Platoon's renewed energy. They were suffering from cuts, bruises and rope burns, yet Packman continued to push his comrades hard. The gap was down to less than a minute and a half as they crossed the marker for the last kilometre.

Packman's demands for yet more effort were greeted with angry protests. Lane, who was enjoying his ride perched on the end of the barrel, was causing discord, provoking a string of comments calling for him to get off and push the gun. Packman knew that Lane was probably more useful on the barrel than helping to push the 25-pounder. Initially, the complaints were ignored as he hoped they would disappear, but they returned with greater ferocity. The new commander was in a difficult position. If he continued, there was a slim chance of winning the race, or at least closing the gap to a respectable margin. If he changed Lane with someone else, he would lose momentum and effort. Dwelling on making a decision, his peers became increasingly boisterous, forcing a premature answer.

'OK, OK. Mathews, get ready to change with Lane; when I shout "change", change! Stop the gun, get ready with the ropes. Change! Change!'

However, only one side of the gun reacted, skewing the gun into a turn off the track and into a large shrub, throwing Lane off his perch in the process. Several students were bowled over like skittles as the gun ran out of control. Luckily, they all escaped injury. The gun came to a halt jammed in several thorn bushes. A frantic panic to extract the gun was futile – they had blown the opportunity.

Captain Dunn found it hard to keep eye contact with me. Disappointment and frustration were written all over his face. With a great team spirit, the students set about getting the gun moving at pace, but too much time had been lost. Despite a determined final kilometre, the students had come second. Demoralized and angry as they crossed the finish line, arguments boiled over as the internal inquiry into why they had failed began. Packman accused several people of slacking, causing some of his peers to threaten him with violence. It was the heated exchange of words we fully expected. It would serve to strengthen resolve and intensify the desire to succeed next time around.

Major Gray called for silence. Balancing precariously on the carriage of the winning gun, he officially declared Paddy's students the winners. What surprised everyone was the time gap. One minute and thirty seconds was the lead, meaning the winning margin was just thirty seconds. This only added to the pain of the defeat. As the OC read out the score – twelve points to zero – Paddy's students jeered and danced in celebration. A jealous glance at Paddy, who was surrounded by his jubilant students, had me deflated. They were calling his name as if he was a rock legend or film superstar, and Paddy seemed to relish this adulation. For a brief moment, priorities appeared confused and principles twisted. Paddy was giving me the impression that he was as keen to win the competition as his students were. For a short while, the celebrations clouded my thoughts and suspicions crept in. Once the worm of envy grips, it is difficult to suppress. At that very moment, focus and composure gave way as the inquest into another failure began.

'Anyone want to explain why we lost this race?' I ventured.

No one answered. Heads bowed to avoid eye contact, the only noise was that of individuals coughing and spluttering as lungs burnt in the cold air.

'Haigh, you started this farce! Tell us all, what the hell went wrong?'

'Commensurate with other competitions, the dichotomy in persuasions made control untenable, Colour Sergeant. Salutations for the brave attempt, but …'

'Shut up, Haigh. Fuck me, you're talking crap! I have met some people who could torture nursery rhymes out of Rambo, but you have brought a whole new meaning to the word for me. Stop torturing the language and speak in plain English. What did we do wrong?'

The platoon fell quiet. Heavy breathing still dominated the silence, which I broke:

> 'If no one is prepared to speak the truth, let me unpick the points of failure. By God, there are enough of them. Firstly, you bunch of whiners became fixated on one issue. You thought Lane was having it easy and used peer pressure to convince Packman to change him over. This single act of selfishness resulted in the gun coming to a grinding halt. Agreed?'

Most of the platoon nodded, and Captain Dunn reinforced my point. He had calmed down sufficiently to take over the debrief.

'The Colour Sergeant is right. It failed because your precious opinions mattered to Packman. Well, let me tell you this.' Captain Dunn was animated and angry as he wound himself up for a no-holds-barred debrief.

'Packman, you and Haigh are the reason we failed to win. I am tired of repeating myself. Command is a lonely place. If you don't have the courage to stick the mission in front of your popularity, fuck off and join the boy scouts.'

If Captain Dunn swore, we knew it was going to be a bad day. He never lost his cool. Such a gentleman in every respect, any swear word seemed to have a greater impact. He continued:

> 'Packman should have driven you all harder. He should have told you to keep quiet and focus on the execution. Stopping the cannon would cost you valuable time. Even a 3-year-old would have figured that out. Secondly, Haigh, why on earth did you change the plan seconds before the start of the race? Your indecision added alarm and misunderstanding, which gave way to dissent and rebellion. There was no conviction in your decision; it was all contradiction and chaos before we started. Then, at the point you should have been thinking of re-evaluation, you decided to just pull the gun, leaving the task without command and control. That's why the Colour Sergeant removed you from command, and that's why we lost the race.'

Like a wrecking ball making its final hit on a crumbling tower, the words brought home a crushing truth. Whilst it was a hard decision to make, an experienced leader would have resisted changing Lane with a fellow runner. You don't need to be an evil, single-minded, egotistical lunatic whilst in command, but you do need to be decisive and possess an agile edge when dealing with your subordinates. There is a time to be fair and a time to be committed. Had they won the race, they would have forgotten that Lane had an easy ride.

Breaking the silence, Watson raised his hand and suggested that maybe they didn't understand what was meant by coordination and discipline while running with the gun. Captain Dunn glanced at me, as if to suggest this was a valid point.

'Well, Watson, let's rectify that here and now.'

Without answering further, Captain Dunn gathered the students around the gun. He explained that having come second in the race, they would be punished with a second gun run. Splitting the students into two groups, one group pushed 'Pain' whilst the others pushed 'Gain'.

'We will run the last kilometre again,' said the boss, going on to explain what discipline looked like. 'It's about the rigid application of the commander's instructions! Resisting the urge to do your own thing! Maintaining a unified effort. No insubordination, no whingeing, just drive and effort. Discipline is about working hard for a common goal. Working collaboratively towards a unified purpose, that's the solution.'

Captain Dunn finished by demonstrating how to organize people at close-quarters. A two-minute warning was given, and the platoon was split in half.

'No commanders. Colour Sergeant will run with "Pain" and I will run with "Gain". We will organize, command and control, so you understand what "good" looks like.'

After such a valiant effort over the final 2km, it was understandable that the second effort lacked emotional energy. On more than one occasion, both guns came to a crashing halt and the students struggled to get them restarted. Encouragingly, this time it was not due to lack of coordination or discipline, it was more to do with the effort expended on their first attempt. The physically weaker students offered less and less effort with each step – Barns, Stone, Lane, Haigh and Williams became a severe handicap to their teams' efforts. It took over thirty minutes to travel a kilometre, most of which was at walking pace. They were dead on their feet as they crossed the finish line.

Captain Dunn had one last thing to say before putting the students on to a truck destined for a distant training area:

'During the next few days, there will be several more races, the loser of which will be punished. Take heed, if you end up taking these punishments, you won't last the week. Absorb the pain you feel. But fellas, there is much worse to come. My message is simple: increase your effort, work collaboratively or fall by the wayside. Your choice!'

The deflated group climbed aboard the 4-ton truck. Stone, the duty student, received his instructions for the night. As the tailgate of the truck slammed shut and the security chain rattled, a brief angry exchange quickly died down as the exhausted bodies settled into their seats. It was clear they were hurting. If we were looking for some positives, this brutal and angry self-examination was it.

The boss and I sat in the back of a Land Rover, with one of the guns hooked up to the rear. For the first time, we questioned our approach to the competition.

'Boss, we are in need of some social engineering with the next few races. If we don't do something soon, it will become a one-horse race.'

Captain Dunn took a deep breath to acknowledge my statement. He was hurting just as much as the boys he commanded. Like all quality leaders, he was passionately connected to those under his charge.

'Yeah, Colour, you're right. It's unusual to see the platoons so poorly balanced. This is new to me. Never has it been that one of the platoons wins all the events. The OC will have this on his radar, you can guarantee that. He may juggle the manning about and give Captain Watts some of our weaker students.'

My expressions compromised my thoughts.

'Do you not agree, Colour?'

'Well, boss, Captain Watts has his fair share of weak students. I'm not sure why we've lost every race, but it just appears that they always have the edge. For example, on today's gun run, they put someone on the barrel from the start. Now I have done my fair share of pulling 25-pounders over the years, but I didn't figure that out before we got underway. It was genius. How did they figure it out? Unquestionably, that was the key to getting the gun moving freely. Maybe we just need to win one or two races to give them some confidence. Maybe we just need a slice of luck.'

'Well let's see what tomorrow brings us, Colour. If things don't improve, then there will be little option other than to speak to the OC.'

We arrived at Minley Manor training area long after it had got dark. Lethargy had gripped the students. Hungry, tired and wallowing in self-pity, there was no space for kid gloves. A short, sharp shrift served to kick-start their motivation and after twenty minutes, every student had set up his basher. For those who had failed to pack their emergency rations, they would go hungry after Pete explained to the course that evening meal was on a truck that had broken down. Furthermore, he informed everyone that he needed to organize the recovery, and that could take some time. With the students huddled together, they looked around for confirmation of what this implied. Still not attuned to the unorthodox style of training that Rowallan used, the students sympathized with Pete, thinking he would be put out by the additional work this would bring him.

Once Pete had finished spinning his tales of woe, Captain Dunn briefed the platoon on the following day's activities:

> 'Stone, you will remain on duty. Make sure everyone is up and ready for a "Type A" inspection by 0630hrs. For those suffering cuts and bruises from today, sick parade will be with the Colour Sergeant before the inspection. Breakfast will arrive at 0700hrs if the CQMS has managed to get the truck recovered and fixed. Most importantly, park the events of this afternoon. Tomorrow's another day. Make sure you do your feet!'

With that final statement, we left the boys to get a good night's sleep.

The morning was due to start with a 'Type A' Field inspection, but before we had a chance to begin, Stone greeted me with a list of names of people who wished to see the medical orderly. Goldson, Lane, Barns and Haigh all stood behind Stone, sheepishly hiding in anticipation of the response.

'What's wrong with them?'

Stone fiddled with his notebook, looking for what he had written. Frustrated with Stone's slow reactions, I confronted the trio one by one.

'Goldson! What's your problem?'

'Headaches, Colour Sergeant. I think I have an awful headache. I doubt I can continue.'

'Explain further – what do you mean? Do you have a headache or not?'

'No, I mean yes. I mean I'm struggling with my ability to concentrate. It's like I have a hangover, but I haven't been drinking.'

Goldson had a familiar expression on his face: a mixture of confusion and bewilderment, accompanied by mumbling monotones. He continued to try to explain his symptoms, but each time failed to construct a comprehensible sentence. They were clear signs that something was troubling him, and it wasn't physical.

'Why does a headache stop you working? Surely it is something you just put up with.'

'I keep hearing voices in my head. They distract me from whatever I am trying to concentrate on. Last night I woke up four or five times thinking that I was in the process of bugging out. I just can't retain any length of concentration.'

Goldson's symptoms worried me. It was hard not to be suspicious, given the circumstances. His body language hadn't displayed anything untoward, but his comments indicated this was not a normal sick parade.

I had seen this sought of behaviour before in a soldier under my command during a tour of Northern Ireland, when a 'coffee jar grenade' exploded a few feet away from him. He was a very experienced and mature soldier who had always been the backbone of the platoon. Only by the grace of God did the entire patrol walk away with nothing more than ringing in their ears. The terrorist had thrown the device through the narrow gap between two detached houses. This was a common tactic used by terrorists, as the defilade angle made it almost impossible to counter the attack. Luckily, the glass jar clipped the corner of the furthest building and the explosion was caught between the gable ends of the houses. By the time I had got to the scene of the explosion, the terrorist was long gone and my priority turned to intelligence gathering. Eventually, we extracted the four lads who had been the target of the grenade attack so they could undertake a quick medical check. It was only twenty minutes after the event, but they recounted the attack with clarity before declaring themselves fit to continue soldiering. Yet there was just the slightest of concerns with the Rifleman nearest the point of detonation.

Physically he looked fine, but in a conversation, he failed to make any sense of what was actually happening. In hindsight, it was foolish to speculate that he was just shaken, and that very soon he would be back to normal. Thinking work was the best way to keep his mind occupied and distracted from the recent events, we decided to send him back to duty. There were civilians who needed evacuating from the area, and all hands to the pump were required. This proved to be the straw that broke the camel's back. Within ten minutes, this normally quiet and reserved lad had beaten up two bystanders and one of his closest friends. The look on his face still haunts me. He was struggling after the attack, but I didn't recognize the symptoms. We struggled to understand his behaviour. Standing in front of Goldson, he was wearing that same expression. I wouldn't make the same mistake again.

There was no alternative. Without further hesitation, he was directed to skip the triage and go directly to the Medical Officer back at Sandhurst.

'Who's next?' Lane took one pace forward.

'I am shocked to see you – not! What's your big ailment then, Lane?'

'It's my heels, Colour Sergeant. I have the biggest of blisters on them. I'm at the limit of endurance in pain. There's no way I can continue.' Lane removed his boots to reveal the two biggest ruptured blisters ever seen by man. Both of his heels had virtually worn away, matting the sock to the dried blood and soft tissue. To make it worse, the heel had been rubbing on his boot, ripping away the skin high up the back of his heel. It was as bad as it could get.

'This hasn't happened in one day, Lane. How long have you had these blisters?'

'Since the day we were given these boots. They don't fit at all well.' If this statement was meant to encourage empathy, it failed. In fact, it provoked an angry response. On so many levels, this was Lane's own failing.

'How could you be so bloody stupid? At what stage of this military course did you think you would not need comfortable boots? To tell me now that your boots don't fit is irresponsible and reckless!'

Wet, cold and in no fit state to continue, effectively there was now nothing he could take part in. Lane had finished the exercise before it had started; it would take him at least a week to recover sufficiently to be able to wear boots again. Moreover, Pat was going to throw a track at me. I had checked feet forty-eight hours earlier and never saw these blisters. This kind of thing should never happen, yet somehow it had. In this case, the fault was all mine. He would have to return to Sandhurst to receive professional medical help.

I looked up for the final member of the trio, only to discover he had vanished.

'Haigh!' I shouted. 'Haigh!' Eventually he reappeared, with his head held low, mumbling when quizzed about his injury.

'Where did you go to, you nutter?' I demanded.

'Nowhere, Colour Sergeant. I'm fine. I mean, well at first, but now I am fine.' I had fully expected Haigh to go sick during the exercise. His constant need of attention and encouragement was indicative of his character, but if he had the urge to go sick, there was a reason for it and we needed to identify what it was.

'What was the problem, softlad?'

'Blisters, Colour Sergeant. They appear to be covering the whole of my heel.'

'Well get your boots off and let me see!'

'No, Colour Sergeant, I really don't want to waste your time.'

'Haigh, shut up. Sit down and remove your boots! Where are these blisters then?'

'Right here, Colour Sergeant, on my heel.'

Haigh pointed out two small red marks, both of which were the beginnings of a blister. The slightest amount of fluid could be seen underneath them, but no more than you would get on your hand after ten minutes of manual labour.

'Don't patronize me, Haigh, I am standing right here looking at your heels. There is the faintest of abrasions, and the tiniest amount of fluid. What's the complaint. You need to know, if you see the medic he will take you off today's events. Is that what you want?'

Haigh began to drone on about the viscosity and diffraction, none of which was understandable. So, whilst he was distracted, I whipped a safety pin from my pocket and stabbed Haigh's small blisters. He shot to his feet in a nanosecond, dancing around on one foot.

'Sit down, Princess. It's a blister, not a gunshot wound. There is worse to follow.'

I was beginning to sound like Pat. He had such a funny repartee, and shamefully I was stealing his quips.

'Worse! You just cut me with a knife, what is worse than that?' Haigh asked.

'Dry your eyes, Princess, it won't hurt. Let me explain how to deal with this kind of blister. Firstly, we drain away the fluid by piercing the skin, then create more holes in the skin to prevent the blister from healing itself and refilling with fluid. With a pin, not a knife, but hold that thought! You must prevent it from sealing, so you may need to use the knife to remove surplus skin before covering it in potassium or iodine spray.'

'What's potassium iodine?'

Haigh couldn't have set me up better. With a splash of iodine to the exposed fresh skin, Haigh took off like a rocket.

'Ahh! Oh my bloody God. Fucking hell! Ow! Fuck! What is that?'

It did give me a hint of satisfaction seeing Haigh move so quickly. He held his foot and hopped in a circle, breathing like he was about to give birth. Tears rolled down his face with pain, and tears rolled down mine with laughter. His heel was then wrapped in zinc tape and he was as good as new! It was nothing other than the basics of self-preservation he had been shown, but he felt euphoric and stayed away from the medics. In these legislative times, combined with a society fixated on pampering and convenience, medical staff dish out sick chits as much for protection as they do for a cure. This is not a criticism, just an acknowledgement one must adjust to. Medics knew that before a student could see the medic, the DS would have conducted triage, something they didn't always agree with. Haigh had seen how bad Lane's feet were, and immediately realized that he had little to complain about. Nevertheless, he was right to go sick. He learnt much in those ten minutes: getting a practitioner's view on dealing with blisters was worth a million sick chits.

With sick parade dominating our time, we missed the opportunity to conduct the 'Type A' inspection. 'Thank God for small mercies,' said Captain Dunn, but the inspection would have been pointless having lost so much time dealing with medical issues.

'Stone, get the lads ready for the day's first event – more navigation.'

'Yes, Colour Sergeant. Can I ask, what time is breakfast turning up? We have not yet eaten.'

'Funny you should say that, Stone. There has been a problem with transport. We may not get fed this morning. I'm sure you will cope. Let's get to it. Two minutes, ready to go!'

Stone set about gathering the troops together. Shortly after, Minley was filled with students navigating from one hill to the next. By midday, we had finished the basic navigation and began to congregate at a centralized feature. The DS gathered around a Land Rover and slowly began donning an assortment of blue Row-Co T-shirts and sweatshirts. The OC was wearing the string vest. Seemingly he had said 'well done' to a student at some stage during the gun run, and Pat confirmed it warranted a handover of the vest of shame. It must have confused the hell out of the students, who were huddled in small groups speculating about what was going on.

When Staff were seen wearing their blue T-shirts, it signalled a fitness session. There was no disbelief or shock when Pat screamed out the order to put on their rugby tops. The sound of rucksacks being plundered for their red shirts was sobering. The gentle rustle amplified forty times merged to create one louder sound. As the quick-release buckles clipped into place and drawcords whooshed tight, the atmosphere was tense. Fixed with glares of determination, the platoon massed at the base of a large hill waiting for their instructions.

'OK, you lot, hush up,' said Major Gray. 'Keep quiet and listen to the instructions for your next competition.'

Major Gray climbed onto the bonnet of a Land Rover, his face red raw with wind-chill and his bare hands white at the knuckle. As ever, he rubbed them continuously to generate heat as he announced 'the yellow handbag race':

> 'This event is simple. You will run from here to the base of the large hill behind me. When you get there, you will pick up two yellow burdens, then follow the track up the hill, along the ridge, down the far side and finish back here at the start point. Once you arrive back at the start point, you only have one more lap to do. So, two times around for the slow ones amongst you. Or 2km, whichever you prefer.'

The students had experienced the yellow burden before. It featured in their first encounter of the Mean Machine. The H83 ammunition box was filled with flint and sand. Over the years, these ingredients had congealed to make a concrete-like filling.

'This is a straight race. But the winner will be the platoon to complete the course in the quickest average time. The time is measured between the first and last man across the line, and the average time calculated. In simple terms, it's about the fastest man being faster than the other platoon's fastest man, and the slowest man being faster than the slowest of the other team. No. 1 Platoon having won the last race, it is your right to go first. Staff, you have five minutes to ready your platoons.'

Captain Dunn cornered me at the rear of the Land Rover, wearing one of those expressions that betrayed his thoughts. He was gearing up to say something that would be uncomfortable.

'Shall we pull Haigh out of the race? With his blisters and in his present state of mind, the OC would probably agree. He is just a millstone around the platoon's neck, and we need to win one of these competitions.'

For many reasons, this made sense. But we both knew that Haigh could get around this course. It would not be easy, but the zinc tape on his heel would hold out; he could do it. Desperately keen to agree with the boss, but unable to say the words, the silence dragged on too long. Captain Dunn sensed my unease and changed his mind.

'Clearly you're not comfortable with that, Colour. Fuck it! Let him run! It would be a hollow victory without him running. They will just have to push him around the best they can. They know they need that vital first victory.'

Winning is as much about mental strength as it is about your physical conditioning. As a team, it is about the chemistry, the collective desire, the leadership decisions, the collective mental strength and, every now and then, a slice of luck. How did Greece beat Portugal in 2004 to win the European Championships? How did little old Wimbledon beat the invincible Liverpool to win the 1988 FA Cup? Defying the odds is not luck, it's maximizing the human agile edge. The simple explanation is team chemistry, and the formula for understanding this is not over complex. Most military instructors have it in abundance. There are sceptics about team chemistry, but a simple piece of analysis has consistently proved it is a real thing. A formula calculating friction, predicated on relationship histories and conflicts of personality, can accurately predict the likely outcome of a competition. In the case of Haigh, he was proving to be a millstone, but he was not the single point of failure. There were other dynamics that needed to be realized.

Major Gray set Paddy's platoon on their way as the boss briefed our students on the need to win. Captain Dunn spoke for a full five minutes about determination, the psychological mastery required to overcome pain and fatigue. His tone was calm and calculated, his speech consciously unexcitable. As was common, after he finished talking, he invited me to summarize the event.

The pamphlet sent to students prior to arriving at Sandhurst was designed to reassure participants and simplify the training objectives. © MoD, reproduced with permission.

"Develop character first and military leadership will follow"
Lord Rowallan, 1941

Adventurous Training

The next stage involves the great outdoors – including exercises in the Brecon Beacons, sea canoeing and rock-climbing.

Training the Individual

The key to the Rowallan course – activities that build confidence, awareness and self-reliance. Everything from first aid and rescue work to basic construction techniques, from navigation to trapping!

Training the Group

The confidence and the knowledge that have been gained are now put to work in the group. Teamwork is the order of the day, but between the group tasks and debriefing sessions there is time to relax – or to enjoy the exhilaration of a stretcher race!

Rowallan Student balances at the top of the trainasium.

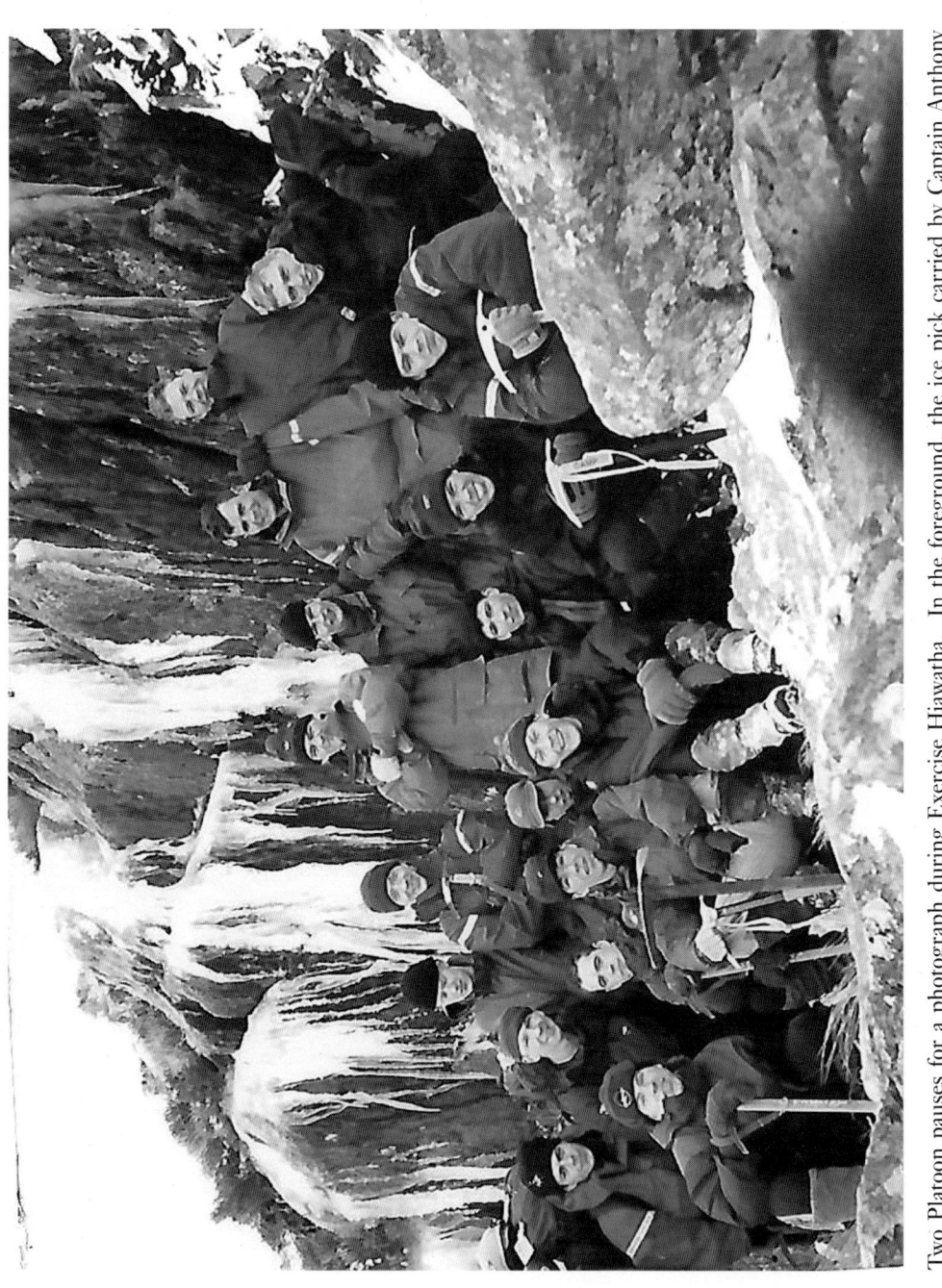

Two Platoon pauses for a photograph during Exercise Hiawatha. In the foreground, the ice pick carried by Captain Anthony Streather on the failed Haramosh Expedition.

Survivors of course Number 963 celebrate with their 25lb Artillery Gun and newly named stretchers 'Pain & Gain'.

Students reenact the leap from the Pontoon as they begin their search for fish in the Wish Stream lake.

'There is only one way to win this race. That is to pick up the yellow burden and run. Run so hard your stomach shrinks and you vomit, your eyes glaze over and your head becomes light just before you faint. If you don't win this race or collapse attempting to win, don't come back. I heard you blame each other for the gun run defeat. Well put your money where your mouth is because this one is an individual effort. The only person to blame this time around will be you. There is no place to hide. Stone, let's get them warmed up.'

Stone raised his hand to ask a question.
'What's up, Stone?'
'Is the 4-tonner with breakfast here yet, Colour Sergeant?'
'Is that all you wish to say after the advice you just received? That is why we keep losing: you're full of self-pity! Always the victim, Stone! "No" is the answer. Now get a grip and ready the team.'

Stone turned his attention to corralling the students into a large circle and the platoon began to stretch off their muscles. So distracted with his task, he failed to notice that No. 1 Platoon had completed their run.

'Stone, it's time to go!' yelled Pat. The students gathered at the start line and Pat instructed them to lie on their stomachs spread-eagled. Arms and legs were splayed, then raised in the freefall parachute position. It was some perverse tribute to his beloved Parachute Regiment that no one quite understood.

'Marvellous! Bloody marvellous! Eighteen minutes, thirty-two seconds to beat. Stand by. Stand by. Go!' Pat screamed at my students, and instantly Captain Dunn and I targeted those who were slow out of the blocks.

'Barns, get to the front you useless toe-rag! Francis, Danner, you bunch of tarts, move it. Come on, sprint.'

Rideout and Moore took the lead. Mathews remained at the rear as the self-elected policeman. He was shouting at his slower peers, desperately trying to keep the platoon in a tighter formation.

'Withers! Withers! Come on, mate. You can do this.'

Struggling with his own two burdens, Mathews thrust his head into the centre of Witherspoon's back and began to push him faster.

Remarkably, and without warning, Rideout appeared from nowhere, pushing Barns. It was an encouraging sight, and proved to be extremely effective. At the halfway point, exactly nine minutes had passed; we were thirty seconds ahead. Mathews repeated the time, calling it out so everyone could hear. This had a morale-boosting effect which galvanized the platoon and the tailenders.

'Come on, we can do it!' screamed Mathews. 'Nine minutes to go, come on. Withers, Dan, come on. You can do it!'

A surge of enthusiasm raced through the platoon. With the finish in sight, the effort being expended was phenomenal. Students were vomiting, coughing and spluttering, yet still running hard. Mathews was last to cross the line, having pushed Barns the whole way. Ironically, it was Barns who threw up several times while Major Gray calculated the scores. Paddy's students stood expectantly as they stared at Major Gray. They knew it would be close, as did the DS. On tenterhooks, we all listened to Pat call for silence.

Balancing on the spare tyre bolted to the bonnet of the Land Rover, Major Gray encouraged the Company to get closer to the front of the vehicle.

'Close in everyone, close in. There is some extraordinary news for you all.'

Major Gray had run around the course with both platoons. Forehead dripping with sweat and breathing heavily, he announced the results.

'No. 1 Platoon, eighteen minutes thirty-two seconds. Before I read out the next score, please give No. 1 Platoon a round of applause. They have broken the course record, which has stood for eight years.'

Paddy's boys began jumping and cheering as they congratulated themselves. The sound of their celebrations tore through me like fingernails on a chalkboard. Clapping as instructed, there was little sincerity on offer from No. 2 Platoon.

'Hush, everyone. Hush.' Major Gray called for order, and silence fell on the Company.

'Regrettably, No. 1 Platoon, your record has lasted less than twenty minutes. With a new course record of eighteen minutes twenty-six seconds, No. 2 Platoon are the new holders of the course record and win today's competition. Congratulations No. 2 Platoon; about time! The score is now 12–3 to No. 1 Platoon!'

Major Gray raised a huge smile and clapped his hands as the DS joined in, less Pat, who declared the OC could wear the vest again for congratulating the students.

No. 2 Platoon let out a deafening cheer, and an outbreak of emotion followed. With hugging, high fives and much back-slapping, the feeling was exhilarating. It was their first taste of victory, and they didn't hold back on the celebrations. Experiencing the absurd reward of being a spectator to a punishment came with just a hint of satisfaction. Captain Dunn called for order as he issued a debrief on their performance.

'Two kilometres, two burdens weighing not much more than 15lb each, you should be able to do that in seventeen minutes. Some of you are still cruising, and this week will find you out! Colour, do you want to add anything?'

'Yes please, Sir.'

It was hard to remain dispassionate, as the urge to stand up and praise them for their achievement was all-consuming. We knew there had been some outstanding performances, especially by those who pushed the weaker runners all the way around. Standing in a semicircle, faces portraying their endeavours and sufferings so far, the golden threads of success beamed brightly. For the first time, fatherly pride washed over me. Fighting my emotions, I chose my words carefully:

> 'You lads have lost enough times to know what it's like to be punished for losing an event. Don't let the euphoria of this victory cloud that feeling. When the other platoon return, no sarcastic comments; applause and respect only. Then you can move into the woods, set up a shelter and get ready for the night-time activities.'

As the other platoon descended from the crest of the hill, they were being hounded and berated by Captain Watts and Paddy. It was a familiar scene, but we were grateful not to be part of it. At the finish line, my instructions for respect had been rigidly adhered to, with the exception of Stone, who had thought it funny to heckle the losing platoon with comments of a derogatory nature. That one act of immaturity reinforced his unpopular status as he drew internal criticism for his lack of decorum.

'Colour Sergeant!'
'Yes, Moore?'
'Is there any sign of the transport with breakfast on it?'
'Moore, it's 1200hrs. You have missed breakfast.'
'So it's lunch, Colour Sergeant.'
'Bloody hell, Moore, anyone would think you hadn't been fed for twenty-four hours.'
'Well, it's not far from that, Colour Sergeant.'
'Pete, any sign of the transport with food on it?'
'No, not today, Gaz!'
'There's your answer, Moore. Maybe tomorrow.'

By 1600hrs it was dark enough to begin the evening's activities. After a short period revising basic night navigation skills, each student was assessed on his ability to command and control a large group at night. Moving around the training area as two patrols, students took turns in navigating between checkpoints. It was a formal assessment, but not a particularly difficult one. Along the route, they received further tuition on escape and evasion techniques, as well as trapping and tracking by moonlight. It was near midnight when the last of the platoon passed through the final checkpoint manned by Eddie and the Sergeant Major. In typical fashion, Pat teased everyone by cruelly frying hamburgers and bacon at the control tent. Sarcastically, Williams asked if there was any news on the food arriving. It had been over twenty-four hours since their last meal, and desperation was creeping in. Pat instantly jumped on the opportunity to increase the misery Williams was feeling.

'Hungry are you, Princess? Tell you what, seeing as you are so keen to get involved in the administration of the Company, you can be the duty runner tonight. How's that for an answer? Get all your kit and set your basher next to mine.'

Pat would spend the next few hours sending Williams out on spurious tasks. Firstly, he sent Williams to the water's edge and told him to decide if the tide was coming in or going out. An hour later, Pat had to send a few people to find him. Williams was still standing by the edge of the water trying to figure it out when Moore arrived to explain the physics of waves and tides. Disparagingly, Williams returned to Pat and was promptly dispatched to draw a sketch map of the stars. It was going to be a long night for the lad as Pat toyed with his emotional reserves.

With everyone else settling into their bashers, the boss and I reviewed the students' performance over the first twenty-four hours. It had been a tough start to the exercise. The weather was abysmal, the physical training tiring and food was not forthcoming. For the boss, his group cruised through the night navigation with no problems, but my group had several near misses. We were still recalling these events when Pete arrived fresh from an admin run to Sandhurst. He was accompanied by the students who had been taken back to the medical centre at the start of the day to see the MO.

'How are my two lads, Pete?'

'Lane has told the doctor that he was made to run wearing ill-fitting boots. The doctor has gone ballistic. He is on the warpath. Apparently, there is a letter already on the way to the College Commander! Oh, and Goldson has been kept in for observation.'

'Bloody hell, boss, that's crap. Lane has dropped us in it from a huge height.'

'I know. To make it worse, the doctor is no fan of Rowallan. He will be quick to blame the course for any injury. You know, the closest he should ever get to soldiers is in the morning with his soft-boiled eggs!'

Major Gray interrupted the conversation.

'How's Goldson, Q?'

'Strange; very strange in fact,' replied Pete.

'What did the doctor say?'

'Not a lot really. He was not prepared to discuss it with me. It is serious enough to keep Goldson in for observation.'

Silence took hold while we thought of the possibilities. Major Gray, arms folded, looked towards the sky. Gently rocking forwards and backwards on the rear legs of his green army-issue camping chair, he was deep in thought. Captain Dunn scratched at an insect bite on his face as he too pondered the outcome.

'Woof! Woof! Woof woof!!' Pat broke the silence with repeated barking, that morphed into howling like a wolf. 'He's as crazy as a mad dog – barking mad.

You know it, I know it, and after a few hundred wasted man hours, the doctor will know it.'

'More like Tooting you mean, Sergeant Major,' said Captain Watts.

'Tooting? What's Tooting?' Pete asked.

'When someone goes beyond Barking, he's Tooting. You know, two bus stops further down the road than Barking!'

'Oh, and you're perfectly normal,' replied Captain Dunn. The comment gained him instant laughter and applause, sparking off a loud bantering session to draw the day to a close.

Pleasantly, the following morning saw a thaw in the temperature as the platoon paraded for a 'Type A' field inspection. Looking dirty and exhausted, Williams stood in front of his peers and presented them for inspection. His lethargic stance spoke volumes for his present state of mind. Pat had kept him up most of the night. Deprived of food and sleep, his face portrayed self-pity. It was the exact reaction the DS expected and wanted. The previous forty-eight hours were designed to erode resilience and smash fortitude, leaving students desperate and vulnerable. Their determination and drive had reached the bottom. For the next event to succeed, it was imperative the students experienced how bad things could get. In time, they would learn how to cope and not let it affect judgment. We were aiming to give the course a feeling of desperation, a condition that generates plenty of opportunities to learn much about someone.

Rowallan is about leadership. To teach this complex subject, you must try and replicate every conceivable scenario in which an officer could find himself. Understanding how hard it is to inspire and lead thirty soldiers who are broken, low on morale, hungry, cold and losing faith in you is the hardest lesson of all. Firstly, before you can learn to be a leader, you need to experience life as a disciple.

'OK, Williams, ready to go?'

'Yes, Colour Sergeant.'

'Have you checked everyone's kit? Made sure they have washed, shaved, powdered feet etc?'

Failing to catch my eye, Williams nodded with agreement. It was blatantly clear that the students had resigned themselves to punishment and decided not to put too much effort into preparing their equipment, prompting an education in motivation.

Standing in front of Witherspoon, his kit poorly laid out, I saw he'd failed to wash and shave. Boyle was the next in line, and at a quick glance, he was in a similar state to Witherspoon. This theme repeated itself throughout the inspection. Without exception, every student was in a poor state of self-administration. Captain Dunn confronted the whole platoon and asked why they were in such a poor state. Only after repeating the question several times did someone offer an answer. It was futile. The platoon had lost its drive, and it was time to demonstrate that despite how poorly they believed they had been treated, they hadn't experienced any real hardship at all.

'Colour Sergeant, please remind everyone why they are here,' Captain Dunn said.

> 'My pleasure Sir. So, just because you are cold, you stop putting the effort in? Because you are hungry, you stop trying? And because you are slightly damp, you feel hard done by? Has the world come to a grinding halt because you are out of your comfort zone? Well if you think things are bad now, in ten minutes you will be wishing for the comfort of your damp boots and the easy tasking of cleaning your kit, standing still for inspection. Turn to your right and follow me.'

Captain Dunn chased those who were too slow on the pick-up. 'Get going. Follow the Colour Sergeant.'

It took less than 100 metres running at a fast pace towards a large stream for the students to realize what was coming next. With no pause, we jumped in and turned left before struggling upstream. A hundred metres further on, the students were struggling to keep pace. The point had been made, and we scrambled out of the freezing water and headed towards the base of a large hill. For twenty minutes, we ran up and down the hill until the students could do no more. All that remained was to explain the balance between sleep, administration and preparation:

> 'You people need to digest this. Working hard will prevent things from going from bad to worse. By letting a problem grow, it will snowball, as it did just then. We wouldn't have run through the stream had you tried harder on the inspection. That is why you are here! Just because you have missed out on food and sleep, it doesn't mean you stop putting the effort in. It means you dig deep into your mind and find that extra something that makes a positive attitude – the attitude that separates the men from the boys, the leaders from the disciples. It is all about mental strength. So, I ask you all now, and this time you will answer: do you want to lead soldiers?'

To a loud chorus, the students replied: 'Yes, Colour Sergeant!'

'Good. In that case, stop feeling sorry for yourselves. Pull your socks up, and start searching for a positive attitude. When you return to your kit, powder your feet, and put on dry socks and underwear. You also need your red rugby tops. Meet me here in ten minutes. Go!'

The on-the-spot punishment had the desired effect. The students returned in the time allotted, bringing with them an improved attitude. They had received what is commonly referred to as an injection of motivation, or an old-fashioned kick up the backside, mixed with a hint of education. But while it appeared to be working, the acid test was just about to be taken.

'I asked before if you wanted to lead soldiers, and you all agreed that you did. I'm now giving you the opportunity. Who wants to lead on the next event?'

Without hesitation, Mathews, King, Murphy, Moore and Rideout threw up their hands.

Although the students never knew it, the appointments had already been predetermined. Captain Dunn was responsible for ensuring each student had equal opportunity to demonstrate his ability by plotting appointments on a complex matrix chart. The matrix was the product of our analysis, and would be used to micromanage performance and development. By giving the student the opportunity to volunteer, we retained the perception of chance and chaos.

'Me, Colour Sergeant.' Murphy was full of aggression. He was desperately keen to make amends for his failed stretcher race on Monkey Hill.

'Good, Murphy. But you had your chance and screwed it up. Why should you get another go!'

Murphy's body language cried out with hurt.

'Colour Sergeant, that is unfair. It was the first attempt. I can do much better.'

'That's a confident statement, softlad! Let's hope you have the ability to back it up. March the platoon to the Company Sergeant Major so he can give you the brief on the "P Company" stretcher race.'

Anything remotely connected to tests used by P Company had Pat excited. He had enjoyed several successful years as a P Company instructor and loved to talk about these antics. With the two nominated students standing in front of their teams, Pat explained the rules of the race to all the students. The race was just over 5km long. It followed narrow sand tracks, which meandered up and down several large hills. Each platoon would carry a cast iron stretcher loaded with six full sandbags. In the absence of the OC – who had returned to camp to speak with the doctor about Goldson, and probably Lane – Pat played master of ceremonies:

'Right, low life. Staff Sergeant Dazzell will lead the frontrunners round the route, so all you have to do is run and carry the stretcher. Both teams will set off at the same time. It is a team race, so the first platoon with all its team members across the finish line wins. Finally, all is fair in love and war, but take care; if you are knocked down by one of these stretchers, you may not get back up. So if you fannies are ready, adopt the freefall position.'

Daz ran to the top of the first hill to avoid being trapped between the stretchers as they battled for the lead. Captains Dunn and Watts followed, while Paddy and I stayed with the platoons.

'Stand by! Stand by! Go!' shouted Pat.

Taking a back seat and hoping Murphy would do well, I realized it was critical to capitalize on the momentum of our first win. It was imperative to Platoon morale; they needed to win this race. If there was just a hint of suspicion that Murphy would fail, we would need to replace him. Side by side and stride for stride, the stretchers clashed along the first stretch of the narrow sandy track. Murphy had organized his team better than he did previously, but his command lacked authority. Maybe his need for food denied him the aggressive streak that was required. With less than 50 metres gone, it was starting to look like his first effort on Monkey Hill.

Both teams struggled to secure the lead as they continued to clatter into each other, hemmed in by the embankment straddling the track. The sand footholds sapped their speed, and both stretchers were forced into a quick walk. The time was ripe for a breakaway. This was the moment Murphy needed to identify. By mounting a decisive assault, he would break the will of his opposition. As the track became narrower and the banks became higher, the tangled stretchers collided and crashed to the ground. A frantic few moments saw Paddy's boys emerge first from the sea of bodies. Murphy was losing control, and Mathews became frustrated at the lack of progress. I'd seen enough; sensing this was a defining moment, Murphy was replaced by Mathews. Like a man possessed, he rallied his team together in an effort to keep in touch with No. 1 Platoon. After 2km, the gap had closed and less than 20 metres separated the teams. It was imperative that Mathews took measures to close the gap now, so he could mount an assault before the finish. A moment later, Mathews began to bark out instructions.

'OK everyone, listen up. When I say "go", I want you all to sprint for ten seconds; no one shirks. Get ready. Stand by. Stand by. Three, two, one, go!'

Mathews counted down from ten as the students sprinted with the stretcher. Captain Dunn looked at me in amazement.

'Ha! Well I never. I'm impressed with that, Colour. If they keep that up, they will catch the other platoon.'

The success was instant, as our stretcher merged with the tailenders of the lead platoon. Mathews' initiative had inspired his team, who were by now pushing weary students out their way as they sought to press home the advantage. Despite the amount of hard work they had put in, they still found themselves in second place. Their progress was being held up by the stretcher in front. It was becoming frustrating as time ebbed away and the opportunities to get ahead dwindled. The full extent of Mathews' knowledge in leadership had been exhausted – it was time to introduce him to another skill in leading men, how to 'influence change'.

The lad from Herefordshire needed simply to pass the stretcher in front of him in order to succeed. His problem was that he had all but spent his reserves. Having pushed everyone to their limit, few people had any more to offer.

Running alongside Mathews, the knowledge he needed was imparted just as the gap was on the cusp of reopening: 'Mathews, it's time you influenced the change in position, and the only way to be sure of success is to lead by example. There is a time and a place for perspiration, and this is it. Don't get the balance wrong, but every now and again, the commander needs to get his hands dirty.'

I hoped Mathews understood what was being said. It was one thing to give him the knowledge; it would have been an entirely different thing to tell him what to do. He was left to figure out what had been said and make his own interpretation of 'lead by example'. It felt like a lifetime before he made his move. Amazingly, he did it exactly the way we would have hoped. Shoving Murphy out of the way, he gripped the front of the stretcher. With a burst of explosive energy, he began an assault on the front platoon. Seconds later, both groups were once again side by side, fighting for space on the narrow track. In a repeat of what happened at the start, they became entangled in a mass of bodies as they both strove for superiority. It was now impossible to see who was who. Stragglers, runners and relief runners were all mixed in a gaggle of students.

In a cloud of dust, both stretchers smashed into the ground. With no time to stop, the runners following fell like skittles as they ran into the rear of the stretchers. First to emerge from the maul was one of Paddy's platoon. Confused and disorientated, he started to help out on our stretcher. Quickly, Rideout dragged him off and threw him back to the ground. The tension had gripped everyone. Captain Watts was berating his students for idling. I turned to look over my shoulder to see who was getting an ear bashing, and thought I saw Paddy pushing the rear of his stretcher. But there was no time to hang around and confirm my suspicion; this was a critical stage. For the next two minutes, with students losing their footing, the lead changed hands several times. Like two Spanish galleons broadsiding each other, students exchanged blows with their rivals as they fought for the lead.

With the finish line in sight, Mathews let out a war cry and dragged the stretcher out of the crowd, taking the lead in the process. The realization that a second win was in sight, the mental battle won, renewed confidence and turbocharged their efforts. With just a hint of arrogance, Mathews and his stretcher bearers began to edge away from No. 1 Platoon. Once in the front, he relinquished his position on the stretcher and went back to commanding. As so often happens in command, once you become fixed by a micro-problem, the macro issue becomes unhinged. Mathews had produced a new problem – the absence of Stone and Lane. Both had failed to keep pace with the stretcher. So, in textbook fashion, he balanced his weak and strong runners on the stretcher before sending his fittest men back to retrieve his stragglers. It was an inspirational piece of leadership. Moreover, it was confirmation that our teachings were being assimilated, just the reassurance Captain Dunn and I needed. Lane, Stone and Haigh crossed the line with No. 1 Platoon's stretcher, way ahead of Paddy's stragglers.

Mathews had won the race because he applied his new-found skills of leadership, but there was no celebrating, back-slapping or euphoria, just the expression of sheer exhaustion. Both platoons were spent. Haigh was hobbling badly, while Danner was as pale as a sheet and looking severely undernourished. The second win had come at a cost, but if possible, worse was still to come. Captain Dunn enjoyed his debrief and revelled in the mini-renaissance by repeating the score several times: at twelve points to six, there was a renewed hope. Whilst the students listened intently to the boss, I returned to the Company control tent. The next lesson of the day had just arrived on Pete's truck, and it was not for the faint-hearted. Students were about to get a lesson in managing desperation, tolerating discomfort and developing new levels of mental robustness to survive.

Pete was busily offloading large green food containers, known as hay-boxes, from the back of his truck. You could hear the excitement ripple around the course as the boxes were stacked three high. Tea and coffee urns, bread, butter and condiments all came from the rear of the vehicle. The sight of the food containers brought anticipation and raised morale. The prospect of their first feed for over twenty-four hours was irrepressible. Pat rounded up all the students and ushered them towards the food containers, occasionally barking at an inattentive student. Simultaneously, Pete was busy organizing two queues in front of the hay-boxes. He carried two large serving ladles, which he banged together, causing the students to fantasize about what they would be served.

With eyes fixed on the large green boxes, the students stood in total silence, drooling in anticipation and waiting patiently for the next words of command. Pat began to giggle to himself before he addressed his audience.

'Right, ladies, I'm sure you are all hungry! If you want to eat, you're going to need your mess tins and mugs.'

Excitement bubbled uncontrollably from the crowd as they balanced themselves in two equal queues, eating utensils at the ready. First in the queue was Danner. He had shed a significant amount of weight in the last few days, and it was no surprise to see his cheeky grin beaming from the front of the line. Pat was quick to spot Danner's excitement, and as normal, capitalized on the opportunity by inflicting his warped sense of humour on the unsuspecting giant.

'Danner, what would you prefer for dinner, beef stew or pie, chips and beans?'

'Well, Sir, currently the thought of what particular type of food I would prefer is far from my mind. It is more the quantity that one's concerned with. I would eat a scabby horse given the opportunity.'

'Yeah, yeah, Princess. Stop waffling and pick a queue! Left for beef stew or right for pie and chips.'

The course quickly shuffled into a queue of their preferred choice. Tapping the serving ladle on the metal box to attract everyone's attention, Pete slowly cracked open the lid of the first food container. With forty pairs of eyes burning down on his every move, he reached into the food box and pulled out a fluffy white rabbit, complete with long ears and bright red eyes.

'Rabbit! Rabbit! That's rabbit!' exclaimed Mathews.

'No shit, Sherlock, you have found a use for your first in biology!' replied a dejected Boyle, who was by now developing the Rowallan humour.

'No, I mean that's Rabbit, my pet rabbit from Sandhurst. Look, it's still wearing his collar and tag I made for him!'

With instantaneous sobriety, the students collected the very animals they had been caring for during the previous two weeks. Given they were being pulled from the food container, there was no requirement to ask why they had been brought out on the exercise. Hunger pains subsided as an undercurrent of distaste for the Rowallan sense of humour bubbled at the surface of idle talk.

The platoon collected one animal between two and gathered in a small wood to build cooking fires. Assembled in one large circle, I reminded everyone about the need to execute a swift kill. It was vital that the fatal blow was delivered with ruthless efficiency to prevent the creature from suffering pain. Failing to do so would cause great stress to the animals and other students. For peace of mind, each kill would be micromanaged. Captain Dunn needed to guarantee we had taken suitable measures to prevent any mishaps or needless suffering.

'OK, who wants to start us off?' I asked.

Most of the students avoided eye contact. There was a tangible fear of being selected first. It was exactly what we had expected. On this occasion there were no volunteers, so we nominated.

'Danner, out you come with your rabbit, lad!' I ordered.

With an almost expectant look, Danner walked to the centre of the circle cradling his rabbit.

'OK, Danner, do you recall how Captain Watts demonstrated this to you?'

'No I don't, Colour Sergeant!'

'OK, grab the rabbit by his hind legs. Hold it upside down.'

Danner's large frame made easy work of holding the agitated rabbit.

'Good! Keep calm. Now slowly rub the blunt edge of your machete up and down his back until he arches his neck at a 90-degree angle. The moment he does that, strike swiftly. You must hit the crux of the neck with the blunt edge. Full power; it must be a strong blow.'

With the rabbit surrendering to the inevitable outcome, its neck in a prime position, Danner raised his machete high above his head and paused too long.

'Now!' I screamed, to jolt him into action. The pause allowed the rabbit to lower its head and Danner's blow missed the crux of the neck, impacting with the skull. The rabbit gushed blood and wriggled violently. Danner flapped and began swiping frantically as the rabbit convulsed and dodged each subsequent attempt. Blows rained down on the animal's body, causing large open wounds, ripping fur the length of the rabbit's body. Each blow was accompanied with a yelp of pain and a cloud of candy-striped fur being flung into the air. The remaining students stared in horror as the other rabbits appeared to pick up on the plight of their pain-stricken mate.

Preventing further stress to all, I removed the rabbit from Danner and finished the job for him. His once white rabbit was now crimson red and covered in ugly scars. The big lad's face said it all. Horrified and ashen, he had got it wrong in a big way and lost a great deal of confidence in the process, as well as making skinning the rabbit a great deal harder. The unpleasant sight of watching a kill go drastically wrong gave the next few students an incentive to get it right. Concentration was heightened as the next member of the platoon prepared to dispatch his rabbit.

Having seen most of the rabbits meet their fate, it was now the turn of the chickens. In the same manner we had used for the rabbits, careful supervision was exercised. The first to attempt a kill was Witherspoon. He fought to retain control of his chicken as it flapped and wriggled to break free. With his face covered in fear and trepidation, he began to slowly stroke the chicken's neck to calm it down before coaxing it into full extension, ready for snapping. With a hint of the Norman Wisdoms, Witherspoon fluffed his attempt at snapping the bird's neck. The twist and forward thrust motion lacked aggression; it was under-extended, and the animal's neck was only partly ripped from its socket. Expecting the chicken to die, Witherspoon relaxed his grip. Surprisingly, in a cloud of feathers, the chicken broke free from Witherspoon's arm. With its neck broken and limp, it scampered around the dumbfounded students. Snapped but not detached from the body, the head dragged along the ground between its legs. Surreal was the sight of the animal playing keepie-uppiee with its own head! For nearly thirty seconds, the students held their breath and watched in horror as it continued to run out its last seconds of life. Witherspoon gave chase in an effort to stop the suffering, but instead, just added to a weird situation that made him look even more like Norman Wisdom.

Seeing chickens run around headless was not new to me, but this was a strange experience. Some students shielded their eyes from the trauma suffered by the chicken. Others were keen to help Witherspoon and joined in the chase, but inevitably they crumpled in a heap several times, outmanoeuvred by an all-but-dead chicken. Sheepishly, Witherspoon eventually brought his kill back to the centre of the platoon. In a sombre moment, we revisited the need to be ruthless and that developing this skill could potentially save their lives. The focus was waning, and it needed to be re-established.

It wasn't long before we had the first refusal to kill. Boyle stood silent with a chicken tightly secured under his arm. Having been coached in the technique, Boyle was given the command to dispatch his chicken, but he failed to respond.

'Boyle!' I shouted. 'Don't stress the animal any more than we already have. Kill that bloody chicken before it catches a cold and dies.'

Boyle raised his head and spoke incoherently.

'Speak up, softlad, what are you saying?'

'My arm, Colour Sergeant.'

'What about your arm?'

'I think I've pulled a muscle. I don't think I will be able to pull and twist the chicken's neck. I am worried that I may cause the animal undue pain.'

'Are you saying that you have full use of your arm, but you can't twist and push?'

'Exactly, Colour Sergeant.'

Pleased with his excuse, Boyle smiled and nodded at me.

'Who has a rabbit left?' Francis raised his arm. 'Give Boyle your rabbit and take his chicken.' A wave of defeat washed over Boyle's face as he finally executed his evening meal. There was little to enjoy about this particular duty – the discomfort on his face said it all.

Night had truly taken hold by the time all the students began to cook their kill. Haigh was hunched over a fire, cursing at the archaic nature of the training and the liberal adherence to the hygienic preparation of his evening meal.

'What's wrong with you, Haigh?'

'The demise of an animal is not something to rejoice in. We shouldn't be killing animals, Colour Sergeant. I never joined the Army to do this. Barbaric and needless, is my view. I admit to feeling decidedly uneasy with myself presently.'

This was reassuring to hear. If it was an easy test, you would be invited to do it in every job interview you attended. If he found it easy, it would be a concern. Most normal people would feel the same way, so Haigh's observations warranted a careful response.

'Well the good thing is, Haigh, I had you figured as the type of character who would petition the Queen to save the whale. It's good to see you haven't proved me wrong. But you are right, you should be upset after being made to kill an innocent animal. We don't do these things for fun, but the facts are these. When you become a leader of men, you will be forced to constantly make hard and uncomfortable decisions, and you must learn to live with them. Critically, do not allow it to cloud your judgment. Guilt, annoyance, pity, confusion and anger: all these emotions are currently coursing through your veins. Am I right?'

'Yes, Colour Sergeant.'

'So you will not be feeling hungry then, softlad.'

Dipping my hand into the improvised boiling pot, I made off with his well-cooked chicken. It wasn't long before he was up off his perch chasing after me. Danner joined in. He was urging me to return the food, fearing that Haigh would come calling for scraps if he didn't come to his senses. With food on the stove and hot drink spilling out of their black mugs, morale was on the up. We had given them a taste of desperation that would galvanize them like no other event they would ever experience.

As dawn arrived the following morning, it brought back the rain. Despite the misery of the wet climate, the temperature change suggested the big freeze suffered by the UK was nearing its end. The change was bittersweet. The warmer weather made life a little less miserable, but the rain made it more uncomfortable. None of this was noticed by the students suffering another 'Type A' field inspection. The conditions had got the better of everyone, and even the most enthusiastic of students found it hard to smile. Fortunately, it was the penultimate day of the exercise and the main event was a 10-miler, or in other words a 17km march across a number of training areas around Aldershot. The route stretched from Minley exercise area along several small back roads before crossing the M3 and back into the Barossa training estate. Because this would be their first real test of endurance wearing full marching order, carrying rucksacks, the students would not be forced to march at a specific speed. They would navigate and set their own pace.

The DS bunched together in a small circle, waiting for Major Gray to arrive. He had spent the night at home after speaking with the doctor about Goldson. Yesterday seemed a lifetime ago and the issue was far from my mind. Pat was the first person to begin talking about Goldson.

'I wonder if the OC had any luck getting the doctor to rid us of our man Goldson? Hah, speak of the devil and he shall appear. Morning, Sir, a good night off?' Irrespective of rank or standing, everyone suffered sarcastic comments from Pat.

'Yes, thank you kindly, Sergeant Major. I popped round to see your wife. She sends her regards! *Quid pro quo*!'

The OC was just as quick as Pat, and his riposte earned him a belly-busting chorus of laughter as Pat realized he had just been outwitted.

'Are we ready to do the 10-miler, Sergeant Major?'

'Yes, everyone is present, with the exception of Goldson,' replied Pat.

'How do you mean "with the exception of Goldson"? I thought the Company Quartermaster brought him back last night?' said Major Gray.

'No!' snapped Pat. 'You said you were going to visit Goldson last night!'

'Yes. That was my intention, but when I got back to camp, Q said he wasn't at the MRS any longer! I assumed you had picked him up!' said Major Gray calmly.

Pat screamed for Pete, who was busy packing away the food containers.

'Pete, can you shoot back to Sandhurst and find out where the hell Goldson is? Have a chat with the Medical Centre receptionist; she should know. There seems to be something of a miscommunication between the OC and himself!' It was a not-so-veiled dig at the OC for missing valuable detail. Pete headed back to Sandhurst as we prepared to start our 10-mile bash.

This event was a formal assessment, and as such, students would be given a leg to command. For no reason other than his name was on the appointment matrix to start first, it was Watson who received the detailed brief. He would need to be at his very best to navigate and lead his weary charges. Attentively, he listened to the instructions given by Captain Dunn before getting fifteen minutes to brief the platoon prior to crossing the start line. Nonchalantly, Watson surveyed his map, paying little attention to detail. Failing to mark his map or plot way-points that would create a progressive route, he saw himself too cool for a route card. Eventually, he announced himself ready and Captain Dunn gave him permission to lead on. Standing at the point of departure, Watson issued the students a half-cocked brief with his usual arrogance. Every fibre in my body knew that it was going to be a long day.

Two hours into the tab, the platoon had covered 3km. Like watching a blind date unravel, Watson's command style made for uncomfortable viewing. Platoon cohesion crumbled beyond rescue as one mistake snowballed into another. Frustrations boiled over as Watson's poor navigation and command vexed everyone. Having taken several wrong turnings, the platoon had walked for more than 3km before hitting the 1km checkpoint. Despondency gripped everyone, and in response, Watson took his frustrations out on his fellow students. Instead of concentrating on navigating, he scurried up and down the platoon line shouting irrational commands. Captain Dunn, trying to work out the cause of his shouting, concluded that it was simply because he felt that was the best way to command. Typically, he was masking his own failings by distracting everyone with idle accusations.

There was a marginal improvement over the next 3km, but the pace was agonisingly slow. At the four-hour point, we had yet to hit the 6km checkpoint. There had been several major navigation errors, and the fact we had hit the 4km checkpoint was more down to luck than judgment. It had been tedious watching Watson take one wrong turn after another before shouting at his peers. By virtue of the fact that no one was answering him anymore, the indication of worse to come should have been identified. To add to the frustration, he had twice overruled his check-navigator, despite irrefutable evidence that he had made a navigation error. Captain Dunn and I had twice stopped and made hot drinks on our Peak stoves while Watson argued himself into yet another error. He was so entrenched in his own ability that he could not see his failings. This was the moment we were waiting for – the one defining opportunity to use irrefutable evidence that Watson had got himself into a pickle because his ego was greater than his ability. As Captain Dunn sipped his hot chocolate, we discussed the timing of our intervention.

As the first full moon of the year made its appearance, Watson seemed to be taking more advice. For a moment, things began to look up. A warm glow beamed from Captain Dunn as he confessed to feeling a little disappointed with himself having not intervened in the hours leading up to this moment. But as he massed his colleagues in a tight huddle under the thick canopy of the Minley woods, we were confident he was about to change tack and our patience would be rewarded.

'Not before time, hey, Colour? He has clearly realized that he is struggling and looks set to re-evaluate, just as we taught him.'

'To be honest, boss, I am too tired to listen to what he has got to say. We should have sacked him by now!'

'We have done the right thing. He has to learn the hard way. This will do him the power of good. Admitting he has got this wrong will humble and focus him in equal measure.'

Captain Dunn was absolutely right. The Rowallan way was to suffer your mistake so badly that you never repeated them. With hot drinks in our metal mugs, we listened to Watson as he addressed the platoon.

'OK, guys, the situation is this,' he began. 'We've been moving now for some time. I appreciate that you are all getting tired and the rain is not making this easy, but there is something you must all be aware of. Having studied the map extensively since we started, I have concluded that the map is wrong!'

A barrage of calls for Watson to explain himself came from most of the students, most notably Francis, who was struggling with a knee injury.

'Well chaps, the map is wrong,' repeated Watson. 'There shouldn't be a main road close to our current location, but it appears there is. That means the map is wrong. Best guess is, the DS may well have given me a defective map on purpose. This is some kind of leadership test. I am sorry you have all been messed around, but if I had a proper map, this wouldn't have happened.'

Mathews didn't hold back. A mixture of tiredness and aggravation culminated with a tirade of abuse. Savage with his words, his swearing caught everyone by surprise. We would never have used the words Mathews did, but Watson was overdue a few home truths, and it was brutally delivered by one of his peers.

'What are you accusing me of?' Watson demanded. 'You think I am geographically embarrassed, Mathews?'

'No! I am saying you're bloody well lost, you dick. There are drunks with dyslexia who could read the map better than you. The road was built last year, and the map is ten years old, Sherlock! It doesn't make everything else wrong! You need to hand over the fucking map before I feel the urge to take it.'

Mathews was feeling aggrieved, and rightly so. There was much sympathy for Mathews and his fellow students. They had all worked their socks off during the week, but were now suffering at the hands of a man whose ego was out of control. Several students agreed with Mathews as the overture of mutiny played loudly in Watson's ears.

Captain Dunn watched, transfixed by the reactions of the remaining students. Lane was slumped backwards, leaning on his rucksack with a look of abject misery, his eyes firmly shut. Moore, who had been check-navigating, shook his head in disgust, his loyalty to the patrol commander hanging by a thread. After a few minutes, we decided to step in and give Watson the final chance to recover from his mistake. Having silenced the lynch mob, Captain Dunn offered the lad an opportunity to explain how he had gone so wrong.

'Sir, it's the map. It's so far out, someone needs to write to Ordnance Survey and complain.' Watson was that type of man who would argue that black is white, leaving Captain Dunn with no alternative but to embarrass him once again in front of his equals.

'So, it's a dodgy map we issued you! It's a leadership test, is it? You are so special that we chose just you to give the dodgy map to? Well, here you go, have my map and crack on to the next checkpoint! It's even marked with the route for you.'

Watson took Captain Dunn's map and studied it for a short while. I hovered over Watson's shoulder to ensure he had identified where he was, and the map was orientated with at least three points of confirmation. Once he knew as much as we did, he was left to crack on. Without any further conversation, he made off into the dark, closely followed by a dejected rabble of men.

After thirty minutes had lapsed, Francis collapsed on the floor. He was curled up in a small heap and squashed by the weight of his rucksack. Watson arrived to see what the problem was.

'I can't go on,' said Francis. 'You'll have to leave me. I am shattered.'

Danner tried to get Francis to his feet, but after several attempts he gave up.

'Watson, how much further?' asked Danner.

'About six-Ks. Maybe seven.'

Rideout, who very rarely spoke unless spoken to, appeared at the side of Watson.

'How do you mean six? We only had five at the last stop, and that was more than an hour ago.'

'I didn't say that. You must have misheard me,' Watson claimed.

Mutiny again surfaced amongst those students who could muster the energy to argue. This only served to divide the group further as Watson's denial sunk deeper and deeper.

Francis, despite sitting on the floor, demanded to see the map. He had found a renewed energy, having realized that the prospect of further map-reading errors loomed large. The random statements Watson had issued were clearly hiding his lack of competence, and he had been compromised by his peers.

'You are making the walk harder than it need be,' Francis said. 'We have boxed around the edge of these woods for over an hour, when a beeline would have been much quicker.'

Francis pointed repeatedly at the map, but Watson didn't pay attention. His stubborn attitude would drag everyone further from the intended target unless one of his peers decided to intervene.

Murphy was the first to suggest a change of leadership. They were all tired and angry, but the remaining students demanded that someone else read the map. This was a perilous situation for Watson. His command appointment was already in the red. Openly insulted, publicly berated and his navigational credentials compromised, yet inexplicably, he stood in total defiance. As tempers flared to a point of violence, Captain Dunn directed me to step in and calm everything down. It was regrettable, but the damage was done.

'Everyone cool your jets and calm down,' I ordered. 'Watson, just point out where we are on the map and show me the way-points between here and the finish.'

'We are at the base of this hill, Colour Sergeant, on contour 95.'

'Wow! Watson, look over my left shoulder. Can you see the church about 50 metres from here? Show me where that is on the map.'

'It's not on the map.'

'Incredible, Watson. I am staggered you have made it this far on what can only be described as a "wing and a prayer". You are actually 1km further west than you think you are! The wood you are boxing around is not the one you are pointing at.'

The situation was not as bad as everyone thought. We had walked nearly 5km the wrong way, but at least it was not in the opposite direction! The error was recoverable, and the going would be easier from this point forward. The true location was pointed out on Watson's map. For a second time, he was shown three points of orientation. We were desperate to succeed with him and there was still a glimmer of hope that he could earn a deferred pass for this assessment, but we needed to win back the support of his peers. I ushered him out of earshot with the intention of giving him advice on leading a rebellious group of disgruntled soldiers. Selfishly, there was a desire to get everyone to the final checkpoint early so they got a decent night's sleep before tomorrow's competition. Having calibrated my own disappointment at being dragged miles in the wrong direction, the advice Watson was about to receive was an amalgamation of military and life experience. Staggeringly – and to my complete amazement – before the words left my lips, Watson shoved his map under my nose and contested the location he had been shown on it.

'Colour Sergeant, the location you gave me is not correct. We can't possibly be in that spot; it's miles from where we are.'

So convincing was Watson that doubt crept into my mind, forcing me to take a second look at the coordinates. It was a combination of tiredness, loss of patience and the returning rain that broke my composure as I exploded at him:

'Are you a qualified clown or just serving an apprenticeship? You have just taken nearly five hours to walk 7km; an accomplishment that defies explanation. But for the record, let me state that you have achieved an average speed of less than 2kmph. Ironically, that's not the worst factor in this debacle. That accolade goes to your ability to continually walk in the wrong bloody direction! To summarize, you think we gave you defective maps, and to add insult to injury you are now questioning my ability to navigate! Watson, you are lost. No, in fact, you are fucking lost! Let me spell that out – L.O.S.T., lost. You are deluded! A bloody liability. You refuse to take advice from your peers, accuse the Platoon Commander of deceit and insinuate I have set you up to fail! Give me the map, you are sacked.'

Rideout didn't wait for the offer. He stepped out of the shadow and snatched the folded map from Watson before it could be handed over. Within ten minutes, we were heading in the right direction and began to make up good time.

'What happened there, Colour?' asked Captain Dunn. 'You told me you were going to give him a gentle piece of advice?'

'Boss, sorry, but we are all on our chinstrap. If we let him carry on any more, either one of the students would have killed him or one of us would have.'

We followed behind the platoon at a much-improved pace. With so much to think about, my mind searched for the reason why Watson had been sent on Row-Co. Unquestionably, he was a very arrogant individual with an equally unpleasant persona. It was very easy to understand why his friends called him Vic. But his greatest failing was his inability to listen to people's advice and filter it into useful information. This kind of attitude had cost so many lives in the First and Second World Wars, and Watson was in danger of sleepwalking into the same mould. Previously, he had been publicly humiliated, but since then, he had displayed no signs of improvement. We were left with no other choice but to take official action. After a brief chat with Captain Dunn, we agreed, Watson would be placed onto a Platoon Commander's warning as soon as it was convenient.

Rideout had made good speed. Despite being soaked to the skin and tired, the platoon arrived at its destination without anyone falling out. There was just enough time to fit in the final serial of the day and get some sleep before the next competition. Our home for the next five hours was the boating lakes of Farnborough training area. The lakes were used by the Royal Engineers' Phase Two Training Regiment to perfect 'watermanship' skills. As a matter of priority, we instructed everyone to concentrate on drying feet, treating blisters and managing chafing. Finally, the students were given one A4 sheet of paper and told to write an essay on why they thought they had been chosen for Row-Co. Unsurprisingly, several students suggested it was little more than an extension of the subterfuge the Staff love to employ. Suffering from sizeable blisters on their heels, friction burns on the balls of their feet and covered in bruises, the platoon settled into their bashers to write an essay. The dwindling morale was hovering just above zero, so this was a good place to assess their powers of communication. The first of many essays they would be invited to write whilst exhausted, this one was made easy if not a little personal: 500 words on why they were selected for Rowallan Company.

Pat stepped out of a Land Rover, engine still running and heater on full blast.

'What kept you, Gaz?' he enquired.

'Watson. I swear he is a menace to society. He took us 5km in the wrong direction.'

'Why did you let him go so far wrong?'

'We wanted him to succeed, so we offered him every chance possible. We corrected him a number of times, but he is just in complete denial and thinks all this is below him.'

'I'd like to tell you how noble of you that was, but that would be bollocks. Look at the state of you! You're piss wet through and clearly hanging out. Two stops past Tooting!'

It was hard to know if Pat had intended to say this or was mixing his metaphors, because it was funnier than the real thing. Either way, his message was as right as it was hurtful.

'Seriously, Gaz, I have said this before and I will say it again. Don't let mistakes snowball too far. It's about balance. Don't punish yourself to the point that it's detrimental to your performance or decision-making as the instructor. It's fine to nudge them in the right direction once or twice; after that, you need to increase your influence and take over if necessary.'

Pat zipped up his fleece jacket, turned up his collar and got back into his heated Land Rover. He had a fair point. Watson had been afforded too much grace, and it was fair to say that the event had taken more out of me than perhaps it should have. Sitting in my basher, peeling off the sodden clothes before sliding into a crisp, dry sleeping bag, I was vexed at my own failings. Balance or Barking, it was a lesson that would repeatedly be revisited and a skill that is not easy to master. Learning when to cut your losses was proving a difficult lesson for me.

Captain Dunn was the first to wake the following morning. Lifting his head out of the basher, it looked like the frost had sprinkled the land with a coat of icing sugar.

'Bloody nora, Colour, it's Baltic out here.'

His Edwardian delivery made me giggle. Back home in Liverpool, young people never mixed their words. They are direct and blunt in their observations. Childishly, words like damn, blast or bloody nora would always provoke a mischievous giggle deep inside my subconscious, knowing that at home, such words were only encountered in comic strips. Peering from inside the warmth of my sleeping bag, my morale plummeted as the Polar Vortex that had gripped the UK turned the large lake we resided by into a massive open-air fridge-freezer. So much for Michael Fish and the end of the 'Big Freeze'! More fool me for trusting him ever again after the horrendous hurricanes of 1987! The poor weatherman took a pummelling of abuse from all the DS as we gathered around the tailgate of Pete's Land Rover, drinking coffee and recounting stories of that dreadful stormy weekend, made famous by Michael Fish's miscalculation.

King was responsible for ensuring the students were roused and ready for battle on time. Acknowledging the punishment their equipment had taken in recent days, the morning inspection was downscaled to a 'Type B'. With fewer items on display and fewer things to unpack, the 'Type B' inspection was a blessing. Surprisingly, morale was high and their efforts kept the DS happy. Although we were not being fooled, as most of this was down to it being the last day of Compass Rose and the students knew it. Predictably, Stone and Witherspoon stood out with their nonchalant demeanour. Both fell short of the inspection standards and paid the price with fifty names each. With the kit packed away and essays handed in, the platoon appeared ready for the final event of the exercise. The sense of improvement was slowly beginning to show. The number of punishments had reduced, and despite the lethargy induced by the cold climate, we had much to be positive about. Specifically, learning to deal with the cold and wet was a by-product of our teaching. As much as the DS could teach about equipment husbandry and minor injury management, dealing with the cold is about mind over matter. For a sizeable number of the platoon, they were coping much better than first term cadets on the Commissioning Course.

Overlooking the lake, Major Gray's briefing followed a trusted format. The event was simple and fun. The mental and physical exertion would be equal, but this race was all about command and control. An improvised raft race across a boating lake presented staff and students alike with plenty of opportunities to demonstrate, assimilate and assess amidst the fun of this military classic. The student in command was told to build a raft, then transport his complete platoon to the far bank. To ensure maximum activity was created, only four men at a time were allowed on the raft. There were plenty of sarcastic comments as the OC explained that for safety reasons, everyone needed to pass the obligatory open water swim test.

Dressed in lightweight green trousers and red rugby shirts, students waded into the water and swam out to a point 20 metres from the bank, ducked under a canoe manned by Daz and then swam back. The shock of the icy water on the body is no easier to take despite the number of times you do it. Leading by example is what we taught, so Captain Dunn was first in the water, leaving me to encourage the slower students. Those swimming close by could hear me berating myself with unrepeatable expletives, much to the amusement of Rideout, who loved every minute of it. Having completed the swim, Boyle was put in command of the race. Frenziedly, he organized his team. His blend of Liverpool wit and overzealous effort was infectious. Students fed off his enthusiasm, buzzing around a plethora of large oil drums piled up next to several long ropes and large planks.

Boyle's command presence was raw with emotion. When he couldn't articulate a command, he demonstrated it. He was using all his skills to get the platoon to build the raft in quick time. Every word carried a sense of urgency. Pithy, concise and speaking in imperatives, this was what we needed. Ten minutes into the race, his raft was the first to be assembled and make contact with the water. Without fuss, the sturdy structure began to ferry the first load to the far bank. As Paddy's boys hit the water, Boyle had secured what appeared to be an invincible lead. Victory was in the air as the platoon called out each stroke to a chorus of 'in-out-in-out'. But to my bewilderment, as Paddy's students made their first trip across the lake, they had attached a long length of rope to the raft. Several ropes tied together stretched the full width of the lake. They had engineered a dumb waiter system, allowing them to pull the raft from one side to the other without the requirement to paddle. It was a great piece of initiative; the system proved to be ten times as quick as paddling, and in no time at all, they had overhauled Boyle's valiant efforts.

The celebration was animated even before the OC announced that Paddy's lads had won the raft race. Their lead was fifteen points to six. We fully expected Boyle to be devastated by the defeat, but his expression displayed more than despondency and disappointment. There was a look of pure anger, full of suspicion and muted accusations. It was not the reaction we had anticipated, but worryingly, this was reflected on the faces of the majority of his colleagues. It was difficult to identify the cause of this mood change within the platoon, and to my total disbelief, I detected an attitude that bordered on contempt. Keen to get to the bottom of this mood, the platoon was summoned to answer for their failings.

'Boyle, you have been outthought on that particular event, and that is what caused you to turn in second-best, do you agree?'

Boyle said nothing. He just stood still, in silence, looking down at his feet. Out the corner of my eye, I saw Danner shake his head in disagreement.

'Got something to add, Danner?'

'No, Colour Sergeant.'

Francis mumbled, and Mathews shook his head in approval.

'Francis!' I snapped. 'Like to share your secret with everyone?'

Francis refused to answer my challenge several times before he eventually spoke.

'We are wondering when you will start to give us a helping hand on these races, Colour Sergeant.'

The inflammatory comment was initially misunderstood. Responding to his request, Captain Dunn explained that a victory would mean nothing if it wasn't earned. But the response wasn't greeted with the normal receptive attitude of previous answers. Silence fell for a short time before Danner added to Francis's remarks.

'Colour Sergeant. The only reason we never won that race is that Colour Sergeant Jones told his students about the trick with the rope. That was as much as they needed to clear us out.'

'I hope you are not suggesting that Colour Sergeant Jones has cheated on the raft race, Danner,' I said. 'Questioning the integrity of a Colour Sergeant is a grave issue?'

But Danner's expression said it all; the accusation was extremely serious. A Colour Sergeant accused of infringement of integrity would be kicked out of Sandhurst. Danner was challenged to repeat his statement, but he replied with only a blank look. The failure to repeat this accusation led me to believe it was all down to sour grapes and poor sportsmanship. Paddy would not help his students to win a competition; there would be no point in it. Yet as the platoon suffered another punishment for failing to win the raft race, which inevitably resulted in everyone fully submerged in the freezing lake, the seed of doubt had been sown in my mind. Coupled with the suspicion of him pushing the platoon stretcher at the start of the week, this was going to be hard for me to dismiss.

Soaked, exhausted and clearly angry, the students crammed onto the rear of a 4-ton truck and headed back to Sandhurst camp. Normally the end of an exercise would be greeted with a hint of jubilation, but an ill feeling bubbled below the surface. Having arrived back at Sandhurst, the students were ushered quickly into their study hall. Each student sat soberly mulling over the past week of activity. There was an intensity to the atmosphere that suggested betrayal. They would need to serve many years before they understood that we shared their pain.

'Two things to do before the week is complete,' I told them.

'Firstly, if you look on your desk there are several forms. They are called "peer assessments". You are to complete these forms, describing the performance of your fellow students. Once you finish, put your forms into an envelope and seal it, then place it on my desk as you leave the study hall. Let me be crystal clear about the peer assessment. Fail to be honest and we will see right through your lack of moral courage. Try to throw us off the scent of someone's failings and we will suspect a lack of integrity. Follow the format on the paper, don't mince your words and don't play games.'

Grabbing my bag and a file from my desk, I made for the door before King grabbed my attention.

'Colour Sergeant! What is the second thing you were going to say?' asked King.

'Oh yes! The other form on your desk is a leave pass. After you have finished the peer assessments, you can go home for the weekend.'

Boyle raised a smirk before asking me if this was a Row-Co joke being played on everyone. His wisecrack brought a brief outbreak of laughter before it was confirmed that they were all going home for the weekend. The information was greeted with a wave of relief and sporadic clapping.

After lunch, the students departed for a much-earned break, leaving Captain Dunn and me to read the peer assessments. There were the normal groans of bitterness and sarcasm leaping off the page. Several individuals claimed that Faraday Hall academics had suggested that the students would perform better if the Staff relaxed their approach. Ironically, this only had the reverse effect. Writing to influence was fully expected. It was no surprise to see Stone, Lane and Goldson were the most vociferous. Having read over 100 assessments between us, we sat down to work out our strategy for improving our students' performances, targeting the worst and highlighting the best.

'Colour, have you seen what they all write about Witherspoon?'

'Witherspoon, boss, has been as wet as a wet thing bought from Wet-R-us!'

'Yes, but the assessments sing his praises. In nearly every assessment, people pick him out as the most reliable and the most considerate. We need to get a better look at him next week and see if we can identify this.'

'Understood, boss. Is this our Progress Board or are you wanting to sit down before the Company board?'

'No, I think a quick mind-dump will do. Only if you have time?'

'Boss, there is always time in a Colour Sergeant's schedule. But the wife would like to see me at some stage this week, so a down-and-dirty exchange would keep me in her good books!'

'Brilliant, Colour, what have you got?'

'Danner. We must continue to subject him to additional fitness; he is still off the pace. There is progress but it's not arriving quickly enough.'

'Fair comment, Colour. Let's increase the tempo next week. What do you think about his back-chatting?'

'Well he can be cheeky at times, but he has the makings of a good leader. He won't be intimidated, and I like that. During the exercise, Colour Jones gave him an almighty telling off because his boots were minging. Paddy said: "Danner, look down at the state of your boots, they are hideous. I'd no do my garden in those boots." Danner looked skywards, shook his head and replied: "Nor would I, Colour Sergeant, it would bloody ruin them."

'Captain Dunn burst out laughing. There was no malice; he was just cheeky and witty. If Paddy was stupid enough to engage in a duel of wits with a sharp Etonian, he needed to be at his best or he would be made to look stupid.'

'Agreed, Colour. Who else is on your radar?'

'Watson!'

'Well, Colour, the comments about him in the assessments were pretty damning. They are consistent with our thoughts. No matter what, Monday morning he will be the first to be placed on to a Platoon Commander's warning. His navigation is appalling, his attitude stinks and above all, he is just not listening. There is no concern that he could become Machiavellian as a commander, but there is a real concern he could become a danger to himself or others. I will give him this advice when he is placed on a warning. Let's hope it sinks in.'

'Haigh, boss,' I continued. 'He is high up on my list of potential failures!'

'He's destined for a Platoon Commander's warning at some stage soon! Send him to me early on Monday as well please, Colour. He is overthinking stuff and stifling any hope of leadership development. A lack of decisiveness is the main cause of his pontificating. He is workable, but only just. Now let's deal with the top students, like Lane.'

'Lane, did you say, Sir?'

'Calm down, Colour! Just making sure you were listening. He's not going to pass this course, is he?'

'In summary, no! Never! But we must work hard to give him every chance of success.'

'Monday morning for a chat please, Colour. Platoon Commander's warning for him too.'

'Shall we finish with Stone? He has been virtually non-existent on this course – always on the sick.'

'Do you want him in on Monday?'

'No, unfortunately not. If I put him on a warning, the College Commander will just say to me if he's been on the sick for so long, how can we assess his ability?'

'But what if he goes all the way through the course on and off a sick note?'

'He will probably pass the course! It won't be the first time someone has schemed a pass. Maybe you could apply some pressure to test his resolve.'

'OK, boss, I'll see him on Monday if he turns up. But understand, I struggle to make sense of putting Haigh on a warning for participating, then letting Stone go free for failing to participate.'

Just as I was getting into the flow of a rant, Pat flung open the double doors like Lord Flashheart from *Blackadder*. He stood at the end of the corridor with his legs astride and hands on hips, with waist thrust forward.

'Marvellous, bloody marvellous! Gaz, we've found Goldson. The stupid git had only bugged himself out from his room. Would you believe it, one of the chefs found him at the back of the cookhouse with his kit laid out ready for a field inspection.'

'Oh my God. What's going to happen with him, Sergeant Major?' asked Captain Dunn.

'He's history, Sir. The lad is barking. The OC has more details. Apparently, there is a history of drug abuse and it's coming back to haunt him. Haunt him! Get it?'

Pat disappeared to complete the paperwork, barking and howling all the way to his office. Twenty minutes later, the accommodation was empty, and the weekend was underway. During the long drive home, my mind buzzed with everything that had happened over the past few weeks. Would Paddy really give away information that would help his platoon win races? Could Stone transit through the course on a sick note?

* * *

Scamming a pass is not new. During the early 1980s, as an instructor delivering basic training, I had experienced an extremely deceitful and vindictive recruit who had similarities to Stone. Cheating his way through life by blaming, claiming and lying was a professional vocation for him. Dishonesty is a poison that denies the instructor an opportunity to engender camaraderie and an esprit de corps. The inability to nurture meaningful friendships is not a recognized failing and doesn't warrant dismissal. Removing him from training, despite numerous attempts, had failed, and no reasoning with the system would change this. It was hard to prove his dubious character, and even harder to get him to do more than four days of consecutive work. His constant accusations against various NCOs had turned him into a political hot potato. He had tied the training team up in knots, and he knew it. Through vexatious accusations, several instructors had been suspended pending further investigations and disharmony had fractured the training team. He was using every possible underhand trick to discredit the

Staff, including faking an assault by his Platoon Sergeant. A professional and experienced fraudster, he was too clever for the clumsy military judicial system.

On the morning before we deployed on the final exercise, my Platoon Sergeant informed me that the troublesome recruit had gone absent during the night. The Regimental Orderly Sergeant had found him absent on the roll call and had informed the chain of command. We were all baffled. There were less than two weeks before he completed training, and with a posting to sunny Cyprus on the cards, it was hard to fathom out why he went AWOL. He had won his battle. The OC had instructed everyone to stay off his back; the lad had a free pass right to the end. Nevertheless, the news was welcome – we were all pleased he had gone. One month later, and long after his platoon had finished training, he reappeared at the camp guard room. When he proudly announced his name, the Regimental Police placed him into custody for being AWOL, despite protesting his innocence. He claimed that Corporal Thomas had come to his room during the middle of the night, gave him a train ticket home and explained that he had been given three weeks' leave as compensation for previous ill-treatment. He claimed he was then driven to the train station, given £20 for food and drink and told to report back to the guard room in four weeks, ready to go to Cyprus. The story was so farfetched that he was dishonourably discharged for deceit and absenteeism. He even alleged that the corporal told him he would be promoted to lance corporal if he could stay away for the month.

At the end of that year, during the annual Christmas ball, the truth about his mysterious disappearance was explained. After a few beers, a friend confessed that the young recruit's claims were all true. He had assisted Corporal Thomas, the victim of two vexatious allegations. The claims had brought him great hardship, even had him removed from a promotion course and took his marriage to the brink of disaster. Paying for a ticket out of his own pocket, the pair woke the recruit up once everyone had gone to bed. On the journey to Winchester train station, Corporal Thomas explained that the Commanding Officer wished to compensate him with a month's leave. Putting him on the red-eye mail train to Sunderland, he knew that when he returned, no one in their right mind would believe such a crazy story. Even if they had chosen to do so, Corporal Thomas had been posted back to Germany and was by now impossible to bring back for questioning. It was a daring stunt that could have backfired horribly. On this occasion, the widely used military philosophy 'if you are going to be a bear, be a grizzly' worked for him. It was easy for me to understand the anxiety of suffering vexatious allegations, and my bias sided with the fellow instructor. Right or wrong, there was a part of me that thought the plot was genius. Although it had been induced by deceit, it was the truth that brought about his demise.

Compass Rose Reflection
by L.J. BARNS

During the burden race at Minley Manor, all bodily functions shut down. My legs knotted, my arms were frazzled and my eyes rolled backwards with every blink. Come the finish line, I was barely conscious. The narrow handles on the ammo boxes cut my hands to shreds. Worse still, the sharp corners bashed my thighs with every step. It was an absolute killer. So steep was the first hill, it induced panic and a fear of failure. I could hear the Colour Sergeant running just behind me screaming, 'Do something about it! Influence change! Come on, make a difference!' I was just about to demand he leaves me alone before I realized he wasn't shouting at me, he was shouting at the others to do something about me!

Angry, embarrassed and failing dismally, my fellow students set about pushing me from behind. Tears rolled down my face as an overwhelming feeling of belonging energized my desire. They weren't going to leave me behind, and I wasn't going to let them down. Whoever it was that pushed me around the course on that day, he saved my life. The emergence of unrivalled intimacy, loyalty, courage and commitment, it was indescribable. I ran myself into the ground on that event.

Not easy to identify at that time, the lessons of Compass Rose had laid the foundations for success a few weeks later. During the final stages of the night navigation on Dartmoor, the Colour Sergeant told me it was my turn to map read. The unexpected appointment knocked me for six. Why me? Why now? I was too tired to map read, let alone lead the rest of the platoon. I headed off in what I thought was the right direction, but after less than 200 metres, the ground no longer fitted the map. The Colour Sergeant was on my back as my torch failed and the incessant rain collected in small puddles on my map. I set off again in a different direction, but the Colour Sergeant exploded with a diatribe of abuse. By now everyone was fairly peeved off with me. Then it came! 'Get a grip, Barns, or I will sack you, softlad! If you take me more than 5 yards in the wrong direction once more, you're finished.'

I panicked, guessed at the heading and moved. In an instant the Colour Sergeant erupted into a fit of rage. He snatched the map from my hand and slapped me around the head with it.

'Use your shagging compass! Last time! One more step and you're through.'

It had the desired effect. My concentration levels hit overdrive. My numerous blunders provoked an impromptu lecture on leadership and command, which seemed to calm the Colour Sergeant's mood! Then, completely shocked by his change in tone, he dragged me away from everyone's earshot and gave me a final warning. He pointed out my exact location on the map and watched me set my compass bearing. Before being dragged back to the group, he casually said, 'You've been here before, haven't you? You are not going to fail this appointment, provided you apply the leadership qualities we have taught you. When you get back to the group, convince them that you have it all under control. You need to reassure them or you will lose their trust! Use your team to buffer your decisions or confirm your thoughts. Make the pace counter work hard, force the check-navigator to brief you at every feature.' His sincerity was inspiring.

Although grateful for the help, I was feeling under immense pressure. With the check-navigator and pace counter beside me, we marched in a southerly direction. Praying and hoping it was the right path, I was desperately searching for any recognizable feature to confirm my bearings. I could see the Colour Sergeant checking his own map; he was just hanging on to his temper. Then, just at the point of exhaustion, I caught a glimpse of a bridge over a small stream. The wet grey slate, illuminated by the intermittent moonlight, was the most incredible apparition ever. It was the only one for miles, and it located me precisely where I wanted to be. Revitalized with confidence, the assurance lifted everyone. The Colour Sergeant was wearing a big smile as he winked at me. Despite the innocuous nature of this gesture, its emotional impact was infectious. Words cannot describe my feelings when my success became apparent. Even the Sergeant Major's venomous insults couldn't dampen our spirits as we crossed the finish line.

As we began to walk the short distance to our 'bivi' site, I overheard the Colour Sergeant talking about me to the other DS. He was telling them that he was thirty seconds away from sacking me. But in the same breath he explained how I had held things together in such appalling conditions. The thought of winning the Colour Sergeant's praise fuelled my confidence. For the very first time, I felt there was a chance that I could get through the course, but I had also realized what it would take: pain, tolerance, attitude and 100 per cent effort every time. When we finished the exercise and returned to Sandbags, there was an overwhelming urge to shake the Colour Sergeant's hand and thank him for keeping the faith in me. If he would have sacked me, I would have VW'd that weekend. I had learnt to be decisive, to think quicker with clarity and logic; truly a defining moment.

Chapter Eight

Dear John

Heavy rains arrived and the snow departed for another year, but the change didn't benefit the students, or the Staff. The roads at the rear of Old College had flooded, forming giant black mirrors across Chapel Square. The orange glow of countless security lamps bounced off the floor and into the murky grey sky. It was Sunday, 1800hrs, and time for the roll call, the first after the students had returned to normal life since the start of the course. The Sunday evening check was more to gauge people's mental health than it was to ensure their attendance. Wandering from room to room making small talk with my students, it was a very useful way of offering them an informal opportunity to chat about any problems they had collected over the short break. Haigh was the first to admit to having a disastrous weekend. His lazy tones gave away his feelings while we chatted about the horrendous train journey he had just completed. Eventually, he felt comfortable enough to say he was thinking of voluntary withdrawing. This was half expected and didn't come as a surprise. Sitting on the end of his bed, I listened to his reasons and found myself agreeing with what he was saying. He had a sound argument for wanting to leave. His state of mind hinged on two things: an ultimatum from his future wife and the promise of an excellent job in Europe.

Making myself comfortable in his room we talked through his predicament. It was understood that he had just had a bad weekend. His fiancée was serious about dumping him if he stayed in the Army, and although he didn't know it yet, we were going to test his resolve by placing him on a Platoon Commander's warning. For an age, we spoke about the trials and tribulations of an Army officer and the relationships that are won and lost in the process. I reminisced about the overwhelming feeling of being accepted by soldiers as their commander and the inevitable outcome of distant relationships. In his current emotional state, it was difficult for him to digest the powerful bond soldiers formed with their commanders. Having won the respect of a soldier, you can count on his loyalty for a lifetime. This sort of male bonding is not replicated in any other profession. A soldier will go to extreme lengths to protect the safety or reputation of his boss, taking great pride in the camaraderie induced by good leadership. Ironically, it is not replicated between officers; this undiminished devotion is exclusive to an officer and his soldiers.

The reason why people become professional soldiers is not a difficult conundrum to understand. A simple piece of analysis will identify that those who join the service have many similarities. Regional, domestic and vocational parallels are key components, but it is the development of shared values that transform a civilian into a soldier. These shared values become the glue that binds relationships at all levels, but nowhere can it be equalled like the relationship between an officer and the soldiers under his command. Recounting stories to exemplify the joys of platoon command, Haigh listened attentively as one example followed another, before I finally left him with an invitation to withdraw on Monday morning if that was what he really wanted. No soldier deserves to be commanded by an officer lacking commitment and dedication, so there was no sales pitch, just a cerebral stretch. His expression told me there was doubt; maybe the debate was already lost. It would save us all a difficult conversation if he was standing outside my office bright and early the following day. Haigh had potential. If he gave us the opportunity, we would find it, but he had to be a willing participant.

Mathews was the next person to receive a visit from me. The look on his face spoke volumes. He was a young man hanging on by his emotional fingertips.

'How the hell did that happen, Mathews?' I asked. It was a stupid question in hindsight, as the black eye he was sporting could only happen one way.

'Girlfriend dumped me, Colour Sergeant! Ran off with a mate from uni, so we needed to straighten some stuff out and one thing led to another. Am I in trouble?'

'Mmm. Let's see what tomorrow brings! For now, just concentrate on making sure you are up for PT in the morning!'

The Army officer is a peculiar beast. Whilst there may be similarities with other services, when it comes to discipline, atmospherics and personalities can swing decisions. When dealing with an issue of officer indiscretion, akin to the predicament faced by Mathews, one officer would view this as honourable, yet another could take the view he had been thuggish.

An officer in my unit wrecked the Chelsea Flower Show in the early 1990s. So bad was his behaviour and so drunk was he, that the story made the national newspapers. He had caused significant embarrassment to his regiment, not to mention the Army. Astonishingly, he was forgiven and thereafter elevated to hero status as a result of his boyish antics. On another occasion, a young officer working with me was taken to the threshold of dishonourable discharge because his car tax had expired. Apparently, the Commanding Officer told him he was irresponsible and deceitful. Whilst neither event would have undermined unit cohesion, it is testimony that the benchmark for deciding if an officer has breached values and standards is not black and white. Despite the reams of papers spelling out what is acceptable, it will always be open to an individual's interpretation. There are countless examples of extramarital affairs undermining fighting spirit that go unpunished. The truth is, our moral standards are as deep as the pockets of the guilty and as precious as the relationship with the victim. If we can afford to sack someone because of an abundance of resources, we will set the benchmark high. When manpower is tight and the loss of a soldier will reduce our capability, standards are interpreted to suit. For Mathews, we were on the cusp of not enough and this would help his cause.

Walking home in the rain, I decided to turn back and speak with Mathews. Not wishing to take the chance on how this would be perceived should a senior officer inquire as to how he obtained his black eye, an intervention was required. Bursting into his room, he was caught off guard by my reappearance!

'Rugby, Mathews. Is that what you said to me?'

'No, it was fighting, Colour Sergeant.'

'So that will be someone punched you at the weekend while in a scrum, during a charity game of rugby, playing for your old uni then!'

'Yes, Colour Sergeant.'

'You stick to this story, softlad. Know that you have made a huge error in judgment, and a career in the Army will help you make better decisions!'

It was now down to me to circulate this story as early as possible in order to deter anyone quizzing him on his condition. I headed back to my room with my fingers crossed, hoping no one would get a good look at Mathews before the swelling went down. But I couldn't take that chance. It was reasonable to believe that he had been given a punch in a scrum, but if they took a look at his knuckles, there was evidence he had been doing a fair bit of punching himself. It was a great risk asking him to evade the truth, which went against every sinew of my being. Foolish or not, Mathews had great potential. It would be a real travesty should a sanctimonious commander decide to pass judgment. Effectively, we had just put our careers on the chopping block, something we both realized.

It is hard to understand the mixed emotions a Rowallan cadet experiences when he returns to normality. Life in an environment as intense as Row-Co brings intolerable discomfort to every aspect of an individual's character and causes behavioural change. Such institutional desensitization comes with consequences, so it is no shock to see them behave in strange ways during their first weekend off. Having slept with one eye open for three weeks, suffered induced anxiety, never knowing where or when your next meal is coming from, emotions are heightened. It is inevitable that the process of decompression has its bumps. The course takes the brain to new levels of alertness and tunes the body to cope with near exhaustion. All these new experiences are normally only forced onto a potential commander at the later stages of a long course. At Rowallan, time is at a premium, so the learning curve is more acute and the risks greater. Cause and effect analysis would help make sense of this, but few senior officers would accept this in mitigation for a lapse in self-discipline.

The first morning back, and the programme would pick up just where it left off, with hard physical fitness. Typically, there would be doubt and fear in the minds of all those who made it back. Add this to the inevitable 'Dear John' and you have all the ingredients of a crisis in morale on your hands.

'Gaz! Paddy! Are you two ready?' Pat screamed down the corridor.

'Daz is at the Mean Machine ready to welcome the girls back! Is everyone back?'

Captain Dunn jumped in.

'Yeah, sorry, Colour. Totally forgot to ask, has everyone returned?'

'Yes. Well done, boss, that makes me look efficient! Is that you demonstrating the caring father figure you bang on about?'

It was only 0700hrs, and already the banter had started to fly. Daz swung open the door into the main corridor and began screaming at the students just to confirm to everyone that Monday morning had arrived. Like rabbits scattering from a farmer's gun, students scurried out to the Mean Machine. With everyone less Stone, who had gone sick again, the whole course stood in their start positions. Daz set them to work, sparing no one any sympathy as the DS increased the misery. Pat continued to berate people as they moved between exercises, while Captain Dunn competed against two students doing press-ups. Keen to see how individuals were coping, I studied the faces of those under our charge. Understandably, no one was overly excited at doing a hard fitness session after a weekend full of fun, food and booze, but there was much more apathy than expected.

Time restrictions forced the session to last little more than twenty-five minutes, but it served the purpose of being a short, sharp shock and just enough to get the neurological pathways firing. As soon as Daz had blown his whistle to finish, Haigh made a beeline to speak to me. Standing to attention and trying very hard not to wave his hands around as he spoke, Haigh stated that he still wanted to leave. There was little conviction in his voice or urgency in his request. Having lost Goldson last week, there was a desire not to lose someone so early in week four. Thinking that Haigh would change his mind as the week progressed, I promised him an interview with Captain Dunn during the week. I felt sure that once the rest of the students heard he wanted to leave, they would rally around him and persuade him to stay. It was a strange predicament I found myself in. Here I was, trying to convince a student to stay, yet there was a realistic prospect of him failing the course if he made it to the end.

By 0830hrs, Major Gray was briefing everyone on the intricacies of the next competition, Exercise Klondike. Just as the name suggests, this was a treasure hunt, an exercise in command and control that demanded the students to conduct an estimate to understand the task. Upon completion of their estimate, they would need to analyse the mission, draft a scheme of manoeuvre, then execute a search operation. The mission was to recover more treasure than the other platoon. They were both given a series of cryptic clues that guided them to a mysterious location somewhere on the camp or training area. When they arrived at this location, they would find a house brick painted gold. The bricks were worth anything from ten points to 3,000. The harder the clue was to solve, the higher the number of points the brick was worth. Additionally, the further away the brick was from the camp, the greater its value. So, a brick that was hidden with a hard clue 3 miles away would be worth 3,000 points, while one with a simple clue hidden close to the control room would be worth only ten.

The idea of this exercise was to practise the students in their ability to assess a problem, strategize a solution, turn it into a logical plan and then command and control the recovery of the bricks whilst under pressure induced by competition. The students were given all the information they needed to formulate a plan to reach a target of 10,000 points inside three hours. There was the obligatory hidden surprise to be discovered on the route, but other than that, we had taught the students all the skills they needed. All that was required from them was an injection of ingenuity, enthusiasm and good leadership. The students conferred as to the best way to tackle the problem and then set up a control room ready to start the competition.

'Watson, this can be your task. You are in command!' announced Captain Dunn.

Keen to see if he had learnt anything from the previous week, we watched as he busied himself ordering people about in every direction. Initial impressions could fool the passer-by into believing that he was extremely confident and capable. But the boss and I knew full well that it was just a masquerade; the truth of the matter was that his understanding of the tools of command boiled down to shouting loud. It wasn't an unusual failing with a Row-Co student, but Watson's problem was that his irritating, conceited leadership style had become hard to address. Moreover, all his peers were at their wit's end with his flaws and tolerance was low. Watson's greatest problem was that he could not inspire a collegiate approach, so galvanizing any meaningful relationships would be difficult.

With the study hall transformed into a small operations room, Major Gray issued Watson and his opposite number in Paddy's platoon with their instructions.

'What's it say, Vic?' asked Rideout, unable to contain his enthusiasm. Watson shot him down with a sarcastic comment bordering on insulting. Captain Dunn logged it down in his notebook: Watson had not gone more than thirty seconds before scoring a default. It was frustrating to witness his behaviour, and bizarrely a feeling of personal failure subdued my mood. Had I failed him? Was I not astute enough to find the correct approach? Given the fact we had identified his problem over three weeks ago, the solution should have been found by now. The failure for anyone to arrest his arrogance was hard to understand; maybe it wasn't just me! But my knowledge and experience were exhausted. Maybe his character flaws were irreversible; possibly there was nothing that could be done. Watson was speeding towards a fail, and unless we could do something to alter his attitude, he was likely to cause real disharmony amongst the team.

The estimate and mission analysis contained impressive deductions that could lead to a logical plan and execution. Despite this, Watson had pre-situated the estimate with his own answers, and contrary to all the information he had to hand, he made judgments based purely on his own thoughts. Forcing the findings to fit his solution, he decided to ignore what other people thought. After a brief assessment of the Exercise Klondike problem, Watson despatched the students to several speculative grid references in search of the first bricks. In groups of two, armed with map, compass and a few clues, they disappeared into the undergrowth of the Barossa training area. Watson assumed his tactic of swamping the ground containing high-value bricks would work by dominating the probability of success. He gave each pair a question and sent them off to decipher its meaning, hoping they would deduce the exact location of the brick as they made their way to the far end of Barossa. There was the slightest alignment to concurrent activity, but in a classic military blunder, he confused activity with progress. For a short while, he did nothing apart from pestering his workforce on a walkie-talkie to learn of their movement. To compound his poor leadership, it was not long before everyone had moved out of radio range, leaving him with no one to guide or command.

'Is there anything I could be doing?' asked Francis.

'If there was, don't you think I would have told you by now?' snapped Watson.

Captain Dunn stepped in to give his uncensored opinion on Watson's attitude, but the strong burst of criticism was not well received. In response, the lad nonchalantly offered Francis the opportunity to suggest something for himself to do.

'Can I look at the question paper?' Francis enquired.

'Why?'

'I thought that two heads would be better than one!'

Watson pushed the questions into his hand, commenting, 'Most of these questions are in Latin!'

Francis continued to study the paper.

'Well done, Sherlock, that's why I never used them,' snapped Watson.

'But it's only the last bit, and I think that they may well all be flowers,' suggested Francis. 'The clue is saying that the brick is located near or amongst these flowers.'

'As I said in my brief, if you were listening, I figured that much out Francis, but no one knew what these flowers looked like.'

'Other than the Academy's mammoth library! They have books on wildflowers, and it's bound to give you the Latin name. Why don't I take a quick walk over there and grab a book for reference?'

'Well, you're wasting your time, but you can try it if you must.'

Having aggravated an old injury on the Mean Machine that morning, Francis limped 100 metres to the Sandhurst library. Within five minutes he returned, clutching a red house brick with numbers painted on it.

'That was simple. Look what I found,' he chirped.

Watson smirked before he passed comment on the first acquisition.

'Not of any great use on its own, really, is it? And why is it red with only thirty points?'

'Well, there is a clue attached to the brick that offers another seventy. If I find it, we would have enough points to buy the boat mentioned in the instructions. I know there will be a pile of bricks on the island!'

'What are you talking about, Francis?'

'Look, here in the instruction, it says that there is a selection of equipment you can exchange for bricks via the Company Quartermasters Sergeant – climbing ropes and harnesses, rubber dinghies and life vests.'

'That means nothing,' scowled Watson.

'Well, one of the clues states no swimming allowed, and the value of the brick is 3,500 points. I haven't deciphered the clue, but there is only one place where no swimming is allowed, and boats are used, and that's on the boating lake.'

Watson waffled for a short while before suggesting it would be a good idea to get on the island by making an improvised raft. In an unfathomable attempt to appear in control, he claimed credit for the concept as he meddled with Francis's idea. It was a classic example of poor command, a characteristic of toxic leadership: bastardizing someone else's idea and then selling it back to them is divisive. Then, without committing to any form of action, his attention switched to the radio as a garbled message blared from the Motorola.

'Hello, is anyone there? This is Rideout, can anyone hear me? Over. This is a wild goose chase. Where else do you want us to go? Over.'

Without waiting for approval, Francis disappeared in search of more bricks.

Stone had quietly sat in the study hall, avoiding any involvement. Watson ignored him in his usual aloof manner, but between the pair of them, their lethargy and arrogance were grating on me. Both students intentionally obstructed further development of the scheme of manoeuvre by aimlessly talking in riddles. If it wasn't so infuriating, this encounter between Mr Uppity and Mr Lazy would almost be funny. Watson would ask an extraneous question, which Stone would misunderstand. He would reply with something that was even less connected with the initial question. Remarkably, because Watson didn't wish to appear less intelligent than Stone, he would answer with another question even less relevant. It got to the stage where neither the boss nor I had a clue what they were talking about. It was obvious the pair were deliberately being disruptive, prompting me to find them work to do.

'Stone, why didn't you go with Francis?'

'Colour Sergeant, my injury is causing me concern and he may run too fast for me to keep up. My ankle isn't strong enough to do anything too physical just yet. Leastways, that's what the doctor told me this morning.' Stone showed me his sick chit.

'Well, I'm sure the big bruise Francis has on his knee is slowing him down considerably, but he still appears to be contributing,' I countered.

Characteristically, Stone failed to respond, which alluded to his guilt. Winston Churchill said the price of greatness was responsibility. By failing to assist Francis, Stone was consciously trying to avoid failure through association. While this behaviour was tolerated in the City, in the military it was the most poisonous of character traits an officer could possess. While businesses live and die on decisions, the military lives and dies on consequences.

Stone could not be told to do anything, but the guilt was beginning to show and he eventually left the hall on his own accord in search of Francis. To wind me up to the point of internal combustion, Watson congratulated me on motivating Stone before explaining that if it was down to him, Stone would have been put on the Mean Machine for his lethargic attitude. Stunned into silence, it took all my inner strength to control myself as he uttered his patronizing comments. Deflated, my ego melting under self-induced heat, it was best to keep my distance from him. It made sense to cool off by visiting the students running around the training area.

Barns and Moore had married up with Francis and were carrying an inflatable dinghy to the boating lake. The smell of a possible success broke through my black mood. Buoyed by their enterprise, I walked out towards Barossa. There was a small gathering of students standing at the large metal gates that give access to the training area, and they were deep in discussion.

'How are we doing with the search, lads?' I asked.

'Not good, Colour Sergeant.'

'How many is "not good"?'

'One, worth 200 points,' replied Witherspoon. 'We should have planned this better before we left. I've been running around like a headless chicken with only one clue.'

The other students nodded their agreement, adding to his comments with comparable stories. With time running out, there was no answer other than to tell them to return and get a quick task from Watson.

Walking back to the study hall in something of a daydream, Paddy drove past me with a few students in his car. I assumed that there must have been a serious incident or injury and he had jumped in his car to take the student to the hospital. Despite seeing it with my own eyes, there was disbelief that he was helping his lads win the competition, although the comments made by the students in the previous week still played over and over in my mind. In fact, they hadn't gone away over the weekend. My brains searched for alternative reasons, convincing myself that it was pure luck that his students knew they had to counterbalance the weight on the gun run and there was nothing sinister about it; or that it was a student that came up with the ingenious idea of a ferry rope on the raft race. Now, here we were, facing another defeat, and Paddy was carrying students in his car.

Back in the study hall, Captain Dunn sat in the corner with a look of abject misery. The exercise had been a total washout for Watson. Once again, the lad displayed every problem we had warned him about over the past three weeks. It was not the start to the week we would have liked, knowing morale was on the slide. In a familiar tone, Major Gray announced the winners of the event, and it was no surprise to anyone that it was Paddy's platoon, giving them an incredible eighteen points to six lead. As the students took their first unsupervised lunch break, a conversation with Pat was overdue. It was too late: Paddy was already in Pat's office receiving a friendly debrief about adhering to the rules of the competition. Innocently, Paddy claimed not to have realized that his lads were looking for bricks and he had only given them a short ride. He added that it would not have changed the outcome of the competition, which was quite possibly true. But the damage had already been done. My students were convinced that Paddy was taking part in the competition and the whole thing was rigged.

Irrespective of the innocence of intent, the impact of Paddy's actions were undermining everything I believed in. The pressure inside me began to build, and once again the question of my suitability of being at Sandhurst gnawed away at me. The evidence certainly suggested that Paddy was helping his students to win. Maybe if Pat knew about the 'gun run' and the 'raft race' he would have taken a different view on the matter. How on earth did Pat believe that Paddy didn't know his students were looking for bricks? He would have delivered exactly the same brief as me to the students. Like a marble rattling in an empty tin, my thoughts became erratic and loud.

The greater problem that needed urgent attention was the fact that our students were twelve points behind in the main competition. If the concept of the contest was to replicate the pressure a student may feel during real-life command, it was in danger of becoming ineffective. Captain Dunn confessed that he was suspicious of No. 1 Platoon's success early on during the course, but didn't wish to cause ill-feeling. It was clear that he was disappointed to learn that his suspicions were right, but there was little that could be done. Disheartened, he announced he would go and speak to the OC and thrash out a way to rectify the imbalance between the two platoons.

At the end of the Second World War, Sir David Sterling DSO, founder of the Special Air Service, introduced adventurous training to the Special Forces. He did this to replicate the intensity of combat that had been lost after the war came to an end. Sir David recognized that induced fear helped to sharpen the qualities required by the Special Air Service. In the absence of conflict, the challenge of climbing K2 brought with it significant risks, including loss of life. It is this concept that Rowallan sought to replicate on a lesser scale. Like David Sterling, Row-Co staff understood that achievement needs a balance of effort, intelligence and fear, but above all else, something valuable to lose. In Row-Co, this was achieved using competition. The competition was only an aid to help the Staff simulate pressure under command and replicate the consequences of losing. But this concept was certainly being diluted by gamesmanship. A win at any cost was expected, but at the expense of a student's education, just to massage the ego of the Staff, was difficult to stomach. I was stuck for words as Captain Dunn coaxed me out of my coma with some light banter.

'We will put it down to you coming from Liverpool, Colour!'

It was hard to respond. Coming to terms with this was going to be difficult.

'There are a few ways we could deal with the points difference, Colour.'

'I am all ears, boss, as long as it doesn't involve fixing the event so that we win.'

'Well, let's not discount anything just yet. But I was going to suggest one of two things. We could ask the OC to transfer some of the fitter members of the other platoon into ours, or transfer some of our weaker students into theirs.'

Captain Dunn took these ideas to the Company Commander while I marched the course to Faraday Hall for a study afternoon with the gorgeous Emily.

The long walk to the academic centre gave me time to analyse what went wrong on Exercise Klondike. This wasn't quite a crisis of confidence, but there was some serious soul-searching required. My understanding of people was better than most. Years of youth development and instructing students of all ranks and from various countries had exposed me to some difficult characters, but there was always a means to get them motivated. But Watson was neither an 'X' or a 'Y' character. Nor could he find a niche within John Adair's Action-Centred Leadership model, despite the Row-Co syllabus being perfect to do just that. If this was the perennial case of 'nurture versus nature', I should have cracked the code by now. Having studied many inspirational, ingenious and unconventional leaders, Watson shouldn't be presenting me with such a problem. These thoughts consumed me so much that I marched the Company way beyond Faraday Hall, and would have continued walking but for a student speaking out!

Two weeks earlier, students were given a number of leaders to research. Each of the leaders had been involved in notable moments of military history, displaying fortitude, strength of character and unrivalled determination amidst the most desperate of scenarios. Several students were then selected at random to examine critical decisions made by their character and told to analyse that individual's leadership qualities. For No. 2 Platoon, Witherspoon had been chosen to head up a team of six, all of whom had studied a failed climbing expedition in the Karakoram range of mountains of Pakistan. The expedition included only one military leader, a young captain called Tony Streather. Hugely experienced, the Army officer had a burning ambition to conquer Mount Haramosh in 1957. Along with an international gathering of experienced climbers, Captain Streather planned the climb with due diligence and professionalism. But bad weather caused the young captain to halt the assault on the summit, having hit an impasse just short of the peak. Witherspoon explained that the disappointment was too great for Streather's American colleague, Bernard Jilliot, to bear. Not wishing to be denied some form of success, he and his tethered partner decided to push their luck and climb a large cornice adjacent to the summit. Almost inevitably, the cornice collapsed and deposited the pair in a deep crevasse. It was disastrous. In the fall they had lost equipment and one of the climbers was badly hurt. The young captain was faced with two courses of action: mount an improvised rescue attempt or return to camp and collect the correct equipment to achieve a successful rescue.

Streather knew if he made a rescue attempt without the correct equipment, the likelihood of success was slim. If it failed, they would all be stranded with no means of escape and certain to die. Alternatively, he could return to camp and collect the necessary rescue equipment. This would significantly enhance the chances of a successful rescue, but base camp was a day's march away. The American and his partner would have to survive at the bottom of the ice bowl for over twenty-four hours, with no equipment, and would possibly die. With the weather getting worse, the Englishman was stuck between a rock and a hard place. There was no time to waste. Their 1950s equipment was little more than waxed cotton, with limited thermal retention qualities. As Captain Streather looked down into the ice bowl, he knew that death had come calling, but for whom?

It was a brilliant problem to analyse, and the very reason why Sir David Sterling endorsed this kind of training. Expeditions test every facet of character and leadership; moreover, when things go wrong, lessons exploitation helps the rest of us improve our understanding of why. Only by studying characters who have endured harrowing ordeals like this can we understand how to survive in the face of adversity. This academic training was as critical as the practical stuff the DS delivered. The challenges that Streather faced were comparable to those of combat. This was an exhausted party at the end of their ability, engaged in a Mexican standoff with Father Time. The third-man factor, sometimes called 'divine intervention', is a real thing. Although Witherspoon explained this phenomenon, he was not able to paradoxically compare and contrast it with the same feeling experienced by soldiers during brutal periods of fighting. Death in combat brings an intimacy similar to that experienced by adventurers who've lost partners in pursuit of unrivalled achievements. Also similar is the solitude and emotional pain endured at the moment you realize that death is imminent for someone under your immediate command. Irrespective of what decision you make next, death will befall someone. Life will pass to death in front of your eyes and there is nothing at all you can do. Climbers describe this as the widow effect; for soldiers, it is similar but mostly manifests itself post-incident. All these emotions are experienced in combat, and for Witherspoon plus his six team members, articulating what went wrong on that fateful night was an invaluable lesson in leadership.

Having impressed the tutors at Faraday Hall, Witherspoon's team were chosen to deliver their presentation to a selected VIP audience in Old College auditorium. After supper, Witherspoon and his crew re-enacted the story of the ill-fated expedition. Having done their best to recreate the critical decisions that led to the deaths of all members of the expedition but one, a sombre debate ensued. The presentation was attended by the senior tutors and other interested parties. A packed lecture theatre was treated to an hour of light-hearted acting and thirty minutes of soul searching and thought-provoking analysis which unpicked the decisions made by Captain Streather. The emphasis laboured heavily on the decision of Bernard Jilliot to climb the cornice, with Witherspoon summarizing that Streather should not have let the climb happen. He suggested that Streather had lacked authority and should have been more insistent. Summarizing, he concluded that as a direct result of failing to be more commanding, only one of the five original climbers returned from the expedition. It was a moving presentation and very poignant for the audience to listen to. We had been walked through the decisions, the nature of the characters and analysed the reasons why four men lost their lives.

At the end of the debate, there were thirty minutes of random questions. Students and visitors bombarded Witherspoon and his team with questions of all natures. Every answer was met by yet more questions as the debate quickly hit fever pitch. The atmosphere was tense as the audience argued the intricacies of command and control in such circumstances. With no end in sight, the OC stood up, walked to centre stage and called proceedings to a halt. He congratulated everyone on a debate well held before discussing why there was an emphasis on the young captain's decision to allow the cornice climb. Deliberately, he coaxed the students to reflect on leadership styles and how to manage difficult characters in multifaceted situations. One student then announced that the expedition was destined to fail because a clear chain of command had not been established.

The OC thrived on the contribution and allowed questions to flow back-to-back without reply. Question after question, he stood in front of everyone, just saying, 'next question, next question'. As the new boy, I didn't have a clue what was going on. It all appeared a little bizarre. Then, like being hit by a thunderbolt out of the blue, Major Gray hushed the audience and said, 'Please give a warm welcome to retired Colonel Antony Streather.'

You could have heard a pin drop. The expression on Witherspoon's face, who had thus far been unabashed with his interpretation of Streather's leadership, was priceless. The retired officer stood up and thanked Witherspoon for his explanation before speaking candidly about commanding the climbing party. Captivating and brutally honest, the sole survivor and commander of the disaster humbled the audience. During Witherspoon's presentation, we had all relived the moment when his whole climbing party died. Now it was time to hear how it really occurred, as we were treated to Streather's version of events. With fascinating insightfulness, he reflected painfully on the effects of being deprived of food, sleep, warmth and, in the days after the deaths of his colleagues, companionship. Invaluably, we received a first-hand account of the dynamic characters that formed the climbing party. A mixture of arrogance, passive aggression and subversion caused internal conflict detrimental to cohesion and, consequently, success. It was an extraordinary glimpse into the effects of team toxicity conspiring against the leadership.

His explanation of isolation, grief and his incorporeal experience drew gasps of disbelief from the audience. Streather's cultivated inner-character resonated with many students, for despite their limited exposure to hardship, they had felt his pain. Time flew by and in the blink of an eye, it was 2100hrs. Before leaving, the retired colonel offered a final word of advice:

'Command is the loneliest place on the planet when things go wrong. There is no Colour Sergeant to encourage you to keep moving, to think clearly. Remaining calm, calculated and focused is the best way to recover a failing situation. It's essential to know that failing situations can get worse, and they often do. There may be no end to how bad they can get, and don't think it can't get worse than death, because it can. If there was a skill you should fine-tune whilst at Rowallan, it would be that of "perpetual evaluation".'

Major Gray stood up and called an end to proceedings by thanking the retired Antony Streather for recounting such a distressing experience. It was an astonishing twist to the debate, catching the students totally by surprise; a truly remarkable couple of hours. Listening to total strangers who had no experience or understanding of leadership, debate the mistakes that sealed the fate of all his climbing party, required extraordinary levels of emotional intelligence. He was the epitome of a quality commander. Gentlemanly, modest and courageous, few people could have remained as calm as he whilst listening patiently to his decisions being discredited and misrepresented. He could balance his grief in the knowledge that, after the cornice collapsed, he had done everything correctly. His analysis was logical and the execution as good as it could have been, given the circumstances; maybe for that reason, he was the only one to survive.

The following morning, the boss arrived bright and early to discuss the outcome of his conversation with the OC. There was a provisional agreement to move one of our weaker students to the other platoon, but he couldn't come to a decision as to who it would be.

'Easy, boss, Lane,' I interjected. 'He is by far our worst student.'

'That's exactly why we can't get rid of him, Colour. It would be viewed as an intentional attempt to scupper the other platoon.'

With Major Gray agreeing to the move, payback would be adequately sanctioned. I took a long look at Captain Dunn but knew he wouldn't agree to send Lane, no matter my logic; he just had too much morality about him to deliberately deliver No. 1 Platoon a hospital pass.

'OK, boss, who do you think?'

'Well, Barns is one of our slowest runners.'

'No, we don't want to send Barns, Sir!'

'Why?'

'Firstly, we are getting somewhere with him. There are promising signs, albeit small. Secondly, he is good for the boys' morale. I like him.'

'You are not supposed to like these lads. You should be striking fear into the very heart of their soul.'

'What can I say, boss, I'm just a big softy. Anyway, you will have to excuse me, the platoon have an appointment with the Mean Machine.'

'What's that for, Colour?'

'Not sure yet, but there will be something wrong with their rooms after we finish my inspection.'

As always, it was a planned session made to look like a random punishment that achieved its multitude of requirements. Daz was at his evil best, hounding and pushing students on each crude item of the Mean Machine. Pat arrived and berated Daz for starting without him, before adding a higher authority to the session. Stone stood at the side of the courtyard, once again taking no part in the event, in stark contrast to Francis, who limped from exercise to exercise determined not to go sick. Daz was itching to give Stone a good dose of fitness but knew, whilst he was hiding behind a sick chit, there was no touching him. It had crossed my mind that he could be the one we transfer to Paddy's platoon. But knowing that he was unlikely to participate in any competitions, it wouldn't change a thing. If he wasn't taking part in anything, he would just do nothing for Paddy's platoon. Suddenly, the answer became blindingly obvious. Watson was not the worst student, but he caused so much ill-feeling in the platoon that getting shot of him would at least bring some harmony to the team. While we couldn't label him a toxic leader, his disruptive nature caused toxicity that oppressed and obstructed a unified spirit. Given our efforts to adjust his attitude had failed, maybe it was time for someone else to have a look at him. His stubbornness and arrogance were masking his ineptitude, but he was convinced it was nothing more than a character clash. It was time he heard this from someone other than me.

Captain Dunn interviewed him a few hours later and explained that for his own self-realization, he was moving to Captain Watts' platoon. There were no punches pulled as the boss informed him of his failings. Watson had displayed hollow leadership, patronizingly inviting his subordinates to contribute to the process of decision-making even though he would never diverge from his own entrenched thoughts. He was meddling instead of inspiring, complaining instead of motivating, and accusing instead of taking responsibility. Irrespective of this being the right decision, there was a sense of personal failure as Watson packed his bags. In fairness to Watson, he wasn't the cause of the platoon being so far behind in the competition. Deep down inside, I knew Paddy had interfered with the outcome, so if we had one less person to carry, and Paddy had one additional burden, it may just compensate for the scheming that was contributing to the deficit.

Sitting in his room, Captain Dunn glanced down the remaining names on the course.

'We are getting through a lot of students, Colour! Trollope, Weston, Puddick, Hays, Goldson, now Watson.' Repeatedly, he scanned the enlistment photograph.

'One more and the OC will start asking questions about our ability. Even worse, you just know that Academy Headquarters are sharpening their knives, getting ready to cut the course.'

It probably wasn't the best time for me to chat with him about Haigh's desire to leave, so quickly I changed the subject.

'Boss, the Sergeant Major said we were expecting a few Back-Termed students. How does that work?'

'Yes, he is right. Tomorrow we're likely to get at least one or two. If there is sympathy to be dished out, it should go here. These people will be in a world of hurt, and normally they don't stay too long.'

'They will not have long to settle in before the next major event, boss!'

Captain Dunn nodded and glanced once more at the names of those students we had lost. At any stage of training, being 'Back-Termed' causes a serious loss of morale. But being sent back to Rowallan was even worse, mainly because you would have scoffed at their predicament as you saw the Row-Co students being thrashed from breakfast to sundown. Now, you would find yourself as one of them and your mates would be looking on from their large single-man rooms laughing at you! The Commissioning Course Colour Sergeants often threatened their students with Row-Co, using it as a tool to scare the platoon into improving their performance. The threat of being sent to Rowallan was more than some could cope with.

By mid-morning, the course had taken the short coach journey to the old home of the Parachute Regiment in Aldershot. Browning Barracks had long been closed to the recruits of the famous elite fighting force, but the equipment remained serviceable. The once daily-used assault course and steeplechase circuits bore the scars of thirty years' wear and tear, but they remained as imposing as ever, no more so than that of the old Trainasium. The tall scaffolding poles, locked together and towering 40ft into the air, created an imposing challenge. The intimidating apparatus sat menacingly in the shadows of the empty prefab accommodation blocks. Prior to the reconstruction of the Army's recruit training system, it had been the stumbling block for many a potential paratrooper. Anyone failing to complete one of its multitude of high-altitude confidence tests would immediately and unceremoniously be kicked out of training, with no second chances. Undoubtedly it was a great test of character, and in the quest for such challenges, Rowallan students found themselves as one of its few visitors.

With the course assembled at the foot of the Trainasium, Pat and Daz climbed to the top of the primary hurdle, the parallel bars. The 40ft-high structure offered the protagonist an excellent view of Aldershot and its surroundings, although few chose to take the opportunity. They resembled the parallel bars that one would find a gymnast exercising on, but were made from scaffolding and elevated high into the air. Pat and Daz stood 10ft apart at opposite ends of the tower. With the students captivated by the appearance of these two key personalities perched high in the grey skies, Daz was ready to demonstrate the first test, screeching in his Liverpool accent: 'Right, you bunch of ugly creatures,' Daz screeched. 'You will be sent up the ladder by your Colour Sergeant. When you get to the start of the parallel bars, you are to adopt the squat position and hold on to the bars until you are told to let go.'

Daz demonstrated the position after each instruction.

'On the command "Up", stand up straight with your arms outstretched. Once you are steady, scream out your number, rank and name. Then advance across the bars until you reach the other side. Watch the Sergeant Major as we demonstrate the drill.'

Forty feet in the air, Pat was squatting down, legs astride and locked into the parallel bars, playing the role of a student.

'Student! Stand by! Stand by! Up!' screamed Daz. Pat nervously twitched on the bars, appearing to struggle with his balance. Twice he tried to stand up but failed.

'Stand by! Stand by! Up!' Daz screamed once again, but this time with more aggression.

Pat failed to move. Bewildered by what was happening, the students nervously looked around at each other. What was so terrifying that a Sergeant Major in the Parachute Regiment struggled with the test? Daz repeated his command, and apprehensively, Pat stood up. He swayed in the wind and repeatedly grabbed out for the safety of the bars at his feet. Daz issued a warning.

'Touch the bars with your hands again and it's a fail. State your number, rank and name?'

'24644199 Private Hardman, Sir.'

'Stand by, Hardman. Advance!' yelled Daz.

The bars stretched for approximately 15ft. The physical effort required just keeping the legs locked-out wide against the bars to stay upright made it arduous. Pat inched his right foot forward, followed by his left, his arms flapping frantically to keep himself balanced. Staff and students were craning at the neck as all eyes were fixed on Pat's every move. At the midway point of the parallel bars lay two large clamps. Offset and designed to force the navigator to break the security of having two legs locked into position, they forced him to pick up his feet and take a long stride over the problem. It was a crucial moment in completing the short journey. As you lifted one foot up to step over the obstacle perched 40ft in the air, with just your toes resting on the opposite round bar, balance and composure were compromised. A mistake at this height would certainly result in broken bones. It was a test of mental courage; shifting the balance of your body for that brief moment to step over the clamp was terrifying.

Pat dithered at the first clamp and Daz barked a warning at him. Several times he raised his foot and failed to step over the obstacle.

'Last warning, Hardman. Move over the clamp on the next attempt or you fail.' The intensity of Pat's arms flapping began to panic the students. Hesitantly, he stumbled over the first clamp and shuffled up to the second on the opposite rail. Pat lifted his foot and began to wobble. Beaten by the laws of physics, he began to fall forward. Heading for the gap between both bars, 40ft in the air, the students gasped in disbelief. But just as it looked like he would fall through the bars down to the maze of scaffolding below, he stretched out both arms, grasped hold of the parallel bars and, with a flick of his legs, turned his stumble into a perfect handstand. It was an amazing feat of athleticism. To a spontaneous round of applause, Pat began to show off with an array of stunts and tricks.

Dropping his body through the bars and performing one regain after another, he swung majestically on the apparatus. He executed press-ups and pull-ups before running from start to finish on just one bar. He showed off his agility for nearly five minutes, with the intention of disarming any fears the students had.

Before serving at Sandhurst, Pat had been a Sergeant Instructor on P Company, preparing soldiers and officers before they carried out their parachute course. He later instructed on the All Arms version of P Company, taking non-Parachute Regiment soldiers through the Trainasium. No stranger to the crude confidence course, Pat had mastered the art of frolicking high up. Standing in the centre of the parallel bars, hand on hips without a care in the world, Pat announced that the next to negotiate the high bars would be the DS. All had experienced the Trainasium at some stage in their careers, except for the OC. He was petrified of heights. Despite loving the assault course and thriving on the fitness, he didn't enjoy being off the floor. For two weeks before the course started, he repeatedly practised this event to avoid embarrassment on the day. As Commander of the Company, it was the place of Major Gray to go first. Daz called for him to stand up, and the OC called out his number, rank and name. He shuffled across the bars, doing the bare minimum, his body working overtime to conceal his discomfort at height. It was kidology of the greatest order. Leading by example sometimes can be just that. Convince people you are invincible, and they will believe it. Sometimes that's all you need to inspire people. If the OC had failed to take part in the event, he would struggle to convince the students of his credentials, undermining everything Rowallan represented. The Directing Staff put great emphasis on the phrase 'I don't ask you to do anything I can't do!'

With the Staff having completed the course, it was now the turn of the students. Francis was the first to make the parallel bars, despite needing several attempts and loud verbal encouragement from Staff Sergeant Dazzell. With an air of confidence, he moved onto the second obstacle. The illusion jump consisted of two planks separated by a gap of less than 3ft. The deception is achieved by placing one plank 20ft in the air and the second approximately 4ft lower. This gives the student the impression that the gap between the planks is huge. The fear factor was further increased by the planks' narrowness and wet condition. With nothing more than the plank and fresh air between the jumper and the ground, it was common for people to refuse to jump. Francis took a deep breath and hurled himself into the air. With knees bent to cushion the landing, he cleared the illusion jump with little more than a stumble and a sigh of relief.

Next up was Williams. He stood at the edge of the plank, gazing at the size of the gap. Pat stood below, screaming at him to jump.

'If you don't jump, faggot, you will fail this event, and you can pack your bags and go home, you big pussy. Stand by! Stand by! Jump!'

Williams remained motionless, placing his hands over his ears to shield himself from the increasing levels of abuse Pat was delivering.

'Jump!' Pat yelled as he ran out of patience, his veins bulging around his neck and forehead.

'Williams, jump. Now!' Captain Dunn spoke in a calm voice.

'Fail! Get down, you spineless creature,' Pat bellowed.

But Williams remained fixed to the spot, further antagonizing Pat.

'Let me get him down.'

'No, Gaz. You can't keep wiping his arse. Leave him there. He's a fanny.'

Pat began to work himself into a frenzy at Williams, hurling insults and abuse at the lonely figure stuck on the end of the illusion jump.

'Pat, I think he is suffering from fear of heights,' I intervened. 'It's probably best I go up and get him down.'

In a verbal blaze of swear words, Pat agreed. I climbed up to Williams, who was visibly frightened by the combination of the height, the prospect of the jump and now an angry Sergeant Major. Williams was displaying symptoms of the phenomenon known as 'crag-fast', which can cause the body to freeze when faced with a daunting manoeuvre at height. Normally, it is induced by traumatic experiences such as an accident or injury.

Crag-fast should not be underestimated. The most experienced of climbers can succumb to its symptoms, and recovery is tricky. A few months earlier, whilst climbing Tryfan, a substantial mountain at the start of Ogwen Valley in Snowdonia, my climbing party found itself involved in a serious accident. We were traversing the mountain just below the snow line when we became conscious of a four-man climbing party trying to ascend an ice chute. The narrow passage no wider than a suburban alleyway sandwiched between two huge boulders looked intimidating. Packed ice and below-zero temperatures made the climb technically challenging, but it was their lack of ice-climbing equipment that caught our attention. From a distance of 200 metres, we watched the climbers negotiate a critical point in their climb. Passing through a bottleneck high up, the ice chute would see them finish the ascent. More through morbid curiosity than interest, we stopped to see them reach the peak.

In ultra-slow motion, we watched on as the lead climber lost his grip and slid agonizingly slowly towards the rest of his party. Gaining speed, incapable of arresting his fall, disaster had struck. Stuck in the narrow channel, there was no escape: he crashed into the three climbers below him, and one by one they lost their purchase and began to slide in unison. The first climber was hurtling towards the end of the ice chute at high speed. He flew off the end of the chute and landed in a puff of red spray on a large boulder just below the snow line. The second climber tumbled out of the chute halfway down. Like a doll tossed from a child's playpen, he cartwheeled uncontrollably before coming to rest at the forward edge of a bluff. Fortunately, climbers three and four were knocked in such a way they spun to the side of the ice chute and became lodged in a rocky outcrop halfway down.

Our party set about helping the stricken climbers and headed for the two who had fallen the furthest. They both had serious head injuries and horrific breaks to every limb. Having stabilized their conditions and called mountain rescue, we made our way up the ice chute to help the remaining climbers, one of whom was suffering crag-fast. A combination of shock, fear, isolation and guilt, he could see the red splashes dotted at 5-metre intervals marking the impact landings of his friends leading to where they had come to rest. His vacant look, fixed on one spot, was a clear indicator that he had lost connection with reality. It took over an hour for the mountain rescue to airlift the seriously injured climbers off Tryfan, and in that time we had failed to convince the fourth man to let go of the rock he was clinging to. As the helicopter disappeared into the distance, the professionals took over the counselling, but there had been little progress. The man was still clinging onto the rock.

Williams remained stuck at the edge of the jump, mirroring the symptoms of the fourth climber on Tryfan. He had that detached look in his eyes and was dislocated from his surroundings. Both Pat and I were hanging onto the scaffold poles either side of the jump, trying to explain the illusion.

'It is designed to create the appearance of a huge gap,' explained Pat. 'You must overcome what you see and deal with what you know. This is a 3ft gap. This is a 4ft drop. Once you have rationalized this concept, you can deal with the fear and jump.'

It was the first time I had been in Pat's presence when he was not berating someone or something. Williams understood that it was only a small gap and it was the height that was intimidating.

'Williams, you have made all the rational conclusions as to why this is fooling you into not jumping. It's time to jump. Jump before it's too late, and you fail this event.'

By now I had joined Williams on the plank, hoping to instil confidence without increasing his anxiety. The young lad continued to stare at the gap, but there was no movement. With his toes just hanging over the edge, he was in a prime position for me to give him a shove and force him to jump. My mind raced with the thought. If I pushed him, flight or fight instincts would kick in, and probably it would be fine. He would most likely land safely. Pat, Daz and Paddy all stared at me, fully expecting me to give Williams a quick nudge. With the pair of us balancing at the edge of the plank, my hand gently placed on his shoulder, it was decision time.

'Williams, I am going to turn you around and walk you off the obstacle.'

There was no encouraging him off the end of the plank. Convinced he was suffering crag-fast, carefully, Williams was guided to the escape route. To have shoved him off the end of the illusion jump would have caused irreparable mental damage. A few minutes later, he was back on terra-firma and his ordeal was over. Pat was clearly upset with Williams and me. But pushing him would have achieved nothing. If he made the jump or not, it would still have been a fail. As soon as he got down to the ground, Captain Dunn placed him straight on to a Platoon Commander's warning. In what was dubbed 'cowards' corner' by Pat, he was then forced to watch the rest of the course make their way around the remainder of the Trainasium.

Lane enjoyed a trouble-free run over all the obstacles before arriving at the cargo net jump. At a height of 15ft, a gap of 6ft separated a taut cargo net and the end of the assault course. The student was required to take a fast run down a long plank and leap into a vertical cargo net. Preventing the elasticity of the net bouncing you back from where you came required a specific technique. Twisting mid-air, the student had to hit the net sideways on and punch through the square holes, simultaneously hooking his arm around the ropes to secure himself to the obstacle. Fail to execute this manoeuvre correctly and you endured a painful tumble to the safety net 10ft below. Bizarrely, success was equally as painful! Smashing into the cargo net ripped muscles and bruised arms, ribs, thighs and occasionally the face. As a bare minimum, there would be rope burns and bruises guaranteed. Injuries were inevitable, but get the technique wrong and it was truly going to end badly.

Lane stood at the start of the run-up to the cargo net, slowly rocking back and forth like an Olympic athlete preparing for the long jump. His hesitation was causing a queue to form behind him. A combination of frustration and procrastination sparked unhelpful comments from his peers. With a little encouragement from Pat, he eventually began to run towards the net.

'Faster, Lane! Faster!' Daz screamed, with a real sense of urgency. He could see that Lane achieved insufficient speed to clear the gap between the net and the plank. Lane also realized this and tried to stop. It was too late; he was going too fast to stop and too slow to make a safe recovery. With a loud scream, he toppled over the edge. This was possibly the worst scenario. The safety net was there to catch those who bounced off the cargo net, not for those who failed to jump. There was no safety measure for the man who had done the unexpected, such as falling off the end of the run-up! To compound his error, he landed on the heavy oak supporting frame that kept the safety net taught and secure. A thud followed by a muffled scream accompanied Lane's mistake. The frame of the safety net had prevented a 15ft fall to the ground, and although Lane wouldn't recognize it, hitting the safety frame may have saved him from an even worse fate. Pat was the first to reach Lane, who was curled up on the floor clutching his ribs in a semiconscious state.

'Marvellous! Bloody marvellous! The lengths some people will go to, just to get out of doing the Trainasium.'

Pat stood over Lane, hands on hips, offering more insults. As two paramedics tended to the young student, who was poleaxed and breathless on the floor, Pat delivered the final cut: 'You can count that as a fail, Lane.'

Pat instructed the two medics to take him over to 'coward's corner' for further treatment, before screaming at the next in line.

As the medics swarmed around Lane trying to assess his injuries, he was clearly in no condition to be moved. In what can only be described as a horrendous fall, we all felt sure he would have a number of broken bones. The medical staff called for their ambulance to back up onto the Trainasium, and the sirens wailed all the way back to the medical centre in Sandhurst. In his absence, Pat proceeded to verbally abuse Lane for his lack of aggression. Addressing the whole course, most of whom were stuck at various stages of the assault course, he used Lane as an example of why they must follow the instructions. Finally, he warned everyone that they would suffer the same ignominy if they held back with their efforts. His warning worked well: the students who were stuck behind Lane before his fall ran so fast at the net that they nearly knocked it out of the frame.

Completing the Trainasium normally gave the students a great sense of achievement, which transferred into confidence, eventually resulting in higher morale. Such events are designed to engender camaraderie and cohesion, to give a feeling of uniqueness and elitism. But surveying the faces of our platoon, we could see our key characters were subdued and submissive. In any unit of men, there is one key principle for success, and that is high morale. If by our actions we were incapable of guiding the students to a mental serenity, we were in danger of failing. As the students boarded the coach to return back to the Academy, Haigh, Danner and Mathews all appeared dejected, while Witherspoon, Moore and Williams looked close to quitting.

In an effort to get to the bottom of why the trip to the Trainasium failed to produce a spike in morale, we gathered the platoon into the study hall. Captain Dunn left it to me to try and crack the problem. Sitting on a table at the back of the room, I cracked a couple of jokes about the day's activities, mainly at the expense of Danner, who was sure to take the bait. Not my normal *modus operandi*, but I judged he was able to take a bit of comical criticism and thought it may induce a response. It served its purpose, breaking the ice and starting a bit of friendly banter. I let it roll for a bit and contributed when the opportunity arose, trying not to be the one dominating the session. Already people were beginning to ask questions that would allow me to discover what was causing the current atmosphere.

'How is Lane, Colour Sergeant?' inquired Witherspoon.

'He is OK. His ego is more damaged than his ribs, but the good news is there are no breaks.'

'Will he be kicked off the course?' asked Murphy.

'I think you will have to do more than bounce off the cargo net if you want to get sent home.'

'How bad does someone have to be before you kick them off the course, Colour Sergeant?' asked Haigh.

'No one gets kicked off the course without good reason. But to answer your question, if it is clear that you are not attempting to achieve the course requirements, you will be kicked off. It is as simple as that. But from my experience, the student normally knows long before he is told. Failing something comes as a surprise only to the deluded.'

'Do you know why we have been selected to do Rowallan, Colour Sergeant, or why we never went straight on to the Commissioning Course?' asked Moore.

'We have a good idea, and it's not what most of you have written in your essays! It's clear-cut in some cases. In others it may be the RCB selectors got it wrong. But regardless of why you are here, let me tell you that if you pass this course, you will be better placed than your contemporaries to serve with soldiers and more accepting of the world's most hostile places. Don't look back and regret this, or you will be bitter and twisted forever and miss the true beauty of what you are doing. If you can handle this, you can handle anything.'

'"Got it wrong", Colour Sergeant? Can you expand? Do you mean I am here because someone has made a typing error?' said Danner.

'Firstly, Danner, you can rest easy. With you, the selectors got it spot on. You are a tubby snob who is too cheeky for his own good, and before we let you loose with real people you need an education in reality. Secondly, no! Not a clerical error, more an error in the assessment of character. There are people on the Commissioning Course who should be here. That being the case, there are people sitting in this room who "maybe" should have gone straight to the Commissioning Course. It is such a fine line and we don't know what side of it you fell!'

'Is life in the Army as hard as this for real?' Rideout asked, inquisitively.

'It can be. I recall doing a survival course in the middle of winter, living on mushrooms for a week, with little more than a black plastic bag for clothing. That was no fun! Each day consisted of a 10km forced march, and a further 5km during the night. That was certainly a hard time for me. It rained constantly, my ankle was swollen after a bad tackle sidelined me in the final of an Army Cup game, and the day before the course started, my car was stolen. All this played second fiddle on learning that my long-term girlfriend was cheating on me with some spotty faced druggy. Emotional and physical challenges had mounted just days before the "Escape and Evasion" course began. These things don't last forever. It is just as conceivable for Lane to have fallen out of a ski lift while on holiday. If you are having a wobble because of what happened to Lane, the only way to avoid a similar experience is to wrap yourself in cotton wool and stay in bed.'

'Surely things like that must have a lasting effect on you?'

'The thing is, Rideout, apart from the fact that mushrooms are off the menu as a result of the survival course, I have fond memories of the camaraderie struck up with other lads on every course I have done. Fond memories are forged in fire.'

'How about your wife, Colour Sergeant. You spend most of your time with us. Do you miss being at home?' Mathews asked.

The proverbial penny dropped. Having just returned from a weekend off, these lads were suffering from the phenomenon known as post-leave blues. I kicked myself for not aiming for this problem. It was a cheeky comment, but the fact that he asked the question proved to me that the students were becoming comfortable in my presence.

'To answer your question, my wife likes to see as little of me as is possible.' The students burst into laughter.

'Is that because you give her room inspections?' yelled Mathews.

'Yes, every morning before the kids go to school. There is a formal parade so I can check their shoes are polished, homework done, then they are marched to school in two ranks. The wife gets the same treatment. If she hasn't pressed her work clothes, watered the plants and cleaned the house before she leaves at eight in the morning, she is put on my home-made Mean Machine!'

Most of the students gasped at my statement.

'But Colour Sergeant, you don't have any kids, and you only see your wife at the weekend.' Francis was quick to remind me of my domestic situation previously declared.

'Yes, Francis, there is no pulling the wool over your eyes! You've caught me out. I do as I am told or face the prospect of being kicked out. My wife is stunning, and I am punching above my weight with her. Added to that, she earns more money than me, so it's not even an equal partnership.'

There was more laughter, followed by the comment that Mathews was an expert in being kicked out. The students began to openly discuss who had split with their girlfriends over the weekend. In total, there had been five splits and two declared cool-off periods. It was the ideal time for me to explain that this was not an uncommon story, and that anyone considering a long-term future with the Army needed to be prepared for it. Military careers are only successful if the girlfriend, partner or wife can tolerate the stresses of a distant relationship.

'Has it ever happened to you, Colour Sergeant?' I was asked.

'Yes. On more than one occasion!'

'How did you cope?'

'Well, the first time not too good. While serving in Germany, my girlfriend was back in Liverpool and ran off with a local shop owner. For about two weeks, drink was the answer. That led to wallowing in self-pity and dreaming up ways to get even. Stupidly, I placed an advert in a gay magazine for her new boyfriend. It said, "Shy, retiring gay hiding a secret from a new girlfriend seeks young male for fun and discreet relationship." His business was swamped with calls for months after. Then his name and address were entered on to the list of every Sunday supplement subscription plausible, in an effort to cram his house with junk mail.'

'Did it work?'

'I'm not sure, but the thought of my ex receiving post from *All things leather and tight Plc* and other weirdo magazines made me giggle for months after. She obviously cottoned on to the fact it was me. The next time I went home, the police constantly stopped me whilst driving around Liverpool. Each time, they arrested me for car theft. Someone kept reporting my car stolen, making it impossible for me to get around town. The police said the caller was Asian-sounding, and so was her new boyfriend, and my ex had used that trick on the bloke who dumped her just after we met.'

'But how about if there was a chance of reconciliation?'

'OK, this is the solution. If you want to see her again, you get everyone in your platoon to write to her, telling her that since the split you have been unbearable to live with. Also, they need to add that you are still mad about her and what a great fella you are. Then add that since the split, you have given all your fortune to the poor and needy. She becomes so guilt-ridden she takes you back. You get a second chance.'

'And live happily ever after, Colour Sergeant,' giggled Rideout.

'No! Then you dump her so she knows what it feels like, because if it didn't work the first time around, it's unlikely to work the second time.'

The unexpected response had the platoon laughing out loud, prompting banter to flow freely.

It was the first time we had talked about anything other than the Army, and they caught a glimpse of my true identity. We left the study hall on a small high. It was a successful talk, giving us a slim hope of re-cultivating sub-unit cohesion ahead of tomorrow morning's competition. There was much more to my words than just chit-chat with the students. Surreptitiously, I was desperately trying to demonstrate that leadership is not all about issuing orders from afar. Nor is it commanding remotely through conduits of oppressive implementation. The best leaders are capable of conveying vision, intent and instructions during informal encounters. Known as 'the light touch', it is the ability to get subordinates to execute the most difficult duties through personable communication. General

Custer was rumoured to have invited the lowest rank in his personal protection party to read the order he was about to issue to his troops. If the soldier couldn't understand it, it was rewritten. Soldiers idolize commanders and trust them emphatically. But if they can't communicate and manage soldiers on a level playing field, that blind loyalty is unpicked and the predictable shift through the gears of leadership will drift towards toxicity. Like a loveless marriage, they can coexist, but no one will be inspired, incentivized or enthused.

The day had ended well. A feeling of recovery was gently hovering over the students as they vacated the study hall and went about their night-time routine. With the briefest of updates into my diary, another day had passed.

The following morning, the first man to greet me was Haigh.

'Haigh, what can I do for you?'

'Well, firstly good morning, Colour Sergeant. I was wondering when my interview with Captain Dunn was happening so that we could discuss the possibilities of leaving?'

Despite him telling me at the start of the week, it was a total surprise that he still wanted to leave. For the strangest of reasons, I felt betrayed. After last night's 'love in', it was hard to accept that there was still doubt in anyone's mind.

We walked out to the courtyard and sat on the dwarf wall that surrounded the Mean Machine. Relaxed and keen to learn what had brought this on, I listened as Haigh began to explain himself. He continued to repeat the same excuse as he had previously. Lost in a myriad of pathetic vindications, my frustrations bubbled up deep inside my psyche. Before it was possible to control my disappointment, swear words and angry gestures flowed in abundance:

> 'You're just a fucking quitter, Haigh! Everything you do is by half. You put in half the effort of everyone else! You should change your name to Arfa, because everything about you is only ever arf-done. You can go in front of Captain Dunn. But I promise you this, thirty minutes after you see him, you will be in front of the College Commander. Thirty minutes later you will be out of the Academy with a tag around your neck saying: "My name is Arfa-man Haigh. I will only ever do half a job and apply half the effort because I am half the man I could be!"'

The lad stood in silence, intensely staring at me with his teeth grating and nostrils flaring. Momentarily, there was a concern he was offended enough to take a swing at me. My words hit home, and they clearly hurt as I continued:

> 'If you walk away from this course, you will always be a quitter. When you get to my age, there will be nothing other than regret in your life. Whether you like it or not, this course is shaping your identity and who you are as

a man. For the rest of your life, you will continue to live with that "nearly man" attitude. It is better to have tried and failed than to have left halfway through. I can get you through this course if you really want to succeed. It's your choice. Don't base it on the discomfort of the moment. Be outside Captain Dunn's office in ten minutes or rejoin the platoon.'

Ten minutes later, Haigh was standing to attention outside the Platoon Commander's office. The anger still showed on my face as he was ushered in for his interview. Closing the door behind him, I made my way back to my room, but no sooner had the door closed, than it opened and Haigh came straight back out, followed by Captain Dunn.

'Wow, that was quick. Is everything alright, boss?'

'He's changed his mind. He apologized for wasting my time and asked to rejoin the platoon.'

It was pleasing Haigh had made a U-turn, but with the assault course competition about to take place, maybe this was an own goal. We were still considering if we should place him on a warning; we could yet regret his decision to stay. Of course, the irony of him changing his mind was further evidence he lacked a decisive streak. Once again, he had only half done what he intended to do. It was the strangest of feelings. Changing his mind did little to reassure me. Nevertheless, for now, he was committed to getting through the course.

Dressed in red rugby tops, helmets donned, carrying a water bottle and a toggle rope, the course assembled at the Sandhurst outdoor assault course. Tucked away in the woods at the gable end of New College was the traditional old-style assault course. Daz had rehearsed the whole Company in the techniques required to successfully negotiate the main obstacles to mitigate potential injuries. This included tactics required for climbing the 10ft wall, methods for clearing the monkey bars and rules for staying safe. It was a minimum of two times around the course in preparation for what would become competition number nine. Standing with the OC, both Pat and Pete had come dressed for the occasion; they were going to run with the students. Our platoon was now much smaller than Paddy's, since Stone was still on the sick, Lane was still in the medical centre recovering from his fall and Watson had been transferred. Despite the perceived advantage, this event would be won and lost at the bottlenecks and choke points. Speedy negotiation relied on technique, organization and holding vital ground. Pat instructed all the students to adopt the freefall position, and the students dutifully fell to the wet ground: arched backs, feet in the air and legs astride, arms outstretched and heads forced back. With everyone adopting the freefall position, Pat called out, 'Stand by! Stand by!' Two seconds later, Daz gave one long whistle blast and the race was underway.

The woods filled with screams of self-motivation. Both platoons set off at a frantic pace, understanding that the key to winning was securing the prime breaching point of the first obstacle. Moore had been given the task of leading this event. Cunningly, he chose King as his chief of staff, simply because he would have done this event many times before. King intuitively knew what Moore was thinking when he assigned his strongest team members to stay close to the weaker students in a man-marking system. Shrewdly, he had also employed Barns as a human ladder. His tall gangly frame was making light work of the 6ft and 10ft walls. King's enthusiasm inspired a committed team performance as Moore directed him to fight for the prime real estate at the foot of each obstacle. Francis, Murphy and Mathews had latched onto Williams, Witherspoon, Packman and Danner. Astonishingly, Haigh was like a man possessed as he threw himself at every obstacle in an effort to demonstrate his commitment. Angry, focused and full of energy, we were seeing a side of him we thought didn't exist.

No obstacle proved too daunting. Even the flooded culverts failed to slow down the platoon as they pushed and pulled each other over everything that stood in their way. Fifteen minutes later, Moore was celebrating a vital, morale-boosting victory. Caked in mud, soaking wet, knuckles and knees cut and grazed having smashed against the concrete obstacles, Moore loved every minute of his command. The platoon danced and cheered as Major Gray declared No. 2 Platoon as the winners. Captain Dunn turned his back on the boys and, with a clenched fist, motioned a covert fist-pump into the air. It was a tough task for me to demand the platoon show some respect for the losing team and calm their celebrations. If Paddy's platoon had been receiving help, and it was still hard to believe this was the case, the boys were within their rights to be overanimated with this win. The gap on the scoreboard was beginning to look a little more respectable – eighteen points to nine – and thoughts of recovery were tangible as cohesion amongst the group seemed to have appeared overnight.

Winning the assault course race, combined with Haigh's improved attitude – neatly complemented by Watson's transfer – was clearly the formula for improvement. High on morale and success, they rolled into their accommodation, where they were greeted by a solitary figure deep in thought. Standing in the centre of the corridor, feet awash with a collection of bags, a young man struggled to muster an acknowledgement. There were no smiles, no greetings offered by either party, as the reason for his sudden appearance in the accommodation dawned. His demeanour was the epitome of self-pity and dejection. In a rare declaration of empathy, the returning students suppressed their triumphant mood as they brushed passed him on the way to their rooms. One look at the way the lad held himself indicated he was low on confidence. Clothing creased, hair tousled, he resembled a young Ken Dodd, minus the buck teeth. He snapped to attention, half expecting a telling-off when he caught sight of me. Avoiding eye contact, the back-termer offered me his name.

'Officer Cadet Norris reporting from Blenheim Company, Colour Sergeant!'

His eyes began to well up as he braced himself for my response.

'Danner! Danner!' I shouted.

'Yes, Sir. Sorry, I mean yes, Colour Sergeant.'

'Here is your new roommate. Move out of your current room and move into Hays' old room together. Norris is his name. Once you have dropped off his bags, take him to the Company Quartermaster's stores for a kit issue.'

If anyone could pick up the new lad's morale, it was Danner. His Etonian idiosyncrasy and upbeat disposition could make the sinking of the *Titanic* appear to be little more than a hiccup on what was otherwise a perfect holiday.

Friday came and went in the usual frantic manner, with command tasks, fitness and the inevitable session on the Mean Machine. Notably, the strength and conditioning of Barns, Williams, Danner and Packman were improving. Physically they were more capable of dealing with the pain, and emotionally more tolerant of Pat's continuous ridicule. The platoon was getting mentally stronger, with a marginal improvement in everyone's self-confidence. For the students, the final stages of the day were committed to interviews and the issuing of Platoon Commander's warnings. Captain Dunn and I reviewed the names of those we had singled out for a formal warning.

'Watson, Colour! This one is easy. Let's pass the file to Captain Watts, and it's up to him.' A comedy giggle leaked from his composed exterior.

'Agreed, Sir. Let's hope that he gets a fresh start and it gives him the opportunity to absorb all we said to him.'

'Williams?'

'Boss, he is already on a warning, remember?'

'That's easy then. Of course, he failed to attempt the illusion jump, so this is just formalizing what was said to him back then. Let's have him in for a confirmatory chat as early as we can.'

'OK, Sir. Although it's sad it has to be that way. He seems to have been trying harder since then, but if we fail to follow it through, all our words will be seen as idle threats hereafter.'

'That's the way the cookie crumbles, Colour. Williams will feel hard done by after a sterling performance on the assault course. But not everyone can be a paratrooper, Colour!'

'Not sure, boss; surely Lane is stupid enough to jump out of a perfectly serviceable plane?'

'Yes, Colour, maybe! First, he needs to be released from the med-centre.'

'That is later today, Sir.'

'We need to officially serve him a warning. If possible, can you set him up for an interview at the earliest opportunity?'

'Understood, Sir. That's the lot, isn't it?'

'No – Haigh. We said we would place him on a warning for his lethargy and ad hoc application.'

'Boss, this is tough. We have turned a corner today. He is a changed man. My fear is a Platoon Commander's warning will undo our own efforts and push him over the edge. Can you give him a warning that doesn't amount to a Platoon Commander's warning?'

'Colour, it doesn't work that way. If he goes back to his old ways, you will be demanding we kick him out; am I right?'

'Yes, but …'

'The College Commander will demand to see the evidence, and that includes the Platoon Commander's warning! He goes on the warning. Your protests are noted, but trust me, it is for our own protection.'

'OK. Stone – are we putting him on a warning?'

'Again, Colour, it's tricky and you are not going to like my answer. But what is the reason for putting him on a warning?'

'For playing us like fools. For being on the sick since he arrived!'

'Colour, you are getting too emotional. Don't let the process get to you. Stone has done nothing wrong. He is on a sick chit which runs out close of play today. If he struggles next week, we will deal with it. For now, no warning for Stone.'

It just didn't make sense. The bureaucracy was driving me to distraction. Although it wasn't the case, it did feel that my efforts to retain Haigh were being thwarted by our own self-imposed morality, whilst simultaneously we were protecting a charlatan like Stone. This was not going to end well. Placing Haigh on a warning and not Stone was crazy. It was a high price to pay to ensure our collective reputations and ethos remained pure.

Captain Dunn and I walked into the OC's office for the first official Progress Board. Captain Watts, Paddy, Eddie and Pete were all waiting on our arrival. Unquestionably there was a tense atmosphere. This was the first time the DS had gathered collectively since the Exercise Klondike car incident. This had not gone unnoticed by the OC, who sought to ease tensions with some light-hearted banter by poking fun at Captain Watts and his failure to win the last competition. Pat jumped on the comment and berated Paddy.

'Hah, Paddy, you should have taken your car!'

'That's unfair, Sir. Sure I'd no idea they were collecting bricks.'

Captain Dunn glanced at me with a wry smile, but neither of us said anything.

'OK, just to remind you all, the Progress Board is designed to identify those failing the course and facilitate a path for their success. We will battle through names at random so there is no prejudice. Please let me know if you have issues.'

Major Gray eventually came to our first student as he called out King's name.

'He is doing OK. We were appreciative of his leadership on the assault course race, even though it was as second-in-command. He has the ability to organize and command well. If there is a concern, it is that he may still be relying on his soldiering skills, but we have this in hand.' Captain Dunn spoke with authority, and the OC nodded sagely.

'Fine, I am sort of content. Please can I see his journal? Let's see how he performs amidst academic pressure. Also, can you give him an essay to write after one of the long marches next week?' Captain Dunn nodded in acknowledgement.

'Barns?'

'Improving slowly. Very slowly. We can't make too much of him until we can get him to a point where we can examine his resolve under intellectual and physical pressure, but he is getting there. He had a good Exercise Compass Rose with a valuable regain after a massive navigation error, but he's developing.'

'OK, another student from No. 2 Platoon. Lane, first name Gareth. That's two things he shares with the international footballer Gareth Southgate.'

Bemused, Pat asked what was the other?

'Neither of them can hit the net!'

I spat my tea out with laughter, and looked around to see no one else was laughing.

'Missed the net! Come on!' I said. 'You must have watched the game? Gareth Southgate missed a penalty! England is once again knocked out by Germany in the Euros!'

The remaining DS looked at me as if I had two heads. Football was my choice of vehicle to teach leadership outside of the military. For me, football was all about nurturing team spirit, camaraderie, humility and selfless commitment. In a rugby-mad Academy like Sandhurst, this wasn't always welcome and frequently got me into hot water.

'At least you got it, Colour!' laughed the OC.

Captain Dunn flicked through his file and summarized Lane's performance to date.

'Lane is due out of the Medical Centre any time now. He will go straight on a warning when we get time for an interview. The command matrix has him down for an appointment early next week; sadly, this is likely to confirm our fears. It would be prudent for the College Commander to get a look at him. He is not demonstrating any leadership qualities, and while he is trying to contribute, we have already seen the best of him and it's short of the minimum requirement.'

'Understood. Let's put him first on the list for a visit. Please ensure he is in a command appointment between 1000hrs and 1200hrs on the second day of Exercise Plain Jane. OK, move on. How about Danner?'

'Danner. Cheeky, has a sense of humour and there is a suspicion of lethargy. We have him fixed in our sights and he is kept under pressure by the Colour Sergeant. Content he is going in the right direction.'

Paddy jumped into the conversation to give his opinion on Danner. Although he had no authority over Danner, at Rowallan we subscribed to 360-degree reporting. Anyone could say anything if they felt it would help with the development of an individual.

'There's something about that big lad that's no good,' Paddy said. 'He has an arrogance about him that says he would be a better politician than an officer. See the way he looks at yee; I swear he thinks he is a cut above the rest of the students.'

A telling glance from Captain Dunn was enough to raise everyone's suspicions. That was not the Danner we knew. Sure, he could be cheeky, but he was the most affable character you could come across. If he had taken a dislike to someone, there was possibly a good reason, and it wasn't a class divide. Captain Dunn was quick to defend Danner, and the OC sought to calm the waters.

'Thank you, Colour Sergeant. We shall all keep an eye out for that. If he has any delusions of grandeur, the weekend's events will bring him down to the ground with a huge bump. James, how is Francis doing?'

'After a shaky start, he is doing well,' replied Captain Dunn. 'There have been a few injury issues, but provided they don't get worse, we have a steady development plan for him. He is yet to have a command appointment, but we have no concerns.'

'Moore – is he the slightly effeminate character?'

'Well, I couldn't possibly comment, but he does occasionally pout his lips! That aside, there is an underlying assured quality about the lad. He is fit and possesses mental robustness that he is just learning how to use. Great effort in command of the assault course race. Potentially a talent in the making.'

'Good. Moving on – Boyle please, James.'

'Boyle is proving popular. He has bags of character, it just needs steering in the right direction. Bounced back after his disappointment on the first competition. Positive outlook and keen to impress. His mental agility is improving, as is his mental strength. Occasionally he gets nervous, but that will be knocked out of him in the weeks ahead.'

'Watson next please, James.'

'Ah, he's no longer ours. He moved to Tom's Platoon.'

'So he did! Yes of course. Tom, have you had time to analyse Watson?'

Captain Dunn excused himself to refill his coffee cup, and that was my cue to join him. Standing in the kitchen with a face like thunder, searching for a clean cup, he was pleased to see my appearance.

'What the hell was that about? Has he got an issue with Danner or is he just trying to cause trouble?'

'Boss, it can only be something that has happened between them. I will press Danner on the issue later. But you are right, there is more to that exchange than meets the eye.'

We both returned to the Progress Board and sat quietly as Captain Watts and Paddy discussed more of their students. Strangely, the temperature had risen in our absence and a sense of disharmony had crept in as the OC and Captain Watts finished discussing the last of their students.

The OC searched his notes and resumed by asking for our thoughts on Stone.

'He has done nothing since he arrived, Sir. It's been one long sick chit for him. I think he is scamming us.' I was quick to leap in before Captain Dunn had the chance to speak.

Pat turned the pages of his discipline book to see how many days sick Stone had taken. Between the OC and Pat, they made a brilliant team. They could be as devilish as each other in many ways, but very little escaped their attention.

'Eight working days. Two groups of three days and one of two. I have to agree with Colour McCarthy, it looks like the lad is playing the odds.'

With Pat's damning summary, the OC surely had to put Stone on a warning. But, just to confirm that Captain Dunn was right in his initial assessment, the OC nodded and glossed over it, repeating that sick notes would only support the College Commander's claim that we couldn't make a sound assessment on someone who hadn't had the opportunity to show us what he was made of. He did, however, ask Pat to point Stone out to him during the next event.

'Here's an interesting character – Haigh. What do you make of him, James?'

Captain Dunn paused and looked at me, smiled, took a deep breath and answered. 'We have placed him on a warning. Much to the dismay of the Colour Sergeant, who has offered me his reservations, but if we are to show evidence later in the course, this week must count towards his dismissal. He had the gun run as his initial command appointment, and after a good start, he made a serious error in judgment. We are edging forward, but it is painfully slow. Yes, we have a concern, but not one for your attention just yet.'

'Colour; not happy?'

'Sir, I don't disagree with Captain Dunn, but Haigh is fragile. There is a lot of effort expended on Haigh and we are just making progress with him. There is a part of me that is reluctant to push him unnecessarily. Just maybe the warning will be a kick in the swingers when what he really needs is a hug!'

'Hug! Did you say hug? Fuck me, you're lucky we only have one string vest. If we had two, you'd be wearing both of them next week.' Pat was properly offended.

'I see, Colour. I agree with the Sergeant Major, a hug is too much,' said the OC. 'But this is tricky. It's prudent to place him on a warning. It's easier to de-escalate than it is to escalate late. Please direct him to me for an informal chat. I would be keen to question his resolve and see where it takes us. Sergeant Major, can you pencil him in for an interview please? Oh, and can I hand over the string vest to Colour Mac, I am fed up of the sight of it?'

Pat scribbled in his book, got out of the chair, returned with the string vest and promptly slammed it down in front of me.

'Packman – who is Packman; what does he look like?' The OC offered a cheeky smile as the vest sat on my notebook.

'That sums him up well. He is hard to nail down. I think he is just one pace ahead of us. Maybe he is bluffing his case, or it's just luck, but he is deliberately avoiding the limelight. This could be his way of dealing with things. On the other hand, maybe he's just not a natural leader.'

'Well, nothing new there, James. What's your plan?'

'He is in an appointment next week. This will give me the opportunity to analyse his leadership and develop a SMART plan.'

The OC nodded wisely, but we all knew he didn't have a clue about SMART objectives. He enjoyed hands-on leadership, but was a little too long in the tooth for clever mnemonics.

'Very well. Mathews – is he the lad with the black eye?'

'Yes, Sir.' I quickly blathered out a heap of nonsensical rubbish to distract any further reference to the black eye. Luckily, Captain Dunn knew what was going on and left no space for further discussion as he endorsed Mathews' good progress.

'Yes, I like Mathews. He is consistently trying hard – seems to be everywhere. Top bloke. He has taken full advantage of his opportunities. He has been in command on two occasions and impressed both times. This guy is here for all the wrong reasons, but we are grateful for it. His efforts on the stretcher were fabulous.'

'Stop drooling, James! And let's get back to reality with Witherspoon.'

'Bump! Witherspoon; that will bring me back to earth. We see glimpses of hope, but they are too infrequent. He has a good brain; we saw that during the Haramosh debate. And the confidence course demonstrated his ability to think straight under pressure. We just need to develop his character to go with it. We will be in a better place to comment on his progress after the next seven days have passed. There is a good man in there and he earns great reviews in the peer assessments. We are quietly content.'

'I think that's it, James?'

'No, not quite – Rideout and Murphy. There isn't much to say, other than we know Rideout is a little jittery and we have it in hand. Murphy has yet to show his real character.'

'Fantastic. Well, let's summarize No. 2 Platoon. Started with twenty-one students and you are down to fifteen. Williams and Haigh are both on a Platoon

Commander's warning, and Lane is to go onto a warning when he gets out of the hospital. When you put it like that, it doesn't sound great, James!'

The OC grinned, and Captain Dunn responded with his own version of the truth.

'Well, technically we are at sixteen, as Norris has just arrived. If we count Hays as a defect on enlistment, we only started with twenty. This gives us a current pass rate of nearly 80 per cent. That's about average. Things have never been better. Not so bad when you put it that way.'

The OC raised a very knowing smile. It is clear to me now that they were both hardwired into the same mainframe. This short clash of academic swords was eye-opening, with differing views cordially exchanged and not a cross word between them – leadership exemplified.

We walked back to the accommodation, where students prepared for their evening meal. By now they had established a clandestine intelligence-gathering network. They exploited their good relationships with the chefs, drivers and gate guards to syphon any snippets of information that would compromise our activities. They had become experts in analysing the patterns of life, piecing together information indicating the date and time of their next bugout. Drivers, wash-hands and past students would all be quizzed to within an inch of their lives. It all mounted up to a game the students called 'tease the time of the next bugout'. Whilst other members of the DS frowned on it and never indulged, Captain Dunn and I loved to join in.

Mathews stood in the corridor, half-dressed, polishing his civilian shoes and smiling like a lunatic.

'What's up with you, Mathews? You're looking fairly pleased with yourself.'

He continued to smile, while increasing the effort expended on cleaning his left shoe.

'Well go on, softlad, spit it out. What are you itching to say to me?'

'I was just going to ask you if you had anything special planned for the weekend, Colour Sergeant?'

My arrival sparked a mini-commotion as a number of students appeared from out of their rooms, keen to hear my response. Not for one second did I believe that Mathews was bothered about my recreational interests. He was fishing for a clue or a hint that would indicate the time of a pending bugout. His cheek made me laugh, prompting my small audience to laugh with me.

'Football is the answer to your question, Mathews. You all know that I am the Academy football coach. We have fixtures every Saturday, and this weekend we have a tough game against RAF Cranwell. On Sunday, my own team are in the semi-final of the Wiltshire District Cup for small clubs. Other than one or two other work-related things, that's about it.'

Mathews smiled as he scratched his head, thinking of something else to say.

'Colour Sergeant. One wouldn't toy would one?' Danner asked, appearing from behind me.

'Sorry, Danner, but you will have to translate that into a language understood by normal people because I don't have a clue as to what you're asking me. Boyle – what did he say?'

Danner tried again: 'I simply asked, Colour Sergeant, if there was a hint of prevarication in the synopsis of your weekend's activities.'

'No, you will have to do better than that, softlad. Try to use words that you are likely to hear on the TV. That way you can be guaranteed they will be understood.'

Danner smirked, unsure if I was being serious or deceptive by pretending not to understand his questions. We all knew there was a bugout imminent, and sticking to my word, no lies were issued, nor was anyone misled, despite Danner's educated play with words.

'I'll see you Sunday night then, Colour Sergeant.' Danner smiled, believing his questions had predicted the next bugout correctly.

'I'm sure there is a good chance of that, Danner. But there is also a good chance you'll see me before.'

That was not the answer he expected, and the students looked stunned. They hadn't contemplated an early bugout! They had convinced themselves that it wouldn't happen until late on Sunday. Now there was doubt. With nothing else to say, Captain Dunn and I wished them good night and walked out of the door in the direction of the car park. Following close behind us, the students made their way to their evening meal. The privilege of making their own way to meals was granted after week three. Despite the timings remaining tight, the concession was gratefully received. Watching them disappear through the doors of the canteen, we waited until the last man had vanished from sight. With the unsuspecting students happily engrossed in their evening meal, the DS returned to the accommodation.

With less than twenty minutes to prepare, we frantically set the study hall up for Exercise Helping Hand. As each student made their way back from a reasonably leisurely dinner, they were absolutely dumbfounded to discover the DS had all returned to work. As each student reached the entrance, he was filtered into the study hall. Haigh was the last student to join his peers. Exasperated by the appearance of the DS, he struggled to comprehend what was going on, and for a brief moment the old Haigh emerged.

'Welcome to Exercise Helping Hand everyone. This is a bugout.'

The students gawked at me in bewilderment.

'Are we being bugged out? it doesn't feel like a bugout.' Haigh's impetuousness rattled my cage, but now was not the time to confront it.

'It's a bugout, but just a gentle one. Go pack your kit and prepare to go somewhere that you weren't expecting. Grab your crash out bags and return back here for a brief. Ensure you have your washing-shaving kit and don a pair of chinos or smart slacks and a shirt. You have fifteen minutes to be back here seated, ready to go, or it's the Mean Machine.'

There was no dissent, just a sense of urgency as the confused students busily achieved my demand. In an orderly fashion, bags were placed at the rear of the study hall and all students sat attentively at their desks as I spoke:

> 'The following people are off to Woking Police Station to help them deal with drunks and vagrants for the weekend – Stone, Barns, Witherspoon and Mathews. The following are going to the Thames Valley Disabled Adventure Centre for the weekend to help disabled children enjoy a taste of outdoor activities – Williams, Lane, Francis and Murphy. Next, it's the Dellow Hostel for the homeless – Rideout, Packman, Boyle and King. That leaves Haigh, Danner and Moore – you lucky dudes are going to the Samaritans' soup kitchen in London. At midday tomorrow, Colour Sergeant Edwards will come and collect you. He will take you to a new location and twenty-four hours later, the rotation will be repeated. Enjoy your weekend!'

Standing on the grass outside the Memorial Chapel, with a smile and a wave, we watched the students depart with just a hint of satisfaction. The first minibus, destined for the Samaritans' soup kitchen, honked its horn to acknowledge our gesture as Danner pressed his nose hard up against the window and smiled with excitement. He knew we had sent him to the soup kitchen as part of our warped sense of humour. It dawned on us all that he was going to be a big hit at the Samaritans. Helping Hand was a humbling exercise, uniquely designed to ensure those who had enjoyed a privileged upbringing got close to those who lived day-to-day in desperation and despair. Thames Valley Police enjoyed Row-Co visits, if only for the opportunity to poach our most talented students. Whilst there was always a risk involved in this kind of franchised training, the rewards far outreached the penalties.

Chapter Nine

Plain Jane

Sunday evening began with the usual flurry of DS packing their kit in preparation for yet another trip away with the students. The side door swung open and the corridor filled with laughter as Eddie regaled the OC with stories of Exercise Helping Hand. He explained that he was due to send three students to a home for delinquent children, but when he got there, the kids had burnt it down. As he got within earshot, I overheard him inform Major Gray that one of Paddy's lads broke his leg when the police car that he was in crashed while chasing a stolen motorbike.

'Bloody hell, Eddie, was he badly hurt?'

'It's a broken leg, Gaz! It doesn't get much worse than that. The good news is, the break was clean, but he won't be taking any further part in the course.'

'Anyone else hurt?'

'No. Lane was given a bit of a roughing up by a few tramps at the soup kitchen on the Embankment. Apparently, he was also mistaken for a hungry tramp by one of the permanent soup kitchen helpers.'

'How come?'

'Well, firstly, the thick idiot wore his Sandhurst blazer, and while serving soup to a few winos, they decided the poor little rich kid helping the homeless deserved a kicking. They roughed him up, ripped his blazer off his back and searched his pockets before someone detected his northern accent. Apparently, it all calmed down after that. Then he showed all the winos the bruise on his chest and ribs he acquired from his fall from the Trainasium. Before he knew it, he had everyone in tears of sympathy. Half-dressed and scraggy, the old lady serving the soup thought he was a new visitor!'

Pat chuckled as he bounced in and out of the DS rooms looking for food. He had that expression on his face that indicated a lack of sleep over the weekend.

'Where I come from, you normally beat people up because they have a northern accent, not stop them from getting beat up. What has the world come to?'

Pat was still moving at 100mph as he offered his view on the world order.

'I'm sure you beat people up regardless of how they speak where you come from, Sergeant Major,' replied Captain Dunn.

Pat erupted into laughter, but it wasn't at the dig Captain Dunn had just delivered.

'Look at that poor sucker. Is he wearing paisley pyjamas? My God! Who is it, Gaz, and why isn't he out on Helping Hand?'

'Ha, that's Norris. We didn't send him on Helping Hand. He needed to move out of his room in Old College and hand back his equipment, so we let him stay home and pack his kit for this week.'

'Weak; wouldn't have happened in my day. What is happening to Row-Co. Was that your idea?'

Fearing that this was yet another 'string vest offence', the blame was firmly placed at Pete's door as he was in charge of kit and equipment. Pat shook his head as he laughed louder. Pointing through my office curtains, across the courtyard, there were no words of sympathy afforded for our latest arrival.

Norris was solemnly mooching around his room in his pyjamas. He would have heard the rumours of a bugout and knew it was imminent. The height of his anxiety would have been incomprehensible, but there was nothing that could prepare him for what was about to come. As sympathetic to his plight as I was, he would just have to find the mental resilience to get through it. The lad looked forlorn, as vulnerable as a mouse living in a cattery. Anyone with a hint of compassion would stick their arms around this chap and give him an encouraging welcome. Before Pat's comments, I was on the verge of asking the boss about the possibilities of giving him the week off. It made sense to give him time to adjust to his new surroundings. He was about to receive what would undoubtedly be the worst treatment of his life. If he was teetering on the verge of submission after being Back-Termed this would surely see him over the edge. Fighting with my conscience, this issue was going to niggle at me until we had thrashed out a plan to minimize the discomfort he would be subjected to. Taking it too easy would do him no favours. Others would sense blood and ostracize him as a special case. He would have to suffer the next few hours like everyone else. Go too hard, and we would lose him to another service. His transition from zero to hero needed great orchestration if he was going to earn his stripes and win the respect of his new peer group.

Deep in thought, Pat slapped me on the back and proceeded to rip into Norris' silk paisley-patterned pyjamas before returning to the matter at hand.

'Fifteen minutes before the coach returns with the last of the students,' Pat bellowed the warning to all the DS. Paddy and I switched off all the lights and settled down into our rooms, ready for the start of Exercise Plain Jane. The Platoon Commanders both headed for the Officers' Mess in search of some posh coffee. With the accommodation in darkness, the first mini-coach pulled up next to the front entrance. Quietly, the students disembarked and filtered through the swing doors and into their rooms. They were oblivious that an ambush had been set, and that in just a few hours their whole world would come crashing down around them.

The busy hum of the students regaling their exploits dwindled, and slowly all the accommodation lights were doused as midnight approached. Just the occasional dull reading light illuminated the odd room as five camouflaged Army Land Rovers came screaming into Chapel Square. Engines roaring, tyres screeching, lights ablaze, the vehicles mounted the kerb before coming to a halt outside the main entrance. A heartbeat later and the accommodation was mobbed with twenty-five members of the Parachute Artillery Regiment (7RHA). The assault was lightning quick as they descended upon the students' rooms with precision. In a well-rehearsed night raid, the Paras split into three assault groups and destroyed the tranquillity of the day's end. Holding nothing back, the experienced soldiers dragged the students from their slumber and manhandled them into their respective study halls. The ferocity of the expulsion was unrelenting, deliberately harsh in pursuit of an effect. The aim of the ruthless intimidation was to induce the shock of capture.

Dressed in camouflaged tactical clothing, faces blackened, weapons loaded and with turbocharged levels of aggression, it was enough to bring several students to tears. If the sight of the gun-toting muscular menaces wasn't enough to strike fear into the heart of every man, they had brought with them two enormous attack dogs. It was irrelevant that they were both muzzled: when one of these furry beasts lunged at you, it was impossible to remain composed. Nearly 6ft tall stood on their hind legs, they leapt up at everything in their way. Frantically trying to break their chains and maul the students, they were terrifying. Saliva flew everywhere as the snarling dogs lunged at everyone in their path. The noise never relented for a second. You could hear grown men whimper as they cowered behind each other for protection. If it wasn't so frightening, it would have been funny. The weight and ferocity of the dogs were sufficient to pin the likes of Danner up against the wall. In war, these dogs would be used to apprehend and subdue their targets. Armies not governed by the Geneva Convention would consider using dogs as a form of torture. As we watched the tears of fear roll down the face of Lane, it was easy to understand why dogs were used by enforcement agencies.

The Paras had arrived in five stripped-down reconnaissance vehicles, each one of them packed to the gunwales with surveillance equipment. Rowallan course number 4/93 had just met the 'Hunter Force' for Exercise Plain Jane, and they were under no misapprehension; these boys meant business. They had been drafted in by Pat, who was good friends with the Battery Sergeant Major of 7 Sphinx Special Observation Post Battery. The Battery Sergeant Major was only too keen to offer the services of all available paratroopers. The unit is synonymous with Special Forces operations and revelled in the opportunity to dish out a little rough justice to potential officers. This was a once-in-a-lifetime opportunity and they were going to make the most of it.

By two minutes past midnight it was full-blown chaos. Students were running back and forth from rooms in every kind of state imaginable. The Hunter Force screamed loudly at everyone to induce fear. The attack dogs barked frantically as the handler encouraged erratic behaviour. Despite having done escape and evasion training previously, the act of being captured still got the pulse racing. This was the most effective bugout so far, and it didn't matter that they knew it was coming. There were real tears, real concerns on the face of the students. This was fear personified. We stood and watched as the students were dragged from the study hall to their rooms and back again. They were given two minutes to finalize their equipment before being wrenched from their rooms and into the holding pen. Bullied and intimidated, they were frogmarched to the courtyard for searching.

We had left every aspect of the bugout to the Troop Sergeant. He was a bear of a man. Six feet tall and just as wide across the shoulders, his presence was not to be messed with. Sweating buckets under the strain of his heavy kit and busy nature, he played the role of villain brilliantly. In typical Para fashion, he couldn't complete a full sentence without threatening violence or spitting out a dozen expletives. At one stage, Captain Watts found himself caught up in the melee. With his youthful looks and short size, the Troop Sergeant inadvertently mistook him for a student, grabbing him by the collar and hurling a tirade of insults. It seemed like the world stopped revolving as these two Special Force ninjas exchanged daggers in a 'Mexican standoff'. Thankfully, the big man realized his mistake and thought best to apologize for his eagerness. Fortunately, Captain Watts laughed it off and we all breathed a sigh of relief.

The Troop Sergeant had lined everyone up against the wall of the Mean Machine enclosure. His team had positioned two Land Rovers with their lights ablaze illuminating the courtyard, so his soldiers could begin the process of escape and evasion.

'Sit down on your rucksack and shut the fuck up!' he screamed, standing high up on the bonnet of the Land Rover.

> 'We will now bring you forward to the personal search area. You will be told to relinquish the following items: money, phone cards, credit cards or cash cards, spare food or water. You are warned of the consequences should we find prohibited items during the search. This is your only opportunity to surrender contraband. If you are in possession of anything that is not on the packing list, stand by for pain! After you declare yourself sanitized for inspection, you will be strip searched. You are warned not to resist. This will only result in you being forcefully restrained and searched anyway. From head to toe, every part of your body will be searched. That's every part, and by the look of some of you, it won't be the first time someone has searched your back passage!'

In a regimented fashion, the students were stripped of all their clothing until they stood completely naked waiting to be searched. The heat coming off the halogen headlamps offered a hint of warmth for the individual standing 2ft away from the front of the Land Rover. The bright white light bounced back off the anaemic body of Stone. Mercifully, there was no rain and the temperature wobbled marginally above zero. Systematically, the 7RHA soldiers processed the company, mimicking the techniques used by the Special Forces. Once the shock of capture had been achieved and disorientation was confirmed, everything was done in silence. There were no words used, just manhandling, clicking of fingers, tapping of magazines or gesticulation. Occasionally the silence would be broken when a student tried to buck the system and the Troop Sergeant's outburst would clear the air. For assurance, once the student had been searched by the RHA soldiers, the DS conducted a sanity check to make sure all safety equipment was packed in accordance with Row-Co instructions. Getting it wrong on this particular exercise would be disastrous.

Slowly, the company filtered through the individual search point. It was no surprise to see that the first person to be caught breaking the conditions was Stone. It was the first time we had got Stone to a point where he was not deploying on a sick chit. For him, this was like day one, week one, all over again and he was displaying much anxiety. His agitated behaviour caught the eye of the corporal in charge of the body search, which prompted greater scrutiny. Wrapped in a condom and hidden between the cheeks of his backside was a £20 note. The searchers took enormous pleasure in ridiculing the lad for his failed attempt to smuggle money. The depth of Stone's unpopularity was affirmed by the loud cheers from almost everyone in the courtyard. It appeared that everybody was laughing at and enjoying Stone's disposition, but more alarmingly, so were the DS. It would have been easy for me to defuse the situation, but Pat was just laughing harder, saying that he hadn't had so much fun since the day he slept with two lesbian porn stars during a trip to Vegas.

No mercy was shown as they continued to poke fun at Stone long after they had finished searching him. Unwittingly, Stone was giving us more ammunition to secure a Platoon Commander's warning way before we had even started the exercise. If Captain Dunn wanted to, he could sack Stone on the spot for lack of integrity. Although this would be harsh, it had been done many times before. Major Gray would, however, sniff a witch hunt, and we all knew it. As the students put their clothes back on and repacked rucksacks, we discussed the advantages of keeping Stone on the course for the duration of the exercise. It was a tough call. Losing students this early would heap disproportional stress on the rest of the team, so as unpalatable as this was, it would be best to leave this issue until we returned at the end of the week. It made sense to me, and we were both aware the OC would want to see more evidence before agreeing to such drastic measures.

With the searching complete, Major Gray issued the instructions for the next phase:

'Gentlemen, from here on in, consider yourselves as fugitives. You are on the run. You have escaped from Alca-bags. Your DS will issue you with a route card that will lead you to the partisan organization who will smuggle you over the border to the free state of Curnow. You have specific timings and grid references to adhere to. You will also receive a detailed brief on how to conduct yourself during the exfiltration. Once we are content that you understand the aim of this exercise, you will be loaded onto a truck and taken somewhere in the South-West of the country. Your first checkpoint is approximately 13km away from the drop-off. Navigate cross-country and avoid the roads. You should use the emergency telephone number, should everything go pear-shaped or you need help. If you fail to make the checkpoint on time, again call the emergency number. You must complete your move from the drop-off point to the checkpoint before 1000hrs tomorrow morning. I reiterate, if you are not going to make it for any reason, use the emergency number. Most importantly, thirty minutes after you are released from the start point, 7RHA will be dispatched to hunt you down. If they catch you before you reach your checkpoint, you will be given a fairly unpleasant lesson in the art of concealment and moved backwards 5km. Finally, there is to be no contact with civilians at all. If you are caught fraternizing with the civilian population, you should expect to be placed onto a College Commander's warning!'

Without further instruction, the students were hurried onto the vehicles destined for the long drive to Dartmoor.

'Colour!' said Major Gray. 'Stone is a creature, isn't he? His pathetic attempt at cheating says a lot about him. How crazy to think he could get away with such an obvious stunt. They would have all known this was imminent, but trying to cheat like that was pitiful.'

If it had been anyone else, I would be screaming for clemency, compassion and understanding, yet Stone had brought this on himself. Once again, he had brushed off another public humiliation as if it was par for the course. When his report was written at the end of the week, the Commanding Officer would have no choice but to raise the issue of integrity. Effectively, this action would see Stone perched precariously at the threshold of the exit door. It would take an astonishing performance to reverse this decision or one of those bizarre scenarios that just worked in his favour.

At 0430hrs, the trucks had arrived at Sheepstor, a sleepy village on the west edge of Dartmoor. The students quickly dispersed and by 0500hrs, Plain Jane was running at full speed. As dawn washed across the moor, several students had been caught by the hunter force. Captain Dunn and I walked towards our first checkpoint, listening to the Para Artillery commanders coordinating their search on the security radio. The infiltration had been going for just over an hour and someone had already called the emergency telephone number. This was understandable; it was the first real test of their navigation in unchartered territory, the first time they would walk without the DS lurking in the shadows behind them. It was reassuring that the weather was slightly warmer this far south. If nothing else, it was dry with clear skies. Dartmoor is an unforgiving land that has seen its fair share of misadventure. The probability of disasters were dramatically reduced in mild weather.

We moved at pace once the last man left the start point. Having set off just behind the students, it was imperative to make good speed, mainly because we were manning checkpoint one. Fortunately, unlike the fugitives, we didn't need to avoid choke points, roads and obvious features where the hunter force would be gathered. Consequently, our route was unhindered; even the rain abated as a cool coastal wind kept the skies clear. We arrived by 0730hrs and predicted the first students would be less than thirty minutes behind us. Pitching a tent on the eastern slope of Fox Tor, there was just enough time to get into our sleeping bags to stay warm before the first visitors were expected to arrive. Sure that the first man was imminent, I fired up the Peak stove, made hot chocolate and sipped it slowly whilst still wrapped in my sleeping bag.

The sun was high in the sky before either one of us questioned the length of time it was taking for the first student to arrive. We turned up the radio and listened to the Paras having fun as they hunted our students. The chatter was lively and excitable as they tracked down targets just as they would if they were tracking the progress of a rogue dissident. They were not holding back their efforts as they obstinately chased every suspected sighting until they caught it or it got away. It was close to their finish time and the Troop Sergeant's booming voice issued a Charlie Charlie One call (a message to everyone listening) instructing the Hunter Force to gather their belongings and join him at a central crossroad. His overtones indicated they had done as much as they could. The vehicles could be heard in the distance, all heading to the RV, and it appeared that the chase was over. But just as the radio was about to be switched off, it burst back into life. A sighting! Someone reported a student stepping out of a car. The violation and audacity angered the Para Commander as his shouts bellowed out of our radio. Attentively, we listened as the excitement of the pursuit mounted – another sighting, and then another. They were getting close. The Troop Sergeant sent instructions via burst transmissions: 'Go north! Go north! Stop! Stop! Stop! Too far, you've overshot the target! Drop 50 metres. On your left now. Blue coat. Just entered a shop! Left, left, left. On your left, on your left.'

He was guiding a Land Rover full of burly soldiers, all desperate to get their hands on the young potential officer. Every one of his men had been dispatched to look for the student, who was now running for his life. It was the most excitement we'd had in months.

'This is brilliant, Colour! Do you wish you were with them?'

'Being chased or doing the chasing?'

'Either! I can't help feeling envious of the fun they are having!'

Like errant teenagers, Captain Dunn and I giggled as we put ourselves in the shoes of the escapee evading twenty-five angry Paras. If he got caught, he would be in for some double jeopardy: the Paras would work him over and the OC would put him in front of the College Commander for cheating. The radio continued to crackle with the frantic sighting reports. The intensity of the chase had us both sitting bolt upright, willing the students to escape. No one likes to get caught, and despite the defiance and contempt for the rules, we were both rooting for him. An excitable call-sign called for assistance and confirmed the student was cornered in a local shop. Elation broke out across the airwaves as the search teams congratulated each other on the good work. They surrounded the shop and waited for the Troop Sergeant to make the arrest. As he entered the shop, we were buzzing with anticipation to learn who it was he had caught. Then in a moment of pure drama, the radio spluttered into life and declared it a false alarm. The man they tracked to the shop was not the student who got out of the car; spookily, he was just wearing a similar jacket. The momentum was lost, and slowly the reports died down until eventually the last of the Hunter Force acknowledged they had also been given the slip. We both cheered. The student had run the gauntlet and triumphed. No matter how much we disagreed with his actions, there was a hint of satisfaction that he wasn't caught.

Mathews and Francis were the first to arrive at the checkpoint. As always, Mathews wore a smile and Francis hobbled behind. They were wet from the midriff down, confirming they had crossed rivers and avoided bridges and roads. Despite this wet and ragged condition, they were both in high spirits.

'What are you doing together?' Captain Dunn asked.

'No one said we couldn't, Sir!'

He had a fair point. There was nothing in the brief that said students could not link up and share the navigation.

'Get caught?' I asked.

'Yes, Colour Sergeant!' giggled Mathews.

'Did they give you a hard time?'

'Did they ever! I mean they did at first until, you know!'

'No, I don't know! Until what, Mathews?'

'Until they asked me what regiment I was going to join. So I said I was going to join the Para Artillery. After that, they stopped roughing me up, threw us into the back of a Land Rover and drove forward 5km. They even gave me a mug of coffee!'

'You're not joining the Artillery, Mathews! Aren't you down to join the Engineers?'

'I know, Sir, but when the Para lads were dipping my head in a flooded cattle trough, it seemed like a good thing to say.'

'Well, I dare say I would agree with that statement, Mathews.'

The boss raised a smile at Mathews, suggesting he had done the right thing. His partnership with Francis was prudent and the pair made a strong team. Here were two young men who had all the right ingredients to inspire young soldiers. They giggled at adversity, they battled against the odds, but most importantly they were focused, intelligent and committed. They were given another checkpoint to navigate to, which mercifully was only 5km away.

'Mathews. The Colour Sergeant has something for you!'

'Brilliant. Thank you, Colour Sergeant, what is it?'

'100 Names. "I must not take a lift." What, did you think you could cheat and get away with it scot-free? Even if it was the Hunter Force that gave you the lift, it was still against the rules!'

Francis did push-ups. We sensed his knees were just holding on, and the squat-jump burpee motion would not be kind to him. Cheekily, Mathews thanked me once more as he got just out of gripping range.

Major Gray's voice came on the radio and we paused to listen. He was talking to the operations room based in a camp to the west of the training area. The local police had received a phone call from a student's mother. The concerned parent told the police that her son had got lost and walked all the way to Plymouth! Apparently, the student had mistakenly plotted the emergency telephone number on his map instead of the grid reference. Eerily, the numbers were a good match for the Ordnance Survey map, but took him in the opposite direction. When he arrived at a supermarket car park on the outskirts of Plymouth, he became suspicious that something was wrong. Even then, he didn't understand what had happened. Only after no one else arrived did he feel compelled to call the emergency number. When it didn't work, because it was the grid reference, he phoned the only number he knew, which turned out to be his mother's. She called the police. Everyone found it funny, apart from Pat, who had to take the long drive south to collect him.

The sun was warming the south-facing slope with all the attributes of a spring morning. As each student passed through our checkpoint, Captain Dunn and I engaged in some light-hearted banter. Matching the ingenuity of the students who liked to invent games, we invented our own game called the 'Horror Box' challenge. Before the student set off on his next leg, he was invited to play the game. It was very similar to the card game 'find the lady', but played with two white cardboard lunch boxes. One contained five Blue Riband chocolate bars, while the other had orange peel and rubbish inside. The student watched closely as the boxes were mixed up for 30 seconds whilst we all sang the *Sesame Street* song 'One of these things is not like the other'. When the song was exhausted, the student was invited to pick a box. It looked very easy. With only two to choose from, and sitting less than 2ft away from the action, excitement and expectation were palpable. Surely it was easy to identify the box with biscuits; it would be difficult to get it wrong. But whatever box they chose, it always had rubbish and orange peel in it. Watching their faces go from bristling with expectation to desperation in the blink of an eye was fascinating and hilarious. Nearly all of the students laughed at their predicament. It was the oldest trick in the book. There was a small hole in the ground, which was hidden by the groundsheet of our tent. As the Blue Ribands were placed into the box, they were pushed through a slit in the floor of the box and disappeared out of sight. Whatever box they chose, it would not contain the biscuits.

The first victim of our cruel trick was Danner. He fell for the hoax hook, line and sinker before protesting heartily. Physically and emotionally hurt by the scam, he was keen to let everyone know of his disdain for our antics.

'Incredibly cruel, Colour Sergeant, not to mention grotesquely perverse!'

He demanded another go. When he realized it wasn't forthcoming, he asked for some food anyway. Like a drunk annoying the policeman outside a nightclub after kicking-out time, he outstayed his welcome to voice his dissent. He was desperately hungry, and the tell-tale signs were shining through. We had raised his expectations, then mercilessly dashed them for our own amusement. Incapable of containing his emotions as he walked away, Danner mumbled insults at nothing specific. The lad had the right to be as boisterous as he was, so we rolled with the punches and humoured his protests before he eventually disappeared from view.

Moore was not in a good mood when he arrived. He just screwed up his face, pouted his lips and sighed in disapproval at our game. Refusing to join in the *Sesame Street* song, he half-heartedly selected a box and exclaimed 'what a shock' when it contained orange peel. Not one to overstay his welcome, Moore stormed off, calling us childish. Captain Dunn giggled as he agreed, but this just seemed to upset him further. Barns and Williams nearly broke down in tears when it was their turn. They never saw the funny side at that moment in time, but later in the week, Barns confessed to laughing for about an hour afterwards. There is a fine line between fun and mental torture, and on this occasion we had got it right. Even Haigh, not renowned for his sense of humour, found it funny. By midday, all the students but one had passed through the checkpoint. Stone had yet to arrive or phone, and neither the boss nor I were surprised. The checkpoint was due to collapse at 1400hrs and move to the Company assembly area. Having hung around for as long as we could, at 1430hrs we had no choice but to leave.

In the assembly area that would be our home for the next twenty-four hours, the DS considered conducting a full-scale search. It's a hard call to make when you find yourself in a situation that has serious implications such as the one we faced. Stone could have been injured in a ditch, close to death, or maybe just totally lost, although it was more likely he was shying away from the hard work ahead by hiding out in a barn or a derelict building. The problem this presented the training team with was what to decide? At what stage did we alert the civilian authorities and the chain of command back in Sandhurst? To inform people too early could cause a panic, yet to do it too late would demonstrate lack of appreciation for the seriousness of the situation. The OC listened intensively to our character assessment of Stone. We knew he was work-shy and had the ability to scam and scheme his way through specific issues. The lengthy discussion bought Stone an additional twelve hours before we involved the emergency services. It was a brave decision by the OC to gamble on our assessment of Stone, including my suspicion that he may be in hiding. If it were my decision, I would have called the Mountain Rescue and started searching now. But as the OC would say, he was paid to make this sort of decision. He wasn't going to be panicked into a decision too early.

As night fell, the students were being tasked to write a short essay on the Newbury bypass. Topical, tricky and emotive, there was much to discuss. The bulldozers were revving up to mow down 10 miles of outstanding natural beauty to link Winchester and Newbury. The link road would improve the UK economy, reduce pollution and ease congestion on the M4, but protesters built tree houses and Vietnam-style tunnels in an effort to block the construction. The Battle of Newbury essay was designed to test the students' academic skills whilst tired and exhausted, not to mention their awareness of current affairs related to defence. Different to the essay on Compass Rose, this simple event looked to test intellectual ability whilst under stress. Haigh's lengthy essay disapproved of our demands, choosing to voice his opinion on why he shouldn't be writing an essay and offering not one word about the Newbury by-pass. It was entertaining, well written and inexplicably as left-wing as you could get for someone wishing to join the Army. There was no debating the might of his pen; he was good with his words. Pithy, concise and articulate, it was a crying shame he couldn't match these skills with a hint of foresight and intuition!

In contrast, Danner, who was schooled at the world-famous Eton College, failed to drum up one reasonable point of view. His paper was full of sarcastic quips and witty comments, with great structure and perfect punctuation, but even a second read didn't help me understand if he did or didn't agree.

Most significantly, we were interested in what King had to write. We needed to scrutinize his academic resilience. Could he stay awake all night and deliver a sensible report to a Brigade Commander on the eve of a battle? His essay suggested so. It was gratifying to hear the OC pass pleasant comments on the tight argument he forged. Although King was blissfully unaware of what we were doing, he had all but secured his passage through the course, provided he stayed the distance.

By midnight, Captain Dunn was busy reading and marking the rest of the papers. Inviting officers and senior NCOs to plan and conduct operations on the strength of a report compiled in similar circumstances is a realistic scenario. After any operational patrol, the commander will immediately write his report on everything that happened. Time-sensitive, this document could set the conditions for execution later in the war. Although the students would never be able to understand the significance of the written exercise, this would prepare them well for the future.

The following day started with a 'Type A' field inspection and a return of the rain. It was 0700hrs, and the bemused expression on the face of Norris said it all. This was his first real taste of Row-Co, and it was no surprise to see his equipment in total disarray. I took a long, hard look at the young Scotsman. His eyes portrayed a sorry tale of disbelief and dejection. There was nothing for me to say as his kit was overlooked. Next to him stood Williams, who had by now mastered the art of keeping his equipment at a decent standard. He was pleased with his efforts, greeting me with confidence and a smile.

'Good morning, Colour Sergeant.'

'This is a very good effort, Williams. Are you pleased with what you have achieved here?'

'Yes, Colour Sergeant!'

'Well, it will come as a surprise to know that it's been a long time since we have seen this sort of performance. Have a look at Norris' kit and tell me what you see!'

'He is in clip, Colour Sergeant,' Williams said, with an ever-increasing smile.

'Wrong! Very, very wrong. You are not looking beyond the end of your nose. This is a course in leadership and the art of command. It's about selflessness, commitment. The man standing to your left or right is your most important responsibility. What kind of man allows his comrades to falter so greatly in the hope that their errors will make him shine?'

The smile slowly drained from his face as my point hit home.

'If you haven't understood what I'm talking about, let me make it very clear. You are a selfish little toe rag. You knew that the new lad didn't have a clue, and yet you have offered him no help. Is this a sign of things to come? Is this the real Williams, the one who's just interested in himself? Do you see this as good leadership?'

'No, Colour Sergeant.'

'No. That's correct. This is Jack. It's hard to see how anyone would see it otherwise. Or do you think Norris didn't need help?'

'No, Colour Sergeant. I should have helped him.'

'Jack! Lieutenant Jack Williams. Captain Jack Williams; fuck me, Colonel Jack Williams! There is no end to it. Not a nice thought is it, cupcake? If you continue in this vein, it will shortly be Mr Jack Williams. Fifty names! "I am Jack!" No, sod it, 100 names. Go!'

Amongst the inner sanctum of a soldier's barracks, this selfish character trait can bring widespread disharmony to a well-balanced team. Cohesion and trust are the golden threads that bind the hidden contract that sees a soldier lay down his life for his country. It's never about the realm, nor is it about the country of origin; it's about the men you serve with or for. No matter the consequences, this behaviour needs to be eradicated as soon as it is identified. When it appears in a private soldier, it becomes a form of self-isolation, but when a commander shows this selfish outlook, the repercussions have far-reaching consequences. Occasionally, this selfish behaviour can be confused with ambition or elitism, but the difference is that ambition and elitism are underpinned by team ethics and ethos, without which you just have narcissistic individuals. Conversely, egotism can look like ambition; it's easy to hide, and for this reason, any suspicion must be confronted. If it gets beyond the early stages of leadership, it will flourish unchecked. Although he did not clearly understand what he had done so wrong to rattle my cage, it was a point that needed to be explained to Williams. We were warming to Williams. He lacked knowledge, but there was no malice in his actions. He had sufficient raw ingredients for us to make something of him. This indiscretion was hugely disappointing, and he now had my full attention. If he had any hope of being taken off the Platoon Commander's warning, he would need to do something special during the week.

Standing next to Williams was Witherspoon. We were still not seeing enough of him to make an informed assessment. Along with a few others, whether by design or accident, he had mastered the art of hiding in the shadows, avoiding the Directing Staff and keeping out of the limelight.

'Where is your shaving mirror, Witherspoon?'

'Don't need one, Colour Sergeant.'

'How did you shave then?'

'From feeling my face each time I went over it with my razor.'

'Do you think that is the only use for the mirror?'

'Yes, Colour Sergeant.'

I pulled out a pencil from my pocket and curled up his top lip. Using the blunt end of the pencil, the clotted sticky yellow plaque was removed from the top of the young lad's teeth.

'What do you think of this then?'

'Not good, Colour Sergeant.'

'Well, by the tone of your voice, you think I'm being a bit pedantic. So, consider this scenario. You are on operations somewhere in the world. Every time you eat, you ingest this yellow gunge; eventually, it renders you ill. We must now take you off the battlefield to get you to medical aid. While needlessly travelling around a battlefield, we are unprotected and vulnerable, thus get picked off by the enemy, all because of your poor personal administration. You have become a serious liability. That, Williams, is a true fact and history is littered with people dying whilst taking a needless journey in a combat zone. That is the consequence of gungy teeth.'

Searching deep into my small rucksack, I produced a compact mirror in order to allow Witherspoon to look at his face.

'Look in the mirror and tell me what you see!'

'A useless individual, Colour Sergeant!'

'Agreed, but it's more about the state of your face. It's not been cleaned for over forty-eight hours! There are blackheads and yellows spots everywhere. Tell me how you inspire twenty young men when you look like a walking advertisement for Pizza Hut? Personal hygiene! If you are going to demand it from everyone under your command, you must exemplify the concept at all times. Fifty names. "I am not an animal, I'm a human being!"'

By the end of the inspection, the platoon was busy counting out their punishments. Captain Dunn and the OC were in deep conversation about the still-missing Stone. This was surely going to bring an end to the day's training as we were diverted into a search.

'Colour Sergeant Mac!' With a wave of his hand, Major Gray summoned me into the conversation.

'As you are aware, Stone has yet to arrive. To make things worse, the Colonel is on his way to visit us. This leaves me in a bit of a jam.'

I recall thinking to myself how remarkably cool the OC was with all this, but his next comment took nerves of steel.

'The Colonel is arriving by Gazelle helicopter at 1000hrs. When he arrives, I will ask him if we can use his Gazelle to recce a few training areas. If we get a "yes", I want you to fly over the route in, starting from the drop-off point, in an effort to find him.'

'What if he says "no"?'

'Well, I'll tell him I have lost a student and he will change his mind. Simple really.'

'And how about if we don't find him?'

'I will simply have to tell him anyway. Look, we are damned either way, so let's give ourselves every opportunity. And don't worry, at some stage, whatever the outcome, the College Commander will be told.'

The College Commander had a reputation for sacking people on the spot. Some months later, it came to light that he handpicked me to serve at Sandhurst because he was keen to dilute the doggedness of the instructor cohort. He was attracted by my lack of rigidity and desire to go beyond the script. As flattering as it was, if he thought I was complicit, he would have a different opinion. My mind rehearsed every possible scenario, including the one where he sacked me.

At exactly 1000hrs, the unmistakable whining of the turbine engine belonging to a Gazelle helicopter crested the hill. With all the grace of the animal the helicopter was named after, the Colonel landed and, with no fuss at all, we were granted permission to use his helicopter for twenty minutes. After a spurious brief issued to the pilots explaining we just needed to recce our route out, off we flew in the direction of the ground we had just covered. As the minutes ticked by, the pilots politely agreed to my requests, but it was obvious that Stone was not on the intended route. We had criss-crossed the northern end of Dartmoor, and there was little place to shelter. Every hill was barren, each one similar to the next. My growing interest in areas of danger such as sheer drops, large holes and derelict buildings had begun to arouse the suspicions of the pilots. They had done enough flying to know the difference between a recce and a search. I dodged a number of questions, wishing a swift end to this charade, but the pilots were growing impatient with me.

Having used as much fuel time as we were allowed, the pilots returned to the exercise area and shut down on the LZ. The OC and the College Commander were deep in conversation as they watched a command task being run by Captain Watts. Dreading the thought of telling the OC that the search proved fruitless, the opportunity to inform him was proving tricky. The College Commander was on his first official visit and keen to cast his eyes over those we had identified as possible failures. Like Montgomery at El Alamein, the College Commander strutted around the exercise area, hands clasped behind his back, listening intently to the OC's brief. Eventually, they arrived at the first of our command tasks. It was being managed by Captain Dunn, who had placed Lane in charge. I hovered around the rear of the gaggle, waiting for an opportunity to impart the bad news to Major Gray. The Colonel was armed with a printout of our weakest students, coupled with the results of the last Progress Board. They were discussing the failings of Lane when the College Commander asked my opinion. The Colonel was a man of few words. Each sentence began and finished with a blow of his nose using a polka-dot hanky. There was no flowery language; he got straight to the point.

'How do you see Lane's progress so far, Colour Sergeant?'

'Poor to middling, Sir!'

'Why?'

'He lacks drive, motivation, interpersonal skills, command, control and a desire to succeed.'

'So, nothing we can't work with?'

'Sir, the only difference between Lane and a slice of toast is we stand a good chance of turning toast into a soldier!'

'You know what they say about sarcasm. The highest form of wit, the lowest form of intelligence, Colour Sergeant. So, I shall not waste my words. Negative attitudes bear negative results. You are not paid for negative results, so pull your socks up. I expect him to pass this course, and if he doesn't, I would be keen to learn where we failed?'

He blew his nose, stuffed his hanky into a pocket and smiled. You could have cut the atmosphere with a knife. If that was how he spoke to me whilst pleased with my performance, God knows what he was going to say when the OC told him we'd lost a student.

The Colonel returned to search through the pages of his Progress Board brief. He studied a page for a few minutes before asking Major Gray about the next problem.

'Stone! Yes, I thought you would have trouble with this young man. They can be hit or miss, but it's normally clear in the first twenty-four hours. How is he doing?'

My heart sank in anticipation of the answer. Major Gray turned to Captain Dunn and asked him for a summary of Stone's performance.

'I concur with your initial assessment, Colonel,' said Captain Dunn. 'Stone is a typical Welbecksian. He is potential officer material; however, despite our greatest efforts, the rigours of the course will deny us the privilege of his company come the end. His greatest failing is the inability to apply the simplest of command tools, principally the art of communication and evaluation. Socially he is awkward, and this has him at a disadvantage when trying to forge collaborative partnerships with his peers.'

The Colonel nodded in agreement and I smirked at Captain Dunn, envious of his smooth talking. He had said exactly the same as me not five minutes before, but without the humiliation of a public rebuke.

'Good, let's take a look at him,' suggested the Colonel. 'Reading your programme notes, he is due to take charge of a command task shortly.'

I braced myself for what was about to come.

'Certainly, Colonel, he's on task seven; it's this way.'

Shocked by the OC's answer, I pulled on Captain Dunn's coat tails as we walked towards task seven. 'What's going on?' I mimed to him.

'Don't panic, Colour, Stone turned up shortly after you departed. Apparently, he got lost on the moor, but he's lying. He's clean, dry and looking refreshed, so you don't have to be Albert Einstein to figure out that he has been hiding out somewhere.'

My face flushed red as expletives thundered under my breath during the brief walk to the command tasks. He had done it again, and would probably do really well in front of the Colonel. The lad had the devil's luck, which was enough for him to scrape through to the next stage of the course.

'Boss, what was all that garbage you spieled to the Colonel. "Yes, Sir! I concur, Sir! Three bags full, Sir! Do you want your boots polished, Sir?"'

'Now, Colour, don't get all aggressive. I said everything you said previously, it was just a better choice of words.'

'Yeah, you're right, but it doesn't mean it was enjoyable to suffer. God, how I wished Stone had not shown up. I bet your answer would have been different then.'

Captain Dunn laughed, knowing he was holding all the trump cards in our battle of banter, but it didn't stop me altering the story later that day as Pat received my corrupted version of this encounter in an effort to see the boss wear the string vest.

Stone's command task was fairly simple. He was given three 50-gallon oil drums and two planks to construct a contraption that would allow him and his teammates to cross a make-believe shark-infested river. The solution was simple: position the oil drums in the right place, then build a bridge using the planks. It required only short commands, complemented by strong control. Typically, his brusque monotone instructions irked his peers. Within the secret world of the students, they resented his continued scamming and had a good idea where he had been during the escape and evasion. Now the College Commander was watching him, which was an indication he was in trouble. There was a noticeable air of ill will, which gave rise to arguments and dissent during the task. Stone's impetuous behaviour provoked a near mutiny as he argued over the practicalities of his plan. The other students had detected that all was not going well and made every effort to scupper his appointment. The sheer simplicity of the task, however, was in Stone's favour, and he had completed the job well inside the allotted time. Despite his success, it had been a personal disaster for Stone. The true nature of his character had been laid bare for the College Commander to witness. Above all, the inability to build successful relationships and apply command tools was a huge failing.

The Colonel had seen everything we reported in the brief. He had been guided to observe the performance of the weaker individuals as we primed our case to remove him from the course. Captain Dunn debriefed Stone on the practical aspects of the command task, explaining why certain phases went wrong and how best to improve his command. After he had finished, he offered the Colonel an opportunity to address the students. A large smile covered my face in expectation of the savaging Stone was about to receive from the Colonel.

'Thank you, James. Let me add one thing. It is essential you master the tools of command, like a carpenter masters his chisel. In this case, we witnessed indifferent communication! If you don't communicate effectively, you can't command efficiently. Communication takes many forms: body language, voice tones and correct use of the Queen's English. You will come to learn that 90 per cent of what you wish to achieve is conveyed through the passion and belief during the delivery of your directions. Tempo, timing, temperament, tone; keep this at the front of your mind when speaking to subordinates. If you get this wrong, it will lead to your downfall, as we have just witnessed. Success is not quantifiable purely on the outcome of one issue. You should reflect on the valuable lessons gleaned from this task. I don't just mean the commander; this applies to everyone. Still, it is early days and I'm sure you will get a chance to rectify these problems as you progress. Well done everyone, stick at it.'

With a big smile, the Colonel wiped the dew from his nose and shoved the hanky back in his pocket before he set off in the direction of Paddy's platoon. Dumbstruck by the debrief that left Stone thinking he had done well, the red mist was descending as the OC and College Commander disappeared from view. I wanted him to publicly humiliate Stone, to shock him into shape, hopefully succeeding where we had failed. The overwhelming urge to rip into Stone for putting me through two days of worry knotted my stomach. He had not even remotely thought of the consequences of his actions, and we knew that he had been hiding out in a warm, dry place. Even more annoying, so did everyone else, and our inability to prosecute his endless scheming threatened DS credibility.

The students relied on us to ensure fair play for all. They expected straight-talking and punishment for those who failed to make the standard. Allowing people to progress without achieving the standard undermined everything that had gone before. More importantly, it recalibrated the students' minimum threshold of effort. If Stone could get away with this, he would prove that the whole thing was little more than idle threats and bluff. They knew Stone was playing the system and getting away with it. We just needed to be patient – one of two things was going to happen. Either Stone would realize he couldn't keep up this charade for a year and a half just to get through Sandhurst, so he would leave of his own accord, or he would see that his performance needed to improve and grow with the course. But for now, the DS had to demonstrate to the remaining students that we knew what Stone was up to. We needed to make his life as uncomfortable as possible without compromising our integrity or showing bias. Whilst the remainder of the platoon distrusted Stone, it was not their place to snitch on a fellow student, regardless of whether they liked him or not. It was the responsibility of the system, the Platoon Commander and Colour Sergeant to prove he should not have the privilege of progressing.

'Stone, what happened to make you twenty-four hours late?' I demanded

'Got lost, Colour Sergeant. I wandered around the moor until I found a spot to get a bearing from and identify my location on the map.'

'Well, I'm absolutely amazed at that. You see we are all soaking wet because of the early morning rain, but you, you're bone dry! It must surely be a miracle! How do you explain that?'

'Just lucky, Colour Sergeant. I slept under my poncho because the Hunter Force had blocked my way. I just looked after myself like you taught us to.'

Stone was lying through his teeth. It was a catch 22 predicament: accuse him of cheating, and he would claim victimisation; fail to prove he was cheating, and he would undermine everything we were achieving with the rest of the platoon.

By early afternoon, the College Commander had gone. The crazy weather had brought bright sunshine and clear skies as we welcomed the first platoon race of the exercise. The wheel race was another event demanding high levels of command and control, exercised through the application of strength and determination. The key to success was to keep it simple. Each platoon would push a large combat tractor wheel (complete with tyre) around a field. The wheels were huge, 5ft in diameter, clumsy and awkward to handle; disrespect them at your peril. Fail to treat them with caution and they would bite. The object of the race was to push the wheel around a course of approximately 2km. The first kilometre was downhill, and the return leg uphill. Major Gray explained to both teams that this was a straight race, side-by-side, so there was to be no funny stuff. As he issued a two-minute warning, Captain Dunn seized the moment to issue a few words of encouragement:

> 'OK, chaps, there are only nine points in it. This is the one to win. As it stands, No. 1 Platoon has eighteen points and we have nine. You've done well to claw it back. You are in with a shout of closing the gap to a respectable margin. I am putting Norris in charge. I want you to show him how we fight to the death in Rowallan. He will not have experienced anything like this on the Commissioning Course, so dig in deep. Don't let him down.'

There was sufficient blue sky to justify Daz wearing his singlet vest as he issued a safety brief. With goose pimples on his arms and blue lips, the sun was out but the wind chill kept the ground temperature only just above freezing. There was a real art to handling the wheel, and Daz went to great pains explaining the duties of the brake man, the actions on turning the wheel and, most importantly, how to avoid being run over or losing control. The combat tractor wheel, with a tyre fitted, weighed nearly 900lb. If it was mishandled, injuries were certain. Using my platoon, Daz demonstrated how the wheels would not stay up straight whilst travelling at slow speeds. Momentum was the key to stability. Finally, he demonstrated various methods of controlling downhill speed. A few sarcastic jokes later, both platoons were lying flat on the floor in the freefall position. With the DS poised to follow the students, Daz screamed the dreaded words: 'Stand by! Stand by! Go!'

Norris was undertaking his first appointment. This was part of our deliberate ploy to achieve integration at the first opportunity, also known as the 'hero to zero' moment. Coincidently, it was the first time the wheel race had been used on Plain Jane. But it was a familiar and well-practised exercise, so there was nothing we were concerned about. On previous courses, it worked well on Barossa and Minley, but to prevent students knowing what to expect next, all exercises were routinely rotated between locations. Standing at the crest of a large hill, we both watched as Norris scowled at his new peers as he delivered his first commands. In response, they challenged his authority in an attempt to override his instructions and tactics. Rideout and Murphy tied their toggle ropes through the centre of the wheel to manufacture a crude braking system. Fastidious and a little patronizing, Norris was not going to rush off the start line. Paddy's lads had opted for the more direct approach. They placed many students in front of the wheel to regulate its descent, then allowed their wheel to run free. The conservative approach chosen by Norris caused Packman to complain about the slow start. Lane and Murphy sensed he was wobbling and tried to oust him from command.

The two conflicting approaches produced hugely different results. No. 1 Platoon's carefree method had a quick impact as Paddy's boys freewheeled at speed down the hill. The tactic of employing students to run in front of the speeding wheel as it bounced was risky. Using men to contain its acceleration appeared brave, if not a little careless. The more conservative Norris was just getting the wheel moving by the time No. 1 Platoon had secured what seemed an unassailable lead. The distance between the two wheels was unnerving, but both the boss and I were more concerned that Norris was not coping with the contest of his peers. Misplaced allegiances, an uninhibited desire to win and tangible desperation emanated from the group he commanded. This event was about observing his command skills and identifying where we could help him. We were just about to discover how much he had assimilated from the Commissioning Course. He was losing ground rapidly, but the race was not the most important issue at hand. This appointment would be the only tuition Norris would receive on the course, as the teaching phase had all but finished. If we were to stand any chance of getting the young pretender through the course, we needed to maximize every opportunity, and this one was golden.

Captain Dunn ran alongside the Scotsman, quietly coaching his thought process. In the space of 100 metres, he had been given the tools of command, Row-Co style. Of all the tools he was introduced to, the skill of constant re-evaluation was the one he needed to master first. The situation was already changing, and the boss was piling on the pressure for him to find greater urgency. Simultaneously, I was quick to see that no student held back on commitment. It was make-or-break time for Norris. If he failed dismally, the pain of another disappointment would crush him. He would surely VW, suffering death by a thousand cuts. But with just a hint of luck and a fiercely contested race, irrespective of the outcome, there was a chance of retaining him. A courageous defeat would still offer valuable experience in command and control, subsequently enticing him to stay longer. It would boil down to his mental resolve, the desire to overcome a mountain of defeat and the humiliation of being sent to retake three long months of training.

Every now and again, a soldier will momentarily develop a sixth sense, a time when no words are required to describe a predicament, no raised voice is needed to enhance the will to succeed. This was one such occasion. Apart from the perennial skivers, every student worked extra hard in support of Norris. They knew he needed an injection of confidence. Empathy for Norris was not flowing from cups, but it was as tangible as plausible. It was just unfortunate that the bold decision of Paddy's platoon to freewheel was proving the difference. In anticipation of a defeat, the debrief was already formulated in my head: 'Unlucky, lads. Good effort, lads. Out-thought again!' Dishing out compulsory punishment to Norris and the rest of his team would not bring any comfort to my dark mood!

'Colour! Colour, look!' shouted the boss as he started to laugh loudly.

I looked up just in time to see Paddy's platoon lose control of their wheel as they got close to the bottom of the steep hill. The wheel was bouncing freely, unabated, and gathering momentum. It was unstoppable, leaving its carers trailing in its wake. We watched as it bowled over the small group of students employed to arrest the speed. Travelling in excess of 20mph, it hit a draining ditch, propelling it upwards towards a drystone wall. Catching the edge of the boundary wall, the wheel took off into the air and spun forward, gaining even more speed. It must have been travelling at over 30mph when it bounced onto the main road and hit the top of a passing minivan. It was the perfect strike to slingshot the wheel forward with added momentum and height. As the wheel came crashing down, it narrowly missed a motorcyclist travelling in the opposite direction before steamrolling into a farmhouse fence. With a splash of standing water and a spray of broken wood, the large green and black wheel spun to a halt. It resembled a clip out of *You've Been Framed*. Cars screeched, drivers screamed abuse and an old lady came out of her house to discover a large wheel poking out of the remains of her fence. It was just the slice of luck that Norris needed. With Paddy's lads busy managing a major incident, Norris slipped quietly past the halfway point and up the hill to win the race.

Despite the race developing into a walkover, the pace remained at full pelt. The decision to employ toggle ropes to prevent the wheel running away was now the tool being used to drag the wheel up the hill. Crossing the deserted finishing line was an anti-climax. The little amount of euphoria that broke out amongst the platoon was overshadowed by the fact that there was no one there to acknowledge it. Every available person was at the bottom of the hill recovering Paddy's wheel. Pete was controlling traffic, Pat was dealing with the insurance of the minivan driver, Paddy was trying to mend the fence before the cattle escaped and Captain Watts was comforting the farmer's wife. Although we had been denied a celebration, Norris' morale was given a massive boost.

Captain Dunn debriefed the platoon on the event, deliberately heaping grand praise on the new lad. Justifiably, he had deserved it, not on his performance – because that owed as much to luck as it did skill – but more for his emotional tenacity and fortitude. Not many people would have coped with being Back-Termed to Row-Co, and this had not gone unnoticed by his peers. He had brought the score to a deficit of six, eighteen points to twelve. In the process he had gone from zero to hero, just as we hoped.

With morale at a high, it was unfortunate that Stone's transgressions still needed to be addressed. Standing before me was the complete platoon. My plan was to concoct a bluff witness to force a confession out of Stone, which at the time seemed a good idea.

'Quiet!' My shout filled the valley, and the platoon's rowdiness fell silent.

'There is some bad news for you all. You can recall, before you started this exercise you were told that contact with civilians was strictly prohibited. Well, we have a witness who says he saw one of you get out of a car close to a checkpoint, then return to the car shortly after. You will agree that this is clearly an organized effort to get around the checkpoints by cheating. I don't have to remind you that integrity is a golden strand of an officer's DNA! So, to save everyone the embarrassment and heartache of an ID parade, would the individual like to own up? I'll give you a few seconds to think about it. I want to know who took a lift in a car during the march across the moor?'

Confident that Stone would hold his hands up, there was little more to do than stare at the shell-shocked faces as their eyes scanned left and right, waiting for someone to flinch.

'OK. Who was it?'

Ten hands drifted up into admission. Worse still, not one of them belonged to Stone.

For the first time during my service career, I was cursing the honesty of my students. This was not supposed to happen. In the cold light of day, it was expected that maybe one or two students would have taken an offer of assistance, but more by luck than a calculated effort to cheat. Francis, Danner, Norris and Mathews were amongst the guilty. This placed me in a very awkward position. If the OC found out how many students cheated, he would go bonkers. But worse than this was the fact that Stone now knew that a number of his peers had also cheated, giving him a sense of equal standing. If, at the end of the week, we tried to kick him out for cheating during the exercise, he would just quote this incident and claim discrimination. In the grand scheme of things, he now knew that he was safe from punishment for all crimes categorized by deceit.

Too deflated to give them an old-fashioned bollocking, and too confused to think straight, my moral calibration had lost its orientation. In times like this, physical exercise was my panacea. Principally, it is a punishment that affords benefit to the recipient, but it also offers thinking time while the mind searches for solutions. I separated the guilty from the innocent and set out on a run around the training area. After twenty minutes of high-tempo exertion, the answer still evaded me, so escalating the current level of misery seemed to be the solution. At the top of the hill, there was a small pond that would fulfil this requirement. Without hesitation, I jumped into it, and the students dutifully followed. There was an expectation that the water would be shallow, but to my surprise the pond was extremely deep. There was no wading to be done, and instead we all took a short swim to the other side. Dripping wet and shivering, their sorry state was all down to my poor handling of Stone's indiscretions. I had failed to deal with the problem effectively at the start; consequently, it had snowballed to include half the platoon.

Captain Dunn giggled at me when I returned.

'That will be the return of a very unhappy Colour Sergeant. What went wrong?'

'Yeah, Sir! A number of our lads had cheated on the walk in, so we went for a little jog and found a not-so-little pond.'

'I like the sound of that, Colour,' said Captain Watts, who was sitting next to Captain Dunn. 'Where did you say the pond is? We have a number of students who cheated on the insertion as well. We were going to wait till we returned to Sandbags, but if there is some water here, we can deal with it now.'

Captain Watts leapt up, his face full of enthusiasm. There was a glint of mischief in his eye: he didn't need much of an excuse to inflict a few hardships onto his students. His years with the Special Air Service had rubbed away any feelings of sympathy and only served to enhance his slightly warped sense of humour. This attitude helped to ease the self-torture over my actions, having previously thought they were a bit extreme.

'Who was it, Colour?' inquired Captain Dunn.

'Murphy, Mathews, Francis, Williams and Norris. Plus many more.'

'Stone?'

'Seemingly not!'

'Fuck!' declared Captain Dunn.

It was the expression on his face that told the story, as he joined the dots and ended up with the same picture as me. Sitting under my basher with the boss, we talked about the problems this presented; explicitly, the misery that Stone was inflicting on us both.

'We are in danger of losing sight of the ball here, Colour! Stone certainly is starting to wind the pair of us up, but while we waste time on him, there are a number of students who we really need to concentrate on: Lane, Witherspoon, Haigh, Barns and Williams, not to mention Norris!'

Balance and harmony were proving illusive, and the cause was absolutely Stone.

With irksome issues like this, my coping mechanism was to quietly swear at anything and everything. For me, it was cathartic. It had been pointed out to me many times before that this behaviour was a little weird, but it helped me manage my frustrations. From my wet clothes to the broken zip on my rucksack, it all got a good tongue-lashing. If all my swearing was exhausted on inanimate objects, the living would get off scot-free.

'Don't take it to heart, Colour. It's really not that bad.'

'Yeah, boss, you're right, but it doesn't feel that way. It's hard to accept Stone is getting away with so much. It seems like he has nine lives. Every time we think he has cooked his goose, he comes up smelling of roses. If the little fucker fell from the window of the fourth floor, he would go up!'

'You're letting him get to you. If the truth be known, he will slip up again and again, so it's really just an issue of when, not if. Let it go before it consumes you.'

Captain Dunn was once again right. Although five years my junior, he was capable of outsmarting me on a regular basis. Unfortunately, this only served to fuel my frustration. Needing to calm down, I grunted like a caveman, broke into my emergency chocolate stash and fired up my Peak stove in preparation for the evening meal. To spoil myself, both sachets of chocolate powder were emptied into my drink, and just for good measure, I added three packets of sugar.

Sipping out of a black metal mug, rimmed with green cloth tape to protect my lips from the heat, my priorities were beginning to realign. Looking through the exercise instructions to remind myself of the events programmed for tomorrow, the last line of the remarks column caught my eye.

'Bollocks! Bollocks! Bollocks!' I had a full-on hissy-fit and punched my folder several times before slamming it into the ground.

Captain Dunn burst out laughing.

'You've just seen the amended route for tomorrow's march, haven't you?'

'Yes!'

'Thought you had! Long, isn't it!'

'Bloody hell, Sir, what was your first for at uni – stating the obvious or cartography?'

'Now now, Colour, I didn't go to uni, but I do have a degree in last-minute changes.'

Having complimented myself on how diligent my preparation was just five minutes before, I kicked myself for not reading the programme as closely as required. There were two long navigation exercises listed, but that was not the surprise. What I failed to read was a small asterisk in the remarks column of the programme, detailing the fact that both exercises would run back-to-back. The total distance was nearly 50km, with thirty during the day and twenty during the night. My group were the first out at 0630hrs. For two or three minutes my cursing hit a new level as the boss continually laughed at my inaptitude. He received every halfwit comment and joke in my repertoire, along with a few friendly insults. Having calmed down, Captain Dunn split the platoon in half and suggested they were evenly balanced groups. Finally, we analysed the routes we anticipated the students would select and confirmed who needed the most attention during their command appointment. In total, there were eleven legs to negotiate, and each student would navigate and lead at least twice. For safety reasons, we would be walking close by, but only *in extremis* would we interfere with a student's command and navigation.

For my group, Moore was in command first, navigating a leg covering 5km. As he briefed me on his route, my heart sank as he explained he wished to take a direct route on a single bearing to the first checkpoint. In theory it was a good idea – we had taught this skill – but the ground he intended to walk was full of hidden bogs and marshland. Whilst Moore may not have seen this, it was important he was given the opportunity to experience the consequences of his decision-making.

'Moore, there is logic in your choice of route, but the checkpoint is called Buckland Ford. Is there anything in the name of this place that is sounding alarm bells for you? Before you answer, that's not Ford as in Escort Van.'

'Maybe we will find a "ford" there, Colour Sergeant?'

'Is that it?'

Moore looked at me with a blank expression. That was as much help as was allowed. From this point forward, the young man needed to learn from his mistakes. The low ground looked good, but in reality this was going to be a nightmare. Buckland Ford was going to be flooded with the fresh rain, all of it waiting for our arrival. Having issued a comprehensive brief, Moore set off at pace. Once he was heading in the right direction, I shadowed his movements before taking a longer path to the south, via the opposite hill. The devil in me wanted him to get stuck in the bog, just to teach him the benefits of intellectually interrogating the map and not just looking at the obvious features.

Walking on my own, it was now possible to get to the destination much more quickly than it would take in a group. From my vantage point, the view down to where Moore and his team walked could not have been better. The group were fighting their way through the peat bog and the myriad of hidden puddles at the base of the hill. They were moving painfully slowly as I stopped just short of the first checkpoint manned by Pat. Wandering over to my vantage point, he stood beside me, giggling as the misery unfolded.

'Hello, Gaz, how the devil?'

'I'm good thanks, Pat. How long have you been up here?'

'Left early last night to get a bit of peace and quiet under the stars. How are your Biffs getting on down there?'

Even in their absence, Pat insulted the students. In the unlikely event that one of the students impressed him, he would blame it on the full moon!

'Not too bad. Moore is leading this leg. He is a good lad, but he has chosen the direct route straight through the bog. You can see they are struggling already. If he has any sense, he will backtrack and come up the side of the hill like me.'

'Moore! The fanny with big lips? He is a big tart, Gaz, he's not a good lad! I wouldn't let him loose with a garden hose for fear he would drown himself. You're a brave man letting him out of your sight like this. You clearly have faith in him.'

We both sat at the forward edge of the hill, where we could see the students holding a Chinese Parliament. The peat would sap their energy and the cold water would accelerate their demise. Inevitably, we watched as Moore began to walk back the way he came as he extracted himself out of the bog and headed for the rear of the large hill. Unexpectedly, and to my surprise, Paddy's group were the first to appear at the checkpoint. They had set off thirty minutes after Moore.

'Hey, Paddy, you made good time.'

'Aye, Gaz. The wee fella is doing grand. They watched your boys get stuck and opted to go the long way around.'

Fortuitous as it was, it still irked me. The lingering suspicion that Paddy was not playing with a straight bat would always colour my thoughts, even if he was totally innocent.

'Your boys were in a world of pain at the bottom of that hill, Gaz!'

'Yes, we just watched them extract out of the bog and move around the side of the hill. It won't be long before they arrive. Still, it was good your lads never made the same mistake.'

'Aye, Gaz. Every now and again they can surprise you, eh!'

Paddy set off to his next checkpoint, while Pat threw small stones at the tail end of the group. To ramp up the tension, he told Paddy that Moore and his group were just about to catch them up. But to my astonishment, the next group to appear over the crest of the hill was the second group from our platoon. Led by Boyle, they had virtually run all the way from the start point. Captain Dunn appeared from the rear of the group, grinning like a man possessed.

'Hi, Colour. Where's your group?'

I shook my head with disbelief, thinking to myself they couldn't get lost. This was the only big hill for 2 or 3km. They couldn't mis-navigate, they were nearly here before they had to turn around and extract from the bog.

'You haven't lost them, have you?'

'Of course he's lost them!' chirped Pat, never missing an opportunity to stir up trouble.

'We'll see. Moore is about to appear over the crest of the hill at any moment. They're a fit bunch and we will make the ground up quickly.'

Time crept by with no sign of the group. Incapable of containing my frustrations any longer, I took a walk back down the hill to chivvy them along. It had crossed my mind to sack Moore for wasting so much time, but that would be pointless, knowing he would be changed at the checkpoint anyway. It had been over an hour since we last saw them at the bottom of the hill, and the fury was beginning to sidetrack my concentration. Halfway back down the route, I caught sight of a group on the opposite hill, approximately 2km away. To make things worse, it appeared as if they were walking away from checkpoint one. Surely that could not be Moore! Reaching into the back pocket of my daysack, my trusty binoculars gave me a better look at the group.

'For Christ's sake! It's them! The stupid little fucker.'

There was no one around to listen to my protestation. How could he be so bloody stupid? How could they walk past this massive hill? The questions kept coming. With the situation deteriorating by the minute, there was no alternative. Dropping my kit on the spot – my fleece, showerproof jacket and daysack – the only answer was to run the 2km to the next hill. After less than 200 metres, the contours took me below their line of sight and committed me to running the full distance. It was twenty minutes before the crest of the hill they were on levelled out. Cutting a solitary figure against the darkening sky, Moore caught sight of me running towards them and stopped. By the time we had regrouped, they had travelled just over 3km in the wrong direction. Soaked to the skin from sweat, and my calves cramping up, there was little to be said as the students initiated their own Spanish Inquisition.

There was little for me to shout about. Having seen me running up the hill towards them, wearing nothing other than a thin thermal shirt, they knew something had gone dramatically wrong.

'Show me where you think you are, Moore.' It was impossible to get out any more words. Air was proving hard to take in and the cramp was beginning to bite.

'I think we are here, Colour Sergeant,' he said, pointing at the correct place on the map.

'Well that's fucking great, isn't it! How come you know where you are now? Why has it taken two hours, and my intervention, for you to figure out that you've gone miles in the wrong direction?'

'It wasn't until we saw you running up the hill that I felt the requirement to check my bearings, Colour Sergeant.'

Absolutely flabbergasted and professionally embarrassed, I snatched the map out of his hands and threw it at Francis before turning around and making our way down the rocky hill towards where my kit lay. It was a pathetic symbolic gesture of dissatisfaction.

Francis merrily followed behind me, knowing where I was going. By the time we arrived at checkpoint one, everyone else had long gone. A little more composed, a sombre debrief issued to the group was humbly accepted. At great length, we discussed the skill of map interpretation versus reading contours and map symbols. In this case the word 'ford' needed little explanation; in hindsight, Moore knew it. There were numerous indications telling Moore to choose a different route. Walking at the bottom of a valley was naïve, and this failure was going to cost us dearly. The group had no idea we were walking 30km, and conservation of energy was pivotal if we wished to get there in good order. Every minute wasted was a minute of rest denied before the night march. Francis was told to take charge of the second leg as we set off for checkpoint two.

The next two checkpoints went smoothly, with both King and Francis having relatively easy legs to navigate, but we were still losing time. As Packman reached the 10km mark at checkpoint four, we were nearly two hours behind. In true Rowallan tradition, this tardiness was going to be punished. With enormous pleasure, the OC welcomed the students into his checkpoint. He was now accompanied by Pat, who had driven the safety vehicle around the edge of the training area to join the OC. The checkpoint was at the side of a road at the base of Brockhill, just east of Avon Dam reservoir.

'Marvellous! Marvellous! Absolutely bloody marvellous! This is my favourite checkpoint of all time. I love this part. Gaz, give these late Muppets a burden. In fact, no! This was the group that kept me hanging around at checkpoint one. They made me miss the Company Commander buying the coffee and cakes. Give them two!'

On the floor next to Pat's feet was a stack of large burdens. The cousin of the smaller H83 container, the large burden was reserved for endurance events like this. Once holding 105mm howitzer ammunition, these C572 boxes were filled with shingle, painted yellow and weighed about 50lb each. Either end had a narrow handle just large enough to get four fingers through, and they were designed to be carried no further than a few hundred yards. The thought of carrying these awkward and ungainly boxes sent shivers down the spines of Barns. He was much taller than his peers and knew instantly that he would end up carrying more than his fair share of the dead weight. It would have been understandable had the group broken down in tears at the sight of the heavy boxes, but Francis broke out giggling at the disposition he found himself in. Along with the boxes, Pat issued them with their instructions for the next leg.

'You have one hour and fifty-five minutes to make it to the next checkpoint. If you make it on time, you can ditch the boxes. If you fail to make it on time, you get another box. Your choice! Stick the effort in or collect another box. Your time starts now!'

Stone was commanding this leg, but failed to pay attention to Pat's words. After a brief pause where Stone said nothing, Francis began to organize the group into two teams, each being responsible for one burden.

Checkpoint five was at the top of Ryders Hill, 4km as the crow flies, but 6km if they stayed on the high ground and avoided the valley, which was covered in tumps of elephant grass and hidden mud holes. Using Naismith's rule of hiking, the journey was easily achievable. Add the misery of carrying two heavy ammunition boxes and the awkward ground, and the task was just about achievable if maximum effort was applied. Stepping off at speed, the burden quickly drained their energy and the students began feeling sorry for themselves. With every 40 or 50 metres covered, Stone ordered everyone to rest. He resigned himself to failing even before they started. The meagre power output he was demanding from his team would not have lit a light bulb. If it had not been for the intervention of Francis, we would probably still be sat back at the checkpoint. It was the perfect start handed to Stone, and all he needed to do was keep the momentum. Perhaps predictably, Stone gave up quite quickly. Having not done the same amount of fitness as the rest of the group, he lacked stamina. Using his command appointment as an excuse to stop and rest, the progress was pitifully slow. It was clear to me that he had come to the conclusion that this was all a bit of kidology. Surely no one would make them walk another leg with these heavy boxes. I was bursting at the seams to help him out, and it took every ounce of self-control not to get involved. His petulance was accumulating a number of life lessons just waiting to tumble down on him all at once. If he was thinking the worst that we could do would be to make him carry the box further, it was going to come crashing down in a wicked dose of reality.

Ten minutes late, Stone ambled up to the checkpoint. Daz was waiting for him with an ever-increasing grin. Playing tunes on his thermos flask, sitting on the tailgate of the Land Rover smoking a cigarette, Daz dished out insults to everyone in the group as he poured me a coffee.

'Who's in charge of this shower of garbage?' Daz snarled.

Stone limply raised his hand. 'Me, Staff Sergeant.'

'I might have known it was you, "Mr I am too fit for all this"! I'm chuffed you are late. It couldn't have happened to a nicer man. Do you know you are late?'

'Yes, Staff Sergeant.'

'Oh good, I am pleased your brain is still working. What do you think the punishment will be for failing?'

'Carry the boxes to the next checkpoint, Staff Sergeant!'

Without a care in the world, Stone sarcastically gave Daz a flippant reply. He had not carried the boxes on the last leg. As the commander, he chose to navigate, and his frivolous flirting with Daz's authority suggested that Stone thought he would be punished and left in command for the next leg.

Daz giggled at the answer. He took a long draw on his smoke and exhaled the residue forcefully high into the air.

'If only life was that easy, eh, Stone! A punishment by its definition is to make something worse. Making you carry the boxes to the next checkpoint would be more of the same. No. No. No, Stone. I am going to give you another box and half your time, Stone. And finally, should you fail to make the cut-off time, there will be another box waiting for you. To be crystal clear on what is happening here, every time you fail to make the cut-off, we give you a box. This will continue until you have one box each!'

Daz thoroughly enjoyed giving the students unwelcome news. He revelled in his hard-man attitude. Even when Norris went to receive his instructions for the leg he was about to lead, Daz never tempered his comments. Imitating Rab C. Nesbitt, he goaded the young Scotsman.

'See you, Jimmy. You still here? Didn't you no git the message first time around? This is no for you, wee man. See if it waz, you would still be on the Commissioning Course!'

Norris took it in his stride as Daz kept trying his Scottish accent whilst issuing the grid reference of the next checkpoint. Down Ridge stone circle was about 3km away and mostly downhill. It was marginally achievable, but there could be no slacking. If they wanted to ditch the boxes, they would need to fight through the pain barrier.

Norris canvassed opinions before reordering the group to carry the three boxes. He spoke quietly in the hope it would not heighten the apprehension. The lack of smiles caused me to break out my flask and offer everyone a sip of hot chocolate before imparting a few words of encouragement:

'Norris, you would have received much tuition on dealing with difficult command conundrums. This is your opportunity to right some wrongs. You must be under no illusions. There is another box waiting for you at the next checkpoint. There was a little luck in winning the wheel race; this is all about you. My advice is, jog all the way. Don't stop and rest. As commander, sometimes you need to physically contribute. This may be one of those times. Choose the moment wisely. When you need to get physical you must inspire, but don't lose sight of the fact you are in command. Make a difference, don't rely on others.'

Norris sensed the urgency in my voice. He would have detected my peripheral concerns, or maybe there was an inclination of what lay ahead, but he was like a man possessed when the order to go was given. The first 500 metres fooled me into thinking that this was easier than it looked, as every student worked to the maximum. Then, inexplicably, despondency broke out amongst the ranks. Norris called for continuous effort with no rest, while Stone claimed to be exhausted. With maximum pressure applied to all characters, it didn't take long before tempers flared. Danner threatened to bang together the heads of Norris and Stone if they continued to argue. Seconds later, he promised to beat up everyone if they failed to make the next deadline. Witherspoon questioned Norris' tactics and called for short sprints, with rest in between. It was critical that this exchange was allowed to develop without interference. This was a learning point, and it needed to be realized. Threats and gesticulation warned of imminent violence, and my money was on Danner to get the better of any exchange. Emotions were at their peak as the burdens were dropped to the ground and the students postured for physical exchanges.

With Danner and Witherspoon standing toe-to-toe and on the verge of blows, group cohesion had vanished. Not wanting to get dragged into confrontation, Francis picked up one burden on his own, hitched it high onto his shoulder and started walking. There were a few relieved faces as calm was called for and everyone's attention was directed to Francis. His single act of defiance amplified the need to focus on the task in hand. No one wanted another box, and that included me.

'OK, before Francis kills himself, pin your ears back and listen to my ten-second burst and my only words for the next fifty minutes. You are one minute ahead of schedule. You have just lost thirty seconds and I am now taking ten seconds to speak. Do what the fuck you wish to do next, but the reward for your lethargy and childish behaviour will be more pain. Work as a team and share the responsibility. Or do what Francis is doing and try this on your own. Your choice! Resolving conflict is an art of leadership.

You need to regain cohesion. This race is your unifying purpose, any fool can see that!'

Norris broke out into angry shouting. His encouragement helped to forget the insults issued seconds before as he motivated the team to concentrate on arriving in the time. The bust-up had done them good. With the atmosphere reduced to one of 'let's just get there on time', they began to swallow up ground. More by chance than judgment, Norris stumbled onto an old footpath. Just when he really needed a helping hand, a cinder path lay just below the moss and offered the team an unimpeded route to the next checkpoint.

'Right, let's open up the pace!' shouted the Scotsman.

Ten minutes previously, that very command would have caused a mutiny, but now, in unison, they dutifully obeyed. Slowly, the pace built up as the shuffle became a jog, and despite the large yellow boxes, the speed was impressive. Francis was limping heavily, yet astonishingly he was leading the way.

Chasing us from behind, Daz caught up to the group. His driver had moved the Land Rover to the farm by Down Ridge stone circle, allowing him to follow our progress and keep the time. As he jogged alongside the group, he told them to look up and see where the vehicle was now parked in the distance.

'That's your checkpoint, fellas. I will walk at the pace that you need to achieve if you want to get there on time. Provided you stay with me, you will make it.'

Daz broke out into a fast walk, which quickly became a speed march. At this pace the group could keep up with him. With 200 metres to go, Daz began to run-walk. Slowly, he eased passed the front man, five steps running, then ten steps walking. The boys chased hard. The groaning became unbearable as the team sensed Daz was out to make them fail. Norris screamed obscenities at everyone, trying to squeeze every ounce of energy out of the group. But Francis wasn't moving any faster. Hobbling at best, he couldn't gain any more speed if he had it in him. His rucksack weighed 30lb and his share of the burden another 25lb. Add this to his wet clothes and he was 70lb heavier than Daz, who was still wearing little more than his singlet vest. Despite their best efforts, they arrived twenty seconds behind Daz.

Standing on a rocky outcrop at the finish line, Daz counted out the seconds loudly. As the last man crossed the line, he stopped the watch.

'Nineteen, twenty, twenty-one. Stop. Gutted! Absolutely gutted! Well, you have just ruined my day.'

Daz walked to the rear of the Land Rover with his thermos flask in one hand and a cigarette in the other. Dropping the tailgate to make an improvised bench, he poured himself a coffee and sat on the back of the vehicle, surveying the forlorn students. Francis, Moore, Danner and Witherspoon lay where they fell, panting like Siberian Huskies tethered in the ranks. Norris stood hands on hips, eyes fixed on Daz.

'Did we make it, Staff Sergeant?'

'Don't know how you've done it, but you have made it with four minutes to spare!'

There was no praise from Daz. He spun around on the tailgate and reached deep inside the cavernous storage space of the Land Rover. A metallic scraping sound shrilled through my ears as two more yellow boxes were dropped to the floor.

> 'Look hard at these boxes. These had your names on. We weren't bluffing when we promised to give you another box. It would have been my pleasure to give you one of these bad boys. It is massively disappointing that you made it on time. Gutted! But take this as a warning. Gamesmanship is for politicians. It's not for us who bear arms. So, if you think we are just playing, these boxes tell you we are deadly serious.'

Daz had his failings, as we all do. Occasionally, he would say things that could be overly cruel, with no desired outcome other than to be mean. But his little speech at the conclusion of the 'heavy carry' was perfect. Sadly, it would have been lost on Stone, who was the target of his lecture. A few short checkpoints later, and mercifully the last daytime leg was underway. Having given each member of the group one leg to command, we were back around to Moore. By this stage we had been walking for eight hours. The route to the final checkpoint paralleled the main road that dissected Dartmoor training area. At the halfway mark there was a natural choke point dominated by two bridges, and of course a huge country pub called the Two Bridges Hotel. The sun was enjoying longer periods of cloud-free interruption, which gave the impression of a warm summer's afternoon. As we got closer to the pub, we could see all the Directing Staff in the beer garden, eating and drinking. The students didn't know it yet, but this was their final check point of the first phase.

'Oi! Billy back-bearing! Glad to see you could make it!'

Pat was in the pub garden sitting on a large oak bench with table. His comments signalled the green light for the remaining DS to hurl sarcastic abuse at me. No matter how righteous my actions were by letting the group make mistakes, the comments still hurt. It would have been foolhardy to contest the issue, so swallowing my pride, the barrage of mocking and torment just washed over me.

'Fancy a beer, Colour?'

Captain Dunn walked out to the side of the road and quietly asked me to come and join the rest of the team.

'They have the most stunning Cornish pies. I'll get you a pie as well.'

'Yes, OK, but best get me five Mars Bars too. No beer; I need some sugar, so a full fat coke please, Sir.'

My words were not heard. He stopped listening after I said 'yes'. Predictably, he returned with two lagers and no chocolate.

Pete appeared from the rear of the pub and called for my group to follow him. By kind permission of the landlord, the support team had set up a small canteen in the rear garden, out of sight of prying eyes. He provided all the students with hot tea, coffee and fizzy drinks, as well as some locally purchased fish and chips. It was intended to be lunch, but with so much time being lost with poor navigation, it was closer to evening meal. This was one of Pete's finest moments. However, devilish at heart and loving the opportunity to get directly involved, the crumbs of deception were being laid. This momentary pause in proceedings was Pete's opportunity to administer the next phase of the exercise, otherwise known as the sucker punch. From the moment the students arrived, Pete gave them the impression that the exercise had finished for that day. But he then arranged everyone into groups of four and told them that they would be moved to Willsworthy Camp on the western edge of Dartmoor. True to his word, a fleet of vehicles turned up and transported everyone to Dartmoor's newest transit camp.

Willsworthy Camp had only just opened, and was in pristine condition. Modern facilities and the smell of clean bedding mixed with fresh paint was graciously received. Pete delivered a central brief to everyone, explaining meal times, shower times, fire escape routes and what to do in the event of an alarm being raised. Finally, he sealed the deal by writing a guard force roster and allocating everyone a two-hour shift, starting at midnight and finishing at 0700hrs the following day. No detail was left unaddressed; the charade was perfect. Pete followed the standard procedure for entering any camp. These actions gave our cover story great credibility. With the students settling in for the night, Pete left one student in charge of the guard roster before bidding everyone a good night's sleep.

As my watch vibrated on my wrist to tell me it was 2200hrs, I climbed out of my sleeping bag, packed my kit away and joined the rest of the DS at the front of the accommodation. The deception plan had well and truly worked. Morale was sky high, with students already swapping stories of great escapes, near misses and double-burden carries. Laughter filled the accommodation as students set about their personal administration. Rucksacks, soaking wet clothing and towels adorned every available space on radiators and heating pipes. Queues formed in conformance with allotted shower times, while others busily cleaned mess tins and mugs in preparation for breakfast. The atmosphere drifted into that of a relaxed self-congratulatory love fest, confident and assured that a decent night's sleep awaited and nothing would happen to them in the middle of nowhere at such an ungodly hour.

'Bugout! Bugout! Bugout! Outside now, move it.'

The DS charged through the accommodation, shouting the order in stereo. Students had dropped their guard and were caught entirely unawares. It was the first time this scenario had been played out for real and we expected the shock to generate an explosion of activity, but instead we got a reaction of stunned silence and disbelief. Disappointed by the lack of urgency, Pat resorted to throwing people about by force in order to provoke a response. It did just that. Total carnage ensued. Blind panic gripped everyone, students racing through the accommodation gathering personal belongings. Half-dressed, covered in soap suds or woken from their sleep, students bounced off each other trying to escape Pat's attention. Fifteen minutes later and the last student appeared in the courtyard of the Dartmoor camp. The grey slate stone-chip car park complemented the threatening black sky. A solitary white halogen security light beaming through the rain illuminated the start point of the night navigation.

Stupefied and assembled like cattle going to market, the students wandered around the car park trying to remember what comes next. Eventually they formed the obligatory hollow square for an inspection as the DS gathered their thoughts on the next stage. Then, like a scene from a sci-fi film, the accommodation door opened and a blinding light swamped the hollow square. Stepping from the light, Stone nonchalantly walked out wearing nothing but a pair of boots, a towel and a huge grin.

'What the hell are you playing at, Stone?' yelled Pat.

'I was in the shower, Sir.'

Pat's eyes bulged with disdain. He knew that no one was in the shower when the bugout was called; it was the first place he cleared. Stone had clearly decided that it would make a good excuse for not getting involved with the pandemonium of the bugout if he jumped in the shower. Pat's fists clenched as he processed his courses of action. For a few seconds we feared that a haymaker would be unleashed on the young lad. If it had, we would have fully understood the reason. It was hard to recall such insubordination in all my years of service. It wasn't arrogance, nor was it a lack of ability; it was pure contempt.

Pat stood at the point of no return. Stone had professionally embarrassed him, and now the whole course stood watching as Stone back-chatted the Company Sergeant Major. It was an extraordinary display of stupidity that was hard to comprehend. Pat moved to within a whisker of Stone.

> 'You would like me to give you a good kicking for back-chatting, wouldn't you? It's the excuse you're looking for just so you can get off the night march. You are just one of a hundred wannabes that have passed through my administration in recent years. Revel in the knowledge that you are

by far the worst specimen I've ever had the displeasure to encounter. Get dressed, get packed and rejoin your squad.'

Pat, sensing that Stone was trouble, deliberately guarded his words, knowing that this may end up with a complaint, yet another tactic in Stone scamming his way through training. Walking away from Stone and stewing on the moment, Pat snapped at everyone in his path, including Captain Dunn, me, Pete and Paddy.

At 2300hrs on the dot, my group set off in search of six checkpoints. Fur Tor was 6km away. Criss-crossed with streams and re-entrants, it was a formidable first leg. The black clouds occasionally separated and offered us a sporadic glimpse of a full moon. When it appeared, the silver light bounced shadows around Dartmoor's matt grey landscape. The rain came and went, but other than this nuisance, the conditions were good for navigation. Still, it didn't take long for Lane to get us lost. With less than a kilometre covered, Lane had led us up a blind alley. He made the common mistake of following a valley, thinking it was heading in the direction he wished to go. Tired from the morning's activities, it would be irrational to let him go until he discovered his mistake.

'Lane!' My voice shattered the dark silence.

'Yes, Colour Sergeant!'

'Before you take one more step, be sure you know where you are going or this will be a very long night. Now, we have travelled about a kilometre. Half of that is in the wrong direction. So, have a good look at your map. Chat with the check-navigator and identify where the fuck you are and where you went wrong. The re-entrant we have entered is a blind alley; don't try and push on through it.'

A combat indicator that my temper had drastically shortened was the early use of swear words. Snapping so early at Lane wasn't great, but it was imperative to fix this before we went any further.

While Lane looked at his map, the remainder of the group listened to me complain that they were all complicit in the dismal start:

'Every person here has a map, compass and can map-read! We have taught you all you require to know. Yet you all choose to stick your thumbs up your backside and leave it all to one man. Take heed, go wrong again between here and Fur Tor and we will end up walking to Plymouth! The next time you get lost will be the last time you get lost. Stop feeling sorry for yourselves and start helping with the navigation, or you will suffer.'

The warning was a sign of my desperation that the lack of application was becoming a threat to the good order of the patrol. Cognisant that they were tired and susceptible to mistakes, we needed to maintain a sharp sense of alertness. It hadn't been a great success thus far, and of all the challenges we faced, this was going to be the hardest. Kneeling down about 20 yards away, I listened to the students argue over who was check-navigating and who was checking the checker. After several false starts, we finally set off, this time heading south in the direction of a large spur. It was the right move: contour around the steep slope, traverse slowly on to the ridge and avoid the bogs in the lowland, a textbook solution. It was a tougher route that would pay dividends later during the march. But it was not down to the leadership of Lane. Pushed to the rear, he was effectively sacked by his peers as they navigated for him. Francis and Moore picked their way through several small tors until they had a clear run to Fur Tor. Watching Lane fall further and further to the rear of the group affirmed my assessment. He displayed zero leadership ability, being ineffective as a commander and incapable of assimilating instruction or forging meaningful relationships. At Sandhurst, if someone was not going to make it as an officer, we had the option of inviting them to join the Army as a soldier, but Lane was as poor as the worst recruit ever to fail in training.

After a brief stop at the top of Fur Tor, it was the turn of Francis to take command. Even though he had already been leading, this was his official opportunity to affirm his status as a top student contender. His checkpoint was 4km away, and unquestionably the most undulating ground on the moor. It had not been lost on me that he had been struggling with his knees. At our current location we were as far away from a road as you could possibly be anywhere in England. Impressively, Francis appointed a pace counter, a check-navigator and a bearing checker. As he set off, there was a calmness that assured everyone that this leg would go smoothly. Then, just as things appeared to be on track, Lane fell to the floor, complaining of stomach ache and dizziness. It was the worst possible place for him to fall ill. We set up an emergency shelter and boiled some water to make hot chocolate. This had the potential to become a serious problem. To carry him off the moor would take a gargantuan effort. The other option was to leave him here and send for help, which would be incredibly risky. Thirty minutes passed, and it was decided that it was best to leave Lane with a few other students and go to get help. However, just before the emergency group departed, Lane declared he was feeling better and ready to continue. With absolutely no hint of illness, he picked himself up and slotted into the middle of the group as they carried on with the leg. The delay had cost us dearly. We had lost time and momentum, and the intensity of the rain had increased. It had just turned 0200 hours as Francis made it to Whitehorse Hill.

Yes Tor was the next target, the highest peak on the map, some 5½km away as the crow flies. It was the turn of Danner to navigate, but he was slowly losing interest as tiredness set in. Long gone were his witty comments and jovial inputs. It was a huge struggle for him to keep his concentration. Stopping to check his location every 50 metres or so was becoming exhausting for everyone.

The constant stop-start induced cramps and accelerated fatigue. As we neared the highest part of the moor, the rain reached peak ferocity and the wind howled at our every step. The environment was unforgiving, and this was proving a fantastic test for the students. At the base of a long ascent, Danner stopped to confer with Moore. The discussion seemed to go on for ten minutes or so before the team started to move again. It had been a joint decision to use the rocky scar as a handrail to gain access to the crest of the tor. They always knew that at some stage they needed to pick their way through the escarpments to get to the knife's edge. Risky as it was, it made sense to skirt around the prominent feature. Cresting the southern end of Yes Tor brought a small cheer from the first three to join Danner. After a minute passed, Francis appeared, but there was no one after him. Danner called out to Haigh, who was behind Francis.

'Haigh! Haigh! Lane! Lane! Haigh.'

Danner's voice became louder and louder, dissipating quickly into the darkness.

Nauseous with the thought of Lane having a reoccurrence of his earlier episode, a mild panic flushed through my body. After his little incident, he could have relapsed. Even worse, he could have fallen as we weaved our way through the crags of Yes Tor. It was for this very reason that the DS walked with the students. This had all the hallmarks of a disaster, and it was prudent that Danner should now let me take charge.

'Danner, Francis, Moore. You three wait here. Switch your torches on and keep them on. Keep them pointing south-west and remove the red filter. Norris, you are coming with me. Danner, in the event we do not return within the hour, you are to walk north until you hit the checkpoint. It is manned by Colour Sergeant Edwards. Read back!'

Danner repeated my instructions to assure me he understood everything precisely.

Norris kept close to me as we scurried down through the rocks. The wet surface made the descent much more treacherous than going up. Travelling at speed increased the frequency of slipping, so for our own preservation we slowed to a sensible walk. Several times Norris called out, fearing my groans indicated a fatal fall, but it was just the jarring of my knees and ankles. I became desperately worried about what we were going to be confronted with. That was if we even made it, for Norris kept falling as he remained hot on my heels. Almost comically, each time he fell, he apologized profusely as if he had somehow let me down. His polished Edinburgh accent was oddly comforting as he repeated his apology numerous times.

'Sorry, Colour Sergeant, the rock was very slippy there. Sorry, Colour Sergeant, I didn't see that one. Oops, sorry, Colour Sergeant, that caught me out.'

Nearing the bottom of the tor, we both began shouting to locate the rest of the group.

'Haigh! Stone! Switch on your torch!'

Nothing. Not a peep. I bounced my thoughts off Norris, more as a sanity check than a need for advice. In situations like this, it helps to air your thoughts. In a similar fashion to advanced driving techniques, if you keep repeating aloud what you are thinking, what you are seeing and what your next move is, those with you can contribute and increase your situational awareness.

In the valley running north to south, we paused to catch our breath and re-evaluate the issue, desperately trying to second-guess what they would have done had Lane become ill. If it was me dealing with a sick student, separated from my group, what would my actions be?

'Norris, what would you be doing now if Lane was ill and you couldn't move him?'

'Well, Colour Sergeant. First thing would be to stick up an emergency shelter. After that I'd go back to the last emergency RV.'

Norris was following protocol. It was not the best option, but he was thinking like a student and not like an instructor. After a quick assessment, it was the course of action Norris suggested that shaped the next move. Setting my compass on a back bearing, we headed back to Whitehorse Hill. Both torches on full blast, with filters removed for white light, we scoured the terrain as we moved. Then the luck of the gods shone brightly as the reflective strips of the waterproof jackets worn by our students flashed my torch beam back at me.

'Haigh! Stone! Is that you?'

The lack of response frightened me. Moving as fast as we could, every second would count if Lane was down.

My torch was now picking out multiple reflective strips on several jackets, but still no light being shone in my direction. The nearest student to me was flat out on the ground. Face down and motionless, it was impossible to see who it was. A few feet behind him, another student slumped backwards, resting on his rucksack.

'Who's this?' I placed my hand on the first student in line. There was still no response. With care, I rolled him over onto his back to discover who it was.

'Lane! Lane, can you hear me?'

Lane opened his eyes.

'Who's that?'

'It's me. The Colour Sergeant. Are you OK? What happened?'

'Oh, not sure. Are we going?'

'Are you ill? Did you fall?' My voice began to rise. Norris walked beyond me to check the other students.

'I must have fallen asleep, Colour Sergeant.'

Stone, Haigh and Witherspoon appeared from the darkness. It became obvious that this was the last place we stopped to check-navigate before we turned up to attack the rocks. The stop was prolonged as they faffed about debating the route, and the group not helping with the navigation had obviously sat down on their rucksacks and fallen asleep.

It wasn't the right time to deal with what happened or who was at fault. Mixed emotions were clouding my thoughts. Relief that Lane was not ill and that there would not be the need to call out the emergency services, and huge relief they had not moved and compounded the problem. This was sufficient for me to do little more than organize them into a tight group and lead the way to the top of the tor to rejoin Danner, Moore and Francis and then proceed to check in.

'Hey, Gaz, how are you getting on, buddy?'

'Well, Ed, it's been rough. They are exhausted. Are we the last through? We had to stop a few times'

'No, Gaz. The other half of your platoon with Captain D has been through, and so has Paddy.' There was still Captain Watts to come.

Ed produced his thermos and offered me steaming hot chocolate. He complimented it with a few Blue Riband biscuits. Desperate to tell someone of my misery in leaving behind half my group at the bottom of Yes Tor, it took every ounce of my emotional strength to hold my tongue and not inform Eddie. Despite the serious nature of what had just happened, if Pat found out, he would just extend my ownership of the string vest.

Williams would navigate the next leg. The vacant look in his eyes was telling as he struggled to draft his route card. The students needed to recharge their batteries before continuing. Williams led everyone off the top of Yes Tor and down the north-west slope to take a break. Stopping beside a small bluff that offered respite from the elements, the team were told to make a hot drink. Working in pairs, they fired up the Hexi stoves and boiled the last of their water to make hot chocolate and coffee. This small injection of morale would help them cover the remaining 10km. Our final destination was Okehampton camp, where transport was scheduled to pick us up at 0900hrs. The final leg was on a well-beaten track, which would make the march less tricky. Slurping my coffee watching Williams plot his route to Sourton Tor, approximately 3½km away, it was imperative he selected the right route. There was a huge valley between our current location and the tor; getting it wrong here would swallow up the last of the students' energy. Not wanting him to take one step in the wrong direction, his route card was discussed in detail. It was prudent to contour around the base of Yes Tor and Sourton Cairn before attacking it from the north. This would save energy and be less treacherous. It would add an additional kilometre to the march but present a less demanding climb wearing full kit.

We hit Sourton Cairn at approximately 0445hrs. It was an unmanned checkpoint that contained just an orientation marker, which Williams dutifully used to stamp the team card. Symbolically, he gave the card to Barns, who was to navigate the penultimate leg. Like the rest of the students, Barns was struggling to retain focus. He was barely conscious as he scribbled down the coordinates for Meldon reservoir. Fortunately, the rain had eased and the temperature peaked at a comfortable 8 degrees. Occasionally, the sky would clear and the full moon bathed the hills with extraordinary levels of ambient light. These were ideal conditions for reading the contours and features, yet Barns still set off in the wrong direction to test my dwindling reserves of tolerance. A short, sharp shrift was issued, and Barns once again muddled up his departure. Along with his peers, Barns was exhausted. Another bollocking would have been futile. Mustering as much patience as possible, I showed Barns where he was, checked his bearings and explained the importance of leadership when everyone else was spent. Despite walking in a dog-leg, Barns hit the handrail he needed to lead us home. Maybe it was more by luck than judgment, but there was a sense of relief when we arrived at the checkpoint. Pat was sitting on the bonnet of the Land Rover, twirling a Leatherman knife. Wrapped in Gortex waterproofs, he looked me up and down to assess my condition.

'Gaz! You made it and you're not last for a change.'

Such backhanded compliments were gratefully received. If for no other reason, they stopped Pat haranguing anyone else.

'Only just, Pat! And we are not there yet.'

'Well, not far from here! The last leg is on the Roman road with a fence either side – even that dick Stone couldn't get lost.'

Ironically, it was Stone's turn next.

As the first strands of daylight broke over our heads, we could see the glowing lights of our destination in the distance. Okehampton camp is a busy place, frequently used by the Royal Marines and Special Boat Squadron. During my two previous visits to Okehampton, the camp was covered in mist, but the students had been lucky with the final three legs. There was no requirement for extensive map reading. The pale white roofs of several large hangers caught the morning sun, and the route home was well defined. It was all downhill after Sourton, but the cobbled Roman road played havoc with tired joints and limbs. Like walking on hot coals, the heat blisters on my swollen feet repeatedly burst and reformed as we headed south of Meldon. Shortly after 0700hrs, we arrived at the large hanger that marked the finish point. Pete was there with a large tea urn, distributing a hot drink to all that wanted it.

'Hi, Gaz, how was the walk?'

'Bloody hard, Pete, I can't lie; my feet are throbbing. That last stretch on the cobbles brought tears to the eyes of a few of them!'

Pete giggled and made several jokes about his busy day sat in the warm cab of his truck, but fatigue had the better of me and his banter flew over my head.

'You might as well get some sleep, Gaz, the transport has been delayed until 1000hrs. But I can't see us leaving on time. Captain Watts has not reached the halfway point yet.'

Pleased for once it was not me holding everyone up, my attention turned to the students. Kit checks, first aid, food and morale all accounted for, there was just enough time to get some sleep before the long journey back to Sandhurst.

The warning tones emitted from a reversing coach woke me from a deep sleep. Disorientated and struggling to open my eyes, it was a while before my full cognitive state returned. My whole body ached as it slowly stretched out of the sleeping bag and into the new surroundings. The hanger was almost full of people and vehicles for the return trip home. I was amazed that anyone could have slept through all this activity. Pete saw me wake and wandered over with a mug of coffee.

'Nice snooze, Gaz?'

'Yes, Pete, not bad. Is everyone back OK?'

'No. Still waiting on Captain Watts. He passed through Meldon about thirty minutes ago, so he is on the Roman road; he shouldn't be too long. Pat has told me to get everyone onto the transport in the next ten minutes so that we can make a quick getaway when he arrives. If we don't make it to Yeovilton in time, we will miss the next serial.'

'Colour.' Captain Dunn's voice echoed around the hanger as he peered out of his sleeping bag. 'Have you got your PB head on?'

'PB! What for? What PB, when?'

'The post-exercise Progress Board. The OC wants to do it in the minibus on the way to Royal Naval Air Station Yeovilton.'

The unexpected task annoyed me; it would have been handy to have known this before my nap. Now there was a pressing need to get my notes together! Slurping my brew, kit packed away, we jumped on the minibus, leaving Pete to corral the students.

An angry Captain Watts boarded the minibus. He had a face like thunder. If the night march had gone bad for me, it had been much worse for him. One of his students threw his hand in at the top of Whitehorse Hill. The rebellious trainee refused to soldier on and sat on his rucksack, unwilling to take any further part in the exercise. Adamant he was not going to walk one more step, Captain Watts and his students had to carry him off the moor to the emergency RV. It had added four hours to the march and a further 15km. Having been dragged 8km in the wrong direction as they made a beeline for the emergency extraction point, his students assumed they would miss out a few checkpoints, but Captain Watts was having none of it. He made them all walk back to Whitehouse Hill to pick up the original trail.

We all settled into our seats, removed our warm clothing, rummaged for our personnel briefing packs and listened to the OC.

'The College Commander has requested a list of names by close of play today of those students we wish to escalate to a College Commander's warning. So by exception only, please. In reverse order, James, your boys. Let's start with those I am aware of. How did Haigh perform, and is he showing signs of improvement?'

'Not seen much of him this week. He has been with the Colour Sergeant. So maybe it's better he takes the lead.'

Looking at my notes and trying to think fast, this was going to be tricky. Haigh had done little wrong. However, he must have been complicit in the sleeping incident at the base of Yes Tor. In my mind, this issue had to be placed in context. This was not a tactical exercise. There was no enemy out to get us and this wasn't a military patrol. As far as the world was aware, this was nothing more than a group of people walking the moor at night. Wrestling with my conscience lengthened the gap before I offered an opinion. If the OC learnt of 'snooze-gate', it would be difficult to prevent Haigh moving onto a Company Commander's warning. The consequence of defending Haigh meant that Stone also benefited. It would not be possible to condemn one and not the other.

'Haigh has done sufficient to be removed from his Platoon Commander's warning, Sir,' I ventured. 'He hasn't put a foot wrong. In the interest of rewarding him for a positive approach, this would be the right move.'

'OK, Colour. James, are you content?'

'Yes, we have worked hard on Haigh. We are making progress, but he is still a risk. The Colour Sergeant makes a valid point. We reward as often as we punish, so he should be removed from his current warning.'

'Good news, James. That's a good start. Williams, he was another one of yours, wasn't he?'

'Again, it's best the Colour Sergeant answers. Williams was in his group.'

'Williams, Sir, yes. He has not done enough to be removed from his current warning, but he has done just enough to avoid an escalation. There is a danger of falling below the standard required, but given we have three weeks left, we have sufficient manoeuvre space to develop him further.'

'OK, James, keep him on a Platoon Commander's warning. It would be good if we could work hard on him to help him off it. How about Stone, please?'

'Not looking good for me, is it? This is going to look suspicious, but, again, the Colour Sergeant had Stone in his group!'

'Hah, Colour, did you know you were getting all the problem children in your group?'

'To be honest, Sir, no. But looking back on how we divided the group, Captain Dunn had my eyes out! Now it's easy to see why he bought the beers at Two Bridges! He must have been feeling guilty about it.'

'Whoa, steady on everyone! Let me start with Stone!' Pat interrupted the banter. His tone was serious and focused. 'This little scumbag needs to be put straight onto a College Commander's warning. The little shit is toxic. We can't be pussyfooting around with this fucker. On a different day, he would have been 6ft under after his little stunt at Willsworthy Camp.'

'Colour?'

'Sir, the Sergeant Major is right. He is so immature it is hard to comprehend how he got through RCB?'

'Well that's easy, he didn't do RCB because he has been assessed at Welbeck. But the College Commander will demand evidence. Other than his poor attitude, what do we have? Before you answer, the MoD investment at this stage in Stone has been significant. Your justification needs to be watertight.'

We were over a barrel. Silence fell inside the minibus. There was much to think about as Pat mumbled obscenities whilst becoming increasingly animated at the lack of support. Eventually, Captain Dunn broke the hush.

'Sir, he should bounce from my warning to yours. If he puts one more foot wrong, he can go in front of the College Commander having stepped through the required hoops. When he gets off the bus at Yeovilton, I will place him on a warning for failing to call the emergency number having not made the initial infiltration on time. This will leave you to place him onto a Company Commander's warning for failing to exit Willsworthy camp in a timely fashion during the bugout.'

Pat remonstrated louder: 'Bollocks! Don't play games with this fruit-bat. The contempt he displayed warrants discharge, not a warning.'

'OK, Sergeant Major, we hear you. In the interest of fair play, let's keep it to what can be proved. Place him on a Platoon Commander's Warning. On Monday, get him in for an interview with me. He can go onto a Company Commander's warning. If, during the interview, there is a hint of arrogance or contempt, he can go direct to the College Commander. James, anyone else you wish to discuss?'

'Erm, yes please. Lane, but he too was in Colour's group.'

'Wow – really! Are you two still talking, Colour?'

'Lane, Sir, has gone from bad to worse. Really, there is not even a glimmer of hope here. At best he is a disciple. At no stage has he offered himself as a potential leader. Worryingly, he is susceptible to feigning injury and illness.'

'That's fairly damning, Colour. OK, he goes on a Company Commander's warning Monday. Is that it for No. 2 Platoon, James? Anyone on the peripheries we should worry about?'

'Sir, there are fears over Barns and Packman. Barns is by far the worse of the two. He is jittery and nervous around the Staff and indecisive in command. His navigation needs constant encouragement. We have contemplated a Platoon Commander's warning previously; it may be time we do it.'

'Barns! Is he the really tall gangly chap?'

'Yes, Sir, a little anaemic-looking. Jet black hair.'

'Your business, James. But if he is truly indecisive, maybe he should go directly on to a Company Commander's warning. Places on the Commissioning Course are at a premium. If he is incapable of making a decision and we allow him to progress, we will have wasted a place. Give it a little more thought, please. We can discuss it further Monday if needed. Finally, who are your runners and riders for the Highland Trophy.'

Captain Dunn tapped his pencil nervously before he turned the page to show me a list of names. Moore, Francis and Mathews had been highlighted. Prising the pencil out of the boss' hand, I circled Mathews.

'No. 2 Platoon would like to nominate Mathews.'

'Good choice, James. Thank you. Let's move on to No. 1 Platoon.'

It was a struggle to stay awake as we discussed Paddy's lads. As the warmth of the minibus permeated through my body, the windburn throbbed horrifically, as did the chilblains and blisters. The heater on the minibus was on cold, but compared to what we had just endured, it felt more like being on the receiving end of a hairdryer. Fighting the snooze monster as Paddy and Captain Watts briefed the OC, nothing registered until they got to Watson. Captain Dunn and I listened intently as the OC of No. 1 Platoon repeated how Watson had a meltdown and refused to soldier. He just sat down and gave up. Captain Watts walked off several times, threatening to leave him to the beast of Dartmoor, but the boy didn't care. Eventually, he had to drag him to the emergency RV. This was welcome news to me. Not because he had failed the course, but because it was confirmation that our original assessment was right. We could relax, knowing it wasn't me or Captain Dunn holding Watson back or failing to identify the best route to development. It was vindication of our decision to send him to No. 1 Platoon. He would have sucked all the enthusiasm out of me, as well as robbing the others of their fair share of mentoring had he stayed much longer. The Army would be a better place without him; the course syllabus had done its job. Content, my eyes closed and before too long, the snooze monster had swallowed me whole.

Two hours later, we arrived at HMS *Heron*, better known as RNAS Yeovilton. It was used by Rowallan as yet another test of character and nerves. Amongst other duties, the training staff at HMS *Heron* were responsible for ensuring all pilots and aircrew were sea-journey worthy. This was achieved by teaching them how to survive an aviation crash on water. The 'dunker', as it was euphemistically known, was the cabin and cockpit of a Lynx helicopter dangled over a deep indoor swimming pool. The doors, windows, seats and restraints all functioned as they would do on a real helicopter. The hoist that controlled the actions of the aircraft shell was programmed to simulate crash conditions and replicate how the helicopter would react in water.

After the mandated safety brief, the DS showed the way by being first to take the plunge. We had all done this training before and enjoyed the opportunity to demonstrate our composure under crash conditions. The dunker had six set programmes. Firstly, it would drop onto the water and float. Next, it would drop and sink halfway. It continued to escalate the severity of crashing, until eventually it hit the water at full pelt and sunk to the bottom of the pool, turning and twisting all the way. If that was not scary enough, it was done in total darkness with all the windows and doors firmly shut. After each dunking, Pat would emerge first and shout at the Navy staff, telling them to make it tougher. He goaded them to increase the crash speed and spin it around under water for longer. Captain Dunn enjoyed the water, and on one particular occasion, just held his breath and sitting in the pilot's seat until the helicopter was dragged out of the water and back into the starting position.

The first ten students were dressed in pilot jumpsuits and helmets, briefed and ready to go. Amongst the first to take on the dunker were Packman, Danner, Murphy, Haigh and some of Paddy's boys. Haigh claimed the seat nearest the main door, so he could be the first out. This was met with a tired rebuke from Danner, who protested that his size warranted the seat closest to the exit. We watched as the helicopter carcass was populated, with doors and windows fixed in place, before gently ascending into the rafters. A deafening siren reverberated off the walls as the helicopter came splashing down on the water. But even before the body of the aircraft made contact with the surface, the main door window was kicked off its hinge and Haigh dived out. Shortly after, the rest of the occupants followed. The Navy staff gripped Haigh and lambasted him for failing to follow instructions. They explained that had there been turning rotors on the aircraft, he would have been decapitated.

They were sat back in the helicopter and winched high in the air, before the Lynx body was dropped again, just a little faster. As soon as it hit the water, Haigh was once again out before the helicopter stopped moving. This time, the Navy divers lost their cool at him. He was panicking, and this was causing alarm and despondency in the cab. For the next serial, he was placed on the rear bench, behind everyone else. By now the whole course had become aware of Haigh's troublesome behaviour, and watched with interest. With a large splash, the helicopter hit the water and immediately began to sink and rotate. There was a pause before the door was ejected, allowing the first student to appear, and it was astonishing to see that once again it was Haigh. We couldn't help laughing, knowing that for Haigh to be the first one to the surface, it must have been pandemonium under the water as he grappled with those in front of him. He must have released his four-point harness, jumped over the lateral bench and triggered the escape hatch, all before anyone else moved. The Navy divers were apoplectic with his behaviour, so for the next time, Haigh would be held in place until it was his turn to escape. This time they did just that. He came out last and was debriefed by the Navy divers. Thankfully, the divers had seen it all before and were well versed in dealing with those who panic underwater.

Similar results followed as each group of ten went through the drill. It was mostly uneventful until the last group undertook the task. Barns slowly slid into the water, but refused to board the airframe. Stricken by fear, he spiralled into a panic as the divers tried to encourage him onto the helicopter. With nearly everyone waiting to get dried and changed, the last thing they wanted was further delay. Barns was now receiving a barracking from all sides, which only exacerbated the problem as he became more vocal and physical with the divers. The DS had gathered to discuss what was happening, and the OC became irritated by Barns' failure to get in the helicopter.

'James, is that Barns?'

'Yes, Sir.'

'If he can't get in that helicopter, there is no point in him staying on the course! You can't serve in the armed forces if you have a fear of water or helicopters.'

A conversation broke out between the OC and the boss that edged closer to deciding to kick Barns off the course. It was heartbreaking to think he had come so far only to falter at such a simple exercise. Whilst the boss continued to debate what to do next, I slid into the water and swam to where Barns had latched on to the aircraft door. Squeezing between the two divers, my presence seemed to calm him down. I spoke quietly to him:

'Barns. Listen very carefully and focus on how serious this is. You have just worked your way onto a Platoon Commander's warning. Whatever happens next, that is the best outcome. From this point on, it can get worse. Alternatively, you can prevent the issue from snowballing. That's not what you wished to hear, but cast your mind back to the advice Colonel Streather gave you. You must focus on preventing things from getting worse. I'm here to tell you that unless you get in the aircraft, you will be kicked off the course by the time you get out of the water.'

My comments would make or break his next decision, but he had less than ten seconds to answer.

'We will get in the helicopter together and you can sit alongside me,' I continued. 'If Haigh can do this, you can. Let's go.'

Grabbing his hand, I peeled it backwards to release his grip on the edge. As he broke free, I moved my grip to the front of his jumpsuit, so it couldn't be seen by his peers. Slowly, we edged close to the seats and his fellow students pulled him into the cab. There was no room for me, but the divers inside the cabin had read my mind. The first diver fastened Barns' safety belt, whilst the other replaced the escape hatch and locked the door. Seconds later, the aircraft was lifted to the start point.

Sitting at the edge of the pool, we all watched as the first serial was executed. My heart raced as it hit the water and the door was flung off. If Barns freaked out, we would all see it and it wouldn't change the OC's mind. I liked Barns; he had truly developed into real officer material. He had passion and compassion in equal measure. If he appeared in my regiment, he would be a huge success. It was desperate to think this could be the end of the road for him. First out of the door was a diver, followed momentarily after by Boyle. Last out was Barns. Brilliant, I thought. Wow, he must have stayed calm. I kicked the water in joy as one of the Navy divers appeared from beneath my feet.

'How was my lad?' I asked. The diver laughed at me, wiping his face mask clear. The divers wore nothing more than a clear mask. It was too congested to wear breathing apparatus or fins. They were physically fit enough to hold their breath and work underwater until the airframe was lifted.

'The tall lad you mean?'

'Yeah, he was sat by the door, but he came out last.'

'He came out last because he had only undone half his four-point harness and got stuck in the door. The helicopter was on the way up by the time he got free. He will be fine on the next run. Now he knows he can hold his breath for as long as the helicopter is underwater, he could just sit still and not bother getting out.'

Barns got back in the body of the Lynx and finished the rest of the exercise without incident. He was within a hair's breadth of being kicked off the course, and secretly it was the best news of the week for me.

By the time we all arrived back at Sandhurst, most of the post-exercise work had been completed. The drive to Camberley via Yeovilton was made worse by the rush-hour traffic. Captain Dunn and Major Gray continued to debate the reason for carrying on with Stone and Lane. Their arguments were way beyond my understanding at the time. Later in life I would come to learn the complexity of managing defence as a business and the monetary cost of training and recruiting. At that time, however, my perspective was so localized that I couldn't care about the business; I just didn't want to see either Stone or Lane ever get close to wearing a Queen's Commission. It was frustrating for everyone, but the final decision was not going to change. No one would be kicked off the course at this stage, but we had prepared the ground for the removal of Stone and Lane, while Barns had worked his way to the forefront of everyone's concerns.

Chapter Ten

Calm Before the Storm

It was Monday morning, 0715hrs, and the weekend had flown by. The students had been left alone to recover from the week-long exercise. Deliberately, the DS stayed away from the accommodation, leaving the students to enjoy Saturday and Sunday to themselves. They had seen plenty of us over the past seventy-two hours, and most of that time had been spent working at high levels of intensity. For everyone's mental health, we needed to put some distance between each other. For the students, they were allowed out of the camp, and most had chosen to visit Tesco's and momentarily take in the hustle and bustle of life in the real world. For the DS, it was a weekend of enforced fun. The Academy Sergeant Major was retiring, and attending his leaving party was compulsory. Being stuck in Sandhurst for another weekend had its advantages. Come Sunday morning, all my personal administration was complete, allowing me the opportunity to remind myself that there was life outside of the gates.

There was little said during Monday morning's 'return to work' fitness session. A flat 10km run with Daz and his replacement ushered in the winds of change. The time had come for Daz to move to his next appointment – it was prudent he escaped the intensities of the Sandhurst gym. On Plain Jane, there was just a hint of fatigue creeping into his mannerisms. It may have been the fact he had been at the Academy for three years or something else, but he was losing the love for his job. There was venom in his criticisms that went beyond banter, and occasionally his flippancy was unhelpful. Having been forced to stay one extra year, he was blameless for the swing in attitude; he would be the first to admit that three years was one year too much. Standing in front of the students, who were dressed in red rugby shirts, green lightweight trousers and boots, he introduced everyone to their new Physical Training Instructor.

'Sadly, it's that time in my career to move on. This is my last run with you ugly bunch. But don't worry, I have with me my replacement. Staff Sergeant Heal has just successfully completed Corps selection and this is her first assignment as a fully-fledged member of the PT Corps.'

Paddy and I had met Tracy Heal at the Academy Sergeant Major's dining out on Saturday. She was approximately 5ft tall and a size eight dress: there was very little of her. Standing alongside the rest of the DS, she almost disappeared in the mass of bodies. It crossed my mind that she was not going to be capable of delivering the flavour of PT we had been used to under Daz. The intense, unforgiving and slightly masochistic but hugely beneficial physical punishments demanded a hands-on approach. Shivering in her brand-new singlet PT vest she had been awarded only days before, the DS glanced around with concern. For the Staff, PT sessions were becoming more enjoyable. The fitness standards of the students had increased to a reasonable level, and with the exception of a few, who still needed to lose or gain weight, we could all just concentrate on getting as much out of the session as we could. The emphasis on PT was set to take a change as we shifted from cardiovascular and fat-burning to endurance.

Running at a pace of 'six minutes a mile', the Company was stretched out over 500 metres as we arrived at the far end of Barossa training area. With 6km completed, the Jack Wagon received its first guest, and shortly after the floodgates opened. Danner, Stone and Lane all dropped out within a hundred metres of each other, along with a few of Paddy's boys. Daz didn't stop: this was his last run with the Company, and he was going to break as many of them as he could. As we turned around and started to head home, the pace was unrelenting as the students started to fall further behind, but we just kept going. It was a straight track all the way back to the rear gate, and everyone knew the route. By now there was no room on the Jack Wagon; if you didn't keep up, you were walking home.

For just the briefest of moments, we stopped while Daz and Pat took stock of who they had lost. There was a quick chat with the OC, then those who had kept pace with the leading group departed for the accommodation. Paddy and I hung around to make sure everyone had made it back onto the camp safely. We rounded up the stragglers and grouped them together before running them back to the Company lines, where Pat was waiting.

'Straight onto the Mean Machine, you fatties!'

There were at least fifteen students to put through the Mean Machine. Pat, both Platoon Commanders, me and Paddy all joined in. There was no shouting at the student; it was just encouragement and demonstrations. Their improvement was obvious. Although none of them could compete with the DS, at least they were capable of completing each exercise without breaking down between rotations. Whilst the Mean Machine session would benefit all who participated, it was truly nothing more than a demonstration for our new PTI, Sergeant Tracy Heal.

Showered, changed and sitting in the study hall, it was time for Platoon Commander's interviews, the first of which were for those receiving warnings. Barns was inconsolable, having been given a warning for failing to get into the helicopter dunker at Yeovilton without DS intervention. He felt he had overcome a major hurdle in conquering his fear of drowning, and maybe he was right to feel aggrieved. But conquering fear was not what Rowallan was after; not showing fear was what was needed. After he came out of Captain Dunn's office, it was evident his morale had taken a kicking and he needed further explanation. We sat on the wall outside the Mean Machine and discussed his performance to date. He had come a long way, but there was much more he could do to prepare himself for the Commissioning Course. Our conversation centred on making it to the next stage, with no mention of failure. It was pivotal that he understood that this was as much his safety net as it was ours. There is nothing like the fear of losing something to channel someone's energy and squeeze out every morsel of effort available. As he stood up and left, there was determination and desire oozing from every sweat gland on his gangly body. He probably thought my smirk was one of contempt, but in truth, it was a demonstration of confidence. Barns had what it takes – he just needed to realize it and feed on inner confidence.

Next to be marched in to see Captain Dunn was Stone, who smirked as he received the formal brief outside the Platoon Commander's door. Standing rigidly to attention, uniform pressed and starched to death, he seemed at ease with the procedure. It was proving harder to figure him out. Was this nervous energy or arrogance? Or didn't he care? Maybe he was just deluded? His self-assured persona was shallow, and he needed to see how perilous his position was. Standing in front of the Platoon Commander's desk, Captain Dunn reminded him that during Plain Jane he was verbally placed on a warning. This interview was official confirmation of that warning. It was explained that despite the records showing his censure was for failing to call the emergency number at an appropriate time, his conduct was below that expected of a Sandhurst student. Stone continued to smirk as he acknowledged the boss's words with a simple 'Yes, Sir'. His nonchalant response rattled the boss, which heightened the intensity of the next comment:

> 'Stone, you may feel you have a rite of passage through Sandhurst, but you are deluded. We are but a whisker away from kicking you out. You may have been told that you are too valuable to be rejected, but this is not the case! To help you understand how perilous your plight is, you are going to be placed on a Company Commander's warning after this interview. This means you are just one more indiscretion from discharge.'

Stone marched out with a changed expression; not one of disappointment, but of anger. It was becoming increasingly difficult for me to treat him fairly. There were few redeeming factors about Stone. He had received some fantastic tuition from the DS, but still thought this was just one big game. I marched him down to Pat's office in preparation for his interview with the OC, yet still there was no change in his demeanour. Standing quietly in the corridor waiting for the OC to arrive, he cut a forlorn figure.

Williams was next in line to see the Platoon Commander. He was already on a warning and this interview would review that status. His performance during Plain Jane left a lot to be desired. Since his arrival on the course, Williams had repeatedly been told to embrace the opportunity, but to date, he had failed to do so. He marched in to see Captain Dunn.

'Williams, at length we have discussed escalating your warning to the next stage. Your performance on the exercise fell short of the requirement to rescind the warning you are currently on. But, you will be relieved to learn, we are not putting you in front of the Company Commander. Have you anything you wish to say?'

'No, Sir. Other than to confirm I can perform much better. I am learning and getting fitter. The next exercise will allow me to prove myself, Sir.'

After letting Williams out, the boss called for me to come back into his office.

'Bloody hell, Colour! I wasn't expecting that!'

'Me neither, but it was a pleasant surprise. I thought he would crumble. He must have been fearing a Company Commander's warning, so it is understandable that he feels reprieved.'

Waiting outside Captain Dunn's office was Lane. Trousers only half-pressed, shaved, but not as close as he had been taught, he was looking defeated even before he received the news. It was a straightforward conversation. The Platoon Commander confirmed that Lane had no ill effects after his brief stay in the MRS after his fall from the Trainasium before discussing his poor performance on Plain Jane. For a brief moment, Lane debated his ranking within the platoon. He listed Packman, Williams and Francis as a few of the people who were performing worse. There was no holding back as he slated his peers. But when requested to explain his own lethargic approach to his duties, there was little defence on offer. Asked why he had failed to iron his uniform, he looked at the boss blankly before Captain Dunn thanked him for exemplifying the reason for recommending that he be placed on a Company Commander's warning. Lane saluted, turned about and marched down the corridor to the Company Commander's office.

There was just Haigh left. Nervously, he raised his eyebrows then smiled awkwardly. His arms moved from behind his back to his sides, then to the front. He was uncomfortable and agitated to the point of distraction as he marched in to see the Platoon Commander.

'Good morning, Haigh.'

'Good morning, Sir.'

'Why is it you find yourself in front of me today, Haigh?'

'Probably because you are going to kick me off the course or put me on a Company Commander's warning, Sir!'

'Interesting, Haigh. Why do you think that?'

'Firstly, everyone else that has come in here so far has been placed on a warning or gone to see Major Gray. Secondly, you have to fail at least one student a week so you can keep the pressure on everyone else on the course.'

'Wow! Wow! Do you believe that is the case, Haigh? Do you really think that people are sent home or fail the course just to massage our self-esteem?'

'Everyone does, Sir. The only reason Lane is still here is that students can't be thrown off the course if they are in the MRS. So that leaves me.'

Captain Dunn burst out laughing. He found Haigh's comments hilarious.

'Haigh, you do know I did this course ten years ago? Don't think I haven't heard every rumour and half-arsed story ever invented on Row-Co. God knows, most of them were invented by me. The Company Commander and I haven't been plucked from obscurity to be here. So yes, we can throw people off the course when they are in the Medical Centre, in fact, we did just that two weeks ago. And no, we don't have a target to kick people off so that we can maintain a reputation of being cold, heartless, merciless people. You're here to be taken off your Platoon Commander's warning, but having heard you pedal this pitiful wives' tale, maybe you should stay on it?'

Haigh struggled to find his words. He spluttered excuse after excuse before pleading his innocence. Had Captain Dunn not enjoyed Haigh's pathetic attempt to backtrack, he could have found himself on a warning for one more week.

The next two days were spent at Faraday Hall. There was no spare time between now and the end of the course. Every waking minute would be packed with busy activities, and this week was all about preparing for 'test week'. Concurrently, there was an air of nervousness as the rumours of a trip to Wales circulated. The academics were helping the students craft their essay submissions and individual leadership presentations. Whilst they had previously done similar tasks as a group, this was significantly different. During test week, students would need to impress a panel of senior officers and confirm they understood the fundamentals of leadership. It was the ideal time for the rest of the DS to prepare for the week ahead checking equipment and packing vehicles.

To the delight of the students, Wednesday's PT session was their first ever outdoor run wearing training shoes. Facing the familiar heavy black doors of the Academy gym, wearing white vests, blue shorts and Silver Shadow training shoes, there was a confident mood permeating the ranks. Murphy was smiling and whispering as we patiently waited for the new PTI to appear.

'What's funny, Murphy?'

'Nothing, Colour Sergeant.'

'Yes there is. You wouldn't have giggled and whispered if there wasn't. Are you a man or a mouse? Share your thoughts, big lad!'

'Things are looking up, Colour Sergeant. We are in training shoes, not boots. Staff Sergeant Dazzell has gone, and best of all we have got a lady PTI. I am thinking it's a really good start to the day.'

'Hold on to that thought, Murphy. Let's hear your thoughts when we return from this jolly.'

Sergeant Heal appeared on the doorstep of the gym. Standing on her tiptoes to see the heads of the students in the rear rank, she waved to the DS to acknowledge she was ready.

'Good morning, gentlemen. The syllabus requires you to undertake a 6km steady-state cross-country run. A gentle warm-up between here and the back gate, followed by an easy route through the firebreaks. It's dry underfoot so you should achieve a good strike. Regulate your breathing and stay close to me. Any questions? Bring your heels together and turn to face your right. By the left. Double march!'

Captain Dunn and the OC exchanged glances. It was a stark contrast to Daz: polite, pedestrian and far too nice to the students. Even Lane was smiling as we set off on the run.

Sergeant Heal brought the course to a halt just short of the training area. The back gate marked the start and finish point of the cross-country route, and as the sun's gentle rays warmed the northerly breeze, it appeared Murphy was right.

'Gentlemen. Move into two ranks. Keep pace with me. If you break ranks, we will do continuous loops until we are ready to crack on. Any final questions?'

The DS fidgeted at the rear of the Company as the students filtered from three ranks into two. This was looking more like the Commissioning Course with every passing minute, and for a few seconds we discussed Daz and missed his unorthodox style.

'By the left, double march.'

Tracy flew out of the blocks. She set a five-minute mile pace. Within 500 metres, the Company was strung out all the way down the road. The OC beamed a huge smile, as did Captain Watts and Dunn. We hit the first mile point at five minutes exactly, before she glanced rearward to see the course strung out in the distance.

'Jogging on the spot, begin!' Tracy paused her stopwatch.

'Turnabout!' Still jogging on the spot, the ten or so students that kept pace with her turned to face the way they had just come.

'Forward!'

At the same pace, we ran down the hill we had just run up. Every student we passed was instructed to join the rear of the Company. Only after we had collected the last student did we turn around and head back up the hill. At the start of the second mile, she paused proceedings.

> 'Gentlemen. Your first mile was eleven minutes and nine seconds as a Company. My mother could do better, and that's no joke. I am embarrassed for you. You should be ashamed. Greater effort on the second mile. There needs to be a dramatic improvement on this mile, or there will be punishments. All you have to do is keep pace with me. How hard could it be?'

Tracy set off at a fierce pace, and for the first time on the course, my pulse rate eased beyond its comfort zone. We were flying! At the 3km marker, she paused her watch, turned around and once again ran back to collect the stragglers.

If there were doubts over her credibility at the start of the run, they had vanished by the sixth kilometre. Not only was Tracy far fitter and faster than Daz, but she was also just as evil. Her words were few, but cutting. No threats of violence, no insults, just well-chosen words and punishments. She never smiled, never engaged in banter, she just ran hard. It was frightening! The students pulled themselves apart as they continued to do endless loops to pick up the weaker runners. Tracy never intervened. She left the students to insult each other and moan at the same old faces failing to keep pace.

'Keep up gentlemen. Stay level with me.' Every thirty seconds she glanced over her shoulder and repeated the requirement. Occasionally she stepped up the pace just to demonstrate to the fittest of the Company that at any stage, if she wanted to leave them behind, she could. Rideout challenged her in the last kilometre or so, but even he was left watching a clean pair of heels disappear into the distance. By the time we arrived at the finish point, we had covered 6km in forty-nine minutes. Given the stragglers, the size of the group and time spent doing press-ups, burpees and star jumps, this was impressive. Glancing at my watch, she had completed the session with twenty minutes to spare. The prospect of a leisurely shower before the next lesson seemed a fair reward for our efforts. But to the surprise of the DS, we returned through the gate and headed for the large hill behind the assault course.

At the base of the hill, the students caught their breath and focused on Tracy, who was perched on a fallen tree halfway up the hill. Psychologically, it was a masterstroke. Fifty minutes ago, the students looked upon a diminutive character, thinking life was a breeze. Now they were sweating profusely, craning at the neck and listening intently to what she had to say. Celtic overtones and pithy sentences hit the mark quickly. Standing victoriously in a commanding position, she was the double of Boudicca.

'We will finish off with a few hill reps. Again, keep up with my pace. If you beat my time you don't have to run again. Easy! Any questions?'

Tracy covered 50 uphill metres in fifteen seconds, and not even Captain Watts stood a chance of staying with her. Ten minutes felt like an hour as she thrashed every student, doing shuttles up and down the hill with no rest. With five minutes of the session left, she marched the Company back to the camp. Bang on time, she brought them to a halt outside the gym.

'Gentlemen. I am not sure what you have been doing for the last couple of weeks, but you are miles off the pace. Bring your 'A game' tomorrow. It would be nice if you could make it worth my while next time.'

With not so much as a wave, Tracy turned around, pushed open the heavy black doors and disappeared into the gym.

'Murphy!' I called out. 'Murphy, stick your hand up! Where's Murphy?'

Captain Dunn quietly pushed past a few of the DS so he could speak to me.

'I have sent him to the Medical Centre, Colour. It's just a precaution, but he was looking decisively ill after the hill reps. Oh, and Danner's with him.'

'Bloody hell, boss! Call Staff Sergeant Dazzell back. Sergeant Heal is just evil.'

For the first time during a PT session, the Directing Staff were dripping in sweat. It had been a thrashing for all involved, and Murphy's words would be ringing in his ears at the MRS. Tracy was an accomplished athlete in her own right. She held the record for the academy fitness test, which was eventually beaten by another Row-Co Instructor, Colour Sergeant Craig McBurney.

Friday witnessed the one and only deployment from Sandhurst everyone knew about in advance. Of greater interest, it was the only correlation between the course and the pamphlet the students received prior to their arrival. Adventure training week was the culmination of leadership and fitness training. During the week, students would have the opportunity to put into practice all they had been taught and test themselves in a less oppressive environment. Comfortable coaches and orderly kit checks paved the way for a leisurely trip to Capel Curig in North Wales. Peculiarly, the sun was making regular appearances as morale soared to an all-time high. And there was more good news to come for the students.

The long journey to North Wales took most of the day. After the routine camp administration issued by Pete and a discipline brief from Pat, it was time for Tracy to divulge the programme of events for the next seven days. There would be four days of single events, followed by a two-day expedition, known as Exercise Hiawatha. The evening of day six was ring-fenced for a Company barbecue and games night. As she flicked through her PowerPoint presentation, the students' smiles grew larger. Pictures of magnificent summit ascents and white-water rafting encouraged enthusiasm and engendered a real sense of belonging. She concluded with an explanation of Values-Based Leadership and the theory of adventurous training. Elegantly, Tracy dissected each activity into the building blocks of character development. She captivated the audience by explaining that stretching our goals beyond our reach was the route to discovering our failings and weaknesses. Only by knowing where we needed to improve, she stressed, could we start the process of knowing what to develop. She was a bright lady. We had misjudged her massively, and whilst she had quickly earned the respect of the students on the epic cross-country run, her value rocketed with this intellectual understanding of character development. Her last PowerPoint slide simply had a picture of the Coach and Horses pub and the words 'free Sausage & Chips 2100hrs every weekday'.

The first question came from Mathews. As he raised his hand, everyone knew what he was about to ask.

'Are we allowed out to the pub, Staff Sergeant?'

'Allowed out? It's vital you go out! Sitting in the Coach and Horses sharing your experiences is the best way to learn from each other. We insist you go. If you can't afford it, I urge those who can to take those who can't. Please do not misunderstand me. Every day will be physically tough, emotionally draining and most certainly dangerous. So, don't get hammered, but swapping stories of victory in the face of adversity is the best way of doubling your reward.'

Tracy articulated the point superbly. Teams bond best in adversity, and it was her job to ensure that the adversity was delivered in a controlled manner. One of the golden threads that bind the military brotherhood is mutual attainment. From the most junior member to the most senior commander, when every step of the way is shared, the value of success is amplified. Recalling the challenge in the comfort of a country pub, drying your socks by the open fire, face glowing with windburn and extremities tingling back to life as they thaw, is invaluable.

On Saturday morning, Captain Dunn and I had exchanged groups. It was pleasing to get respite from Stone and Lane, but the witty antics of Danner would be missed. Our first day was a beautiful walk up Tryfan. Stepping out of the minibus and staring up at the grey granite rock, it was hard not to recall my last encounter with this mountain. We would walk right past the very spot where the men fell as we headed to our first objective. The aim of this climb was to reach the famous stones known as Adam and Eve by midday, and gain the freedom of Tryfan by leaping between the two gigantic rocks. From the car park on the A5, the route would take us over Tryfan, then Glyder Fach, and finish by descending back to the A5 via the small lake of Llyn Idwal, a route of approximately 12km, or six hours' walking.

Boyle navigated to Adam and Eve. He struggled to interpret the contours and rocky outcrops, but had cleverly employed both King and Murphy to check-navigate. Two-thirds of the way up, we stopped at Cannon Rock to enjoy the stunning views back across the valley. Perching on the edge of this iconic tourist feature evoked an all-consuming feeling of adventurism. Even Packman stopped complaining as he nervously peered over the edge and into the valley below. He took a long pause before he raised his arms like a champion boxer and let out a huge victory cry. Although his celebration was premature by four-and-a-half hours, his cheer was warmly applauded by his peers. The experience had triggered his enthusiasm as he scrambled to the front of the group to engage in pleasant conversations and some gentle teasing about what lay ahead. Ego and bravado filled the air as the group discussed Adam and Eve. Tales of chivalry and heroics interjected with mythical dragons and the legend of King Arthur's sword fuelled their excitement. King stated he would be the first to jump, and an argument broke out over the right to go first. The childish dispute continued, right up until they saw the rocks for the first time. When they saw the enormity of the monolithic stones for the first time, their eagerness dampened.

'Are you doing it, Colour Sergeant?' Boyle asked.

'Values-Based Leadership, Boyle. If I don't do it, I wouldn't expect you to do it.'

The leap between the rocks is not so terrifying; it's the view that gets the pulse racing. Its ability to psych you out is unexplainable. Despite having done it several times previously, disco legs still make an appearance in the seconds before the leap. Although I was the first to make the jump, the adrenaline kept pumping around the body long after the rest of the group had successfully cleared the challenge.

Inevitably there would be one heart-stopping moment. Packman failed to make a clean jump and, for a second, the world stopped revolving. My mind's eye saw every conceivable outcome flash before me. He had taken several steps backwards to accommodate a run-up, but jumped too soon and failed to make the gap. Luckily, he fell between the stones and slipped to the ground without injury. For a moment we held our breath, until Packman swore and stood up, shaking his wrist and cursing the rock. With the fear of serious injury past, he was subjected to a merciless outburst of abuse by everyone. Despite his protestations, it was prudent not to let him have a second attempt. Instead, his reward for entertaining us with his pathetic attempt to jump the small gap was more navigation: a trip to Glyder Fach and on to the iconic tourist attraction we had come to see. After an hour, his sulking and complaining subsided as he peered over the false crest to be confronted by the remarkable sight of Cannon Rock.

The journey to this stage of the course had been gruelling. So much had been crammed into the weeks leading up to this moment, but only memories of misery existed. It all seemed fair penance for the privilege of walking through this inspiring Welsh valley to stand on the cantilevered stone. Staring at the sight below, the granite rocks fused with the lush green grass to illuminate the sides of the mountains. Ice-blue water mirrored the clear skies, and only the occasional bird could be heard in the valley below. Sitting on Cannon Rock, full of contentment, the group was applying the finishing touches to their male bonding. They were comfortable with each other's failings, a real sign of camaraderie amongst soldiers. We were achieving everything they previously thought impossible. Physically stronger, mentally more robust, a glance at this young group of men had me brimming with pride. With their legs dangling over the edge, they chatted about nothing in particular; they seemed to be consumed by the enormity of their surroundings.

The walk off the granite ridge and back down to rendezvous with the minibus provided more opportunities to take in the stunning scenery. We had been out for six hours and it felt like fifteen minutes. There were no complaints of tiredness, blisters or other aches and pains, just enjoyable banter and idle chat. Later in the evening, the DS visited the Coach and Horses to exchange stories and enjoy the wildly exaggerated interpretations of how Packman fell between Adam and Eve. As funny as we found it, Tracy issued a warning to everyone not to jump the stones on future expeditions. Tales of 'derring-do' filled the pub. The students slowly relaxed in our company, the youths showing off their exuberance. Occasionally there would be a brave encounter with the DS as a student would try to break into our inner circle. Their surreptitious visits were a charade to assess how much alcohol we were consuming. This was their barometer for gauging how difficult the following day's activities would be. Although they were not to know this for a few days, this was exactly what we wished them to do. Overtly, we solicited their approach and grasped every opportunity to explain that we were limited to two drinks due to the physical challenge of the day ahead. Critically, we would say to the students we would be able to enjoy a more social drink on the last day. It was a bait we knew the students would take.

Captain Dunn and I joined forces for day two as we took the platoon canoeing. The weather had flipped in a way that is only ever experienced in North Wales, and snow had settled across the land. We both loved the water. Several scuba diving qualifications gave me the confidence to enjoy every other water sport. We spent an hour at a time paddling around the students as they took instructions from Tracy, who was also an Army canoe instructor. Barns still suffered from his fear of water. It didn't help that his long legs made life in a canoe extremely uncomfortable. He quickly became acquainted with his 'Jesus Christ' handle on his splash deck when he started to roll. Whilst negotiating some slow rapids, his canoe rolled left and he ripped the splash deck off, thinking he was going under. Then, as quickly as it rolled, it righted itself and smashed bow-first into a stopper. The water ran over the top of his canoe and in through the cockpit. Seconds later he was swimming for the side as the boss and I retrieved his paddle and canoe. Five hours on the water had taken its toll and most students opted for an early night, skipping the opportunity for a cheeky beer.

Two days later, the platoon came together again for the two-day expedition. Following the Rhyd Ddu path, we would walk over Mount Snowdon on day one and sleep over at a Llanberis campsite. Day two would be an easier walk over Glyder Fawr, finishing off where Queen Guinevere reputedly raised Excalibur from Llyn Ogwen. However, shortly after we set off, the snow fell so heavily it became clear that our expedition was not going to follow the plan. Visibility was reduced to 50 metres, with blizzard conditions looking certain. Halfway up the Rhyd Ddu path, Captain Dunn took over the navigation as I moved to the rear of the group to ensure no one got lost. The true snowline was now difficult to identify. Two days ago there was no snowline at all, but now the whole area was covered. At 850ft, the Rhyd Ddu path merges with the Watkin path and we paused to check-navigate. We discussed the risk of continuing. Although the pace had been slow, and the students had not struggled, there would be a significant danger in continuing to the summit. Haramosh was at the forefront of my mind during our re-evaluation. Did we need to reach the summit of Snowdon to make this expedition successful?

With no ropes, ice picks or crampons, the sensible decision was to take the Watkins path down, but I sensed the boss wanted to crest the peak. With an increased sense of seriousness, we discussed the benefits of attempting the summit. Tentatively, we agreed to try to reach the top, but if we encountered packed snow or ice we would not look to traverse it; rather, we would turnabout and climb down. Sticking to the path was not as easy as it sounded. The beaten track had disappeared under a thick blanket of snow and there was an increased danger of being blown over the knife's edge by the strong northern wind. The final section before the peak was fraught with fear and angst. Williams, Witherspoon and Lane moved at a snail's pace. There was real worry in the voice of Lane. Moving so slowly, we would be separated from the main group. With conditions treacherous underfoot, he was beginning to panic with every slip. He was conscious of the precipice to the south and the craggy drop to the north. Keeping three points of contact with the rock at all times, he mumbled to himself as we edged closer to the end of the path. The voices in front of us had now disappeared and we were split from the main group. This was a good time to panic. I couldn't see what route the rest of the platoon had taken and wasn't sure that the boss had continued to the summit. Cursing and swearing to myself, I was seconds from taking emergency action by turning around to descend when an enormous chunk of electric blue sky swept over the mountain. It was a heavenly intervention. The trodden snow path was suddenly visible all the way to the false crest before the mountain railway station.

Lane walked in front of me, and it seemed like we were serenely enjoying a day out in the hills as we rejoined the platoon. At the top of Mount Snowdon, the skies cleared and visibility extended for miles. The disappointment of the closed cafe was overcome by the stunning scenery that greeted us as we stood at the cairn. The cloud in the valley had been blown seawards and the coastline was just visible. Had it not been for the horrendous wind that battered us from every angle, it would have been the perfect place to stop and have lunch. My old-school altimeter and barometer indicated a drop in pressure and the imminent arrival of a storm. After a short conversation with Captain Dunn, we agreed to get down as quickly as possible. Without further delay, we descended via the quickest route and made camp at Gwern Gof Isaf. An hour later, we were sitting in the pub half-naked, clothes hanging from the oak lintel over a roaring fire. Like one massive family at Christmas time, we swapped stories, joked and got to know each other a little better. Surprisingly, Stone was not drinking. Sitting on a moth-eaten velour chair next to a comfy leather long back I had made home, he kept trying to catch my eye. Eventually, he summoned the courage to ask for some advice. Despite appearing unflustered by being placed on a Company Commander's warning, the realization of his perilous situation had dawned on him. It was the first time Stone had opened his mouth and not irked me. Candidly, we spoke about his awful attitude, and he confessed it had been unacceptable. Although still lacking in sincerity, it caught me unawares. He was pressed on why it had been so poor. With no answer forthcoming, it was suggested that he thought he was indispensable, having done so well at Welbeck.

No punches were pulled as we revisited all the stunts Stone had tried. On several occasions, he was close to breaking Daz and the Sergeant Major. We recalled the times both had been taken to the brink of violence. We also revisited the times his peers had threatened him. Disturbingly, he had been subjected to more than we had realized. It was hard to have sympathy for Stone. He was clearly very bright and wanted to be in the military, but leadership and command are not about intelligence alone. If he was to get through the course, there would need to be a dramatic improvement in his overall view on life. He quizzed me on the likelihood of him failing, his eyes welling up. The answer of 'highly likely' hit home. It was potentially the most productive thirty minutes we had spent in each other's company. He was given three simple things to address immediately, and even then, passing the course would be tight: try harder, contribute positively or not at all, and stop being selfish. Stone gathered his warm kit from around the fire and headed for the campsite, leaving me to contemplate a change in my attitude towards him. Maybe there was a glimpse of potential.

The predicted storm lasted no more than six hours. As dawn broke, fresh snow had covered our tracks and the massive drop in temperature created numerous ice zones. Captain Dunn and I sat around our boiling kettle, poring over the map looking for an alternative route. It was too dangerous to go over the top of Glyder Fawr; the packed ice would be lethal to our ill-prepared group. Instead, we would pass through the saddle to the north of the Glyders. With clear skies, mountains coated in sparkling white snow, we set a course for home. The cold temperatures quickly sapped the energy out of the platoon. Before we hit the plateau between the peaks, we had already stopped twice for a tea break. By lunchtime, we had experienced all four seasons. At one stage, we had removed jackets as we navigated the sun-trapped saddle. No sooner had we reached the shadow of the mountain, the sun had gone and sleet arrived with a vengeance. With four hours of walking still ahead of us, it was going to be a long day.

It was our last night at Capel Curig. Pete issued his instructions for the students to pack all their surplus equipment and place it on the baggage truck. Corporal Davis issued weekend leave passes before Pat briefed the students on the final night's activities. No adventurous training week would be complete without the obligatory barbecue, and despite the obvious weather challenges, we would eat something close to summer food. To cap off a week of fun, each platoon was to provide some form of entertainment by performing a short play. The venue would be the Coach and Horses, and curtain-up would be 2000hrs. Pat selected Boyle from No. 2 Platoon to take charge of our play, and he was given directions on acceptable levels of mickey-taking. In order to make it funny and entertaining, Pat announced that he and the OC would judge the plays and that it was part of the inter-platoon competition.

The end-of-exercise party was in full flow when No. 1 Platoon delivered their play-let. The fact it was a competition had focused their efforts, and they had drafted two-thirds of their strength to contribute. Typically, it was aimed at mimicking DS characteristics and behaviour. Students played the part of Captain Watts and Paddy during a platoon competition. With expert performances, they had mastered the mannerisms of Paddy and the excitable nature of Captain Watts. The play refashioned numerous stories since the start of the course. There was no denying the admiration the students had for both Captain Watts and Paddy. They were both held in high regard, a warm affection shining through the performance. A series of scenes saw gentle teasing of Paddy's desire to interfere in command tasks and tell students how to do it. The room was bursting at the seams with laughter as they reconstructed the infamous Exercise Klondike car saga. Even my students found it hilarious, but I couldn't help suspecting there was more than a trace of truth in what was being said. In the grand scheme of things, it didn't matter; we had our own styles and we just needed to work with it.

Captain Dunn and I braced ourselves for the legitimized abuse we were about to receive. Similar to No. 1 Platoon, our students played out a number of competitions and exercises, with Boyle imitating me and Danner playing the boss. Then they introduced students to play the role of those who had failed to remain on the course. To rapturous applause, Hays (played by Stone) made a reappearance. He fell onto the stage, fell off a chair and fell out of the door, crying almost the whole time. Every thirty seconds, Boyle would produce a map from his pocket, hit someone on the head with it and say 'Softlad, you're sacked.' Meanwhile, Danner wandered around the pub with a stupefied grin, continually repeating 'alright fellas', much to Captain Dunn's amusement. The final instalment saw the platoon erect a tent and recreate the infamous 'Horror Box' challenge game we had invented during Plain Jane. Vengeance being a dish best served cold, they called for two members of the audience to participate, and, encouraged by the rest of the platoon, Captain Dunn and I duly obliged.

'The Horror Box challenge is a game of skill and observation,' Mathews explained to the rest of the audience. 'In one box we have a Ritz dining experience. In the other, an experience to forget. Watch and see, look!'

Mathews was tipsy. Slurring his words and mixing his metaphors, he couldn't keep a straight face as he fondled inside the first box to show the audience its contents. Like the magical carpetbag belonging to Mary Poppins, there was no end to the stuff he pulled out of the small white cardboard lunchbox: two bottles of champagne, two jars of caviar, two cans of Heineken lager and a bag of cheese and onion crisps, 'because the Colour Sergeant wasn't posh enough to drink champagne and appreciate fish eggs', he claimed. There was also a radio, soft toilet rolls and some dubious reading material. In the second box were empty crisp packets and coke cans. As Mathews rotated the boxes, he forgot which one was which. Painfully, it took him three attempts before he eventually got us to pick the right box so he could deny us the luxury items. He gave out the champagne to the audience and enjoyed handing me the empty coke can. We took it on the chin, even giving him a round of applause at the end. The night could not have gone better. It was a side-splitting hour of 'close to the bone' fun-poking and frolicking.

But if the students thought this would be it, there was more to come. Knowing that the DS would be slaughtered, the Staff had prepared their own play-let. Pete and Corporal Jarvis played the role of students failing to keep up on a platoon run. Then they re-enacted a Company Commander's warning, with the OC and Pat playing themselves. It all failed excruciatingly, and the students were damning in their criticism. The only laughs came from the DS as the truth got in the way of the fiction. Sensing the audience had been lost, Pat brought an end to proceedings and, to raucous cries of 'fix!', declared the DS had won the competition. Of course, there was never going to be points awarded for mastering jazz hands on a course like Row-Co! It was just another ruse to heighten performance levels and effort.

Boyle weaved through the crowd to assess our reaction to their skit. Mathews, in tow, offered to buy us both a drink. But this was no ordinary offer: this was to gauge how much we were drinking, to see how safe it was for him to overindulge. The theory was that if the Colour Sergeant had a lot to drink, there would be no way the DS could spring a surprise in the morning. With a knowing smile, we accepted the drink, and the next three thereafter. The more beer the students had, the braver they became. By 2300hrs, we were surrounded by students who were obstinately asking questions and offering opinions. Mathews and Danner were pushing hard for answers.

'Colour Sergeant, I heard there was going to be a bugout this weekend. Is it the night we get back or on Monday morning?'

'Danner,' I replied. 'This is adventure training. Everything is planned in advance. Areas booked, agencies informed. Routes submitted. Coaches paid for! It is a deliberate operation. We must conform to the regulations and we have done just this. You have a leave pass signed for the weekend – what does that tell you? Come on, figure it out yourself, softlad!'

Boyle jumped in.

'It tells me that we are getting bugged out when we get back to camp, Colour Sergeant.'

'I promise, you will not get bugged out as we get back to Sandbags. Just enjoy the moment. Stop worrying about the next bugout and chill.'

Captain Dunn was well on his way to being giggly, as was I. The students revelled in the moment, and if there was any lingering suspicion that we were planning a surprise, it disappeared as the OC called for everyone's attention.

'Everyone listen in. Listen in. Hush! Hush!'

A little worse for wear, he called out above the din, 'There is a problem with the coaches tomorrow. They won't get here until late in the morning or early afternoon. You can stay in your rooms until after breakfast. Enjoy the rest of the night. DS, you can have a lay in.'

The cheers could be heard in Merthyr Tydfil as Captain Dunn cheered and asked whose round it was next.

From nowhere, one of Paddy's students produced a guitar. He sat in the corner with Moore, Francis, Witherspoon and Rideout, frantically scribbling and strumming. After twenty minutes they took centre stage, where Boyle was playing master of ceremonies.

'For one night only. By popular demand. No expense spared. Please put your hands together for Row-Aces!'

Like the good old days in the Liverpool Cavern, everyone – including bar staff and random visitors – squeezed into the small function room. Adamson from

No. 1 Platoon strummed the cords to *Wonderwall* by Oasis and the whole course broke out into song. Cunningly, they had altered the words to reflect their days at Sandhurst. Renaming the song *Row-Co Wall*, the changed words were well-chosen and poignant:

> 'Today's going to be the day they are going to bug us out at two.
> 'By now you should've somehow realized what they're going to do.
> 'I don't believe that anybody feels the pain we do, I bet you now.
> 'Backbeat, the word is on the street that Major Gray is drinking stout.
> 'I am sure you heard it all before but you never really had a doubt.
> 'And all the roads they make me run are winding.
> 'And all the blokes that lead me there are blinding.
> 'There are many things that I'd like to say to you, but I am not that brave.
> 'Cos maybe, you're going to be the one to save me.
> 'And after all.
> 'You're my Row-Co Wall!'

Their impromptu rendition of the Oasis classic tune could not have been better. They sang it over and over until they were hoarse, dancing, singing and making up new words whenever the chorus came around. By the end of the night, the whole pub was joining in with the chorus, bar staff and all. Crashing down on the green plastic mattress in our poky little room, Captain Dunn giggled, 'Mission achieved methinks, Colour. Mission achieved.'

Chapter Eleven

Exercise Red Light

Eddie and Pete sneaked around our room with several cups of strong black coffee. Waking the DS one by one, they shoved the pungent antidote into our hands and whispered, 'it's time'. From bed to bed, Eddie and Pete gently repeated the process until we were all out of our beds. Pat walked up and down demanding, 'No light, no light, keep it black! Don't switch on your torch. No noise. Keep movement to a minimum.'

We had been asleep for less than two hours, and this was the start of Exercise Red Light, one of the most revered exercises in the Academy, if not the whole military. An unbridled assessment of resolve, initiative, enterprise, determination and British doggedness, the exercise brought shivers down the spines of all who knew of its existence.

Eddie, who had not participated in the party, along with Pete, who had attended but was teetotal, secretly watched as all the students returned to camp. Once they had been in bed for approximately four hours, Pete roused the Directing Staff so we could set the conditions for the start of the exercise. Firstly, we established search rooms to sanitize the students' personal belongings. Then we set out holding pens and conditioning cells so we could manage individual movement. Finally, we arranged briefing rooms, back brief rooms and a control room where we could synchronize the exercise's implementation and deployment. It all had to be done when the students couldn't see and wouldn't suspect what was about to happen. Had we done anything remotely suspicious, the exercise would have failed even before it started. Operational security was Pat's business as he crosschecked the arrangements, then checked them again and again. This particular part of the exercise was the most vulnerable – if something was to go wrong, it would be here. He counted the escape packs twice, the nominal rolls twice and then counted the Staff twice. This exercise had a history of mishaps, and he was keen to prevent any from being attributable to him. Once he was ready, he nodded at Eddie and said, 'Red Light on.'

'Bugout! Bugout!' Rattling mess tins and ringing manual fire alarms, the DS raced through the billet to wake the slumbering students.

'What? Who said "bugout"?' slurred Danner.

'I did, you big lump! Now get out of your sack and bugout.'

'Well hold on, Colour Sergeant. This is hardly fair. We are all slightly pie-eyed after a fabulous evening. Surely you can't be allowed to make such unreasonable demands. Can't these shenanigans wait until sunrise?'

'I'll forget you said that, Danner, and put it down to the beer talking. Final warning! Get yourself outside. Now!'

Danner stumbled out of his bed as he continued to complain, whilst Witherspoon started to pack his bag.

'Stop packing. Get dressed into your suits and get outside. You just need to be dressed in your best clothes. Nothing else.'

Murphy was in disarray. Hair standing on end, face rubberized and folded with pillow marks, he was still suffering the effects of too much alcohol.

'Do I need my rabbit, Colour Sergeant?'

'What? Did you bring a rabbit?'

'I don't know, Colour Sergeant. I'm not sure. Is it Friday?'

'Fuck me, Murphy, wake up! You are talking gibberish, and if you pull a rabbit out of your bag I will freak out. Get dressed. Get outside.' Murphy pulled on his trousers and searched through his bags for a shirt. It was surreal watching him fumble around his bed space trying to coordinate his movements and stay upright at the same time. It was as close as you could get to a Charlie Chaplin film.

For thirty minutes, chaos rained down from all angles. Norris was still wrestling with the concept of a 'bugout'. He grabbed as much as he could carry before running off into the nearby woodland. Running so deep into the forest, it took me fifteen minutes to locate him. Getting out of the wood was not as easy as getting in. Stumbling over leaf-fall, walking into branches, we both exited with cuts, scratches and bruises from our repeated tumbles.

'What were you thinking, Norris?'

'I don't know, Colour Sergeant. It spooked me. I wasn't sure what to do! Why do you have to do that? Really, is there a need to come crashing through the billet like a man possessed? Banging mess tins and shouting, you nearly gave me a heart attack.'

It was possibly the slowest bugout to date. Considering the students needed only to get dressed and move to the holding pen, it took forty minutes before we could start the next stage.

Major Gray surveyed the room before issuing the exercise instructions:

'When the Sergeant Major calls your name, you are to come forward and collect a brown envelope. Inside, you will find an instruction that invites you to complete ten extraordinary tasks. These tasks are a test of your resolve, intelligence, initiative and determination to succeed. Read them in detail. Make your plan and decide how you are going to achieve them. Once we are content and you are in a fit state to leave Capel Curig, you will be driven somewhere in Wales and dropped off. From there on in, you are on your own. Figure out your location, get yourself orientated and achieve as many of the tasks as you can! Return to Sandhurst at exactly 0900hrs on Monday morning and not before. Your written instructions explain all the rules. Importantly, this is an individual task. There is a small card in the envelope with emergency contact numbers should you need help, so do not contact your family or friends during the exercise. Nor are you to break any rules of civilian law. You will not be given leniency should you break the law in the name of the exercise. Nor should you make a nuisance of yourself. Finally, on Monday afternoon you will be delivering a presentation on those tasks you achieved. It must be accompanied by evidence. As proof of accomplishment, we will accept photographs, signed letters and physical items that can only be obtained from the location you have visited. Does anyone need clarification on anything you have just heard? Good. In which case, Sergeant Major, take them away.'

Pat divided the course into four groups and sent them into search rooms. During the process, he whittled out anyone he thought had taken too much alcohol on board. This small group were held on camp until deemed fit enough to travel. Everything but the envelope was removed from the students. They were allowed to keep their wallets with £10 and any personal effects such as photos or identity cards. All credit cards, cash point cards and other useful items were removed. Dressed in suits, reminiscent of a scene from *The Great Escape*, the students were smuggled into the rear of several trucks and vans before being dispersed to all four corners of Wales. Each vehicle was driven for a few hours in random directions to buy the student sufficient time to sober up – one north, one south, and the remaining to the east and west. Students were dropped off in villages, towns and cities, with no two students within a 10-mile radius of each other. Despatching students into the cold morning dawn had a sobering effect. Whilst there is no doubt that there would have been a number of headaches as they stepped off the vehicle, apart from those held back, they would have all been sufficiently sober to undertake the task. By 0700hrs that morning, all the students had been released and would be deciphering the instructions, thinking how the bloody hell any of it could be achieved.

Tasks varied from person to person. A weaker student was given a less ambitious task sheet, allowing him a good chance of success. Conversely, the overconfident characters were given the near impossible to achieve. If the students applied a degree of effort, Exercise Red Light would reinforce success and build a different flavour of self-belief and confidence. The exercise sought to achieve a unique blend of military leadership and streetwise enterprise that would exploit human nature, conformance and survival. Much of this would only be realized if students were kept from visiting their previous social environments. To prevent this, those who lived in the north were given tasks in the south, and vice-versa, although it was hard to prevent contact in totality. Completing tasks was made more complicated by removing access to money and forbidding access to family and friends, but when the chips were down we knew that's what they would do; the trick was not to get caught.

During Red Light it wasn't uncommon for students to get into trouble, as they sometimes misjudged their authority to pursue completion of a task. This was the key reason for ensuring they departed well-dressed and not looking like a vagrant. Their only hope of being protected from prosecution came in the form of a letter addressed to the police. If someone found themselves in trouble with the authorities, the students could hand over the document explaining that they were Officer Cadets from Sandhurst on an authorized initiative exercise. Along with our telephone number, the letter also included a request not to help the student any further!

With the camp abandoned, we set about gathering the personal belongings of our platoons. All items were placed into large clear bin bags and marked with the students' names so we could place them back in their rooms at Sandhurst. For most of the Directing Staff, the week was complete. Eddie was back in Camberley manning the operations room, ready to deal with all the problems associated with this style of exercise. For the remaining Staff, it was the last free day before the end of the course.

The Monday morning offered a leisurely start for the Staff. With the students banned from camp until 0900hrs, most of the Staff stayed away until one hour before. Eddie had run the operation all weekend and was kept busy with phone calls and inquiries from all around the country.

'Any of my guys get into trouble, Ed?' I asked.

'Yes, of course they did. Danner, Francis and Witherspoon. There were a few calls for other members of the platoon, but it was niff-naff and trivia.'

'Anything we need to worry about?'

'Erm, oh yes! Pat is on the phone to Thames Valley Police dealing with an incident involving Danner, but it's best he explains. Oh, and there are ten faxes in your pigeon hole from Haigh!'

Pat was nowhere to be seen. He was clearly busy with an issue that had now escalated to the new Academy Sergeant Major.

Looking like they had just returned from a wedding reception that went on through the night, at exactly 0900hrs on Monday morning, all the students dutifully walked through the front gates of Sandhurst. Bedraggled and baggy-eyed, they marched proudly to the front doors of the accommodation, as instructed in their written orders. Eddie counted the students in and issued them the simple instruction to change into their red rugby tops in preparation for fitness. Tracy had organized a special event to welcome the students back to camp; as usual, it revolved around water obstacles.

Menacingly, sitting on the grass in front of the Royal Memorial Chapel were four enormous logs. Tracy drilled the students in log fitness.

'Pick up the log. Up-down, up-down. Place the log on the floor. Pick up the log. Raise it up over your head. Hold, hold, hold. Down! Up-down, up-down!'

The intensity of the exercise was exhausting, but this was just the warm-up. The students were sweating profusely well before we started the PT session. With five men on each log, Tracy issued her final safety instructions. Carrying a 15ft, 200lb dead weight is tricky at the best of times, but Tracy intended to race these logs around the camp. With the logs resting on their shoulders, the students began to run out towards the sports pitches. The continual bouncing of the log shed splinters every time it bashed against the shoulder. A heavy dose of creosote rubbed up against the open sweat glands, administering a toxic coating to the chafed skin. But the splinters and creosote burns were little more than an irritation compared to the demanding cardiovascular output that quickly numbed the legs, arms, heart and lungs. This was their first organized fitness for over a week. Despite walking through the hills of Wales being physically demanding, it seldom had the heartbeat over 110 bpm. Tracy showed no sympathy as she demanded a fast pace, accompanied by the familiar hounding from the Directing Staff.

After twenty minutes of non-stop running, we arrived at the first water catchment outside Academy HQ. Tracy waded through it several times, with the students and DS following in her wake. She went out of one lake and into another, causing the logs to become virtually impossible to hold. After forty minutes of battling with the logs, the Company arrived at a wide gap in one of the deepest lakes of the Academy, where Eddie had positioned an A-frame building kit, with ropes, poles, clamps and pulley wheels – sufficient equipment for the students to make a large rope bridge. The fitness session had paused for a command task. All students and their logs had to cross the gap using the rope bridge, which each platoon needed to build. Only one person was allowed in the water; after that, everyone and everything needed to remain dry, including the logs. Against the clock, they had twenty minutes to achieve the task. For every minute they were late, they would be given a yellow burden to take on the rest of the run. The sight of the dreaded large yellow boxes on the far bank generated a sense of urgency and desperation to succeed.

The reasons for such a punishing physical exercise straight after returning from the weekend is well understood by the experienced leader. Primarily, it is to re-establish authority and good order or to prevent complacency. In addition, on this occasion, we added a command task so both platoons could set the conditions for the College Commander to take a sneak preview at the men we thought would compete for top student. For our platoon, the main nomination was Mathews. He stood the best chance of winning the coveted Highland Trophy. Dynamic, with a genuine passion for people, his personality oozed 'leader-in-the-making'. His adversary in Paddy's platoon, Staples, was an old-style charismatic leader, but truly idle and unwilling to get his hands dirty, not to mention being only half as fit as Mathews. If there was a concern with this two-horse race, it was that the impressive charisma Staples possessed masked his lack of leadership, but there was a chance he could fool the College Commander.

The military has its fair share of charismatic leaders. They are fabulously entertaining and socially intoxicating. They succeed through powers of persuasion and seek to grow their support by dividing and conquering. Frequently there is a trail of destruction in their wake, but the most disturbing characteristic of the charismatic leader is that they can be incredibly successful. This success is built on convincing people through passion and conviction, and no matter how barking mad their thoughts are, people trust and believe in the charismatic leader. History records a succession of cult leaders as charismatic. Just before assuming the role of an instructor at Sandhurst, my military education teacher tasked me to write an essay on flawed leadership. As my subject, I chose David Koresh and his Davidians, mainly because there was a global fascination with the disaster at Waco and the world's media had produced reams of information on the inner circle of the cult and its leadership. Koresh was charming, tall and good looking. He had convinced well-educated men and women to join him in a death pact using charismatic leadership. It had dawned on me that if a man could convince seventy-five people to kill themselves for such a warped belief, what could he do with a half-convincing argument and an army? Whilst we now categorize charisma as a characteristic of leadership and not a type, it remains a threat to the good order of any hierarchical industry. Binding various types of leadership and their differing characteristics into one that is compatible with a complex and multifaceted job, such as commanding a brigade of soldiers, will always be susceptible to setting the conditions for charisma to out-compete true leadership.

Both Mathews and his opposite number, Staples, were given the task of commanding the bridge across the lake. The event was orchestrated so the College Commander was present for their opening briefs. Mathews knew little about constructing A-frames, but Stone was an award-winning Welbecksian who had excelled in engineering. If only Stone's stinking attitude could be harnessed, he would be a real asset during this task. We could see Mathews go through the process of distributing tasks. His mind clunked like a naked grandfather clock as he stalled his announcement of chief of staff. He was buying himself time so he could analyse the risk of trusting Stone. Then, with a killer stare, Mathews put him in charge of building the bridge, placing Danner alongside him as a semi-quasi commander, tasked with ensuring Stone didn't slouch and the team worked hard for him. Stone thought through the task and took an age to come up with a solution. For a while, it looked as if he was deliberately idling. Mathews was becoming agitated at the sight of No. 1 Platoon's building activity. Just before he let loose on Stone, the young Welbecksian quickly made several large prusik knots and tied them on the rope at intervals of 3ft. With the help of Danner, they stretched the rope across the lake and high into the air on the A-frame. Paddy's boys had their bridge erected in quick time, and we could see the College Commander was impressed by the decisive leadership Staples demonstrated.

With the race nearing its climax, both platoons just needed to get their logs across the bridge. No. 1 Platoon was the first to attempt to carry their first log across the gap. They had constructed a hybrid version of the classic Burma bridge, with a top rope used as a bannister rail. They fought frantically against the laws of gravity as they tried to walk the log over the top of their rope bridge. The physics of the flimsy rope construction and weight of the log inevitably resulted in an almighty splash as the heavy pole toppled from its precarious height. At a slower pace, but unquestionably more successful, Mathews watched as his logs were threaded through the prusiks that dangled below the bridge. An ingenious technique saw men and logs cross the gap with three minutes to spare. So impressed was the College Commander that he clapped as Stone crossed the bridge last. It was the rarest of moments to see such a sombre character overtly show his pleasure.

'Stone. Wasn't he one of your risk candidates, James?' the College Commander asked whilst still wiping his nose.

'Yes, Sir, he still is.'

'Good. It looks like you are getting the best out of him. Good show. Well done.'

While the platoons tidied up the equipment, the College Commander took the opportunity to talk to the Staff about the students in danger of failing. This time I kept my mouth closed and let Captain Dunn do all the talking. It all appeared to be well received until the College Commander asked me to take a short walk with him. With his hand on my shoulder, we moved 20 yards away to get out of earshot of everyone else.

'Colour Sergeant, how are you getting on here at Sandhurst?' It was a peculiar question, and one that caught me off-guard.

'I like my job. I try hard. I keep myself to myself. There is little more to add, Sir. If you are worried that my part-time job as a youth worker is interfering with my work, I can give it up!'

'No, Colour, I am pleased you are working in the community. You are winning high praise from Woking Town Council. I wanted you to know you have the uncanny ability to upset the Foot Guards. Are you aware of this?'

It was hard to answer the question. The previous Academy Sergeant Major didn't like me, but there were others who suffered that ignominy. The new

Academy Sergeant Major hadn't even met me – if there was a conspiracy forming, it would be news to me.

'Sir, possibly my lack of love for wearing service dress, or marching up and down the drill square has sometimes irked certain quarters of the Foot Guards, but it's not intentional. I am even scruffy naked, so I know there will be Guardsmen who don't like me. But in my defence, some of my best friends are in the Foot Guards!'

'Good. As long as you have identified all this. You need to be more tactful when it is required. But it is imperative you are not deterred by what I have said; just find a solution for doing it in a different way or you are in for a bumpy ride, Colour. You are an easy target for reproach, which detracts from your good work. Sadly, people will not appreciate you until it is too late. By the way, well done getting Stone back on track. Tricky young man.'

The Colonel smiled and winked at me as he walked away. From being elated to being utterly deflated in a heartbeat, my thoughts spiralled out of control. He left me unsure whether he agreed or disagreed with me. Analysing his words, trying to pick up on the hidden meaning, my brain was beginning to cook. Where did that conversation come from, and more importantly, why did he feel the need to say that to me? Did he dislike me, or was he wishing to get rid of me? Failing to find a hidden meaning, my only option was to share the conversation with Captain Dunn in a hope he could decipher what was said.

'Colour, he doesn't dislike you,' Captain Dunn said. 'It's not so much what he said, but more what he didn't say. If he had thought that you had a difficult manner, he would tell you. There have been rumours that he sacked a Colour Sergeant for blasphemy, although it is only hearsay. If you had upset him, you would know. Trust me, you have nothing to worry about. If anything, he is trying to protect you from unwarranted criticism.'

Following quietly behind the students, we continued to walk for a while before I broke the silence.

'He said that I had upset the Foot Guards.' Captain Dunn nearly burst into tears laughing at me.

'Come on, Colour! Get real. You ride around on a mountain bike to avoid carrying a pace stick! You run around the camp in your sports kit to avoid wearing a jacket and tie! You are the only Sandhurst Colour Sergeant Instructor in the history of the Academy who ever dared coach the cadets football team. And if that didn't upset the Guards, you then have the audacity to take them to watch football at Wembley. Maybe if it wasn't done at the expense of not going to functions in the Warrant Officers' and Sergeants' Mess, they wouldn't be so offended! You draw criticism quicker than you draw your pay.'

'By Christ, boss, that hurt! You make me sound like a maverick!'

'That's not what I mean, and you know it's not! You are different from the archetypal Sandhurst instructor, and that will rattle cages. People don't like different, you know that! Hey, you are the leading edge of change. The College Commander wishes to reform the instructor cohort by ushering in the new breed of Colour Sergeant. The Guards are brilliant at what they do, but they are an institution in their own right. The Guards have run Sandhurst since time immemorial, and you will be seen as a threat to this stronghold. The College Commander is a wise man. He knows change is uncomfortable. Don't think the man delivering bad news is your enemy, and don't think the man promising salvation is your ally.'

Still carrying the logs, the Company walked back to the accommodation. It had been a hard morning for all concerned, including the Staff. Mathews had done well; we had great hope for his chances of winning the Highland Trophy. There was a purpose in his every action, but it was his emotional intelligence that separated him from everyone else. Selecting Stone to build the bridge was genius and brave in the same breath. We knew he was a Welbeck prodigy, we just hadn't been able to get the best out of him – but Mathews did. However, it was the employment of Danner as an enforcer that proved his leadership qualities. Mathews displayed a fantastic understanding of his human terrain. Whether he knew it or not, he had just impressed all the Staff, not just the College Commander. Inadvertently, he had just thrown Stone a lifeline that could change the final outcome for this socially awkward character. Quietly, it was heartwarming to watch Stone respond so well to all we discussed in Wales. With this week being our last in camp, the majority of the time would be dedicated to testing and assessing how well students had assimilated information. This would start with a test of verbal communications, a forty-minute presentation by students examining their own performance during Exercise Red Light. They had to demonstrate analysis supporting their Scheme of Manoeuvre and link their assessments to prove their success. For tasks that went uncompleted, the student was told to identify valuable lessons he had learnt during his failure to succeed.

Rideout was the first to present his Exercise Red Light presentation. Standing in front of his peers, there was no sign of the nerves that once plagued him. His demeanour had changed: steely-eyed, focused and no hint of the old Rideout, this new-found confidence brought a smile to my face. Physically, the young man had filled out around the chest and arms. He was beginning to fit the part of potential officer. Spread out on the table was a raft of documentary evidence and pictures that explained how he attempted his tasks, of which he had to complete eleven out of fifteen. Having been dropped off in the pouring rain somewhere near Anglesey, he decided to take shelter until the sun came up and people started heading to work. Rideout went on to explain:

'I read my task sheet a hundred times, each time thinking, "I must be dreaming, who makes this crap up?" It was just bewildering. My tasks were: score a goal on a Premiership football ground; milk a goat; appear on foreign soil; appear on stage in the West End; work for a charity; swim with dolphins; interview a lady performer; interview an overseas harbour master; appear at a height of over 3,000 ft; drive a car worth £100,000; open the door for a famous person; serve food at a famous restaurant; ride on a fire engine or locomotive; appear in an article for a Fleet Street newspaper or on a TV programme; sketch Hampton Court; and have tea with a Chelsea Pensioner. There were sixteen tasks in total on the list. Cowering from the elements in a bus shelter, dressed in my best suit, reading a scrap of paper that was directing me to attempt the most preposterous of things, I could have cried. That was until I got to the bit where it said, "don't talk to a member of the Royal Family". At that stage, you knew someone on the previous course had done just that. I got a grip of myself and imagined the Colour Sergeant standing in the bus shelter with me. He would say, "Analyse the problem, Rideout; do a SWOT! Work out where the opportunities are. Isolate the threats, mitigate the weakness and focus on your strengths." I sketched a SWOT table and listed them in their respective quarters. From here, I developed a plan. The SWOT pointed to the most obvious task achievable in Anglesey, which was to interview an overseas harbour master.

'I bluffed a ride on a bus and made my way to Holyhead port. I wasn't 100 per cent sure what I would do when I arrived at the port, so I planned on talking with the local fishermen, asking if they knew of such a man. After endless rejections, one fisherman explained he was just about to cast off and would be fishing the Irish Sea, eventually stopping in Dublin. We would find an overseas harbour master there. "Excellent," I thought, so I took him up on his offer, thinking he would return the same day. After a full day at sea, having worked for my keep, I interviewed my man. But then disaster struck. I had somehow lost my military identity card. I frantically searched the boat, but to no avail, eventually deducing that I must have lost it at the fish market whilst de-frocking from my sou'wester. Standing on top of a few empty fish crates, I whistled loudly across the hanger to attract everyone's attention. At the top of my voice, I shouted: "I am a British Army Officer Cadet from Sandhurst on an initiative exercise. I have lost my ID card here in the hall. Please could you have a look around your feet to see if it is here?" Before long, the whole market was looking for my identity card, and by a stroke of good fortune, it was located amongst the discarded baskets.

'My second task also appeared to be impossible, but by now I was beginning to enjoy the challenge. The paper simply said, "appear at a height of more than 1,000ft". I chatted with a few friendly deckhands to see if there was a mountain this high in Dublin, only to be laughed at. Taking sympathy on my plight, one of the fishmongers, who was driving his stock to the Belfast market, suggested that I should catch a plane. It was the ideal solution to my problem. A flight to London would see me home and get me over the prescribed height. He took me to Belfast International Airport, having given me dinner at his brother's and a guided tour of the city. With £20 to my name, pay for a day's work on the fishing boat, I bought a disposable camera to record my success and set about trying to get a flight to the mainland. Having tried to scrounge a flight from several desks in the departure terminal, I was arrested by security. I explained my situation, handed them my letter and they duly phoned Sandhurst to check my story. It was at this point that one of the officers decided to explain to me the dangers to servicemen travelling in Northern Ireland. The police refused to believe that I had twenty or so people in a Dublin fish market helping me find my ID card. They listened in incredulity before explaining that some of those workers in the fish market would not be sympathetic to my cause, and that such a document as a military ID card carried a high value on the black market. An RAF officer arrived from Aldergrove airbase and assessed I was a risk to myself and possibly others. In the best interest of everyone, he secured me a flight out on the next BA shuttle. I did have to sign a letter promising payment in full within thirty days. But three tasks done by Saturday afternoon was good going: appear on foreign soil, appear at a height of 1,000ft and interview an overseas harbour master. It was a good start.

'By 10 o'clock that evening I was in London, clutching onto the three items that proved my success – a letter from the Dublin harbour master and a British Airways flight ticket with my name on it. Next on my agenda was task four, to open a door for a very important person. Thinking that I would best achieve this at one of London's top hotels, I paid a visit to the Dorchester. The manager listened to my story with what appeared to be a look of total boredom, but then, to my surprise, summoned one of the bellboys to escort me to the back of the hotel. Making our way through a maze of lavish marble corridors, I was escorted to a lower ground floor hotel room. The bellboy rapped a loud knock on the door and, to my complete astonishment, Packman answered it. We were like long-lost brothers as we both screamed at each other in excitement. Then Daniels from the other platoon stepped out from behind the door. He was the first to have spoken to the duty manager. Making good use of his First in Drama, he gave him the full story and the manager told him he had heard it all before; ten times before, to be precise. The manager was well versed in Rowallan Company students asking to open the door until someone famous came along. "You lot do this three times a year," he said! This explained the reason for the uninterested look on his face as I pleaded for help!

'Kitted out in a Dorchester uniform, we all completed shifts at the front door. We looked the part dressed in the official uniform, waiting for someone famous to walk through. But most importantly, I had food and accommodation for the night in a five-star hotel! By the end of my shift, I had opened the door to a number of people who carried the title of Sir or The Right Honourable, although I didn't actually recognize any of them. Cunningly, knowing that the comfort of my accommodation hung on the fact I would need to leave once my task was complete, it made sense to drag it out until after breakfast. Packman and I then tried to join forces for the remaining tasks, but although there were similarities, his task sheet was different from mine.

'Four tasks down, seven to go as Sunday morning dawned. The remaining tasks could all be accomplished in London, so it was just a case of finding the best place to achieve them. I had to drive a car with a value of £100,000 or more. I decided to stand by the traffic lights at Piccadilly Circus and wait until someone with just such a car stopped there. After only ten minutes, a gentleman driving an Aston Martin pulled up at a red light. I jumped at the opportunity and quickly explained my actions before the lights changed to green. I won't repeat exactly what he said to me, but he would have made the Company Sergeant Major blush! Conceding the fact that the man was right to suggest I was mad, I walked to the Mercedes garage on Cave Street. My patter was perfect by this stage, so after a swift explanation, the manager and the sales team worked a little magic for me. They allowed me to sit in the garage's pride and joy, a 1955 300SL Gullwing Coupe, worth a reported £1 million. With the engine running, and one of his salesmen sitting in the passenger seat, I drove the car from one side of the showroom to the other. It was a dream start to the day. Next was task five, "serve food at a renowned restaurant". This was easy. Walking into a McDonald's, the idea was to hang around and wait for someone to request a large order. The cashier eventually told a client to sit down and the food would be sent over. At the ideal moment, I stood up out of my seat and offered to carry the food. The cashier was grateful for the assistance, the customer was pleased with the food and task five was over.

'Number six proved to be great fun – take a ride on a fire engine or steam train. I followed some directions given by an off-duty firefighter in McDonald's and ended up at a fire station near Covent Garden. The lads at the station were an immense help. They fed me and told me stories of other students from Sandhurst who had asked for the same thing. There had been at least three others who visited the night shift over the course of the weekend. All we needed was a "shout" and this task was done. After an hour, they could sense my angst to get moving. In the absence of an emergency, they kindly decided to take the engine out for some fuel. A short ride, lights and sirens included, and they kicked me off in the West End. It was the weirdest scenario imaginable. In a strange twist of circumstances, just before we parted, they requested a picture of me. Apparently, they need to advertise their efforts to reach out to the community and help people in different ways.

'Walking around the streets of the West End, I had to find a show to appear in. Firstly, I tried a few small shows but to no avail. I was about to re-evaluate, then I bumped into five lads from the other platoon. One of them had a brother who was a choreographer on the show *Cats*. He had arranged for them all to walk onto the stage in costume. Cheekily, I tagged along and was lucky no one contested me. Although we never took part in the show, we did appear on the stage of a West End play. It was with great amusement to some of the cast, who took pity on me as they got ready for the real thing. Task eight was to be charitable to someone. Easy, really. I returned to the Embankment, where we went during Exercise Helping Hand and worked for a Salvation Army soup kitchen. The women there weren't so surprised to see me, as only ten minutes before I had arrived, Lane had just left. Again, this task provided me with a meal.

'My final two tasks were proving to be unattainable. I had to appear in an article published by a prominent newspaper from Fleet Street or appear on a TV station. Initially, I targeted the BBC at Broadcasting House and tried to get in with a few wild excuses, but was thwarted by the gate guard. Thinking I needed to speak with an editor of one of the big papers, I made my way to Fleet Street. But then it dawned on me that the instructions said nothing about it needing to be an authentic article, or how long the article needed to be. Using the last of my money, I had my picture taken in a photo booth, picked a Sunday newspaper out of a bin and began searching for a topic in which my picture could be used. Having found an article about Robin Williams and the film *Jumanji*, I carefully removed the page and stuck my photo in the place of Williams, took the page to a late-night Xerox shop and reproduced the original article. With the help of the staff, who found the whole thing exciting, we reconstructed the newspaper. In full colour, the article appeared as if it was from the original print with my picture and name substituted as the author.

'All but one task complete, there was no hope of finding a goat to be milked, so with the time quickly approaching midnight, the next challenge would be getting back to Sandhurst. Standing at Paddington Station, with a total of twenty-five pence, the railway guard informed me that the next train to Camberley wasn't until 0530hrs the next morning. Not wanting to take the chance of being refused a train ride so close to the reporting time, hitch-hiking seemed a better option. It took a while to get to the A3, but just at the start of the Richmond section, two Officer Cadets from the final term of the Commissioning Course stopped to give me a ride home. They dropped me off at the front gate, where I joined a large number of the course that had made the same decision as me. Because the instructions stated that we were not allowed on the camp before nine o'clock, we crammed into the small bus shelter by the small strip of shops and exchanged stories about our weekend.'

The class burst into a round of applause, as did Captain Dunn. Although the students only had to select eleven of their allotted tasks, we would have been pleased if he had achieved five. We looked at his photographs and the other items Rideout had collected on the way. Having finished the formalities, we examined his plan. It was faultless, apart from the trip to the Republic of Ireland. I understood his innocence, but this didn't prevent me from issuing him with a warning to apply a bit more thought to what he was doing. He had travelled to a foreign country without a passport and could have caused an international incident. Notwithstanding this one indiscretion, the exercise was a complete success for Rideout. He had learnt a valuable lesson in concentration in the face of excitement and realized his ability to achieve the near impossible with no resources to hand. Now was the perfect time to teach him the next stage of analysis. For ten minutes we talked through the process of converting the SWOT into 'outcomes and outputs' before charting the end-state through 'means and ways'. Had there been time on the course to teach him how to use this planning tool, he would have generated more than one way to achieve each task. Maybe, just maybe, he would have identified that travelling to the Republic of Ireland was a bad idea! Rideout had learnt as much about himself as we had learnt about him.

Danner was next to present his findings. Pat had told me that he was in jail over the weekend, so we knew this would be brief. Danner explained:

'My first task was to interview a model. The best place for this is absolutely Soho. I knew a few places that provided this kind of service and thought to pay one of them a visit. It all seemed to be going smashingly. The gentleman at the entrance to this renowned club was very amenable when he learnt of my quest. My request to interview one of his girls was granted and he showed me into a little room at the rear of his establishment. Shortly after, two lovely women obliged my desire for no more than the cost of a drink. In my innocence, I genuinely believed what was being offered was the chance to talk with two women who were exotic models and nothing more. We chatted for about ten minutes, taking a photograph for evidence, then I made a polite excuse to leave.

'Having ordered two Coca-Colas for the girls, the manager presented me with the bill on my way out. When it arrived, I thought it was £4. That was expensive, so I complained to the barman, protesting that £4 did not represent a fair price for two halves of coke. I gave the barman a £5 note and explained that I would be wanting the full amount of change back. You could imagine my reaction as the barman explained I was short of £395. By this stage it was obvious that there was to be trouble, so the barman called for the bouncers, predicting that this was turning ugly. Firstly, I tried to fight my way out of the bar, only to be swiftly restrained by more bouncers. Then I demanded to be allowed to call the police, but the bouncer suggested that would not work out well for me. He advised me to phone a friend first or they would be forced to find the money in other ways. So I called my brother to come and bail me out. When he arrived, about three hours later, he was so incensed by the behaviour of the manager of the establishment that he punched him. A massive fight broke out and the police arrived. This may have been our saving grace. Had they not arrived, things could have taken a turn for the worse. We were taken to the station and remained there overnight. On my release, I was told to stay at my brother's and not attempt any other tasks. Apparently, that message came from Sandhurst.'

There were no cheers, no applause, just stunned silence as Danner finished. On display, there were two pieces of evidence: a receipt for £400 and an evidence tag from the police station. Although we didn't need any more evidence than we currently had, the logbook in the operations room manned by Eddie gave a blow-by-blow account provided by the police. The Academy had been dealing with this incident for most of the weekend. Danner was great officer material, but once more he demonstrated the ability to start a riot in a phone box. If anyone was going to be misunderstood, or was likely to misjudge the moment, it was him. He needed to be accompanied by a counterbalance at all times. This was not an issue for me. Every officer in command has a Non-Commissioned Officer serving alongside him. This would unquestionably provide the yin to his yang. He would be fine with a strong Platoon Sergeant when he got to his regiment, if he made it through the rest of the year!

In typical fashion, Lane had failed to realize the main emphasis of the exercise. He claimed to have tried very hard before deciding to ask someone for help. Using his emergency money, he called a friend who offered to spend the weekend doing the whole thing with him. Seemingly, his friend only did the driving and Lane had done all the negotiating, but all his photographic evidence suggested otherwise. We enquired as to what he thought the overall aim of the exercise was, but Lane just looked bewildered by the question. He was truly pleased by his efforts, having achieved ten tasks in a comfortable environment. At the halfway point of Lane's account of the exercise, the Academy Commandant entered the classroom. General Deverell knew the exercise had taken place and was invited by the OC to attend the presentations. He was keen to hear the students' adventures at first-hand, having undoubtedly been informed of a number of encounters with local authorities. It was not forecast for him to come and listen to anyone particular, but it was unfortunate for Lane to be the student in the hot seat for such a high-powered visit. After Lane had finished telling his story, Captain Dunn unpicked his efforts. There was no hiding the disappointment as he told Lane that he had wasted a wonderful opportunity to discover valuable personal lessons. General Deverell added a few observations at the end. With a look of thunder, he summarized, 'Simply calling a friend is a betrayal of personal values. If anything, it's a real lack of initiative. Like water escaping its catchment, you have taken the path of least resistance. This is not the kind of qualities that will endear you to soldiers under your charge.'

Notwithstanding Lane's ineptitude, most of the students' stories had us all in stitches. I hadn't laughed so much in years as I listened to each adventure, and at times felt jealous as they repeated their successes. Boyle had been tasked with scoring a goal at a Premiership football ground. He had turned up at Hillsborough Stadium in Sheffield on Saturday afternoon and explained his situation. With open arms, they accommodated his madcap request. They walked him onto the pitch at half time, announcing him as a special guest. In front of 25,000 people, he kicked a ball into an open goal and the home fans cheered.

It was Witherspoon who recalled the most cunning of plans. After showing us his SWOT analysis, which he had sketched out on the back of the envelope we had given him, he walked us through his weekend. Firstly, he went to B&Q and standing on Irish fertilizer, and claimed he stood on foreign soil! He videoed an interview with a stunning young lady. The film focused on the lady's lips – crimson red and pouting. The conversation was about how long she had been stripping, and the lady spent a minute or so talking about how hard it was. Flicking her golden locks back, fluttering her long eyelashes, she whispered to the camera that she had been at this game for five years. Slowly, the camera panned out. With a full chest filling her dungarees, we suspected the camera was about to reveal a half-clad lady stood in a lap-dancing bar. But instead, the screen blurred in and out of focus before it came to rest on a paint scraper held in her left hand. The beautiful lady was stood next to a wall stripped back to the bare plaster, with woodchip paper crumpled at her feet. A stripper is a stripper, no matter what they strip! Ingeniously, he interviewed a harbour master over the phone and then opened the door for Mickey Mouse at the large toy store on Oxford Street. Whilst buying lunch at Tesco's, he took a ride on a kiddies' fire engine located in the lobby. There was nothing wrong with what he had done, as he explained he had followed the instruction verbatim, just with his own unique interpretation.

Williams, who had too much to drink before the start of the exercise, was still suffering the effects the following morning when he boarded a train he thought was heading to London. Five hours later, he was woken by the train guard at the end of the line, in Newcastle! Having spent most of the day trying to hitch a lift on the motorway, he eventually got a ride in an old Bedford Army truck heading to the annual classic military vehicle rally. The driver was an ex-National Serviceman who was only too keen to help; it appeared he had landed on his feet. One hour and 60 miles later they broke down and, predictably, the recovery wagon towed them back to Newcastle!

It was now nearly 2000hrs on Monday evening, and test week would start again in earnest the following morning. Despite the fantastic results, that had captivated us all, it had come at a cost. Rowallan Company had hit the headlines for all the wrong reasons. Although it escaped the attention of Fleet Street, an Army officer on exercise landing in a foreign country unannounced was a serious violation of international law, no matter how innocent or accidental. If Rideout had been arrested, it would have ended up at Number 10 Downing Street. Even worse, had he bumped into an Irish Republican with links to terrorism, the outcome would be tough to contemplate. Eventually, someone would question the madness of Exercise Red Light and, given the risks, it would be hard to defend its aim and objectives. Making my way back to the Warrant Officers' and Sergeants' Mess, it was amazing to think we had been so lucky. Except for Lane and Haigh, everyone tried their hardest and had learnt some valuable lessons. However, my fears for Haigh had once again increased. It would be a restless night for us all before testing continued the following morning.

Tuesday morning's first round of mandated tests was formally designed to confirm that we had achieved the prescribed aims of the course. For efficiency purposes, all programme information was published on the Company noticeboard. It was the first time the students had seen such detail published for general consumption. Timings, date, location and even test criteria information were listed for all to read. The first test was a repeat of the 3-mile basic fitness test, the very same one they had attempted at the start of the course. If anyone was to fail this test, they would be sent home and kicked off the course. This test would be the yardstick for forecasting a student's performance during the final exercise. If he couldn't pass this fitness test, he certainly wouldn't cope with the rigours of the Welsh mountains and would probably not deploy. Additionally, comparing the score from day one against the new score, it would help the Company Commander convince the Academy Headquarters of the benefits of Rowallan.

Tracy greeted the Company outside Sultan Qaboos gymnasium and reminded everyone of the test: two minutes of press-ups, two minutes of sit-ups, followed by a 3-mile run. The first mile and a half would be as a squad, the second as an individual. For added value, Tracy announced she would lead the course around the circuit for the first and second half. It was a cheeky claim that caught everyone's attention. Rideout was highly likely to make it around the course in eight minutes or under. His fitness was good before he arrived, but now he was like a racing snake. There was the briefest of warm-ups before the test began. Dark green exercise mats were laid out along the full length of the gym floor. Tracy then split the course into two groups. Group one started doing sit-ups while group two counted. The students were told to complete as many repetitions as possible in two minutes. As Tracy walked up the line of exercise mats collecting the scores, she stopped and examined Danner's results. He scored just enough to pass the test. Two minutes later, the whole process was repeated, but this time it was press-ups.

The running circuit looped around the huge lawn in front of Old College, down to the back gate past the transport squadron and back to the gym via the gap between New College and the swimming pool. It looked a long way when you were standing at the start line. Even before we set off, Danner was having a wobble.

'What's the issue, Danner?' I enquired.

'Nothing, Colour Sergeant!'

'Crap! He is worried he is going to fail.' Mathews jumped into the conversation. 'We won't let you fail,' Mathews then added.

'Yes you will, Mathews" I interjected. 'You have your own issues to consider, you are not waiting for Danner. You make your own way around the course and make sure you beat Rideout.'

Danner had a look of fear on his face. He was psyching himself out long before we had even crossed the start line.

'Danner, you are not going to fail, provided you throw everything at this. And please rest assured, should you fail to do just that, it is me you will answer to.'

Tracy counted down from five. As she did so, Major Gray and Captain Watts nudged their way to the front of the crowd. There were forty-seven runners, and getting a good start was critical to getting a good time. Rideout was being blocked by the masses and was certainly disadvantaged as they crossed the start line. By the time we had reached the halfway mark, the front runners were out of sight and Danner was firmly stuck in last position. His legs were pumping hard, but lifting his body off the ground with each stride was sapping his energy. At the halfway point, his time was five minutes and forty seconds; he was ten seconds off the pace, and the second half had a steady incline. Unless he increased his pace, he wouldn't make it. The temptation for me to put my hand in the middle of his back was overwhelming. But doing that on a test would be cheating, and achieving success that way was meaningless. The best he could receive was verbal encouragement.

'Twenty seconds off the mark, Danner. Open your legs! Further yet! More yet! Harder yet, harder, push it harder.'

Running and clock-watching, Danner was making up the time, but this was going to be agonizingly close. With less than 100 metres to go, we could hear Tracy call out the time.

'1015. 1016. 1017. Come on! 1018.'

The distance was too great for Danner to make up. Five seconds over the cut-off mark, the lad crossed the finish line. He was the only one to fail the running part of the test. His eyes welled up as his platoon comrades offered comfort.

Captain Dunn and Pat stood at the finish line talking with Tracy. Although Danner was the only student not to make the ten minutes and thirty seconds pass time, two of Paddy's boys failed to make the minimum number of press-ups and sit-ups. One student scored forty-nine sit-ups, one below the required fifty, while the other was ten push-ups shy of the forty-four required.

'Danner failed, Colour!' said Captain Dunn.

'Boss, it wasn't for the lack of trying. If he had started at the front of the squad, he may have stood a better chance.'

'Colour, that's rubbish. If he didn't make it, it's because he didn't try hard enough.'

The boss was right. Danner had come on leaps and bounds with his fitness, but ultimately, he had not tried hard enough. Without so much as a by your leave, I scurried off with my tail between my legs. It was hard to accept that Danner would now be kicked off the course. He had knocked two minutes off his first attempt, and that was good going.

I had learnt much at Sandhurst. With every passing day, there was a new dynamic to the business for me to understand. Be it training, leadership or the politics of defence as an industry, learning never stopped. Comprehending how this massive machine worked was something never previously contemplated, but for the first time ever, I took a deep breath and calmly reflected on what was happening. Would the OC really kick all three of those who had failed the test off the course? The OC was a bright man, and secretly we all knew he was trying to stop Rowallan becoming the victim of budget cuts. Of course, he wouldn't throw them off the course if he felt they could be saved. Having kicked myself up the backside for sulking, I returned to my office in the Company lines.

'Better now, Colour?'

'Boss, I am sorry. There is a lot of effort invested in a number of these boys, and Danner is one of them. The thought of him being kicked off or not doing the final exercise in Wales got the better of me.'

'Colour, I wouldn't want it any other way. So there is good news and bad. The OC will give them all a second attempt on Friday, but if they don't make it, they are off.'

It was harsh, but if the standards of Rowallan were to be upheld it had to be this way. To be fair to all the other students who had achieved the required standards, we could not fudge this issue. But if Danner was feeling under pressure before, his stress levels were going to go ballistic when he was told.

Captain Dunn briefed Danner at the start of the next assessment. Understandably it unnerved him. With five assessments to undertake, it would be hard for him to concentrate on the week ahead. The next assessment would play to his strengths: he and his fellow students were to design a command task. Danner's forceful personality and colourful thinking would help him design a command task that could be used by junior commanders learning to apply the tools of command, control and leadership. Designs needed to be simple, interesting and capable of setting conditions that allowed the Directing Staff to analyse how a group of ten people interacted. The task would need to be multifaceted and produce obvious points of contention to test a commander's ability to resolve internal conflict and create cohesion amongst a group of individuals.

The assessment lasted four hours. Should a student feel so inclined, he could collect the stores from Pete and test his concept with a trial run. After the assessment was complete, the best example from No. 2 Platoon would be tested by Paddy's boys, and vice-versa. The OC would choose the best from the Company and it would be used to assess the leadership of students during the next Rowallan course. The first submission came from Boyle. His design included some very clever weight-to-power ratios that combined to make a grappling hook for scaling a wall. Whilst it was clever, it failed to generate concurrent activity and demanded the protagonists have a detailed understanding of physics. Witherspoon submitted a task very similar to the first command task he took charge of during Plain Jane. It was reliant on the parbuckle technique generating the opportunity to practice command and control, but overall it lacked originality. Francis, Rideout and Moore all had similar tasks. They had focused on generating maximum activity, allowing the Directing Staff to assess the commander's control. Yet once again, there was little originality about their entry.

Danner's draft drawing and designs were complex and hard to build. It was not so much the level of difficulty, but more a case of the time available. The task needed to be accomplished in twenty minutes, allowing ten minutes for a debrief by the instructor. With Danner's submission, he had allowed the participants ten minutes to build a complicated lifting hoist. The concept was sound, but it failed to meet the criteria. It was going to be a close call whether he passed this assessment, let alone impress and build some self-confidence. It would take Eddie a full day to mark the submissions, and Danner would have a long wait to discover if he had failed two out of two on day one of test week.

The following day was known as Navigation Day. Unsurprisingly, it comprised a full day testing the complete range of navigation skills, with theory exams all morning confirming the understanding of compass bearings and protractor transfers. The second part was even more complex, working out inter-visibility and intersections as well as route calculations using Naismith's theory. This was swiftly followed by a daytime orienteering exercise. To ensure the integrity of the practical assessment, the Company were bussed to a new training area in Aldershot. Although the Sandhurst area was large enough, the students knew it so well they would find it all too easy to navigate around it during daylight. The 6-mile circuit was relatively easy to achieve in the timeframe they had. With the exception of Williams, everyone from No. 2 Platoon made it in time. Given they had endured so much navigation in recent weeks, it was something of a surprise that Williams had failed to make the cut-off time. They were all proficient in daytime navigation, making his failure a real cause for concern. If he failed the tougher night test later that evening, we would have to consider him failing the course. There was no point getting emotional at the lad; it was a test, and for whatever reason, he had failed it. No amount of shouting was going to fix it. Yet the Army would not suffer an officer who could not navigate. No one would entertain his excuses; he had failed a simple test and his future hung in the balance.

We returned to Sandhurst for the night navigation test. Eddie issued the navigation control cards and his standard brief. The circuit was no greater than 3 miles, depending on the sequence you visited the control points. Unusually, it included an urban section around the married quarters of the Academy. Whilst this wasn't particularly difficult, we had not taught urban map reading and it could present some students with a problem. Dotted around the circuit, the DS would patrol the likely approach routes to ensure no one strayed outside of the safe area. Although no help could be offered, it was plausible to encourage a student to adjust his thinking or to remind him of the techniques he should be using. The test needed to confirm assimilation, and helping someone to achieve a better score would be increasing his chances of winning the Highland Trophy. It was critical to the award's veracity that the winner achieved it on his own merits. We watched with enthusiasm as Mathews and Moore flew past me and Captain Dunn. One of those two lads had a valid claim to the top student award, and the week of assessments would place one of them in a prime position.

On the walk back to the rear gate, Captain Dunn passed comment that Lane had done well on the previous two assessments. Should his performance continue to improve, his chances of success would increase. It was the most perfect statement for the moment. We had just reached the ammunition compound, about half a mile into the training area, when Lane appeared from the scrubland behind the illuminated courtyard. Dishevelled and not carrying his safety equipment, he pulled out his map as we approached him.

'Lost, Lane?'

'Er, no, Sir. I know exactly where I am.' Pointing at his map, he indicated his location to Captain Dunn.

'How many checkpoints have you collected?'

'Two, Sir.'

'What time did you leave?'

'2115, Sir.'

'It's 2230 now! Bloody hell, Lane. You are not going to make the remaining eight checkpoints and get back within the two-hour cut-off. Maybe you need to re-evaluate the situation before you decide what you do next. Remember, the back gate is locked at 2330 on the dot.'

'Lane!' I snapped.

'Yes, Colour Sergeant.'

'Where is your webbing belt with your emergency kit?'

'I dumped it at the front gate, so I could run faster, Colour Sergeant.'

'Is that what we taught you?'

'No, Colour Sergeant, but it was a risk worth taking.'

'Excuse me! The risk of getting caught cheating is punishable by immediate discharge, Lane.'

'That's not what you did to Francis, Colour Sergeant! He did it and so did Witherspoon, Williams and Boyle.'

Captain Dunn snapped at Lane with a short reprimand. He told him to get on with his assessment and not to waste any more time. With Lane disappearing into the distance, we both headed back to the command and control tent. Lane had me over a barrel. Francis had made a mistake and I chose to punish him Rowallan style. Punishing Lane in any other way would support his claim of victimization. As I regaled Captain Dunn with my story about forgetting that Francis was running around Chapel Square for nearly two hours, the boss calmed the waters.

'Don't stress, Colour! He is not worthy of a place on the Commissioning Course, and it is obvious to anyone with a pulse. If we are patient, he will cook his own goose!'

Despite the calming influence of the Platoon Commander, this was a problem of my own creation. The decision to treat people differently is not always the best use of emotional intelligence, and Lane was the case in point. When you are in a position of authority, standards and rules can't vary depending on personalities – you must treat everyone equally. It was a lesson well learnt that served me well some years later when faced with a similar incident on tour in Cyprus. I decided to punish an individual using due process for a trivial misdemeanour and my decision was met with widespread criticism. The soldier was widely respected and in line for promotion; consequently, my decision to bring a formal charge against him would jeopardize his chances of advancement. Even the Company Commander complained that disciplining a good soldier with a minor infringement was pointless and bad for Company morale. But six weeks later, when a perennial 'problem child' committed exactly the same offence, he was treated the same, yet as a repeat offender with a chequered past, it proved to be the final straw. He was dishonourably discharged, and the Company had rid themselves of a millstone that had constantly besmirched its reputation. Due process is there to protect us not only from ill-discipline but sometimes from ourselves. Two years elapsed before the Company Commander acknowledged that disciplining that particular soldier for a minor infringement was the right thing to do.

Eddie was counting the control cards when we returned to the camp. He confirmed that Lane was the only student not to make it in time.

'Colour, we are more interested in who came first – Moore or Mathews?' Captain Dunn hovered around Eddie as he mumbled incoherently. It was most unlike Eddie. He was dynamic and forthright, so my suspicions were immediately aroused.

'Sorry, Ed, who did you say came first?'

'Staples from No. 1 Platoon. Maybe!'

'Maybe, Eddie? Maybe? Surely it's black and white. He has a scorecard! He has a recorded time! If they are better than everyone else's, that's it, isn't it?'

Eddie handed the boss the control card used by Staples.

'Looks good, Colour. All boxes filled; time is quick. What's the issue?'

'Look at the punch holes closely on checkpoint two, three, four and five. Now compare them to the rest of the punch holes. The card has scuff marks made by the impression of the stamp. However, two, three, four and five just have clear puncher marks, no compression marks left around the edges by the stamp! I have my suspicions, is what I am saying. So, the Company Sergeant Major needs to take a view.'

Staples was the chosen man for No. 1 Platoon. If he wanted to be in with a chance of winning the top student award, he needed to win more of these events than Mathews and Moore. It was easy to cheat a control card, but it does demand experience and know-how. Instead of going to the checkpoint, you divide your efforts with a friend. You split the course into equal distances and meet up at a convenient point to copy each other's scorecard. In the knowledge that Staples may have cheated with someone else, there may have been another card with similar marks on checkpoints six to ten belonging to his accomplice. Excited by my 'Inspector Clouseau' findings, I dashed out of my room to visit Eddie, but just before I opened my mouth the consequences of getting this wrong washed over me. Tensions had been fraught since the revelations of 'car-gate', when Paddy gave his students a lift during an exercise. If we wrongly accused his nominated top student of cheating, life for the remaining weeks of the course would end up intolerable for all. It was best to trust Pat. If he thought there was a scam, he would unearth it. It would be better if he discovered it rather than me.

On the penultimate day of test week, the students were to deliver leadership presentations and essays to the academics at Faraday Hall. Unlike previous presentations, the students delivered their findings on their own. They were required to provide evidence and examples supporting their analysis, whilst making it interesting and insightful. Each student had a forty-minute slot, and Captain Dunn would sit as part of the judging panel. It was not my responsibility to stay and listen, but it was useful for me to understand the strengths and weaknesses of all those in the platoon. The first student before the panel of Academy tutors was Stone. Slumped in my seat at the rear of the classroom, I listened to his evaluation of Lieutenant William Calley, a young American officer imprisoned for his part in the Mai Lai massacre during the Vietnam War. It was unbelievable to listen to Stone identify in Lieutenant Calley all the failings that Captain Dunn had recognized in Stone. His depiction of Calley was perfect, articulating his failings with remarkable clarity before concisely summarizing his failing characteristics.

We were all pleasantly surprised. Was this Stone comprehending what the qualities of a good leader look like, or was he just repeating words we had used on him? Either way, he impressed the academics. There was much to talk about with Lieutenant Calley, and Stone had somehow identified the salient points that we all like to discuss. He had singled out the Toxic leadership style that had consumed Calley's command. Impressively, he suggested that prolonged exposure to horrific levels of violence had eroded empathy and all perspective on the value of life was lost. Stone stated that Calley was a product of his environment, and he could not have chosen a better example to prove this theory. Of all the presentations that day, Stone's had struck a chord with the panel. Despite the suspicion that Stone's words were not his own, the pendulum of pass-fail no longer favoured one particular side. Yet his reputation still clouded our thinking and it was a challenge to believe he had turned the corner.

The final day of test week started with a room inspection and kit check. This was not a test of tolerance like all the previous room inspections that Pat conducted. This was a test of attention to detail and discipline. Pat inspected every room with all the attributes of a Dover customs officer searching for contraband. Perturbingly, Pat executed his duties in total silence, with nothing torn from its rightful place, nothing strewn across the floor. It was pure torture not knowing what Pat was thinking. After two hours of note-taking, Pat repeated the process, but this time he inspected the students' equipment. The silent treatment was getting to Haigh. Increasingly, he fidgeted and frowned as he stood to attention waiting his turn to be inspected. For Danner, the slow morning was the ideal preparation for his fitness retest, but Lane would need to wait until it got dark for his second attempt to pass the night navigation test.

Danner would be running the Basic Fitness Test with two other students from Paddy's platoon. Dutifully, we all reported to Tracy at the gymnasium five minutes before the start. She was just finishing circuit training with one of the senior terms. To a man, they were all dripping wet with sweat. Whatever she had been doing with this particular Company, it looked to have taken its toll. She whisked the three students away and put them through the sit-ups and press-ups phase. Shortly after, Tracy reappeared clutching a stopwatch and filling out the scores on her clipboard.

'I will run around with him, Gaz. You can stay at the start line and keep the time.'

'No, Tracy, he needs to pass this test, I will run with him.'

'Gaz, I know he needs to pass. I see how important this is to you both. Trust me, you should leave this to me. Unless you are going to tell me that you are a qualified Physical Training Instructor that is?'

Tracy was quite forceful. She may have been as small as a dormouse, but her authority and confidence were compelling. Standing clutching a stopwatch, I stayed put as instructed at the finish line.

It was deathly quiet as Danner set off. Tracy allowed Paddy and his boys to sprint off as she ran with Danner, happily chatting away to him like they were running buddies. Her chat was calming and random, without so much as a hint towards the importance of the test. The pace looked slow and my stopwatch appeared to be working double time as Danner disappeared behind the tennis courts at the far end of Old College lawn. Unable to contain my desire to check on his progress, I cut through the stables behind the grey stonewashed building, hoping to get a glimpse of how the lad was doing. Instead of getting a glimpse of Danner, I ran into the rest of No. 2 Platoon. They had sneaked out of the accommodation to roar Danner on. For a microsecond, they looked at me knowing that they shouldn't be there, before they turned their heads to see Danner appear on the main road just before the swimming pool.

'Get a move on, Danner!'

'Come on Danner, you can do it!'

Mathews ran after him to get closer to the action, but as he neared, Tracy turned and issued an angry warning. She was full of venom, with piercing eyes cutting deep into the burly figure of Mathews. Like the child from *The Exorcist*, her head spun 180 degrees. Spittle flew ferociously with her words as she carried on running and shouting. Adhering to Tracy's warning, the platoon thought better of chasing Danner. Instead, they cut through the gap between Monkey Hill and the cemetery to get to the finish line before Danner. Foaming at the mouth and filling every inch of his lungs with air, he flung himself across the finish line, panting like an exhausted Grand National winner.

'Up, Danner!' Tracy demanded. Her tone towards Danner had changed. She was back to her assertive self.

'Get up! Get up, Danner! This is not Ibiza and that's not a beach.'

Gingerly, Danner rose to his feet. The platoon, led by Mathews, crowded around Tracy trying to get a sight of her watch.

'Ten minutes, seven seconds,' she said. 'I don't know what all the fuss was about.'

The platoon mobbed Danner. It didn't take too much effort for the big lad to crumble to the floor. For a brief moment, it was important they celebrated his success. Danner was a born leader, but whilst there were many admirable qualities with his style, there were just as many failings. Prudently, this wasn't the moment to discuss them. Tracy issued a warning for everyone to get a grip and stop celebrating mediocrity.

'If you children don't get up off the floor in five seconds, we will run the route again – five, four, three …'

The platoon were up on their feet and standing in three ranks way before she finished counting down. Tracy scared me, let alone the platoon. She would have run us ragged and we all knew it. We marched back to the accommodation before Tracy changed her mind. Steely-eyed and grinding her teeth, her demeanour was Hulk-like. If there was any nagging doubt that she would not live up to Daz's reputation, it had been banished forever. She was fitter, faster and twice as scary. Just what Rowallan needed.

After lunch, the Company assembled in the Academy swimming pool to compete against each other for the last time before the final exercise. The swimming gala was run by the students, with the winning platoon earning a vital three points. Captain Dunn corralled the platoon in the changing room for the obligatory pep talk.

'Fellas, you know this is the last competition in the camp and there are only two races left after today. It is all over if you don't win this event. By hook or by crook, you must win.'

There was no wry smile, no hint of tongue in cheek. He was deadly serious, we had to win this race. The morale in the platoon was high, confidence oozing from everyone as they took to the swimming pool. This was because No. 2

Platoon had a secret weapon: Rideout was an accomplished swimmer at county level. In every race, he was several seconds ahead of his nearest rival. On the relay competition, he swam twice because No. 1 Platoon had one more member than we had. Instead of this being a disadvantage, Rideout romped home on the last leg with a huge advantage. Single-handed, he delivered the win, reducing the deficit to just three points, eighteen to fifteen. It was not lost on his peers that his performance had won the day. Euphoric, and singing like drunken football supporters on the way home from a cup final, the celebrations were raucous and unbridled, much to Paddy's annoyance.

It was 1630hrs as we left the bright lights of the swimming pool and entered into the dark and cold of deep winter. Cars left the Academy in their droves as Friday afternoon got into full swing. For the Academy, it was the start of another long weekend and most people had left as Lane prepared himself for his navigation retest. Having not heard any news about the mysterious hole-punching that appeared on the card belonging to Staples, I thought it prudent to ask Pat what he had thought.

'Pat, did Eddie chat to you about the control card Staples handed in?'

'Staples! Gaz, come on! You have nothing to worry about. He has nothing on Mathews. If you have concerns about the Highland Trophy, you needn't worry. Mathews needs only to stay out of trouble next week. He is the clear favourite. However, we will change the marking system for the next course. We won't have a repeat of that issue again.'

Pat grabbed his fleece jacket and left his office, screaming obscenities at students idling around the accommodation. He left without answering the question, but his evading tactics said more than his explanation. For all his rough edges, Pat was insightful and tactful when required. It would take me many years to learn how much Pat really knew about what was going on behind the scenes, but nothing escaped his attention.

Eddie had just finished taking Williams through his daytime navigation test. It was a close-run thing, with just a hint of help from the other two students sitting the same test, but Williams had scraped through. With little time to transition, Eddie ran the night navigation re-test for Lane. Whilst the young student ran around the circuit, I watched from a distance until it was clear that intervention was required. By the time he made checkpoint six, his allocated time had lapsed, with two checkpoints still to visit. There was little for me to do other than to call an end to the exercise and save us all the pain of finding checkpoints seven and eight. Dejected and frustrated in equal measure, I walked slowly behind him and contemplated where it all went wrong.

As promised, Eddie was waiting at the rear gate, albeit because he had to lock it up. The orange glow of the neon security light amplified the low mist and drizzle, creating a rainbow-like halo around the fence.

'Has Lane come through, Eddie?'

'Yes. I told him he failed, but he already knew that. I had to bite my tongue with him, Gaz. If the lad was devastated, he would get some sympathy. But he just shrugged his shoulders and asked me what he should do with the map. I swear I could have knocked him to Bracknell and back, the cheeky little git!'

Eddie and I walked back to the accommodation together. The awkward silence was broken as the topic of Staples and his magic scorecard surfaced. It was hard to let it go. Deep down inside, we all knew he had received help. But if we couldn't identify the culprit by his card, maybe it was not a fellow student! Conspiracy, treachery, treason and suspicions – my mind bounced as intensely as a Sumo wrestler on a trampoline. Quizzing Eddie to the limit of our friendship, he declared that he didn't want to get his hands caught in the mangle. He offered an insight into conversations held by Pat and Major Gray over the past few days, hinting that the navigation exercise was a hot potato best left alone. But like a dog with a bone, there was no letting go for me.

'Do you think the lad acted on his own? Do you think he could have received inside help? Do you think the whole platoon was in on it?'

'Gaz, you are in danger of making yourself look stupid here. There is nothing to be gained in pursuing an outcome, apart from giving you the moral high ground on the next episode of car-gate. If you bring this up now, you risk poisoning the well you drink from. Let it go! Move on before you become the villain and not the victim.'

It was insightful from Eddie. He wasn't known for his emotional intelligence but his comments were intuitively correct, even if they hurt.

With the students busy preparing themselves for the week ahead, it was a rare Friday night off for the DS, except for Pete and his storemen. They had long since departed for Wales in preparation of the final exercise. Wasting little time, I made the short trip from Sandhurst to the M3 in my battered Peugeot 206 and promptly joined the rush hour commuters in stationary traffic. The torrential rain being wiped away by the drone of worn-out wiper blades and a busted radio created the ideal conditions for my mind to wander. There was much to contemplate. Stone, Haigh, Lane, Williams and Danner all gave me cause to analyse my own performance. But it was my obsession with Paddy's antics that gripped me to distraction. Unquestionably, Paddy had been influencing the outcome of events. But for what reason? Was it within the spirit of the competition? Did it even matter? So what if Paddy's platoon won? It wasn't going to change a single thing for me or my students, so why did it consume me so much? What was nagging me? Was it a sense of injustice or the fact that Paddy had beaten me? Did I lack the killer instinct, the 'win at all costs' mentality? Maybe Sandhurst wasn't for me? This issue plagued me all weekend. It had knocked my self-belief, and now it was harder to deal with. There were more doubts and suspicions, and now angst.

Trying to find the right path whilst understanding the second and third-order effects of confronting such an intangible issue was full of danger. I understood what Eddie was saying, although it added to my complaint; this was a battle that could not be won. As the traffic eased, the solution seemed even further away. Wrestling with a conundrum never got easier over the weekend! The only way to maintain my concentration was to busy myself with greater conviction.

There was no way to have known that these events were shaping and defining who I was as a soldier and as a person. Ultimately, analysing events like these would inadvertently equip me to deal with similar conundrums in the future. But at that moment in time, learning to stay focused on issues within my control and ignoring those that weren't was alien to me. It would take a further ten years for me to properly learn how to manage emotional turbulence amid dynamic scenarios and make balanced decisions. Learning to compartmentalize and categorize that which is important, whilst filtering a plethora of distractions so as to inform actions and anticipate the likely outcomes, is derived from life experience and self-analysis. This is the cornerstone of emotional intelligence and a skill very few professions require. It took me many years to identify these as the ingredients that created the agile edge and generated mental agility. The realization was not an epiphany, but more a blundering recognition of why this skill is mostly unique to soldiering.

* * *

As the fighting lulled in Iraq, the Commanding Officer of 29 Artillery Regiment requested help from the Brigade Intelligence services to investigate rumours of a mass grave in his area of operations. The regiment was responsible for control of the Az Zubair oilfields, and Allied forces had long chased stories of huge prison camps, mass graves and hidden chemical weapons. On this particular occasion, it was my turn to investigate the claims. After a detailed brief, a reconnaissance patrol arrived to escort me to a building complex halfway between Az Zubair and Al Shaibah airfield. The patrol consisted of two soft-skin vehicles, each manned by four men: one commander, a driver and two soldiers providing protection with machine guns mounted on the roof. The target was somewhere in the middle of the Az Zubair oilfields, and with the Commanding Officer's final instructions, we set off to find a prison housing hundreds of people just waiting to be freed.

After a thirty-minute drive, we arrived on the outskirts of what was undoubtedly a military camp of some description. Although I was not the patrol commander, the Warrant Officer in charge recognized that I was the only one with the right qualifications, knowledge and experience to lead a combat patrol into such a dangerous situation. So, at a distance of half a kilometre, I suggested we stop and conduct a short overwatch. We needed to build our situational awareness, study the ground and identify any signs of danger. With large walls adorned with barbed wire, abandoned defensive positions and empty watchtowers, there was little doubt we were in the right place. The main gate was busted from its hinges. Inside the camp, many doors had been jammed open and no window remained intact. On the southern edge of the main complex, there was evidence of an airstrike and the tell-tale signs of looting. Disappointingly, it was clear that we were not going to be releasing prisoners from this location.

Standing behind the vehicle, surveying the ground through my binoculars, there were no obvious signs of a threat. Between us and the building complex lay hundreds of square oilfields. Resembling a massive chessboard, the fields were cut into perfect squares approximately 100 metres across. Some were covered with a white crust of salt, others filled with liquorice-black sand stained by waste oil. Around each field there was an elevated track, giving the appearance that each field was sunken to a depth of 6ft. Our Pinzgaeur vehicles offered no ballistic protection; consequently, the sight of these sunken fields immediately attracted my attention. They were the only protection available should we be attacked by the enemy. A combination of the soft sand and sunken terrain would offer some shelter from most forms of small-arms fire.

With the binoculars shoved up hard against my eyes, I began to read the signs dotted around the camp. Entrance, exit, training stores, admin office, guard force, police office – there was nothing suspicious jumping out at me. Turning to declare it safe to move closer, the unmistakable whoosh and thud of an explosion knocked me off my feet. In quick succession, a further three deafening detonations had the patrol scurrying for the safety of the sandbanks. Being subjected to a bombardment of any kind is like nothing else you will ever experience. From the very first thud, your mind speeds out of control. It is mentally tortuous and utterly terrifying as you wait to discover if you will survive the next explosion. Irrationally, you convince yourself that the next bomb will land next to you as you cower and curse. Even when logic returns, the fear of a random shell landing by you is a thought you struggle to suppress. It's not like being shot at. When bullets fly, there is an illogical mindset that suggests you can predict where they are falling. Of all the miserable ways to die in war, being shot was the lesser evil. Thrust tight up against the sandbank, we waited in anticipation of the barrage finding its range and creeping closer.

For a minute there was nothing, then, in the distance, the roof of a building within the camp exploded, shooting debris high into the air. From behind the safety of the sandbank, we could see that two sides of the building had disintegrated. Smoke billowed from the ruins and the unmistakable signature of burning propellant spat orange flames ferociously up the sides of the two remaining walls. A degree of calm descended upon us as we took stock of what was happening. The explosions continued in the area of the burning building.

A pattern was emerging: four or eight detonations in close proximity less than a minute apart. They were missing the characteristics you associate with mortars or artillery. If this was an enemy mortar attack, the fire would be edging towards us by now. There would be no flames, just the flash of detonation followed by the black cloud of spent explosives and flying fragmentation. After four more detonations, my ears were attuned to what they were hearing. No longer was there a whoosh that accompanied mortars. No crack or flying fragmentation that followed the thud of the round arriving. This was now something different. The situation had changed.

Peering over the lip of the sandbank, squinting through the sight of my rifle, there was a commotion coming from the area of the explosions. Emerging from the smoke, an orange and white taxi with three people in it was heading in our direction. Our weapons were poised, and the patrol commander shouted a target indication.

'Section! Two hundred metres! Reference burning building. Taxi heading this way on the track! Rapid!' He paused and waited for the taxi to get closer. The next time he opened his mouth, he would shout the word 'fire' and over a thousand tungsten steel bullets would rip through the Toyota Corolla taxi. Every ounce of emotion told me this was not a suicide bomber looking to conduct a follow-up attack. We had five seconds to make a decision – brass-up the taxi or take cover? All the doors of the cab were wide open, and a young man was hanging out of the front door, frantically waving. With the car speeding towards us, a decision needed to be made. Fire or not?

'Stop! Stop! Stop! Everyone. Apply safe, check fire. Check fire!' The patrol commander screamed out his instructions. He was spot on. Despite its sinister appearance, this was not a suicide bomb attack; this was something different. The car slid to a halt beside the Pinzguaer and a badly burnt young man fell out of the back door. Hysterical and unintelligible, the front passenger ranted and pleaded in the same breath. He was too agitated for me to understand, but the most pressing concern was the young man sprawled on the dust track at my feet. His burns were horrendous. The fibres of his thawab had melted and fused to his skin. It was hard to tell where his garment ended and his skin started. One side of his face had been burnt to the bone. The dull shine of his cheekbone protruding from a cauterized hole on the side of his face was stomach-churning. So sickening was the sight, it was hard to focus on saving his life. The patrol commander made a request for an evacuation using a helicopter Medical Emergency Response Team. Concurrently, I set about finding a vein on the casualty that would accept a cannula. A combination of open wounds and burns made administrating an intravenous drip a gruesome task. The lad was in hypovolemic shock, and his veins had all but disappeared. The only way to get the cannula in was to dig deep into an arm. Simultaneously, two of the patrol members broke into their own first aid equipment and dressed his open wounds in wet bandages.

Almost immediately, the explosions began again with greater ferocity. We had to move. The patrol commander demanded we all mount up into our vehicles and extract to a safer distance. We loaded the injured man onto the rear of our vehicle and the patrol geared up to leave. But the young taxi driver began to wrestle with me, demanding we don't go. He was emotionally charged and determined not to leave. 'We have to go,' I explained in Arabic. But the moment he knew I spoke his language, he clung to me like a limpet mine.

'I am not leaving my baby brother! My brother, my baby brother. He is there, next to the building! He is hurt. The explosion got him. Please save my baby brother!' he pleaded.

There was an overwhelming desire to ignore him. But his words were very clear. Occasionally he burst into broken English and there was no misunderstanding what he was saying, but I asked him to confirm it anyway.

'Where is your brother?'

'By the building. He is hurt. Please help him. It is my baby brother!'

'No, there is nothing we can do. Look at the explosions. We can't do anything.'

The patrol commander was waiting to drive off. As I tried to mount up, the young lad wrapped himself around my legs.

'In the name of God the merciful, don't go. Please help my baby brother.'

Another attempt to get on the vehicle was thwarted by a grappling session as he desperately tried to prevent us from leaving. The eyes of the patrol commander compromised his need to get the vehicles and his men out of harm's way. We agreed that he would drive the patrol out of the oilfields and clear a landing zone for the helicopter while I consoled the young man. In my mind, I convinced myself that he would come with us once he saw the vehicles drive off.

With the vehicles disappearing into the distance, I tried to convince the young lad to come with me, but he just became more agitated. When he motioned to walk back in the direction of his baby brother, I put my hand on his arm to stop him passing beyond me. In a flash, we broke into a wrestling match. He could not have been older than 16, but he was strong and agile, as well as being physically fit. For thirty seconds we rolled in the dust. Laden in all my equipment, it took every ounce of strength to gain an advantage before pinning him into submission. As quickly as it started, it was over. His arms pinned down by my knees, the lad surrendered and burst into tears.

'My mum and dad are dead. My big brother is badly injured. Please! Please save my little brother. You have a bulletproof vest. You have a helmet. If you don't want to save him, give it to me. I will wear it. Let me save him.'

The patrol was now a kilometre down the long straight track. If there was any hope of saving his little brother, it rested with me. His desperation was raw and evident. I looked at the building, which continued to spew out smoke, and for a moment contemplated if this could be achieved. There was a track leading to the building. By virtue of this feature there was a 6ft sand bank handrailing it all the way to the front door. Theoretically, it would be possible to get right up to the building with minimal risk. The vulnerable part would be crossing the tracks and picking up the child. My mind was processing all the permutations when he raised his hands and placed them on my cheek. He fixed his eyes on me and he pleaded once more.

'I am finished. There is no one left but you. In God's name save my brother; please, please, save my little brother.'

Still undecided, my brain could not cope with so many competing priorities. I needed time to think.

'OK, OK. You walk towards my colleagues. Let me think about getting to your brother! But nothing is happening until you are 500 metres away. Do you understand?'

'Yes. Yes. Understood. His name is Mohamed. But go quickly – he is badly injured.

It fell silent once the young lad ran up the track in the direction of the patrol. This was the time to do a sanity check! Was this the right thing to do? How likely was death? What were the chances of him still being alive? In what can only be descried as an out of body experience, autopilot took over without me being in cognitive control. Before my full faculties returned, I was on the far side of the track at the base of the sand bank. There was no going back. Looking across the first of the five oil fields that separated me from the injured child, the plan was to keep the sand bank between me and the explosions. Skirting around the edge of the field was energy-sapping. The loose sand, plus all my equipment, made progress slow. At the first crossover point, I listened to the rhythm of the explosions. They continued to detonate in groups of four, with an interval of less than a minute between each group. Predicting the gap between explosions, the first track was crossed. Three tracks later and there was less than 100 metres to go before reaching the building. The heat was taking its toll and it felt like an age to get to this point. Along the route, it had dawned on me that no one knew of my decision. My ill-advised choice left no opportunity to brief anyone. My greatest fear was for someone to follow me and risk their life trying to help. Time was running out. Standing inside the last field, my launch point was 50 metres away as the crow flies. With the sweat constantly dripping into my eyes and my mind tiring, an easier option was considered.

It was maybe 100 metres contouring around the edge of the field. But making a beeline for the launch point would reduce it to 50. It was contrary to good military training – leaving a proven surface was not recommended. Yet the pressure to get this done quickly clouded my judgment. Faced with dwindling energy levels and running out of time, the shortcut was too hard to resist. The ground was a little moist, crisp white like a salt plain. The first few steps saw my boot gently fall through the crust and settle neatly on a spongy surface. Then, after nearly 10 metres, the edge of my foot clipped something metal. A nervous glance down and my worst fear was confirmed – the opposite edge of an anti-tank mine was protruding through the surface of the sand. My heart seemed to stop. The mine was complete and the fuse assembly in place. A million scenarios filled my head. Incredibly, my concentration levels leapt into hyperdrive as the next decision was analysed. My body was screaming 'run!', my heart was crying 'why did you agree to do this?', whilst my head was trying to compute what next.

It had not gone 'bang', and I realized there must be a reason for this. After a better look at my predicament, things began to make sense. Now I was looking for them, there were mines everywhere: some on top of each other, some even lying in the open. Before they were banned, laying minefields was one of my responsibilities in preparation for the arrival of Brezhnev's Third Soviet Shock Army in the Minden Gap in the old West Germany. Taking a long look at the surface, it was obvious now! The scattered nature of the mines could be seen underneath several layers of sand. However, it made little sense for anti-tank mines to be here, as this was the least likely route for an armoured vehicle. By now feeling composed and thinking straight, my assessment was that this was not a minefield, but more a field with mines in it. The grouping pattern, coupled with the lack of anti-personnel mines, indicated that this was either a dumping ground or a migrating field caused by sand shift. This logic helped me stay calm. Painfully slowly, ensuring each foot was placed into the exact same imprint it had previously made, I walked backwards. It was ten minutes before the safety of the sand bank was reached. My hands were shaking, as were my legs, making forward movement tortuously slow. At best it could be described as crawling, but all movement induced cramp in every part of my body. Scurrying around to the launch point opposite the building, sand breached every gap in my clothes – it was like wearing a boiler suit made of sandpaper. With every movement, sand scratched me red raw, with sweat facilitating the effectiveness of the irritation. From my armpits to the crack of my arse, the pain came from everywhere!

The building was now just 20 metres away, and the moans of Mohamed drifted across the track in between the explosions. My plan was simple: launch myself over the track in between detonations, grab the baby brother and haul him back to the safe side of the track, then stabilize his condition before carrying him back to the helicopter landing zone. Psyching myself up, it was vital that the plan was rehearsed in my mind so there was no time wasted trying to think about what needed to be done. I made one last nervous check. With rifle strapped tight around my back, pouches closed and chinstrap taut, all that was left was to count myself into the breach as the explosions occurred. Boom, one. Boom, two. Boom, three. Boom, four, up and over. It was working well until I crested the track and caught sight of Mohamed, the baby brother. He was enormous. Eleven or not, he was not a baby, nor was he small. To make it worse, he was horrendously burnt.

There was about thirty seconds before the predicted next round of explosions began. Under normal circumstances, a rescue using a fireman's carry would be the answer. But his muscles had cooked through and there was little for me to hold onto. If his arm was to be pulled with the force that was required for a fireman's carry, it would come away from its socket, just like ripping a chicken wing from the breast. My plan was in tatters. Tiredness slowed my thinking speed and stole every spare second from me. With no plan B, and the next round of explosions brewing, my only option was to lay flat next to Mohamed and ride out the upcoming explosions. With each detonation, body fluids squeezed their way out of my body, induced by the pressure wave. On the fourth explosion, I snuggled under Mohamed and wrapped him around my neck like a large duvet. First carrying him like a mule on all fours, then getting to my feet to negotiate the bank, a successful rescue seemed plausible. The flat track was a welcome sight, but there was no way of getting down the far side; it was just too steep and Mohamed was too heavy. Physically, it was beyond me; emotionally, the fight had gone. The track was now my plan B. From here on in, I thought, whatever happens next happens! Shuffling down the track with all my kit, body armour, rifle, helmet and Mohamed, the detonations started again. This time they came with the familiar whistling sound of flying shrapnel. My calves tensed and cramped as they braced, ready to be torn apart as the white-hot metal fragments kicked up dirt on the track ahead of us.

Close to exhaustion and losing my vision, the unmistakable whine of the independently sprung portal half-axles of the Pinzgauer appeared from nowhere. The patrol commander was reversing his vehicle in our direction with two members of his patrol, coming to help us. In a heartbeat, we were all on the vehicle heading to the safety of the helicopter landing zone. But Mohamed was in a bad way. The patrol set about attempting to keep him alive as the commander explained that it was too dangerous to bring in a helicopter, so a combat ambulance was inbound. By the time it arrived, my strength had returned. Two medics were busily trying to save the lives of Mohamed and his brother. With my faculties back in full working order, the patrol commander suggested we had been here too long and needed to move. We were damned if we did and damned if we didn't. The two casualties were not as stable as we would have liked, but the patrol commander was right; we had to move.

'OK, team, we can't spend any more time here. You need to get these boys back to the hospital. Come on, let's get going,' the patrol commander demanded.

'Well, about that, Sir! We were told there was only one casualty,' the medic said, sheepishly.

'So what?'

'So we only deployed with two people. If we wish to keep them both alive on the trip home, someone needs to drive the ambulance so we can work on them in the back.'

There was only one person without a clear responsibility, and that was me!

Sitting behind the wheel of the ambulance, lights blazing and sirens wailing, it was surreal. We cut our way through the narrow streets of Az Zubair en route to Shaibah airfield, making good progress until militia groups began to shoot at us. It was another twist in this horrific ordeal all of my own making. Not only had I placed the patrol commander and his team in danger, now we were risking the lives of two young medics barely older than the two dying Iraqis in the back of the ambulance. Bullets passed through the soft-skin vehicle without making a sound. The report of the shot dissipated in the urban mayhem. Only the noise of the air vacuum collapsing behind the bullet as it passed warned you of the danger you were in. Occasionally, when the bullet hit a part of the vehicle's rigid structure, the noise could be heard above the drone of the road wheels humming in tune with the road surface. As we flew past the gunmen, their rifles tracked our movement, with muzzles blazing. Black tarmac splashed up in front of the ambulance as bullets tried to hit us. My body tensed in anticipation of being struck as we drove through the hail of bullets. A second later and it was over. The moment had passed, and we were now in the shadows of another building and out of reach of the AK47s. Comically, it dawned on me that my eyes had been closed for the last 100 metres. There was just as much chance of me dying in a head-on collision as there was being hit by a bullet! It made as little sense as the nervous laughter that accompanied us as the airbase appeared in the distance.

We arrived at the Role 2 hospital at Shaibah airfield, and with a sense of calm and composure, a number of medics and nurses stood at the main entrance waiting to relieve us of the casualties. For a moment, euphoria and fear collided, and my eyes welled up. There was a fixed partition between the driver's cab and rear of the ambulance, so there was no way of knowing if everyone had survived the ambush. As the trauma team pulled open the rear doors, both medics were busy treating the casualties, blissfully unaware of our perilous situation. They had been focused on keeping the two young boys alive and never had time to consider their own safety.

The following day, as we were leaving the front gates of Shaibah airbase, our vehicle was stopped by the taxi driver and his younger brother. They had been queuing at the front gate, hoping to get into the hospital. As soon as he recognized us, he rushed over and stood in front of my Toyota Land Cruiser. No sooner had the door opened, than he wrapped himself around me and burst into tears. Then another relative, followed by another and another. The air was being squeezed from my lungs by a crowd of ten people or more. It was humbling and heartening in equal measure. Faisal formally introduced himself and thanked us for what we had done. He then introduced his mother and father.

'You told me your mother and father were killed!'

'No, my brother, not correct. I said they will kill me if Mohamed dies!'

I had convinced myself to risk life and limb because Faisal was facing a life with no living relatives. Maybe if my understanding of what was being said had not been corrupted by my own inability, his brother would not have survived. It wouldn't be the last time my language ineptitude would have profound consequences.

Two months later, in the most bizarre of scenarios, I found myself interpreting for the Prime Minister. Tony Blair was visiting a local school in Basra, where I was gathering intelligence for the Provost Marshal. In the pre-operation, the Military Police and Black Watch had locked down the area ahead of Blair's arrival, inadvertently denying the duly appointed interpreter access to the area. In something of a panic, the visit coordinator asked me to stand in as the official interpreter. We rehearsed nursery rhymes and songs before the Prime Minister arrived, a precaution to avoid me misunderstanding what was being said. It had gone well, exactly as rehearsed, right up until we were about to leave. Then the headmistress of the school requested she give the Prime Minister a gift. From out of the crowd, young Adnan Abbas walked forward with a bunch of flowers. As Tony Blair bent down to receive the flowers, Adnan paused with nerves. I moved close to reassure him it would be fine, and instructed the lad to give the Prime Minister a hug.

'Hug him, hug him!' ('TAnNaq! TAnNaq!'). But Adnan gazed at me, confused. Maybe he didn't understand my accent, or maybe the word was not colloquially suitable. In something of a panic and desperately trying to prevent that awkward silence, another phrase was required.

'TQbeel, TQbeel.'

His eyes lit up as my words made sense to his young mind. With a huge smile on his face, and to everyone's astonishment, Adnan planted a huge kiss on the side of Tony Blair's cheek and the crowd roared with joy.

That wasn't in the rehearsal, nor was it expected, and many of the official press missed the kiss, apart from one journalist, Ross Benson.

'Oi, mate, get him to do that again!' shouted another journalist. But it happened so quickly, it was hard for me to know what Adnan had understood. The moment was slipping away, and the angry press were demanding a repeat.

'You need to get the boy to do that again,' several people shouted at me.

'Do what? I am not sure what I've done!'

The press sniffed a rat. They suspected foul play as Adnan disappeared back into the crowd and we all headed for the exit. One of Blair's aides thanked me, and Ross Benson slapped me on the back as he flicked through his digital screen. But not everyone was happy. One angry journalist brushed passed and paused to give his assessment of my performance.

'Not sure what you have done, eh? Let me help you figure that out. You just got him re-elected with that kiss. That's what you have done!'

Indeed, Tony Blair won the next election and the photograph of him being kissed by little Adnan was shown the world over. I had used the word 'kiss' when I meant 'hug'!

Twenty-four hours after we had rescued the two Iraqi boys, it was time to return to Az Zubair for another intelligence-gathering task. Lying on my American camp cot, 'mozzie' net draped over the top, my thoughts played havoc with my emotions. Dried blood stained my desert boots. The smell of burnt flesh hung around my jacket and the images of both lads remained vivid in my mind's eye. It was hard not to contemplate different outcomes for the young Iraqi brothers, the soldiers in the patrol, the medics or myself. The events of that day were replayed in my mind over and over for weeks after, and still do today. There was a desperation to appease myself that my decisions were the product of logical analysis. Endangering life because of my self-centred aspirations would have been unforgivable. Equally inexcusable was my impulsive decision that had come close to turning a wonderful wife into a widow and denying my 5-month-old daughter the opportunity to know her father. Some explain this as survivors' guilt, but this was different. It was a decision made of my own free will. Knowing my actions were right, they needed self-justification. Repeatedly, my days at Sandhurst were examined. All that was imparted, and that which was learnt, was analysed hourly. Revisiting many decisions, as well as the conversations with high quality officers and future leaders, had furnished me with a complex matrix for processing information to achieve success. Even the bumps and bruises caused by the turbulent relationship I had with Paddy and the rest of the Foot Guards had contributed to my decision-making. Unquestionably, the lives of the brothers had been saved nearly ten years before we ever met. The actions I took on the day were forged on the training areas of Sandhurst and Wales. It was a realization that, as much as I thought I was at the Academy to develop and nurture the next generation of generals, Sandhurst was there to shape me as a professional soldier.

MEMORANDUM

To: Cadets

From: The DS
Rowallan Company
Old College
RMA Sandhurst
CAMBERLEY
Surrey
GU15 4PQ

Tel: Camberley Mil Ext
Fax: Camberley Mil Ext

Date:

Your Ref: Our Ref:

Subject: Exercise RED LIGHT

1. Welcome to Exercise RED LIGHT!

2. Attached is a list of tasks which you are to achieve in the next 24 hrs.

3. You are to complete as many tasks as possible, bearing in mind points may mean prizes!

4. You must obtain documentary or photographic prove that you have achieved each task (1 hr & 12 hrs photo booths are available!)

5. In order to achieve any tasks there is no requirement to spend any money, credit will be given to the team which spends the least money.

6. Be prepared to give a 5 min presentation on you exploits in Pl HofS at 100 hrs.

7. You must all be aware that whilst this exercise tests initiative the conduct of this exercise is sensitive and there are several important rules:

    a. Do not BREAK THE LAW.

    b. Do not appear in the press, on radio or on television.

    c. Do not approach any of the following:

        (1) Members of the Royal Family.

        (2) Members of Parliament.

        (3) Senior officers of the Armed Forces or Military Establishments.

EX RED LIGHT TASKS

Task No	Task
1 ✓	Visit the cockpit of an operational Concorde aircraft.
2 ✓	Stand on foreign soil of a neutral country.
3	Interview a media celebrity (+ signed photo) Avoid BBC TV Centre.
4 ✓	Drive a car valued at #50,000 or more.
5	Milk a goat by hand.
6 ✓	Sweep a street within SW 1.
7 ✓	Ascertain the size of a Brontosaurus Egg.
8 ✗	Draw a full sketch map of Hampton Court Maze.
9 ✓	Swim with a Dolphin.
10 ✓	Work at a 5 Star Hotel as a Doorman.
11 ✓	Pose with a live, respectable female Model.
12	Have tea with the Chelsea Pensioners.
13 ✓	Sell programmes at a Major West End Show.
14 ✓	Drive a Thames pleasure Launch.
15 ✓	Act as a Guide in a Military Museum.
16	Man a Salvation Army (or other Charitable) Soup Kitchen.
17 ✓	Assist with the Distribution of a Major Fleet Street News Paper.
18 ✗	Obtain the signature and stamp of the Guard Commander The King's Troop RHA
19 ✗	Obtain an elephants foot print.
20 ✓	Travel 300m below ground.
21 ✓	Have breakfast in a Fire Station.

Chapter Twelve

Brecon Brenda

The United Kingdom had suffered one of its worst winters in recent memory; if it hadn't rained, it snowed. Floods, storms and the Polar Vortex punished the countryside and anyone venturing outdoors. With the final week of the course upon us, the forecast suggested there was much worse to come. Arriving back at Sandhurst after the weekend, my first port of call was to see if the platoon were ready for their final exercise. It was the penultimate Sunday of the course and there was no hiding the fact that this was going to be their final exercise. The students had developed a well-tuned intelligence-gathering system. They knew that Monday would see them deploy for the final time, but what they didn't know was where or when. It was important to the course integrity that we released no information and retained an air of mystery about everything we did. On this occasion, the students held most of the cards, so this called for innovation and deception on our part.

Operation Mincemeat, the most famous deception plan British Intelligence ever deployed – involving the disguising of the 1943 Allied invasion of Sicily – was mimicked in a calculated attempt to generate just enough doubt in the students' minds. The deceit was initiated the week before. During an idle moment amidst the chaos of test week, an exercise instruction was accidentally left on my desk in the study hall. It looked as authentic as it could get: a task matrix populated with the right names, a visit plan, maps with checkpoints and the main events list. Critical to the deception was the coordinating instructions page. It listed the timings, as well as the transport and feeding plans. Meticulously prepared, this fake document gave every detail of the imminent exercise with a clarity that made it look genuine. But knowing the students would remain suspicious, another ingredient was added. To give the fake instructions further credibility, we also employed a military driver to turn up at the accommodation early on Sunday morning. He was briefed to wander around the building looking for the DS. Playing ignorant, he told the waiting students that he was booked to pick up all the baggage and drive it to Dartmoor. So convincing was his role-play that Danner paid him to sneak in some food from a local shop during the exercise.

At 2000hrs, the accommodation was buzzing with activity. Walking through the accommodation doors caused blind panic. First to see me were Williams and Witherspoon, and both instantly began screaming 'bugout!' at the top of their voices.

'What? No, you fool. No, don't bugout,' I reassured them. 'It's just a check to see if you are ready for the week ahead!'

The commotion had generated much interest, and the corridor filled with students half-dressed and carrying rucksacks. The chaos was only arrested once they knew that my check was authentic and not a bugout.

'Calm down, softlad! Calm down!' Danner appeared from his room, impersonating me with an exaggerated Liverpool accent. It was quite impressive, and as I laughed, the rest of the students assumed it safe to join in and laugh with me.

'Well done, Danner,' I said. 'At last, we have found something you are good at! Tell you what. If you can impersonate the Company Sergeant Major, you won't be punished on the Mean Machine for being a cheeky little shit.'

Danner thereupon walked into King's room and threw his bed into the corridor, then his rucksack, followed closely by the contents of his locker. He emerged from the room with two roll mats under his arms and his chest pushed out.

'What are you looking at, you moron? Hoy! Hat, try harder. Marvellous, bloody marvellous! Dry your eyes, princess, and pick up that burden like you want to!' The quips rolled off his tongue as smooth as silk. This wasn't something he could just do; this was something he had been practising.

'Who else can you do?' I ventured.

'OK, fellas. Got to do better, fellas. Right, fellas, well done!'

Dancing around on his tiptoes to make himself appear taller and thinner than he was, Danner had all of Captain Dunn's mannerisms off to perfection – the cheeky smile, the frantic rubbing of his hands and the manic energy in everything he did. Danner was on a roll. He had everyone in stitches with his impression of Pete and his Somerset accent. Despite Pete never saying anything of the sort, Danner made pun after pun to rapturous applause.

'Do Colour Sergeant Jones!' Murphy yelled.

'I will, I will, to be sure, wee man! We'll no win this race walking at that pace I'll tell ye, get in me car! Aye, wee man, stop thinking and do as I tell ye or we will lose the race see.'

The gasps and muted giggles said enough. Right or wrong, Danner misjudged the moment. There's many a truth said in jest, but chivalry is the better part of valour. Of course, we all suspected that Paddy had assisted his platoon on several occasions. In his defence, most Colour Sergeants at Sandhurst did the same. It was not unusual for the DS to employ 'black economy' tactics to achieve acclaim. For me, it was plain that the students could see this and thought no less of me because it was not my style. It was unfortunate that Danner chose this moment to say those words. It had plagued me all weekend; now the first thing to greet me was a reminder of the issue.

Perchance more worrying was Danner's ease at undermining authority. His aptitude to inspire his peers was palpable. In his short time with Rowallan, his ability to manage people using command tools had developed better than anyone else. At times his pithy sarcasm proved just the right words to motivate and inspire. Despite his language being designed to divide and conquer using the perennial 'us and them' theme, his uncanny knack of galvanizing the platoon just when it needed it the most was not lost on me. There was something of the General Patton about the lad. With a commanding presence, bullish and dynamic, his size could intimidate and convince simultaneously. Uniquely, his polished banter could charm the devil into freezing hell over just for shits and giggles! This dangerous combination conspired to prevent him from making balanced judgments. All too frequently, he would cuff his analysis and bungle into a dilemma before charming his way out of it. While this would get you so far in the military, sooner or later, it would lead to a disaster. Was Danner capable of slapping two soldiers in a fashion similar to that of General Patton? Absolutely, but would he? Amidst today's tightly controlled performance standards, it was unlikely that Danner would reach such dizzy heights as Patton, but on a smaller scale, he would need to work harder if he wished to avoid an ignominious demise to his career in the Army.

Despite Danner's overstepping of the mark, morale was high as the main door swung and clattered behind me. To escape the rain, I made a quick dash across the flooded Chapel Square and into the warmth of my car. Sitting behind the wheel, looking at the shadows fleetingly appearing at the windows of the accommodation, the question of my approach once again gnawed at me. Who was this journey truly about – me or them? Watching my car's underperforming wipers swoosh back and forth, barely clearing the water from the windscreen, it was too late to change. The question was too big to answer and too complicated to tackle at that moment. There was an urgent need for me to park the issue and not let it distract me any more than it already had. This is something of a human condition. We never focus on our accolades, but instead, torture ourselves when we learn of criticism. Alas, tucked up in my bunk that night, fatigue had gripped me and there was no time to dwell.

At 0500hrs the following morning, the DS gathered in the pouring rain behind the Royal Memorial Chapel. Major Gray said little other than to report that his phone call with Pete late last night warned of floods across all of the Beacons. With the coaches due to collect us at 0530hrs, the bugout needed to be swift. Paddy and I entered from the rear of the accommodation, while the officers led by the OC burst through the front entrance.

'Bugout! Bugout! Five minutes, outside!'

It was hardly a surprise, and in less than ten minutes they were standing in a hollow square awaiting inspection. Most students had slept in their walking clothes and boots. They simply woke up, grabbed their rucksacks and walked out of the front door. Huddled together on the only spot that wasn't flooded, the inspection was brief. Emergency first aid kit, dry bags and a change of clothing all accounted for, the last check was the all-important command kit: compass, notebooks, protractors, pencils and maps.

'Where are your maps, Lane?'

'In my pocket, Colour Sergeant!'

'What? All five of them?'

'No, Colour Sergeant. Just my Dartmoor map!'

'Why is that? Since you have been on the course, the instruction has always been, we carry all our maps so we are ready to go anywhere at any time. What are you going to do if we end up in Wales?'

'One of the drivers told us last night we were going to Dartmoor. I didn't see the sense in needlessly carrying any other maps!'

We hadn't expected the deception plan to work this well, but before we boarded the coaches, most of the course would return to the accommodation to retrieve their other maps. Although it was Lane who had been caught out, at least 80 per cent of the course were equally as guilty.

The early start ensured we beat most of the traffic to the Severn Bridge. By 0800hours, we had entered South Wales. Mystically, the rain seemed to increase the moment we paid the toll fee to cross the bridge. The spray from the roads made it all but impossible to see anything from our coach window. There was water everywhere. Leaves and broken branch ends rode high on the torrents of water running down the gutters of every road we travelled on. Gathered at the grates guarding the drains, foliage and debris indicative of a brutal storm caused localized flooding. If Bristol and South Wales had been hit by some extreme weather, you could bet the Brecon Beacons had it worse.

The coach pulled into the car park of a disused quarry about 30km south of Usk reservoir. This was the start point of the exercise, and the first task was to navigate to Usk as quickly as possible. Captain Dunn split the platoon in half. King, Danner, Lane, Stone, Packman, Murphy, Boyle and Mathews were in the first group, while Barns, Norris, Haigh, Williams, Witherspoon, Moore, Francis and Rideout were with me in group two. For a pleasant change, my group would be the last to set off, and Haigh would take command. We huddled under the branches of a small copse as everyone else departed. Haigh marked his route and organized his team – Moore as check-navigator, Norris as pacer and Rideout as tail-end Charlie.

Haigh's target was approximately 5km away. Foel Fraith, a hilly escarpment on the foothills of the Brecon Beacons, located on the southern edge of the mountains. Despite its lowly height of just 600 metres above sea level, the climb was steep from the start. The base of the ascent was green scrubland, which quickly gave way to a large open expanse before hitting rock crags leading to the crest. Hiding from the driving rain in our little huddle, it appeared to be a straightforward leg: head north, pick up the obvious re-entrant and follow it to the crest. But in practical terms, this was going to be Haigh's biggest ever challenge. The driving rain would become his worst nightmare, energy would quickly ebb away and concentration levels would drop with each kilometre covered. To compound the issue, visibility was down to less than 500 metres, and you could guarantee it would be less than that once we left the scrubland and headed up the hill.

Haigh dithered as we set off on the first part of the route. At the base of the re-entrant, he boxed from left to right looking for an attack point. Stupidly, he dragged his group with him each time he walked up and down the myriad of tracks at the base before he eventually selected a route. Although the distance wasn't great, the constant stop-start, get up, get down began to take its toll. At the point which we broke clear of the scrubland, we had been walking for over an hour. It was painfully slow and tedious progress, not to mention incredibly frustrating. Occasionally, someone would snap at Haigh and his constant procrastination. His response was typically flippant, dismissive and random, which served to do little more than fuel his critics. Thick-skinned or desensitized, it was hard to fathom out if he was aware of other people's opinions. However, it was crystal clear that he had been subjected to similar criticisms previously.

Two hours had passed before we walked into the open expanse of Foel Fraith. Howling winds smashed the rain through every nook and cranny of our clothing. Even before we had reached the halfway point, cramp and cold were affecting the group. The squelching of boots could be heard in between the gusts of wind and dancing rain. Water ran freely from the escape holes in rucksacks and waterproof pockets. It was almost like wading through a chest-high stream as the water continued to pour in from the east. The higher we got, the more intense the rain was. By the time we hit the 300-metre contour, visibility was less than 20 metres and our speed had dropped to less than a kilometre per hour. Eventually, we stumbled upon the grey slate of the escarpment that led to the crest of the hill and up to Haigh's finish point. It had taken four hours and we had expended much energy in getting there.

Williams was the next student in the hot seat. We gathered for a brief moment to confirm the location he was to navigate to and the route he would take. Standing at the apex of the hill, there was no time to waste; we needed to get moving before the elements caused casualties. This command appointment was critical to Williams. He was sitting on a Platoon Commander's warning and he knew that mistakes at this stage of the course would be costly. Biting my lip as I watched him draw up his route card, he was working at a snail's pace.

'Do up your jacket, Williams. The bloody rain is pouring through that gap. Consider a short leg first to get off the crest and out of the elements.'

Williams called on Norris to check-navigate, and between them they plotted a route along the crest.

With less than 400 metres covered, we had stopped more than ten times to check-navigate. Each stop presented the weather with an opportunity to take a chunk of resilience out of the group. Sensing that the navigation was becoming more than Williams could cope with, he called for Moore to assist. It was a prudent move. Moore was recognized as the best navigator in the platoon. As far as I was concerned, this was a good use of human resources at this stage. For the next 2km, the pace picked up. We were closing in on the second-highest peak, Picws-Du, from where we would begin our descent and take a respite from the elements. But just as there seemed to be progress, Williams stopped. For a while, the three decision-makers chatted as the rest of the group cowered in the wind and rain. It must have been less than a minute before my patience with Williams broke.

'What's the holdup?'

'Nothing, Colour Sergeant, we are just checking the map,' said Moore.

'I was asking Williams. What's the holdup?' Williams didn't answer. His eyes had glazed over and he was unsteady on his feet. Worse still, he was becoming unresponsive. This was serious. Williams was on the edge of succumbing to hypothermia and we needed to do something right now.

'Moore, Norris – plot me a route to the north of Fan Fach. We need to drop off the crest and into the bowl on a direct bearing. Rideout, Witherspoon, get up here and remove Williams' rucksack. The remainder of you, get around Williams and keep the wind and rain off him. It's about 900 metres to the bowl of Fan Fach. We are going to walk him to the bowl so we can make an assessment on what to do next.'

Francis made his way to the front to assist with the navigation. Employing a technique for limited visibility, Francis walked in front of Moore so that he could be used as a fixed point to lay the compass onto. It was an impressive demonstration of assimilation. Captain Dunn had taught this technique only once during the early weeks of training, but now these young men were using it during an emerging crisis.

Fifteen minutes later, we handrailed the lip of Fan Fach to the north and descended to a rocky outcrop. The grey slate knife's edge would afford us the slightest protection from the wind and allow the group to erect a temporary shelter. Williams was stripped naked and shoved into a sleeping bag. Witherspoon boiled endless cups of water to make hot chocolate, and forced it down Williams. Francis, Moore and Norris worked on planning a route to Usk reservoir via the lowland. The pair busied themselves with conducting a SWOT in anticipation of not moving Williams if his condition deteriorated. To date, there had been doubts over a number of these young men. Could they manage in a disaster? Would they prevail under fire or cope with serious pressure? From the embers of this developing situation, it was an unequivocal 'yes'.

Darkness had enveloped our position to bring visibility down to five metres. Although the mist was still present, it was less relevant. After an hour, Williams' condition improved. He was coherent and cognitive in his response, if not overly apologetic. The team dressed him ready for the final leg into Usk ravine and on to the reservoir. We were approximately 5km from our destination and 4km from the nearest road. Although the SWOT analysis had already informed the team that the only answer here was to head for Usk, it was worth re-evaluating the problem once we knew how Williams was coping with the march. He would need to walk as much as he could before we made an improvised stretcher to carry him. It was imperative we eked every inch of his mobility out of his body before we tapped into our own reserves to get him off the Fan.

At the 4km point, we met Pat in a Land Rover on the track to Usk. He had driven as far up the path as was possible.

'What's happened, Gaz?'

'Williams. He's gone down!' Pat took one look at the lad, who by now had begun to slip into a semi-comatose state, and declared he would take him to hospital.

'He's not the first today, Gaz, and if they don't get a grip of their personal admin, he won't be the last. You need to stay on top of them!'

Pat sped off in the Land Rover as we walked the last kilometre to Usk reservoir. As we arrived, it was clear that Paddy and Captain Watts' group had taken casualties. Major Gray was holding a long chat with the rest of the DS by the time my group arrived.

'Colour, the medics have taken Williams to the hospital and we are just discussing the need to curtail the programme amidst this foul weather. I think we cancel the night navigation.'

Nodding in agreement, Captain Watts supported his fellow Platoon Commander's recommendation. But the look on Major Gray's face compromised his reluctance to approve.

'I am not keen to cancel anything, but it would help if we shortened the course.'

Eddie's eyes opened wide as he focused on Major Gray.

'Colour. Could you shorten the course and keep the route in the shelter of the trees, so they are protected from the weather?'

Eddie paused. He had spent a full day laying out the circuit, none of which was accessible by track. Setting up a new circuit would firstly involve recovering the checkpoint markers scattered around the hills of Usk.

'It's a pain in the arse but not impossible, Sir!'

Captain Dunn and I jumped into a vehicle and headed off to the hospital to check on Williams at Merthyr Tydfil. By the time we got through the rush-hour traffic and endless car accidents caused by the horrendous weather, Williams was tucked up in a bed on a ward. Fortunately for us, the doctor doing the rounds was familiar with the military, having done some service as a young man.

'The lad has been suffering from hypothermia. You got him here just in time. His feet are trashed, suffering from trench foot and frostnip, maybe frostbite!'

From the far side of the room, a thunderous voice rumbled down the ward.

'Did you lot see the forecast before you decided to play silly buggers with these cadets?'

An angry staff nurse appeared from behind a surgical curtain at the far end of the room. Stereotypically matriarchal, and hell-bent on making her feelings known, she stomped purposefully across the shiny floor. As she closed in on us, her body language became increasingly animated, so I took two steps behind Captain Dunn and hid!

Captain Dunn was cornered. The nurse blocked his exit and unleashed a diatribe of accusations as the boss rolled with the punches. By the time the nurse had spent her energy complaining, Captain Dunn had spun the conversation around 180 degrees by explaining the need to push servicemen to the limit of their ability.

'Lives will be saved. The world will remain free from tyrants, and the oppressed can move out of the shadows of evil. Inevitably, there will be bumps and bruises along the way, but he will be better for it, so will the rest of the free world.'

He countered the nurse's argument with a serenity beyond my understanding. Seconds later, the nurse's demeanour was in reverse. Smiling and agreeing with our 'train hard, fight easy' philosophy, she had been charmed into submission. Unbelievably, Captain Dunn then suggested the nurse had been a little too eager to berate those who protected her democratic right to criticize whomsoever she desired. Seconds later, the nurse duly apologized with sincerity and gratitude. It was a joy to watch him at work. His ability to manage heated discussions and disarm people with a gentle nudge was the sign of a brilliant leader. The privilege of watching the most gifted officers do this is a rare treat and not something you get to witness that often.

During the early 1990s, whilst serving as a Rifle Company Platoon Sergeant in Northern Ireland, my area of operations was the Republican stronghold of Strabane. There was never a dull moment in this border town as terrorists sneaked across the River Foyle and routinely carried out bombings and shootings. My platoon had been gated after an informant had tipped off the RUC that a gunman was lying in wait for us in the Head of the Town district. After four dull days, with boredom at its peak, a policeman burst into the operations room and announced they needed help to capture a fleeing gunman. After a quick map brief, the Chief Constable requested we deploy to our cut-off positions. The platoon sprang into action, and just as we rounded the corner, we saw the gunman trying to escape. After a frantic fifteen minutes of chasing him, we had him pinned down in a house on the border. The police were called and the gunman was apprehended.

The feeling of capturing a gunman is intoxicating. Supercharged euphoria courses through the body like the elixir of life. A sense of accomplishment and pride intermingled with excitement and emotion displaces rational thinking. Passions rocket through the roof until the nerves subside and the realization of what you have just achieved is digested. With the man in custody, the boys withdrew back to Strabane Police Station. My young Platoon Commander and the rest of the Riflemen were merrily slapping themselves on the back when the Commanding Officer arrived. Lieutenant Colonel Nick Cottam was a calm, assured character with the easiest of personalities. He congratulated us on our endeavours before announcing that the man we captured was a local farmer carrying a legally held shotgun. From what he had discovered, the man had been deliberately trying to tease out a reaction from the security forces. He concluded by saying that from his experience, the man we had caught was nothing more than a patsy. Calmly, the Commanding Officer guided the conversation towards our tactical procedures in search of any flaws in our plan. He listened attentively, keen to include his subordinates in the process of 'identifying lessons'. Too inexperienced to understand what he was doing, it felt like we were just backslapping and congratulating each other. Eventually, we discovered that we had inadvertently left our flank unprotected and vulnerable to a cross-border attack. Had the terrorist decided to shoot from within the Irish Republic, there was no way we could have responded.

The Colonel had not said much. He gently steered our conversation to a point where we realized this huge mistake. Our eagerness could have cost lives, and he knew it. With a smile on his face, he politely requested that should we be faced with such pressure in the future, it would be prudent to seek advice before embarking on an unsupported operation. However, he once again congratulated us and the Riflemen as he left our base. It was the most extraordinary telling-off I had ever received. Colonel Cottam's words kept me awake for weeks, as he suggested that the Provisional IRA may have used this incident as a trial run for the real thing. To affirm his suspicion, two weeks later, the IRA ran the same incident again, but this time using more terrorists and assault rifles. It was undeniably because of his intellect and insight that the terrorist attack failed. Colonel Cottam would have been justified in blaming me for giving the IRA the information they required to mount the follow-up attack. But one of the greatest characteristics of his leadership was his 'no blame culture'. If something failed, the inquest started with him. It was an infectious approach that forged loyalty and respect.

Captain Dunn had all these qualities too. Wherever he was destined for in life, he would enthuse and inspire those around him. Never once did the tone or pitch of his voice change during his conversation with the angry nurse. He remained humble and grateful for the care the nurse was affording Williams. But most impressively, he never backed down or shied away from confronting the issue in hand. So jealous was I of his ability to defuse tensions that, pathetically, I suggested he had gone soft. Such a betrayal of Rowallan DS values warranted punishment, and I urged him to confess his crimes to the Sergeant Major. As the bare minimum, he should volunteer himself to wear the string vest for not dragging the nurse back to Sandhurst for ten laps of the Mean Machine! But Captain Dunn just winked at me as if to say, 'if you've got it, flaunt it'.

Many leaders listen to what is being said, but few hear the words. It is a skill that is hard to master, but once you have met an officer who listens intently but hears nothing, you will know how rare it is to meet someone who can listen and hear what is being said. Captain Dunn was just such a man. It wasn't through a sense of duty he thanked the nurse for her paternalistic rhetoric, but because he was hearing her words and identifying with her character and profession. Every word he used was delivered with all the sincerity of a proud parent, with not a hint of the uncompromising Platoon Commander he played previously.

The journey back to Usk was tortuous. The roads were littered with minor traffic accidents and water flowed wildly down the verges and gutters. The only positive result of the day was to arrive just in time to witness the end of the night navigation. Major Gray and Eddie manned the control point and were happily chatting about fitness routines and interval training as we checked in.

'Anyone lost or not back?' Captain Dunn asked.

'Lane got lost,' said Eddie. 'He only made four of the six checkpoints. The lad broke me, again. There is no helping someone who doesn't try. It is like he has given up. Even the slowest of the rest made it back with fifteen minutes to spare. It couldn't have been much easier!'

The boss wore a look of disappointment before suggesting we walk around the bashers to see how the students were coping. Lane was already in his sleeping bag.

'Lane. Have you eaten?' I asked.

'Yes, Colour Sergeant.'

'Dried your feet? Powdered them? Got yourself ready for tomorrow?'

'Yes, Colour Sergeant.'

It was a blatant lie. His peers were still cooking, all of whom arrived back at camp long before him. But it was prudent to let him think he knew best. Foregoing food for sleep is akin to a criminal offence in the military. If he hadn't eaten, tomorrow's performance would suffer. We made our way around the remaining students, and to a man, they all asked after Williams. We hadn't noticed this before, but Williams was a popular student. They all recognized he wasn't brilliant at anything – in fact, he was distinctly average – but he worked tirelessly for his peers. He never complained to his fellow students or dodged a shift; he was just the 'grey man' we first met. It was going to be a tricky conclusion for Williams. Failing to take part in the final exercise whilst on a Platoon Commander's warning would certainly spell an end to his time in the Army.

The following morning arrived sooner than we would have liked, and the rain had not relented one bit. The water flooded the tracks around Usk Forest, with mini mudslides forming around the embankments. But the rain was not a consideration Pat would listen to; he was keen to get on with the first serial of the day. In fact, the heavy rainfall had just given Pat another opportunity to inflict misery on the students. He and Tracy had set out a log race around the tracks of the northern forest of Usk reservoir. It was an undulating circuit which started off with one long uphill stretch. There was a small surprise at the end, but in the interests of fair competition, Pat said nothing to the Staff, other than 'be prepared!'.

Tracy warmed up the muscles of the students. She gently jogged the course up and down the tarmac road at the head of the reservoir. Once the muscle memory had sharpened the senses, Tracy revised the skill of 'log carriage'. It was essential to refresh the drills before they took part in the race. Notwithstanding the fact these logs were thinner and light enough to be carried by just two men, they were still long and cumbersome. Carrying such an awkward dead weight in such close proximity to other people is dangerous. Add to it weary minds and wet conditions, and you have a recipe for disaster. Dwarfed by Captain Dunn and Eddie, Tracy stood before the course in the pouring rain. She briefed the students on the route, reiterating the need for caution on the narrow, wet tracks. In bullish fashion, Pat cut her off before she finished.

'Blah blah blah blah! Don't get hurt and all that good crap. Get in the free fall position you bunch of fannies!'

Instantly, all the effort Tracy had put into keeping people safe was undone. For the briefest of moments, I thought Pat was joking.

'Don't just stand there, you bloody morons! Get on the road and adopt the freefall position!'

Witherspoon took charge of the race for No. 2 Platoon. He had done everything we had previously taught him. Rideout and Moore would set the pace, tasked with securing a lead before they entered the narrow tracks. There would be Danner and Francis on the first change, then King and Murphy next. The lad had thought this through. Seconds before the Sergeant Major started the race, Major Gray shouted out the scores.

'No. 2 Platoon, you have it all to do here. Fifteen to eighteen in favour of No. 1 Platoon. There is only one more race after this, so if you haven't figured it out, this is a must win.'

It felt like an age before Pat gave his familiar cry to start the race. Deliberately seeking to heighten tensions, he dragged out the start.

'Stand by! Stand by! Stand by! Stand by! Go!'

Both platoons were neck and neck as they squeezed into the first of the narrow tracks heading north up the hill in the forest. Paddy's boys had edged the lead as the track narrowed to a single path, and Captain Dunn asked Witherspoon for his thoughts.

'What's the plan, Witherspoon? How are you going to recover this?'

'Just going to keep with them until the road opens up, Sir.'

At the halfway mark, the two platoons were bumper to bumper. Provided the road opened as Witherspoon predicted, this race wasn't over. As both groups began the tricky descent, Witherspoon tried to overtake, only to be foiled by the terrain each time. He issued his final plan. In the last 100 metres, he would outsprint his opponents. He refused to allow Rideout and Moore to get on the log, explaining he was holding them in reserve.

'Are you sure, Witherspoon?'

'Yes, Sir! I am sure.'

We broke out of the woods with 300 metres to go and the two logs began to draw level.

'What's the plan now, Witherspoon?'

'We are going to launch soon, Sir.'

Witherspoon called for his sprinters just as Pat unexpectedly appeared from a gap in the hedgerow. With Paddy's team having their noses in front, they were first through the gap. Manically, he directed the lead log through the bushes and into a flooded irrigation ditch. The banks were high and slippery, and the width scarcely big enough for one log. There would be no overtaking. No. 1 Platoon crossed the line, which was marked by a flooded culvert at the start of the road.

The celebrations from Paddy were once again overzealous. He punched the air triumphantly several times before letting out a huge victory cry. Captain Dunn placed his hands on his hips and glanced over at me. There was no disguising his disappointment. He had given Witherspoon as many hints as possible without telling him that he needed to get ahead of the other platoon before they got in the water. Fortune favours the brave, and on this occasion, Witherspoon misjudged the definition of 'brave'. Tough as it was, the loss deserved a punishment. Witherspoon was invited to pick up both the logs and instructed to take his team back across the last kilometre of the race. As we disappeared down the bank and into the drainage ditch, Paddy could be heard celebrating the win. Chants of 'We are the Champions' cut through the soul of the platoon. It was unbearable to watch the morale physically ebb from the collective spirit of the students.

With a hint of empathy, Pete was ready to receive the logs with the truck as we returned.

'The OC needs you and your boss, Gaz. There is some kind of problem with the visit!'

Major Gray was frantically scribbling in his folder as all the Staff gathered around his basher.

'The College Commander's flight is cancelled, so tomorrow he is travelling by car instead. This means his visit is slashed from four hours to one. Before you all jump for joy, you need to whittle down your list of who he needs to see. So, only the very worst and the very best. James, very worst, very best please. Who are they?'

'Lane and Mathews.'

'Thank you. Same question, Tom?'

'Staples and Carter.'

'Brilliant, team, thank you. Here is an adjusted MEL [main events list]. You have about ten minutes per person. Twenty minutes each platoon. He must see the right people. If you waste time, you will lose the opportunity to convince him of your argument at the final Progress Board. Make sure you are clear with him on those you feel will fail, and your Highland Trophy nomination. So be warned. Just manage the time sensibly; he has to be in the car and back on his way home by 1200hrs to make his next appointment.'

Captain Dunn and I pored over the MEL. We needed to adjust our appointment matrix to ensure Lane and Mathews were both midway through their respective command tasks when the Colonel visited. It would require some cunning choreography to get him in the right place at the right time without over-orchestrating the visit.

The College Commander turned up five minutes ahead of time. After a few pleasantries, Major Gray ushered him to watch Lane take charge of a Command Task. It was a simple par-buckle mission requiring little thinking, but lots of coordination and communication.

'Hi, Colour Sergeant. I note the weather has been troublesome over the first two days. How is Williams?' the College Commander enquired.

'We left him in good spirits last night, Sir.'

'Good. That's reassuring. Now, how about Lane?'

'Well, Sir. He is failing to engage or communicate with his group on this task. We have made some progress over the last two weeks, but much of his body language appears to suggest he doesn't want to be here!'

For a few minutes we stood quietly watching Lane exercise his Command and Control skills. Lane stood silently, watching his peers figure out the best way of achieving their task. Occasionally he offered advice, but for the ten minutes the Commander witnessed, Lane was ineffectual and unfocused. As time ran out, the group failed to achieve their aim. The College Commander invited me to debrief the task before he took Lane to one side and quizzed him about his desire to be an Army officer. For all the money in the world, we couldn't guess how this was going to pan out. It appeared calm and cordial, and it looked like the College Commander would cave in and give him another chance.

Captain Dunn looked at his watch. He was anxious and agitated, as the conversation went on for some time.

'He is not going to get to see Mathews. Look at the time, Colour!'

Just as he said that, Major Gray and Captain Watts arrived to escort the Commander away.

'Ah, it's fortuitous you are all here,' the College Commander said as he joined the group.

'Lane. Regrettably, I have informed him that the Army does not require his services. He has been given the option to complete the course and leave with dignity, rather than drag him off unceremoniously right now. This way, he can leave honourably and earn the respect of his peers. Alternatively, he can leave now. The choice is his.'

You could see Pat's blood boil. If he had his way, it would be a dishonourable discharge followed swiftly by public humiliation as the whole Company kicked him up the backside before he boarded the train home. But there was much to be learnt from the Commander's management of this event. He had been understanding and respectful in acknowledging that not everyone was cut out for the demands of military service.

'Sadly, I am nearly out of time,' he continued. 'I can make one more visit. Is it Carter who is on a Company Commander's warning?'

'Och, he is no that bad, Sir.' Paddy looked at Captain Watts and gave him a small nudge with his elbow.

'The Colour Sergeant is right, Sir. Maybe it would be more beneficial to watch Staples.'

'Fine, Tom. I am in your hands, lead on.'

As the group turned to walk in the direction of No. 1 Platoon's command tasks, I tugged at Pat's smock.

'What the fuck is that about? He has done nothing but complain about Carter from the day he arrived. Here is the best opportunity to get rid of him and instead he is showing off his prize puppy!'

'Gaz, he is doing what's right for his platoon. There is nothing wrong with what he said. Maybe you should have changed the order to ensure Mathews was seen first. But don't panic. The Commandant is coming out for the final race, so we will ensure he runs with No. 2 Platoon. And don't forget, the OC still has a dog in this fight. He will make the final recommendation to the Commandant of who is a worthy recipient of the Highland Trophy.'

It had been a lousy morning, and it was hard to see how it could get much worse. But five minutes later the medics ran past us, heading in the direction of our students. By the time we had caught them up, they were already attending to a forlorn figure crumpled on the floor. As the young medics parted to break open their respective first aid bags, Mathews could be seen clutching his ankle. He had fallen off a rope bridge and landed awkwardly, and the initial assessments were not good. The medics had called for a stretcher, and Pat arrived driving the ambulance. Gingerly, he was loaded into the back of the military ambulance and by the end of day two, we had two casualties residing in Merthyr Tydfil hospital!

As night fell, the students were writing essays in their bashers. As part of their final grades, the essays needed to be coherent and clear. To ensure there was no cheating, the DS patrolled the basher area and answered questions on the problem they had been invited to analyse. Lane was busy writing his notes. He was content and fairly chirpy when we exchanged comments on the day. The College Commander had implied that no one was to know about the decision he had made until Lane had decided it was time to go. In keeping with this wish, there was no hint given that we knew what had been said. It was uncomfortable keeping secrets, but this was for a good reason. Allowing Lane to leave on his own terms was genius. He would leave with no recriminations, while we would declare ourselves the epitome of professionalism. But collecting the essays, we could see Lane had subconsciously given up. He was the first to finish and the first to go to sleep.

Wednesday morning's field inspection was telling. Lane had failed to shave, brush his teeth or cover his boots with polish. If this pretence was to remain credible, he would need to suffer the same fate as he had throughout the course.

'Fifty names, "My boots need polishing". Fifty names, "My teeth need cleaning". Fifty names, "I must wash and shave".'

With apathy seeping through his every movement, Lane began his punishment. You could see the confusion in his eyes. Maybe he had understood the College Commander's words differently to me. This was not a free hit! If he wished to leave with respect, it still needed to be earned. There were only two others who deserved punishment during the inspection, and the fear that Lane had been compromised dawned on all the DS.

'Not sure he can stay much longer, Gaz,' Eddie whispered in my ear. 'If he continues to put in so little effort, his own mates will end up filling him in!'

This was now a real concern, but one we felt Lane had identified. If he wished to take up the offer the College Commander gave him, he still had to apply himself. The irony was it was the lack of trying that had got him into this predicament. It was like watching car crash TV; there is some enjoyment, but you wince all the way through it. It was hard to see how he was going to survive the next forty-eight hours.

Immediately after the last student had repacked his rucksack, the course undertook a forced march to a small ravine 2km north of Usk reservoir. As we arrived, we were greeted by Pete and a large 4-ton truck. On the back of the vehicle were two equipment packs with sufficient stores to build a Burma bridge – scaffolding poles for the A-frame that would support the ropes spanning the gorge, pulleys, winches, jackhammers, pegs and wood planks. Each platoon was tasked with constructing a rope bridge that could carry every student from one side to the other and back again. There would be heavy lifting and a degree of engineering required to accomplish the task: geometry to calculate the gap, measuring to formulate the lifts, an initiative to build a contraption to get to the far bank before the second A-frame' came across.

It was yet again another competition, but this time the prize was not three points – it was the right to begin the final race with a three-minute start. The size of this generous lead was indicative of the length of the race, although at this stage, the students knew nothing of what lay ahead. For Boyle, it was not about the reward, it was about the desire to win. This was his moment in command, and he wanted to demonstrate his grasp of all he had learnt. His first action was to gather the platoon and confess to knowing nothing about engineering, maths or geometry! Instead of trying to bluff his way through the task, he invited others to come up with a solution. Firstly, he nominated a second in command, then he split the platoon into three groups and gave them five minutes to identify possible Courses of Action (COA).

Murphy spoke for group one. His team had made a number of assumptions with their calculations and deduced there was sufficient equipment to make a tightrope bridge, with one rope at the top to hold on to and one at the bottom to walk across. But their solution for getting the first man across the gorge to build the bridge on the far bank was to fire him across by making a trebuchet! For a brief moment, the conversation continued as Boyle listened intently to the building of the ancient weapon of war. Captain Dunn giggled and, spontaneously, we all burst out laughing.

'Boyle! Just so we are clear – because at the moment, I am worried that you are actually considering this COA – under no circumstances is anyone getting fired across the gap in a trebuchet!'

He nodded and professed to knowing that it was not going to be allowed, but he had a duty as a commander to listen to the plan!

Witherspoon spoke for team two. He waved his arms like a windmill as he pointed out where the bridge would sit and what it would fix up against. His proposal didn't involve the use of any scaffolding poles or winches; it was just two ropes strung across the gap. Interestingly, both ropes were at the same height and running parallel, 2ft apart. The concept was to shimmy across using legs and hands for purchase and propulsion. This novel idea had some credibility, but it lacked the ingenuity we were hoping for. Although their solution for getting the first person across the gorge, so they could tie their ropes to the trees on the far bank, did have some imagination, the chance of success was minimal. Witherspoon explained they would make a lasso and hook it around a tree on the far side, before swinging across like Tarzan. When quizzed about the strength of the branch they would lasso, he simply replied that they would send the lightest member across and hope it didn't break.

It was not looking good for Boyle. The two COAs he had listened to thus far offered him little to work with. Worryingly, his final group consisted of the less effective members of the platoon, led by Stone. The past few days had not been kind to Stone, with an outbreak of acne and a black eye after a wayward bungee-cord on the first night snapped and hit him square in the face. His jacket was ripped and his trousers were hanging off him like an American gangsta rapper. He doodled in his notebook as Captain Dunn snapped at him for daydreaming, but then announced:

'Our plan is to build a double A-frame, lash three of the four planks together and make a drawbridge. This will get us three-quarters of the way across the gap. One man will then carry the final plank across the drawbridge and place it on the edge of the bridge to reach the far bank. He takes with him a rope and ties it to the trunk of the large tree. We use this rope to make a dumb waiter and deliver the A-frame to the far bank. After that, we can build our Burma bridge, Sir.'

We were all stunned into silence. It was brilliant. Stone had pulled out a solution that was better than the DS answer. What was more, he delivered his brief with a conviction and maturity that had thus far been missing.

As Witherspoon set about following Stone's plan, Captain Dunn questioned our assessment of the lad. What we had just witnessed was as good as we could have wished for, and despite his scraggy appearance, there was something about his thought process that stirred doubt in our minds. If he could reach this level of intellect more frequently, he could possibly make it as an Army officer. We both sat on a fallen tree, watching the platoon lash together planks, and discussed the chances of Stone passing the course. He had made some monumental mistakes in his short time with us, but he was also maturing quickly. The end of the course may come too soon for him, or maybe we needed to take a risk. For ten minutes, we debated the possible outcomes. We discussed every extremity, from winning the Sword of Honour to making a poor decision that led to the deaths of hundreds of soldiers or millions of pounds. Sitting quietly, contemplating our conundrum, we watched Stone orchestrate the task. If we were intending to convince Major Gray to fail Stone, it would be near impossible after this performance.

With the double A-frame reaching high into the air, the platoon lowered the bridge unit into the horizontal position. The planks swung gently from side to side as Norris walked to the edge. Placing the final plank between the gap, he crossed the gorge as planned. Boyle ordered King and Barns across with ropes and pulleys, and Norris recovered the loose plank before the home bank team retracted the bridge. Minutes later, the dumb waiter was ferrying poles across the gap and enthusiasm was high, full of hope, that is until Pat arrived.

'You lot on a go slow? No. 1 Platoon are already making their bridge.'

We all walked over to see how Paddy's boys were doing, and of course, they were in full flow building their bridge. We had been at the task for nearly an hour and a half, and they were close to finishing. Although there was a time limit of three hours, it looked as if Paddy's boys would be finished in under two.

To tell the truth, it was no longer affecting me. We had lost the platoon competition and my best student could not win the Highland Trophy whilst sat in a hospital bed in Merthyr Tydfil. It was my turn to feel resigned to my fate. There was little to be said as we walked back to see the progress our boys had made. Even if Paddy had helped his students find the solution, it was not going to change the outcome. There was little to be gained for Paddy, other than massaging his ego. Winning every event would be worthless to the students later in life. Getting my head around this never-ending desire to win at the cost of student education was a fool's errand. Again, it took me to the point of distraction and the bridge was completed without me realizing it. As the last man made the journey across the improvised structure, the platoon high-fived and hugged Stone. They were truly thrilled with their achievement, even though they already knew they had come last. It was the second time Stone had demonstrated his engineering prowess. Maybe we needed to overlook his other failings. There was no denying that this lad had a rare talent; it just wasn't fully compatible with the military.

With the bridges dismantled and the stores placed back on Pete's truck, Packman was given a grid reference and told to lead the platoon to the described location and set up camp for the night. Francis was simultaneously told to attend a Company Commander's Orders Group upon arrival at the new location. The campsite was 3km away as the crow flies. A large wooded area just south of Cray reservoir in the shadows of Pen-y-Fan would be home for the final night out for the course. It would take two hours to get there now that night had descended, and as soon as they arrived it was time to get busy planning the final race of the course.

With all the students gathered around Francis' basher, there was a mood of determination in the air. It was 1900hrs on day three of the final exercise, and

Francis issued his plan for the following day's race. We had put him in charge because he had demonstrated some fine leadership qualities over the past two months. Moreover, the final race was a marathon and it needed a calm, analytical approach and a coherent strategy, and Francis had these qualities. The platoon had landscaped a model of the ground the race would be run across, using mud and branches to replicate the undulations, main roads and rivers. Like Montgomery issuing his orders for the D-Day landings, Francis stood in front of his model with a stick clutched in his hands as a pointer. Describing the route as if it was their last ever journey, the enormity of the task was evident: 20 miles across the Brecon Beacons. Worse still, every hill between here and the finish point would need to be conquered. But Francis didn't wince in his delivery. Focused and determined, he quickly cut to the heart of the problem. Even when he explained that there was a 7km walk carrying full kit, just to get to the start point, he didn't miss a beat with his conviction.

Captain Dunn congratulated Francis on his delivery. Before he gave the students his final pep talk of the course, he pulled out a bag of jelly babies and offered them around. With a huge smile and the occasional use of some light-hearted banter, the tone was congratulatory.

> 'Fellas! Whatever happens from here on in, you should be proud of what you have done. Just the fact that you are still here is testimony to a unique resilience. But fellas, tomorrow is all about you. It is about applying all the lessons we have taught you. Stay focused and ready for the unexpected, because you all know we like to challenge your resolve by testing your sense of humour. Above all, show determination to win with a positive attitude when things go wrong. Don't amplify the problem; rectify it before you decide to make the next move. Always remember, things can, and often do, get worse. Colour Sergeant, do you have anything you wish to add?'

I could have talked for an hour. There was so much to say. The route was horrendous, the surprises in store were hideous and, most of all, they had a three-minute penalty before they could cross the start line.

> 'Let's reflect on what we've learnt during the course. I have attempted to break your resolve, smash your spirit and press you to quit. Repeatedly, I have demanded the unachievable, tricked you and deliberately deceived you. I have deprived you of food, sleep and privacy, actively sought to cause agitation and friction. You have been ushered to the precipice of hell's valley just so you could appreciate the view! I did this to cultivate the ingredients of inspirational leadership. It was essential you undertook this journey, so you discovered those characteristics that separate the ordinary

from the great, to gift you the qualities to think straight under stress, to cope with intolerable pressure, to survive in the most miserable of physical or climatic conditions. So, if you are looking for inspiration, look no further than the end of your nose. You have the individual fortitude to endure unrivalled misery, the unity to defeat a concerted effort to unpick your emotional strength. You have demonstrated it all. You are an inspirational group of young men. Apply Captain Dunn's advice. Evaluate and re-evaluate constantly. A blend of command tools and a unique character will bring success. I will see you at the southern edge of the wood at 0430hrs, ready to walk to the start point.'

Chapter Thirteen

Brecon Bimble

The apprehension and nerves had the better of me. It was 0300hrs, and less than two hours of sleep had been achieved. Sitting bolt upright, sleeping bag wrapped around me, the students could be heard shuffling around the wood, packing kit and encouraging each other not to be late. Having packed my kit, Paddy and I waited for the students to assemble. We both stood on the edge of the wood chatting about the route as the students slowly made their way out of the forest. The sound of twigs snapping and branches swaying echoed around the woods as the course broke out onto the track. They were relieved to discover that there would be no field inspection. The faff involved was tedious and time-consuming, something we could not afford on this event. Paddy reminisced about the previous course.

'See this, Gaz, it's a killer. Aye, it hurt last time, so yee can no let them make a map reading mistake. See if yee do, there is no recovery.'

It was prudent to take heed of Paddy's comments. Pat had consistently said something similar. Despite our differing philosophies, Paddy knew what he was talking about and this was not the time to exercise my principles. It was not a place to teach people how to win; if anything, it was the opposite. Learning from mistakes is culturally difficult in any walk of life, but when mistakes are made in the Army, they're viewed as a failure. But by learning from our mistakes, we discover the true formula for winning. As we staggered around in the dark, encouraging students to move more quickly, there was no guarantee that either Paddy's or Pat's advice would be taken.

The course walked one behind the other. Like a large snake slithering across the landscape, we weaved our way through hedgerows, fence lines and gravel tracks before arriving at a lay-by on the road somewhere between Trecastle and Sennybridge. The long section of elevated road, normally used for emergency vehicles, hid the first surprise. Pete had set up a field kitchen and the students were treated to a cooked breakfast served by the DS. Much like the last breakfast of the condemned man, despite the luxury of eggs, bacon, beans and fried bread, there were no smiles of delight, just gratitude. The welcome intake of high-calorific foods was just what they needed ahead of the biggest challenge they were ever likely to face.

As the students placed their rucksacks on the back of the cargo truck, Pete and Corporal Davis removed two telegraph poles and placed them on the ground.

Fifteen feet long, freshly coated in creosote, the poles were the heaviest Pete could find. Laid out on the floor, the size of the task that lay ahead was clear for all to see. The Company Quartermaster's team busied themselves with loading stores on to the truck and tidying away breakfast. Pete rushed around the students, relieving them of their rucksacks. Meanwhile, Major Gray and the rest of the officers were involved in a heated debate. Paddy asked Pat what was going on, and he shrugged his shoulders before berating everyone within earshot.

'Stop gibbering, you fanny! Hey, cupcake, get those gloves off; it's not cold enough for that shit! Princess, put your kit on the truck before a real man does it for you!'

Slowly, the students moved away from Pat's line of sight and the OC brought an end to his fun by asking him to round up all the DS for a chat.

Major Gray greeted us with a huge smile. His face was white and devoid of colour, which compromised the real temperature and not the warm morning Pat pretended it was.

'How did they all sleep last night, Colour?' he asked.

'Aye, Sir, fine. You know it was a wee cold but no that bad.'

Paddy and the OC reminisced. They had done this exercise in December, three months earlier. Then, the landscape was covered in thick snow and several parts of the Beacons had been placed out of bounds. But instead of provoking happy memories, Pat destroyed the romance of the moment by accusing the OC and Paddy of being 'fannies' for following rules made up by lame civilians. At times it was hard to know if Pat was joking or serious. His hard-man image was impressive and annoying at the same time. It was easy to see why he had been such a success in the Parachute Regiment.

Major Gray invited Pat to gather the students for a brief before the final race got underway. There was a tension in the air that was hard to identify. Pat was even more hostile than usual as he picked on Corporal Davis and Pete for nothing in particular. Captain Watts and Dunn stood together. Arms folded tightly, faces like thunder, there was something going on; you could have cut the atmosphere with a knife. Not even the comical sight of Haigh wearing his trousers back-to-front could ease the mood. Major Gray edged his way up a small embankment so he could see all the students.

'Good morning, team. I trust you all slept well and enjoyed a full-hearted breakfast? Welcome to Brecon Bimble, a simple jolly across a few hills, full of surprises and loaded with fun!'

Despite the huge smile and energy in the opening statement, there was no reaction from the students. The two enormous logs that lay at their feet didn't look like they were there to deliver fun! The road to Sennybridge sat at the base of the valley, and everywhere you looked there was a hill disappearing into the clouds.

'I have much good news to tell you of,' the Major continued. 'Firstly, Major General Deverell is going to join us for the Bimble. Secondly, you will know that the points gap between the platoons is six! Well, this race has a value of seven, so it is all to play for.'

The reaction from the students was telling. No. 1 Platoon openly protested, while our students chatted excitably. A glance over my shoulder to where both Platoon Commanders stood told its own story. If there had been any doubt as to the content of the debate just after breakfast, it was confirmed by the shocked look on Paddy's face as he made his way through the crowd to complain to Captain Watts. It was evident that Paddy was aggrieved by the OC's decision, and as he gesticulated and remonstrated out of earshot, Pat could be seen giggling with Major Gray.

There was no sub-plot to derail Paddy. Pat would later remind us all that the course was 'all about the student', and it mattered not which Platoon Commander and Colour Sergeant won, only that we created the conditions for everyone to excel. By adjusting the scoring system for the final race, Major Gray increased the opportunities and induced a desire to win right up to the final moments of the course. No one saw this coming. It was a masterstroke, and as insightful as it was cunning. Pat glanced at me and winked. He said nothing, just nodded his head sagely as the OC continued to talk about how the previous two months had been building up to this day. Notwithstanding the fact that there was still a monumental task ahead of us all, morale was on the rise. Not that it needed another boost, but as the students became excited by the news of the seven points on offer, Mathews and Williams appeared from the cab of the 4-ton truck. No. 2 Platoon went wild with excitement as jubilant scenes greeted both lads. After a brief exchange of banter, Mathews explained that neither he nor Williams was allowed to participate in the final race. Instead, as punishment for receiving hospital treatment, they had been drafted in to clean the pots and pans used for breakfast. If Mathews thought that his statement would earn him some sympathy, he had misjudged the transformation of his fellow students.

'Serves you right for taking a sabbatical!' Danner blurted out.

'Can you do my mess tins while you're at it?' requested Haigh.

The floodgates opened, and both lads were verbally pummelled by the abuse thrown at them from every angle imaginable. Once the words had been exhausted, Danner put Mathews in a headlock and accused him of malingering, while the remainder of the platoon wrestled them to the ground in one huge heap.

In this one defining moment, the platoon had come of age. They had found the ingredient that becomes the elixir of success. In their own unique infantile manner, they had stumbled upon the elusive formula that binds a band of brothers. It is greater than respect and more powerful than love. It is something that is not easy to identify when you are young and still asking awkward questions about life. With soldiers, their duty hangs over their heads like the sword of Damocles, for they know that they will one day stare death in the eye. When Frederick Wilhelm Von Steuben – who wrote the influential drill manual for the Continental Army in the American War of Independence – spoke of loving soldiers under his command, his message was lost amidst the complexity of his own sexuality. He was not referring to the intimacy of sharing a bed, but one of the golden threads of command. Learning to love those whom you command reduces toxicity and endears soldiers to go beyond the call of duty. Pivotally, it is the agent that prevents a commander from becoming frivolous with the lives of those under his charge. The first step along the way is failing and winning in training. Watching Mathews endure this playful expression of endearment was the cornerstone in building a bond that is unbreakable. It was a warming endorsement of the harsh training regime we had used. Erwin Rommel would tout that the best training was the only way to deliver a professional army. He was nearly right. If he understood what we know today, maybe things would have turned out differently for him!

Other than the three-minute penalty, the pre-race conditions could not have been better. Francis had galvanized his charges, Major Gray had given them something to play for, and Mathews' presence, even if only to wash the dishes, had fuelled the tank of morale. Amidst all this distraction, No. 1 Platoon was preparing for the off. Paddy was at his most animated, bordering angry. Just as animated was Captain Watts. There was fire in their bellies, and we instantly knew that whilst we were incentivized by Major Gray's decision to award seven points for a win, Paddy's students needed no motivation after this perceived injustice. If Paddy kept his nerve, this could inadvertently become the catalyst to their success.

We watched No. 1 Platoon disappear down the road carrying their telegraph pole. Their screams of encouragement filled the valley and reverberated from every direction. Major Gray counted down the three-minute penalty, and just before he despatched our students, he gave us a huge smile that said everything. He had known all along that there had been a slight imbalance, but it worked to his advantage. It had been kept in check throughout the course, even if it hadn't looked that way at times. It was the best example of playing the long game that I would ever experience, an example that wouldn't be bettered by any of the more famous or celebrated officers I would later serve under.

Pat and the OC waited at the start line. The Academy Commandant had not arrived by the time we got underway. Even if everything went to plan, the likelihood of arriving at the finish point in the dark was high. To delay the start of the race would be to heighten the risks involved, so there would be no waiting for him and his entourage. The first mile of the race involved running along the A40, and we needed to be clear of it before the morning traffic arrived. Francis had thrashed his teammates down the tarmac before cutting through a bridle path dividing a series of farmers' fields south-east of Trecastle. He would now pick his way through the undulating ground and arrive at a checkpoint perched at the top of Fan Llia.

The distance between Paddy's platoon and ours had increased. At first glance, it appeared that this was down to the efforts of the students. Paddy and Captain Watts were walking way ahead of their platoon. It was inconceivable that they could influence their boys from such a distance. For all the tea in China, it appeared to be old-fashioned hard work. But as Francis negotiated a succession of five-bar gates, Danner openly remonstrated that Captain Watts was navigating and No. 1 Platoon was once more doing little more than following their instructors. Despite the good weather, navigating through a maze of streams and fields would demand total concentration. If someone was pathfinding for you, it would be much easier to apply your efforts to the physical aspect of winning the race.

'Fellas, for God's sake, stop complaining,' Captain Dunn urged them. 'What did we discuss last night? This is not about them, it's about you.'

Francis paused to look at his map. Calling for Rideout and Moore, the three of them discussed the route that No. 1 Platoon took. They had made a beeline for the peak of Fan Llia through the low ground, following the River Afon Senni. After a flashback to the hard-learnt lessons during Plain Jane, the team decided to contour around the high ground of Fan Bwlch Chwyth and stay clear of the wet bogs, elephant grass and hidden quagmires. It would mean walking nearly 2km further, but the going in the valley looked horrendous.

Francis knew that this would be a gamble. He would need everyone to throw everything at it for the next hour, or it would fail. United under his command, the platoon followed behind Francis as Moore forged ahead on pathfinding duty. He and Rideout ran ahead to identify the easiest route for the log. Every 200 metres or so, one of them would go back and put a shift in on the log. It was an admirable display of command by Francis. Under pressure, he was making leadership look easy. His peers were operating on their own initiative in an attempt to achieve his intent. There was an air of confidence oozing from Francis, until it was pointed out that Lane was now 100 metres behind the log and failing to try.

'Your leadership skills are about to be fully tested, Francis!' Captain Dunn giggled.

Francis called to Norris, and between them, they began to push Lane in an effort to repatriate him with the group. They took it in turns to put their hands in the middle of Lane's back and drive him forward until they could push no more. Initially, it appeared to work, but after three sprints apiece, their energy was draining. In return, Lane demonstrated no desire to contribute. After a succession of similar incidents, Francis knew that this race was not going to be over after his leg. There was not a hope in hell that they could keep pushing Lane for the rest of the day – he had become the proverbial millstone.

It was crunch time. Lane had made the mental leap to leave, and from experience, that is the point to cut and run. In war, you must be capable of detaching the emotion from the desired outcome. You accept casualties and recognize when you can do no more without risking failure. If we allowed Francis to push Lane any more, Francis and Norris would be spent before they completed the first leg of this marathon.

With approximately 2.5km to go before we hit our waypoint, we came across the Academy Padre. He had made his own way to Brecon in the hope of seeing the students start the race and then meeting them at the end. Having missed the start, he parked his car between the two lower hills west of Fan Fawr and walked up towards the first checkpoint. Fortunately for us, his navigation was as poor as his timekeeping and he appeared on the northern edge of Fan Nedd, not far from where Francis looked to turn east and over Fan Llia.

This was fortuitous. Captain Dunn glanced at me, as if to confirm we were both thinking exactly the same. The Padre would offer us a golden opportunity to rid the platoon of their greatest burden. We stopped Norris and Francis from pushing Lane any further. They had done enough. Lane fell to the floor; there was nothing left of him to give. There was no sweat, no tears, no disappointment, just relief. The Padre was quick to intervene. With no explanation required, he offered to take Lane the rest of the way in his car, and as quickly as the Padre arrived, he disappeared with Lane in tow. It was heart-warming to see the relief on the face of Lane as the Padre rustled a packet of Liquorice Allsorts under his nose. Like a proud parent comforting his child after finishing last in the annual egg and spoon race, the Padre praised him for making it up the steep hill. The change in Lane's demeanour was instantaneous. How could the Padre, with only four weeks' military training on the Professionally Qualified Officers course, be capable of transforming a soldier's outlook on life within a second of meeting him, yet for me it took months, sometimes years?

Historically, most soldiers have viewed the Padre with great suspicion. His office has frequently been exploited by those lacking in morality. By hiding behind the Padre, soldiers have escaped wars or returned home early. Feigning illness or pleading domestic catastrophe is a disease that plights most employers, but in the military there is utter disdain for people complaining about life's glitches. In a combat unit, you are highly likely to receive more sympathy mourning the loss of a faithful labrador than you would crying over the loss of a parent or bleating about a failing marriage. Seeking help from the Padre instead of your peers or commanders is frequently perceived as weak. But it is not just the humble soldier who has failed to understand the mosaic landscape of a Padre. Many

Commanding Officers and directors of drill and discipline continue to carry a hint of suspicion of the Padre's efforts to help with spiritual unity.

During the period of Operation Panchai Palang in 2009, the British suffered the heaviest casualties of the Afghanistan campaign. At a time in which we witnessed an overstretched pastoral capability, repatriating large numbers of fallen soldiers and officers, their leadership stood firm. Despite the overwhelming emotional pain and grief, a succession of male and female Padres somehow found an inner strength to galvanize a UK force in pain after nine years of fighting. What is most intriguing is how they could inspire and stimulate in a manner like no military commander or politician. How could a Padre influence hundreds of soldiers with little more than a few well-chosen words? What ingredient of leadership had they that no one else possessed? Ashamedly, my connection with the church had always been a one-way relationship. Lead flashings on spires and steeples shone like gold to a poverty-stricken kid surviving on the streets of Liverpool, and this was easy money for a wayward child. Later in life, as conflicts came thick and fast, God was the focus of my disputations. Accusations, idle private conversations and promises made in desperation (none of which have subsequently been kept) were my only spiritual connection. Ironically, some years later, Rolly-Rolland, an inspirational Army Padre who left the Coldstream Guards as a Colour Sergeant to join the clergy, helped me better understand faith in the military. He explained that we had morphed from a Christian Army into an equal opportunities employer. As a consequence, most soldiers had turned into 'Supermarket Christians'. Faith had been diluted to a modern-day convenience. Like microwave meals sitting on a Tesco's shelf, we pick up our need for God's help only when we are desperate. Spiritual guidance has become little more than an inanimate object, waiting futilely for the next disaster so it can advertise its utility.

Despite the devastation of realizing this was true of me, it was highlighted that at least there was still a belief in Christian values, and this was a substance that military leadership relied on. It hurt to be reminded that God was only called upon when it was convenient to me; it somehow questioned my loyalty. Although it didn't imply inferiority or a loss of spiritual patronage, it did spell out the links between the conflicts raging in the Middle East and the changing culture of the Western world. Notwithstanding this demise, the religious values and identity of a soldier are a golden thread tightly wound around the tiller of the army he serves. A religious leader amongst the ranks can invoke a reaction on a biblical scale. For the Padre, the skill is all about pulling on that golden thread.

After years of ignoring this golden thread, it is now clear to me that the church doesn't weave it, rather it can be found within our inner selves. Most humans are compliant, conformant, and goodness exists in the very essence of our characters. This the Padre recognizes as Christian values, and he needs only to offer a soldier the opportunity to let these qualities shine without prejudice or judgment.

Lane's best was not good enough for me or his peers, but for the Padre, Lane had done his bit and for this, the world of conformity and compliance was grateful. At that moment in time, as Lane walked down the hill, my suspicions remained for him and the Padre. The leadership of a military chaplain is unique and multidimensional, and seldom understood by senior military leaders. Commanding Officers often clash with their pastoral component. There is a conflict of interest that is not replicated in any other form of employment. One man is a master of violence and the other a prophet of peace. Accordingly, this clash of purposes corrupts the intentions of unity at unit level. When it comes to dealing with the Padre, many commanders and soldiers remain suspicious and anchored to their prejudices. It is only during the misery of war that the value of this 'vanilla' style of leadership becomes valued and understood. Maybe this is just another form of command that Frederick Wilhelm Von Steuben described, and one that a modern army struggles to fully comprehend. However it is dissected, there is much about leadership we could learn from the Padre if we could park our self-conceited views on leadership.

Both the Platoon Commander and I needed to catch the students before they went through a control point. Having ditched the millstone that was Lane, the platoon was motoring along at pace. We arrived in time to see Francis and his team get to the control point just behind Paddy's boys. Both platoons fought for the rite of passage through the cattle gate. It was satisfying to hear Paddy's platoon complaining about the direct route they had taken to the checkpoint. The steep hill had inflicted a casualty, and it was significant. Keating-Wells was a shining star for No. 1 Platoon. Physically strong, charismatic and bursting with energy, he had hurt his back pushing the log up the hill. So serious was the fear for his health that he was being helped off the hill by Captain Watts, leaving Paddy to push the boys on. It was a huge loss to his group. Keating-Wells was the nearest rival to Rideout for the fittest student award, and his absence would be significant in the closing stages. Despite having lost one student each before the first checkpoint, we were still two students fewer than No. 1 Platoon. As both groups broke out of the checkpoint, Major General Deverell arrived with a small entourage. By virtue of a prearranged appointment, the Commandant attached himself to our platoon for the next phase of the race.

It was less than a kilometre to the end of the log carry and Francis found himself at the tail end of the platoon. It was unfortunate for Francis that a fit, energetic Major General had not witnessed his endeavours to keep Lane in the race. Had this been the case, Francis may have escaped the berating he received from the Commandant as he followed on at the rear of the group.

'What's your name and why are you at the back, lad?'

'Francis, Sir, and I am trying to encourage people to keep up.'

'Do you mean you are in command?'

'Erm yes, Sir.'

'Well, Francis. Best you get your thumb out of your arse and start leading from the front!'

'With all respect, Sir, I haven't got my thumb up my arse because I am breathing out of it!'

Captain Dunn struggled to contain his laughter before he realized that the Commandant didn't enjoy the quip from Francis. To prevent intervention from the Academy Sergeant Major, the boss grabbed Francis by the arm and dragged him to the front.

The change of appointment could not have come soon enough for Francis. He had spent much energy making up the two-man tag team dragging Lane the first few kilometres. The students had carried the logs for more than 7km and taken a physical battering in the process. With bruised shoulders, wood splinters, battered ears and chafing cheeks red raw, it had been a ferocious start. But there was no time for reflection as Pat kept the tempo high by warning the platoon to prepare for a 3km double-burden carry. Pat called for the commander of the second leg and issued him with a grid reference along with seven heavy yellow boxes. The return of the howitzer ammunition boxes was sickening. The race would follow a large valley floor before arriving at the southern edge of Fan Fawr, the start of the notoriously challenging Brecon Beacons. Carrying the two-man yellow burdens would be painful on already sore hands and energy-sapping from start to finish. In a cruel twist of inevitability, the sun broke through the clouds and bathed the landscape with all the heat of a summer's day.

Stone was placed in charge of leg two. Back in the planning phases of the exercise, this was supposed to be the appointment that we used to demonstrate that Stone was not ready to be trained for leadership. But his late rally had us rethinking our appraisal. He had little more to do than encourage his peers and navigate a linear feature through a series of checkpoints. This was made easier by the fact that Fan Fawr was hard to miss, and No. 1 Platoon was spread out in a long line on the valley floor, marking the route to the next checkpoint. Barns and Norris shared a burden. The mismatch in height twisted the loosely hinged handle tight against the knuckles of the much shorter Norris. Within less than a kilometre, he had lost most of the skin, covering the end of his burden in blood. A kilometre later and his other hand was in the same condition as he and Barns switched sides to rest arms during the carry. It was Plane Jane all over again. Comically, Barns apologized for being so tall and Norris replied in kind.

It was proving to be an easy appointment for Stone. With Major General Deverell watching on, he was close to securing himself a pass. It had been a remarkable turnaround for the Welbecksian. The maturity on display was sufficient to suggest the transition from child to man was near complete. Gone were the sarcastic overtones and irritable inflictions that caused him to be ostracized by his peers. Although he was not out of the woods just yet, Stone was winning over his critics. His diminutive size was struggling to carry the heavy box, but he had chosen to share with Danner in the knowledge that his large frame would carry more than its fair share.

As the platoons reached the halfway mark, they were inseparable. A combination of the unexpected heat and the burdens had slowed progress down to a snail's pace. It was impossible to identify who was truly leading this leg. Moore and Witherspoon were out in front of the course, but Packman and Haigh occupied the rear position. The decisive moment would come as they transitioned and received their instructions for the third phase. If Stone wished to secure his place on the next month's Commissioning Course, this was his moment to shine. The Academy Commandant, the Company Commander and the Academy Sergeant Major would all be watching as he demonstrated his understanding of leadership in one bite-sized chunk. I owed Stone some encouragement. For the majority of the course, he had irked me to distraction, but with this new-found attitude, we wanted him to succeed. There was no undoing the things he had done during his time at Row-Co, but there was a golden opportunity to convince everyone he was worth a gamble. I strode alongside Stone as he concentrated on his navigation.

'Now is the time to grip your charges, Stone. You can see the checkpoint and you can see where Packman and Haigh are! Take the advice we have previously given you. It is the commander that makes the difference. It's obvious what needs to be done! Go make the difference.'

Stone sought council with Danner. The big Etonian was in no mood for games and told Stone exactly what he needed to do. Stone called for Rideout and Francis.

'Lads, you need to take my place and help Danner. Form a three-man team and carry two burdens at once.'

It was a humbling gesture. Danner didn't like Stone, but at that moment, he knew there was a need to park their differences in pursuit of a common goal. By forming this three-man team, Stone was released to chase up the stragglers and motivate those lagging behind. If he put sufficient energy in racing up and down the line, there was a slim chance that his plan could work. Captain Dunn and I stayed with the group of three. Danner was pulling out all the stops as the centre man of a three-man team. Watching him endure the pain of the heavy carry was bizarrely comical. In the space of 100 metres, he spat out over fifty swear words. Randomly, he would shout out the name of an old school teacher and berate him for a punishment long-since spent.

'Curse you, Mr Narroway. They were never my cigarettes and you know it! I hate you, Mr Painting. I should have been captain of the firsts! Henderson was never as good as me. Ask anyone!'

By the time we arrived at the checkpoint, we must have learnt the names of all the teachers at Eton! If nothing else, it did exactly as it was intended: he had distracted himself from the pain and suffering.

No sooner had Barns and Norris crossed the finish line and dropped their burden at the feet of Pete, than they both ran back to help Packman and Haigh. It was a defining moment for Barns. He had gone from scrawny tall kid to potential officer of great promise, and all his new-found confidence broke through at the most opportune moment. He grabbed hold of Haigh's handle and encouraged Norris to replace Packman. Together, they sprinted over the finish line to draw level with the last of No. 1 Platoon. The Commandant wore a huge smile, delighted by the effort of both lads, particularly that of Norris, who had been one of the first people he had agreed to back-term to Row-Co.

'Is that Norris, Colour?'

'Yes, Sir.'

'That is pleasing. He looks twice the man he was a few weeks back. Who is the other chap?'

'Barns, Sir.'

'Fabulous effort, Colour. Truly impressive!'

For a second, General Jack became caught up in the moment. He encouraged Norris and Barns as if he was the Platoon Commander. Willing both men on with so much enthusiasm, you could be forgiven for thinking he was part of the student cohort.

For all Stone's endeavours, both platoons remained inseparable on arrival at the end of the second phase. It was midday and we had covered a total of 16km, and it was showing on the faces of each and every student. But instead of the usual self-pity we had previously seen emanate from the likes of Packman, Stone and Haigh, there was a desire to get on with it. As the race instructions were once more issued to the new commanders, it was Boyle's turn to take charge. After receiving his orders from Pat, the young student decided to conduct a SWOT analysis. This afforded No. 1 Platoon the time to break clean from the checkpoint. Getting away first incentivized Paddy's boys. They exited the control point enthused by being the first to depart, further spurred on by the return of Captain Watts.

'Boyle, you need to speed up. SWOT will only work if it is timely delivered. Dwell on it too long and you will lose the initiative,' Captain Dunn snapped.

The prompt worked, but the gap between the groups had been re-established to the three minutes it began with. For Boyle to recover this would take a phenomenal effort. Conditions for navigation were perfect. Fan Fawr arced around in a giant U shape, and navigating to the top was simple; you just kept heading up, keeping the edge of the feature on your left.

The pace picked up significantly after shedding the burdens. Norris had administered some first-aid to cover up the sores around his hands, Haigh and Francis had both developed a limp and Packman was complaining of knee problems and back pain. Danner, not to be out-moaned, reminded everyone he had just carried two burdens for the last kilometre. This light-hearted banter amused the General. He was an accomplished team player and recognized the chemistry that was seeping out of their efforts to keep up the pace. Ever the leader, the General offered Boyle a few words of encouragement.

'While morale is high, exploit the opportunity, commander! Make the most of it; the opportunity may not come again.'

Slowly, the penny fell through the mechanical mind of Boyle. You could almost hear the cogs whizz around his head as he processed the advice. The General's intelligence carried higher authority, prompting an immediate response. Boyle started to walk backwards so he could see where his team were.

'OK. Listen in! We are going to run-walk-run until we catch the other platoon. Only we need to do it with stealth. No shouting, no complaining. My aim is to catch the other platoon before they realize what we are up to.'

'Not a hope!' I mumbled to Captain Dunn.

'Colour, you don't know. It just might work if they can pull it off.'

Boyle began to run. Fifty metres later he walked, then the same again, and again and again. The gap became noticeably less. The General walked alongside Boyle to heighten the pressure. Having listened to me badger him for the whole duration of the course, it appeared that after just a few simple words from the Camp Commandant all our problems were solved. Where an incline was less dramatic, he ran the platoon all the way. Where the Fan was steep, they force-marched. The gap had been reduced from 300 metres to just short of 20 metres. We were on the limit of noise propagation. If we got much closer, the other platoon would bolt before we had time to rest.

The expansive plain of Fan Fawr opened suddenly before our eyes. The view across the Beacons was breathtaking. It had taken two hours to make it to the far side of this gigantic feature, and the effort was waning. No. 1 Platoon had been alerted to our presence, and predictably had countered the endeavour with a burst of effort. Admirably, Boyle pushed just as hard. There was still 2km to go before we finished the penultimate stage, and the platoons were as close as ever. Captain Dunn shuffled alongside me to chat about the General and how his presence had eked extra effort from the platoon.

'He has to be at least 54 years old you know, Colour! Surely he can't keep this up for much longer?'

'I know. He has ditched his whole entourage and is just happily chatting with the boys. I will confess to being impressed. Carrying his own kit, up at the front with the commanders, he puts most others to shame. Do you think he will make it to the end or finish at the Storey Arms?'

'I don't know, but best we show him the map before he starts the final phase. It just may kill him if he doesn't know what comes next.'

As we reached the Storey Arms, the Commandant took a sip of coffee from my flask, pored over the map and joked about the Padre getting lost in God's Country. The energy he was exuding was infectious. General Deverell had reached into the very heart of his charges and offered insightful advice, without being overbearing, arrogant or condemnatory. It was a pity the students could not bottle the moment. They were too tired to examine his leadership style at the base of Pen-Y-Fan, but it had not been lost on Captain Dunn or me.

The tail end of No. 1 Platoon had merged with the frontrunners of No. 2 Platoon, the first of whom was King. His strength and conditioning had paid dividends during the course, and as a consequence, he was in better shape than most as phase three ended. For the first few minutes at the Storey Arms it was pure chaos. The final surprise of the race for the students was to be given back their rucksacks. To add to the confusion, there was no selected commander, just the Sergeant Major shouting 'collect your rucksack and navigate to the grid written on the side of the Land Rover.' King had seen this all before. He collected his rucksack, pulled out his map, plotted the grid reference that Pat had scrawled in white chalk down the side of the Land Rover, and was just about to depart.

'Oh, softlad! Where the hell do you think you are going?'

'The grid, Colour Sergeant!'

'You do that! But just before you set off, ask yourself what course you are on!'

King looked embarrassed. His eagerness to prove himself as a competent individual overshadowed his ability to lead and command. In his defence, it would take a while for him to make the transition from soldier to an officer, and eagerness is not the worst quality in a young officer. He returned to the melee of bodies scrambling at the rear of the 4-ton truck trying to identify their rucksacks, all of which were heaped in a muddle on the floor of the car park. It was telling that he called Moore, Francis and Boyle together once they were ready to go. The group conferred and mutually agreed to tackle the last leg as a formed platoon. It was the right decision; anything else would have been disastrous.

The finish line was 6km from the famous Storey Arms car park. Selecting the right route would be the difference between winning and losing. There were two plausible options. The first option was to head directly up Gryn hill and across the saddle separating it from Pen Milan. Option two was to follow the Taff trail around the base of the Beacons and climb Pen Milan at the most northerly point to get onto the plain that led to the final checkpoint. Option one meant a slow, arduous start. Additionally, it was slightly longer but mostly good ground. Option two offered a flat, fast start. The drawback was the need to climb a nearly vertical slope littered with rocky outcrops at the end of the trail. This would be the defining decision of the course.

Barns offered his course of action as the preferred option. He wanted to climb first, explaining he had little left in the tank so an ascent late on in the route could spell the end for him. Moore, Rideout and Francis agreed, but Boyle was keen to follow No. 1 Platoon. He couldn't let it go that the DS had already set off down the Taff trail and the students were just following. He was convinced that if the DS of No. 1 Platoon thought it was the best way to go, they should follow. Danner supported the notion. Haigh and Packman looked at the big hill and also voted for the easier option first. It was a Mexican stand-off. The boss was desperate to say something, as were the rest of the Staff who were all stood watching. Then Barns walked off in the direction of Gryn hill and the decision was made. King followed and Rideout sprinted to the front. General Deverell beamed with excitement. He knew that the race was hanging in the balance, and if he admired one quality in the officers he commanded, it was decisiveness. Barns had come of age. Choked by his transformation, words failed to come out of my mouth as Captain Dunn asked me to explain how this change had come about. For long periods of the course, he was in danger of being kicked off, but now he was everything you would hope for in an aspiring young officer.

Packman crossed the first sty and winced with pain. The race had inflicted significant stress on his young body. Lingering at the rear, it was surprising to see Witherspoon appear from nowhere to drag him along. A few hundred metres later, Captain Dunn grabbed me from behind and pointed back at Packman. He was walking without his rucksack. Astonishingly, it was being carried by Witherspoon. Captain Dunn rubbed his eyes with disbelief. Witherspoon must have been carrying nearly 90lb. Even more astonishingly, he kept pace with everyone else. Occasionally he would stop, re-shift the load on his back and push on another 50 metres. Repeating the process, we watched Witherspoon as he made his way to the top of Gryn hill, a height of 600 metres.

'OK, enough heroics, Witherspoon,' I said. 'Give Packman back his rucksack or get someone else to carry it.'

For all Witherspoon's failings, he was a team player. He was now showing leadership quality, all of which had been deep inside him somewhere, just waiting for the moment to get out. But the effort had taken its toll. He was now breathing heavily and not contributing to the debate about the best path to take across the crest of the hill. Norris gave him water and Stone pulled out his emergency chocolate. As the majority of the platoon gathered around Witherspoon, they could see No. 1 Platoon way out in the distance. Although they had not yet begun to climb, they were miles ahead. Moore and Barns became agitated. King was less reserved. The cursing and swearing increased commensurate with the attrition rate. What they needed to do at this precise moment in time was to nominate a commander, issue roles and responsibilities and organize themselves into a team.

Captain Dunn walked away deep in conversation with the Academy Commandant. They glanced at Witherspoon and issued a few words of encouragement. Francis waited until they were out of earshot before pleading with everyone to get a grip. His comments had the opposite effect, as old conflicts were resurrected and despondency crept in. Just as it appeared to be falling apart, Barns cried out: 'For fucks sake. We are going to lose if we don't get moving.' His blast of anger did the trick. King recognized the cancer of discontent, offered to navigate and invited Moore to path-find. It was just the nudge they needed. Francis again offered his thoughts, only this time he crafted his words better.

'Guys! Someone needs to take command. We need to get organized or this will go to rat-shit.'

Danner appointed himself as Chief of Staff.

'Norris, Stone, Haigh, Barns, you need to keep Packman going. Share his rucksack between the lot of you. Kingy, you and Riders cut a path to the finish line. Boyle and Withers can do pacing and timekeeping and check navigating. I will help out where needed, so that leaves Francis to command. Are we happy? Let's go, before we lose any more time.'

Throughout the course, Danner had frustrated and inspired in equal measure. Such a volatile spectrum of command would always be susceptible to erratic decisions and adverse interference, but there was no doubting his presence and ability to command in a crisis. Seconds after his authoritative outburst, the platoon was moving with renewed determination. Remarkably, even the DS were buoyed by Danner. All that was left was for Francis to make the right decisions from here on in, most important of which would be the pace and tempo. The mini-crisis had cost ten minutes. In travel time, this equated to just short of a kilometre. Everything would hinge on how No. 1 Platoon coped with their climb once they reached the turning point on the Taff trail.

In the saddle between Y-Gryn and Pen Milan, the magnitude of the event was showing its true impact on the platoon. Norris appeared to be wearing red gloves as blood continued to weep through the makeshift bandages. Haigh's gait had deformed to that of a mechanical robot gone rogue. He had stopped striding forward and was now wobbling side to side to avoid further chafing on his crotch. Occasionally, the effort to keep walking in this manner would succumb to the lack of energy and he would take several steps in a traditional fashion, wincing in pain with each stride. Francis' limp was more pronounced than ever, and Danner lumbered like a laden pack mule. Character traits that Stone had become known for began to resurface as he complained at Witherspoon's efforts to offload Packman's rucksack at regular intervals. But for the energy of Rideout, yet to feel the effects of the long march, the sight of the platoon heading for the crest of Pen Milan resembled Napoleon's retreat from Moscow.

At the top of Pen Milan there is the smallest of saddles, more of a dip in the ground than a true topographical feature, just before the final rise. Stretching about 50 metres in length, the platoon disappeared from view and headed to the east of the summit. As they exited the dip and traversed to the peak, they encountered the middle order of No. 1 Platoon. Remarkably, after nearly eight hours of racing, the course was inseparable once more. It was now a straight race to the finish line. Rideout struggled to contain his excitement. From the apex of the feature, he could see every facet affecting the result. The front men of No. 1 Platoon were in the lead, but they were spread out over 200 metres. The finish line was less than a kilometre away, all of which was downhill. No. 2 Platoon were in a tight group, and as they began their descent they would merge with the middle order of Paddy's boys. This was going to end up a one-on-one shootout.

Tensions and anxiety levels rocketed once the situation became clear to both groups. This would now develop into a battle of character and come down to who wanted it more. In a fit of excitement, Rideout ran back up the hill towards the tail-enders. Bouncing with excitement, he turned away and crashed to the floor, falling and rolling around – it was like he had been struck by lightning. Screaming in pain, he shot his leg in the air and clutched at his toes. Charley Horse had gripped him in the calf. Desperately bending back his toes, he called for help. Witherspoon, with his knack of appearing from nowhere, bent Rideout's foot backwards to ease the pain. Pulling him to his feet, the pair charged forward and started the descent. By the time they had rejoined the rest of the group, No. 1 Platoon had realized the danger. Collectively, they began to scream and corral each other, searching for greater effort.

With the tail end of each platoon emerging from opposite sides of the reverse slope at exactly the same moment, the effort required was as much emotional as it was physical. For the first time, we got a look at the state of No. 1 Platoon as they jogged alongside our students, desperate to stay ahead of Haigh, who was now the last man of the whole course. They too were scarred, battered and bruised by their contribution, as well as being three men less than they had started with. The first of the students were crossing the finish line, and Pat refused to allow any to return to encourage the stragglers to increase their efforts. Both Paddy and I ran beside our final runners. There was little more than 200 metres left to go, and like a jockey frantically whipping the winner during the final furlong of the Grand National, Paddy was animated in the extreme as he cajoled and screamed at Butler and Jacobs. Both were just a yard in front of

Haigh, struggling to stay upright. Spittle flew wildly, words blurring between encouragements and insults, but neither Paddy's students nor Haigh found the energy to break away. Paddy went to put his hand on Jacob's back, and in an outburst of oppressed rage, I screamed at Paddy to get his hand off him. With as much anger as embarrassment, Paddy stared at me with pure hatred in his eyes.

For Haigh, this would be the defining moment of his young life. He had repeatedly allowed challenges to get the better of him, and now at the final moment of this epic adventure, he was about to be the man who failed himself and his teammates. Before I could control my own emotions, I let loose on Haigh with my assessment of how his future looked.

'Same old Haigh, here we go again. Mr Fucking Nearly-man. If you fail to overtake Butler and Jacobs, it will haunt you your whole life. You will not recover from this failure. It is over for you. Let down all those lads who have carried you through this course, and it will be unforgivable! Being the man who nearly won is like being the man who can't be bothered. Is that you, Haigh? Is it?'

The scowl from Haigh belonged in a Halloween film. With every word that left my lips, he became angrier. Incensed by my words, he sparked into life. Berating himself, with fists clenched, the raw nerve was fully exposed. Snot flew out of his nose and the wind blew it back over his face. His crazy awkward running style ceased as he broke out into a full-on sprint. The chafing caused his face to contort as each step removed another layer of skin off his inner thigh. Shocked by his response, I was left behind, struggling in his wake. Within 50 metres he was level with Jacobs, who himself was enjoying a mini-revival. After such a long journey, it could never have been imagined that this race was going to be won or lost by a margin of metres.

Moaning in pain, Haigh reached deep into his reserves to find the resolve to match Jacobs. His rucksack bounced up and down on his back, and the clanging of mess tins and cutlery along with half-filled water bottles reverberated with each step. Jacobs was becoming unresponsive to Paddy's torments, which were by now being matched for intensity by the inaudible words of Captain Watts. If Haigh could get in front for just a second or so, the emotional impact would break Jacobs and the race would be won. With 50 metres to go, Haigh's strangely long arms pumped across his chest alongside Jacobs. A sideways glance at his adversary, and Haigh's peculiarly large feet edged into the lead. I was struggling to deal with my own excitement. The emotional investment in this young man was substantial, and it was now within his gift to repay this endeavour. The sight of Haigh's flailing arms and goose-stepping strides were comical, but it was having the desired effect. The cheers of his comrades fixed behind the finish line fuelled the final push. Inside the last 10 metres, Haigh's long strides put daylight between him and Jacobs. By little more than a hair's breadth, Haigh crossed the line first and promptly crashed to the floor with exhaustion.

The elation released by the students was palpable. Irrepressible emotion was vindication for the perceived injustice suffered throughout the course. Haigh had hardly hit the floor before he was mobbed by every member of No. 2 Platoon. But irrespective of their achievement and euphoria, there was an expectation of mutual respect and Pat was keen to restore order.

'Get up, you bunch of fannies. What do you think this is, a game of kiss ball? Get off each other and stand up. Fall in. Three ranks now before we run you around the course again!'

The raucous behaviour vanished as quickly as it arrived. Pat had restored order with his typical no-nonsense approach, but he couldn't suppress the smiles and the inner glow that shone brilliantly from the platoon as they stood silently to attention. To Paddy's annoyance, Danner glanced across the short divide between the platoons, pulled a huge grin and winked at him. Had it not been for the presence of the Commandant, Paddy would have exploded.

The Sergeant Major ordered the platoons to gather in a semi-circle around the Commandant, and the course duly obliged. Still wearing a huge smile, General Jack rubbed his hands and cracked a few jokes about how he remembered the hills being much harder. He pulled a card from his pocket to read out some statistics:

> 'Over the period of the course, you have run or marched 869 miles. Had twenty-two nights out of bed and munched your way through 3,000 packed lunches. You started with a course of forty-four and you have finished with twenty-seven. Some of you may not filter through to the commissioning course, but irrespective of the final outcome, you should be immensely proud of your achievements. All that is left for me to say is congratulations No. 2 Platoon, winners of the Inter-Platoon competition. You are all invited to a cocktail party tonight at the Indian Army Memorial Room to celebrate your achievements.'

Bridling my emotions proved difficult. There was an irrepressible pride radiating from the group which was being enjoyed by the DS. Notwithstanding the distractions, the students had achieved the best they could. My differences with Paddy were little more than a dichotomy of ethos, but the variance was hard to accept. He had done nothing wrong and chosen to deliver his instruction in a way that was mutually beneficial to him and his students. Had the outcome been different, maybe my frustrations would have morphed into jealousy.

Paddy was incredibly popular with everyone within the Warrant Officers' and Sergeants' Mess. No one would care that his platoon failed to win this marathon competition. However, had he won, it would have been celebrated for months to come.

Pat called the DS together at the behest of the OC. He was in no mood for getting carried away. In fact, Pat really didn't care who won or lost. He was driven by keeping everything on track.

'We need to sit the final progress board and balance the books before the cocktail party.'

Tiredness had dimmed the OC's smile. Clothes covered in white sweat stains, and, face red with windburn, he cut right to the chase.

'Notes at the ready. As soon as we get on the minibus, we need to craft our submissions to the Academy Adjutant. The results need to be with the Commandant ahead of his arrival at the Indian Army Memorial Room so he can avoid any embarrassment whilst discussing the past few weeks with the students in a social environment.'

It was essential that we briefed the General. It would be devastating for the Commandant to raise the hopes of a student. He needed to be fully appraised of who would fail and those who would be considered for prizes.

Pete took control of the students as the DS boarded an eight-seater minibus. We had not even moved before cramp snatched at its first victim. Captain Watts kicked out to straighten his leg, and in sympathy, Paddy and I did the same. Pat, who as usual was the self-elected driver of the bus, snapped at our predicament, demanding we got a grip of ourselves and worked harder on our fitness levels. Despite the muted giggles, Pat was being serious. Captain Dunn waited patiently while No. 1 Platoon was discussed in detail. There was not much for us to say. Even when it came to the winner of the Highland Trophy, there would be little point in representing a case for Mathews. He had not been seen by the Commandant on the last exercise, and the College Commander would dismiss his claims as 'unfortunate'. On this occasion, it was better not to pick a fight we would lose. Eventually, it was our turn to discuss winners and losers, and first on the table for review was Williams.

'OK, James. Where do you stand on Williams?' Major Gray started the discussion.

'Fail. Scraped through the navigation after a retest. Failed to keep himself administrated on this exercise. As a result, we didn't get to see anything of him during the final week. He was on a warning at the start and he failed to finish the first event. I can't see how we can recommend any other outcome.'

'So he has not failed an assessment, but you wish to fail him because he fell ill?'

'No, I wish to fail him because we cannot confirm he reached the standard!'

'Do you think he would have reached the standard?'

'We don't know. To speculate either way would be foolhardy. The fact is he never demonstrated he can achieve the standard we demand.'

'Agreed. However, he didn't get the opportunity to demonstrate that he could have made the grade. The warning he received on Plain Jane would not be sufficient for me to use against him when we invite the College Commander to fail Williams. Unless we have a stronger case, he will go through with a pass.'

Major Gray didn't invite a response. His tone and expressions said as much about his intentions as his words. He was not in the mood for discussing the issue further.

'Stone please, James?'

'The Colour Sergeant can take this if you don't mind, Sir.' Captain Dunn's tone compromised the moment just passed. He was pained by the fact Williams was going to pass by default. There could be no doubting Major Gray's understanding of the bigger picture. In the grand scheme of things, Williams still had a full year of tuition on the Commissioning Course to get through.

'OK, as you wish. Colour, pass or fail Stone?'

'Fail. He is a wretch of the highest order!' Pat slammed the dashboard with his fist.

'This is tough, Sir,' I countered. 'In the last seven days, he has matured a lot.'

'Bollocks! Gaz, listen to yourself. You are being scammed and you know it. He is a wheel short of a unicycle. It's a waste of a place on the Commissioning Course. If we don't fail him, we might as well all go home.' Pat was not calming down.

'Sergeant Major, be careful what you wish for,' warned Major Gray. 'We may all need to go home if the wastage rate continues to spiral out of control. But thank you for your frank assessment. Colour, continue please?'

'Sir, if it had not been for the past few days, I would agree totally with the Sergeant Major. But there is a spark of hope and if we are seeing the real Stone, he deserves a shot at the real thing. Pass.'

'Bollocks, Gaz,' Pat continued. 'Are you telling me that you would be happy with that lunatic if we made him your Platoon Commander today?'

'No, of course not.'

'No! Well no one else should be forced to suffer that dick. The lad has no leadership qualities at all. None. If this is a leadership course, he failed it several times over.'

Pat ranted and swore as the OC tried to placate his outrage. He warned repeatedly that we had been mugged by Stone consistently. If we let him filter through to the Commissioning Course, it would come back to haunt us. Eventually, Pat cooled his temper and switched his frustrations to the traffic.

Major Gray could not ignore Pat's comments. After nearly three years at Sandhurst, Pat had seen it all. It would be foolish to think Pat didn't have a detailed understanding of a particular student. Possibly Captain Dunn and I were suffering Stockholm Syndrome – we had come to know these characters very well and wanted them all to progress. Pat, on the other hand, was detached from the emotions of it all.

'Sergeant Major, without swearing or crashing the minibus, why should Stone fail?' asked Major Gray.

'I am not his Platoon Colour Sergeant, but there has not been one moment when Stone has even come close to showing he could command respect from any of his peers. At the age of 22, if he is still trying to bluff his way through life, he will do it until he dies. He can pass the tests. He can make a bridge. But he can't lead people.'

The minibus fell silent. Major Gray was caught in the middle of polar dynamics. If he agreed with his Colour Sergeant, he could lose the support of his Sergeant Major. Yet, by supporting his Sergeant Major, he could endanger the support of his Platoon Commander.

'Tricky,' said Major Gray, typically balancing a cataclysmic situation. 'All things taken into consideration, we should let the College Commander take a view. I shall inform him of our thoughts. Given that he will be his Commanding Officer if he progresses, there is merit in offering him the chance of carrying the risk. I shall put him down as a "provisional" pass.'

On reflection, this was genius. No one was happy, but more importantly, no one was disenfranchised. Major Gray had found a route to keeping the peace and maintaining harmony amongst his team.

'Packman next please, James.'

'He is a real risk. There is little to suggest he is going to make it through a year on the Commissioning Course, but there is little evidence to issue a fail. If we could defer his pass for a year, I would be comfortable saying pass.'

'Well we can't. Unless you give me solid evidence and explain why he has not been flagged as a serious risk in the previous eight weeks, it's a pass. He has a place on the next intake. Pass.'

'Rideout next.'

'Best at PT nomination and a solid pass.'

'Yes, I like the lad. He was a bag of nerves when he arrived. He called me Colour Sergeant every day for the first week. I had to tell him I wasn't that important! You and Colour have done a good job on him, he is just nervous now!'

'Surely if he is nervous he shouldn't be awarded a prize,' suggested Paddy.

It was a furtive attempt to discredit Rideout; his hidden agenda was as clear to see as the nose on his face.

'No, can't agree, Colour. That's a little disingenuous. He is super fit. Consistently first in the PT assessments. Had it not been for Sergeant Heal's arrival, none of the Staff would have beaten him on the final assessment. He will be my recommendation for the fittest student.'

The OC stared long at Paddy and nodded sagely as he delivered his verdict.

'Francis?'

'Strong pass. Colour, you have seen more of him, but there is only one recommendation we can offer here, and it would be that he goes forward with a strong recommendation.'

'Barns – was he on a warning?'

'Yes, Sir. He had a wobble on the dunker during the helicopter water escape drills. You may recall it was only for that.'

'OK, Colour, thank you. I couldn't quite remember. How did he fair?'

'Contender for the most improved student,' Captain Dunn chirped.

'He could barely carry his own body weight when he arrived,' I recalled. 'Spoke to no one and mumbled most of the time. Today you would have seen him be decisive, strong and committed. He took plenty of praise from the Commandant on Fan Fawr and at the Storey Arms. I don't see the Commandant complaining at that award.'

'Agreed, James. We did see him wobble a few times during the course; he is not hard to miss. But it was a changed man we saw today on the hills above the Storey Arms. The transformation has been remarkable. Let's stick him in the pot with the other nominations for most improved. Strong pass. Good work you two, it did look shaky for a while.

'Mathews. Now this is unfortunate.' The OC glanced around the minibus.

'Got to be in it to win it!' shouted Captain Watts, giggling menacingly at the same time.

'Mmm. I beg to differ,' voiced Captain Dunn.

'I know we never got him in front of either the College Commander or the Commandant, but there can't be a single man on this bus that hasn't been impressed by him,' I ventured.

'Yeah, but, James, you wouldn't say to Steve Cram, "I am impressed by you so here, have a gold medal". More importantly, I don't think that he would wish to win that way!' Captain Watts was quick to set out his stance, but his words were not well received by Captain Dunn.

'Don't be ridiculous, Tom. There is no correlation between elite athletes and potential officers on a leadership course. It's as illogical as judging a student on one event out of sixty. Mathews has been the outstanding candidate from day one.'

The temperature on the bus began to rise. It was right that the issue was debated to ensure we all did what was right by our students. Maybe doing so after such an emotionally charged event was not ideal. If Major Gray let the debate rumble on further, it would inevitably descend into a playground argument.

'Wow, team – time out,' Major Gray intervened. 'Nominate him, James, it's not a problem. The gift is the College Commander's to issue, so let's not fall out over it. If we agree with a strong pass, we will put him in as a nomination for the Highland Trophy and move on. Happy?'

'No. I think they should "mill" for the trophy,' said Pat, lightening the mood, although he probably did wish to see 'milling', the jungle rules boxing that was used on P Company.

'Can we discuss Moore next?' I suggested.

'Sure, James, why not! Moore; he is up there, as I recall!'

'Certainly is, and given Mathews is out of the running for Highland Trophy, Moore should be considered?'

'Really! This again? I thought we were nominating Mathews? It's one or the other.'

'Sir, that's all well and fine, but if we knew Mathews was going to end up in hospital, we would have ensured the Commandant was briefed about Moore.'

'I hear you, James. But the Commandant has not been briefed that Moore was ever a contender. He stands no chance! But if you wish to change your nomination, that's your business!'

The dull hum of the engine revving to maximum and trundling down the M4 filled the silence of the minibus. Both Captain Dunn and the OC wore an expression of defeat. Unsurprisingly, Captain Watts sunk back into his chair with a knowing grin.

'Pass or fail, James? And it's one or the other for the Highland Trophy nomination! Which is it?'

The mood on the bus was tense, not helped by Pat deliberately driving over the cat's eyes whilst making a heartbeat noise to put pressure on Captain Dunn to make a decision.

'Well, I am loathe to subscribe to this, but strong pass without a recommendation for the Highland Trophy.'

'Thank you, James, we live and learn. Norris – our only surviving back-termer. You have done well to retain him. I can't recall the last one that made it all the way to the end!'

'Strong pass. After the shock of capture, he has been bright. He may need to be hospitalized when we return to Sandhurst. His hands are shredded,' laughed Captain Dunn.

'Danner?'

There was a long pause before the boss answered the OC. It was obvious to me what he was thinking. There could be no doubt that if we put Danner on the Commissioning Course, he would be fine. It was what comes next that gave cause for concern. But was it our right to judge that which we could not know? Like driving a classic car across Europe, the journey would be spectacular, and people would comment on the splendour of it all. But it would be troublesome, impractical and on occasions leave you in precarious situations, needing someone to bail you out of trouble! Danner would unquestionably inspire and command with passion and commitment, and we had no right to read his tarot cards. Provided he had a strong mentor upon arrival at his unit, he would be fine(ish).

'Strong pass. But it may be worth an interview with you before he progresses. He has all the makings of a great Platoon Commander, but it won't take much to derail him.'

Captain Dunn, waiting for the OC's response, commented: 'No. James, if it is obvious he is going to be a problem child, we shouldn't advance him to the next stage. We can't enter into an arrangement where we micromanage students at the conclusion of the course!'

'Understood. Just a thought. Strong pass, and the Colour Sergeant will interview him after me.'

'Marvellous! Then send him to me. Danner, he's the tubby Etonian, right?'

Pat laughed as he explained that the interview would take place on the Mean Machine!

'Sergeant Major. Look at your eyes light up! I am thrilled you are still so passionate about officer development, but please concentrate on the road. You nearly doubled the speed limit when you started to talk about fitness and the Mean Machine!' The bus erupted into laughter as the OC delivered a quick put down.

'Witherspoon. Still can't picture him!'

'He was the lad carrying two rucksacks today when you walked past him on the way up, Gryn!'

'Are you sure? Was that not Williams?'

'No, Sir, Williams was the spotty biff skiving in the hospital all week. The one whose fruit you stole when we visited him.' Pat spoke loudly so we could hear him at the back of the bus.

'Now that makes sense! He does look like Williams, doesn't he?'

'No, Sir. Not even close.'

'Anyway, he impressed today. Two rucksacks; good man.'

The OC flicked back through his notes and adjusted the comments before noticing it had not been the first time he had written something about Witherspoon thinking he was Williams. The lengthy pause compromised his actions and the DS ridiculed him mercilessly!

'Pass. The Colour Sergeant may wish to add something, but he responded well to the encouragement we gave him. He is still too quiet, but he is incredibly popular. On all the 360 reporting, Witherspoon wins credit for his repeated selflessness. I can see him progressing well. Colour, do you agree?'

'Yes, Sir. There is a hidden strength to Witherspoon that took a while to identify. Occasionally it has been masked by insecurity and a lack of confidence. In the right conditions, he would make a brilliant leader. If there is a fear, it would be the fact he will suffer in silence before becoming decisive. He doesn't self-advertise and will happily wait his turn to shine. In the wrong hands on the Commissioning Course or in a regiment, this could go horribly wrong.'

Captain Dunn nodded in agreement. Witherspoon was easy to misjudge. Dutifully, he would share the blame for failings unattributable to him. In as many ways as this was a strength, in a toxic environment it would be disastrous. He was easy to inspire, hard to break down, but Witherspoon was a mentally resolute character searching for a purpose.

'Haigh. Hero of the hour, eh, James. Pass?'

'Yes. Pass.'

'No way! He is two clowns short of a circus!' Pat couldn't resist it; he needed to comment. 'Surely you cannot allow him on the Commissioning Course? Can you imagine if Prince Charles asked him a question on Sovereign's Parade? It would be nightfall by the time he finished answering!'

'Eyes on the road, Sergeant Major.' Captain Dunn imitated the OC's voice.

'Fuck me, Sir, I think I have just found one of those missing clowns here in the bus.' Pat looked over his shoulder and gave Captain Dunn a death stare.

'In all seriousness, pass. It looked for a long time that we were trying to nail jelly to the wall, but I have to hand it to the Colour Sergeant, he has nurtured this young man and today we saw the potential unlocked.'

'Couldn't agree more, James. Well done both of you. For all the world I thought he would fail, but the effort he put into the last kilometre was payback for months of perseverance. Big pat on the back for getting him through.'

'Mini McCarthy?' said Major Gray.

The bus burst into cheers. Up until that moment, it had been a closely guarded joke that Boyle apparently looked like me and possessed some similar mannerisms. Apart from living in the north-west of England, it was hard to see any resemblance. But as the bus broke into every memorable sound bite from the television drama *Boys from the Blackstuff*, it was plausible that there were similarities.

'In which case, strong pass, best student, most improved and best at fitness, as well as winning the Inter-Platoon competition single-handed!' In for a penny, in for a pound, I thought.

'OK, Colour, don't get carried away. A pass will do just fine. Move on to King, please, James.'

'Pass. He continues to show all the makings of a good soldier, but can he make the grade as an officer? Maybe the Colour Sergeant has a view?'

'Sir, he can be a little self-absorbed at times, but that's four years in the ranks for you. He has done both P Company and the All Arms Commando course. These courses condition you to behave in that particular way. If he arrived at my unit, he would do fine after a little tuition.'

'Colour, that's fine,' said Major Gray. 'Fully understood. It is a pass all day long. The Commissioning Course will polish him up a little more. Any more to add, James?'

'Yes, Sir. Have you missed Murphy?'

'Oh, of course, sorry. Murphy.'

'Pass. We somehow lost Murphy amongst the weeds of other issues. He came out of the blocks well. A number of good performances kept the heat off him. We lost him amongst the shadows after Compass Rose. Possibly we are guilty of not investing in him as well as we could have.'

'How do you mean, James?'

'Well, Sir, sometimes it's the problem children that get all the attention. You know, the squeaky wheel gets the most oil.'

Major Gray scribbled in his notebook before asking Captain Dunn to chat about how this had occurred during the end-of-course review. There was little point trying to analyse why it had occurred with tiredness kicking in. Captain Dunn closed his P-Files and sunk deep into his seat. Captain Watts had already nodded off, and Paddy's eyes were rolling back as he struggled to remain awake. The next time my eyes opened, the minibus was parked outside the accommodation back at Rowallan.

At 2030hrs, gathered in the Indian Army Memorial Room waiting for the General to arrive, we surveyed the students who had made it. Lane was present and, despite failing the course, he appeared chirpy and content with his efforts. The remaining students all wore the same weather-beaten, wind-burnt look of fatigue masquerading as a happy partygoer. When the General arrived, he looked like he had just been on holiday for a week. Refreshed, smiling and joking with everyone, it was in stark contrast to the rest of the DS, all of whom looked blurry-eyed with chapped lips and sore throats.

With most senior officers, these kinds of events are strictly controlled and tirelessly rehearsed before the VIP arrives, but with this Commandant, he liked to stay in touch with reality. He mingled with everyone and offered his thoughts on everything from Armageddon to the opening batsman at the next Test match. As he gate-crashed my little group, one of the DS asked if he found it difficult getting over the hills that morning, to which he replied, 'no, not at all'. He was about to say something else before being stopped in his tracks by his wife, who reminded him that he fell asleep in the bath whilst getting ready for the cocktail party. The Commandant could not have appeared more human if he had tried. As we left the grandeur of the Indian Army Memorial Room, which only a few months ago had hosted the mothers and fathers of all the students, it had not been lost on anyone that, bar the presentations, it was all over. Watching each student file quietly out of the huge double doors, every one had earned the right to stand at the top of the white marble stairs a month later and begin the next phase of their officer development. They would sleep well on their last night of the course.

The following morning, all those who had been awarded a pass were gathered in the Old College presentation hall. Major Gray awarded the Highland Trophy to Staples of No. 1 Platoon, the most improved award to Haigh and the fittest student award to Rideout. Then, to rapturous applause, Major Gray invited all of No. 2 Platoon to come down to the stage and receive the Inter-Platoon Trophy. Gingerly, still bearing the scars of the long marches throughout the week, the platoon made their way onto the stage. Francis collected the small stag's skull mounted on a wooden plaque from the OC. Like the winner of the FA Cup, he stepped forward and thrust it high in the air. It was choking to see them all so delighted, and with good cause. Yet as soon as there was a hint of pleasure seen to seep out of the platoon, Pat cut them all down to size.

'Right, that's enough of that crap. You have done nothing more than I would expect of my granny. It's time to get your bags packed and go home so we can prepare for the next victims. You are to report back here to start the Commissioning Course on the 16th of April.'

We walked back to the accommodation to see the platoon off. Parents had arrived in cars to collect their sons, and others were cramming as much as they could into one bag ready for a long train journey home. As each student left, we shook their hands and congratulated them on an amazing achievement. It was impossible to hide my pride. In most cases, the students could sense approval. Having passed the course, they were now granted 'Officer Cadet' status, and for this, as they left, I afforded them due respect and called them 'Sir', as with all other Officer Cadets. As they exited the building, most thanked us both for the influence we had exerted on them during the course. This did little to enhance my mace-wielding persona, and Captain Dunn was quick to point this out to me! Skulking in the corridor was Haigh. He had been packed for a while, but it was obvious he wanted to be the last to leave.

With a huge smile, we both greeted Haigh. Gripping his hand firmly, there was a huge emotional connection between the pair of us. Haigh had received my all, and at times he had replied in kind. Getting him to the end of the course was, to date, my finest hour.

'Colour Sergeant,' he said. 'Firstly, please accept my most sincere gratitude for helping me through this monumental challenge. It has been a journey of self-discovery, much as you had explained several times during the course. I came here blinkered and confused, but I leave with humility, pride and a self-belief never experienced before.'

'Haigh, it is my job, so don't thank me. Recognize that we just helped you realize what you are capable of.'

'Yes, Colour Sergeant. I thank you now because what I am about to say may cause you distress.'

'Ha, Haigh, you stressed me to the moon and back. You couldn't cause me any more stress than that!'

'I have decided not to return. The Army is not for me. Maybe you can't understand, but it has been clear to me for a while. I just didn't want to walk out and let anyone down.' With this, Haigh handed me a letter and walked down the few steps of the accommodation before getting into his parents' car, which was ticking over in Chapel Square.

Amazing! That was as much as my thoughts could stretch to. From the first day of his arrival until the last, he had baffled me. My emotions were mixed. So much effort had been expended on Haigh, and to see him walk away at the end of the course was heart-breaking. He had given me a taste of my own medicine. I must have told him a million times to finish the course or become the nearly-man and regret it for the rest of his life. He had done just that. I turned and walked back through the accommodation doors, dragging my morale along the floor behind me. Within two steps of entering the corridor, Pat slung the string vest in my face.

'Ha, Gaz! I saw you clapping when your man got the "most improved" award. That's a string vest offence. Make sure you're wearing it on Monday when the new lot arrive. Marvellous! Bloody marvellous!'

Chapter Fourteen

Where are they Now?

A few months after my tour of Sandhurst was complete, the Academy was forced to close Rowallan Company as part of cost-saving measures. It just was not cost-effective to take forty or more students and only see 50 per cent of them make it through to the end. We had been warned several times by Major Gray that the course was under close scrutiny. Few senior officers approved of the Rowallan leadership course, and despite a succession of previous Commandants defending its value, those who owned the training engine at that time took a different view.

The course reopened a few years later with a new look. Gone were the intensity and high attrition rate. Gone also were the phases that demanded initiative and free spirit. Most changes were truly for the better. Reflecting on Francis losing his military identity papers in Dublin still frightens me to this day! That incident could have resulted in a fatal outcome of international proportions. And how different the result could have been when Danner had his run-in with the Russian Mafia in Soho. The course had been lucky not to make the national newspapers. Had we lived in today's age of social media, the exploits of these students would have made for a reality TV programme of their own. Whilst the new-look course was risk-averse, it still retained some of the old characteristics.

For years after Sandhurst, I never saw any of my former students or colleagues. Wars in the Balkans, Iraq and Afghanistan fixed us all in one place and our paths never crossed. In the twilight of my career, the central hubs of Army HQ and the Army Personnel Centres came calling. Here I learnt the progress of my seniors, peers and the students I trained.

Major Gray: After a successful tour as Commanding Officer of a Royal Engineer regiment, he was promoted to full Colonel. He settled down in London before taking up a full-time Army Reserve post at the Permanent Joint Headquarters in Northwood. Today, he can still be seen running during his spare time. One particular lunch break, we met at the door of the gym, so he invited me to join his daily run. Thinking he would have slowed with age, I agreed. After 3 miles, my body was hurting so much I faked a meeting that needed my presence. Without so much as a bead of sweat falling from his forehead, he left to run a few more circuits of the camp. At 55-plus, he was still incredibly fast and fit. Ageless and loving life, he still wears that huge grin. Unquestionably, he could have gone on to make 'One-star' rank, but for most people it is more about the quality of life than it is about rank and standing.

Captain Dunn: The former Rowallan student commanded a regiment within the Royal Logistic Corps and went on to be promoted several more times. Nearly twenty years later, he made the dizzy heights of Major General and it is likely he will be promoted further. From our first encounter, it was clear that Captain Dunn had a natural ability to lead soldiers. Humble, dedicated and interested in others, his core leadership skills were exceptional. Most remarkable was his humble approach to his profession. Many military officers with only half his quality used arrogance to mask ineptitude, but Captain Dunn had a raw mental strength that didn't need an artificial crutch to support his thinking. Above all, his transactional style of leadership had the perfect balance of key characteristics. He could be dynamic, charismatic and decisive, all in one sentence. He had broken new ground for the non-graduate officer cohort, and may well have members of the newly formed Army Officer Selection Board rethink their commissioning strategy.

Captain Watts: After returning to the Special Air Service, he spent much of his time on Operations behind enemy lines in Iraq, Afghanistan and Libya. He distinguished himself on active service several times before being promoted to the rank of full Colonel. Much of his later years were spent advising NATO allies on counter-terrorism measures before returning to instruct at the Joint Military Staff College, Shrivenham. It came as no surprise to me when he left the service earlier than he needed to. The turgid work of a Staff Officer would not have played to his strengths once he became too old for the close-quarter combat he had previously enjoyed with the Special Forces. He was a man of action and adventure; there would have been little excitement for him after he turned 40. After leaving the Army, he took a senior role with a bank dealing in high-risk security investments.

Sergeant Major Pat Swift: Pat became Regimental Sergeant Major of a Parachute regiment before taking a Late Entry Commission with 1 Para. We met each other briefly in 2003 in Iraq, where he was in charge of the Motor Transport Platoon. As mad as ever, he still refused to be polite to anyone who was not a member of the Airborne forces. During my visit to see him at Abu Naji camp in Maysan Province, Pat repeatedly called me a 'hat' and demanded I do five 'names' before he gave me access to the coffee machine. There was much to be learnt from Pat's approach to soldiering. His experience was sagely employed, and although at times his articulation succumbed to his passion, in the cold light of day he was an outstanding leader and a brilliant counterweight to military bureaucracy. Sadly, after a very short battle with illness, he died a few years later.

Colour Sergeant Paddy Jones: After the final day of the course, Paddy returned to his parent unit and we never spoke again. Sometime later, he transferred from the Foot Guards and took a Late Entry Commission with the Army Air Corps as a non-technical officer. He enjoyed a successful career before retiring as a Major. As the years passed, I came to better understand our differences. There was little wrong with his way of doing business, and in the grand scheme of things, maybe there was some merit in his style. Although there was nothing I ever sought to emulate from his practices, our encounter did help me to recognize some of my own failings. Learning to play the long game was the most valuable lesson, as well as understanding that, sometimes, despite your best efforts, things still don't always work out fairly. Dealing with irrelevant distractions is our biggest downfall as humans. We obsess about other people so much that it drives us to distraction. This issue has become a phenomenon with the emergence of social media, and one as yet we don't fully understand.

Packman: After a shaky start on the Commissioning Course, Packman made it through at the first attempt. When we last met, he was serving with the Adjutant General's Corps as a Lieutenant Colonel. We saw each other in Army Headquarters, Andover, in 2017. He had piled on the weight after endless desk appointments. Despite his bulky appearance, he kept fit. He became a specialist in Human Resources and a master of crafting policies. Always keen to discuss his importance, he was particularly proud of his performance during the Army redundancies a few years previously and was keen to tell me he was on the cusp of commanding a unit. The working-class socialist in me resented his efforts during the recent rounds of redundancies. Not only because we saw some high-quality people ejected too early, but simply because redundancy in the military is the catalyst to making those who remain work harder for less reward. Simultaneously, we turn off the recruiting tap and scratch our heads at why the Army is undermanned a few months later!

Barns: He took the Commissioning Course by storm and was proving very popular. His days on Row-Co had given him the confidence to lead without fear and the belief he could achieve anything if he put his mind to it. We saw each other briefly during his first term as he helped me craft my thoughts on writing papers on leadership. Out of the blue, Barns gave me a hand-scribbled piece of A4 paper and said, 'just in case you ever write a book'. The concept of including 'Reflections' was all his. A few days afterwards, Boyle, King, Francis and Danner all added their thoughts, some of which was too graphic to include! Tragically, he died whilst he was still at Sandhurst in an incident not connected to training. Although two wars would rob me of many outstanding young leaders and friends in the years ahead, the loss of Barns seemed to have a greater impact.

Maybe it was my emotional connection, or maybe it was that no one ever got to enjoy the style of leadership he was developing.

Boyle: Military life suited Boyle right up to the point where he had to spend more time behind a desk than behind a rifle. Despite narrowly missing out on winning the Sword of Honour, he enjoyed every aspect of his time at Sandhurst. He joined the Royal Artillery and we failed to meet each other in 2009 whilst we were both serving in Afghanistan. Despite successfully converting his Commission from Short Service to Interim, he left before it was time to apply for a Regular Commission. Much was made of his desire to spend more time with his wife and young family. He and his wife set up their own business growing organic fruit and vegetables. It has long been a problem for the Army to retain their young talent. At some stage, the soldiering and adventure have to come to an end and the officer cohort needs to focus on defence as a business. In realizing that Boyle faced an imbalance of fun, work and life, he chose a different path to follow. A free spirit, learning he had left was disappointing. Leaders like Boyle are succeeded by those less talented, and for this, the Army is a lesser place.

Danner: Predictably, the Commissioning Course caused Danner a few discipline problems. His second term Colour Sergeant was a dogmatic young career Guardsman and their relationship was fraught and turbulent. The Colour Sergeant had a reputation as a tyrant who was desperately keen to make a name for himself at Sandhurst. The Warrant Officers' and Sergeants' Mess knew he was a bully, and Danner returned to the Rowallan DS looking for advice. We had frequently talked about tackling toxic leadership; less than four months later, Danner faced the challenge for real. Reluctantly, Pat intervened. He brought a temporary end to the Colour Sergeant's errant antics to ensure Danner made it to the end of the Commissioning Course without being kicked out or back-termed. Popular and great company, he stole the limelight right up to the day he left the Academy. After enjoying early success with his unit, his facetiousness brought an ignominious end to his career. Despite his demise, every soldier who knew him spoke affectionately of his command. Never one to stop thinking, he set up an enterprising business in London shortly after his service which is now listed on the FTSE Index.

Francis: After commanding a company of Royal Scots on operations in Iraq and Afghanistan, Francis' last appointment was as a Staff Officer in Army Commitments. Responsible for sustaining the manning efforts in conflicts across the world, he was in his element, enjoying life and hoping for promotion to Lieutenant Colonel. His functional style of leadership was the backbone of success in places like Dogwood and Bastion. Loyalty would, however, become his

Achilles heel. The epitome of a team player, he filled a succession of unglamorous jobs at the behest of his manning branch, and as a result failed to receive due recognition. At the end of the Afghanistan conflict, the Army Retirements board selected him for compulsory redundancy. It dawned on me that Packman would have been the man who processed his selection.

Haigh: Despite many people trying to remain in contact with Haigh, no one ever heard from him ever again. Searches of social media platforms have yielded no reward. No one shed a tear over his decision to leave. Few of his fellow students thought he would have made it through the Commissioning Course, a point of view that was easy to understand. For me, the encounter with Haigh remains my biggest disappointment. There was a place in the Army for Haigh. He was an unconventional butterfly thinker. Not that this would help him go far in the military, but as part of a small team, his confrontational thought processes would have been invaluable in certain quarters of defence. Employing a counterweight or someone to counter concepts and ideas is healthy. Haigh would have done this brilliantly. With this young man, there was a formidable thinker desperately trying to find a place in society.

King: He returned to the Royal Engineers and served in the same regiment where he had once been a Sapper. He proved to be a very popular officer, saw action in Iraq and Afghanistan several times and made it to the rank of Captain. Failing to convert his Commission, the rules forced him to leave after only six years. This is a risk that is not always realized by soldiers who cross the divide between enlisted men and officers. Had he remained in the ranks, unquestionably he would have served twenty-two years and taken a Late Entry Commission, giving him a thirty-seven-year career. It was unfortunate that he chose to return to the Royal Engineers. Succeeding in such a competitive regiment was always going to be difficult for an ex-ranker. In hindsight, a commission with an Infantry regiment, where his abilities would be appreciated, may have been prudent.

Moore: Successful at every turn of the handle, he was quickly drafted into the top echelons of the Army Staff and was on the shortlist for Brigadier at the first time of asking. He remains popular with all who work for him and committed to those he serves. Moore was always going to make it in the Army. We bumped into each other at the MoD Main Building during 2005. He had been married and divorced twice. It was not hard to see the cause of his domestic misery. Wedded to the job, few women tolerate the demands the service puts on their husbands. In his third relationship, the next Mrs Moore was a serving officer equally committed to the cause. By all accounts, this is the dream pairing.

Mathews: As a young officer, Mathews attended P Company and the All Arms Commando course. His reputation grew as a tough and capable leader with a refreshingly light view on Army life. Having successfully converted his Commission at the first time of asking, he was quick to rise through Command Appointments to become Commanding Officer of an Artillery regiment. Along the way, he ironically became commander of 7 Sphinx Special Observation Battery, much to the bemusement of the soldiers who had roughed him up during the escape and evasion phase of the course. We narrowly avoided bumping into each other on several occasions whilst he was attending Advanced Command and Staff College at Shrivenham. Promoted to full Colonel and posted to Larkill, he is certain to make Brigadier.

Norris: Second time around he breezed the Commissioning Course. He also found the Infantry Platoon Commanders' Course easy, where he won the binoculars as the top student. He was quick to earn the respect of his young Guardsmen by deploying on operational duty five weeks after arriving at his unit. Although we would never physically meet again, the stories of his service remain legendary. A close friend retold me the story of the time he watched a DVD with the Queen and Prince Phillip whilst in charge of the Queen's Guard at Buckingham Palace. Apparently, it is well known that Her Majesty will invite the Commander of the Guard to join her and Prince Phillip for supper, after which they settle down to watch TV or discuss current affairs. Norris was invited to choose a film and he selected, *Love Actually*. Reportedly, he was teased by the Queen who suggested he needed to be a little more manly! True story or not, everyone who served with him had nothing but praise and admiration for the diminutive character. He was shaped by his back-terming. Humble, with bags of empathy, his soldiers would have crawled across hot coals if he told them to. His leadership style was forged in the fires of unjustness; we knew he should never have been back-termed. Had his first Platoon Commander and Colour Sergeant been a little less vainglorious, the outcome would have been significantly different.

Rideout: After a relatively trouble-free year on the Commissioning Course, he enjoyed the first few years of service. On the Platoon Commanders Course at the School of Infantry in the following year, like Norris who was on the course before him, he also won the prestigious Bino's award. Successive deployments to Kosovo and then Iraq gave him credibility by the bucket load. Like others, converting his Commission proved elusive. Consequently, he left the Army as a Captain after just six years. It was strange to learn he had not successfully converted his Commission. Perhaps he relapsed to his former self once he reached the real world. More likely, he failed to impress those who wrote his reports and made recommendations on his future employment. Rideout was fiercely loyal, but only if he felt it was reciprocal. It was easy to envisage him having problems with a chubby Staff Officer who had little combat experience or had not been subject to hostile fire.

Stone: After much deliberation, the College Commander issued Stone with a pass. Then, just as Pat had warned, it came back to bite him. It appeared that Stone had reverted back to type once he made it on to the Commissioning Course. He struggled to appease a succession of Colour Sergeants and was back-termed twice. He had become infamous for his poisonous nature and disingenuous comments. Although he excelled on his Platoon Commanders Course, he never converted his Commission and left at the rank of Captain. Retraining Stone on two occasions was everything Pat had warned us of. Stone would always be able to impress in small doses, but his selfishness would always shine through. He worked alongside Francis in Iraq in 2003, where he repeatedly bent the truth to appear well informed and ahead of the power curve. In truth, he had become the master of irrelative narrative and inviting inaccurate synthesis. It was rumoured that he joined the Canadian Army as a private soldier and is currently still serving with them. Irrespective of the truth, Stone should never have been allowed at Sandhurst without going through RCB.

Williams: In the first few weeks of the first term, he fell off the 6ft wall of the assault course and broke his ankle. He spent nearly a year on the Y-List before restarting training long after everyone had moved on, including me. To add to his woes, he was back-termed in term two and in total spent two years at Sandhurst before taking a Commission in the Royal Logistic Corps. He failed to earn an Interim Commission and after a few poor annual reports, he decided to leave having only completed four years' service.

Witherspoon: On the Commissioning Course he partnered up with Danner. They both endured the stewardship of a tyrannical Colour Sergeant. Despite Pat convincing the Colour Sergeant to change his aggressive and bullying style, the intervention arrived too late for Witherspoon. He had fallen out of love with the military and voluntarily withdrew himself from the Commissioning Course. His departure had a huge impact on the other students, none more so than Danner, who frequently came close to exchanging blows with the Colour Sergeant over the treatment of Witherspoon. This would not work out well for either of them. Shortly after Danner was commissioned, his Colour Sergeant was unceremoniously kicked out of the Academy for repeated infringements of Army Values and Standards. Reportedly, he had exploited his relationship with a rich Arab and was found to be receiving expensive gifts in return for favours. Witherspoon later confessed to several members of the platoon that it was not the Colour Sergeant's corrupt and narcissistic behaviour that caused his premature departure. It was the realization that the Army was not full of officers like Dunn and Watts, and this was too hard to take. When he complained about his treatment to the Royal Tank Regiment officer in charge of his platoon, alleging that his Colour Sergeant was a corrupt bully, the RTR officer dismissed his claims as deluded. Even when Witherspoon delivered irrefutable evidence that even a 10-year-old could decipher, namely a shiny new high-performance vehicle beyond the means of a soldier's pay packet, his cries went unheard. Whether the Platoon Commander was arrogant, idle or just too weak to confront an aggressive Colour Sergeant, Witherspoon lost faith in the officer corps. All the values and standards we had preached to him on Rowallan Company had been unpicked; it was too much for him to take.

Murphy: Another young man who spent a year longer at Sandhurst than he would have wished. Murphy broke his foot halfway through the first term during a foot drill competition. Typically, he tried too hard to impress the adjudicating DS and slammed his foot into the ground with more enthusiasm than was required. He spent two terms on the Y-List before rejoining training the following year. The extra year at Sandhurst placed him behind his peer group, and it took him a while to catch up. He chased adventure and excitement in his early years, and enjoyed an exchange appointment with the US 101st Airborne Division at Fort Campbell, Kentucky. Eventually, he took command of an Army Reserve unit. Bizarrely, we crossed paths whilst we were both out running across Salisbury Plain. Apparently, he had seen me on a number of occasions but was apprehensive to approach me. He giggled as he explained he was worried I was going to make him keep running! When we last spoke, he was serving as a Lieutenant Colonel at PJHQ (Permanent Joint Headquarters), hoping to secure another appointment in America.

Acknowledgments

When an officer pulls on his Oxford Blue Rowallan T-shirt, yellow stag guarding the heart, he is wearing the UK Kitemark of 'leadership in adversity.' The stag represents qualities some officers lose sight of in pursuit of greater authority. Stamina, instinct, dedication, independence and nobility are characteristics of leadership that can't be found in the Staff Officers Hand Book. They are ingredients forged in fire, tailored to lead the bravest of warriors during the darkest of times. If there is one thing, I can be certain of, it is this: any officer who successfully completed the Rowallan Course will have inspired every soldier he went on to lead. This unique small band of men, are amongst the most genuine leaders ever to serve their country and epitomise the Sandhurst moto 'Serve to Lead.' To all those young men who survived the course, I acknowledge your remarkable achievement.

I will forever be grateful to the precious few people who have encouraged and supported me in my endeavours to publish this account. Whilst I will never be able to repay their kindness, I have donated the first royalties of this book to a serviceman's charity on their behalf.

General Sir Jack Deverell KCB OBE
Andy McNab CBE DCM MM Darts
Colonel David Wakefield OBE
Lt. Col (Rtd) John Pentreath

Additionally, I must acknowledge the kindness and sincerity of Tara Moran and Harriet Fielding of Pen & Sword. To remain focused and committed during a pandemic, has required, courage, resolve and commitment of an extraordinary nature. On behalf of every Row-Co officer, we thank you for ensuring that this historical story has been told.

Finally, I acknowledge the Doherty family, for their collective support, encouragement and help in achieving a lifelong aspiration.

Dr Niall Doherty
Justin Doherty
Lt Col Simon Doherty

Index

A Frame 146, 318–20, 368–70
A&E 52, 127
Abigale, Hurricane 34
Academy Sergeant Major 33, 72–3, 167, 297, 317, 320–1, 382
Adam & Eve 305–07
Adamson, Oct 312
Afghanistan 380, 402–3, 406
Al Shaibah 342, 349
Aldershot 2, 196, 227, 334
Artillery Regiment 251, 342, 405, 407
Avon Dam Reservoir 276

Baáth Party 128
Back–Termed, 10, 226, 250, 384, 407–8
Barns, Oct 30, 60, 64, 70, 74, 86, 96, 100–101, 105, 110, 133, 137,144–5, 152, 169–71, 176–7, 183–4, 210, 219, 225, 239–42, 248, 258, 272, 277, 289, 292–3, 295–9, 307, 357, 371, 382–84, 397–8, 395, 404
Barossa 67–8, 80, 153, 163, 196, 217–9, 268, 298
Basra 18,127–30, 350
Belfast 8, 36, 77, 89, 324
Benson, Ross 350–1
Black Watch, The 350
Blair, Tony 350–1
Blobby, Mr 32, 38–9, 48–9
Board, Progress 79, 165, 206, 241, 244, 263–4, 290, 366, 392
Bosnia 21–2, 89
Boyd, John 134
Boyle, Oct 27–8, 57–8, 62–7, 75, 96, 100, 137, 142, 152, 170, 187, 193–5, 204–205, 243, 247–8, 257, 296, 305–6, 310–12, 329, 333, 336, 357, 369–71, 384–88, 398, 404–5
Broadmoor 162
Brockhill 276
Browning Barracks 227
Browning, Fredrick, Captain 5
Buckland Ford 273–4

Bugout 113, 115, 120–6, 131–3, 144, 165–8, 246–53, 283, 292, 312–5, 354–6
Butler, Oct 389–90

Calley, William, Lt 337
Cannon Rock 305–307
Capel Curig 310
Chapel, Square 19, 99, 100, 114, 138–7, 335–6
College Commander 15, 82, 207, 241–2, 256, 262–3, 256–6, 291–2, 318–22, 366–9, 392–5, 408
Command, Tools 134–5, 165, 356, 373
Commissioning, Course 9–12, 16, 33, 47, 61, 64, 83, 104, 140, 167, 203, 227, 234, 267–8, 278, 293, 299, 302, 327, 335, 383, 391, 393–5, 398–9, 400, 404–408
Compass Rose 167–211, 242
Container C527 277
Container H83 104, 181, 277
Custer, General 237
Cyprus 21–2, 209, 336

Danner, Oct 29, 42, 44, 54, 57, 66–7, 75, 84, 88, 95–6, 100, 120, 145, 160, 165–6, 192–6, 199, 205, 207, 233, 240, 243–8, 251, 258, 279, 285–6, 305, 311–5, 319, 322, 327–8, 331–4, 338–9, 354–6, 364, 376–8, 383, 387–9, 391, 396–7, 404–5, 408
Dartmoor 109–10, 254–5, 263, 281–4, 293, 354, 357
Davis, Corporal 3, 16, 36–8, 51–2, 79, 105, 161, 310, 374–5
Dazzel, Staff, Sergeant, 13–16, 36–8, 43, 56, 59–65, 83, 105–108, 120, 169, 171, 189, 190, 204, 215, 224, 227–9, 231–2, 238, 267–8, 280–1, 297–8, 302–304, 309, 339
Dettingen, Company 51
Deverell, Lt, General, 1–3, 72, 82, 155, 157, 161, 163, 329, 367, 376–7, 381–9, 392, (Commandant) 395–6, 399, 401

Dublin 323–4, 402
Dunn, James, Captain 3–403

Edwards, Colour Sergeant 137–140, 145–7, 151–7, 185, 241, 249, 288, 314, 317–8, 334–7, 340–2, 360, 363–4, 368
Eton 25, 29, 142, 207, 240, 259, 383–4, 397

F, Company 22
Falklands, The 21, 60
Fan Fach 359
Fan Fawr 379, 382, 384–5, 395
Fan Lia 378
Fan Nedd 379
Faraday Hall 61, 142, 206, 221–3, 301, 337
Fish, Michael 203
Foel Firth 357–8
Foot Guards 8, 320–1, 351, 404
Francis, Oct 28, 75–6, 86, 132–42, 145, 152, 168, 170–2, 183, 195, 198–9, 200, 205, 217–9, 225, 229, 235, 239, 243, 248, 256–7, 271–2, 276–80, 285–8, 293, 300, 312, 317, 333, 335, 357, 359, 364, 371–2, 377–9, 381–8, 395, 400, 402, 404–405, 408
FRELIMO 98
Fur, Tor 284–5

Gates, Bill 20
Glyder Fach 306
Glyder Fawr 308, 310
Goldson, Oct 29, 62, 70, 85–6, 95, 100, 106, 137, 144–5, 151, 154–5, 163–70, 177–8, 186, 189, 196–7, 206, 208, 215, 226
Gray, Gordon, Major 4, 7, 12, 16, 20–4, 36–7, 44, 47, 55–6, 68, 71, 105, 107, 114–6, 124–5, 135–7, 144, 157–9, 162–8, 174, 181–4, 186, 196, 203–205, 216, 220, 224–5, 229, 239, 242, 249, 253–4, 257, 262–4, 262, 294, 301, 313, 315, 331, 341, 356, 360, 363, 467–70, 375–7, 392–3, 400, 402
Gulf, War 21–2, 58, 116–7
Gurkhas 72–3, 148

Haigh, Oct 26, 53, 55, 64, 68–70, 79–82, 86, 94–5, 100–101, 105, 120, 124–5, 137, 144–6, 156, 158, 169–82, 192, 195–6, 207–208, 212–5, 226, 233–40, 244–9, 258–9, 272, 286–8, 291, 294–5, 300–301, 317, 330, 338, 341, 357–8, 375–6, 383, 384–5, 387–91, 398, 400–401, 406

Hattin, Battle of 46
Hays, Oct 14–20, 28, 31–9, 48, 50–2, 86, 226, 240, 246, 311
Heal, Tracy, Staff Sergeant 297–8, 302–307, 317–8, 331–2, 338–9, 364
Helping Hand, Exercise 247–50
Hereford 26, 79, 191
Highland Fieldcraft Trg Centre 1
Highland Trophy 23, 293, 318, 322, 334, 340, 366–7, 371, 392, 396, 400
Hill, Monkey 55, 58, 338
HMS Heron 293
Holyhead 323
Hudson, Oct 12
Hunter Force 251–7
Hussein, Saddam 21, 78, 117, 129

Indian Army Memorial Room 3, 7, 391–2, 399
IRA 362
Iraq 3, 7, 391–2, 399, 405–408
Irish Guards 8, 22

Jack Wagon 37–39, 43, 145, 298
Jacobs, Oct 389–91
Jerusalem 46
Jilliot, Bernard 223
Jobs, Steve 20
John Lennon 80
Jones, Paddy, Colour Sergeant 6, 8, 12, 16, 19, 35–6, 43, 45–8, 69–70, 108, 114–6, 120–3, 126, 133, 138, 140, 144, 153–4, 156–8, 162, 167–8, 171, 174, 182, 184–5, 190–2, 204–205, 207–208, 215–6, 220, 226, 231, 238–9, 241, 243–4, 249–50, 266, 268–70, 274–5, 284, 288, 293–4, 297–8, 310, 312, 319–20, 332–3, 337, 340–1, 351, 355–6, 360, 365, 367, 371, 374–8, 381, 384, 389–95, 399, 404

Keating–Wells, Oct 381
Kenya 26
King Arthur 306
King, Guy, of 46
King, Oct 28, 55, 64, 76, 100, 133, 136, 148–51, 158, 170, 189, 203, 206, 239, 242, 248, 259–60, 276, 305–306, 355, 357, 364, 370, 386–8, 398, 404, 406
Klondike, Exercise 215, 217, 221, 241, 310
Knights, Templar 46
Koresh, David 319

Labalaba, Sergeant 169
Lane, Oct 30, 38, 55–6, 62, 82, 105, 123–4, 144 154, 160–1, 163–4, 173–5, 179, 186, 189, 199, 206, 232–3, 235–8, 240, 242, 246, 249, 263–4, 268, 284–8, 296, 298, 300–302, 308–309, 326, 328–30, 335–6, 338, 340–1, 357, 363, 366, 368, 378–9, 381–2, 399
Lee, Emily, Professor 152, 221
Light, Division 22
Llanberis 308

Mai Lai 337
Mathews, Oct 26, 45, 47, 51, 53–5, 62, 70, 79, 96, 100, 106, 122, 133, 136, 152, 154, 158, 170–3, 183–4, 189–94, 198–9, 205, 213–4, 233, 235, 239, 243, 246, 248, 255, 257, 271–2, 293, 305, 311–2, 318–20, 322, 331, 334, 336, 339–40, 357, 366–8, 376–7, 392, 395–6, 407
McBurney, Colour Serjeant 304
McCarthy, Gaz Colour Serjeant 1–2, 6, 12–15, 37–8, 43, 48, 62, 101, 108, 116, 122, 126, 128, 130, 138, 140, 145, 153–8, 161, 185, 202, 208, 215, 230, 249–50, 254, 262–3, 274–6, 288–90, 338, 340–1, 350, 360, 366, 368, 374, 393, 398, 401
Mean Machine 104–108, 126, 132–3, 143, 181, 215, 218–9, 225, 235, 237, 240, 248, 252, 298–9, 355, 363, 397
Medical Discharge 79, 88
Meldon 289, 290
Merseyside 26, 73
Merthyr Tydfil 312, 360, 368, 371
Minley Manor 177, 181, 196, 198, 210, 269
Mirbat, Battle of 169
Mons Hall 21
Moore, Oct 29–30, 44, 95, 100, 106, 120, 152, 158, 162, 166, 170–1, 183, 186, 189, 219, 233, 239, 243, 248, 258, 273–6, 285, 288, 333–4, 336–79, 364–5, 378, 383, 388, 396, 406
Mort, Colour Sergeant 164
Mount Haramosh 222, 245, 308
Mourne Mountains 89
Mozambique 22, 97–8
Murphy, Oct 27, 55–7, 61–2, 74, 133, 164, 170, 189–91, 200, 233, 239, 245, 248, 268, 272, 294, 301–302, 304–305, 315, 355, 357, 364, 369, 399, 409

New, College, 21, 47, 108, 113, 238, 331

Newcastle 42, 330
Nicholas, Cottam, Lt, Colonel 362
Night Exercise Without Darkness 108–109
Norris, Oct 240, 246, 250, 260–1, 267–72, 278–81, 286–7, 315, 357, 359, 371, 378–9, 382, 384–5, 387–8, 396, 407
Northern, Ireland 21–2, 77, 89, 178, 324, 361

Okehampton Camp 288–9
Oasis 312
Old, College, 1, 5, 15–16, 167, 212, 223, 250, 338, 400
Operation Mince Meat 354
Operation Panchi–Palang 380
Oxford 26–7, 81, 350

P, Company 21, 75, 189, 229, 396, 399, 407
Packman, Oct 6, 53, 55, 64, 85, 106, 144, 153–4, 170, 172–5, 239–40, 245, 248, 268, 276, 292, 294, 300, 306–307, 324–5, 357, 371, 383, 384–9, 394, 404, 406
Pain & Gain 168
Pane Jane 242, 249–51, 254, 268, 297, 299–300, 311, 333, 378, 393
Parachute Regiment 1, 21, 183, 227–9, 273, 403
Patton, General 356
Pen–Y–Fan 371, 386
Pete CQMS 8–9, 68, 105, 136, 151, 157–8, 161, 167–8, 177, 186–7, 192–3, 197, 238, 241, 270, 282, 284, 289–90, 298, 304, 310–11, 314, 318–9, 333, 341, 355–6, 365–6, 374–5, 392
Pig Trail 21
Plymouth 257, 284
Police, The 73, 127–8, 131, 162, 209, 236, 248–9, 257, 317, 324, 328, 343, 350, 362
Professionally Qualified Officer 80
Puddick, Oct 27, 56, 64–7, 86, 226

Qaboos, Sultan of Oman 331
Queen, The 12, 22, 43, 89, 162, 195, 265, 407

Race, Stretcher 56–63, 74, 106, 170, 189
Red, Light, Exercise 314–7, 322, 330
Reed, Oct 23
Regular Commissions Board 1, 10–11, 26, 28, 103, 234, 292, 408
RENAMO 22, 98
Rideout, Oct 27, 62–8, 86–7, 93–102, 121, 124, 136, 138–40, 152, 158, 170–1, 183,

189, 191, 199, 201, 204, 216, 218, 234–6, 245, 248, 268, 303, 312, 322–3, 327, 330–1, 333, 340, 357, 359, 364–5, 378, 381, 383, 387, 389, 394, 400, 407–408
Rifle Depot 40
River Foyle 361
RNAS Yeovilton 293
Rolly–Rolland, Padre 380
Rowallan, Lord 6, 13
Royal Engineers 28, 202, 406
Royal Logistic Corps 75, 403, 408
Royal Marines 30, 289
Royal Memorial Chapel 318, 356
Royal Military Police 127
Ryders, Hill 277

Sanders, John 5
Snowdon 21, 230, 308–309
Sourton, Tor 288, 289
South Africa 26
Sovereign Parade 5, 408
Special Air Service 21, 117–8, 221, 271, 413
Special, Boat, Squadron 289
Staples, Oct 319–20, 236–7, 340–1, 367, 400
Sterling, Sir David 221, 222
Stone, Oct 26–7, 48, 55, 57–8, 64, 77, 83, 85, 88, 105–106, 124, 137, 144–5, 165, 170–1, 177, 181, 183, 191–2, 203, 208, 218–9, 225, 238, 241, 244, 253–4, 258–9, 262–7, 270–2, 277–9, 283–4, 289, 291–2, 296, 298–9, 305, 309, 319–21, 337, 370–1, 382–4, 387, 389, 393–4, 408
Storey Arms 386, 395
Streather, Tony Lt Colonel 222–4, 295
Swift, Pat, Sergeant Major *passim*

Tasmanian Devil 97
Taylor, Helen, Captain 128
Trainasium 227, 229, 232–3, 249, 300
Trecastle 374, 375
Trollope, Oct 29, 38–9, 48–51, 54, 66, 86, 226
Tryfan 230–1, 305
Turing, Alan 30,
Type A 122, 144, 153–4, 177, 180, 187, 196, 260
Type B 203

Usk Reservoir 357, 359–60, 363–4, 368

Values Based Leadership 72, 305–306
Vest, String 6–7, 38, 181, 184, 245, 250, 363, 401
Victory College 71
Vietnam 48, 237, 279
Von Steuben, Frederick 377, 381

Wales 91, 123, 251, 301, 304, 315, 318, 333, 341, 357
Waterloo 5
Watson, Oct 26, 45–6, 55, 64–5, 84, 86, 111, 112–3, 33, 137, 169–70, 175, 197–202, 207, 216–220, 226, 238–40, 243, 293
Watts, Tom, Captain 21–2, 45, 58–9, 71, 116–7, 136, 157–8, 167, 176, 185, 190–3, 241, 244, 252, 270–1, 288, 290, 293, 302, 304, 310, 321, 350, 367, 375, 378, 392, 395–6, 399
Welbeck College 85, 264, 292, 309, 319–20, 322, 382
Weston, Oct 25, 44, 48, 51–3, 55, 57, 62, 64, 73, 79, 86, 88, 89, 93, 102–103, 119, 226
Williams, Oct 28, 45, 67, 85–6, 106, 135, 137, 144, 152, 170, 176, 185–7, 229–32, 239–40, 245, 248, 258, 260–2, 330, 334–3, 340–1, 354, 357–64, 366, 376, 392–3, 397, 408
Willsworthy Camp 282, 292
Winchester 26, 40, 43, 102, 109, 259
Wishstream 68, 71, 82
Withdrawal, Voluntary VW 49, 66, 211, 269
Witherspoon, Oct 28, 55, 57, 78, 86, 100, 121, 125–7, 130–1, 137, 151–2, 170–1, 183, 187, 194, 203, 206, 219, 222–4, 234, 239, 245, 248, 261–2, 272, 219–80, 288, 308, 312, 315, 317, 329, 333, 335, 354, 357, 359, 364–5, 369–70, 383, 387–9, 397–8, 408–409

Yes, Tor 285–6, 288, 291

Zimbabwe 26